Fundamentals of Planning and Developing Tourism

Bulent I. Kastarlak, AIA, MCP,
M. Arch, Y. Müh.

Brian Barber, Technical Editor
City and Regional Planner, MUP

Pearson

Boston   Columbus   Indianapolis   New York   San Francisco   Upper Saddle River
Amsterdam   Cape Town   Dubai   London   Madrid   Milan   Munich   Paris   Montreal   Toronto
Delhi   Mexico City   São Paulo   Sydney   Hong Kong   Seoul   Singapore   Taipei   Tokyo

Editorial Director: Vernon Anthony
Senior Acquisitions Editor: William Lawrensen
Editorial Assistant: Lara Dimmick
Director of Marketing: David Gesell
Senior Marketing Manager: Thomas Hayward
Senior Marketing Coordinator: Alicia Wozniak
Senior Marketing Assistant: Les Roberts
Senior Managing Editor: JoEllen Gohr
Associate Managing Editor: Alexandrina Benedicto Wolf
Copy Editor: Helen Greenberg
Project Manager: Kris Roach
Senior Operations Supervisor: Pat Tonneman
Production Project Manager: Debbie Ryan
Art Director: Jayne Conte
Cover Designer: Suzanne Duda
Cover Art: Fotolia
Media Director: Karen Bretz
Lead Media Project Manager: Michelle Churma
Full-Service Project Management: Jogender Taneja/Aptara®, Inc.
Printer/Binder: RR Donnelley & Sons
Text Font: Minion

Credits and acknowledgments borrowed from other sources and reproduced, with permission, in this textbook appear on appropriate page within text.

Library of Congress Cataloging-in-Publication Data
Kastarlak, Bülent I.
    Fundamentals of planning and developing tourism / Bulent I. Kastarlak, Brian Barber, Technical Editor.
       p. cm.
    ISBN-13: 978-0-13-507881-5
    ISBN-10: 0-13-507881-4
    1. Tourism—Management.   2. Tourism—Planning.   I. Barber, Brian. K.,   II. Title.
    G155.A1K33 2012
    910.68'4—dc23

                                                                                                  2011022134

10 9 8 7 6 5 4 3 2 1

ISBN 10:   0-13-507881-4
ISBN 13: 978-0-13-507881-5

This book is dedicated to my wife Jean, and my children Todd and Kim, who enthusiastically supported me in the extensive labors of preparing this book.

This book is also dedicated to the memories of

Evner Ergun

Who introduced me to tourism and trusted me with many of his United Nations tourism projects

and

Theodore W. Schulenberg

Who saw the wisdom in exploring a new approach to tourism development planning.

CONTENTS

FOREWORD

By
Jerome J. Vallen, Ph.D.

Because tourism is the one industry common to every nation of the world, it has been—and continues to be—a tool for change on the global scale. Tourism has morphed from the utilitarian service of travel to serve pleasurable recreational needs and critical economic development. Tourism has been the driving force in the political opening of China. Tourism volume has expressed approval/displeasure of foreign leaders and their politics. Tourism has been the economic crowbar that levered Hong Kong to new heights. Tourism became the second concern, after the human toll, arising from the devastation of the Indian Ocean tsunami. Tourism has always been impacted by the falling/rising value of international currencies, the American dollar among them.

Clearly, tourism is a subpart of all disciplines. It is a subject for the political scientist, the international economist, the behavioral social psychologist, the avid ecologist, and the gracious hotelier. It is business, politics, and socioeconomic issues all rolled into one. It is no surprise, then, that a book on tourism by a well-informed international author, whose background touches all of these issues, has been so well received.

The title of the work, *Fundamentals of Planning and Developing Tourism*, tells much about the book and the author. Only someone with his breadth of experience—from architect to educator, from city planner to engineer, from tourist to tourism manager—could pen a volume as broad, detailed, complete, and sensitive as this work.

Within this academic text and operations manual is guidance for everyone from student to practitioner. Unlike many approaches to the subject of tourism, the work has multiple facets, which is, of course, the very essence of tourism itself. It offers both a macro and a micro explanation; it guides both governments and localities; it reflects on urban and rural problems. The author presents this material with frequent headings and subheadings, with bullet emphases, detail, and structure that only come from good research, practical experience, and a deep understanding of a complete subject.

Good reading!

Jerome J. Vallen, Ph.D.
Dean and Professor Emeritus
College of Hotel Administration
University of Nevada, Las Vegas

PREFACE

Fundamentals of Planning and Developing Tourism brings into focus the growing importance of tourism in developing economies of the world for producing social change, alleviating poverty, and achieving sustained growth. The book grew out of the necessity to organize a quantifiable methodology that employs tourism as a growth agent for planning urban and regional development. The methodological basis of the book is the *BIK System* developed by the author from urban and regional planning principles. These principles include, but are not limited to, economics and marketing, which have often been the focus in many previous tourism publications.

The book is oriented to three groups of readers. The first group is students at college and university levels, researchers, and academicians. It can be used as a textbook for courses on tourism development planning. The book presents an inclusive, comprehensive review of the fundamentals and methods of planning the tourism industry in one source. It describes the steps used for analyzing and planning tourism development in centrally planned economies, mixed economies, and free-market systems.

The second group includes tourism professionals from government and private sector businesses. For this group, the book serves as an operations manual and a planning guide. It presents the step-by-step process of planning and developing sustainable tourism at international, national, regional, and local destination levels. For government officials at the national level, the book specifies steps for developing tourism as one growth sector—sometimes the only growth sector—of a country's national economy. It focuses on establishing policy guidelines, enacting laws and regulations, and building national tourism infrastructure. At the regional and local government levels, the focus is on geographic, environmental, social, and land use aspects of sustainable tourism development. For private business practitioners, such as real estate developers, financiers, managers, architects, and urban planners and designers, it presents the steps ranging from selecting a site, designing, securing various permits, financing, constructing, and completing to occupying a tourism attraction or facility.

The third group includes the traveling public and travel agents, who can use the book for general reading or as an aid to customize vacations for special interest trips. The BIK System is intended to evolve into several types of software and will be connected to databases of selected destinations through the Internet. Eventually, the system can be packaged in a portable device the size of a cell phone for making tourism travel decisions at home and on the road.

Many Web sites are identified throughout the text. They are intended to supplement, illustrate, and provide references for material in the text. Readers who access the text on computer screens and other electronic devices can go almost instantly to the Web sites referenced as they read the book. An attempt was made to keep the Web site references short and nondistracting from the main flow of thought and logical development intended in the organization of the text. Readers should remember that Web sites are constantly being changed and replaced. All Web sites included in the text were tested for access and content at the time of editing and publishing the book. Over time, some may disappear and/or be changed.

Fundamentals of Planning and Developing Tourism is also anecdotal. Personal experiences of the author in thirty-five countries are enriched by examples of historical explorations and consultations from around the world. Several actual case studies are presented to describe the satisfactions and disappointments involved in planning and developing tourism.

The basic principle behind advocating tourism development in this book is that tourism first must be proven to be beneficial as an export industry for the host country, region, or destination and, second, that visitors are welcome as long as sustainable growth of tourism is assured. Conservation of irreplaceable natural environmental features, restoration of unique specimens of the cultural heritage, capacity constraints, and thresholds of social acceptability must be considered in planning sustainable tourism and alleviating poverty. *Fundamentals of Planning and Developing Tourism* attempts to give an understanding and practical application of this process to students, scholars, professionals, and the general public. I hope it succeeds in very useful ways.

Bulent I. Kastarlak

ABOUT THE AUTHOR

The author on assignment in Nepal

Bulent I. Kastarlak (now deceased) was an architect, engineer, and city and regional planner with over thirty years of consulting, teaching, and business experience. He was the founder and principal of Kastarlak Associates, a consulting firm with a diversified professional practice in thirty-five countries, including tourism development planning. He was also a partner of Brian Barber in the planning firm Interchange International, Inc., which did general planning and design and conducted tourism development studies.

Bulent I. Kastarlak received his Y. Mühendis degree in engineering from Istanbul Technical University, and his two postgraduate degrees—the Master in Architecture degree in community design and the Master in City Planning degree in regional economic, physical, and social development planning—from the Massachusetts Institute of Technology. He was a registered architect in the states of Massachusetts and Florida and was certified by the National Council of Architectural Registration Boards. He was an Emeritus Member of the American Institute of Architects. He was a visiting professor at the University of Nevada and a guest lecturer at Harvard University, where he taught a course titled "Tourism Planning and Development." He also lectured on the subjects of world cultures and customs and comparative economic systems at Northwood University, West Palm Beach, Florida.

Upon starting his consulting practice in 1970, Bulent I. Kastarlak wrote the five-volume study *Tourism and Its Development Potential in Massachusetts* for the Massachusetts Department of Commerce and Development. In the study, he postulated his general principles of sustainable economic development and social change through tourism and demonstrated its planning applications. Working with the Harvard University Laboratory for Computer Graphics, he devised the first geographic information system (GIS) for tourism development planning in the United States. His work was first published in the *Proceedings* of the First Annual Conference of the Travel Research Association held in Monterey, California, on August 16–19, 1970. During the conference, he presented the GIS and computer applications of his planning methodology. The title of his presentation was "Tourism Potential and Planning for Growth at the State Level." His work was also published in the February 1971 issue of *The Cornell Hotel and Restaurant Administration Quarterly* in an article titled "Planning Tourism Growth."

His consulting practice took Bulent I. Kastarlak to many places in the United States and to thirty-five countries around the world, where he worked on many tourism and regional development projects for the United Nations, the governments of Turkey, Nepal, Hungary, Saudi Arabia, Jordan, and eight Caribbean countries, and the governments of several states and cities in the United States, as well as for many private clients. Poverty reduction was common to all of these projects. In recent years, he expanded and developed the scope of his principles of sustainable tourism development planning and named it the *BIK System*. He worked on adapting software for computer simulation of tourism planning alternatives and for interactive travel planning over the Internet and wireless communication systems.

Fundamentals of Planning and Developing Tourism is Bulent I. Kastarlak's first commercially published book. It is the narration of his lifelong professional experience and interest in world cultures, tourism, and alleviating poverty.

ABOUT THE TECHNICAL EDITOR

Brian Barber is a practicing urban and regional planner who was a classmate of Bulent I. Kastarlak at the Massachusetts Institute of Technology in the 1960s, and was his partner in the planning firm Interchange International, Inc., in the late 1970s and 1980s. Mr. Barber has a Bachelor of Science degree in geography from Florida State University and a Master of Urban Planning Degree from the University of Washington. He was Director of Research for the American Institute of Planners and has gained extensive experience as a planning consultant in various companies, including Alan M. Voorhees, Skidmore, Owings and Merrill, Camp Dresser and McKee, The Planners Collaborative, and Community Preservation Associates, where he currently is a principal of the firm.

Mr. Barber has written and edited many planning reports including municipal master plans, regional plans, land use plans, downtown revitalization studies, open space and recreation plans, feasibility studies for development projects including tourism projects, environmental and traffic impact reports, and planning information systems reports. He has written papers for, and spoken at, many planning conferences in the United States and abroad. Most of his domestic planning practice has been in New England, but he has also worked on projects in California, New York, New Jersey, and Michigan. His international experience includes projects in Slovenia, Saudi Arabia, and Taiwan. He was a Charter Member of the American Institute of Certified Planners after having been a Full Member of the American Institute of Planners. He has prepared and taught planning courses at the University of Rhode Island, Boston University, and Harvard University.

LIST OF FIGURES

Basic Principles of Planning and Developing Tourism

Part I defines tourism, identifies its elements, examines how it functions in different economic systems, and describes how it is planned for orderly growth. It examines the role of tourism development in alleviating poverty and maintaining sustainability. It presents a general theory for planning and developing tourism and, based on the theory, gives examples of various types of tourism.

1

Understanding Tourism Development

This chapter introduces the elements of tourism and one analytical concept that can be used in understanding the role that tourism plays in centrally planned command economies, mixed economies, and market economic systems for reducing poverty, distributing benefits and costs to the people, and sustaining the quality of the environment and the culture of destination regions. Basic premises of this book are as follows:

- Changes in the world economy affect global tourism directly.
- Sustainable tourism can be a function of national development for reducing poverty.
- All types of economic and social systems can engage in and make use of tourism.
- Sustainable tourism protects the future of the culture and the environment of the destination regions.
- Tourism has a product that can be consumed only at the place of production.
- The principles of economic, regional, and urban development planning also apply to sustainable tourism.
- Planning for tourism development is done at international, national, regional, and local levels, and the most favorable economic, social, and environmental outcomes are achieved by understanding and cooperation among these levels.

1.1 WORLD DEVELOPMENT TRENDS

The World Bank prepares and publishes annual reports about development trends throughout the world and reviews actions taken by the bank in alleviating poverty. *The World Bank Annual Report 2008, The Year in Review*, summarizes the world development trends as follows:

An estimated 2.5 billion people are trying to survive on $2 or less a day. The slide of the U.S. dollar and resulting weakening economy, together with the credit crunch, have led to a global financial crisis, which has clearly and significantly put added stress on the poorest people. Skyrocketing food prices are a harsh reality, resulting in even greater hunger and malnutrition worldwide.

The poor typically lack access to education, adequate health services, and clean water and sanitation. They are more vulnerable to economic shocks, natural disasters, violence, and crime. The World Bank continues to support country-owned development strategies that seek to reduce poverty by expanding growth opportunities. It seeks to improve the ability of poor households to participate in the economy and to have better access to basic services. The World Bank focuses on improving infrastructure and risk management instruments and on creating more accountable and transparent institutions.

Rising inequality over the 1990s has severely reduced the potential impact on poverty from the rapid growth experienced by many countries. On average, between 1990 and 2004, only one-third of growth in output transferred to growth in employment. Demographic trends suggest that the next decades will see growing pressure to create employment opportunities in most low-income countries in response to a sustained growth in labor supply that follows from continuing sharp increases in the working-age population and in female labor market participation.

It is projected that the increase in the gross domestic product (GDP) for developing countries will decline to 7.1 percent in 2008, whereas high-income countries are predicted to grow by a modest 2.2 percent. Globally, poverty is in decline, exemplified by East Asia, where the Millennium Development Goal (MDG) of halving extreme poverty by 2015 from 1990 levels already has been achieved. Progress on poverty reduction and the other MDGs varies widely, however, and conditions are especially dire in Africa, where extreme poverty is expected to grow. Africa, especially its Sub-Saharan nations, is the Bank's priority continent for action.

Source: International Bank for Reconstruction and Development/The World Bank: *The World Bank Annual Report 2008, The Year in Review,* pp.13–15.

This one-year summary does not represent a trend. Nevertheless, it clearly indicates where the developing world stands today and most likely will be in the near future. The World Bank makes the point that although external development assistance has contributed effectively to lifting people out of poverty, the primary responsibility for developing a country lies with its national government.

In recent decades, international aid and technical advice have helped create the conditions necessary for social change and cultural adaptation in many regions of the world. In turn, these conditions have created the economic environment necessary for rising entrepreneurship and a flourishing private sector. As evidence has mounted, reasons for this progress have become clearer. Foreign aid is most effective in countries that have socially and economically responsible policies, efficient institutions, and able and honest governance. As a result, the international community has allocated larger quantities of aid, and the effectiveness of aid in poverty reduction has risen sharply. For some skeptics, however, the largesse of rich countries is politically motivated. It is claimed to be another gesture for perpetuating the practices of colonialism, economic imperialism, and political hegemony.

Simply expressed, national development is a process by which a poor country tries to develop its economy by making institutional reforms, building its infrastructure, and improving the governance of its chosen economic system. Sustainable and effective policies for protecting the country's environment and cultural diversity are aspects of developing tourism. However, they are also parts of the national development process.

Preconditions for sustainable tourism development, its planning and its successful execution, are the subjects of the following chapters. The single most important message of this book concerns the relevance of tourism development within the context of national development in a developing country or region. *If tourism can help reduce poverty and have desirable and sustainable economic, social, cultural, and environmental impacts, then tourism is worthy of resource allocation. Conversely, if tourism fails to pass the sustainability test and its relevance for national development is not proven, resources of the country should not be allocated to developing tourism.*

1.2   THE WORLD BANK STRATEGY FOR ELIMINATING POVERTY

Poverty is a fact of life for 2.5 billion people who subsist on earnings of $2 a day in less developed countries (LDCs) located mostly in Africa, Asia, and Latin America. One billion people survive on less than $1 a day. The gross national product (GNP) of LDCs is less than 1% of the world GNP. Per capita income (PCI) in LDCs is less than 5% of those found in developed countries that are located mostly in North America and Western Europe.

Often, the poor lack opportunity and a voice. They are vulnerable to sickness, violence, and natural disasters. They lack basic services provided to almost all persons in richer countries. These services include education, access to primary health care, livable secure shelter, and clean drinking water. Extending the life expectancy and controlling the population increase are serious issues to be resolved. Other issues awaiting resolution include political instability, exploding urbanization, corruption, slow capital flow, poor infrastructure, low savings, limited exports, ever-increasing foreign debt, and physical isolation of the poor in confined and unsafe settlements.

Theories and strategies for eliminating poverty abound. Some center on promoting economic development by expanding the productive capacity of the country or a region and by producing goods and services that the people want and can afford. Others emphasize land and tax reforms and import substitution. Economic development involves more than working with economic variables. It includes changing the technological and institutional arrangements and modifying certain cultural values and attitudes. Often nongovernmental organizations (NGOs) are required to carry out needed social and relief activities leading to changes. In recognition of the enormous challenge involved in reducing global poverty, the international development community has adopted specific targets. In most cases, these targets have immediate and direct relevance for planning and developing tourism.

Since 1990, the World Bank has embraced continuous basic goals for its development program. The bank summarizes the common targets of the international development community as follows:

Goal 1   Eradicate extreme poverty and hunger.

Goal 2   Achieve universal primary education.

Goal 3   Promote gender equality and empower women.

Goal 4   Reduce child mortality.

Goal 5   Improve maternal health.

Goal 6   Combat HIV/AIDS, malaria, and other diseases.

Goal 7 Ensure environmental sustainability.

Goal 8 Develop a global partnership for development.

Source: International Bank for Reconstruction and Development/The World Bank: *The World Bank Annual Report 2008, The Year in Review,* p. 17.

The World Bank's research indicates that in order to achieve a significant reduction in poverty, the average per capita GDP growth rate for LDCs has to be sustained at 3.6% a year, or twice the 1990s average of 1.8%. This kind of growth rate can be achieved only when a country's overall development policy is sound, its institutions are strong, its private sector is vibrant, its government and people are committed to necessary reform, and cultural harmony and political stability exist within its borders. It is critical for the country's development officials to understand that economic growth depends on four major groups working closely and supporting one another. These groups are the private sector, government, NGOs, and people. Taking this into account, the World Bank's strategy has been to build the social-economic-political climate conducive to capital investment, job creation, sustainable growth, and investment in poor people. This strategy also recognizes that some of the most pressing issues transcend national borders and are best addressed globally. Thus, the first dimension of tourism development is the growing integration of economies and societies around the world resulting from increased flows of goods, services, capital, people, and knowledge.

Some of the fastest-growing LDCs are those that have made serious efforts to increase these flows to and from advanced economies. China in particular, as well as Bangladesh, India, Uganda, and Vietnam, are among the successful examples of this movement. For LDCs and many other developing countries, the strategy for economic development also centers on the second dimension of establishing mixed economic systems and joining the world economic community through global trade. Developing tourism is an important part of this process. Its importance depends on the availability of tourism resources and the comparative advantage that countries have over competing countries for the same international tourist expenditures and visitors. A third dimension of developing tourism is the ability to sustain an optimum balance between the demands of tourism and the resources of the country that can be allocated to tourism without creating social, economic, and environmental imbalances.

The World Bank recognizes that the private sector and poor people themselves are the two major contributors to the alleviation of poverty in the world. Consequently, the bank has established the following strategic priorities for its actions:

- Build the economic conditions for investment, jobs, and sustainable growth.
- Invest in poor people and empower them to participate in development.
- Reach across country boundaries and address issues regionally and globally.
- Improve management and finance practices.

The World Bank's approach to poverty reduction is tailored to each country's particular circumstances. The model is based on the country's vision, a favorable prognosis for the policies proposed, and programs that support these policies. The programs are focused on the investment climate, public sector governance, empowerment, security, social inclusion, education, and health.

Poverty reduction in low-income countries is particularly challenging. Often, where poverty is greatest, institutional limitations are severe, policymaking rigidly restricts private investment, and access to resources is most difficult. Recently, the World Bank has adopted a new poverty reduction strategy. It is founded on the principle that the strategy will be results oriented, comprehensive, long-term in perspective, and designed to foster domestic and external partnerships. The strategy is prepared by the countries themselves, relying on broad-based participatory processes involving their citizens. It will have a simple format at first and will be updated every few years.

In 1999, the British government's Department for International Development adopted the approach and term **pro-poor tourism**. This approach, which stresses paying greater attention to the role that tourism development can play in reducing poverty, has been instrumental in defining various aid policies that international aid donor agencies now use. One of its influences has been to encourage the preparation of written national poverty reduction strategies to guide tourism and other investments in countries receiving economic aid. This topic is treated again as a postscript on poverty reduction following Chapter 17.

A second World Bank primary initiative is to ease the transition of middle-income countries' economies to fully functioning market economies. These countries have access to international capital markets, which enhances the availability of private investment, strengthens the investment climate, and establishes efficient social programs geared to building human capital and providing equality of access to economic opportunities. Market-opening reforms are tied to social reforms; thus, together, they improve the investment climate for both domestic and foreign investors. The bank uses several instruments to leverage the private sector, including offering partial credit and partial risk guarantees.

The complexity and scale of global poverty makes it imperative that governments, NGOs, multilateral and bilateral organizations, the private sector, and civil organizations join forces and work together in harmony. This is a management challenge that countries' governments must succeed in meeting.

It must be noted here that the economic crisis the world is now undergoing can, and probably will, change the structure of this poverty reduction model as we know it. It is impossible to predict where changes will occur and where tourism will fit in the new model. But it is certain that tourism will prevail as a vibrant industry in one form or another during the coming decades. The world economies depend on it, principally because of the very large size of tourism activities.

1.3 SUSTAINABLE TOURISM AS AN AGENT FOR REDUCING POVERTY

In reducing poverty, developing regions have a strong case for promoting tourism. One reliable source, the United Nations World Tourism Organization (UNWTO), counted forty-nine LDCs having an interest in developing tourism. In addition, many more regions and destinations in all developed and developing countries are striving to benefit from tourism. According to UNWTO, tourism is the principal product of 83% of developing countries. "Emerging destinations in developing countries have registered significant advances over the last years. In 2008, foreign exchange earnings generated by international tourism in developing countries exceeded 260 billion US$, six times the amount earned in 1990" (reported by UNWTO in its *Worldroom Travel Digest*).

The *Worldroom Travel Digest* also reports that by 2005, LDCs' share of all international passenger arrivals had grown from 28.6% to 40.3% since 1990. Furthermore, from 2000 to 2005, LDC international tourism receipts grew by 76% compared to worldwide growth of 41%. UNWTO estimates that tourism can generate up to 40% of the gross domestic product (GDP) and jobs of small island states, and for LDCs (the fifty poorest countries, mostly in Africa) the rate of growth in tourism arrivals from 2000 to 2005 was 48%, which almost tripled the global growth rate. By following these trends closely, UNWTO has aided in the adoption of a sustainable approach to long-term tourism development and management for all nations.

The definition of poverty has important implications for reducing it. Often, poverty is described in economic terms—for example, annual household or per capita income. It is sometimes defined as the possession of basic survival goods. It can also be defined as the lack of tangible and intangible elements of well-being. These elements can be expressed in terms of insufficient monetary income or barter opportunities; inadequate access to health care, education, and acceptable sanitary conditions; lack of job opportunities for the unskilled; and a sense of powerlessness, insecurity, and vulnerability.

Substantially reducing poverty in LDCs will require large amounts of public and private capital. This capital will most likely come in the form of investments from private sources in wealthier countries and from international finance organizations. Sources of private capital will seek profitability of investments and repayment of loans. Loans from public funds will have many contingencies and conditions attached to them. Donors will demand that funds given by them achieve measurable results. In turn, the citizens of receiving countries will be impatient to see tangible improvements in their living conditions within a short time. Corruption aside, these expectations will be difficult to reconcile. The quality of investment projects, as well as their location, transparency, implementation, sustainability, and environmental and social impacts, will be closely scrutinized. Ill-conceived, poorly executed projects and corruptive influences will impede the desired effects of tourism development and will test the system.

LDCs not only anticipate material benefits from tourism, but also seek cultural acceptance and parity with the cultures of tourists in exchange for the welcome extended. However, conventional wisdom suggests that excessive cultural pride could turn into hostility toward tourists. The attitude of the host toward guests could change when a certain capacity limit is reached, frictions begin to occur, and hosts no longer welcome guests, albeit paying ones. The message is that indiscriminate tourism growth and opening new destinations without proper planning and development could have serious long-term negative impacts on the environment, social structure, and culture of receiving areas. It is only when the principle of sustainability is applied that tourism can achieve lasting and desirable impacts.

What is **sustainable tourism development?** In 2004, UNWTO defined it as follows:

Sustainable tourism development guidelines and management practices are applicable to all forms of tourism in all *types of destinations, including mass tourism and the various niche tourism segments. Sustainability principles* refer to the environmental, economic, and socio-cultural aspects of tourism development, and a suitable balance must be established between these three dimensions to guarantee its long-term sustainability.

Thus, sustainable tourism should:

1. Make optimal use of environmental resources that constitute a key element in tourism development, maintaining essential ecological processes and helping to conserve natural heritage and biodiversity.
2. Respect the socio-cultural authenticity of host communities, conserve their built and living cultural heritage and traditional values, and contribute to inter-cultural understanding and tolerance.
3. Ensure viable, long-term economic operations, providing socio-economic benefits to all stakeholders that are fairly distributed, including stable employment and income-earning opportunities and social services to host communities, and contributing to poverty alleviation.

Sustainable tourism development requires the informed participation of all relevant stakeholders, as well as strong political leadership to ensure wide participation and consensus building. Achieving sustainable tourism is a continuous process and it requires constant monitoring of impacts, introducing the necessary preventive and/or corrective measures whenever necessary. Sustainable tourism should also maintain a high level of tourist satisfaction and ensure a meaningful experience to the tourists, raising their awareness about sustainability issues and promoting sustainable tourism practices amongst them.

Source: United Nations World Tourism Organization. Web site: http://www.unep.fr/scp/tourism/sustain/

The underlying single assumption behind sustainable tourism for reducing poverty is that the benefits of tourism must be distributed fairly among the regions and segments of the society. To achieve these benefits and ensure their fair distribution, poor regions must plan wisely. Therefore, regardless of their economic systems, they will have to observe certain ground rules in planning sustainable tourism:

- While benefits from tourism are received in the immediate future, natural, historical, cultural, and other resources are protected for the long-term future.
- Tourism development is planned and managed in a way that will not cause social and environmental damage in the near or long term.
- Tourism development enhances environmental quality and social well-being wherever it occurs so that tourism destinations retain their marketability and competitive advantage.
- Tourism development and management is an integral part of the national and regional development process.

In following these guidelines, many technical questions are raised. Determining how, where, and when tourism should be developed requires more than guidelines. Understanding what tourism is, what its elements are, how it grows, and how it impacts developing areas are among the questions to be answered in establishing a theoretical framework for planning its development. More information on sustainable tourism can be found on the Web site http://en.wikipedia.org/wiki/Sustainable_tourism.

1.4 COMPARATIVE ECONOMIC SYSTEMS

The collapse of the Soviet Union and its associated states in Eastern Europe during the late 1980s and early 1990s triggered a transition from command to market economies for one-third of the world's population. The long-term goal of this transition is to build a new economic system following the principles of market economies that thrive and are capable of delivering sustained growth in living standards.

Pursuit of better lives, however, had been going on for many decades before the collapse of the Soviet Union and its satellites. After the demise of the Communist system, adopting market systems was the obvious choice for predominantly poorer countries. Zbigniew Brzezinski, former director of the National Security Council during President Jimmy Carter's administration in the late 1970s, saw the collapse of central planning and the gradual transition to a market system taking place in four stages:

1. *Communist totalitarianism*, in which the Communist Party controls the political system that, in turn, controls the society and the economy.
2. *Communist authoritarianism*, in which the Communist Party controls the political system but society contests it and political supremacy is on the defensive.

3. *Post-Communist authoritarianism*, an authoritarian regime based on nationalistic appeal, where ideology is ritualized and civil society becomes a politicized society.
4. *Post-Communist pluralism*, in which political and socioeconomic systems become pluralistic. This is where the former Communist countries and Communist-leaning poorer countries are heading today.

There were many, and for some, inevitable reasons for the collapse of central planning and the Communist economic system:

- State enterprises placed priority on achieving the goals of the central plan rather than profitability.
- Central planning did not promote improvements in efficiency and productivity in all facets of the economy.
- Central planning created serious environmental problems by neglecting conservation and ignoring safeguards.
- Central planning lacked the backup market-oriented institutions like legal and accounting standards, marketing and strategic planning capabilities, inventory control, and profitability information.

Since the early 1990s, the transition from centrally planned economies to market economies has progressed at different speeds in different countries. Countries of Eastern Europe, including Poland, Hungary, and the Ukraine, and in the Far East, China, have made successful and speedy shifts toward market economies. However, the shock therapy tried in Russia in the early 1990s was disastrous. During privatization, old guard Communist managers of state enterprises transformed themselves into corporate officers and major shareholders. They bid for and bought some of the major state assets for little or nothing. They reaped enormous gains while old pensioners and other salaried Russians became penniless. Crime and corruption were rampant. Toward the end of President Boris Yeltsin's term, experimentation with shock therapy ended. It gave way to a gradual transformation more in tune with the character and conditions of the country. The state assumed a stabilizing and supporting role. This was the beginning of a state-assisted mixed economy.

The process for transforming economies around the world from centrally planned systems to market systems is evolving. The transition stage, or mixed economy, is taking different shapes and shades in each developing country. A four-step process is emerging:

1. *Macroeconomic stabilization and control.* This phase involves developing fiscal and monetary government policies that will stabilize the external and internal macroeconomic conditions of the economy.
2. *Price and market reform.* This phase aims at reducing state controls over the goods and services coming from international trade (including tourism) and reforming the banking system.
3. *Privatization and enterprise restructuring.* This phase involves establishing ownership rights for individuals and private businesses over previously state-owned agricultural, industrial, and residential assets by breaking up state monopolies and closing unprofitable state enterprises.
4. *Creating a new role for the state.* This phase involves changing the role of the state from direct ownership and control of economic assets, production, and distribution to providing support by assuming responsibilities that the private sector cannot handle. This includes reforming the administration of the government, adopting a new legal system, writing new tax laws, providing social and economic infrastructure, and creating financial incentives.

At this stage of their development, mixed-economy systems seem to be a better fit for the needs and abilities of many impoverished countries. Attempting to switch to the free-market system without a transition has proven to be a serious mistake. After choosing their transitional mixed-economy systems, these countries are now turning their attention to the factors causing poverty and to reforming their economic systems.

For these countries, the transition from centrally planned systems to market systems entails many changes:

- Resource allocation made through central planning will be made by the market.
- Resources owned by the state will be owned by private companies.
- Prices established by the state will fluctuate and will be determined by the market.
- Income distribution determined by the state will be achieved by the market.
- Profit determined by state guidelines will be determined by the market.
- Money and banking systems owned by the state will be owned privately.
- Public finance supplied by the state will be decentralized to other sources.
- Industrial organizations owned by the state will be owned privately.
- Agricultural estates owned by the state will be owned privately.
- Centralized government structure will be decentralized to substructures.
- One political party controlling the state will become many independent parties.
- Laws of the system will be changed to recognize business and property rights.
- Dictating economic terms will give way to market signals and competition.
- Paternalistic social systems will become more individualized.
- Labor unions controlled by the state will become independent.
- State-controlled ideological education and curricula will be controlled by local governments and private institutions representing public interest groups.

During this transition, privatized and individualized tourism will be introduced and mass tourism will become responsive to individual preferences. Privately owned resorts and destinations, which the individual vacationer will select from among competing destinations, will replace state-owned and operated recreation/vacation destinations for mass tourism. Resorts where the state elite class, or *nomenklatura*, has received special VIP treatment in the past, and others where busloads of state employees are sent by their organizations to have their vacations, will be privatized.

1.5 TOURISM AS A PRODUCTION AND CONSUMPTION PROCESS

As an industry, tourism is composed of a product and services related to it. The product is the combination of **attractions** and **facilities** from which tourists derive benefits in the form of satisfying experiences and by "consuming" the product through performing **activities** of their choice. Tourism is the result of a production process undertaken by tourism establishments and government organizations comprising the **tourism sector** of the economy. These entities produce the **tourism product** that tourists want to consume. Then tourists perform certain utilitarian and recreational activities to derive the desired tourism experience from the tourism product. Depending on the complexity of the tourism economy, attractions and facilities owned and operated by a large variety of establishments are selected from among primary or extraction, secondary or processing, tertiary or production, and quaternary or service industries.

As early as 1970 and 1971 (see Kastarlak, "Tourism and Its Development Potential in Massachusetts" [1970] and "Planning Tourism Growth" [1971] in the Bibliography), Bulent Kastarlak identified two principal characteristics of tourism that he considered fundamental to understanding the dynamics of the tourism industry:

- The first characteristic of tourism is that *it is not a traditional industrial sector*, at least not presently. UNWTO is in the process of defining what constitutes the tourism sector. For the purpose of this book and the planning techniques presented in it, the tourism sector is defined as an **overlapping sector** composed of establishments selected from many related industry categories. Using the United States, Canada, and Mexico as a model, tourism industries and establishments are selected from industrial categories classified by the North American Industrial Classification System (NAICS). The composition of the industry can change, depending on the characteristics of the tourism product and the socioeconomic circumstance of each particular location around the world.
- The second characteristic that differentiates tourism from other forms of production is that *its product can be consumed only at its place of production*. Unlike other products, the tourism product cannot be physically transported from the place of its production to the localities where tourists have their permanent residences. As an illustration, tourists cannot order the tourism product from the factory, or from the catalogue of a distributor, and have it delivered to their address. Tourists, originating from near or far, internationally or domestically, have to travel to the place of production, where the product is located. After traveling to the place of production and consuming the product locally, tourists can take the **experience**, and whatever other **material acquisitions** they may have made, back to the places where they live.

In light of these observations on fundamentals, planning and developing tourism presents special challenges and warrants reconsideration of classic thinking and research methods. Implications of this rethinking include the following:

- As a reversal of international or interregional domestic trade, tourism involves a destination as an independent economic entity in a country, *exports tourism experiences* and associated material goods from the place of production, and *imports visitors and money* from the rest of the world. The growth of the tourism economy depends, therefore, on increasing the number of incoming tourists and the money they bring to the destination for discretionary spending.
- In understanding the tourism industry, the process of tourism has to be reconstructed from its behavioral origin, that is, the **motivation** to travel and consume; through its phase of selecting the product and consuming it, that is, the **experience**; to its ultimate end result, that is, **satisfaction/utility**. For this, a new vocabulary and definitions have to be developed and a logical chain and a network of corollary elements have to be built, including attractions, facilities, activities, seasonality, levels of interest, and many other factors.
- After dissecting the body of tourism into its elements, the *reverse process* of building a new body from its elements must be used for creating an attraction, a new destination, and groups of activities associated with both for a given location and climate. This reverse process is the essence of tourism development planning.

The following chapters of the book will expand on these subject areas.

1.6   THE DEMONSTRATION EFFECT OF TOURISM AND SOCIAL CHANGE

An important aspect of tourism is its great potential for providing firsthand information about, and exposure to, different cultures. This exchange applies both to traveling tourists and to receiving host populations at the destination. The interaction between the two portrays the norms, values, social structure, and social organization of both parties (tourists and hosts). During that interaction, tourists and their hosts are expected to behave according to the norms of their sometimes vastly different cultures. Where there is correspondence between the two cultures, playing the prescribed roles of "host" and "guest" will not require major social adjustment. Between highly divergent cultures, however, adjustment may be more extensive.

In planning and developing tourism, a lesson learned from elementary sociological inquiry is that from every broadly defined social structure, a different set of relationships, rankings, associated behaviors, and values emerge. Carried down from broad societal characteristics to simple everyday relationships, human contact conforms to certain norms or models of behavior befitting the environment in which tourism takes place. In extremely contrasting cases, bringing the visitor and the visited together through tourism could ignite a clash of cultures, or the contrast could instigate a meeting of the two by moving from both directions to a place somewhere in the middle by a process of social change. The first of such experiences observed by locals at the tourism destination is encapsulated in the **demonstration effect**.

The demonstration effect could take place spontaneously or it could be planned. Relationships, existing social structure, values, and behavioral changes enter into the process of training local population and achieving the desired effects of social change through tourism development. In setting an example, conducting a demonstration, and creating the environment desirable for exposing one culture to another, that of the visiting tourist and that of the receiving destination, both the host and guests have to behave according to certain accepted norms.

Tourism often takes place in an environment where two different sets of values, cultures, and preferences come face to face. These two sets constitute the social ecology of tourism. Tourists enter the environment with some but often limited knowledge of what awaits them at their destination. Expectation of the unknown is one of the lures of tourism. The challenge for tourism development planners is to inform tourists' perception of reality. This is accomplished by tourism marketing. Informing tourists about what to expect from the thrilling or fulfilling experiences awaiting them at the destination and illustrating the traits of the local culture are parts of the familiarization process carried out through marketing.

Tourists can express different sentiments toward tourism experiences in urban or rural environments. They may show a preference for the virtues of rural life, folk culture, and the marvels of nature. Alternatively, they may be attracted to the sophistication and history of urban areas. In both cases, they may be repelled by the masses of people in crowded cities, social disorganization, crime, disease, mental disorder, addiction, and inhospitality or prejudice of local populations toward outsiders and tourists.

At the receiving end, local populations may begin to adopt foreign music, films, dressing styles, food, manners, habits, and even vocabulary. The demonstration effect may eventually lead to a loss of authenticity of local culture and to the destruction of the local environmental and historical heritage. While these changes may be welcomed by local populations, strangely, they may reduce the satisfaction and market appeal for tourists. (The case of Nepal is particularly informative. Please see this case study at the end of the book.)

Rural and urban social structures are based on recurring relationships in a network of persons and designated sets of social units. A social organization functions by having its members engage in relationships to achieve common goals. Agreement and equilibrium between the parties may not be permanent. They are established for a particular mission or for solving a particular problem. Tourism interacts with the established social structure and introduces new problems to be solved.

Efficiency of the social organization requires units and persons to work together and achieve common goals. However, all participants may not always work together or know each other. Different shifts composed of different individuals may carry on the work, yet they may be unaware of what is going on at all times. Within a particular social organization, persons designated as leaders attempt to comprehend and control all causal relations that affect the efficiency of activities in the organization. Going to the top and reaching these leaders makes sense if understanding the culture and expectations of tourists is an issue and changing the attitude of the locals toward them is a necessity.

Within the context of tourism, cultural systems, environmental systems, and behavioral systems are all subjects of social organization and activities. Cultural systems are composed of knowledge, values, customs, and beliefs held by individual persons. Culture is a learned behavior; one is not born with it. It need not be uniform, however, or integrated, or shared by all persons, or transmitted by an inflexible social heredity. Environmental systems contain everything nonsocial. They deal with physics, chemistry, and nonhuman biology. Physical events can affect social behaviors, and behaviors can affect cultural and environmental systems. Behavioral systems are the subject of the social psychology of tourism. Groups or individuals within social organizations manage situations dealing with purposive behavior, learning, personality formation, and perception by using techniques of social psychology.

Bringing all of this together, human ecology has its roots in social sciences. It employs sociology, psychology, anthropology, economics, and political science in explaining human behavior. It explicitly considers social organization and social structures that aggregate social concepts, and it explains the causal relationships between the biophysical environment and social organizations.

A **social structure** consists of a set of consistently repeated social relationships among groups, individuals, or positions. Expanding the concept further, **social stratification** is a subclass of social structure, or a ranking system, among the participants in social relationships. The behavior of each group, individual, or position determines the rank in the stratification system. Direct measures of ranking include the indicative behaviors and values associated with education, income, occupation, reputation, cultural styles or lifestyles, physical appearance, and subjective psychological identification.

What is important in this process is the ranking of decision makers. To achieve social change, the highest-ranking groups or individuals are recruited. Their influence in mobilizing, condoning, and supporting social change, which they consider desirable, is essential. In traditional LDCs, for example, it may not be productive to introduce a new model of behavior toward tourists unless the highest-ranking person or group in the hierarchy of the local social structure, possibly the tribal chief, spiritual leader, local mayor, or minister of the government, endorses such a model.

Tourism can play an important role in introducing and propagating social change where such change is desirable and its consequences are predictable. The opposite is equally important. If social change through tourism results, for example, in placing the population of a destination in a permanently subservient role, resulting in the loss of self-respect, and turning traditional hospitality into commercial opportunism, the price of social change may be high.

1.7 DEFINITIONS OF "TOURISM" AND "TOURIST"

Having briefly considered the relevance of tourism in reducing poverty; touched on the sociology of tourism development related to the sustainability of tourism within national development; and very briefly explored the economic systems in which tourism development takes place, we can now turn to what tourism is and who tourists are.

It is important to clearly define what tourism is and who tourists are as a minimum criterion for statistical purposes. In 1937, a Council of the League of Nations recommended a definition of the **international tourist**. More recently, the 1991 Ottawa Conference of the UNWTO made a series of statistical definition recommendations. Two years later, the United Nations Statistical Commission adopted a set of definitions that many countries and regions used. In 2004, the commission decided that further work and revisions were desirable. Further work was produced, and in 2007 an expert group on tourism statistics met and endorsed the revised recommendations. They were presented in *International Recommendations for Tourism Statistics 2008* (published in 2010). Recommendations include the following definitions:

- **Travel** refers to the activity of travelers. A **traveler** is someone who moves between different geographic locations for any purpose and any duration.
- Travel within a country by residents is called **domestic travel**. Travel to a country by nonresidents is called **inbound travel**, whereas travel outside a country by residents is called **outbound travel**.
- **Traveler**: Those who undertake travel, be it domestic, inbound or outbound, will be called domestic, inbound or outbound travelers, respectively.
- A **trip** refers to the travel by a person from the time of departure from his/her usual residence until he/she returns: it thus refers to a **round trip**. A **trip** is made up of visits to different places.
- An **inbound trip** will correspond to the travel between arriving in a country and leaving, whereas a **domestic trip** or an **outbound trip** will correspond to the travel between leaving the place of residence and returning. A **domestic trip** has a main destination in the country of residence of the traveler, while an **outbound trip** has a main destination outside this country.
- A **visitor** is a traveler taking a trip to a main destination outside his/her usual environment, for less than a year, for any main purpose (business, leisure or other personal purpose) other than to be employed by a resident entity in the country or place visited. These trips taken by visitors qualify as tourism trips. **Tourism** refers to the activity of visitors.
- A domestic, inbound or outbound traveler on a tourism trip is called a domestic, inbound or outbound visitor, respectively.
- Furthermore, the travel of domestic, inbound or outbound visitors is called domestic, inbound or outbound tourism, respectively.
- Tourism is therefore a subset of travel and visitors are a subset of travelers. These distinctions are crucial for the compilation of data on flows of travelers and visitors and for the credibility of tourism statistics.
- A **visitor** (domestic, inbound or outbound) is classified as a **tourist** (or **overnight visitor**) if his/her trip includes an overnight stay, or as a **same-day visitor** (or **excursionist**) otherwise.

Source: United Nations Statistical Commission, *International Recommendations for Tourism Statistics*, 2010, pp. 9–10.

The definitions are broadly stated and are further defined and discussed in the United Nations *Tourism Statistics* 2008 report. Yet, they are definitive enough to separate tourists from nontourists. One element common to all definitions is the act of traveling, which must be present in order for the individual to consume the tourism product at the place of its production. Another common element is the duration of the experience necessary for the act of consuming the tourism product. That duration is qualified, at a minimum, as one night for overnight visitors or tourists (excluding day trippers or excursionists) and, at a maximum, as twelve months for all other tourists. A third qualifier used to be a narrower purpose of leisure pursuits that tourists would have for traveling. The United Nations definition of 2008 continued the 1993 adoption of a broader purpose for tourism including leisure, business, and related activities. This broader definition reflects the worldwide scope and diversity of pursuits in the emerging industry.

Further detailed discussion of the definition of tourism can be found on the Wikipedia Web site mentioned above and, more briefly, on the following Web site: http://www.prm.nau.edu/prm300/what-is-tourism-lesson.htm.

1.8 WORLD TOURISM TRENDS

In view of the above discussion, where does tourism fit in the world economy? Today, domestic and international tourism combined is recognized as one of the world's largest and fastest-growing industries in terms of volume of income and employment generated. One indicator expressing the growth of tourism is the increase in the number of international tourist arrivals. Over the past several years, annual international arrivals were uneven among the destination regions of the world. In 2000, Africa received only 1% of the world tourist arrivals. The Middle East followed with 3%, South Asia with 4%, the East Asia/Pacific region with 16%, and the Americas with 19%. More than half of the arrivals (57%) were in Europe. UNWTO estimates that these shares will progressively change and equalize in favor of all destinations outside of Europe by 2020. Europe will receive 45% of tourist arrivals and other regions, with the exception of Africa, will continue to receive an ever-increasing share of arrivals by 2020.

According to UNWTO, the annual growth rate in international world tourist arrivals will rise from 3.2% in 2000 to 4.5% by 2020. The Americas will receive 4.0%, the East Asia/Pacific region 7.2%, the Middle East 6.7%, and South Asia 5.8% of arrivals. Tourist arrivals will peak in East Asia, the Middle East, and South Asia by 2010 and will begin to decline by 2020. The growth of tourist arrivals in the Americas and Europe will see modest but consistent increases. Only the growth rate in Africa will show a continuous decline between 2000 and 2020.

Domestic and international tourism generated US$3.4 trillion worth of business and personal income in 1995, corresponding to 11% of the world's GDP. These businesses created employment for 212 million people, mostly in service jobs. Government income from businesses and jobs resulted in US$637 billion revenues around the world. Foreign exchange revenues alone amounted to US$443 billion, adding considerable new capital for investing in other sectors of the recipient countries' economies. In most countries, domestic tourism contributed more than international tourism to government revenues and employment.

In its *World Tourism Barometer* of June 2008, the UNWTO reported that international tourist arrivals reached 903 million in 2007, up 6.6% from 2006. Other key indicators from that report are:

- International tourism receipts rose to US$ 856 billion (euro 625 billion) in 2007, corresponding to an increase in real terms of 5.6% in 2006.
- Receipts from international passenger transport are estimated at US$ 165 billion, bringing total international tourism receipts, including those for international passenger transport (i.e., visitor exports), to over US$ 1 trillion, corresponding to almost US$ 3 billion a day.
- The top ten destinations by international tourist arrivals and international tourism receipts did not show any major changes. In arrivals, France was in first place, ahead of Spain and the United States, while in receipts the United States ranked first, France third, and Spain second. China and Italy alternated in fourth and fifth place, followed in both rankings by the United Kingdom and Germany.

- In the top ten ranking by international tourism spenders, China moved up to fifth position, after Germany, the United States, the United Kingdom, and France. Japan moved down to seventh position after Italy.
- Outbound tourism in the past years has been increasingly driven by emerging source markets.

One can draw several conclusions from these world tourism trends:

- *Leisure travel, and to an extent business travel, is a function of disposable income.*   The propensity for traveling increases when income is available for purchasing discretionary goods and services like tourism. As a result, international travel flows from richer to poorer countries. In domestic tourism, travelers originate from richer urban areas and go to poorer but interesting destination regions.
- *As disposable income grows in richer countries, international tourists increasingly demand more convenience and better service.*   In response, destinations must upgrade their facilities and provide better-trained personnel and operating procedures. A typical example is the trend toward larger and fully equipped cruise ships. The ship itself has become the major attraction and destination by offering a rich variety of recreational activities, excellent food, and meticulous attention to service.
- *Standards of facilities and services for domestic tourism may vary widely from the generally accepted international tourism standards.*   The standards of domestic tourism are based on the disposable income of the domestic population. When the difference between disposable incomes of international and domestic tourists is great, several sets of facility standards are used by the tourism industry. This differentiation is particularly applicable to hotels, where standards can range from five star to one star or less.
- *Personal security plays a major role in selecting a tourism destination.*   The steady growth of tourism in Europe, particularly Western Europe, and North America is caused not only by the rich variety of attractions and facilities, but also by a stable political climate and a high degree of personal security. Every travel advisory, political upheaval, violent event, war, and insurgency keeps tourists away from destinations where such conditions exist. Despite their rich environmental and historic attractions and their traditional hospitality, Africa, and the Middle East in particular, are susceptible to wide fluctuations in tourist arrivals.

International tourism is subject to conditions in destination countries and changing tourist preferences. The rate of currency exchange, for example, affects these conditions and preferences. Domestic tourism, in turn, depends on the lifestyles, business and recreational demands, and disposable income of the domestic population, as well as on government policies. For example, in China, government policy has played an important role in expanding domestic tourism. Since the government adopted in 1995 the "long holiday policy" of three-week vacations, the country has witnessed an explosion in the volume of domestic tourism.

When international and domestic tourism have widely different facility standards, they create two sets of tourism subcultures in the destination country. Some of the consequences of having two sets of tourism subcultures are the following:

- In destination countries with lower personal incomes, overnight accommodations built to international design standards of five-star and four-star hotels serve almost exclusively international visitors. Domestic tourists tend to stay at modestly priced three-star or lesser-quality hotels.
- Separation of domestic and international tourists often extends to housing. Gated high-rent housing compounds, sometimes surrounded by walls for extra security, create total

separation between visitors and the local population, and could lead to complicated social tensions and even a reverse ghetto syndrome.

- Free-spending international tourists could create two sets of commercial standards and two sets of prices, one for tourists and another, lower one for locals, thus producing a business ethic predisposed to haggling and overcharging. This practice gives a bad name to local merchants. It could hurt the image of the destination country in the eyes of foreign tourists and could negate the positive impact of tourism marketing.
- Domestic tourists may favor attractions and facilities that may not be the best choices of international tourists. Without guidance from the government, local entrepreneurs may invest scarce resources in poorly designed and built attractions and facilities in the hope that they will also, but often cannot, serve foreign visitors. Only backpacking young international and domestic tourists with little money to spend may find these facilities acceptable.

Justifiable concerns aside, emerging world trends are shaping new forms of tourism:

- As the educational and income levels of tourists increase, tourists are increasingly favoring intellectual pursuits and are seeking the greatest physical comfort in their travels and accommodations.
- An ever-increasing number of older tourists and retirees are traveling in groups to ensure security, convenience, camaraderie, cost savings, and comfort.
- Younger educated and affluent tourists are searching for new destinations where they can pursue new and challenging pursuits like adventure tourism.
- Nostalgia tourism is bringing international tourists back to their ancestral lands and to places where their cultural roots and family connections still endure.
- Sightseeing remains the main recreational activity for most tourists. It is growing in importance as world cultures and regions become increasingly accessible through television, the Internet, videos, and movies by offering previews of the world's best destinations.
- Special interest tourism, including cultural and religious pilgrimages, sports events, health spas and travel for medical treatment, professional meetings, conventions, trade shows, adventure, and ecotourism, is increasing.
- Changing vacation habits are beginning to favor shorter multiple vacations at different locations as opposed to one long vacation at a traditional destination.
- Business travel used to account for a sizable proportion of tourism. Recent technology has made live videoconferencing a common occurrence. As a result, executives may travel less often. Declines in business-related travel by air seem to confirm this observation. Unless face-to-face interaction is necessary for an important business decision, the time and money saved on traveling are increasingly important for business executives.
- Modern communication and virtual technology, including the Internet, are finding increasing numbers of applications in direct tourism marketing, travel planning, and educating both the traveling public and the host communities.
- When tourists bypass environmentally troubled areas in their home country or region, local authorities are learning to compensate by planning sustainable and environmentally sensitive and attractive destinations. In order to remain competitive, many underused and substandard tourist facilities and attractions are being restored or their uses changed to attract tourists.
- Ecotourism is evolving into a culture in itself. It is increasingly attracting environmentally and conservation-minded tourists.

With knowledge of what tourism has to offer in terms of reducing poverty, instigating social change, and sustaining the environment, the next question is, how should one proceed to achieve all three? In this, the invisible hand of capitalist market economies, and government–private sector collaboration in mixed economies in particular, play a guiding role.

1.9 TOURISM AS AN OVERLAPPING ECONOMIC SECTOR

Tourism as a large-scale activity, as defined earlier, is a latecomer on the world economic scene. At the beginning, tourism consisted of visiting a few major attractions and patronizing essential facilities. The process of change and expansion was slow and incremental. The industry started by adopting the three traditional necessities of eating, sleeping, and transportation. In addition to roadside shows, historic and natural attractions, restaurants, hotels, cars, trains, and ships were the original businesses of the tourism sector. Since the 1950s, advances in communication and air travel technology have made reservation and airline systems part of the red-hot tourism industry. When money began to roll in, other industries noticed. Advertising, entertainment, marketing, retailing, communication, and real estate followed to join the tourism bandwagon.

Today, the economic importance of tourism is recognized beyond a doubt. Nevertheless, what makes tourism an economic sector continues to be debated. The economic identity of tourism is still evolving. Various methods, including satellite accounts, are being tested and tried. The UNWTO has an ongoing study on the subject (Figure 1.1).

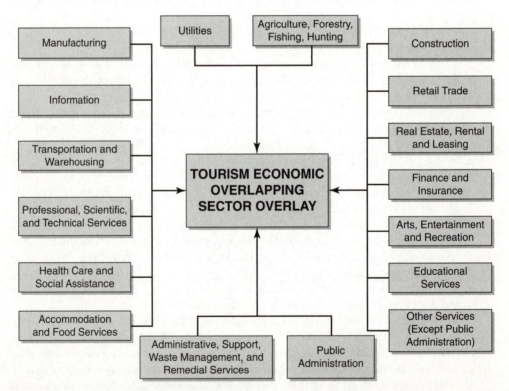

FIGURE 1.1 Overlay of the Tourism Economic Sector. Industries contributing to the tourism economic sector form an overlay sector. A detailed list of 232 tourism establishments selected from seventeen industries is given in Appendix B.

Source: Bulent I. Kastarlak.

Suffice it to say that the boundaries of the tourism industry are still being drawn. For the time being, its economic identity is defined by borrowing elements from various established economic sectors. Hence, the concept of **overlapping economic sectors** is useful. Until the matter is resolved, the tourism industry will continue to be defined differently to serve different purposes. (One such definition used by the BIK System, proposed by Bulent Kastarlak is presented in Appendix B and discussed in Chapter 11.)

1.10 ALLOCATION OF FACTORS OF PRODUCTION FOR TOURISM DEVELOPMENT

Economic development is the process by which scarce resources of countries and regions are allocated in rational quantities, at the right time, and at the right locations to achieve a better life for people. The scarce resources of countries and regions are divided into four categories: **capital**, **labor**, **materials**, and **knowledge**. These factors can be substituted for one another to some extent if one of them is not available in the quantities and qualities needed. In tourism development, materials include natural and human-made assets, as shown in Figure 1.2.

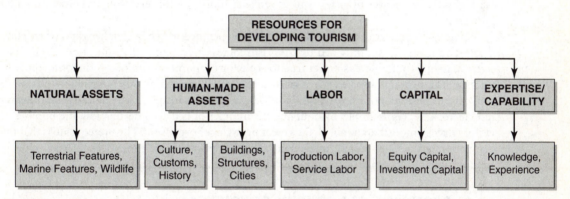

FIGURE 1.2   Resources for Developing Tourism. As in most economic activities, developable resources of tourism are composed of land; financial, intellectual, and human power (labor); and capital that shape available assets, whether they are human-made or natural. Most of these resources are renewable.
Source: Bulent I. Kastarlak.

In allocating its scarce resources, a country, region, or destination must answer six fundamental economic questions:

- *What* products will be produced?
- *How much of each* product will be produced?
- *Where* will the products be produced?
- *How* will the products be produced?
- *For whom* will the products be produced?
- *When* will the products be produced?

Different social systems solve these problems differently. In traditional societies, scarce resources are allocated according to traditions established after many decades of trial and error. As economies progress to transitional and advanced stages, allocation decisions are made by a supreme omnipotent authority or central planning agency, and finally, in advanced economies, by the free market and price system.

Allocation of resources would not be a problem if an infinite amount of every good could be produced, every service rendered, or every human want satisfied. Nor would it matter if the four factors of production were used unwisely, because there would be no scarcity of resources. In reality, however, no resource is available in an infinite amount. Even water, air, and land are available only in finite quantities.

Economic resources are scarce and therefore are not free. Society must choose among them, because not all needs and desires can be satisfied.

Tourism development is part of this selection process. For example, when full employment is the goal of the economic system, scarce resources are allocated for creating the maximum number of jobs that match the skill levels of the labor force. Tourism can create a large number of employment opportunities and thus help relieve the pressure for new jobs. But many of these are lower-skill and lower-paying jobs compared to jobs in other sectors. When the same resources are allocated in different proportions to achieve higher per capita income, jobs and income from tourism will not be sufficient to raise the per capita income appreciably. Another example is the national budget. When the government allocates more funds for building highways and power plants, it will have fewer funds for conservation and environmental protection.

The question is, can tourism development be planned to achieve higher rates of employment? The answer is yes, provided that tourism increases economic diversification. Other concerns remain. Would increasing returns to scale, or economies of mass production, apply to tourism? The answer is also yes. When labor, land, and all other inputs are prepared in the proper proportions and quantities, the result could be a higher multiplier. This is called **increasing returns to scale**. For example, by doubling the number of beds at a destination, the number of visitors may be more than doubled, thus creating cycles of expansion. The prerequisite is that the destination has the high-quality attractions and the capacity to add more beds to accommodate an increasing number of tourists while sustaining its environmental quality.

1.11 ECONOMIC GEOGRAPHY OF TOURISM AND THE THEORY OF CENTRAL PLACES

Economic activity occurs over the geography of the earth. The intimate relation between location and economic activity is evidenced by the flow of people, money, and goods. In 1894, Charles H. Cooley demonstrated that population and wealth tend to collect wherever there is a break in transportation (see the Bibliography). Historically, human settlements were located close to national borders, natural barriers, and transfer points. National borders, however, no longer constitute a barrier, at least in Western Europe, where the European Union removed national borders as barriers to trade and to the flow of goods, money, and people. Theoretically, even if the earth had a uniform surface, it would still have places where people would congregate. These points of congregation form a network of urban or **central places**, each surrounded by a service region, or market area, or hinterland. In advanced stages of congregation, these service regions overlap and create a megacity or metropolitan region.

The city–region service relationship is defined by central place theory, in which the region covers the production, market, and supply areas of the central place. Service functions of the city, like administration, police and fire protection, education, water, and sewer services, have overlapping areas.

- A central place is an urban center where economic activities originate and disperse to its service area, hinterland or region, around it.
- The relationship between the central place and its region is symbiotic. Reciprocal and complementary activities flow in both directions.
- Factors determining the perimeter of the service region may depend primarily on city–region relationships. But they may also be independent of those relationships. Factors determining the perimeter of the tourism region are often independent of these relations.

In a 1933 book called *The Central Places in Southern Germany,* geographer **Walter Christaller** advanced the central place theory (see the Bibliography). He proposed a geographic model showing how and where urban places in the urban hierarchy would be located with respect to one another. He identified the urban hierarchy, expressed as a range from the smallest to the largest urban places, as hamlets, villages, towns, and cities. At the time of his writing, Christaller had witnessed only the beginning of the urban phenomenon of the late nineteenth and early twentieth centuries that we now call the **megalopolis** (also known as **conurbanization** or the **megacity**). For illustration purposes, he pictured a hierarchy of urban centers, each having a hinterland shaped as a series of ever-larger hexagons enveloping the lower-level urban places to form an interrelated network of central places.

Centrality is the primary characteristic of urban centers. It signifies the agglomeration of human activities in one place. Christaller showed that:

- Urban centers have a rank order. Centers of various population sizes form a hierarchy over the geography of the land.
- If one center of this hierarchy is removed, the whole system will readjust itself to compensate for the functions the center had previously performed for its service area.
- Larger cities will be spaced farther apart than smaller towns and villages. The geographic pattern of urban centers is not an accident but a product of particular social-economic-physical forces that create the ordered network.

August Lösch, along with Christaller**,** was a developer of central place theory. In 1954 (see the Bibliography), he confirmed Christaller's theory and visualized an economic region enveloping a network of urban centers and their service areas. He demonstrated that the service areas surrounding every central place also create a hierarchy of their own. He recognized that certain specialized functions, owing to their specific site orientation and configuration, are clustered in certain districts. Tourist destinations and regions became one such type of district. They specialized in tourism. Today, tourism is accepted as a major urban function. The hierarchy of urban centers specializing in tourism, and their rural hinterland, constitute a network of tourism destinations within the independent perimeter of a tourism region. This theory of economic geography was relevant in the 1950s and it is still relevant in the early twenty-first century—that is, until a better theory replaces it or evolves from it. Tourism as a service industry fits in with this theory, because it has geographic and economic dimensions of its own.

Christaller divided the goods and services produced by central places into two classes:

- *Dispersed goods.*   Their production depends on the location of natural resources in the hinterland. Extraction industries like farming, ranching, mining, forestry, and fishing yield such goods. Products are almost exclusively exported and transported to second-level producers outside the region.
- *Central goods and services.*   Their production requires gathering dispersed goods and services from the hinterland. They are produced by primary and secondary industries, the

latter using the products of primary industries. Final products are largely exported and transported to third-level producers and consumers outside the region. Each of the levels adds value to the products processed.

Tourism has a reverse flow of products and consumers. The goods and services comprising the **tourism product** are largely found at the place of production, namely, at the destination region. They are stationary. It is the consumer (tourist) who has to travel and is transported to the destination in order to consume (use) the product. After consuming the product, tourists export or take away their experiences and a few gifts from the region.

The types or ranks of central places identified by Lösch and Christaller are given identifying names. Within the geopolitical context of Western Europe, they are referred to as **progressively larger market hamlets**, **township centers**, **county seats**, **district cities**, **small state capitals**, **provincial head cities**, and **regional capital cities**. The norms of population size, spacing of centers, and extent of the hinterland for these central places in the hierarchy are derived partly from empirical evidence and partly from deductive thinking.

The concept of **rank order of central places** can be applied to tourism planning for establishing a new set of dimensions and a rank order for tourism destinations within each tourism region. This will create a new perspective in looking at simple, noncomplex, and transitional regions where emerging urban centers and tourism destinations are beginning to take shape. Sensitivity to sustainable tourism will be an important consideration in selecting and developing new urban centers as tourism destinations. Existing and new urban centers will morph into a new hierarchy of tourism destinations and will have a new rank order.

Understanding of the system of urban centers as tourism destinations is still evolving. Following Christaller and Lösch, as early as 1955 **Edgar M. Hoover** postulated that any given collection of urban centers constitutes an empirically observable system and that a hierarchy, or ranking, of urban centers as a basis for urban and regional development planning is possible and useful (see the Bibliography).

In 1970, Bulent Kastarlak explored the possibility of applying central place theory to tourism planning. He ranked 351 urban places in Massachusetts according to their population size and correlated them with the size of **tourist attraction and facility mixes** in those urban places (see "Tourism and Its Development Potential in Massachusetts," 1970, in the Bibliography). The emerging geographic and statistical patterns were revealing and confirmed earlier impressions. Kastarlak found that urban centers having the largest tourism potential also had attraction and facility mixes that were disproportionately larger than warranted by their resident population. In other words, compared to nondestinations, tourism destination regions offered more services than their residents actually needed.

Regional planning literature is replete with research papers on the economic importance of urban places and **economic base analysis**. Before the arrival of the information technology age at the end of the twentieth century, the primary analytical concern was with urban functions based on the flow of goods and services associated with extraction, manufacturing, and service industries exchanged between the central place and its hinterland. Economic base analysis, however, did not include a special category for the information flow and the economic activities resulting from it.

The age of information technology added new dimensions to economic base analysis. Now, with the arrival of virtual reality technology, digitized communication, and computer analysis and simulation, it is possible to carry the tourist mentally to distant lands with great realism. As far as tourism is concerned, this realism alters the role of the central place considerably. Now, one can experience tourism and its many activities in distant lands by computer-aided digital imagery found on the Internet and in DVDs borrowed from the local public library. For example, traveling in space, flying a jet liner, and experiencing an earthquake and other disasters are simulated in theme park exhibits everywhere. NASCAR stockcar racing and surfing on Hawaiian beaches are simulated in many theme parks. Even the sail-shaped seven-star Burjalarab Hotel in Dubai, designed by W.S. Atkins, becomes an attraction and a destination in itself due to its architecture, and by simulating exotic experiences and incorporating a multitude of innovative computer-operated features in the building. Many such simulated destinations are found in Las Vegas, where virtual reality technology is serving as a major attraction along with gambling. By transporting tourists to make-believe destinations and experiences around the world, technology is advancing to a new level in tourism planning.

Nevertheless, aside from technological advances, the concept of central place and the hierarchy of urban centers plays an important role in understanding the economic geography of a tourism region. Application of regional planning concepts to tourism research and planning, particularly for economic development and social change, is awaiting further experimentation and adaptation.

In addition to economic issues, tourism development planning focuses on the elements of geography at the national, regional, and destination levels of planning. In addition to spatial and physical elements, geographic inquiry includes cultural elements such as language, food, clothing, political and social organizations, values, attitudes, religion, and visual and performing arts. Marine and terrestrial archeology and anthropology are also important subjects. These subjects are studied separately for their merits in creating new themes and destinations. All aspects of the tourism industry enter into planning at the national, regional, and destination levels to ensure sustainable tourism. These dimensions are explored in the following chapters.

Chapter Highlights

- There are two requirements for tourism development. First, tourism must be proven to have potential as an export industry for the host country, region, or destination. Second, it must be shown that investments in the tourism sector will lead to sustainable growth and socioeconomic change.

- Tourism has a product. However, this product is not transportable in the physical sense. It consists of attractions that draw tourists and facilities that provide tourists with a variety of support services.

- Changes in the world economy affect global tourism directly. The second half of the twentieth century was a period of unprecedented increase in living standards. Progress in communication and transportation technologies, as well as some increase in the amount of leisure time, enabled tourism to emerge as a major industry.

- Sustainable tourism protects the future of the local culture and the environment. It can be included in tourism plans for its own sake, and/or it can be a function of national development planning for reducing poverty. Often, the tourism sector leads growth in many LDCs, encourages entrepreneurship, and provides jobs that do not require extensive training relatively quickly.

- Reducing poverty is an increasingly important objective of tourism in LDCs. Pro-poor tourism has been defined and adopted as official policy by many governments and aid organizations involved in tourism development.

- All types of economic systems can develop tourism. Domestic and international tourism can be developed where potentials exist in central planned, mixed, and free-market economic systems.

- Tourism, like other economic activities, takes place over the geographic extent of a region.

Central place theory helps to explain how these activities interact and how tourism has its own central place and service area.

- International financial aid and technical assistance helped create the conditions necessary for social change, economic growth, and integration of the world economy. Tourism has often played a major role in this process.
- An important aspect of tourism is its great potential for exposure to different cultures. The results of this exposure are called the demonstration effect.
- In its 1993 convocation, the United Nations Statistical Commission adopted definitions for tourism, sustainable tourism, domestic tourism, international tourism, overnight visitor (tourist), same-day visitor (excursionist), inbound tourism, and outbound tourism, among others. These have been incorporated in more recent definitions.

2

Toward a General Theory of Tourism Planning and Development

The BIK System

This chapter introduces an approach to a general theory of tourism planning and development conceived by the author, Bulent I. Kastarlak, and first presented in the United States in 1970 in technical literature and forums. The approach[1] to a theory and its method of application, named by its author the **BIK System** (using his initials), is based on the dynamics of multidisciplinary relations among the elements of the tourism industry, characteristics of the tourism product, using the six-digit NAICS establishments making up the tourism sector of the economy. The system employs both custom and standard software. The software, data, and computer graphics form the essence of the Geographic Information System (GIS) for tourism planning. To review some essential principles presented in Chapter 1:

- Tourism is a series of experiences that make use of its product, which consists of attractions, facilities, and their related activities.
- To experience tourism, one has to travel to places where the tourism product is located. The tourism product is not transportable to places where tourists reside year round.
- The experiences of tourism are made possible by tourists performing certain recreational and utilitarian activities.
- Attractions draw tourists, and facilities serve them.
- Business establishments and government organizations own and operate tourist attractions and facilities that form the tourism sector of the economy.

---

[1]The term **approach to a theory** is used to indicate that the BIK System is not yet a full-fledged accepted theory, but that with work and refinement through applications, it may become an accepted theory for how to best conduct and analyze tourism planning and development.

2.1   FROM NEED THROUGH EXPERIENCE TO SATISFACTION

If one takes the very long-term view, the origins of tourism can be traced to **migration** that was required for survival in prehistoric times. It is commonly known that *Homo sapiens* emerged from North East Africa about one hundred fifty thousand years ago. Some sixty thousand years ago, the climate of Africa began to become less favorable, inducing early humans to move out from places like Olduvai Gorge in Tanzania in search of better living conditions elsewhere. By one account, early humans crossed over from Africa to the Arabian Peninsula over the strait of Bab el Mande. Many generations later, some moved north to Europe and east to Asia, then to Australasia, Polynesia, and the Americas. *Homo sapiens* wanted to explore and find new places where humans could survive. The need to survive led to exploration. Exploration, in turn, generated many experiences and activities. Most of these activities were **utilitarian**, like trekking and hunting. Others were **recreational**, like creating cave art. The cycle was complete when satisfaction prevailed. Many millennia later, both utilitarian and recreational activities have grown in diversity in keeping with social change and technology.

By the accepted definition of the term, tourists always return to their primary place of residence after a period not exceeding one year. Migrants do not. Therefore, the four requisites for tourism are, first, the *intent to return to one's place of origin*; second, the *motivation to travel* temporarily to distant lands; third, exploring distant lands by performing and *experiencing many activities*; and fourth, finding *satisfaction* at the end of this exploration before returning home. For migration, the requisites are different. Early hunter-gatherers traveled far to find food and shelter and never returned. They discovered agriculture, and the first urban settlements rose on the Fertile Crescent in Iraq. Later, when needs changed, human motivation changed with them. People traveled for material gain, conquest, spiritual enlightenment, family ties, and trade or to establish new settlements for controlling the territories conquered. Migration and tourism merged. Even today, some people settle in places they first visited as tourists.

In modern times, conquest and other antisocial behaviors are excluded from the scope of tourism. Only peaceful pursuits are included. The motivation for traveling long distances now derives from a much larger selection of peaceful needs. Compared to advances made in transportation technology over the past twenty centuries, rapid advances of the past two centuries have greatly increased the choices and purposes for travel. The dugout canoe, oared trireme, Chinese junk, horse, and horse-drawn carriage gave way to modern transportation. Trains, clipper ships, vehicles and vessels operating with steam, electric and internal combustion engines, and eventually propeller and jet aircraft were invented and continually improved. More on the history and development of tourism can be found on the following Web site: http://www.answers.com/topic/tourism.

As transportation technology and advancing civilization made traveling easier, new types of peaceful pursuits involving travel emerged. Today, attending a convention, taking a cruise, participating in ecotourism, sightseeing, and even yachting for pleasure are added to the popular activities of the past like visiting relatives, shopping, trading, and participating in a pilgrimage. The motivation to travel for purely utilitarian (i.e., business) reasons is now combined with, and has sometimes been replaced by, the motivation to travel for recreational purposes. The nature of tourism has shifted with changing needs, tastes, and technology. The age of survival and subsistence gave way to the age of affluence with the emergence of modern economic systems. The change is continuing. New modes of transportation, including rocket-propelled space vehicles, and new destinations, including space, are opening new markets for international and, not in the far distant future, interplanetary tourism. Nevertheless, the basic preconditions for tourism, *need-experience-satisfaction*, remain unchanged. The general principles for analyzing tourism emerge from this trilogy. Accordingly, the BIK System has the following definition for planning and developing tourism:

> *Tourism is the act of transporting the traveler to distant locations where his or her recreational and utilitarian needs can be satisfied through one or more experiences. These experiences are the result of certain recreational and utilitarian activities. The traveler is interested primarily in recreational activities, whereas utilitarian activities are necessary for facilitating and supporting recreational pursuits.*

2.2 TOURISM PRODUCT = ATTRACTIONS + FACILITIES + ACTIVITIES

The tourism product consists of **attractions** and **facilities**, which by definition include all kinds of infrastructure, as well as natural and human-made assets, plus recreational and service **activities** that make tourism experiences possible. From the description of the tourism product, the following characteristics of tourism emerge (Figure 2.1):

- The motivation to travel overnight to satisfy a recreational need, or a mix of recreational and utilitarian needs, differentiates the **tourist** from the **excursionist**. The latter takes short (day-long) recreational and utilitarian trips and returns to his or her primary residence without staying overnight.
- The length of travel for a tourist or excursionist is measured in units of time. For a tourist, it is a minimum of twenty-four hours, requiring an overnight stay. The maximum length

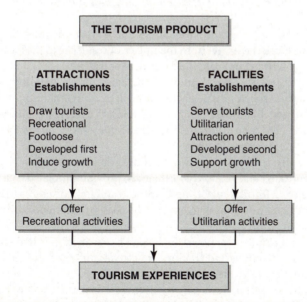

FIGURE 2.1   The Tourism Product. The total number of products and services offered by as many as 232 types of establishments, selected from the NAICS and representing the tourism section of a regional economy.

Source: Bulent I. Kastarlak

for residency does not exceed one year. For the excursionist, the maximum length of time away is less than twenty-four hours.

- When excursionists cannot find the desired tourism product necessary to satisfy their recreational needs at the location of their primary residence, they may be motivated to explore and travel longer distances. When the excursionist travels overnight, he or she becomes a tourist.
- When a tourist travels to a destination where the desired tourism product is located, he or she performs certain activities for consuming the product and for satisfying his or her needs.
- Attractions, and recreational activities associated with them, are the primary objective of tourism and the tourism experience. Facilities, and activities associated with them, provide comfort, convenience, and means for consuming the tourism product and for facilitating the recreational activity.
- Facilities, and service activities associated with them, make attractions function better and increase their productivity by delivering supporting services for the tourist. If they serve purposes unrelated to attractions, facilities do not serve a useful and productive purpose in the context of tourism.
- It follows that *attractions draw tourists* and *facilities serve them*. Facilities depend on attractions, and they support rather than induce tourism growth. However, as will be explained later, some facilities contain, or are combined with, attractions that draw tourists.
- Attractions dictate the location of tourism destinations, whereas locations for facilities are chosen to best serve attractions.
- Most **event attractions** are not geographically fixed. They can take place anywhere and can be created at any place temporarily. By contrast, **site attractions** have specific locations. They cannot be moved elsewhere, but they can be duplicated or simulated at other locations.
- Attractions are growth-inducing economic generators. They are the primary objectives of tourism development. *Without attractions, tourism is limited to those who travel only for travel's sake.*
- An appropriate mix and quality of facilities and attractions must be present to make it worthwhile for tourists to travel from their place of residence to the location of the destination and receive satisfaction from the tourism experience.
- Environmental assets, such as mountains, seas, lakes, forests, buildings, structures and cultural assets, such as social values, customs, and arts, are relevant to tourism planning only to the extent to which they contribute to the tourism experience. *Tourists choose to experience only what interests them,* but their sphere of interest can be broadened by exposure to additional features they encounter.
- Human-made attractions, like theme attractions where environmental and cultural factors are highly controlled and reduced to essentials, provide simulated tourism experiences at an affordable cost. Tourists may choose not to travel long distances to destinations where the original attractions are located, but may be content with reproductions or simulations of them closer to home.
- The drawing and competitive power of a tourism destination is highest where the quality and diversity of attractions and facilities are *blended* and their associated recreational and utilitarian activities are greatest.
- As in any economic sector, business establishments or government organizations own and operate the tourist attractions and facilities. These establishments or government organizations belong to an industry group classified by a system. In the BIK System, the NAICS is used.
- Tourism as an economic sector is defined in terms of establishments listed in the NAICS (Figure 2.2).

INDUSTRY SECTOR 11	Agriculture, Forestry, Fishing, and Hunting	5 establishments
INDUSTRY SECTOR 22	Utilities	5 establishments
INDUSTRY SECTOR 23	Construction	4 establishments
INDUSTRY SECTOR 31–33	Manufacturing	3 establishments
INDUSTRY SECTOR 44–45	Retail Trade	36 establishments
INDUSTRY SECTOR 48–49	Transportation and Warehousing	31 establishments
INDUSTRY SECTOR 51	Information	10 establishments
INDUSTRY SECTOR 52	Finance and Insurance	11 establishments
INDUSTRY SECTOR 53	Real Estate, Rental, and Leasing	12 establishments
INDUSTRY SECTOR 54	Professional, Scientific, and Technical Services	14 establishments
INDUSTRY SECTOR 56	Administrative, Support, Waste Management, and Remedial Services	17 establishments
INDUSTRY SECTOR 61	Educational Services	3 establishments
INDUSTRY SECTOR 62	Health Care and Social Assistance	9 establishments
INDUSTRY SECTOR 71	Arts, Entertainment, and Recreation	24 establishments
INDUSTRY SECTOR 72	Accommodation and Food Services	14 establishments
INDUSTRY SECTOR 81	Other Services (Except Public Administration)	21 establishments
INDUSTRY SECTOR 92	Public Administration	13 establishments
	Maximum:	**232 Tourism Establishments**

FIGURE 2.2 A List of the Overlay Tourism Economic Sector. Currently, the overlay tourism economic sector has not been defined officially by international tourism organizations. In the absence of a definition, the following industries and establishments were selected by the author from the NAICS to suggest the composition of the tourism sector with maximum complexity. Less complex sectors have fewer industries and establishments. Other industrial classification systems may be used where the NAICS is not applicable. A detailed list of 232 establishments is given in Appendix B.
Source: Bulent I. Kastarlak

2.3   THE SITE ATTRACTION AND EVENT ATTRACTION MIX OF THE TOURISM PRODUCT

The *American Heritage Dictionary* defines **attraction** as "a feature or characteristics that attract." *Webster's Dictionary* goes further. It states that "attraction implies the possession of one thing of a quality, or qualities that pulls another thing to it" (Figure 2.3).

Two types of attractions, one fixed and tangible (site attractions), the other movable and intangible (event attractions), draw tourists to a destination and to its tourism product.

- Site attractions have fixed locations, physical characteristics, tangible material substance, and structure. They may be natural or human-made, with attributes that would interest the

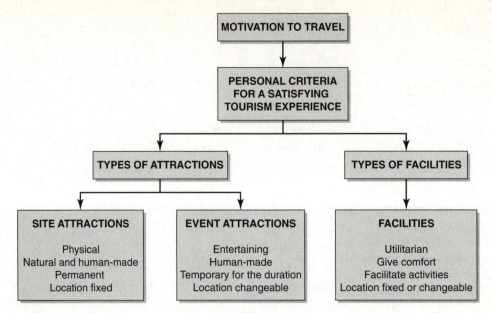

FIGURE 2.3 Why Do People Travel and Become Tourists? Motivation to travel comes from a desire to have a satisfying tourism experience. Traveling a distance in search of that experience is the essence of tourism.

Source: Bulent I. Kastarlak

tourist and are suitable for designated recreational activities. They have three-dimensional environmental qualities.

- Event attractions can have changeable locations. They are human-made or have natural causes. They are temporary happenings that draw tourists. They are staged at a physical venue or facility that can accommodate them.
- Event attractions are movable from one location to another when conditions and timing are suitable. Their organizers control their schedule, content, and availability.
- Event attractions may be substituted for site attractions to quickly draw tourists to locations where there is a shortage of other types of attractions.
- Compared to site attractions, most event attractions have minimum impact on the environment and often require no specialized facility.
- Highly specialized event attractions such as aircraft races may require highly specialized facilities. Probably the limiting example is the Olympic Games, in which, every two years, hundreds of millions and sometime billions of dollars (U.S.) are spent in different locations to host a two-week program of intense international sporting events. However, the facilities created for the Olympic Games become permanent attractions in their own right and continue to attract visitors for many years.

The **site–event dichotomy** underlines an important planning principle for developing tourism: Where tourism is desirable but there is a shortage of site attractions that would be interesting to tourists, tourists can be drawn to the location by organizing and scheduling event attractions. If successful, these events are rescheduled periodically to create a lasting magnet for tourism. When the magnet is established, new site attractions and facilities are developed at the destination.

The United Nations Educational, Scientific and Cultural Organization (UNESCO) General Conference held in Paris in November 1972, recognized the need to survey and inventory the outstanding specimens of world culture and natural assets. The conference initiated the multinational project for compiling the **World Heritage List**. The objective was to identify, study, and safeguard monuments, complexes, and sites—whether natural or human-made—that have "outstanding universal value" and international tourism significance from a historical, artistic, scientific, naturalistic, archeological, or anthropological viewpoint. The list was important for identifying the most important tourist attractions around the world.

The World Heritage List is also significant for demonstrating the common bonds that tie human history and the history of the earth together. Differentiating the cultural and natural characteristics of these site attractions was easy. However, differentiating architectural sites and sites of archeological interest was more difficult. UNESCO has decided to divide the inventory of sites into three categories: **Nature Sanctuaries**, **The Treasures of Art**, and **Ancient Civilizations**. Three sets of criteria were prepared to qualify the sites for the list. As of 2003, UNESCO had approved 730 sites in 125 member countries for listing. They include 563 cultural sites, 144 natural sites, and 23 sites for combinations of both. A sample of 300 sites and their criteria, divided into three groups, are shown in Appendix A. (See *World Heritage Sites by UNESCO*, by Marco Cattaneo and Jasmina Trifoni, in the Bibliography.)

2.4   HUMAN-MADE AND NATURAL ATTRACTIONS

The last dimension of the tourism product is its **composition**. Where they offer extremely diverse and high-quality tourism experiences, attractions draw large numbers of tourists and bring prosperity to a destination. However, the location of many high-quality, diverse attractions in close proximity is an accident of nature and history. Where this combination is not to be found, the answer to the problem lies in creating them. Human-made attractions have proven to be very successful for sustainable tourism development.

Planning and developing a destination starts with an in-depth and sometimes lengthy examination of its existing tourism product. When the analysis of attraction and facility mixes identifies a shortage of worthy attractions and missed opportunities for many recreational activities, the decision to do something about it comes easily. The decision is to supplement existing attractions with new human-made attractions that offer a variety of tourism experiences. *Human-made attractions* are created under controlled circumstances. They are the products of human imagination, which eliminates the redundant and creates what is essential. The process offers many opportunities for creative individuals to pursue the unusual, interesting, beautiful, and other qualities sought by tourists. In this there are no set rules, only a process to follow.

Creating a new attraction is a cognitive process involving a series of logical steps that lead to a new product (Figure 2.4):

Step 1 Select a theme idea from life experience or from the world of fantasy.

Step 2 Develop a message, or multiple messages, derived from the theme idea and select activities to express the message(s).

Step 3 Create the venue, or medium, necessary for transmitting the message(s) through selected activities.

Step 4 Market the new product, its activities, and its message(s).

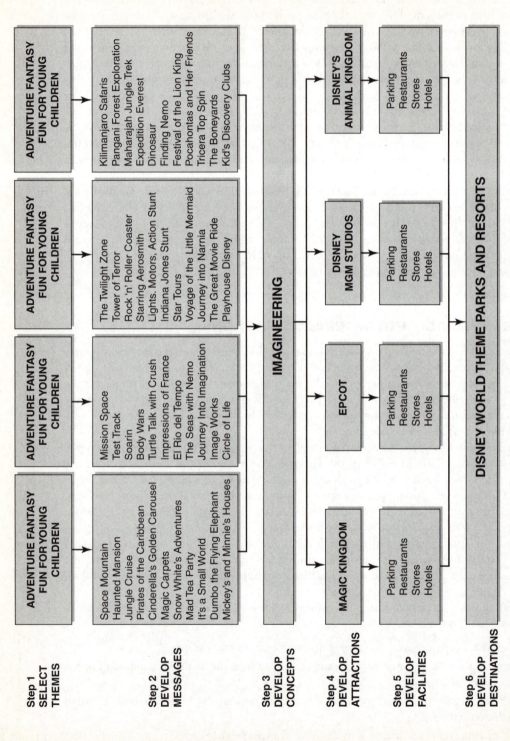

Step 1
SELECT THEMES

| ADVENTURE FANTASY FUN FOR YOUNG CHILDREN | ADVENTURE FANTASY FUN FOR YOUNG CHILDREN | ADVENTURE FANTASY FUN FOR YOUNG CHILDREN | ADVENTURE FANTASY FUN FOR YOUNG CHILDREN |

Step 2
DEVELOP MESSAGES

Space Mountain	Mission Space	The Twilight Zone	Kilimanjaro Safaris
Haunted Mansion	Test Track	Tower of Terror	Pangani Forest Exploration
Jungle Cruise	Soarin	Rock 'n' Roller Coaster	Maharajah Jungle Trek
Pirates of the Caribbean	Body Wars	Starring Aerosmith	Expedition Everest
Cinderella's Golden Carousel	Turtle Talk with Crush	Lights. Motors, Action Stunt	Dinosaur
Magic Carpets	Impressions of France	Indiana Jones Stunt	Finding Nemo
Snow White's Adventures	El Rio del Tempo	Star Tours	Festival of the Lion King
Mad Tea Party	The Seas with Nemo	Voyage of the Little Mermaid	Pocahontas and Her Friends
It's a Small World	Journey Into Imagination	Journey into Narnia	Tricera Top Spin
Dumbo the Flying Elephant	Image Works	The Great Movie Ride	The Boneyards
Mickey's and Minnie's Houses	Circle of Life	Playhouse Disney	Kid's Discovery Clubs

Step 3
DEVELOP CONCEPTS

IMAGINEERING

Step 4
DEVELOP ATTRACTIONS

| MAGIC KINGDOM | EPCOT | DISNEY MGM STUDIOS | DISNEY'S ANIMAL KINGDOM |

Step 5
DEVELOP FACILITIES

Parking	Parking	Parking	Parking
Restaurants	Restaurants	Restaurants	Restaurants
Stores	Stores	Stores	Stores
Hotels	Hotels	Hotels	Hotels

Step 6
DEVELOP DESTINATIONS

DISNEY WORLD THEME PARKS AND RESORTS

FIGURE 2.4 Example of a Strategy for Creating New Attractions and Destinations (Disney World, Orlando, Florida).

Source: Bulent I. Kastarlak

The process may benefit and borrow from all sorts of human knowledge and experience. The theme is selected from among subjects that would stimulate the interests of tourists. The message could be educational, adventurous, athletic, or entertainment. The medium could use advanced technology for creating illusions of reality in detail. The possibilities for creating new tourism products are limitless.

2.5   ATTRACTION AND FACILITY MIXES—THE MENU

The purpose of tourism is to experience the tourism product. One sometimes has to travel long distances to find it, experience it, consume it, and enjoy it. Tourists choose their tourism product from the rich menu of recreational experiences offered around the world. In such a highly competitive market, the host country, state, city, or destination must identify the missing items in its own menu to remain competitive. They have to package the tourism experience in a way that maximizes it for guests and creates the desired economic and social benefits from tourism for the host population. Given the destination and climatic conditions of the region, a two-way analysis of attraction/facility and activity mixes identifies the missing elements in the tourism product and lead to planning and developing more of the same. (This topic is discussed further in Part III.)

2.6   THE RECREATIONAL–UTILITARIAN DICHOTOMY OF THE TOURISM PRODUCT

Nearly all attractions and facilities have *dual qualities*. Some attractions may have utilitarian qualities to serve visitors, and reciprocally, some facilities may have recreational characteristics that draw tourists. Dual qualities are based on the facts that tourists are interested in certain activities and need certain services in others. Generally, *attractions provide the interest* and *facilities provide the service*.

Certain facilities may have features that, by design, are also recreational. Although recreation is not their primary function, these facilities with lesser recreational characteristics could increase recognition of the destination by playing dual roles, serving as a combination of attraction and facility. For example, a particular hotel serves as a utilitarian overnight accommodation. However, it may also have recreational value when it has historic significance and recreational facilities like tennis courts and a swimming pool (Figure 2.5).

To experience recreational activities, a tourist must perform certain utilitarian activities or receive utilitarian services. A tourist needs to travel, feel comfortable, clean and relieved, communicate, and conduct transactions. These associated activities are utilitarian. The means used to perform these utilitarian activities are facilities that support the experience of tourism. Basically, they do not draw tourists to the destination. They serve them when they get there.

The BIK System uses the following working definition of **facility**:

- A tourist facility has human-made or natural features that serve primarily utilitarian functions required by tourists.
- A tourist facility offers primarily utilitarian services and products, but it may also have recreational qualities that allow recreational activities.
- Tourists use a tourist facility directly and personally. Facilities requiring membership generally are not tourist facilities, except when tourists are allowed to attend special events or are invited as guests.
- Tourists use only the first-tier or primary facilities directly and personally to receive primarily utilitarian services. Second-tier establishments supply products or provide services to

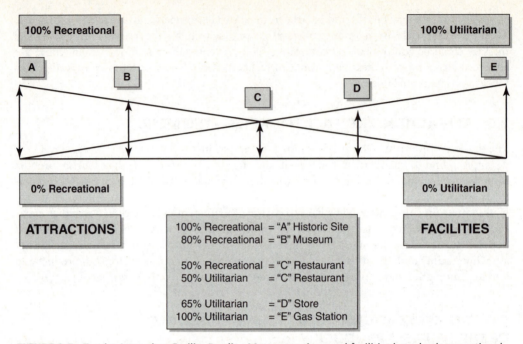

FIGURE 2.5   Tourist Attraction–Facility Duality. Most attractions and facilities have both recreational and utilitarian characteristics. They are rated individually in proportion to their dual characteristics to determine the composition of the regional attraction mix.
Source: Bulent I. Kastarlak

first-tier or primary facilities. Tourists do not use them personally and directly. Therefore, second-tier establishments are not included, in the narrowest sense of the word, in the tourism sector. They do count in calculating the impacts of tourism, since direct spending by tourists results in secondary spending in establishments as money circulates through an economy.

This definition of facility leads to corollary tourism planning principles derived from real-world examples:

• An establishment can serve dual utilitarian and recreational functions. For example, a cruise ship is primarily utilitarian, and therefore it is a facility for transporting paying passengers. However, the ship can also offer a large variety of recreational activities with its swimming pools, putting green, basketball court, sun deck, gymnasium, nightclubs, movies, live shows, shops, and casinos. These recreational qualities can also make the cruise ship an attraction.

• The utilitarian–recreational duality can make a tourist facility strictly utilitarian or an attraction strictly recreational. Other establishments can have more or less utilitarian or recreational qualities. Therefore, they are classified as an attraction or a facility when they pass the threshold in the middle of the range (see Section 11.3 in Chapter 11).

• An appropriate mix of dual-purpose facilities and attractions is necessary for creating a *year-round tourism destination.* In addition to offering winter sport activities, a dual-purpose ski slope can be used for hiking, riding, and even grass skiing during the summer. The recreational qualities of the mountain as an attraction offering a mix of year-round activities enable the ski lodge, restaurants, shops, and other facilities to continue giving services and selling products in all four seasons.

- Seasonality is caused by both supply and demand characteristics of a destination. The local climate may not allow an extended season or tourists may not prefer to travel to the location in all months of the year. Therefore, the seasonality of a tourism destination is determined by the maximum number of recreational and utilitarian activities that can be offered during particular months when tourists may be motivated to travel to the destination.

The BIK System devised a rating procedure to account for these dual qualities. The recreational–utilitarian duality of attractions and facilities—in short, the tourism product—extends along a continuum from purely utilitarian to purely recreational. The position of a particular facility or attraction can be measured between the two ends of the range by assigning a value—0 for purely recreational and 10 for purely utilitarian—making 5 the transition or midpoint from mostly utilitarian to mostly recreational. Values are assigned during the survey of the tourism product for quantifying the tourism potential of a destination. They are based on the draw and marketable quality of each attraction and facility. The **draw** may be measured by *attendance*. The **quality** is determined by industry standards and perception of degrees of excellence.

It follows that:

- Activities can also be utilitarian or recreational. Utilitarian activity is necessary for the comfort and convenience of tourists, whereas recreational activity achieves the experience anticipated by tourists at the destination.
- The uniqueness of a specific mix of utilitarian and recreational activities draws tourists to a particular destination.
- A single attraction may not be sufficient for creating a major destination. Several attractions and one or more dedicated facilities with utilitarian functions may be necessary to support and service the recreational activities associated with the destination.
- The *utilitarian and recreational activity mix* is the sum total of *tourism experiences* offered by the tourism product of a destination. Conversely, a destination is most highly ranked for its tourism product if it provides the desired tourism experience by offering the best utilitarian and recreational activity mix.
- Natural and human-made environmental factors are relevant to tourism to the extent to which they provide the means for undertaking recreational and utilitarian activities to achieve the desired tourism experience.

2.7 SEASONALITY OF TOURISM

Seasonality is the attribute of a particular attraction or facility that allows it to operate during a particular season, or seasons, of the year. Due to favorable climatic conditions, tourists may be able to perform a particular activity at a particular attraction or facility during one or more seasons. Certain activities may be possible during all four seasons, thus allowing the attraction or facility to operate year-round (see Figure 2.6 and Appendix F).

Seasonality plays an important role in planning the tourism experience and selecting a destination. Throughout the world, climate varies during the year in the Northern and Southern Hemispheres, and at various latitudes and elevations. Depending on the geographic location and conditions, this complex climate–seasonality relationship adds variety to the world tourism product. It enables tourism to have a year-round season around the world. By traveling to different

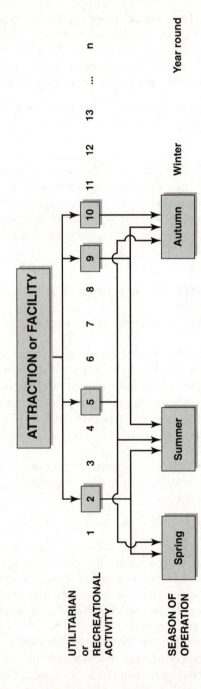

FIGURE 2.6 Tourist Attraction–Activity–Season Correlation. The extent of seasonality for both attractions and facilities is determined by whether recreational and utilitarian activities can be performed during one more seasons of the year or year-round.

Source: Bulent I. Kastarlak

destinations on all continents at different seasons, tourists can find an attraction where they can pursue their preferred recreational activity in virtually every season of the year.

Few tourists, however, have the money or the time to pursue recreational activity around the world in every season of the year. In contrast to excursionists, who take day trips all year, most tourists, by choice or necessity, are able to travel only during a specific month to destinations where their preferred recreational activity is available and the attraction offering that activity is in operation. When the attraction is in operation, facilities that support and serve it will also be operating.

The three-way **attraction** or **facility–activity–season association** is used for identifying the seasonal operation of a particular attraction or facility. The seasonality association is unique for each type of attraction and facility in a particular geographic region of the world. When the survey and analysis of all attractions and facilities for the destination is complete, the seasonal operation and availability of the destination can be determined. If associations between activities and seasons are favorable for all four seasons, attractions or facilities will qualify for year-round operation. If most or all attractions and facilities of the tourism product have year-round operational characteristics, that would make the destination a year-round destination.

It follows that an attraction or a destination does not have the potential to draw tourists year-round if the activities it offers do not match those demanded by tourists during all four seasons. Therefore, the diversity of activities associated with the attraction or destination determines the length of the tourism season at that particular geographic location. To lengthen its tourism season, the attraction or destination must introduce new activities, and it may have to build and operate new supporting facilities associated with these new activities.

2.8   SUPPLY OF AND DEMAND FOR THE TOURISM PRODUCT

The choices tourists make in deciding which destination to go to, which attraction to visit, and which activity to undertake depend on the comparative cost and satisfaction of reaching and experiencing each particular destination. Tourists pay costs in terms of money, time, convenience, and comfort for experiencing and consuming the tourism product of a destination. Moreover, higher satisfaction can result from the experience when the total costs are lower than those associated with visiting comparable destinations and consuming comparable tourism products elsewhere.

Comparative costs vary from one destination to another. This variation affects the demand for the tourism product by reducing or increasing the choice. Demand for the tourism product depends on matching the expectation of tourists with their budgets.

It takes three cognitive steps for the tourist to create demand for a destination:

- First, the tourist feels the *need* for a recreational or utilitarian experience.
- Second, the tourist *compares* alternative destinations in terms of their costs and level of anticipated satisfaction when experiencing their tourism product.
- Third, the tourist chooses the destination with the *lowest comparative cost* and the *highest anticipated satisfaction* and creates a demand for it.

Demand is increased by lowering the comparative cost for experiencing the tourism product and/or increasing the satisfaction in consuming the product. Therefore, planning and developing tourism at a destination depends, first, on organizing the supply side of the tourism product by lowering the comparative cost and increasing the satisfaction level for the tourist. As the comparative cost gets lower, the draw of the destination becomes higher.

Simple methods are used to overcome the difficulties associated with measuring the comparative cost of attracting tourists. One method is collecting **attendance** figures at the gate. These figures are available and reliable for most major attractions and facilities. Another method for estimating the draw is measuring the quality of services offered, that is, the ambiance and structure of an attraction or facility. This is done by **rating** the attraction and facility. Trained poll takers acting as tourists rate the draw of a site attraction or event attraction by using an industry checklist and quality standards. Directories of hotels, restaurants, and other tourist facilities and attractions use this rating method. Facilities and attractions are given quality "stars" ranging from one to five or more. For tourism planning, a rating method is most effective when it is combined with attendance figures. Occupancy of hotel rooms is a reliable measure of the demand for and draw of a destination. Tourism planning and promotion agencies and chambers of commerce periodically survey and collect attendance, rate, and room occupancy figures for measuring demand.

Another method is the experimental application of the **Gravity Model** to tourism. The Gravity Model is a mathematical method used in economic geography, market analysis, and transportation planning. It can be adapted and applied to tourism for calculating the aggregate "gravitational" pull of destinations in terms of the number of tourists drawn to them. The Gravity Model predicts the interaction of a population between two places, such as migration, based on the size of the populations and the distance or travel time between the places. It states that the interaction is directly related to the size of the populations and inversely related to the distance or travel time between them. In mathematical terms, the model holds that interaction is proportional to the multiplication of two populations divided by the distance or travel time separating them. The effect of distance is usually modified by raising a distance or travel time measure to an exponent, analogous to Newton's laws of gravitation. The model is applicable to tourism, because tourism is another form of population mobility, yet it is unlike migration. A variation of the model could measure the gravitational **pull** of a destination (B) from a location (A) where tourists originate. The pull could be expressed in terms of the aggregate quality of the tourism product of one destination compared with the gravity pull and aggregate quality of competing destinations for drawing tourists from location A.

The Gravity Model has not been fully developed and tested for tourism planning. It has the potential, however, to test the suppositions, for example, that cross-regional or cross-national tourism has higher demand flows from origins and to destinations that are not isolated geographically, and that demand flows are higher between regions or countries with cultural and environmental similarities. Once it is ready to be applied to tourism development planning, the Gravity Model could be an important tool for managing tourist flows and maintaining sustainability at tourism destinations. (See Section 16.7 in Chapter 16 for more information on the Gravity Model.)

Another aspect of the demand–supply relationship involves the direction from which the draw comes. Motivation for tourism, largely induced by marketing, could come from **push** factors that originate from the desire of the individual to get away for a few days. Motivation could also come from the lure of the anticipated experience at a distant land, that is, from **pull** factors.

Tourism products are marketed by identifying and targeting push demand from various tourism-originating markets or by publicizing the pull-demand characteristics of destinations. Tourism products could be marketed from either direction to induce a draw. The promotion strategy depends on directing the attention of potential tourists to the pushing effect of demand from origination point A or to the pulling effect of destination B. By measuring these push-pull effects, the Gravity Model could calculate the total draw of a destination from particular tourist markets and even competing destinations.

British demographer Ernst Ravenstein has done studies on population migrations. He used the Gravity Model to measure the interaction between places. He found that the majority of migrants move a short distance. Those who move long distances tend to choose big-city destinations where there are more job opportunities. The lure of the big city—the tourist destination where major attractions are found—holds true for tourists as well. One can assume that the draw between the origin of tourists (A) and their destination (B) is greater for domestic tourists than for international tourists who would travel longer distances in anticipation of larger recreational satisfaction at the same destination (B). When conditions permit, domestic tourism could generate more tourists for a destination than international tourism because domestic tourists and excursionists can take short but frequent vacations year-round.

For examining the distribution pattern of tourists from their geographic origins to their destinations, the concept of **diffusion** is used. Diffusion is defined as spatial spreading, or dissemination of an idea and people who carry it. The science of geography identifies two types of dissemination. In **expansion diffusion**, the idea, and people who carry it, move from a large center gradually in all directions and spread like an advancing flood. By contrast, in **hierarchical diffusion**, the idea, and people who carry it, move from a large center by branching out into ever-smaller channels spreading to destinations like the branches of a tree. Hierarchical diffusion better describes the distribution of tourists from their origins to their destinations. The Gravity Model could be applied to the concept of hierarchical diffusion to study patterns of destination and visitor distribution in a region.

2.9   THE QUALITY OF THE TOURISM PRODUCT AND MARKET SHARE

What draws a tourist to a destination? In one sentence, it is the quality of the tourism product and the value of the recreational experience it offers. It is essential that the destination offer highly rated experiences that match the tourist's expectations. It is essential that the tourism product, and the quality of the experience it offers, are rated according to what would interest tourists, and not according to characteristics that would not interest them.

As noted earlier, the quality rating of an attraction is based on the tourism significance of the particular element of the tourism product, and is done by researchers who sometimes act as tourists. The evaluation of the tourism significance depends, in turn, on the comparative cost and gravitational pull of the destination. Expressed in geographical terms and based on these two criteria, one could differentiate three levels of tourism significance.

- Attractions of *local significance* draw primarily excursionists from places located within the area defined by the daily commuting distance.
- Attractions of *national significance* draw tourists from domestic markets within the country.
- Attractions of *international significance* draw tourists from international markets anywhere in the world.

Higher-rated attractions also draw tourists for lower-rated attractions. Attractions at national and local levels are of secondary and tertiary importance for international tourists. However, having visited the international attraction, tourists may be induced to visit attractions of national and local significance in the same region. Having attractions at three levels of significance, together with great diversity, quality, and proximity of the tourism product, makes a destination a major draw.

2.10   THE TOURISM SECTOR OF THE ECONOMY—THE OVERLAPPING SECTOR

By one account, tourism in 2006 was the sixth largest industry in the world and the largest service sector industry (see Tourism Place, a collaborative blog for tourism and travel research, May 1, 2008, e-mail from Alan E. Lew). Tourism as a global industry in U.S. dollar values in 2006 followed

(1) trade in fossil fuels, (2) telecommunications and computer equipment, (3) chemicals, (4) automotive products, and (5) agriculture. There is a long-standing disagreement about what constitutes the tourism sector. An international classification system defining the sector does not exist at this time. The usual hotels, restaurants, airlines classification is only a fragment of a system. Although it is one of the largest economic sectors in the world—if not the dominant economic sector in many smaller developing countries—tourism does not have an international system of organized industrial classification.

The UNWTO has recognized this problem. It is in the process of developing a universal classification system named **Satellite Accounts** that will identify the types of establishments and government organizations that own and operate tourist attractions and facilities and will classify them by industry groups. The classification will enable tourism economists, planners, and statisticians to perform analytical procedures that will be consistent and comparable throughout the world. Progress toward developing this classification system can be found in "Tourism Satellite Account: Recommended Methodological Framework 2008," published by the United Nations Department of Economic and Social Affairs Statistics Division in 2010. It is identified as Series F No. 80/Rev. 1.

The working concepts of the UNWTO classification system are being tested in Canada. Until the classification is finalized, researchers and businesses will use an interim classification or make up their own. In 1970, confronted with the necessity of compiling comparable and consistent economic data for its tourism studies, the BIK System adopted the **Standard Industrial Classification** (**SIC**; 1970 edition) system as the source for defining the tourism sector. The defined sector was used in Bulent Kastarlak's five-volume study of *Tourism and Its Development Potential in Massachusetts* (see the Bibliography) for inventorying the state's tourist facility mix and establishment types in the state's 351 cities and towns. Three decades later, the SIC was incorporated into and replaced by the up-to-date and greatly expanded **NAICS.** In later chapters, the tourism industry is redefined for the BIK System by using the NAICS. (See Figure 2.2 and Appendix B).

> The history of the SIC dates back to 1937, when the U.S. government established a committee to develop a classification system. It released its first classification of manufacturing industries in 1941, followed by a non-manufacturing classification in 1942. Revisions were made to the system in 1958, 1963, 1967, 1972, 1977, and 1987, the last version. These periodic changes were intended to keep pace with changes in the economy so that the system would recognize significant new categories and eliminate ones for trades that were nearly extinct. With inputs from such data gathering agencies as the U.S. Census Bureau and the Bureau of Labor Statistics, the Office of Management and Budget oversaw the latter.
>
> *Source:* Reference for "Business" in the *Encyclopedia of Business,* 2nd ed., Web site page on the Standard Industrial Classification System.

Read more on the Standard Industrial Classification System (SIC) at the following Web site: http://www.referenceforbusiness.com/encyclopedia/Sel-Str/Standard-Industrial-Classification-System-SIC.html#ixzz1JT9ZXZmW.

The SIC was developed for classifying business establishments by the type of activity in which they are primarily engaged. Its purpose was to facilitate the collection, tabulation, presentation, and analysis of data relating to all kinds of business establishments. It was used to promote uniformity and comparability in the presentation of statistical data collected by various agencies of the U.S. government, state agencies, trade associations, and private research organizations. The SIC system contributed greatly to advances in economic science, most notably in national and regional income accounting and in input/output analysis.

Since 1970, the SIC coding system has been updated several times, most recently in 1987. In 1997 it was superseded by the NAICS, which was developed jointly by Mexico, Canada, and the United States. The NAICS is unique among industry classifications. The single most important characteristic of the NAICS is that the building blocks, or industrial units, of the system are classified according to the *similarity of their production systems.* For differentiating production processes, lines are drawn between industries.

The NAICS divides the economy into twenty sectors, 1,170 industries, and an ever-changing number of establishments in North America. Industries within these sectors are grouped according to the production process they use. Five sectors largely produce goods and fifteen produce services. The twenty major sectors and their code numbers used by NAICS are:

> **11** Agriculture, Forestry, Fishing, and Hunting; **21** Mining; **22** Utilities; **23** Construction; **31–33** Manufacturing; **42** Wholesale Trade; **44–45** Retail Trade; **48–49** Transportation and Warehousing; **51** Information; **52** Finance and Insurance; **53** Real Estate and Rental and Leasing; **54** Professional, Scientific, and Technical Services; **55** Management of Companies and Enterprises; **56** Administrative and Support and Waste Management and Remediation Services; **61** Educational Services; **62** Health Care and Social Assistance; **71** Arts, Entertainment, and Recreation; **72** Accommodation and Food Services; **81** Other Services (Except Public Administration); **92** Public Administration.

As a statistical unit, the **establishment** is defined by the NAICS as the "smallest operating entity for which records are kept, for indicating the cost of resources used to produce units of output." The establishment is counted as having a single physical location where business is primarily conducted and where services and industrial operations are performed. There are thousands of establishment types in the NAICS. They include the factory, store, hotel, restaurant, airline terminal, airline, resort, casino, amusement park, and others. A gift shop operating in a hotel, for example, is identified as a separate establishment. Exceptions to the rule include physically dispersed operations, such as construction, transportation, banking, grocery, or communication branch establishments of a single company. For these exceptions, the NAICS assigns a code to one of the establishments of an enterprise where its primary activity or headquarters is located.

For understanding the first application of the BIK System presented in 1970, the reader may refer to Appendix C. In later chapters, the application of the expanded BIK System based on the approach to a theory of tourism planning and development presented here will be discussed in detail.

Chapter Highlights

- Tourism may have its origins in migration. Primitive humans traveled to find better places to live for survival. In the process, humans also developed recreational pursuits like cave art.
- Tourism consists of a series of utilitarian and recreational activities that form the total experience of tourism.
- To experience tourism, tourists have to be motivated to travel to places where the tourism product is located.

- Attractions draw visitors and facilities serve them. Without attractions, there is only tourism for the sake of travel.
- There are two types of attractions: site attractions and event attractions. The first are fixed in location; the second may be mobile.
- Where attractions are lacking, new ones can be developed from among a large variety of themes.
- Attractions and facilities may have dual characteristics. They may be both recreational and utilitarian in varying degrees.

- All attractions are not equally interesting to tourists. They should be rated as having international, national, and local significance.
- Destinations having the largest variety of quality attractions and facilities draw the largest number of tourists, depending on the season(s) of the year during which these attractions and facilities operate.
- There is a three-way correlation between attractions/facilities, activities, and seasons. The total of these correlations determines the seasonality of the destination.
- The supply of and demand for the tourism product can be measured by using the conventional method of counting attendance or by using the experimental method of the Gravity Model. The latter uses the push-pull effects of the places where tourists originate and the destinations to which they are attracted.
- The tourism sector of the economy is an overlapping sector. It is composed of selected subsectors and establishments drawn from, among other sources, the NAICS. There is no official definition of the sector. The UNWTO is working to develop it.
- Private establishments own and operate most attractions and facilities. However, governments own and operate many public attractions and facilities like national parks.

3

Prerequisites for Sustainable Tourism

This chapter identifies conditions that must be present for government and business organizations in mixed and market economic systems to plan and develop tourism. Decisions to go forward are based on evaluating these conditions and determining that growth of tourism is sustainable and that the needs of present and future generations can be satisfied. The principles of sustainable tourism are:

- Conservation and renewal of tourism resources is the goal of sustainable tourism.
- Continuity of tourism depends on the existence of high-quality tourist attractions.
- Regardless of the economic system, tourism depends on government–private sector cooperation, entrepreneurship, and risk taking.
- Community support and cultural tolerance are essential for tourism to prosper.
- Personal security of tourists and political stability of the country must be ensured.
- Tourists themselves must be prepared to play their part in sustainable tourism.

3.1 INTERNATIONAL AND DOMESTIC SUSTAINABLE TOURISM DEMAND

In 1987, the **World Commission on Environment and Development**, established by the United Nations, defined **sustainable development** as follows: "Sustainable development is progress that meets the needs of the present without compromising the ability of future generations to meet their own needs." The operative concept in this definition is sustainability, which is a key condition for promoting and continuing the tourism demand. Tourism as we know it today, and possibly other types of tourism that will occur in the future, will be more feasible when they are sustainable.

Testing and promoting proper kinds of tourism is challenging. In planning and promoting sustainable tourism, the following issues are considered:

- Natural and human-made cultural and environmental resources comprising the tourism product are conserved, and renewed when necessary, for the benefit of succeeding generations. Presently, tourists are invited not only to consume the tourism product, but they are also made aware of the need to protect it for future generations.
- Tourism must be beneficial for the receiving destination, region, and country. If it is not, receiving destinations will not be prepared to accommodate tourists and hospitality will not be extended when guests have overstayed their welcome.
- Maintaining and renewing the tourism product is critical for sustaining steady tourist flows and ensuring tourist satisfaction. Sometimes, this means limiting tourist flows.
- Benefits and costs must be politically acceptable for the governing entities at national, regional, and destination levels.

Initially, separating the *international tourism demand* from the *domestic tourism demand* is desirable when cultural, income, purpose, and other characteristics demonstrate a considerable gap between the two types of tourism. This would lead to the development of two overlapping tourism economies in the same area. Most Caribbean countries and countries of South East Asia are examples of this type of dual tourism economy. Russia, the Ukraine, and other members of the former Soviet Union transitioning from centrally planned to free-market economies are also recent examples.

When similarities of demand between international and domestic tourism do not exhibit substantial gaps, one set of standards is applicable for all elements of the tourism industry. Western European countries such as Spain, France, Belgium, Luxembourg, Denmark, Germany, and Italy have similar economic and social conditions within the open borders of the European Union; the United States and Canada are other examples.

Tourism demand requires the existence of attractions and, as a minimum, basic tourist facilities. Tourism potential analysis is the initial step for determining the availability and quality of the tourism product. Gradualism is the best government strategy at the time of initiating tourism development. Starting with a few modest but safe and sanitary facilities located near a few important attractions is the first test. Initially, demand for tourism is limited to readily available environmental attractions offering tourism activities like participating in safaris, trekking, swimming, and snorkeling. As a tourism economy expands, human-made attractions are added to the tourism product by restoring historic sites, older monuments, and buildings. Adding higher-quality facilities, like five-star hotels, or human-made attractions, like theme parks, comes later.

Initially, environmental attractions of the tourism product should meet the expectations of tourists. In turn, tourists, through their spending, should match the expectations of local people for creating jobs and improving living conditions. During the start-up period, this strategy limits international tourism to certain specialized activities. Adventure tourism, village tourism, ecotourism in the Amazon rain forest, chasing the wind on the pampas of Patagonia, and trekking the trails of the Himalayan Mountains in Nepal are examples.

International tourists are encouraged to conform to and respect local culture, customs, and living conditions to receive maximum satisfaction from their experience. At the early stages, they should be prepared to expect modest worldly comforts. They are required to carry in and out their personal belongings, and whatever waste material they produce, without leaving a trace behind. Domestic tourists are expected to do even better and protect their country's heritage. A delicate balance between domestic and international tourism is maintained as tourism develops.

Everyone will benefit when this balance is achieved. Nations, regions, and destinations will sort out their assets and promote their specialized tourism. Thirty-seven criteria for sustainable tourism are listed on the following Web site of the Partnership for Global Sustainable Tourism Criteria: http://www.sustainabletourismcriteria.org/index.php?option=com_content&task=view&id=58&Itemid=188.

It is not a foregone conclusion that the demand for international tourism supersedes the demand for domestic tourism. Foreign exchange income flowing into the country from international tourists plays a major role in building foreign currency reserves and improving the balance of payments of the country. However, the demands of domestic tourism could be such that, when encouraged by national policies, it can create the business climate necessary to train and develop a thriving and sustainable domestic tourism industry.

In the past, many destination countries transformed their domestic tourism into international tourism with ease when their social infrastructure and tourism product reached a higher level of proficiency. Even in a changing economic system, in some countries domestic tourism has led the way toward creating international tourism. For example, Russia, the Ukraine, and some other independent states already had large domestic tourism industries for their citizens. Their domestic tourism standards, however, did not match international standards. Their governments are now committed to joining the international world of tourism. They are in the process of inviting many international tourism ventures to their country and upgrading their tourism products. Consequently, their transition from domestic to international tourism will not be difficult.

3.2   ATTRACTIONS AS PRIMARY DRAWS OF THE TOURISM PRODUCT

Some repetition is useful here for emphasis. As noted earlier (see Chapter 2), need and experience are primary motivations for tourism. Transporting individual tourists to the point where that need can be satisfied and the experience can be achieved by consuming the tourism product is fundamental to tourism. Tourist attractions are the raison d'etre of tourism. They are the targets, purpose, and objects of interest. Eliminating attractions essentially eliminates tourism. (With the exception, noted earlier, of those people pushed to travel for the sake of travel itself or simply to "get away." Even these people often choose a destination or series of travel experiences that interests them.)

Attractions draw visitors. They offer experiences that visitors want and need. They must be accessible and have features that are worth experiencing. Their cumulative benefits in one destination must be higher than their cumulative benefits in other destinations. The opposite is true for costs. In making these determinations, costs and benefits are evaluated for each attraction and are rated in comparison with similar attractions elsewhere.

What are the attributes of attractions? They may be *natural* or *human-made*. They may be *fixed* or *mobile*. They may be *new* or *ancient*. They may be *large* or *small*. They may be *temporary* or *permanent*. They may be designed for some type of human *activity*. Most of all, they are *unique*, either by themselves or in association with other attractions as a group. In the eyes of interested tourists, that uniqueness separates these attractions from the ordinary.

What are the things one should look for in evaluating the tourism potential of a country, region, or destination? The search must start by understanding and identifying the elements of the tourism product that are unique in the eyes of tourists. That perceived uniqueness is what counts. Engaged in their daily lives, local people may be indifferent to that uniqueness. The attraction or facility may have only marginal use and significance for them. However, tourists may perceive them differently. They may detect characteristics that are interesting only to them. They may be curious to know and experience them.

Geography and cultural anthropology are two major scientific disciplines used in this search. Geography focuses on the major and unusual elements of the physical world. These include physical characteristics of the climate, vegetation, and landforms that would draw tourists. Their locations as a system of places in the tourism area are particularly important for tourism planning. **Absolute location** is the precise physical location of an attraction or a facility. Two coordinates measured from the longitude and latitude define this point. **Relative location** is the location of one place in relation to other places. It is examined to evaluate the accessibility of an attraction or facility. Both types of location are important for tourism planning.

A tourism planner is concerned only about the tourism significance of locations. When climate, vegetation, and landforms possess interesting features as tourist attractions, they gain in importance. When climatic conditions are favorable, these features offer possibilities for recreational and utilitarian activities. *Seasonality* of attractions and facilities is determined when the seasons for these activities are known in a particular climate zone.

All tourism activities depend on *special climate conditions*. These conditions are found in certain seasons and locations throughout the world. For example, skiing is possible during the winter season in St. Moritz and the Alps. However, the Alps are also suitable for hiking and climbing during the rest of the year, making St. Moritz a year-round resort facility and the Alps a year-round attraction. Other climatic factors, like humidity, precipitation, or the lack of it, could affect the comfort level of tourists and the seasonality of the activity. These factors are noted in planning the tourism product mix of the area.

Patterns of vegetation, climate, and landforms have close causal relations. The combination of landforms (dunes, deserts, mountains, rivers, lakes, beaches, valleys), vegetation (forests, bush, and grasslands), and climate (rain, sun, clouds, snow, temperature) creates an **ecosystem** and several attractions for ecotourism. A parallel ecosystem exists for marine attractions, suitable for scuba diving, fishing, whale watching, and so on. Public consciousness and protection of the environment creates a new form of tourism. Aside from the associations of physical features of the earth with ecotourism, many other associations are established for creating a variety of tourism forms. Many scientific and cultural disciplines study these associations. Among them, cultural anthropology is particularly important.

Cultural anthropology focuses on the totality of socially transmitted behavioral patterns, arts, beliefs, institutions, and all other products of human activities and thoughts characteristic of a community or population. More specifically, cultural anthropology studies human culture based on the archeological, ethologic, ethnographic, linguistic, social, and psychological data of a particular region and historical period. Within this broad spectrum, a great variety of cultural subjects and periods qualify as tourist attractions. Each country, region, and destination decides separately on what qualifies as a tourist attraction (see Appendix A).

Cultural subjects have global appeal. Marine archeology of sunken vessels, whale watching, special events like the Olympic Games, skiing and tennis tournaments, sailing around the world, and nature adventures are among the activities used to create global attractions. Archeology and cultural anthropology are rich in themes for development. Hellenistic towns built by Alexander the Great and his successors in Alexandria, Egypt, and Iraq, as well as the capital cities of Al-Khanum and Kandahar in Afghanistan and Samarkand in ancient Sogdiana, now Uzbekistan, are early examples of urban attractions. Funerary sites of the pre-Islamic Turkic era dot the sandy plains of Central Asia where tourist-archeologists converge and explore. The forgotten and redis-covered city of Petra in Jordan, with its monuments carved from the red rocks of canyons, have

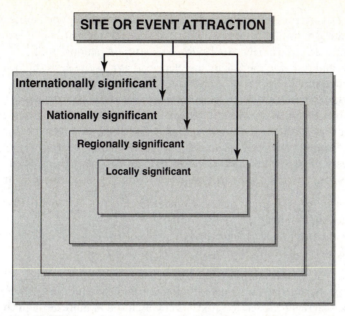

FIGURE 3.1   Tourism Significance of Attractions by Their Market Size. The tourism draw of attractions is measured in terms of the size of geographic areas from which they draw.
Source: Bulent I. Kastarlak

been transformed into global attractions and are now settings for adventure films. All leave different impressions and provide tourists with different experiences.

It is not sufficient to simply classify tourist attractions as site or event attractions. The impressions they make on tourists are critical. These impressions are rated in terms of their *significance* for tourists. The significance of attractions increases as the distance and the area they draw tourists from increase. The wider the area and the greater the distance, the more significant the attractions become. Accordingly, in the BIK System, the attractions are rated as *international, national, regional, local,* or *destination-level* attractions (Figure 3.1).

3.3   AN OPERATING SYSTEM FOR ATTRACTIONS, FACILITIES, AND ACTIVITIES

The tourism industry is an integrated system of many functioning elements. Tourism functions best when these elements interact with one other and with the elements of the world around them. Planning and developing tourism focuses on identifying the elements in the system, organizing them into a cohesive whole, and establishing the guidelines necessary for its smooth operation.

Tourism, in **free-market** capitalist economic systems, operates under one set of guidelines. These guidelines are based on generating optimum **profits** and **costs** that the economy and the environment can sustain. The business establishment is the smallest element in the system. It operates with minimum interference from the government. Profit is the primary motivation for business. Government facilitates the operation of business establishments where necessary and plays a supporting role.

By contrast, in **centrally planned** economic systems, government dictates the operational guidelines from top to bottom. The profit motive is secondary to the higher motive of benefiting the larger society. Government may regard creating employment opportunities as more important than operating a profitable tourism business. For example, national prestige and political image may motivate a government to subsidize an inefficient national airline. Displaying the flag in distant lands and bringing tourists by the planeload at cut-rate fares could eclipse the profit motivation of tourism.

How the tourism industry is organized and motivated has a great bearing on the efficiency of the system. In a free-market capitalist system, operational guidelines can be drawn from the organization theory of the firm. Modern organization theories date back to **Merton** (1940), **Weber** (1946), **Simon** (1947), and **Selznick** (1947). (See the Bibliography for references.) Many works have been written on the subject of organization theory since then. When applied to planning and developing tourism, these theories identify two types of tourism organizations:

- *Private sector organizations* own and operate profit-making tourist attractions, facilities, and service establishments.
- *Government sector organizations* serve tourists by owning and operating public facilities and attractions and by establishing regulatory guidelines.

In recent years, NGOs have multiplied and gained considerable importance around the world. These not-for-profit organizations serve the tourism industry indirectly by providing educational, health, and agricultural services. (NGOs are discussed in more detail in later chapters.)

Depending on the stage of development of the tourism industry in their region, private sector organizations may be numerous and highly diversified. In a free-market capitalist system, private sector tourism organizations become members of the trade associations serving the interests of their respective trades. Hotels, restaurants, amusement centers, retail centers, airlines, and travel agencies, are among those organized trades. In addition, chambers of commerce, business development councils, and regional tourism marketing associations have as their mission serving the interests of their membership. They collect and process basic tourism data and promote the tourism industry for the benefit of their members.

Government organizations also play a supporting role. Municipal, county, and state governments enact laws and regulations for protecting the health, safety, welfare, and security of the public. Local governments pass licensing and zoning by-laws, establish building and environmental regulations, and prepare regional and local comprehensive plans. Tourism becomes subject to these laws primarily as part of building regulations and regulations pertaining to the maintenance of industry standards set for hotels, restaurants, and other places. (This is discussed further in Chapter 9.)

In the private sector, individual entrepreneurs take the initiative and carry the business of tourism forward. Their projects compete for the attention of the marketplace. Attractions and facilities are planned, financed, and developed by private initiative. The ventures are based on the profitability of the project that will amortize the construction and operating costs and make a profit. Commercial banks and private capital finance these projects.

In the United States, when private companies build and operate tourism projects such as resort hotels in other countries, they may receive government assistance. Organizations like the **Overseas Private Investment Corporation (OPIC)** and the **American Export-Import Bank** give direct loans to American entrepreneurs or provide loan guarantees to lenders for funding tourism and other projects overseas. Businesses can also apply for political risk insurance.

In all **market system** countries, large projects like convention centers and hotels can have government participation in the form of tax concessions, fee exemptions, capital investment, and relief from building and zoning codes. Frequently, governments have programs for building public infrastructure that serves the local population as well as tourists. Governments review and approve individual tourism projects, like any other project, with consideration for their benefits and for their impacts on the environment, traffic, and public services like police, education, and fire protection. Sustainability of tourism is not a priority issue. Enabling profit for the entrepreneur, as well as protecting property rights and property values, take precedence over the sustainability of tourism. The invisible hand of the marketplace is the guiding force behind expansion of the tourism economy. In short, expansion is not the result of a grand scheme or master plan in market economic systems. Generally, the private sector leads and government follows.

In **mixed economies**, government is more directly involved in the development of tourism. Government activities involve collecting tourism data at points of entry for international tourists, providing police, security and customs regulations services, developing tourism related national policies and regulations, marketing tourism and providing for sustainable tourism. In mixed economies, the private sector often follows rather than leads the development of tourism. Its projects are given a place in the country's national, regional, and destination-level policies and master plans. Government often gets involved in financing these projects and providing subsidies to emerging entrepreneurs.

In both economic systems, two prerequisites emerge for planning and developing sustainable tourism: **initiative** and **risk taking**. Risk taking in search of profitable business opportunities is basic to the free-market system. Initiative is essential in applying creative thinking to solve old and new problems. In virtually all problem-solving situations, solutions for past problems are known or documented in some form, and they establish precedents.

One element of problem solving is a **search**. The search may be physical, involving finding the right information, object, or person, or it may be cognitive, involving the use of associative steps to locate relevant information stored in written documents, in cyberspace, or in an individual's memory. The search is followed by a **screening process**, which consists of reviewing elements that qualify as possible solutions to the problem.

There is considerable randomness to the sequence of problem-solving steps. This means that the problem goes through a sequence of steps, such as problem formulation, search for alternatives, evaluation of alternatives, and selection of one alternative as the solution to the problem. Successful tourism planning and development blends the creative decision-making process of the private sector with equally creative government decision-making processes. The importance of cooperation between the private and public sectors cannot be overemphasized.

3.4 TOURISM INFRASTRUCTURE

Public infrastructure serves the needs of the resident population as well as those of tourists. Single-purpose infrastructure is often wasteful and should be avoided. What serves tourism is the sum total of basic facilities, equipment, and installations needed for a functioning tourism industry. They include major highways, bridges, tunnels, public parking garages, railways, rail stations, metro subways, airports, airport passenger terminals, ports, port passenger terminals, power stations, power distribution grids, freshwater storage and distribution systems, desalination facilities, wastewater treatment and recycling facilities, telecommunication systems, cybercommunication systems, hospitals, police and security facilities, and many other facilities largely built and operated by governments. In addition to this large array of tourist facilities, governments own and operate many attractions. They include public lands, parks, forests, underwater conservation areas, monuments and memorials, historic sites, and the like. Some infrastructure may be owned privately and may be operated for profit as well as not-for-profit.

Regardless of who builds and operates them, infrastructure facilities are carefully planned and executed as part of the development plans of the country. Infrastructure dedicated solely to tourism is seldom justified. More likely, infrastructure is planned to satisfy the service demands of both tourists and the local population. Tourism, as an economic sector, is a subsystem of national, regional, or destination-level economic systems. It overlaps with, and is subservient to, the rest of the economy. It operates for the benefit of the larger economic system, not for its own exclusive benefit. In addition to serving the interests of an entrepreneur, serving the higher goals of the nation, region, or destination is the justification for developing tourism and tourism infrastructure.

When public infrastructure decisions are made, determining community goals, in concert with the rights of individual citizens and property values, is an early consideration for planning sustainable tourism. This consideration is not a routine review based on preprogrammed decisions like those of many existing development plans. Public opinion is heard and political systems are employed in evaluating the merits of the proposed tourism-related project. With backing from elected officials of the local political system, a project may depend on government support for building some type of single-purpose, dedicated infrastructure. Mistakes are made when single-purpose tourism infrastructure projects are narrowly conceived and rushed through the system for approval. The world is full of ill-conceived tourism infrastructure projects that had disastrous consequences for the environment, economic system, and social structure of their respective areas.

A typical example is a government-funded and -built jet airport facility on a small Caribbean island to provide direct flight connections to major market centers. It was presented as an essential project for developing tourism on the island. It had a long runway to accommodate large jet planes. The developer of the destination resort to be located on a remote beach on the island stated that this expensive airport was a condition for building his resort. In addition, a road built to transport tourists from the airport to the resort required government funding. The road did not continue beyond the resort and had no other useful purpose for the community. The resort turned out to be a high-risk venture with dubious merits for sustainable tourism development. With no plans for follow-up resorts on the horizon, the island depended on the sustainability of this one resort. "Build and they will come," the resort developer and the government said. The airport and the road to the resort remained idle for decades.

Often, **feasibility studies** and **market studies** are required for project approval to evaluate the financial realism and the environmental, social, and economic impacts of tourism development. They often turn out to be overly optimistic. They may ignore factors beyond the profitability of the project by sidestepping impacts like employment generated, tax revenues anticipated, and police, fire, traffic, and environmental issues. Sometimes sustainability at the destination is left outside the scope of these studies.

Another questionable infrastructure, this one hypothetical, was a golf course and a resort located on an arid Caribbean island where an acute water shortage exists. A substantial portion of the freshwater supply was obtained from rain catchments and was disposed of by septic systems. There was no recycling. The golf course would have consumed about 25% of the entire water supply of the island for irrigation. In addition, the developer proposed to import a precut, prefabricated steel structure for the hotel that relied entirely on mechanical air conditioning to cool the resort. Defying good design principles for tropical climates, the resort would have imposed a heavy electrical load on the island's grid. The project was not approved.

In contrast to such questionable infrastructure decisions, there are successful projects. A symbiotic relationship between a larger community and an infrastructure facility serving a tourist attraction may turn a liability into an advantage. For example, a golf resort proposed in the historic and arid Petra (Wadi Moussa) region in the Kingdom of Jordan made good sense. Existing hotels were connected to the regional freshwater distribution system drawing from wells. There was a regional wastewater treatment plant under construction. Recycling the treated wastewater for agricultural, horticultural, and recreational uses also made good sense for the planned golf resort nearby. The wastewater treatment plant would not only send recycled water to irrigate the golf course, but would also irrigate land for growing vegetables and fruits. The excess recycled water would be channeled to a reforestation project next to the golf course and resort hotel. The proposed arrangement was symbiotic and sustainable. (See the case study on Wadi Mousa, Petra, Jordan.)

These examples illustrate the importance of finding multiple uses for proposed tourist infrastructure facilities to ensure sustainable tourism development. Cooperation between the government and the private sector is based on the principle of mutual support to achieve sustainable tourism development by allocating scarce public resources to serve multiple purposes and ensuring benefits for the whole community.

3.5 COMMUNITY SUPPORT AND TOLERANCE FOR VISITORS FROM OTHER CULTURES

Another important issue for sustainable tourism is **cultural harmony**. The world's cultures are rich and diverse. In the context of tourism, **culture** is the totality of socially transmitted behavioral patterns, arts, beliefs, institutions, and all other products of human activity and thought characteristic of a community or nation. Anthropologist **E. Adamson Hoebel** defined culture as "the integrated system of learned behavior that is characteristic of the members of a society and which are not the result of biological inheritance . . . culture is not genetically predetermined; it is noninstinctive . . . [culture] is wholly the result of social invention and is transmitted and maintained solely through communication and learning."

Several characteristics of culture emerge from this definition:

- Culture has numerous and diverse traits.
- Culture is a learned behavior. One is not born with it.
- Culture is the creation of the human mind and practice. It is not intuitive.
- Culture spreads through communication.
- Culture is not limited to human acts, customs, or material possessions. It embraces a large field of human behavior and creativity.

The process of spreading individual cultural traits from their source to other areas is known as **cultural diffusion.** These traits evolve at their source for many centuries. They finally break out of their place of origin and disseminate throughout the world by migration, conquest, trade, and communications. Humans carry these traits with them wherever they go. They prosper when they dominate another culture, and the local or preexisting culture tends to disappear or be substantially modified.

In modern times, culture diffuses through communication technologies that include printed material, computers, television, film and other arts, and audio media acting as vehicles of dissemination. Tourism, which involves traveling, is also considered a means for transmitting culture.

Thousands of years ago, curiosity and need motivated humans to cross the boundaries of their immediate environment and venture out into the unknown. Early explorers who crossed continents and circled the world encountered the exotic cultures of China and Japan in the Orient and the cultures of natives living in the rain forests of Africa, the East and West Indies, and the Amazon. European empires stretched from England, France, Spain, Portugal, Russia, and Holland to the rest of the world through exploration, conquest, and colonization. Mongol,

Chinese, Greek, Roman, Turkic, and Arab invaders built the earliest empires that stretched over the known world of their time from East to West. All brought their cultures with them, and often blended theirs with, or suppressed, local cultures. Crusaders hacked their way to Jerusalem but brought back the wisdom of the Middle East. Arab civilization of one thousand years ago contributed to the Renaissance in Europe five hundred years later.

Geographic circumstances of location, climate, and natural terrain have nurtured human settlements and societies on many continents over many centuries. With each wave of invasion by foreign powers, local cultures have adapted and changed. Colonizing half of the world has led to cultural conflicts that are continuing in our time. True to the cultures of their time, some invaders committed unspeakable atrocities. Colonial powers caused resentment and enduring hostility in the societies they colonized. As empires shrank and former colonies gained their independence and self-esteem, old resentments did not disappear. They fester to this day in many parts of the world.

Clash of cultures often leads to mutual hatred. When the Spanish explorer **Pizzaro** invaded the land of the Incas in 1542, **King Atahualpa** was not worried. He did not know the culture of the invaders. Having traveled a long distance from Spain, Pizzaro had no alternative but to go forward with his two weapons: disease, against which the Incans had no resistance, and sixty-two horses. They helped him conquer an empire of three million people with one hundred soldiers. The Inca Empire disappeared, but resentment of the invaders who supplanted the culture of the enslaved Incas remained.

Unlike the invader, the traveling troubadour of the medieval age was not a threat to the stability of the places he visited. In fact, he carried news from other lands. The troubadour was much in demand. He told stories of different cultures and entertained his audience with music from other lands. Perhaps the best-known raconteur of exotic stories was **Marco Polo**. He told the emperor of China about the ways of the Western world. He also brought back to his home city, Venice, a black powder that changed history and warfare. China used this powder for entertainment and pyrotechnics. The Europeans developed it into gunpowder for shooting destructive missiles from cannons.

In 1620, Pilgrims arriving in the New World aboard the *Mayflower* survived their first winter with the help and hospitality of native Americans from the **Massasoit** tribe. Visitors and natives celebrated the first Thanksgiving together. The natives regarded the visitors as a harmless and misguided group of people seeking refuge on their land and extended their hospitality. Over the course of the following two hundred years, however, the big push to the West by a never-ending stream of Europeans changed the hospitable feelings of Native American tribes toward their visitors. They began to regard their former guests as unwelcome intruders and despaired over their future. Two hundred years later, their native cultures are being appreciated and explored in live and permanent exhibits and museums.

Today, tourism evokes contrasting sentiments and reactions. Often, natives live in poverty and share their country with visitors from distant lands who are far wealthier, far more educated, and far more powerful. Tourists are accommodated in isolated enclaves, resorts, and compounds where natives satisfy and serve their needs. At the extreme, the contrast illustrates the subordination of native populations to the misplaced political and economic policies of their government. How, then, can governments bridge the cultural and economic gap and pursue just and sustainable tourism development policies for their constituents?

The answer lies in establishing a secure and safe environment for tourists where law prevails and local culture is protected. Generalizations cannot be made. But natives frequently talk about law and government in the same breath, usually in the course of explaining their institutions, behaviors, or rights. For them the law is given, but ignored if it is convenient. The law is personalized, and officers of the government are held in high esteem when they protect the interests of natives or are hated when they become instruments of government oppression and greed for tourist dollars.

Throughout history, with few exceptions, the law has been remarkable for its sometime irrelevance to native populations. In the context of tourism, natives may perceive the law as a document that ensures the paternalistic attitudes and culture of tourists toward natives rather than serving as the legal basis for organizing the local community. When law and government conflict with local customs, natives may ignore the law and settle issues according to local customs and by traditional leaders of the community, not by officials of the government.

Riding the waves of cultural diffusion, natives do not easily surrender their customs and traditional occupations in the region. They resist external influences that force them to change their way of life, personal values, customs, and beliefs to accommodate tourists. Nevertheless, leaving their dislike of outsiders aside, they generally show varying degrees of hospitality to strangers and ensure their safety and security for financial gain until such time as their hospitality appears misplaced and their self-esteem and dignity are offended. Sometimes the resolution of these issues may lead to violence. It is important, therefore, that harmony between traditional and foreign cultures is established through demonstration and communication, which will lead to mutual respect between the parties and ensure acceptance of tourism and the cultural changes it may bring.

3.6 GOVERNMENT ASSISTANCE AT NATIONAL, REGIONAL, AND LOCAL LEVELS

Government interest in providing local communities with roads, water and sewer systems, and other tourism infrastructure is closely related to the local, regional, and national political climate. In democratic free-market systems, interest is greatest when elections are near. Political parties play this game to the hilt. Without the support of locals, tourism infrastructure projects, and tourism as we know it, are not undertaken. Entrepreneurs sell the merits of their tourism projects to tribal chiefs, mayors, or governors. These community leaders hold hearings and, when they are convinced, they sell the merits of projects to the public. Their support is a prerequisite for tourism development in their region.

In centrally planned or mixed economies, government support of tourism development originates at the national level. The ruler or governing body initiates tourism development and decides whether, or how, it will proceed. The strategy is then broken down into its components and assigned to various government agencies at the regional and destination levels for implementation. Projects are executed, and measures are taken according to a funding program and schedule. Private sector entrepreneurs from local or foreign countries pay close attention to the direction the governing body wants to take and tailor their tourism projects accordingly.

3.7 PERSONAL SECURITY AND SAFETY OF TOURISTS

It is a rare occurrence when the head of a government agency, given the job of promoting international tourism, declines to do so. This situation arose in Iraq during the war of 2003–2004 when coalition forces invaded the country. The chairman of the Tourism Board tried to keep tourists away until political stability was established in the country. Unable to ensure the personal security of tourists looking for "extreme" experiences, he was quoted as saying, "I understand all about wanting to have an adventure, but Iraq could be a one-way trip. This is not the place for tourists [now]" (*The Wall Street Journal,* October 7, 2004).

Because **personal security** is a prime consideration, war, terrorism, and natural disasters are anathema to tourism. Tourists shy away from countries and destinations where the risk of personal harm is perceived or real. They prefer to travel to a destination country where internal political stability is ensured by a stable government, with passport controls, an effective police force, and friendly natives, all of which have the potential to make the tourism experience worthwhile. The threat of terrorism during transportation and at the destination is a serious negative consideration. Walled-in and gated resorts add to the perception of security, although they do not guarantee actual security. The possibility of extreme violence in the form of suicide bombers leaves tourists vulnerable. Israel is the prime example of a country facing such situations. Travel agencies and governments issue travel advisories and raise the alarm against traveling to certain countries and destinations. At times, governments take extraordinary measures when threats of terrorism are imminent.

In addition to considering personal security, tourists must recognize the probability of **natural disasters** when making travel plans to particular destinations. In certain climates and terrains, avalanches, hurricanes, monsoons, and typhoons are common occurrences during certain seasons. Sailing in open seas carries the risk of being stranded if a sailing vessel is damaged. Other hazards, like earthquakes and tsunamis, are not predictable in destinations located over the fault lines of the earth's crust. Some hazards are not avoided but are actually sought in adventure tourism. When tourists climb the sheer face of Eiger in the Alps, they put their personal safety willingly in jeopardy. Climbing the highest peaks in the world, like Everest, Annapurna, K2, and other peaks in the Himalayas, requires special equipment, guides, and skills. These are destinations where only tourists trained in high-altitude mountain climbing can deal with the risks involved and enjoy the experience of adventure tourism. Deep-sea diving and scuba diving in shark-infested waters are popular but high-risk recreational pursuits.

Access to well-equipped **medical facilities** and competent medical staff is also a major concern. It is important to have emergency first aid and an exit strategy for tourists when things go wrong—for example, when injuries, poisoning, and serious illnesses occur. Emergency evacuation to better-equipped medical facilities may be necessary. A snake bite during an African safari or a shark bite in the Great Barrier Reef of Australia has to be dealt with immediately. In some countries, knowing that a MEDIVAC helicopter with trained medical staff on board can be called by radio to lift them to safety is a comfort for adventure-loving tourists. Naval and air corps services of a country, like the U.S. Coast Guard, are essential for maintaining the safety of seagoing tourists when an unexpected storm catches them unprepared.

No tourist would wish to get hurt or sick while traveling in distant lands. To ensure their safety, government services must be available at a moment's notice on land and at sea. Cruise ships come equipped with medical staff and a clinic on board for medical emergencies. Major cities in all countries have hospitals and poison centers where medical staff know the language of the stricken tourist. Police officers and rescue personnel who attend a traffic accident victim have the equipment to extricate the tourist from the wreckage. The safety and security issues for tourists are numerous. However, travel risks cannot be eliminated altogether. Travel insurance is available to cover some of the risks.

There is a reverse side to the safety and security issue. All tourists must obey the laws and regulations of the lands they are visiting. The laws and regulations of certain countries are lax, while those of others are very strict. Assuming that preferential treatment will be given when one runs into trouble can be a big mistake and a rude awakening for the tourist. In particular, soliciting sex or drugs could land the tourist in jail for months, if not years. When victimized by theft or bodily injury, a tourist may seek the help of his or her consulate. This may take time or could be impossible in remote areas of the world.

Hazardous pursuits, like bungee jumping from a high bridge to the canyon below, may be an invitation to prosecution. The host country, region, or destination may have forbidden such pursuits and may not have facilities or trained personnel to retrieve the risk taker if things go wrong. In such cases, the authorities appreciate common sense and expect responsible conduct from tourists to avoid creating an unpleasant incident and casualties. The expense of retrieval for all parties is another factor to consider.

On the receiving site, local governments must be prepared to respond to multiple crises, including the ordinary and unexpected. A tested and operational crisis management system involving health, police, fire, and volunteer organizations must be trained and ready for action at all times. International assistance can also be activated when a major natural disaster occurs.

3.8   CODES OF ETHICS AND BEHAVIOR FOR TOURISTS

Tourists should extend their respect for local authority to the local population and culture. A gesture, an inappropriate remark, or plain stupidity could create a confrontation with natives in which tourists usually end up as losers. Arrogance and rudeness are not accepted behavior in any society. Petty disputes or behavior that could strain universally accepted host–guest relations must be avoided. For example, the Holy Qur'an of Islam prescribes modesty in personal appearance for both men and women. Non-Muslim visitors in Arab lands often do not know this code of behavior and consequently ignore it. When local sensitivities are offended, exposure of body parts could cause unpleasant confrontations with the authorities and the public alike. Discretion and privacy can prevent these incidents.

Disrupting the local culture or worse, ignoring it, amounts to denying a tourist the pleasure of experiencing diversity. For the curious and responsible traveler, the pleasure lies in being aware of diversity and anticipating the unexpected. If tourism is a social experiment intended to change the local culture, it is not the prerogative of the patronizing tourist to impose the change. It will be up to the natives to decide which foreign influences are acceptable and which are not. The selection can be particularly difficult; for example, when a local culture does not accept the profit motive as a factor in social and commercial interactions. Tourism policies must be aimed at preserving the values and customs of the local culture and ensuring their diversity. They should also make tourists aware of the provisions of local codes of ethics, social mores, and behavioral conventions.

There are many more culture-related situations in which visiting tourists should observe and act accordingly. They include, but are not limited, to the following:

- Do everything possible to make sure that traveling among the people of a different culture is beneficial to and supportive of that culture.
- Make sure that traveling to fragile and threatened societies and enclaves will not overwhelm their culture and environment.
- Wear respectful attire and consider the fact that poverty or choice may prevent a certain segment of the local population from wearing clothing similar to yours and eating your kind of food.
- Communicate in the local language as much as possible, even haltingly, with poor grammar and mistakes. However, take care that seriously misleading miscommunication does not occur.
- Be careful not to accept local customs that would be harmful and unhealthy to you.
- Be prepared to learn and expect the unexpected, which could be good as well as bad.
- Be ready and willing to improvise when things do not go as expected.
- Refuse to participate in the trade of local artifacts prohibited by the authorities.

- Buy arts and crafts produced by local craftsmen and, if known, patronize establishments that are owned by locals.
- Give to beggars selectively, knowing that begging could be a practice sometimes accepted locally as a form of compensation for those with disabilities, elderly men, and single women with children.
- Eat and drink discriminately to protect your health without offending your host.
- Where appropriate, haggle over the price of a good or service for fun and savings, knowing that haggling is a socially accepted practice that local merchants expect.
- Use the black market, where it exists, at your peril, being aware that such transactions are often illegal.
- Use financial enticement discreetly in the form of money, goods, and services as a gift, which may be an acceptable form of supplementary income for local residents.
- Be conscious of the need to preserve the environment at all times.
- Avoid purchasing gift products made from wild animals, which are prohibited by international and local laws.
- If possible and appropriate, leave something behind for the preservation of the local culture and the environment when leaving the country. Examples are monetary contributions to local environmental preservation funds or museums.

Culture includes most, if not all, of the experiences planned and expected by tourists through the act of tourism. If curiosity and the need to know propel individuals to explore, the multitude of cultures around the world exist for them to reach out and discover.

Chapter Highlights

- A country must decide on its own whether to undertake international tourism after making careful analyses of the costs and benefits and after passing the sustainability test.
- Sustainable tourism is best ensured through conservation and renewal of tourism resources for succeeding generations.
- Conservation and renewal of tourism resources must match or exceed the demands of the tourism industry.
- Continuity of tourism depends on preserving and improving a high-quality tourism product.
- Regardless of the economic system, tourism depends on government–private sector cooperation, entrepreneurship, and risk taking.
- Private sector establishments own and operate profit-making tourism businesses.
- Government organizations own and operate not-for-profit public facilities and establish guidelines and regulations.

- Tourism infrastructure is the sum total of basic facilities, equipment, and installations needed for a functioning tourism industry.
- The government usually owns and operates large infrastructure assets like airports, highways, and sanitation facilities, whereas the private sector may own private roads, hospitals, and power generation facilities.
- Feasibility and market studies are required prior to receiving government approval and usually to obtain financing. Often, these studies are overly optimistic in their projections and conclusions. They must be carefully evaluated.
- Community support and cultural tolerance are essential for tourism to prosper.
- Tourists must be prepared to respect the local culture and respond in kind to the hospitality of residents.
- Personal security of tourists and political stability of the country must be ensured for tourism to succeed and flourish.

4

Examples of General and Special Interest Tourism

This chapter describes the characteristics of different types of tourism by giving examples from around the world and by illustrating the activities and levels of interest associated with their tourism product. Several types of tourism can occur simultaneously at the same location. Their collective sustainability could become an issue if their mutual compatibility is not assured.

- Tourism is based on the likes, dislikes, and interests of tourists.
- Depending on the interests of tourists, a great variety of tourism is possible.
- Tourism encompasses all continents, all seasons, and almost all countries and cultures.
- New destinations, new activities, and new types of tourism are created as interests change.

4.1 DEVELOPING AND SELECTING TYPES OF TOURISM

Tourism is based on offering tourism products to tourists at destinations where they will satisfy their general or special recreational interests in appropriate environments.

General interest tourism consists of an array of unsolicited experiences. It does not focus on a particular interest and experience not specifically demanded by the tourist. **Special interest** tourism focuses on a particular interest and experience chosen by the tourist. It is selective and often personalized.

A large variety of special interest tourism experiences can be planned by extracting individual themes from the tourism products of destinations. The selection should be discriminate. Only themes with particular appeal to the connoisseurs of given subjects should be selected and developed. These themes wrap around the specialized group tours and provide the selected experiences. General interest tourism does not have this requirement. Group tours can be planned by packaging several themes together and offering a composite image experience of the destination visited.

Both general and special interest tourism are possible in all continents and seasons. They may embrace a variety of indigenous cultures and environments. As interests may change over time, new themes, new attractions, and new facilities should be created to ensure the sustainability of tourism.

Tourism involves moving tourists, in groups or alone, to sites and events where they experience the subjects of their interest by seeing, feeling, participating, and exploring. They acquire this experience by performing many types of recreational and utilitarian activities. Their satisfaction comes from the diversity and quality of the experience.

The key words are *seeing, feeling, participating*, and *exploring* subjects of interest. Tourism occurs when tourists make contact with the subjects of their interest. Doors to personal satisfaction open by bringing tourists face to face with what they are expecting to find at their destinations. Crossing the threshold from expectation to satisfaction is the object of successful tourism planning and development.

It is necessary to identify what gives satisfaction to tourists for creating tourism demand. The behavioral aspects of tourism demand are key to finding sites and events that would be part of the tourism experience. What tourists like or dislike depends on their personal interests, the activities they undertake, and the level of their interests. Tourism planning and development organizes all these factors and turns them into a productive tourism industry.

This book uses the BIK System for planning and developing tourism. The BIK System defines the types of tourism and corresponding tourism products in terms of site and event attractions and facilities. Site and event attractions and facilities, in turn, are assigned one or more activities and are rated for the satisfaction they offer tourists on a seasonal or year-round basis.

There are many ways of grouping subjects of interest. Each country, region, or destination has its own set of site and event attractions, facilities, and their associated activities, making their tourism product diversified. A sweeping generalization is not useful. Each country, region, or destination must survey its own set of tourism products; classify its own attractions, facilities, and activities; and assign a level of interest for tourists based on a tourism planning classification system. The BIK System provides one such classification.

There are often many possible ways of assembling several types of tourism into mutually compatible groups. Types of tourism are not alternate forms. They do not present either/or choices. Several types of tourism can coexist and can develop into a highly diversified tourism industry. The combined activity mix is what distinguishes the tourism product of a given destination from that of its competitors.

Given its natural and human-made attractions, the activities would be chosen from a list appropriate for the destination region. They would be different for each attraction and facility. However, the level of interest for tourists would be selected from among four levels adopted by the BIK System:

- *International*, that is, attractions that would interest foreign, domestic, and regional tourists, as well as local people
- *National*, that is, attractions that would interest domestic and regional tourists, as well as local people

- *Regional*, that is, attractions that would interest regional tourists and local people
- *Destination*, that is, attractions that would interest local people

Tourists may be interested in attractions at all levels of interest. However, the drawing power of attractions declines as the level of interest diminishes.

4.2 GENERAL SIGHTSEEING TOURISM

Seeing is believing. When tourists go beyond their daily commuting area and enter the world of tourism, they are primed to absorb new scenes and experiences. Experience begins to register when chosen modes of locomotion, whether train, car, motorcycle, bus, bicycle, yacht, sailboat, cruise ship, airplane, balloon, camel, horse, or walking, elicit different sensations. The scenery may be the same, but the experience depends on the mode of locomotion. That is why two tourists visiting the same site but using different forms of transportation may return to their homelands with different impressions and images.

Many factors play a role in giving diverse impressions and images. Speed of locomotion is one such factor. **Kevin Lynch**, while teaching at MIT during the 1960s, named the concept of perceiving and analyzing experiential images **imageability**. He advocated a method of planning and design for maximizing the perception of urban and rural images. He applied his guidelines to creating pleasant and functional urban landscapes.

When the individual is *moving*, Lynch realized that eyes scan and relay images of rapidly changing scenery to the brain at certain speeds. The fleeting images are seen one second and are gone the next. Therefore, it is impossible to catch all the details of scenery from a fast-moving car; whereas, a leisurely walk enables the individual to better grasp the details of the environment. While one is moving, all basic elements of the environment must be used for perceiving the street and landscape. Like a three-dimensional sculpture or a two-dimensional painting, a pleasant street or landscape must harmonize texture, rhythm, color, proportion, symmetry, and balance into a pleasing whole. Driving at fifty miles an hour along Lake Shore Drive in Chicago, for example, is a visual experience. The scenery of downtown skyscrapers, and their perspectives, change every second. New buildings appear while the Sears Tower turns and gives a different view of its massive structure.

In the opposite experience, the individual is *stationary* and the scenery is moving. Observing many ships passing through the Bosphorus Strait, while ferryboats scurry about in the busy harbor of Istanbul, and when the reddening last rays of the sun sink behind the minarets and domes of the Blue Mosque, is an experience in motion. The scenery is moving, whereas the viewer is stationary. The eye catches the moving visual images from a stationary position and registers them in the brain as a visual experience.

Visual experience is reinforced by other sensations. Hearing, smelling, touching, and feeling heat or cold are factors that contribute to the enjoyment of general sightseeing. The aroma of the spice market; the fresh scent of the day's catch at a fish market; the noise of the hustle and bustle and the sing-song of merchants praising their products in the bazaar; and feeling the warmth of the tropical sea and sand, are engaging for the perceptive traveler. He or she absorbs and processes these impressions, storing the experiences in memory and often reinforcing them by taking or purchasing pictures or other memorabilia of the scenes.

In developing sightseeing tours for tourists, tour planners must take into account not only the story that goes with the places to be visited, but also the visual, auditory, sensory, and olfactory experiences that could be absorbed along the way to maximize the pleasure and satisfaction of the visit. When developing similar experiences in new attractions, the tour planner must be creative in duplicating the same sensations.

A sample of activities for tourists associated with general sightseeing includes:

- Riding (e.g., train, car, bus, ship, airplane, helicopter)
- Walking (e.g., street, trail)
- Observing (e.g., rural, urban, coastal, desert, mountain, and other scenery)
- Sensing (e.g., smell, touch, sound)
- Other (e.g., comparing daily experiences with those of other tourists)

Further information about general sightseeing can be found on the following Web sites: http://www.answers.com/topic/tourism and http://www.londontown.com/sightseeing/.

4.3 CULTURAL TOURISM

Experiencing the world of culture and studying its many branches is a challenging and scholarly undertaking. **Culture** is the totality of socially transmitted behavior, arts, beliefs, institutions, and all other products of human work and thought characteristic of a community. It is a style of social and artistic expression characteristic of a society.

Civilization is almost synonymous with *culture*. It is the advanced stage of development in the arts and sciences and is characterized by social, political, and cultural complexity. Regardless of how fine tuning refines these definitions, one thing is common to all of them: Civilization is the history of humankind and the product of the human mind.

One can look at the traditions, wisdom, and civilization of Native Americans, for example, and be impressed with the depth of their perception of the world and the purpose of human existence:

We are the People of this land
We were created out of the forces of earth and sky, the stars and water.
We must make sure that the balance of the earth be kept.
There is no other way.
We must struggle to share our human lives with each other.
We must fight against those forces which will take our humanity from us.
We must ensure that life continues.

AUTHOR UNKNOWN, CHACTOW TRIBE

A visitor to a distant land may want to experience its culture by exploring the environment from which the culture emerged. His or her visit could be short, allowing only a sampling of the culture. Or, the visitor's knowledge of the culture may carry him or her to places widely separated in time. Alternatively, the visitor may decide to stay for a long period at a place of learning and become a student, thus shedding his or her tourist status.

In exploring the lost cities of Machu Picchu, Angkor, Bogazkoy, Pompei, Pergamon, or Persepolis, or the cliff dwellings of Mesa Verde, tourists confirm that they have specialized interests in archeology and architecture. Groups led by a scholar or privately funded scientific expeditions search the origins of a culture, visit remote parts of the world, and produce educational media programs. Their passion and their profession create a special interest form of tourism focused on culture.

Pursuit of culture could take tourists to attractions as diverse as ballet at the Bolshoi Theater in Moscow; a symphony concert at Lincoln Center, in New York City; and the home tour of famous composers of classical music. It could be a museum tour of Europe, starting with the British Museum in London and continuing to the Louvre in Paris, the Hermitage in St. Petersburg, and the Topkapi Museum in Istanbul. Following the trail of an exhibit of rare stamps could be the pursuit of ardent philatelists.

There is no need to enumerate all the cultural products of the human intellect that could become the subject of specialized cultural tourism. Each country, region, or destination can identify potential subjects of interest their land has created and can build a database of cultural attractions using the BIK System.

Proposed activities for tourists associated with cultural tourism include:

- Riding (e.g., car, airplane, helicopter, bus, railway, canoe, boat)
- Walking (e.g., street, trail)
- Observing (e.g., historic, artistic, political, literary, technical, and other attractions)
- Participating (e.g., reading, writing, playing, listening)
- Attending (e.g., concerts, plays, ballets, exhibits, reenactments)
- Other (e.g., eating a new ethnic food)

Further discussion of cultural tourism can be found on the following Web sites: http://www.victoriaculture.org/resource/resource_file/3/WHAT_IS_CULTURAL_TOURISM.pdf and http://en.wikipedia.org/wiki/Cultural_tourism.

4.4 ECOTOURISM

Ecotourism is a reminder for tourists of why our earth is a very special and fragile place and why we must protect it. Conservation of the environment through education and recreation is a form of tourism that has received a great deal of attention from tourists who have a special interest in the environment.

Ecotourism is not limited to observing the natural environment. The earth as a biophysical system is the subject of many scientific inquiries including those focusing on geology, oceanography, volcanology, botany, zoology, and biology. Conservation of artifacts, monuments, buildings, whole cities, citadels, fortifications, parks, and other urban forms is also the subject of ecotourism. These specimens are endangered just like other fragile, one-of-a kind forms of nature. Ecotourism provides the umbrella under which a whole series of conservation programs are organized and seek support. The UNWTO, in particular, takes ecotourism very seriously and recognizes its role in conservation. (See "Nature Sanctuaries" in Appendix A.)

Proposed activities for tourists associated with ecotourism include:

- Climbing (e.g., rock, mountain)
- Hiking (e.g., desert, forest)
- Trekking (e.g., mountain, ox wagon)
- Sailing (e.g., in fresh and salt water)
- Observing (e.g., whales, birds)
- Finding (e.g., endangered species)
- Other (e.g., photographing)

More detailed information and discussion of ecotourism can be found on the following Web sites: http://en.wikipedia.org/wiki/Ecotourism and http://piedrablanca.org/ecotourism-definition.htm.

4.5 GAMING (GAMBLING) AND CASINO TOURISM

Gambling is a game of chance played for stakes with skill and luck. It is not a new form of recreation, although the industry has fairly recently applied the label *gaming* to itself. Casinos, as places for various forms of gambling, have existed as legitimate recreational enterprises in different parts of the world for centuries. High-stakes gambling has been pursued in many casinos around the world for more than a century. In Europe, one of the most prestigious casinos is located in Monte Carlo. Here, the industry is romanticized. A royal dynasty is carrying on the tradition of Monte Carlo with the rich and famous of the world by offering a high level of excitement.

In the 1930s, another gambling center emerged in Las Vegas, Nevada, when construction workers from the nearby Hoover Dam and visitors from Los Angeles began to patronize the open city. After organized crime figures were barred from running many resorts and gambling establishments in the city, a new era was born. The mystique of Las Vegas became ingrained in the minds of the public when one of the richest men in the world and a recluse, Howard Hughes, chose to live on the top floor of the casino hotel he owned. Since then, the "Strip" has been marked by steady building and continual transformation.

Today, Monte Carlo is continuing its legacy of elegance and high-stakes gambling for the elite. Las Vegas has become the American city of lights and a fascinating place where mammoth hotels and vibrant architecture, combined with glittering entertainment and extravagant live shows, provide tourists with one-of-a-kind sensory experiences. Exotic food, liquor, and closely supervised gambling continue to attract tourists by expanding the activity base to include large-scale conventions and amusements for children. This spectacular showcase is now unique in the world. It is a place where the entire family can vacation and find recreation for adults and youngsters alike. Las Vegas has become its own cultural and sensory experience.

In the United States, a more recent development is gambling casinos and resorts built on land owned by Native American tribes. Many entrepreneurs formed joint ventures with a number of tribes to operate gambling facilities. Using provisions in federal laws permitting gambling on tribal lands, they built these casinos on tribal land near major cities. For example, the Seminole tribe is located in the Miami-Ft. Lauderdale-Boca Raton area. The Mashantucket Pequot and Mohegan tribes are operating large casino facilities on their land in the State of Connecticut and are drawing tourists from the Boston, Providence, and New York metropolitan areas. Taking advantage of the proximity of the tribal lands, these casinos seek to attract visitors from cities where gambling is not allowed. The financial success of these casinos has had multiple impacts. With revenues generated from their casino operations, these tribes were able to erase poverty from their lands because net income from gambling was shared by all members of the tribe. Gambling also generated the investment capital needed for the tribes' economic development. However, this pattern has not been duplicated by most of the six hundred Native American tribes, except where laws allow gambling and tribal lands are reasonably close to major urban centers or are located on major intercity routes.

The rest of the world took a similar attitude toward gambling. Gambling was not acceptable on moral grounds. A few countries allowed gambling for foreigners but not for their citizens. With few exceptions, these casinos did not derive the expected economic benefits. Now, cruise ships take gamblers to international waters. Riverboats tied to docks in major cities, horse racing, dog racing, off-track betting, and lotteries add new dimensions to the business and recreation of gambling. From all indications, gambling as a tourist attraction is here to stay. It is worth noting that, in some countries, gambling operations have been infiltrated by criminal elements. Money laundering, fraud, embezzlement, prostitution, drug use, and forms of human slavery are endemic. In particular, the countries of Southeast Asia are vulnerable to these social ills.

Proposed activities for tourists associated with gambling and casino tourism include:

- Gambling (e.g., slot machines, poker, baccarat, blackjack, roulette, horse racing)
- Attending (e.g., comedy, music, dance, other shows)
- Attending (e.g., boxing, wrestling, tennis, football, soccer, other spectator sports)
- Staying (e.g., at a resort hotel, sleeping, eating, playing, viewing fine art on loan)
- Golfing (e.g., at a golf course)
- Shopping (e.g., general merchandise, clothing, gifts, art)
- Other (e.g., swimming and sunbathing)

More elaborate definitions of gambling and casinos can be found on two Wikipedia Web sites: http://en.wikipedia.org/wiki/Casino and http://en.wikipedia.org/wiki/Gambling.

4.6 ENTERTAINMENT TOURISM

Entertainment tourism differs from cultural tourism by the type of experience that the attraction offers. Cultural tourism is generally associated with the fine arts such as classical music, ballet, art, and architecture; whereas, entertainment tourism offers primarily popular music, art, and architecture. Films, theater, nightclubs, rock music, country music, jazz, square dancing, tango and other forms of dancing, and pop art are forms of entertainment tourism. They are popular around the world and have large followings. They draw visitors from far and near, depending on who the principal performers at the attractions are. In effect, the events are the primary attractions, not the sites.

The variety of entertainment types is very large, ranging from sidewalk jugglers to Las Vegas stage shows. With the exception of several universal entertainment forms, most types of entertainment have traditional or local roots. As such, they fill a need for accessible, immediate, rewarding, and participatory entertainment. Universal entertainment may require extensive travel, whereas local entertainment does not.

Proposed activities for tourists associated with entertainment tourism include:

- Attending (e.g., country music, pop music, jazz, and other shows)
- Attending (e.g., theater, including dramas and comedies, concerts, circus)
- Attending (e.g., movies)
- Attending (e.g., nightclub)
- Attending (e.g., celebration, wedding, engagement, reunion, birthday)
- Dining (e.g., eating at a restaurant, picnicking)
- Other (e.g., purchasing audio and audiovisual recordings of performers)

The following Web sites contain more information on entertainment tourism: http://www.bransontourismcenter.com/bransonarticle30.htm and http://entplanet.blogspot.com/2007/09/tourism-entertainment-industries.html.

4.7 VILLAGE TOURISM

For a rapidly urbanizing world, village life is becoming a novelty, and for some a necessity. As an escape from the pressures of living in the city, even for a weekend, vacationing in the country is becoming a high priority. Living in the suburbs is not enough. The simple life of the village, preferably within commuting distance of the city, is considered an ideal combination.

In the United States, farms in general and the Amish farms of Pennsylvania in particular, have strong appeal. Guests participate in the daily life and work of the farm as much as they wish.

They have private bedrooms, but sometimes they share the bathroom. They are served homemade food and share the kitchen table with the host family. They are given a courtesy tour of the farm, riding in the family horse carriage or the sleigh during the winter. A barn-raising event, to which guests are invited, is a very special occasion that calls for the participation of the whole village.

Villages in western Turkey, for example Ozdere, offer a different experience. Following the exchange of immigrant populations in the 1920s, houses of a village abandoned by former Greek villagers were restored by Turkish entrepreneurs fifty years later and marketed as time-sharing vacation and bed-and-breakfast homes. Guests leave their automobile at the entrance to the village, where the paved road turns into a rough cobblestone street. Stone buildings, cobblestone streets, the public fountain at the village square, an abandoned house of worship, and a vineyard complete the local architecture. A modest six-table open-air fish restaurant with a grapevine trellis for shade is the only place to eat out. Guests order fish caught that afternoon only a few hundred yards from the shore. The singing waiter/owner is happy to have his or her only customers and guests for the night, and guests they are. The village dogs lounging outside the door wait for handouts. This represents the idyllic scene and simple life the urban guest is searching for as a temporary respite. If tourists are interested, they are welcome to water the flowers by hauling water from the well outside their cottage. When their time is up, guests pack up, pay the caretaker, and head for the superhighway that will take them to the third major city of Turkey, Izmir, content with the thought that life could not get any better, at least temporarily.

Variations in the two village tourism examples just described are many. In Europe, the United States, South America, South Africa, the Middle East, and the Far East, picturesque villages are selected for village tourism. Cattle ranches in Patagonia, banana and sugar plantations in the Caribbean, dude ranches in Texas, and fishing villages anywhere are promising subjects for village tourism. The primary considerations are proximity to cities and easy access to the services found in cities when they are needed.

Proposed activities for tourists associated with village tourism include:

- Walking (e.g., through the village)
- Riding (e.g., horse, horse carriage, donkey, camel)
- Participating (e.g., farming, building, milking cows, fishing)
- Sightseeing (e.g., village architecture, lifestyle)
- Eating (e.g., at home, restaurant, picnic)
- Other (e.g., learning local customs)

Village tourism is further explained and elaborated in examples given on these two Web sites: http://www.central-java-tourism.com/desa-wisata/en/about.htm and http://www.hotelnepal.com/nepal/program.php?pro_id=29.

4.8 ADVENTURE TOURISM

Jumping out of a perfectly safe airplane with a parachute, or from a tall bridge after being tied at the ankles to a bungee rope, involves danger and risk of life. Exploring the jungles of the Amazon or Central Africa provides a thrill and a learning experience, but it also carries the risk of exposure to serious diseases and compromises with safety. A car or bicycle rally through the Sahara in Africa, Baja California in Mexico, or the Great Outback of Australia is a macho activity. So is hanging from the underside of a jutting rock, holding on for dear life with ten fingers and avoiding the abyss below. Riding the rapids of the Colorado River, scuba diving the "wall" at the Cayman Islands, or diving to the depths in search of sunken Spanish treasures in the Gulf of Mexico make good stories. Climbing Mount Everest without oxygen equipment involves more than sport. Adding to scientific knowledge by exploring caves and underwater cavities is a worthy but dangerous experience. In short, with the exception of undertaking a scientific project, adventure tourism is for those desiring an adrenaline rush and excitement.

Adventure destinations often offer cultural attractions mixed with adventure experiences. They present various degrees of risk to the individual.

Typical **adventure experiences** are found in passages through the tropical rain forests of the Amazon; challenging the whitewater rivers of Colorado; participating in safaris in Amboseli, Lake Manyara, and Serengeti national parks in Kenya and Tanzania; trekking in Nepal between the Daulaghiri and Annapurna massifs; crossing the Sahara in Africa on camel or in auto rallies; crossing the ice cap of the North Pole and reaching the South Pole in Antarctica by plane; exploring the enormous caves of Saudi Arabia; discovering the waterways of Thailand on longtail boats, bamboo rafts, and barges; experiencing the Great Barrier Reef in Australia; climbing the highest Himalayan mountains; and small boat sailing around the world.

Typical combined **adventure and cultural experiences** are found in discovering imperial China and the Yangtze River; visiting the native yurts in Mongolia; observing the Taj Mahal, temples, and tigers in India on foot and by camel, elephant, and bicycle rickshaw; discovering the isolated natural world of the Galapagos Islands; exploring the diversity of Costa Rica by horseback, raft, kayak, and on foot; observing firsthand the relics of the lost Inca civilization in Machu Picchu and Cuzco in Peru; discovering ancient Egypt in Luxor and the Nile Valley; exploring the relics of history in the Middle East dating from the Paleolithic Age; and visiting fifteen thousand historic sites left by Hittite, Urartu, Phrygian, Lydian, Hellenic, Roman, Byzantine, Seljuk and Ottoman civilizations in Turkey, and many others.

Travel companies specializing in adventure tourism claim to offer many advantages. These include an intimate experience, unbeatable value, unforgettable discoveries, unique destinations, maximum mobility, and unique activities involving a variety of animal rides and visits to exotic places. Experiencing local cultures and local thrills are the primary rewards of adventure tourism.

In adventure tourism, experienced guides must lead tourists; proper equipment must be used; and precise procedures must be followed. Tourists must be properly informed and in very good physical condition. Reckless pursuit of thrills and irresponsible stunts are not beneficial for adventure tourism and must be prevented by the authorities and tour organizers.

Proposed activities for tourists associated with adventure tourism include:

- Climbing (e.g., mountain, rock)
- Walking (e.g., trekking, conventional walking)
- Diving (e.g., sky diving, scuba diving, high-rock diving)
- Rafting (e.g., whitewater, ocean)
- Rallying (e.g., auto, truck)
- Exploring (e.g., caves, underwater cavities)
- Riding (e.g., safari, car, animal, raft, canoe)

The following Web sites contain more information on adventure tourism: http://wikieducator.org/Adventure_Tourism and http://adventure.nationalgeographic.com/adventure/.

4.9 CRUISE SHIP TOURISM

Cruise ship tourism is improving every year. The classic tourist crossing the ocean as a paid passenger on a merchant ship has declared his or her independence. When the tourist becomes affluent and the comforts, itinerary, and schedule of the merchant ship no longer provide enough satisfaction, tourists demand specialized marine transport to take them, and others, to destinations that would interest them. During the past one hundred years, ships transporting passengers, rather than cargo, have pursued this specialization. Regular crossing of the Atlantic by luxury liners became fashionable. Maritime companies competed for the honor of earning the "Blue Riband" given to the fastest luxury liner. The ill-fated *Titanic*, where luxury cabins and steerage coexisted, evolved into one-class cruise ships where most staterooms and suites—no longer called *cabins*—have balconies and where all the conveniences and attractions of an opulent lifestyle are available.

The evolution of cruise ship tourism has kept pace with world events, including two world wars when passenger ships carried military troops. During the 1950s, jet airplanes began to capture business from ships that were transporting passengers between two destinations on regular schedules. The passenger ships were transformed into cruise ships when they could no longer compete in terms of speed but could provide comfort. They offered leisurely cruises among many ports of call that were the gateways to exotic places and offered unique vacation experiences. Based on their glorious past, some famous cruise ships were retired to become fixed attractions and hotels. Today, the *Queen Mary I* is resting on a rock bed on the shores of Long Beach, California, as a hotel. Its namesake, the *Queen Mary II*, weighing one hundred fifty-six thousand tons and providing all the comforts for its two thousand six hundred tourists, made its maiden Caribbean cruise in January 2004.

Evolution has also occurred in marine technology and interior design. One generation of cruise ships followed another with ever-larger passenger capacities, more powerful engines, smoother cruising, ever-increasing facilities for a greater variety of activities and entertainment, greater attention to service, excellent food and drink around the clock in multiple restaurants, and shopping on board, including a duty-free shop. Gambling in international waters became an important draw. Floor shows moved directly from Broadway and Las Vegas stages to those of fifteen-hundred-seat theaters in mega–cruise ships.

In 2008, thirty-eight new cruise ships were on order. In 2011, nine even larger and more fascinating cruise ships were being built in Italy, France, Germany, Norway, Japan, and Finland. There are concepts as large as a floating city on the drawing boards. This trend is creating a dilemma for existing ports of call. Few of them can accommodate these mega–cruise ships. Furthermore, fewer tourists are interested in the attractions and facilities these ports of call may offer on land. Increasingly, the cruise ship itself is becoming the attraction. By transforming themselves from a means of transporting tourists between destinations to an unforgettable onboard vacation experience, cruise ships are attracting an increasing number of tourists. They are competing effectively for a major share of the disposable income of vacationing tourists.

More cruise ships mean more demand for ports of call. Today, five or six huge cruise ships drop their anchors off one island or another in the Caribbean every day and ferry more than ten thousand tourists to the harbor. The congestion in the small shopping districts of these islands is substantial and is increasingly unwelcome to tourists. Some prefer to stay on board the ship and skip the land part of the cruise. The answer to the problem of congestion has been to create new destinations and new ports of call owned and operated by cruise ship companies and, not surprisingly, by airline companies. These fully serviced, exclusive, and often remote locations are isolated from the people and economy of the destination countries. The economic impact of cruise ships in helping to alleviate poverty is becoming increasingly questionable.

One possibility for new ports to visit is formerly icebound harbors in the Arctic. Global climate changes have resulted in some northern harbors and waterways becoming ice-free during more months of the year. Studies have been done, and are being done, to determine the feasibility of building port facilities to accommodate smaller but rugged cruise ships in these northern latitudes. Some less luxurious cruises are now offered in both the Arctic and Antarctic in converted icebreaker vessels. These vessels anchor offshore and ferry passengers to shore in inflatable and other small craft that do not need piers and docks.

Another issue with cruise ship tourism is supplies. To maintain its sanitary standards, all provisions are bought and loaded on the ship at the home port between cruises. Local suppliers in ports visited (not the home port) generally do not provision the ship. In these ports of call, ships leave behind only the value of the purchases made by tourists and port fees. These purchases, such as jewelry and electronic gadgets, are usually imported by the stores and could have a large import component. In many instances, excursion operations and larger-scale or high-value gift shops are seasonal and migratory. They set up business in temperate-weather ports in the summer and in tropical-weather ports in the winter. Profits may be substantial, but they are often transferred to home offices rather than reinvested in the local economy. Others, such as taxi services and local gift items, leave only a relatively small residual income for the destination. Locally made handicrafts and gift items, however, use local labor and are made of locally available materials. Their contribution to the local economy may be substantial if the products can be improved and used for other purposes, such as hotel construction, furnishings, and decoration. The pier and docking facilities are additional tourism infrastructure costs that must be borne by the government of the destination port as a condition for attracting cruise ships. These and other benefits and costs are some of the issues to be resolved in developing cruise ship tourism.

There is no question that cruise ship activities have favorable economic impacts on their home ports (usually in developed countries). The Port Authority of Seattle, Washington, reports that each time a cruise ship docks and resupplies for its next trip, about US$1.5 million is spent and circulated in its regional economy. According to the Port Authority of Seattle, 211 cruise ship visits were expected in 2009, generating projected revenues of US$312 million for regional businesses. The cruise ship business grew in Seattle from 6,615 passengers in 1999 to over 800,000 (estimated) in 2009. The Port Authority of Seattle recently spent US$71 million to create an additional docking area for cruise ships. The government of Australia expects eighty or ninety new cruise ship visits in its 2008–2009 season and reports that spending in the country's economy from cruise ship visits increased by 50.3% from the 2007–2008 to the 2008–2009 season (from AUS$376 million to AUS$565million).

Proposed activities associated with cruise ship tourism include:

- Cruising (e.g., ship, yacht, windjammer)
- Gambling (e.g., slots, cards, roulette)
- Dining (e.g., restaurant, café, buffet)
- Swimming (e.g., open pool, covered pool, sea)
- Snorkeling (e.g., sea)
- Scuba diving (e.g., sea, lake, cave)
- Riding (e.g., local port area excursions via horse carriage, horse, rickshaw, aircraft, small boat, train, and bus)
- Sunning (e.g., deck, beach, boat)
- Attending (e.g., shows, movies, lectures)
- Lounging (e.g., deck)
- Shopping (e.g., gift shops, stores)
- Partying (e.g., nightclub, dinner-dance)
- Sightseeing (e.g., historic, recreation, general)

Further definitions and discussion of cruise ship tourism can be found on the following Web sites: http://www.environment.gov.za/HotIssues/2009/cruiseliner/Cruise%20Ship%20Tourism.pdf and http://en.wikipedia.org/wiki/Cruise_ship.

4.10 SPORTS TOURISM

Sports tourism is a worldwide phenomenon. Both participatory and spectator sports bring tourists from long distances, even across continents, for participating in and attending international competitions like the World Soccer Cup or the Summer and Winter Olympic Games. The lure is in the excitement of competition and the sheer enjoyment of the artistry of sport. In 776 BC, the ancient Greeks held a festival of sport to honor Zeus, the greatest of the Greek gods. The games were held in a stadium built in a valley in Olympia. Since the time of the first Olympics, entire destinations, with multiple sport venues, have been built to accommodate a very large number of spectators and competitors. After a hiatus of fifteen hundred years, the modern Summer Olympic Games were held in Athens in 1896 and again in 2004, with shot put and discus events taking place in the historic grounds of the original Olympic theater in Olympia. The Summer Games are now held every four years in different cities around the world. The Winter Games are also held every four years, but are offset from the Summer Games by two years. There is fierce competition among cities and nations to host the Olympic Games, mainly for the prestige and long-term effects they may have. In recent years, the Olympic Games have become very expensive and cannot be justified by the short-term economic benefits associated with them.

The scale and level of interest in sports tourism are high. Hundreds of sports are practiced around the world. Generalization is difficult in understanding sports tourism. For planning and developing sports tourism, however, identifying common characteristics is helpful. Sport activities are classified by climate and season. Certain sports are played in outdoor venues only under certain seasonal conditions at certain locations. Broadly speaking, different types of sports are grouped as seasonal winter and summer sports, particularly in climates and locations where these sports can be played only in certain seasons. However, tradition also influences when, where, and how some sports are played.

Increasingly, venues for sports tourism are climate controlled. Huge arenas seating eighteen thousand spectators and having retractable roofs now schedule ice shows, hockey, basketball, volleyball, and tennis tournaments year-round. Stadiums with retractable roofs seating eighty thousand spectators are common venues for American football, baseball, soccer, track and field events, and rock concerts.

Regardless of how sports, activities, and their venues are classified, each tourist destination must plan its tourism development according to the demands of each sport for the given location. Several sports are illustrated here. Given today's technology and investment capital, many sport venues could be built as indoor facilities, sometimes with striking architectural designs, thus allowing a large number of summer and winter sport activities to be performed year-round.

All sports have fans who attend their favored events. They often practice the sport themselves as a leisure-time activity. However, there seem to be limits to the attention and activity span of many fans. For example, an attempt was made to extend the American professional football season to the late winter and spring with the introduction of a second football league. It was not successful. However, professional basketball has successfully extended its traditional winter season into the summer with the addition of a women's league.

There are also limits to the ability of systems of player development to produce professional-quality athletes for all the professional leagues that exist. However, as countries grow in population and advance economically, more professional-quality athletes will be produced to enlarge the scope of spectator sports and increase the number of people who want to engage in participatory sports.

Proposed activities for tourists associated with sports tourism include:

Fall/Winter Sports

- Snow related: skiing (e.g., downhill, cross-country, board, jumping, acrobatics, and freestyle)
- Ice related: ice boating, ice fishing, skating (e.g., figure, speed)
- Ice and snow related: sledding (e.g., luge, toboggan, skeleton)
- Playing (e.g., hockey, soccer, basketball, American and Canadian football)
- Attending (e.g., winter sport events)
- Other (e.g., lacrosse)

Spring/Summer Sports

- Track and field (e.g., running, jumping, throwing, walking)
- Playing (e.g., golf,* tennis, basketball, volleyball, cricket, baseball, soccer, skateboarding)
- Recreational motorboating (e.g., yacht,* power boat)
- Racing (e.g., automobile, motorcycle, power boat, sailboats)
- Surfing (e.g., long board, short board, boogie board)
- Rowing (e.g., rowboat, skiff, scull)
- Sailing (e.g., sailboat, surf, sailboarding, parasailing)
- Fishing (e.g., sport/recreational*)
- Attending (e.g., summer sport events)
- Other (e.g., field hockey)

Year-Round and/or Indoor Sports

- Playing (e.g., basketball, arena football, baseball, volleyball, tennis)
- Track and field (e.g., running, jumping, throwing, walking)
- Swimming
- Boxing
- Wrestling
- Attending (e.g., year-round events)
- Other (e.g., gymnastics)

*Note: Because of their size and popularity, yachting/sailing, golf, and sport fishing are presented and discussed further in Sections 4.18 (yachting and sailing), 4.21 (golf), and 4.25 (sport fishing).

Additional information about sports tourism can be found on the following Web sites: http://www.onecaribbean.org/content/files/SportsTourism.pdf and http://www.traveldailynews.com/pages/show_page/36066-The-Importance-of-Sports-Tourism.

4.11 THEME AND AMUSEMENT PARK TOURISM

Reality can be fun, but fantasy can be even more fun. Exploring the world of fantasy is a distinct form of tourism. Magic, or combining the unexplained with enchantment, plays a role in this exploration. Small-scale magic, or deception for the sake of amusement, has existed for millennia. It still exists today. Gradually, some small-scale magic evolved into large-scale magic. The thrill that comes from small magic has now evolved into large, thrilling experiences in the fantasy world. Theme parks and amusement parks, with some distinction between the two, are the results of this evolution.

Dreamland in New York City is an example of an early theme park. The idea of a modern theme park has developed from the amusing world of cartoons created by Walt Disney. What started with a big-eared, fun-loving, and kindly fictional animal creature has now evolved into mega theme parks in Los Angeles, Orlando, Paris, Tokyo, and most recently Shanghai. One no longer has to search far and wide to find magic shows. They are conveniently available in a condensed and packaged form in one place. This is the legacy of theme parks. To be thrilled without traveling to distant lands, to experience the fantasy and educational worlds that the human mind can create in a physical form, is what makes theme parks unique.

Over the years, the fine line separating reality from fantasy was crossed back and forth in a multitude of theme parks. Increasingly, what the human mind could imagine and put on paper or celluloid, but could not translate into an operating physical form, is now possible through advanced technology. Computers have played a major role in this evolution. By controlling motion, computers now enable the thrill seeker to duplicate the fantasy experience at will vis-à-vis the "virtual reality" experience.

Robotics can simulate any earthly or otherworldly environment. Still, live actors are needed to complete the experience. In this simulated experience, tourists themselves become the actors. Epcot Center at Disney World in Orlando, Florida, absorbs and surrounds the visitor. Sometimes, other living creatures participate and become the focus. For example, live animals become the center of the theme park in the Animal Kingdom. During a simulated safari, four-wheel-drive vehicles carrying tourists travel over a simulated collapsing bridge, and by doing so add excitement to the scene as real wild animals roam the land. Behind the fantasy or simulated reality, the facilities of permanent resident animals are hidden artfully behind hills and shrubbery where professional keepers attend their needs. At the Magic Kingdom, costumed actors give life to the imaginary kingdom symbolized by the soaring castle with stylized towers rising in the background.

Practically any theme could be chosen for a theme park. History is a rich source of inspiration. Another is technology. Epcot Center is based on both of these themes. Cultural theme parks depicting the culture of Oceania in Hawaii, that of Australia in Cairns, and others are tourist destinations around the world. Reenactment of famous gunfights of the Wild West is a standard attraction at western theme parks in the United States. The history, architecture, and civilization of China were illustrated on a gigantic scale in a model sanctioned by the government of China in a seventy-six-acre theme park called Florida Splendid China located near Orlando. The park was opened in 1993 and closed at the end of 2003. It was a sister park to Splendid China in Shenzhen, China, which is still open and has many visitors. The Florida Park cost US$100 million to construct. The Chinese government owned the Florida park indirectly for marketing international tourism in China. The visitor felt like a giant Gulliver visiting the land of the Lilliputts. Walking around the model was like absorbing a condensed lesson in the architecture, customs, and traditions of China. Back in China, and in some other Southeast Asian countries, a unique form of mobile theme park, traveling from one destination to another, has taken hold. This modern "carnival" has become very popular, particularly with rural populations.

The process of creating a theme park starts with a creative mind and business acumen. What creative minds can imagine, business acumen can make a reality. For turning an idea into a theme park, a new profession has been created and a new term added to the lexicon—**imagineering**. Keeping the expanding horizon of technology in mind, imagineers sketch the idea, build three-dimensional models, compose the scenario of activities, project the flow of visitors, select the technology, and, following the groundbreaking, make the fantasy world emerge. The roadside magic show has now evolved into an international attraction. A monorail running around an artificial lake connects many hotel accommodations with striking architecture, exotic restaurants, fancy gift shops, and popular recreational amenities. At Disney World in Orlando, an entirely new full-service international destination has been created for tourists.

The amusement park differs from the theme park in that the activities it offers are purely recreational; whereas, the theme park offers many educational activities in addition to recreational pursuits. Twisting, dropping, and gravity-defying rides are the mainstay of amusement parks. Old-fashioned, now modernized, corkscrew roller coasters, Ferris wheels, train rides, and pony carousels turning round and round are sheer joy for young and old alike. Knocking over a target and winning a stuffed toy animal for his sweetheart on a date is many a young man's hope.

A new form of amusement park is the water park, where, climate permitting, adults and children can slide down water chutes or frolic on an artificial beach and in surf created by wave machines. Climate does not play a role when the action is moved indoors. The indoor water park simulates the tall waves of Hawaii for indoor surfing and for lounging on an artificial beach. The Wild Wadi Water Park in Dubai, located next to the sail-shaped seven-star Burj Al Harab Hotel, is the latest word in this genre of amusement. The entire complex is a destination drawing visitors from every part of the world just for the multiple awe-inspiring experiences it offers. More of the same has been created in Dubai, including the world's tallest building.

Interestingly, many new hotel-casinos are being built around the world, particularly in Las Vegas. Exotic themes have been chosen for their architecture and interior design. The themes draw the visitors to the casinos and gaming tables. The ancient Fremont Street downtown is now a theme park covered with a vaulted roof with synchronized light shows depicting the history of Las Vegas, since 1931 when gambling was legalized. The story continues.

Theme parks are expensive to build, maintain, and visit. They are not for everyone interested in developing tourism. Countries willing to benefit from the themes of their culture can opt for a form of modified amusement and theme park tourism. They can use their restored historic edifices, ruins, monuments, and palaces as backdrops for staging light-and-sound shows. They can stage reenactments of historic events, with actors or natives posing as historic figures for the benefit of tourists. They can select their themes from their rich cultures. They do not have to fantasize. The reality of their rich cultural heritage is sufficient. They can produce an educational experience that is quite memorable.

Proposed activities associated with theme and amusement park tourism include:

- Riding (e.g., roller coaster, Ferris wheel, carousel, train, safari car, and exhibit)
- Walking (e.g., exhibits)
- Learning (e.g., about nature, science, and history)
- Dining (e.g., restaurants, food stands)
- Swimming (e.g., artificial lake, surf)
- Shopping (e.g., gifts)
- Climbing (e.g., towers, walls)
- Other (e.g., watching light and pyrotechnic shows)

Additional definitions and discussions about theme park tourism can be found on the following Web sites: http://www.hotel-online.com/Trends/ERA/ERARoleThemeParks.html and http://steconomice.uoradea.ro/anale/volume/2008/v2-economy-and-business-administration/113.pdf.

4.12 TRADE SHOW, CONFERENCE, CONVENTION, AND WORLD FAIR TOURISM

Despite claims to the contrary, business and pleasure can mix. People attending business events wish to have time in their two- to five-day schedule for sampling the pleasures of the location they came to visit. After completing the business of the day, visitors disperse to casinos, beaches, golf courses, and many restaurants and nightclubs where the food is good and the entertainment is first class. When a major event is in town, the facilities and attractions of an entire destination are mobilized. Trade shows, conferences, and conventions are such events.

The subjects of these events are quite varied. Membership organizations, special interest groups, political organizations, manufacturers of goods, and service companies of various kinds make up the short list. A large proportion of the people attending these events come from distant lands. The organizer makes all advance preparations, leases the conference rooms at a major hotel, rents the exhibit hall, sets up the exhibit spaces reserves rooms at the hotel, and negotiates special deals with service providers. When the date is reached, trailer trucks carrying the exhibits and hundreds or thousands of attendees and media personnel (if an event is newsworthy) arrive by air and by land. Some distinguished or wealthy visitors disembark from their private airplanes. They are met on the tarmac with a limousine and are whisked to the penthouse of their hotel. Then the fun starts. A cocktail party followed by a banquet serves to get the attendees acquainted with each other and to rekindle old friendships. The evening dinner is reserved for the sponsors and the principal speaker. The next morning, after an early breakfast, the business of the day starts. After a lunch break, some guests stay while others disperse to various venues to pursue their favorite recreation. After a short business meeting sponsored by the organizers, guests convene in the evening for another round of cocktails, dinner, and possibly entertainment.

This scenario is repeated in major trade, conference, and convention centers renowned for their luxury accommodations, live entertainment, interesting sightseeing, luxury shopping, and preferably agreeable climate. The organizers rotate their locations often, creating intense competition among destinations. The success of the symbiotic relationship between the visitor and the visited depends on the desirability of the destination and its amenities. The rewards are substantial. Jobs and income for residents and suppliers are a boon for the local economy. There is competition among major cities for large-scale conventions. Several cities have built ever-larger convention centers and taken steps to increase their hotel space to accommodate the largest conventions. At the other end of the scale, motels and small hotels have added conference rooms with audiovisual equipment and business centers to their facilities to accommodate local small-scale conferences, business meetings, and training sessions for various purposes.

Historically, trade shows in Europe date back to medieval times when local guilds exhibited their wares. They often did this in the town or city halls. These shows have now become renowned annual industrial fairs with permanent fairgrounds. Occasionally, world fairs adorn big cities. Countries and companies take pride in presenting exhibits showing innovative examples of their industries and cultures. Famous Chicago and New York world fairs introduced many new technologies when they were held in times of peace. EXPO 2005, held in Nagoya, Japan, is an example that adopted "Toward a Sustainable Society" as its theme.

Under the theme of "Nature's Wisdom," 122 countries/regions and almost 90 nongovernmental and nonprofit organizations came together at EXPO 2005 to explore the relationship between humankind and nature and to chart a course toward a more sustainable future. The "three Rs"— **reduce, reuse,** and **recycle**—formed the guiding principle of EXPO 2005. The visitors had the opportunity to see some of the technologies that present solutions to the environmental problems facing the world today.

The building, computer, and automobile industries, among others, hold large annual trade shows in cavernous venues like the convention center in Las Vegas, Nevada, to display their latest wares. Political events like party conventions and presidential elections fill the largest venues in interesting destinations. Annual meetings of professional and charitable associations are also major draws.

Proposed activities associated with trade shows, conventions, conferences, and world fairs tourism include:

- Participating (e.g., conference, trade show, convention, world fair)
- Attending (e.g., lectures, elections, parties, shows)
- Gambling (e.g., casinos)
- Dining (e.g., restaurants)
- Playing sports (e.g., golf, tennis, swimming)
- Other (e.g., shopping)

Further discussions about trade show and conference tourism and world fairs can be found on the following Web sites: http://www.ibj.com/convention-centers-tours-part-of-larger-tourism-strategy/PARAMS/article/18382, http://www.conferencealerts.com/tour.htm, http://www.expocentral.com/about.html, and http://en.wikipedia.org/wiki/World's_fair.

4.13 SHOPPING TOURISM

Shopping and acquiring goods and services is one of the pleasurable activities of tourism. A casual walk in the Old Bazaar of Istanbul, dating back to the 1600s, is a unique experience in theater as well as shopping. More than fifteen hundred stores flank both sides of the covered bazaar, where tourists can find every conceivable souvenir to take home. Multilingual greeters at the door of every store show their expertise in guessing the nationality of the tourist and sizing up the sale potential he or she represents. After buying a gift, the tourist is sent on his or her way with a handshake, a business card, and a promise to stay in touch.

More serious shoppers, who are looking for antiques, find them in the oldest part of the Old Bazaar at Ic Bedesten. Upon entering the store, recommended by friends, the tourist is welcomed and offered a courtesy chair. The young apprentice is sent to a nearby tea shop to fetch a glass of sweet tea for the guest. After exchanging pleasantries, the proprietor inquires about the purpose of the visit and begins showing his or her collections. First, lower-priced antiques are presented. After some consideration, the guest may persuade the proprietor to bring out more valuable possessions. These are placed not in the display case but under the counter, lovingly wrapped in black velvet. If the guest is looking for something even more special, the proprietor may bring out a prized possession kept in a secure place, usually at his or her nearby home. When the price is negotiated at some length and accepted, the proprietor may offer to deliver the antique to the tourist's hotel, airport, or cruise ship. Carefully wrapped in protective packaging, the antique is delivered to its owner, together with a certificate authenticating the price and the origin of the antique. This information is for the customs officer who will permit the antique to leave the country and for the customs officer who will assess the import duties when the tourist returns to his or her home port.

This scenario is played out in all parts of the world, with some local variations. Hong Kong, a major retail outlet of China, is a favorite shopping destination. Charter planes of shoppers fly weekly from Los Angeles and Tokyo to Hong Kong. After a short ferry ride, an unforgettable culinary experience on the floating restaurants in Aberdeen follows a "shop until you drop" experience in Kowloon across the bay.

Shoppers make similar trips from both sides of the Atlantic to Paris, Rome, London, and New York searching for art treasures or high-fashion clothing. Where shopping for high fashion and antiques is not the favorite occupation for tourists, there are still the duty-free shops. Perfumes, watches, liquor, jewelry, cameras, and porcelain of all descriptions are found in St. Thomas, Martinique, Cozumel, Georgetown, and other Caribbean destinations, as well as practically every international airport around the world. Specimens of local arts and crafts are also displayed in profusion. Street vendors resplendent in their colorful clothing in Nassau, St Lucia, and Costa Maya, sell straw hats, dinner mats, papier-mâché or porcelain parrots, steel drums, coconut maracas, and inescapable T-shirts. Simulated Mexican relics from the Mayan empire always find a buyer in Cozumel. Brass from India, stylized native figurines from Africa, oriental carpets, and kilims from the Middle East are among the better-known crafts.

Proposed activities associated with shopping tourism include:

- Shopping (e.g., fashion, duty free, decoration)
- Antiquing
- Dining (e.g., Chinese, Indian, Japanese, Italian)
- Other (e.g., bargaining and window shopping)

Information about shopping to attract tourists can be found on the following Web sites: http://www.tourism-review.com/top-ten-shopping-capitals-news2030 and http://www.londontourist.org/markets.html.

4.14   HERITAGE AND NOSTALGIA TOURISM

Exploring one's family heritage is a growing pursuit for many. Professional consultants manage to trace their client's lineage back many generations to some noteworthy ancestor who left his or her imprint for posterity. **Heritage tourism** is sometimes referred to as **diaspora tourism** to reflect the fact that emigration from an area may have been forced or systematic relocation of residents. Elderly tourists, in particular, are curious to find the source of their family lineage. They form clubs and travel to the country of their ancestors in search of information about them. People can take courses and obtain specialized information on genealogy.

Heritage tourism is a special experience, highly personal and spiritual. Traveling to distant lands in search of the remains of revered ancestors and relatives, going through the old birth, death, and marriage records at the town hall or county seat, visiting the cemetery where ancestors are buried, and finding distant relatives separated by a generation and coming from a different branch of the lineage is an exhilarating and often a life-centering experience. This visit may help the individual answer important questions about his or her life: Who am I and where did I come from?

A variation of heritage tourism could have scientific purposes. Scholars exploring religious subjects may organize scholarly expeditions, for example, in biblical lands. Noah's ark has been a subject of continuous interest over many decades. The book of Genesis (Chapter 6) gives clues concerning where to find the remains of the ark, namely, at Mount Ararat in eastern Turkey. Many explorations, however, have failed to find the remains of the elusive ark. Recently, based on three-thousand-year-old tablets found in ancient Babylonia, the attention of scientists and their followers has turned to the ancient cities on the plains between the Tigris and Euphrates rivers in modern Iraq and to the island of Bahrain, where the ark may have landed. This possibility raises questions among many scholars and arouses the curiosity of many others. Unfortunately, heritage tourism cannot prosper in the Middle East until the political climate has stabilized and security in the area is restored.

Nostalgia tourism is about celebrating an event that left an imprint in the minds of its participants. Among others, military reunions, high school and college reunions, fiftieth wedding anniversaries, remembering the place where a military veteran served during various wars, and exploring the sacred lands following in the footsteps of the prophets are possibilities. All participants have one thing in common: Many years ago, they shared one unforgettable experience, like fighting in World War II. Other persons will follow a subject of interest, like joining a team of climbers to trace the path of Sir Edmund Hillary and the Sherpa guide Tenzing Norgay when they climbed the highest mountain in the world, Mount Everest, in 1953.

Nostalgia tourism is sometimes organized into groups. An expert on the subject often accompanies the group and provides information. The organizer of the group charters a bus, a plane, or a cruise ship, and sometimes all three, to bring the tourists to their destination. On location, the group visits the sites and listens to live lectures. Participants have the opportunity to mix with local residents, some of whom may have been present at the time of the event. Visiting war monuments and the cemetery where fallen comrades rest is always a solemn experience.

Proposed activities associated with heritage and nostalgia tourism include:

- Remembering (e.g., an event, place, person)
- Meeting (e.g., friend, former enemy)
- Celebrating (e.g., reunion, anniversary)
- Honoring (e.g., the dead, a comrade)
- Visiting (e.g., site, group)
- Shopping (e.g., gifts, mementos)
- Dining (e.g., banquet)
- Researching (e.g., family genealogy)

The following Web sites provide more information about heritage and nostalgia tourism: http://docstoc.com/docs/11079847/159-Academic-Tourism-Journals and http://www.eturbonews.com/583/tourists-answer-call-nostalgia.

4.15 FAMILY AND FRIENDS TOURISM

Visiting friends and relatives (VFR tourism) during holidays and on special occasions is a favorite form of tourism. It is frequent, usually lasts only a few days, and allows one to enjoy the hospitality of cherished ones in their homes. The purpose is largely recreational or sentimental. Visiting grandchildren, or being visited by them and their parents, is a joy for everyone, sometimes several times a year. Christmas, Ramadan, Kwanzaa, Hanukkah, and other holidays permit vacation days from work and provide frequent occasions for visiting friends and relatives.

This form of tourism concentrates travel on several key days and months of the year. Plans for intercity travel are made in advance. Professional travel agents, who are knowledgeable about where to find plane seats at the best prices, do the bookings. More often, visiting families use their private vehicles for transportation. When they arrive, they embrace their loved ones and stay in their houses as honored guests. Hotels and motels may be used for overnight stays if the number of guests is larger that the capacity of the host's home. Hosts and guests usually go out to dinner often. The economic impact of this type of tourism can be relatively large, particularly when it is combined with shopping and entertaining.

Proposed activities associated with the family and friends tourism include:

- Celebrating (e.g., friends, relatives)
- Dining (e.g., friends, relatives)
- Shopping (e.g., friends, relatives)
- Attending (e.g., religious or ceremonial services, reunions)
- Other (e.g., playing with children, sharing stories with adults)

Family and friends tourism is defined and discussed further on the following Web sites: http://www.tourismknowledge.com/Friends_and_Family_Reunited-VFR_market.pdf and http://www.hotelmule.com/management/html/51/n-2351-2.html.

4.16   RELIGIOUS PILGRIMAGE TOURISM

All major world religions prescribe a visit to holy lands in one's lifetime. The holy places of three major religions—Christianity, Judaism, and Islam—came together in one place: Jerusalem. Situated where Western civilization emerged, the city has played a continuous role in human history. People have settled this land for more than five thousand years. Jews have identified with the city as their homeland. King David conquered the city, and Solomon built the First Temple in about 1000 BC. The Persians, Alexander the Great, and the Romans arrived. Jesus Christ was born nearby, in Bethlehem, about two thousand years ago. In AD 330, Constantine was the first emperor who recognized Christianity as the official religion of the Holy Roman (Byzantine) Empire. Muslims led by Umayyed Caliph Omar conquered Jerusalem during the sixth century AD. The first Crusaders breached the walls of the city in 1099. Saladin arrived from Egypt and took the city back for the Muslims in 1187. Mamlouks, also from Egypt, followed and stayed until 1517, when the Ottoman Empire established its rule and governed the city until 1917. The rest is recent history.

The Old City is only one square kilometer in area, containing twenty thousand Jewish, Christian, Armenian Orthodox, and Muslim residents living in four separate quarters. Gates and walls, last rebuilt by Ottoman Sultan Suleyman the Magnificent between 1536 and 1541, surround the city. Within the walls of the Old City, followers of all faiths have coexisted and practiced their religions in harmony until recent times.

The shrines revered by all believers in the Old City include Haram Ash-Sharif (the Noble Sanctuary), or Temple Mount, where Abraham was called to sacrifice his son, and the Dome of the Rock, the third most important shrine of Islam, where Muslims believe the prophet Muhammad was accepted into heaven. It was built in AD 691 together with the adjacent Al-Aqsa Mosque. Other sacred places include the Western Wall (Wailing Wall), or portion of the retaining wall built by Herod the Great in 20 BC to hold the landfill on which the Second Temple stood; the Via Dolorosa (Way of Sorrows) on which Jesus Christ is believed to have walked to his crucifixion; and the Church of the Holy Sepulcher, the site where the crucifixion, burial, and resurrection of Jesus Christ is believed to have occurred. It is interesting to note that during the centuries of Ottoman rule, it was the daily duty of a Muslim family to open the church doors of the Holy Sepulcher every morning and close them every night. Today, some of these traditions and privileges are still closely guarded.

The first and second holiest places in Islam are in modern Saudi Arabia, where Mecca and Medina are the principal pilgrimage destinations for Muslims. Umra, the short pilgrimage, may be performed at any time of the year and hajj only once a year. In Mecca, the Grand Mosque surrounds the Kaaba, the holiest place in Islam, where the prophet Muhammad cleaned the cubic stone structure built by Abraham from the idols within and declared it the place to pray to Allah (God). More than a million pilgrims pray together in the multitiered mosque and engage in other rituals of Islam during the hajj. Medina is the second stop for pilgrims before or after the hajj. The prophet Muhammad is buried there in the Prophet's Mosque.

Together with many lesser places of worship, pilgrimages to major shrines draw millions of devout visitors from around the world. Visiting these sites is a ritualistic experience involving fellow pilgrims and organized trips. The trips last anywhere from one day to two weeks or more. They occur routinely and sometimes repeatedly. The Holy Qur'an, for example, prescribes only one hajj, or four umras, to Mecca for Muslims. Other faiths have different practices and obligations.

It is important to note that Saudi Arabia does not grant tourist visas for foreigners to visit the country. Only pilgrims and foreign guests invited by the government or businesses are permitted to enter the country and are given limited visas. Other types of special interest tourism involving foreigners are not allowed. Domestic tourism, however, is thriving, with certain limitations. Nudity, gambling, and drinking alcoholic beverages are not allowed in public places by the authorities. Certain foods (e.g., pork) are also not available. Modesty in dress must be observed.

Christianity survived and continues to have millions of believers in Turkey, Greece, Russia, and other countries. Emperor Constantine of the Holy Roman Empire made Christianity legal in AD 313 and moved to Byzantium, where he established a new capital named for him, Constantinople. The Holy Roman Empire later split into the Eastern and Western Empires. After it was invaded by the Huns, the Western Empire collapsed. The Eastern Empire was renamed the Byzantine Empire and survived until 1453, when Constantinople was conquered by the Ottoman Turks and eventually renamed Istanbul. Christianity that developed in the Eastern Empire was called Orthodox Christianity. Emperor Justinian built the Basilica of Hagia Sophia between AD 532 and 508. He dedicated it to Jesus Christ, whose image was depicted in gold mosaics at the entrance to the basilica. The structure was a first in the world, with its 107-foot-wide dome rising 250 feet above the nave below. The dome was a model for many churches and mosques built later around the world. Until the Ottomans modified it into a mosque, Hagia Sophia served as a destination for pilgrims for many centuries. During the twentieth century, the Republic of Turkey converted the structure into a museum.

Another major pilgrimage site is the Vatican in Rome, Italy, for Roman Catholics, where St. Peter's Basilica (begun in 1546) and the Sistine Chapel combine art, architecture, and religion. Michelangelo painted the famous frescoes on the vaulted ceiling and walls of the Sistine Chapel between 1508 and 1512. The frescoes depict the lives of Christ and Moses with the symbolic intention of underlining the concept that the papacy started with and descended from the apostle of Christ, St. Peter. Michelangelo also designed the original architectural plans of the Basilica and its cupola. Both were completed in 1594 after his death. Other major shrines approved by the Roman Catholic Church and the Vatican include Lourdes in southern France, Fatima in Portugal, and the shrine of the Virgin Mary in western Turkey near Ephesus.

As early as 2500 BC, great civilizations flourished on the peninsula of India. Three world religions—Hinduism, Buddhism, and Jainism—originated there. Many temples were built and became shrines for pilgrimage. The Hindu temple Kandariya Mahadeo, with its one thousand carved figures, was built during the eleventh century AD. The multilevel Buddhist shrine Borobudur, also known as a *stupa*, with its eight terraces simulating a hill, has stood on the island of Java in Indonesia since the early ninth century AD. It was built over the remains of spiritual relics. Pilgrims walk along a path around the platform and meditate to reach nirvana.

Siddhartha Gautama, called Buddha or the Enlightened One, was born in Lumbini on the Terai plains of Nepal. There is a shrine where Buddhists come for pilgrimage. In recent years, with financial help from Japan and other countries, a new center and temple for pilgrimage, complete with infrastructure and residential facilities, have been planned to honor the birthplace of Buddha.

The Japanese have turned appreciation of nature into the Shinto faith (*Shinto* means "the way of the gods"). Temples and shrines were designed to blend into nature, not to stand apart from it. The Horyuji Temple complex in Nara was built in the seventh century AD. The buildings are the oldest surviving wooden buildings in the world. This five-level pagoda marks the place where symbolic Buddhist relics are buried and honored. The two-level Golden Hall shelters a statue of Buddha. The political and military organization of Japan since the twelfth century AD also led to carrying out the traditions of pilgrimage. The Japanese warlords, or shoguns, built many feudal castles to protect their rule and shrines. Major castles of Japan include Himeji Castle, built in 1609; Kumamoto Castle, built in 1607; Osaka Castle, built in 1630; Okayama Castle, built in 1597; and the Imperial Palace, built in 1888 and reconstructed after World War II, in Tokyo.

In Bangkok, Thailand, the Grand Palace has been the residence of the kings until recent years. The palace complex includes a Buddhist shrine where pilgrimage is permitted. Since the present king moved his residence elsewhere, the spectacular architecture of the palace has been displayed as a museum and the shrines have continued the pilgrimage tradition. The two-hundred-twenty-year-old Emerald Buddha (made of jade) and the Golden Buddha continue as the foci of the pilgrimage.

In the remote valleys of northern India in Ladakh, where twenty-thousand-foot peaks of the Himalayas dwarf the Hanle Monastery, Tibetan Buddhism thrives. Venturesome pilgrims, if they can get a special permit from the government and endure a twelve-hour drive over rough-cut mountain roads, can visit this monastery. They can visit the crumbling *gompa* (fortified monastery) and read the messages of pilgrims in the Urdu language left behind on slate tablets. They can experience the Buddhist ideals of humility, patience, cooperation, and compassion and be at peace with themselves. The pilgrimage to Hanle Monastery is for the few. It is used to be the residence of the Dalai Lama before China invaded Tibet and he left in exile to India. Visitors are welcome. Their contribution to the local economy of the capital city, Leh, is significant.

Pilgrimages have major impacts on the economy and infrastructure of their destinations. For example, the hajj requires pilgrims to be in Mecca at the same time to perform the rituals together. The government of Saudi Arabia has built a special terminal for pilgrims at King Abdul Aziz Airport in Jeddah, where up to four hundred flights arrive every day immediately preceding the hajj. In Mecca, under the supervision of the Ministry of Pilgrims, more than one million pilgrims can find lodging at the same time in a temporary tent city with all necessary sanitary facilities, drinking water, food catering, and medical facilities.

The examples of pilgrimage given here are one-of-a-kind international attractions. They are not typical. Using the term broadly, pilgrimage travels could be packaged and could be activities around which entire pilgrimage tourism industries could be developed. In addition to their religious significance, pilgrimage places are important for their tourism value. It is important to note that visiting pilgrimage destinations is a spiritual experience. Appropriate personal conduct, appropriate attire, and respect for others must govern the visit at all times. A visit to a sacred place is an uplifting experience for the believers of other faiths as well. Showing due respect and even participating in the ritual in one's own way is welcome in some religions.

Proposed activities associated with pilgrimage tourism include:

- Praying (e.g., in churches, temples, mosques, shrines, or other spiritual places)
- Meditating (e.g., in sacred places)
- Participating (e.g., pilgrimages, processions, rituals)
- Other (e.g., buying religious artifacts, bringing offerings to shrines or holy places)

The following Web sites further explain and provide more historical background for religious pilgrimage tourism: http://hirr.hartsem.edu/ency/Pilgrigmage.htm and http://en.wikipedia.org/wiki/Religious_tourism.

4.17 VOLUNTEER TOURISM

Volunteer tourism is on the rise. It is often associated with international humanitarian programs. Religious organizations routinely send missionaries and maintain missions in all parts of the world. International organizations like the United Nations, UNICEF, the Red Cross and the Red Crescent, Amnesty International, Oxfam International, and other NGOs, and government organizations from the United States, Canada, Great Britain, and other developed countries have thousands of their citizens working as volunteers in distant lands, helping the poor, sick, and hungry, the uneducated, and the disfranchised, who are often victims of natural disasters and inhumane practices. Thousands of volunteers from the Peace Corps, Habitat for Humanity, and similar volunteer organizations, among them retired executives from International Executive Service Corps and doctors, nurses, and engineers, have permanent bases in developing countries where they contribute their knowledge and experience for the benefit of their host country and humanity.

Some would argue that volunteer tourism as defined here is very much like work and is not tourism, but more like a business in which people are sent on organized missions of good will to undertake constructive and humane activities. In its travel and learning content, it is tourism; however, it actually substitutes work for the leisure activities that most often define tourism. But like tourism, these activities are voluntary. The impact of such volunteer tourism is substantial. In addition to knowledge and good will, much money is channeled through these volunteer organizations for achieving humanitarian goals like building and operating education, health, shelter, and infrastructure facilities; improving basic sanitary conditions; or establishing new civic organizations, institutions, and even building nations and improving the government.

A distinction can be made between regularized volunteer humanitarian efforts and natural disaster relief efforts. Many of the relief organizations are the same ones that conduct regular volunteer activities, but in providing volunteer natural disaster relief, they are joined by national government relief organizations that send in paid staff. Natural disaster relief cannot be defined as tourism because it is a grim emergency operation and there is no choice of destinations or activities. Volunteers and paid staff go to the disaster area and perform whatever activities are most needed.

Proposed activities associated with volunteer tourism include:

- Volunteering (e.g., providing physical labor, preparing plans and programs, counseling, social work, management, and other specialized consulting, collecting, transporting and distributing materials, reporting)
- Educating (e.g., students)
- Training (e.g., technicians)
- Other (e.g., temporarily residing with native populations)

The scope and nature of volunteer tourism are further defined on the following Web sites: http://matadornetwork.com/bnt/2007/07/23/the-complete-guide-to-volunteer-tourism and http://www.voluntourism.org/news-studyandresearch51.htm.

4.18   YACHTING AND SAILING TOURISM

Water-related domestic and international tourism has been increasing for several decades. Many countries with access to open seas or lakes have developed major facilities to harbor and service small and large yachts and sailboats. Combined with many auxiliary activities, yachting and sailing continue to grow as a major economic activity. There are many prominent examples of this successful growth.

The splendid royal yacht *Britannia* had shown the British flag all over the world for many decades before it was retired a few years ago. Other heads of state also had the use of government-owned yachts. Among them, the *Savarona* is a special case. The largest nonroyal yacht ever created, it was built for Mrs. Emily Roebling Cadwaller, granddaughter of the engineer who built the Brooklyn Bridge in New York City. The 446-foot-long *Savarona* was built in 1931 at the Blohm & Voss shipyards in Hamburg, Germany, at a cost of US$4 million. After encountering financial difficulties, the owner sold it to the government of Turkey, to be used for official purposes. Since then, the yacht has been sold to a Turkish entrepreneur who, after making extensive improvements, still operates it for charter in the Mediterranean.

The yacht of the shipbuilder Aristotle Onassis, *Christina O*, was named after his daughter. It was highly visible around the Mediterranean for many years. It was built in 1943 in Canada during World War II as a warship for convoy escort. In 1954, at a cost of US$4 million, Onassis bought the ship and modified it into a splendid yacht. At 325 feet in length, the yacht includes eighteen staterooms, each named for an island of Greece. Many notable persons were Onassis' guests, including movie stars, kings, and statesmen. The yacht is still operating as a charter.

Small and large luxury yachts, with all the comforts and technologies that money can buy, are being built in hundreds of shipyards around the world. They are oceangoing vessels capable of undertaking long journeys carrying dozens of guests and crew. Similar comforts and technologies are found on sailing vessels. Tall ships ranging from four-masted barkentines, schooners, or barks to two- or one-masted smaller vessels roam the oceans and create spectacular site attractions in ports they visit. Many of these tall ships were built during the 1920s and are now owned by governments to be used for training young sailors. Tall ships like *Esmeralda* from Chile, *Juan Sebastian de Elcano* from Spain, *Libertad* from Argentina, *Kaiwo Maru* from Japan, *Mir* from Russia, *Amerigo Vespucci* from Italy, and *Eagle* from the United States represent the glorious age of sailing, long gone. When they come together on special occasions, like the five hundredth anniversary in 1992 of Columbus' discovery of America, they create sensational tourism events on land and sea. Their economic impacts on the ports of call they visit are very large.

Smaller-masted sailing vessels for private and charter use are moored in marinas around the world where sailing for trade or pleasure has been a tradition for centuries. Coastal cities around the Mediterranean Sea have marinas with hundreds of slips for permanent or transient docking. Spain, France, Italy, Greece, and Turkey are prime destinations for sailing. The west coast of the United States from Seattle to San Diego is dotted with thousands of marinas. Hawaii is the home port of the U.S. Navy's Pacific fleet and harbors many marinas. The Atlantic coast of South Florida has the largest concentration of yachts and sailing vessels in Florida. Hundreds of public and private marinas are located on the Intracoastal Waterway between Miami and Palm

Beach. Between the two cities, the Venice of America, Ft. Lauderdale, harbors two of the largest marinas in the United States, Pier 66 and Bahia Del Mar, with their own hotels and marine shops.

The eastern Caribbean islands are among the most desirable boating and sailing destinations in the world, where bare boating facilities in the Virgin Islands, Martinique, and St. Lucia are numerous. England, Ireland, and countries on the Atlantic coast of Western Europe, like Spain, Portugal, France, the Netherlands, Germany, Denmark, and Norway, carry on the maritime tradition of their illustrious history with many harbors and marinas. Aberdeen in Hong Kong and Singapore harbor some of the most luxurious vessels in the Far East. Sydney, Australia, and Auckland, New Zealand, are among other major yachting and sailing destinations.

In addition to a protected harbor for large yachts, yachting and sailing destinations have extensive onshore facilities. Marina slips, boat maintenance and storage facilities, hotels, shops, restaurants, marine supply stores, boat charter and sale offices, and parking facilities form large complexes. Examples of these recreational yachting and sailing attractions and facilities are many. Australia and New Zealand are particularly popular. The Caribbean islands offer many opportunities, including bare boat chartering in which the boat is rented by the day to visitors without crew and provisions. If needed, a captain is hired. Generally, private companies operate the marinas. They charge club membership and slip fees. Visiting foreign vessels use the facilities for a fee. Government-owned marinas or mooring areas are also popular.

Yachting and sailing tourism have a twin impact on the economy of their region. Touring with yachts and sailing from one destination to another necessitates extensive onshore facilities. The provisions taken from the port or marina for charter sailing may be extensive. Sailing around the Greek islands, or along the southern coast of Turkey with its hundreds of pristine bays, can make for a long vacation. A longtime maritime tradition, *blue sailing* from Marmaris or Bodrum, Turkey, employs luxury *gulets* with ten cabins, private baths, modern navigation equipment, and plenty of sun and lounging decks. The vessel has a crew of three and is supplied with extensive victuals augmented by fresh fish caught overboard and grilled on the afterdeck for the evening festivities.

Scuba divers join special tours for visiting shipwrecks dating back to the time of the Phoenicians in the eastern Mediterranean and visit the first Museum of Underwater Archeology in the world in Bodrum Castle, Bodrum. In addition to its reputation for yachting, sailing, and scuba diving vacations, Bodrum has a long history. It was the capital of the ancient city-state Carians. It was also known as Halicarnassus, mentioned by Homer in the *Iliad*. Many nations occupied it. It was conquered by Alexander the Great, Romans, Byzantines, and Ottoman Turks. The remains of their occupations are still visible today. This type of high-quality multiple attraction places a destination at the highest level of international tourism.

In addition to the activities and impacts associated with charter, major yachting and sailing events generally create large bonuses for local economies. The 1992 visit of tall ships to New York and Boston attracted more than one million visitors to the waterfronts of both cities during their stay. Regattas and cup challenges also attract thousands of visitors on land and at sea. The memorable America's Cup challenge between two English and U.S. sailing clubs started in 1851 when the yacht *America* rounded the Isle of Wight ahead of its English competitor and won the cup. Initially, one-hundred-foot long J-class boats competed for the honor. The two-time winner for the United States, *Columbia*, was one of these beautiful but expensive boats. The J-class boats were followed by twelve-meter boats and by the more recently used International America's Cup Class boats. The rights to the challenge are given to syndicates from all countries of the world. Built under complicated design rules requiring computer calculations, the high-tech boats now compete for the honor of winning, or keeping, the cup when there is a challenge.

Proposed activities associated with motor yachting and sailing include:

- Yachting (e.g., motor yachting)
- Sailing
- Diving (e.g., scuba, snorkeling)
- Swimming (e.g., at sea, in pools, in lakes, and in streams)
- Skiing (e.g., water)
- Shopping (e.g., provisions, gifts)
- Dining (e.g., at sea, on land)
- Sightseeing (e.g., general and underwater tours)
- Other (e.g., incidental fishing)

The following Web sites contain more information about yachting and sailing tourism: http://www.onecaribbean.org/content/files/Sailing.pdf and http://www.hellenic-charters.gr/.

4.19   CAMPING AND RECREATION VEHICLE (RV) TOURISM

The essence of **camping** and **RVing** is carrying one's own overnight accommodation and living quarters while engaging in tourism activities. The comfort, convenience, and flexibility they offer are more than those basic camping provides. Camping and RVing is a lifestyle. It is about living in an environment shared by others with similar pursuits and interests. The camaraderie, the evening get-together around the campfire, the happy hour with cocktails, communal gathering, and reinforcing family relations are all enjoyable activities that occur with sometimes luxurious camping and RVing.

RVs are permitted to park only in special RV parks or designated areas. Some retail businesses allow overnight parking for RVs. The vehicles can be standard or custom-made to specifications costing very large sums. They can accommodate eight or more persons with sleeping, bathing, lounging, and cooking facilities in often luxurious comfort. RVs are connected to power, water, telephone, cable TV, and Internet outlets and have waste water, garbage collection, and security services. Some RVs have their own patios, awnings, and indoor and outdoor TV and entertainment equipment. The *economic impact of RVing* may be limited to entrance fees to parks, fuel and food purchases, and repairs. Additional expenses depend on the degree of self-sufficiency the RV owner may desire. Luxury RV communities with clubhouses, swimming pools, and other facilities are now being built in vacation areas, sometimes replacing or supplementing conventional hotels, motels, and inns.

The tourism impact of camping is different. Backpacking in Alaska, the Alps, or Nepal during the day, then pitching a tent at night on the shores of a lake or stream or in a mountain meadow, requires little in the way of accommodations. Well-marked trails, food, water, and, in emergencies, access to rescue and health facilities are essential. Backpackers follow the basic rule "carry in–carry out" for protecting the environment. When they are trekking in a group, hired porters do most of the provision and equipment hauling. This gives employment to many local residents. For example, entire trekking economies have emerged along the trails leading to Mount Everest in Nepal. The villages of Namche Bazaar and Kumjung have become tourist service centers accommodating trekking and climbing expeditions. They first provided shelter, food, and porters for higher elevations. Since 1953, **Sir Edmund Hillary** has contributed money and prestige to build hospitals and schools in the remote Himalayan villages of the Sherpas. Now, many Sherpas educated in high-altitude climbing serve as guides, doctors, and pilots in scientific and recreational expeditions.

Proposed activities associated with camping and RV tourism include:

- Camping (e.g., forest, lake, river)
- RVing (e.g., traveling, parking)
- Trekking and hiking (e.g., valleys, mountains)
- Climbing (e.g., mountains)
- Other (e.g., fishing)

The following two Wikipedia Web sites further define and explain camping and RV tourism: http://en.wikipedia.org/wiki/Camping and http://en.wikipedia.org/wiki/Recreational_vehicle.

4.20 RESIDENTIAL TOURISM

In countries where the level of income is high and is getting higher, the population is living longer and often retiring earlier. In the United States, more than half of the population will be above the age of fifty within thirty years. Combined with affluence and early retirement, a significant portion of this population is now facing lifestyle changes. Investments, combined with Social Security income and pensions, have made some retirees financially secure enough to pursue a transitory lifestyle in retirement. One aspect of the transitory life is for retirees to have two or more residences, one for the summer, preferably close to where the extended family lives, and one for the winter, preferably in a warmer climate where traveling and outdoor sports like golfing and sailing are options. A variation of this pattern is for households to own time-share residential accommodations, which typically provide a week's living in another location away from their primary residence. If a household owns four or more time-share weeks, its members can spend at least a month, perhaps more, living away from their primary residence. Another variation is for people to trade homes temporarily, that is, to live in someone else's home while the other person lives in theirs.

Similar trends exist in other countries having similar economic conditions. Second homes for vacations, which often double as future retirement homes, produce the geographic mobility that creates residential tourism. Depending on personal preferences and levels of affluence, retirees have their second homes in different regions, different countries, or even different continents. They are engaged in productive pursuits and travel extensively. Residential tourism allows retirees to live anywhere in the world. They are no longer bound to the location of their jobs. Their Social Security, pension, and dividend payments follow and reach the bank of their choice.

Residential tourism is characterized by the change in season once every six months or so. It involves traveling back and forth, sometimes long distances, to vacation or retirement homes. The population of the receiving area swells to many times the year-round resident population during the "season." The economic impact of this population increase, combined with that of nonresidential tourism, creates large fluctuations in demand for jobs, services, and business income. Shopping volumes increase, and more people patronize restaurants, health clubs, and sports and recreation venues. With this increase comes increased demand for public services. In addition to crowded post offices, highways and parking areas may be overloaded and the demand for water and sewer services may become critical. Demand for police and fire protection may tax local resources. Emergency hospital facilities could be hard pressed. Waterways and coastal waters may experience an explosion of mariners. It becomes difficult to provide reasonably priced housing for employees of the seasonal businesses that serve the seasonally enlarged population.

The most important factor in residential tourism is real estate development. Retirement-vacation neighborhoods, waterfront condominium and time-share apartments, and planned communities with many neighborhoods including golf courses, ski trails, chalets, resort hotels, marinas, shopping centers, and more shopping centers consume land voraciously. It becomes essential for local governments to prevent chaotic land use and manage growth by enforcing strict zoning and growth management regulations. Revenues from property taxes and fees are often used to ensure conservation of the environment.

In countries like the United States, where local property taxes are the primary source of revenue for required public education, local governments have an incentive for developing second-home and seasonal retirement and other residential accommodations. Residents of these accommodations do not normally produce children to be educated in local schools. This results in year-round residents and businesses of these communities paying lower local property taxes relative to communities that do not host residential tourism developments. However, as noted above, there are other impacts that can become critical, and when they become severe enough, a host residential tourism-receiving community begins to become less desirable as a place to live and work. One of the principal purposes for conducting a comprehensive tourism development study is to identify where this has happened, or potentially will happen, and to direct public and private tourism investments to other desirable areas that have not felt the critical impacts of overdevelopment.

Proposed activities associated with residential tourism include:

- Residing (e.g., vacation dwelling, retirement dwelling)
- Shopping (e.g., groceries, household supplies, household furnishings)
- Recreation (e.g., sports, entertainment)
- Dining (e.g., in restaurants)
- Securing health services (e.g., in local medical facilities)
- Other (e.g., participation in local government)

Residential tourism is further explained and discussed on the following Web sites: http://www. cu-again.com/Residential-Tourism.htm and http://www.trans4mind.com/explore/travel-leisure/ 38341.html.

4.21   GOLF TOURISM

In the twenty-first century, golf has become a worldwide sport. It has created its own distinct form of sports tourism. After originating in Scotland, the sport spread to Europe, to the United States, and now to the Far East and the rest of the world. Russia built its first golf course during the 1990s after the collapse of Soviet Union. The very first golf course in the Ukraine has been built, and others are in the planning stage.

The origin of golf is not known. It is conceivable that primitive man acted on impulse and knocked a pebble on the ground with a piece of stick into a rabbit's hole and the game was invented. Some trace the origin back to the game Paganica, played by the Romans. Others trace it to the French Jeu de mail or to the Dutch game Kolven. It is an undisputed fact that the Scots invented the modern golf game. It is known that golf was a pastime in Scotland as early as 1319. The game was first played across the rolling stretches of fine turf among the coastal sand dunes. There is no doubt that golf was played at the links at St. Andrews in the early sixteenth century. The interest of royalty contributed to the spread of golf to the rest of Scotland and beyond. Around 1864, there were some thirty membership golf clubs in Scotland. By 1900, there were more than two thousand golf clubs throughout the British Isles.

From the start of the eighteenth century, a golfer carried eight to twelve clubs. The clubs were made of wood. The earliest clubs were made by bow makers, carpenters, and wood turners.

The development of the modern golf ball had the greatest influence on the spread of the game. The *Feathery* ball took several hours to make and was therefore expensive. It was replaced by the *Guttie* ball in 1848. The *gutta-percha* ball had a core made from the resin of tropical trees, such as the Malaysian *Palaquium gutta*. With the acceptance of the Guttie ball, the design of clubs also changed, becoming heavier and shorter. The *Rubber-core* ball was invented in 1898 in the United States. It was followed by *two-piece* and *three-piece* balls. These balls are still in use.

Nature was the first golf course architect, shaping the links of eastern Scotland out of the undulating dunes lining the shoreline. The sand pits were natural. The grass was cut short by grazing sheep. Initially, the design methods were simple. The trees and greens were marked with colored sticks. Course design continued to evolve, and the modern course matured around the 1960s. Many professional golf players became prominent golf course designers. In the United States, Jack Nicklaus and Pete Dye dominated the golf course design field until the 1990s.

Golf is enjoying a boom around the world as demand for the game increases. Television and professional golf tours with golf superstars playing the game attract thousands of golf enthusiasts. The pastime of Scots has become the passion of millions. The majority of the world's golf courses are located in North America and the British Isles. It is not a coincidence that the majority of championship golf courses were built in former colonies of the British Empire, including the United States. There are about thirty championship courses in the United States. The British Isles account for about thirty championship courses, including the cradle of the game, St. Andrews, to which almost every golfer wants to make a pilgrimage once during his or her golfing life. Canada and South America have four championship courses. The game has expanded to Europe, and the continent now has about twenty championship courses. Africa and Asia account for ten more championship courses. Finally, Australia and New Zealand complete the inventory with ten championship courses. The numbers are growing. Golf is a major and increasing segment of the tourism industry.

Golf tourism is, therefore, universal and thriving. Major golf tournaments draw prominent professional golfers from around the world for large prizes. In turn, they draw thousands of golfers and fans across the borders to observe the tournaments. Many more millions follow the tournaments on television, on the Internet, and via radio broadcasts. The *PGA Tour* in the United States featuring the *Masters Tournament*; the *Ryder Cup* tournament held every two years alternately in the United States and Europe; the *European Tour* in Europe; the *Japanese Tour* in Japan; and similar tours in Canada and Australia are coveted championships. Conventions and product exhibits draw thousands more visitors. Many organizations in the United States are engaged in regulating the game and offering information to their members. They include the Professional Golfing Association, the United States Golfing Association, and the National Golfing Foundation.

In the United States, new residential golf communities, some having five thousand or more housing units, border multiple championship golf courses for their pleasant scenery, but also for their exclusive privileges of membership in the golf club and playing rights on the courses. In Florida, good weather and the retirement lifestyle are major draws for these golf communities. In Palm Beach County alone, there are one hundred fifty public and private golf courses. In the Myrtle Beach, South Carolina, area there are over ninety courses. Major residential golf communities, some of which have commercial facilities and resort hotels, host annual professional tours. Several have championship-level courses. Combining regular play and tournament golf tourism with residential retirement and other living generates major economic and social activity in an area.

Proposed activities associated with golf tourism include:

- Attending (e.g., golf exhibits, golf conventions)
- Observing (e.g., tournaments)
- Playing (e.g., on locally, regionally, nationally, and internationally known courses)
- Other (e.g., enjoying a cool drink in the clubhouse, making an equipment or apparel purchase in the pro shop dining in the golf club dining room)

Further information about golf tourism can be found on the following Web sites: http://www.onecaribbean.org/content/files/Golf.pdf and http://www.marketresearch.com/product/display.asp?productid=1284661.

4.22   ELDER HOSTEL TOURISM

Elder hostel tourism has been enabled by changing demographics. Longevity in developed countries has increased the life span by a decade during the past century. The average life span is now seventy-five years in developed countries and is climbing in the United States and Western Europe. With many more healthy years left after retirement, the elderly are exploring stimulating ideas and fascinating places across the United States and around the world. Curiosity and the desire to learn are at the core of this phenomenon. Knowledgeable guides and interesting local experts prepare the ground for discovery through lectures, visits, and discussions. Educational field trips enable visitors to gain firsthand knowledge of the local history, heritage, arts and culture, and environment. Forging new friendships and associating with people with similar interests is part of the experience.

> *Note*: **Youth hostel tourism** is covered under general sightseeing tourism in Section 4.2. Elder hostel tourism is identified separately here because it is more likely to have structured travel and programs for participants. Youth hostel tourism generally does not have structured programs or travel. Youths usually devise their own programs and activities, and come and go individually or in small groups as they sightsee and visit attractions of their choice.

The organizers of elder hostel tourism arrange comfortable, moderately priced overnight accommodations including hotels, country inns, retreats, lodges, cabins in vessels, safari tents, and college dormitories during vacations. Participants of the program are offered many options for food, including dining in restaurants at their own expense or sharing picnic and cafeteria food paid for by the organizers. Special needs or dietary requests are accommodated. Transportation to the assembly point is usually the responsibility of the visitor. After the participants arrive, the organizer arranges all transportation. Trips range in duration from five to ten nights or more. International group trips are becoming popular.

Typical elder hostel tourism programs include sampling fine arts and liberal arts and sciences, experiencing the history and cultural treasures of major cities, visiting national, state, or local parks, studying birds, engaging in intergenerational exploration with younger learners, bicycling on country roads, participating in creative workshops, developing skills in performing and visual arts, and participating in volunteer projects.

Proposed activities associated with elder hostel tourism include:

- Exploring (e.g., cultural sites)
- Sightseeing (e.g., the countryside)
- Participating (e.g., arts and letters, crafts)
- Attending (e.g., lectures, seminars)

- Shopping (e.g., gifts)
- Dining

Elder hostel tourism is further defined and explained on the following Web sites: http://en.wikipedia.org/wiki/Elderhostel and http://www.oregonlive.com/travel/index.ssf/2009/02/elderhostel_pack_a_bag_then_pa.html.

4.23 CANAL AND RIVER TOURISM

Plowing through the waves of oceans, large inland seas, and lakes may not be for everyone. For those persons, canal and river tourism provides an alternative. Calm navigable waters, with proximity to land and its many attractions and facilities, are turning canal and river tourism into a major form of recreation. The travelers carry their resort hotel and supporting amenities along with them in specially designed and built excursion boats, some of which have become quite luxurious. Daily packing and unpacking in one hotel after another; rushing to the airport; catching the bus; or driving endlessly around the countryside in search of amusement is not necessary. Instead, the boat carries the traveler from one destination to another while the traveler enjoys a 360-degree view of ever-changing scenery, lunching on the sundeck, having cocktails at the lounge, and retiring to the stateroom prepared by the cabin attendant for the night.

Traveling excursion groups generally do not exceed one hundred fifty guests. The advantages of river cruising include docking in the heart of a historic town or major city and taking excursions guided by knowledgeable multilingual guides to nearby historic sites or charming villages off the beaten track; experiencing local nightlife; traveling in comfort and convenience; relaxing with a book in the library; and always returning to the comforts of the excursion boat.

Canal and river tourism has evolved over many decades in Europe and the United States. There is an extensive network of navigable rivers and canals in Europe, where it is possible to travel by excursion boats from the Atlantic to the interior of the continent and from the Baltic Sea to the Black Sea and Caspian Sea. Rivers such as the Danube, the Rhine, the Seine, the Main, the Moselle, the Elbe, the Rhone, the Volga, and the Dnieper, as well as Dutch, German, French, and British canals, offer exciting sightseeing experiences.

In the United States, there are extensive navigable rivers and some canals offering opportunities for exciting river and canal tourism. On the lengthy Missouri, Ohio, and Mississippi rivers, old-fashioned stern-wheeler riverboats still pass by various states, with interesting cities and towns, and offer gambling, accommodation, and excellent service. The charm of canal and river tourism attracts thousands of enthusiasts every year. The economic impact of the attraction is felt all along the river corridors.

There is also a more modest form of river and canal tourism, offered primarily in Europe. Traditional goods-carrying small shallow-draft boats that have been converted to accommodate a few guests, travel on small rivers and canals that the larger ships cannot navigate. These boats offer the opportunity to get even further into the hinterland and stop at small villages of the countries they traverse.

Proposed activities associated with canal and river tourism include:

- Cruising (e.g., lakes, rivers, canals)
- Sightseeing (e.g., cities, towns, villages, scenery)
- Dining (e.g., on board or in towns)
- Sleeping (on board)
- Other (e.g., attending events in towns)

The following Web sites contain more information about canal and river tourism: http://www.canalbargecruises.com and http://www.abercrombiekent.com/discover/small-group-travel/canal-river-cruising/index.cfm.

4.24 RAILWAY TOURISM

The date September 27, 1825, is generally accepted as the beginning of the *railway age.* On this date, the world's first public passenger train, the Stockton & Darlington Railway, opened for business on a twenty-six-mile route between Witton Park and Stockton-on-Tees in northern England, and George Stevenson's steam-operated Locomotion No. 1 pulled out of the station. The steam locomotive was the product of the Industrial Revolution. After the first try, in 1830, the world's first genuine passenger-carrying railway came into existence: the Liverpool & Manchester Railway. Acceptance and development of railways have since been uninterrupted.

Much of the work undertaken by railways involves the complicated task of moving freight. There were always a number of passenger services that nonetheless managed to capture the imagination of the public. This may have been due to the romantic vision of the lonely chain of wagons snaking through the lush landscape of mountains, rivers, and plains. In North America, only one transcontinental train journey for passengers still operates—across Canada, between Toronto and Vancouver. In the United States, with the creation of AMTRAK in 1971 as a federal corporation, the Great Northern and Northern Pacific Railway has continued to serve passengers between Seattle and the twin cities of Minneapolis and St. Paul via the train known as the Empire Builder. Since 1980, the railway has operated with the luxury Superline equipment, including day cars, a sightseeing lounge car with a clear glass dome roof, and sleeping cars. Other passenger lines with names like Lake Shore Limited, California Zephyr, and Coast Starlight continue to catch the interest of the public in the United States.

AMTRAK operates a high-speed passenger service between Washington, D.C., and Boston, Massachusetts, but the United States has yet to operate systems of high-speed rail like those found in Europe and Asia. AMTRAK also offers a passenger train service between Sanford, Florida (just north of Orlando), and Lorton, Virginia (just south of Washington, D.C.), that carries the automobiles of passengers. Car-carrying trains are more common in Europe, where they have been used for many years in tunnels through mountains and under water bodies.

In other countries, famous routes and railways exist on every continent. In Paraguay, the Sierra Madre line runs between Asuncion and Encarnacion. The trip takes about fourteen hours through spectacular landscape. In 1923, the Flying Scotsman began to operate between London and Edinburgh. Since 1862, the Flying Dutchman passenger train, operating between Paddington and London, passes through spectacular scenery. The service that was later named the Orient Express was launched in 1883. Eventually, it linked Paris with Munich, Vienna, Budapest, Belgrade, Nis, Sofia, and Istanbul. The total distance of this service was 1,996 miles, and the journey lasted for sixty-seven hours. Wagons-Lits Austria still provides staff for the sleeper service between Paris and Vienna. Hungarian Railways provides haute cuisine between Budapest and Salzburg. Romanian Railways again operates the sleeper service between Budapest and Bucharest. In 1906, the Wagons-Lits company started the Simplon Express service connecting Calais, Paris, and Lausanne with Trieste after passing through the Simplon Tunnel under the Alps and stopping at Milan and Venice. Now the Euro Tunnel connects London with Paris under the English Channel.

In other parts of the world, many scenic routes are served by famous railway services. The Star of Egypt in Egypt, the Blue Train and Pride of Africa in South Africa, the Trans Siberian Express in Russia, the Shinkansen (bullet train) service between Tokyo and Osaka in Japan, the

Brisbane Express in Australia, and the Coastal Pacific Express in New Zealand are among the better-known and popular passenger services. Train a Grande Vitesse in France offers high-speed train service between major cities. There are counterpart services and systems in Germany, Italy, Belgium, and Spain.

In addition to scheduled intercity railway services with exotic names that serve tourists traveling between major cities of the world, there is a second and a third type of railroad-related tourist attraction. The second attraction involves restored antique railroad equipment. This industry has flourished over the past three decades, beginning when local groups of rail enthusiasts and preservationists banded together to return to service locomotives and rolling stock that have sat dormant and neglected for many years. The mission of these organizations includes educating, transporting, and entertaining the public. The practitioners of the hobby have all kinds of occupations. They restore the equipment tenderly after committing thousands of hours of free labor and spending a lot of their money. They establish not-for-profit companies for providing train rides over abandoned rail tracks to other train enthusiasts. In addition to restored passenger cars, some of the trains have dinner cars for dining service. The trains are displayed in open-air museums, where additional features like repair shops, turntables, and signals are also preserved. These rides and museums are great attractions for children and adults alike. Seasonal train rides can also be popular, such as fall foliage viewing tours in New England.

The third attraction is scale model railroading, involving trains that are accurate scale replicas of real trains. They are made of rugged and colorful materials with authenticated finishes and exquisite details. Collecting and operating model trains is a great hobby in its own right. The distinction between toy and scale trains is often blurred. They are simply two different hobby markets. Scale model trains range from tiny to large. The smallest is Scale Z, with a 1:220 proportion to prototype. Next is Scale N, with a 1:160 proportion. The third, and most popular scale, is Scale HO, with 1:87. The fourth is Scale S, with 1:64. The fifth is Scale O, with 1:48. The sixth is Scale Gn3, with 1:22.5. Building the railroads, layouts, and scenery duplicating the details of the real world is the fun part of putting together the train model. Rails, plastic buildings, and all kinds of scenery material can be purchased from specialty stores, or can be ordered from catalogues over the Internet or custom built. Model making requires manual dexterity, creativity, attention to detail, and some knowledge of electrical wiring. It can be a pleasant lifelong hobby, but in some cases it becomes an obsession. Some enthusiasts have built very large models costing hundreds of thousands dollars and have filled warehouses. These models are displayed in permanent model railroad museums where thousands of visitors, themselves model railroad enthusiasts, are eager to see the master works.

In the United States, there are more than five hundred open-air railroad museums, model railroad museums, and antique railroads giving rides. There are more than two hundred fifty thousand model railroad enthusiasts in the United States and at least one million more model train enthusiasts throughout the world. These train devotees travel long distances, sometimes between continents, to attend conferences, trade shows, and conventions and to ride restored train vehicles and locomotives. They bring their families to these events and start the second and third generations of railway tourism participants. Their economic impacts are substantial.

Proposed activities associated with railways tourism include:

- Riding (e.g., restored trains for recreation, high-speed trains for excitement and to reduce travel time, seeking scenic train routes for sightseeing, riding conventional trains just for the traditional experience)
- Attending (e.g., conferences, conventions, trade shows)

- Visiting (e.g., exhibits)
- Shopping (e.g., souvenirs)
- Other (e.g., swapping stories with other railroad enthusiasts)

Railway tourism is further defined with extensive listings on the following Web sites: http://www.american-rails.com/railroad-museum-and-tourist-railroad-guide.html and http://www.india-travel-agents.com/railway-tourism-in-india/.

4.25   SPORT FISHING TOURISM

The famous oceanographer Jacques Cousteau is quoted in Brad Matson's book *Jacques Cousteau: The Sea King* (see the Bibliography) as having said that "The sea is the crucible of all life on our planet . . . the engine of our continuing existence. Then it follows, more specifically, that humanity is bound forever to the sea; that it sustains us and strongly influences every turn in our lives and institutions. Clearly, our future, even our survival, depends directly on its preservation." Singlehandedly, Jacque Cousteau raised the consciousness of the world and transformed recreational fishing from an act of extraction from the sea to an act of recreational conservation and scientific exploration. This distinct form of sport is now practiced throughout the world. It helps preserve endangered species of marine life and ensures their sustainability.

The Atlantic Ocean, Pacific Ocean, Indian Ocean, and thousands of bays, sounds, and inlets provide bountiful waters for millions of living creatures. These waters are their habitats. The habitats exist in a variety of marine environments. Estuaries are places where rivers meet the sea and where waters are less salty than those of the open sea. They constitute some of the most productive habitats. Recreationally and commercially important fish and shellfish spend part of their lives in these sheltered and fertile waters. The estuaries are often hidden behind barrier islands. Estuarine communities include sea grass, oyster bars, salt marshes, mud and sand bottom, and algal growth. Mangroves and beach habitats, rock and coral reefs, and currents in deep water carry nutrients for a chain of marine species. Fish roam at will in the ocean. Some travel long distances, guided by a navigational system still unknown to scientists. However, their movement is becoming increasingly predictable. With improving fishing technology, one result is overfishing. Many species are now facing extinction.

Many recreational anglers fish only a few times each year and take home few fish. Many gain pleasure from catching and releasing the fish. Serious anglers travel across continents and oceans to pursue their favorite catch. The conservation ethic dictates that one fish can indeed make for a successful day, and catch-and-release practices and size and number limits are necessary for the survival of various fish species. The culture of sports fishing has progressed to the point that fish is more than just meat packaged in skin and scales. Being outdoors, enjoying the sounds and sights of the sea, tasting the salty seawater, experiencing the power of ocean waves, and matching skills against those creatures of the sea with equal skills and tenacity is what the real pleasures of fishing is about. The old adage that "fish are too valuable to be caught only once" can promote the survival of these magnificent species.

There are millions of recreational anglers in the world. There are also different species to catch and different equipment to use at different coastal areas. In the early fall, hundreds of *kayik* with their kerosene lamps hanging overboard resemble a fleet of fireflies over the Bosphorus in Istanbul. The anglers wait with their lines with multiple hooks *(Chaparis)* for tuna, lufer, and mackerel migrating from the Black Sea to the Mediterranean Sea. Elsewhere, the traditional *dow* leave port and head for the Arabian Gulf in search of massive groupers. In Florida, charter boats leave the marina docks early in the morning and head for the Gulf of Mexico or the Atlantic Ocean, where they spread their outriggers in search of sailfish (*Istiophorus platypterus*), blue marlin (*Makaira nigricans*), dolphin (*Coryphaena hippurus*)—not the cute mammal kind—or greater amberjack (*Seriola dumerili*), among others. Other anglers use long fishing piers extending one hundred meters or more into the ocean. Most of the fish caught and taken home are photographic trophies or fiberglass facsimiles of the fish caught and released. Fishing tournaments draw hundreds of anglers. Party boats depart their docks twice a day, each carrying twenty or more anglers.

Inland waters, lakes, and rivers are the flip side of saltwater sport fishing. Although the boats used and the fish caught are smaller, the excitement of catching and releasing a bass, trout, or salmon matches that of the catches and releases at sea. Fly fishing in remote and idyllic rivers is a hobby that starts with tying one's own special lure. In Florida, flat-bottom boats are lowered into canals leading to the Everglades.

The impact of sport fishing is large and wide. Environmental impacts are controlled by regulatory agencies that, through fisheries management, education, and licensing, instill a sense of responsibility in those who harvest marine finfish and shellfish. The economic impact of sport fishing is measured in terms of fees collected, jobs created, boat charter and fuel and repair expenses, money spent in ports, and fishing equipment purchases, which can include boats, engines, and fishing gear that are very expensive.

Proposed activities associated with sports fishing tourism include:

- Fishing (e.g., ocean, river, lake, pier and jetty)
- Boating (e.g., charter, party)
- Conserving (e.g., fish species, catch and release)

The following Web sites further define and discuss sport fishing tourism: http://sportfishing tourism.com/1512.html and http://www.csu.edu/cerc/documents/RecreationalFishingasTourism.pdf.

4.26 HEALTH TOURISM

Health tourism has existed at least since the time of the Romans two thousand years ago. The baths of the Emperor Caracalla, built in Rome in AD 217, are examples of health facilities that attracted visitors from surrounding regions and abroad. The building complex was huge. It was composed of open and enclosed areas for exercise, indoor swimming pools (*frigidarium, tepidarium, caldarium*), take-out shops for food, and a viewing gallery. Gardens, sports fields, lecture halls, and libraries surrounded the main building. Arched aqueducts brought water from distant springs. As many as sixteen hundred persons could have enjoyed the facilities at one time.

The medicinal qualities of hot-water springs, or thermal baths, and mud baths are believed to cure many degenerative diseases such as arthritis, neuralgia, and herniated disks, as well as nervous disorders and circulatory problems. The medical tradition lives on in hundreds of thermal resorts in France, Germany, Hungary, and Italy and follows the volcanic chain to the east, in Turkey. These resorts were built during their most popular years between 1850 and 1900, using the ornate and monumental architectural styles of their period. Statues and works of art are everywhere. As many as seven thousand guests visit some of these resorts every day. Regardless of their medicinal importance, entire vacation destinations were built around these thermal resorts, for they were the places to see and be seen by the elite. In Japan and New Zealand, there are numerous thermal springs resorts. In the United States, there are Hot Springs in North Carolina, Colorado, California, and Arkansas, as well as Warm Springs in Georgia and Saratoga Springs in New York, that are examples of medicinal tourist attractions.

One of the better-known thermal resorts is Warm Springs, Georgia, where President Franklin D. Roosevelt stayed in his modest three-room Little White House and where he received treatment for his polio at nearby springs. He died of a stroke at the Little White House on April 12, 1945, while having his portrait painted.

A typical thermal resort includes covered and open hot water pools as large as five thousand square feet, separate for men and women, individual baths, a carbonated swimming pool, a wave pool, mud baths, massage rooms, showers, lockers, and dressing rooms with a couch, a *buvette* or mineral water drinking fountain, a hairdresser, and service areas. Usually, an adjacent hotel with full facilities provides overnight accommodation for patients receiving long-term therapies at the baths. Resort names like Evian and Gellert are well known in Europe, where many royals, aristocrats, and affluent people frequented the resorts almost daily for therapeutic, recreational, and social reasons. In today's terms, an evening hour spent at the baths is considered to be better than an hour spent at a favorite bar before heading home. Thermal baths provide healthier alternatives.

There are other types of destinations for medical tourism in the United States and elsewhere. Centers for drug and alcohol detoxification and rehabilitation are voluntary destinations for many. Sometimes, entire retinues arrive and stay with the patient during his or her therapy period. Certain medical centers and hospitals associated with medical schools are big attractions for medical treatment. Cancer treatment centers are particularly prevalent. Open-heart surgery is another specialty that many well-known hospitals around the world offer. Kidney transplants and other lifesaving medical interventions are also major attractions. Specialized medical facilities have been built in South and Southeast Asia and elsewhere where the patient can receive excellent treatment in relatively luxurious but competitively priced environments.

What is affectionately known as "scalpel tourism" concerns cosmetic surgery. Tourists combine surgery with a vacation during their recovery period. One particular medical center in Hong Kong is best known not only for its successful cosmetic treatments, but also for its luxurious recreational facilities and relatively low costs. In addition, health spas exist in profusion all over the world and do a landslide business in various health-related treatments by drawing thousands of patient-tourists from all countries. One must be careful, however, to verify whether these places are licensed and offer treatments that are approved by medical authorities. If the treatment is not successful, the patient-tourist may have little legal recourse under the laws of a different country.

The benefits of health tourism are strongly tied to the reputation of medical facilities and their staff, and to differentials in the cost of health services among countries. With continual advances being made in organ replacement, biotechnology, and other medical sciences, and with increasing numbers of medical personnel being trained, more medical centers will be created and will augment the economic impacts of health tourism.

Proposed activities associated with health tourism include:

• Receiving (e.g., medical treatment, beauty treatment, health treatment)
• Related sightseeing while on trips to receive medical treatment
• Other (e.g., related dining and visiting friends while on medical trips)

Health and medical tourism are further defined and discussed on the following Web sites: http://www.health-tourism.com/medical-tourism/statistics/, http://www.healthbase.com/, and http://medicaltourism.com.

4.27 BUSINESS TOURISM

Business tourism can be described as that portion of a business trip associated with recreation-related activities. The desire to meet face-to-face with a business contact at his or her place of business accounts for more than 25% of the trips taken by all travelers in developed countries. After arriving at their destination and participating in business-related activities, travelers often engage in recreational activities during their stay. This portion of the trip can be very productive for the local tourism economy. Eating in exotic restaurants, playing golf on championship courses, engaging in sports and fitness activities, and sightseeing could enrich the experience of the business traveler and could influence his or her business decisions as well. Business travelers often have expense accounts that allow for some extra benefits such as flying first or business class, staying in luxury hotels, and eating sumptuous meals. Business travelers are usually expected to be equivalent in status within their organizations to the sometimes high-ranking officials with whom they meet.

Conducting business in a leisure setting is a tradition in many cultures and societies. Local custom, protocol, and social grace may demand extending hospitality to a stranger or to a friend from out of town or from out of the country. In traditional societies, getting to know each other as individuals is of primary importance. To expedite this process, the business traveler may attend many breakfasts, lunches, and dinners with his or her business contact. In traditional societies, local culture and custom often attach great importance to cultivating trust and mutual respect first. This is achieved through the process of sharing food and beverages and for establishing rapport before conducting business. Mixing business with pleasure can be demanding. The word *demanding* is used in the sense of knowing how to behave and speak in situations according to local culture, customs, and values and how to avoid rudeness and embarrassment.

In different parts of the world, the ritual of camaraderie may range from offering tea, coffee, or a local beverage—sometimes repeatedly until signaled otherwise—to holding lavish banquets attended by many guests and dignitaries. After conducting business, visiting the shopping district to purchase prized souvenirs for the family back home or taking a special tour of the city and sightseeing is often a required practice. Attending nightclubs, a circus, ballet, theater, or concert or playing a round of golf with the host are also possibilities. All of these activities provide substantial economic benefits to the local economy. They include jobs, income in wages and tips, transportation, and revenues to the government from visa fees, taxes, and other indirect revenues.

Modern technology is now changing the tourist activities associated with conducting business. Because of advances in information systems and technology, face-to-face encounters are no longer required for conducting business. Virtual reality telecommunication with teleconference video connections is replacing time-consuming and expensive travel to distant lands. Instant communication over the Internet and access to all sorts of data with a device in the palm of a hand is revolutionizing the concept of business communication. The impact of this trend on interregional and international tourism industry is evolving.

Proposed activities associated with business tourism include:

- Sightseeing (e.g., general)
- Attending (e.g., receptions, cultural and ceremonial events)
- Shopping (e.g., souvenirs)
- Partying (e.g., business)

- Golfing (e.g., business)
- Other (e.g., dining)

Business tourism is further defined and discussed on the following Web sites: http://www.tradeforum.org/news/fullstory.php/aid/161.html and http://www.businesstourismpartnership.com/pubs/briefing.pdf.

4.28 "BAREFOOT ELEGANCE" AND THE TOURISM OF THE RICH, FAMOUS, AND POWERFUL

This type of tourism is separated from other types of tourism described earlier by one major requirement. The subject or attraction has to be the rich, famous, and powerful personified. In a class-conscious society where traditional royalty is disappearing around the world, the new "royalty" embodies the changing distinction between the elite and the masses. The members of the new royalty are the focus of their followers' ardent attention or disaffection. They are from all parts of the world, with different nationalities, different religious convictions, and different occupations. Weddings, funerals, ceremonies, and other public appearances by traditional royalty are events where pomp and circumstances cause thousands of people to travel long distances to observe and share the ritual and enthusiasm of the events. Some members of royalty have become icons of world society due to their modesty, fairness, leadership, and intellect. Others, however, have attained their celebrity status for their scandalous and tiresome behavior. Either way, they are news for the media and the public, drawing thousands of tourists from everywhere.

The powerful become powerful by inheritance, wealth accumulation, or political and other recognition processes. Celebrities from the worlds of art, entertainment, and sport are sometimes accorded power through their influence on the masses. Leadership of the most powerful democratic countries in the world carries with it the obligation to be responsive to the electorate and to the world at large. This responsiveness is manifested by attending public functions, giving noteworthy speeches, campaigning, sponsoring important events, and appointing officials. The public is drawn to these events by the thousands, sometimes by the millions, and gathers in the largest public squares and forums of the country. Grassroots movements centered on some public cause of national and universal importance also bring very large crowds together from all corners of the world. They remind their leaders of their duty to redress some injustice or promote a cause.

The rich and famous also draw crowds, sometimes for no other reason than that they are rich and famous. They set popular trends with every action they take. Film and theater stars, artists, icons of rock music, and sports figures thrive on the publicity and on the adoration of their admirers. Their every act, appearance, performance, and the like causes large crowds to travel long distances and participate in these occasions. The gossip, media, souvenir, and service industries thrive while the occasion lasts.

However, there is also the private side of tourism that the rich, famous, and powerful seek and cherish. Away from the public eye, they play and let their guard down in the company of the few who share their celebrity status and respect their privacy. The locations of their favorite retreats or playgrounds around the world are well-kept secrets. The Caribbean and Pacific islands, in particular, offer the isolation and comfort that the rich, famous, and powerful seek. Accessible only by private jet plane or yacht, these islands and retreats offer accommodations that the less famous, less rich, or less powerful citizens of the world never get to see. The gentle, soothing, informal, relaxing environment and facilities providing the best service that money can buy are characterized by the term **barefoot elegance.** This label encompasses an ambiance where business tycoons mingle with the royalty, film stars, and top fashion models who add a glamorous dimension to socializing; and sports celebrities exchange stories with rock stars. They entertain lavishly and demand the best. The admiring world waits for their return and follows their activities and those of the next group of rich, powerful, and famous celebrities.

Proposed activities associated with barefoot elegance tourism include:

- Seeking seclusion, security, and privacy (e.g., in remote desirable destinations)
- Mingling with members of the same kind of elite (e.g., royals, executives, artists, entertainers, celebrities)
- Observing large crowd events (e.g., weddings, ceremonies)
- Generating media attention (e.g., TV, magazines, Internet blogs)
- Other (e.g., recovering from their high-pressure exposed life experiences)

The following Web sites further describe barefoot elegance tourism: http://travel.ninemsn.com.au/article.aspx?id=278274 and http://blog.ratestogo.com/top-7-celebrity-vacation-spots/.

4.29   OTHER TYPES OF TOURISM

Depending on the interests of tourists and world events, many other types of tourism are possible. They are planned around one or more themes and activities. Exotic places and exotic lifestyles offer exotic experiences that tourism planners can develop into new types of tourism. A sample of the major types is given here.

A word of caution: Traveling to exotic places and doing adventurous things is pleasurable. However, there is a down side to it. One has to be constantly aware of the consequences of the unknown. For example, experiencing the local culture may involve certain rituals that could be detrimental to one's health and safety. Going along with the village shaman and drinking a concoction laced with narcotics and unknown substances may be carrying the experience too far. Entering the inner chambers of a suspect bazaar may carry the risk of being drawn into the back room and robbed and/or assaulted by criminals. Another serious risk involves dealing with shady characters and soliciting sex with minors. Slave and sex trading involving minors is a criminal offense in most countries. Unfortunately, it has become widespread enough to be combined with other unsavory practices that could be included under the labels **decadency** or **debauchery tourism.**

Last but not the least, petty theft, burglary, purse snatching, and pickpocketing are unfortunately prevalent in some popular tourist destinations. In these areas, tourists are advised to hold on tightly to handbags that close and seal securely; to avoid wearing valuable jewelry on the street; to keep wallets and other money- and document-carrying accessories in their front pockets; and to wrap rubber bands around them to prevent them from being removed unnoticed. Tourists are also advised not to accept invitations to parties or other events from strangers, and to try to avoid taxi rides that do not go directly to designated destinations. Usually, the local police mark a security zone around major hotels that keep peddlers, vendors, and other possibly annoying or harmful individuals at a safe distance.

Chapter Highlights

- Tourism can take many forms. General and special interest tourisms are different. They address different demands and interests of different types of tourists.
- Twenty-seven major types of tourism are identified and defined briefly in this chapter. Others can be defined and may be regionally important for a given country.
- A great variety of recreational themes can be extracted from the tourism attributes of a destination and developed as group tours and other packaged products.
- As interests change over time, new themes, attractions, and facilities should be planned and developed to ensure the sustainability of tourism.
- One should be alert at all times to the pitfalls and risks involved in tourism.

Planning Issues for Tourism Development

Part II introduces issues to be resolved in planning and developing tourism in market economy and mixed economy systems. It presents concepts for promoting sustainable tourism development in the transition from centrally planned to market economies.

5

Market System and Planned Growth

This chapter examines the differences in approach in developing tourism under capitalist market, central command, and government-assisted mixed economic systems.

- The capitalist market system is based on private property rights, the profit motive, freedom of enterprise, competition, individual freedom, and minimum government regulation.
- In capitalist market systems, entrepreneurs own the factors of production, take the initiative, and benefit directly from economic activities. Government plays a supporting role by providing some facilities and infrastructure and ensuring economic stability, including access to capital.
- In command economies, the government owns and operates a significant portion of the factors of production. It owns the infrastructure and major facilities. It controls the amount and flow of capital. Benefits from production go to the government, which allocates them to individuals.
- Mixed economic systems combine features of capitalist and command economic systems. The degrees of capitalist and command elements in a mixed economy often shift back and forth, depending on current political conditions and preferences in each country.
- In government-assisted economies, the government owns many factors of production and enterprises that the private sector has difficulty owning and operating. The government also owns and operates many facilities and infrastructure. It gives guidance and support where they are needed. Private enterprise expands the economy by building and operating the rest of the factors of production. Government-assisted economies often are found in developing countries where the government is trying to strengthen the private sector enough to provide key economic activities. These economies are usually in transition to more market-oriented capitalist systems.

- Command economies, mixed economic systems, and government-assisted economies are sometimes labeled *socialist* systems, which is an imprecise term and is often misunderstood.
- Tourism functions under all economic systems. Planning the growth of tourism follows basic guidelines for international, national, regional, and destination level development.
- Horizontal and vertical linkages, as well as economic leakages from tourism, are economic issues to be resolved in tourism planning.

5.1   DIFFERENCES BETWEEN MARKET AND GOVERNMENT-ASSISTED ECONOMIES

Tourism has existed for centuries. It was practiced in economic systems different from ours today. The nature of modern tourism began to change with the rise of industrial nations and economic systems during the nineteenth and twentieth centuries. The trend was toward less and less direct governmental control of economic activity. **Free enterprise**, otherwise known as **competitive capitalism**, replaced feudal and preindustrial systems. The ultimate result of this trend was the **laissez-faire** (in French, "let it happen") economy, which emerged at the end of the eighteenth century and became more codified in the mid-nineteenth century.

Laissez-faire philosophy assumes that individuals are the best judges of their own interests and that government should minimize regulation of business. The capitalist system is founded on the economic principle of balancing the scarcity of **resources** relative to **wants**. Whereas wants are expandable, the factors of production, commodities, and services are not. The allocation of scarce resources for production (i.e., capital, labor, land, and entrepreneurship) is governed by the **price** mechanism determined by the interaction of supply and demand.

Income inequality is an accepted fact of capitalism. Income inequality results from unequal distribution and ownership of the factors of production. The motivation to engage in economic activities is monetary gain for the owners of the factors of production. Individuals with the greatest ownership of the factors of production and therefore the largest incomes generally save most. In turn, savings are invested where they will achieve additional monetary gain for the investor. The rate of interest serves to allocate the money where it is most productive.

Laissez-faire economy and capitalism are associated with the following principles:

- Private property rights
- The profit motive
- Freedom of enterprise
- Competition
- Individual freedom
- Minimum government interference

In the middle and late nineteenth century, excesses of the laissez-faire system created a large concentration of power and capital in the hands of a few industrialists. In the United States, some of these industrialists were called **robber barons**. After several decades, the sanctity of individualism and entrepreneurship was blemished. These policies were not alleviating social problems (in fact, they were contributing to some of them, such as labor riots) and were not ensuring the welfare of all. Government antitrust laws were passed to reduce some of the excesses of monopoly power. When the stock market crashed in 1929, the stage was set for bringing government more firmly back into the system. Individualistic market capitalism turned into state-guided capitalism, also referred to as **communitarian capitalism**. The balancing act involved financial regulations, subsidies, labor unions, public spending on infrastructure and other projects, and Social Security payments aimed at better ensuring social welfare.

In individualistic **market capitalism**, the "right to govern rests with the governed," said John Locke. "The individual will promote the well-being of all," said Adam Smith. Employees and employers were not bound by common obligations. In communitarian capitalism, however, the success of the system depends on a group process. Government assists the economy by stimulating growth, creating steady jobs for employees, and encouraging employers to think long term. In practice, many variations exist between individualistic market capitalism and communitarian capitalism.

In the United States, the role of the government is substantial. The government ensures and maintains the sanctity of private property (with the exception that it can be taken, with just compensation, for a "public purpose"). It protects freedom of enterprise. It adjudicates disputes of individuals and corporations. In the communitarian market capitalism of Germany, the government establishes welfare programs for public health and for creating jobs. In the state-directed capitalism of Japan, the relationship between government and business is close. Policymaking involves achieving a consensus between the two.

In market capitalist systems, the role of the government in assisting the economy is widely known. However, how much economic life goes on without direct government intervention is less well known. The competitive market and price system works despite its imperfections. There is a certain orderliness to the system. Without the benefit of intelligence from a particular entity or individual, the system resolves complex problems by involving a large number of variables and many more economic relations. It evolves over time and changes its nature, depending on the demands and conditions of human society. In the end, it survives in one form or another. The "invisible hand" described by Adam Smith leads individuals to pursue their self-interest and, through equilibrium-seeking and market-clearing processes, sets the stage for achieving welfare for all with the aid of occasional government intervention.

The market capitalist system is a system of trial and error where successive adjustments made in prices and production bring the two into a balance known as **equilibrium of prices and production**. Firms do not know when consumer tastes will change. Predicting the future of the market is difficult. Firms may overproduce one product and underproduce another. When they learn from their experience, the situation may change again. Without predicting the future, firms sometimes succeed by keeping production high. At other times, monopoly or oligopoly distorts prices and production. It is therefore necessary to assume that perfect competition does not exist. Nevertheless, it is an ideal toward which markets strive, and the market system remains the best approximation of perfect competition. It is still the best economic system available for producing wealth and for potentially alleviating poverty by increasing the overall income available for distribution.

Government, despite its own imperfections, plays an important role, depending on the conditions of the particular economy. Government intervention started with the realization that "nobody's business is everybody's business." Therefore, some entity had to step in and provide national defense, law and order, administration of justice, basic infrastructure, and any other national necessity falling through the economic, social, and environmental cracks that needed attention. The role of government in a capitalist market system lies in finding where its intervention can be most effective.

Command economy systems stand at the opposite end of the economic spectrum. With the collapse of the Soviet Union in the late 1980s, the weaknesses that caused the collapse of its command economy became clear. Command economies are characterized by some form of central economic planning and government ownership of (1) most property, (2) many means of production, and (3) all social and economic infrastructure. As a result, benefits from production accrue to the government, not to individuals. The government then decides how such benefits are distributed among individuals. This is the **allocation** role of the government. The government also decides where, what, and when resources are invested. The government decides how much present consumption should be limited in order to invest in factories, equipment, and productive capacity to ensure a future rise in production.

The governments in market economies as well as in centrally planned economic systems are not immune from the frailties of human nature and society. Not all governments are benevolent, looking after the interests of their people. There may be excesses ranging from incompetence to corruption and other illegal actions. The government's organization might be inefficient or bureaucratic, and its members might be inclined to take advantage of circumstances for personal gain. Their rule might be unjust, autocratic, arbitrary, discriminatory, and even criminally liable. The cures they advocate could be more damaging than the excesses themselves.

The shortcomings of any particular economic system can be corrected. If the cure is a transition from a central planned economy to a market economy, the steps to be taken are tested and tried. However, the transition may not be easy. The *World Development Report* published in 1996 by the World Bank poses the following questions on pages 5 and 6 to determine the right steps for transition:

- Do differences in transition policies and outcomes reflect different reform strategies or do they reflect primarily country specific factors such as history, the level of development, or just as important, impacts of political changes taking place at the same time?
- Are strong liberalization and stabilization policies needed up front, or can other reforms progress equally well without them?
- Must a market economy instantly be a private one? Or, can privatization take place in steps in the early years of reform?
- Must there be a gulf between winners and losers from transition? How can social policies ease the pain of transformation while propelling the process forward?
- How should countries in transition develop and strengthen the rule of law?
- How can countries develop effective financial systems?
- How must government restructure itself to meet the needs of a market system?
- How can countries preserve and adapt their human capital reserve?
- Why is international integration so vital for transition and what are its implications for trading partners and capital flows?
- How can external assistance best support countries in transition?

It would be foolhardy to proceed with planning and developing tourism in countries undergoing substantial social and economic transformation without raising these and other questions concerning the impact of the transition. Although the questions are known, the answers will be individualized for each country. The challenge lies in planning and developing tourism based on the best answers that satisfy the sustainability criteria.

There is one fairly recent entrant into tourism development and the poverty alleviation process. It fills the gap between government and private enterprise. Its adherents call it **social entrepreneurship** by private citizens. It has existed throughout history. What is different today is that social entrepreneurship is establishing itself as a mainstream vocation in an expanded role not only in North America and Europe, but increasingly in Asia, Africa, and Latin America as well. The rise of social entrepreneurship represents the emergence of millions of new citizen organizations around the world.

Examples of social entrepreneurship that came into existence during the past twenty years are many. Twenty years ago, Indonesia had only one citizen organization. Today it has more than 2,000. India has well over one million citizen organizations. In Central Europe, some 100,000 citizen organizations were set up between 1988 and 1995. In Canada, the number of registered citizen organizations was close to 200,000. From 1990 to 2000, the number of citizen organizations in Brazil increased by 60% and now stands at around 400,000. In the United States during the same period, similar growth has occurred and the number of public service organizations registered with the Internal Revenue Service has reached 734,000. The number of registered transnational citizen organizations now stands at 26,000.

Social entrepreneur citizen organizations were previously defined as nonprofit or nongovernmental organizations (NGOs). Today, they are the new economic sector active in the development of countries around the world. In the process of their expansion, social entrepreneur citizen organizations have created more than two and a half times the number of new jobs than those created by other means in the economies they are helping to develop. The expansion of social entrepreneur citizen organizations is also significant for the planning and development of tourism:

- Citizen organizations are expanding on a scale never seen before.
- Citizen organizations are more globally dispersed and diverse than in the past.
- Citizen organizations are offering more systemic approaches to solving development problems.
- Citizen organizations are reasonably free of pressure from government and religious organizations.
- Citizen organizations are entering into partnerships with one another, and with businesses, academic institutions, and governments, in pursuing major humanitarian and economic development projects, including tourism.

On the negative side, the global expansion of social entrepreneurship has its share of inefficient, wasteful, and corrupt organizations in the citizen sector. However, with rising competition from well-run groups, incompetent, dubious, and fraudulent organizations no longer find "business as usual" sufficient for their survival. The supporters of social entrepreneurship find their place in streamlining some of the operations normally assigned to governments, changing practices and attitudes in business, opening opportunities for people to use their creative talents in positive ways, and helping to make social and economic transitions possible. Examples in the tourism industry are organizations that make micro loans to very small businesses so that they can sell souvenirs in tourist areas, and other groups that help organize local artisans to design and make the handicrafts and souvenirs that are sold in tourist areas.

5.2   WHEN IS PLANNING NECESSARY FOR ASSISTING TOURISM DEVELOPMENT?

Different economic systems have different ways of approaching economic development and alleviating poverty. It is clear that, to be beneficial, tourism development has to become an integral part of this process at the international, national, regional, local, and firm levels in all of the variations of the economic systems. Government in the capitalistic market system favors a hands-off approach, relinquishing most responsibility for developing tourism to the private sector.

Centrally planned economic systems look to the government for setting policies, standards, rules, and regulations for planning, financing, executing, and developing projects of all descriptions. In the middle, mixed economic systems try to combine the strengths of both systems and adopt shared responsibility.

The justification for planning and developing tourism depends on the past performance of the public and private sectors in all forms of economic systems. In developed countries where tourism in its many forms has been a recognized economic activity for decades, if not for centuries, issues have been primarily domestic and local. In LDCs, all the issues of tourism as an economic activity have not been recognized, let alone resolved, until recent decades.

With the arrival of the jet age, all this has changed. Worldwide international tourist arrivals increased from 25 million in 1950 to 922 million in 2008 (an increase of about 6.5% per year), according to the UNWTO in its annual reports. The ever-increasing demand for international tourism began to press governments for action at all levels, while the private sector scrambled to meet the demand as they perceived it, sometimes with shortsighted, ill-conceived, and often poorly located tourism projects. In developed countries, remedies for the harmful consequences of rapid tourism development consisted of making marginal adjustments in international and domestic policies and establishing international linkages. In LDCs, however, problems at all levels concerning many subjects needed solutions.

The UNWTO, which itself was a creation of the demand for international action for tourism development, has generally supported the position that planning tourism at all levels is essential for achieving successful tourism development and management. In a few decades, the experience of emerging tourism destinations has demonstrated that the planned approach can bring increased benefits by minimizing adverse impacts and by ensuring satisfaction for tourists. Destinations that allowed tourism to develop without the benefit of planning have experienced serious environmental and social problems.

Depending on local variations, specific tourism-related problems arising at the national level include establishing proper levels of visa and passport control, foreign currency exchange, banking, travel information, telecommunications, overnight accommodations, sanitary and health measures, and social and economic infrastructure. Sometimes, the results are surly and untrained hotel and restaurant staff, as well as local traditions and customs that cause local populations to regard foreigners with suspicion and, at worst, with hostility. If these immediate issues are not addressed at the national level, the consequences at the local level are sometimes dire. Within only a few decades, LDCs, regions, and destinations that allowed tourism to develop without the benefit of proper planning and coordination have found their environment abused and their people disappointed. In more developed countries, some popular destinations have been overdeveloped to the point where the tourism experience is uncomfortable and frustrating.

Tourism and human geography are inseparable. Between them, they cover the fields of urban studies, geology, biology, environmental studies, anthropology, sociology, demography, medicine, economics, political science, business, psychology, history, religion, and linguistics. These mutual interests manifest themselves in the way human settlements are laid out, organized, and located around the world. When resources and products of tourism and human geography are not controlled, shaped, and used properly, they result in misused resources, misplaced facilities, destruction of the environment, and crushed expectations.

There are many examples of ill-conceived tourism projects that resulted in wasted resources and unfulfilled expectations. The future of tourism is uncertain when the foundations of the industry are not sound. Trial and error by both government and the private sector can be a very inefficient learning experience. Tourism planning based on comprehensive inventories, evaluation of tourism potentials, and the use of proven technical methods minimizes waste and inefficiency.

5.3 CAN MARKET AND PLANNED TOURISM GROWTH COEXIST?

This question is not academic. Market and planned growth of tourism are not mutually exclusive. Market and planned tourism development methods are used in various combinations to organize an effective approach to developing tourism. The combination depends on where a proposed project or program is located and on who will provide the necessary leadership in the combined process.

Government can be effective in the international promotion of tourism, establishing policy guidelines for growth and location and investing in appropriate infrastructure. Working in concert, entrepreneurship and the invisible hand of the market system can do the rest. The challenge is in articulating these prescriptions and following the general procedures and requirements of the dual system. By using the elements of both systems, government and the private sector can decide together the scale of their respective involvement in planning and developing tourism and carrying out the process. The important point is that both public and private sectors coordinate with each other and agree on a division of responsibilities, functions, and tasks.

Tourism development planning is the process of setting goals and objectives; formulating policies and strategies; and defining projects and procedures to meet tourism development goals and objectives. The process includes both **long-term strategic plans** and **short-term tactical or operational programs**. These plans and programs are implemented at several levels. At the national level, the process translates goals into multiple long-term national tourism sector policies. In turn, these policies are expressed as specific objectives, short-term programs, and measures to be adopted and executed by the national government. At the regional level, tourism planning focuses on specific regional issues of economic development, infrastructure, and sustainable growth addressed by provincial or state governments. Finally, following national and regional guidelines, private sector companies prepare business plans for designing, building, financing, owning, managing, and operating site-specific attractions and facilities at the local destination level.

5.4 LEVELS OF PLANNING TOURISM DEVELOPMENT

It is important that tourism development planning conforms to an overall growth management system. Planning connects the upper- and lower-level elements of the system. It also connects the elements at each level horizontally. From larger to smaller geographic areas, the connected system consists of planning at the international, national, regional, local, or destination levels. The lowest local or destination-level planning involves the elements of project planning. These elements include site planning, building design, and landscape design (Figures 5.1 and 5.2).

International Level

The global scale of tourism, and the problems created by its development, call for action at the international level. Tourism planning at the international level consists of reaching a common understanding of potentials and problems; researching the nature and extent of these potentials and problems; and taking coordinated actions to ensure a better future for tourism worldwide, including finding better means for international cooperation.

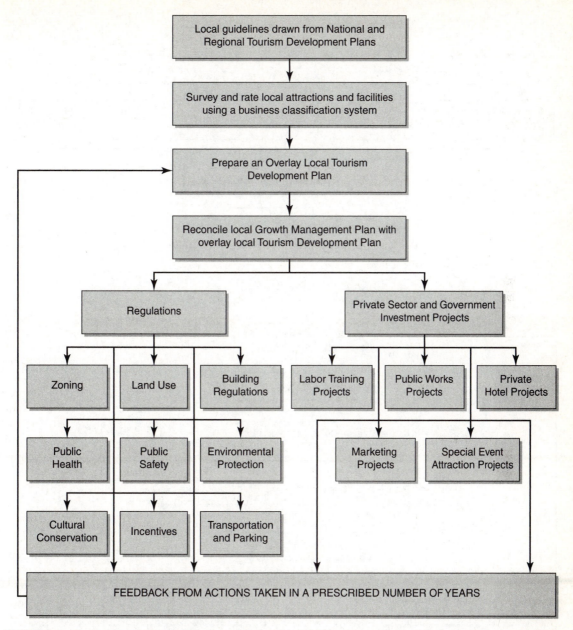

FIGURE 5.1 Tourism Development Planning at the Local Level. The process of planning the growth of tourism at the provincial, state, or municipal level may change from country to country. The planning fundamentals and steps, however, remain the same as the ones described here. Each local government or private marketing organization should adhere to these fundamentals to ensure proper linkages with regional and national tourism development plans and policies.

Source: Bulent I. Kastarlak

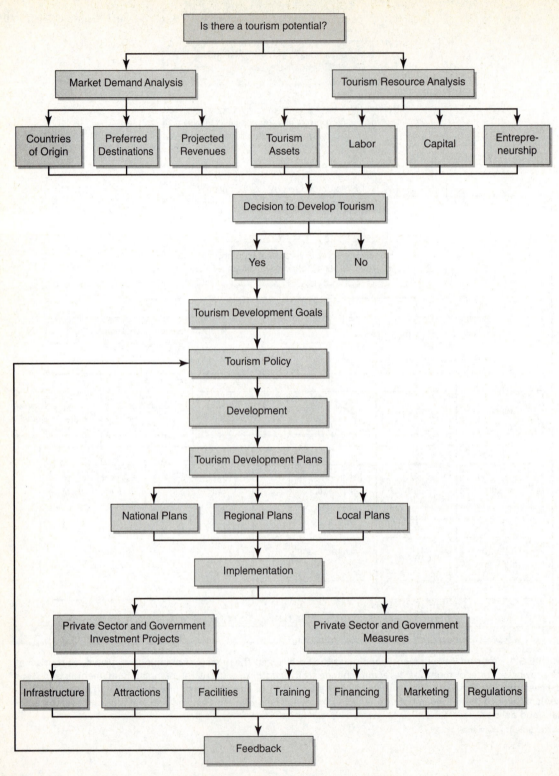

FIGURE 5.2 Comprehensive Tourism Development Process for Sustainable Growth.
Source: Bulent I. Kastarlak

Specific subject areas considered at the international level include conducting surveys and building databases; collecting, preparing, and publishing information on relevant topics; suggesting policies and standards for tourism development; ensuring communication and cooperation among international and national organizations; establishing sources for legal, technical, and financial assistance; participating in joint multinational projects; and providing assistance in marketing tourism.

The lead organization in international cooperation for tourism planning is the UNWTO and its regional commissions around the world. Collectively, they address international, national, and regional growth management issues of tourism. The headquarters of the UNWTO is located in Madrid, Spain. The regional commissions encourage cooperation between private and government sectors and provide policy guidance in their regions.

Another broad-based international tourism organization is the World Travel and Tourism Council. Other international tourism organizations are concerned primarily with their particular subject of interest. They include the International Air Transport Association (IATA), the International Civil Aviation Organization, the Pacific Asia Travel Association (PATA), the Tourism Council of the South Pacific (TCSP), the Caribbean Tourism Organization (CTO), the tourism unit of the Association of Southeast Asian Nations (ASEAN), and the Regional Tourism Organization of Southern Africa (RETOSA). Other organizations interested in global tourism include hotel associations, restaurant associations, and various private membership and government-sponsored tourism marketing organizations. Collectively, these organizations endeavor to ensure orderly growth of global tourism.

National Level

Probably the most determinant actions in planning and developing tourism in mixed economic systems occur at the national level. The need for national policies emerges when governments recognize tourism as a viable economic activity for their country. Committing the resources of national governments for tourism development is a serious political and financial step for governments. Once commitments are made, the entire structure of a government may be mobilized at all levels, principally because tourism cuts across so many traditional sectors. The goal is to develop tourism in the best interests of the country in cooperation with the private sector. The job of representing the national government and preparing policies, programs, regulations, and standards for developing tourism is given to an agency of the national government, sometimes at the ministerial level.

In countries with advanced market economies and well-developed tourism industries, the role of the national government is limited to supporting private sector searches for business opportunities in the tourism sector. This includes collecting and disseminating tourism data and undertaking marketing at the national level. A tourism agency established at a second- or third-layer branch of a government ministry could be all that is necessary for ensuring the continuation of a productive tourism industry at the national level. Western European and North American countries have adopted this practice.

Practices are quite different for countries at the opposite end of the tourism development spectrum. When circumstances in LDCs begin to show that tourism can play an important role in developing their countries, national governments are poised to take major actions for including tourism in their overall national development strategies. Their actions include:

- Establishing goals and policies for national tourism development, possibly including selection of prime locations for tourism development
- Establishing security and safety in the country
- Ensuring protection of the national heritage and natural treasures of the country

- Integrating tourism into the mainstream national economy by establishing linkages with other economic sectors and by preparing a macroeconomic development plan
- Establishing two-way communication for tourism development with the private sector and with regional and local governments; providing technical and financial assistance to private sector and lower-level governments as needed
- Attempting to ensure an equitable distribution of benefits from, and costs of, tourism
- Providing necessary tourism infrastructure for supporting the development and maintenance of tourist facilities and attractions, and for ensuring the comfort and convenience of tourists
- Preparing standards and guidelines that will facilitate the orderly growth and management of tourism
- Establishing an interagency implementation organization for overseeing the execution and completion of tourism projects and measures
- Establishing a feedback mechanism for evaluating the past performance of the tourism sector and recommending adjustments for the future
- Preparing annual tourism development programs, budgets, and projects and passing laws and regulatory measures

Regional Level

The geographic boundaries of tourism planning at the national level are well defined. The plan covers the territories, contiguous or otherwise, defined by the borders of the country. At the regional level, the task is more complicated. Choosing regions for development is a multidisciplinary process fraught with conflicting concepts.

One concept, **comparative advantage** (to borrow a term from economic trade theory), governs the economic development policies of a country. The leading economic sector, having the largest comparative advantage over others in developing the country, is favored for investment. The concept also applies to the leading region of the country. A leading region has a dominant economic sector that, together with its related sectors, ensures balanced and faster growth in the region. Leading investment projects achieve the level of desired growth in the leading sector of the leading region.

Use of the comparative advantage concept seeks to accelerate the development of a few leading regions. In these regions, support is given to economic activities that might offer comparative advantages. The goal is not to equalize growth rates in all regions or in all sectors of a region during the same period. Rather, the aim is to achieve a roughly estimated "critical size" for a few regions or for an urban center within a region. When the critical size or economies of agglomeration is reached, a wide range of internal and external economies begins to take shape.

Because of material, capital, and management skill limitations, the development of other regions and sectors is put on hold. The duration of that holding period depends on its political acceptability. Any extensive development planned for selected regions will take a number of years to get started and more years to be completed. Action starts with preliminary development programs and existing limited knowledge. Revisions are made in these programs when knowledge of the economy and its performance improves.

This government-assisted model of regional development requires strong support from both the national government and the private sector. As regional development programs progress, better information is forthcoming. Government and private investment decisions become more accurate. Training and education measures are gradually refined. Regional development goals are defined, and preinvestment project feasibility studies are prepared. In all, planning organizes and coordinates all development actions by government and the private sector at the regional level. It makes the orderly growth of the country at the regional level possible.

Tourism development fits into this regional growth and development model. After preliminary studies are completed, the tourism potential may rate high. That would qualify tourism as a leading sector. Then regional development is planned around tourism and its linkages with national and other established regional sectors.

Regional planning for tourism development interprets national policies at the regional level. It identifies regional infrastructure needs and prepares government investment projects, regional land use plans, and zoning plans. It prescribes personnel training for regional public services like health, education, security, environmental protection, distribution, and transportation works. Government develops regional service facilities and conserves environmental assets to ensure sustainable tourism. In turn, the private sector mobilizes its resources and, sometimes with government assistance, creates its tourism project opportunities.

At the regional level, many organizations participate in planning and developing tourism businesses and promoting tourism directly and indirectly. Depending on the economic system within which they operate, these organizations take different names and specialize in one or more aspects of tourism-related products and services. Among these functions are providing information to visitors and directing them to their selected attractions, facilities, and destinations. These functions are common to almost all tourism organizations. Other organizations also focus on diversifying and strengthening the tourism industry mix. Local or regional convention and visitors bureaus, departments of transportation, departments of natural resources and/or environment, departments of business/commerce, chambers of commerce, and business development boards often have as their functions providing information on tourism and setting strategies for regional tourism businesses.

Convention, exhibit, and visitors bureaus concentrate on promoting conventions that could be attracted to the principal convention facilities of the community. They advertise the facilities, schedule events, and provide associated information to the public nationally or internationally, depending on their market area. An example of such advertising is shown on the following Web site for a Boston, Massachusetts, convention and exhibit center: http://www.mccahome.com/bcec_ser_pub_er.html.

Departments of transportation operate travel information centers for the convenience of the public. Uniformed, professional travel counselors welcome visitors and provide a wealth of free literature, information, and suggestions to make every trip to the region a pleasant experience. Working with the official travel map of the region, counselors expertly chart routes to the locations in the region desired by the traveler. In addition, they provide telephone numbers to call for emergency road conditions. These departments provide and maintain rest areas with full sanitary facilities, water fountains, vending machines, picnic areas, and scenic turnouts. Mini-parks at these stops are usually equipped with shade, tables, benches, and cooking grills. Information boards provide attractive exhibits that summarize tourism attractions and facilities. Each information board's location is marked on the official travel map. Today, many desktop and handheld computers contain this information and visitors can decide on their own.

Departments of natural resources and/or environment usually own and manage a system of parks, beaches, forest areas, and other recreational attractions such as ski areas or public golf courses. These departments generally publish maps and brochures that provide useful information about attractions, facilities, regulations, and fees. Staff members of these departments operate the sites that are publicly owned. Sometimes facilities are franchised out to private operators.

Departments of business/commerce often include tourism agencies whose main functions are to market tourism attractions and facilities, to coordinate regional and local tourism agencies, and to promote tourism activities within their jurisdiction. Promotion sometimes consists of conducting studies to better inform public and private tourism investments, and to seek out and arrange financing for tourism investments.

Chambers of commerce promote and cross-reference the businesses of their members. The membership consists of leaders in education, small and large businesses, and community organizations. They are committed to building a strong economy and preserving the quality of life in the region. The public relies on these chambers for trusted business referrals. Only chamber members receive referrals from chamber offices. The chamber of commerce is often the only marketing team of the community. Its staff answers thousands of questions about tourism-related and other businesses every year. It publishes the annual directory of the chamber and maintains a web site. Each month it organizes luncheons, workshops, and committee meetings among its members, often with invited expert speakers on topics of interest to members. The chamber monitors and informs its membership about matters affecting businesses in the community. It provides leadership courses to its members. One must keep in mind that business organizations that choose not to become members of the chamber do not benefit from its services, and their names do not appear in the directory and promotion of tourism businesses in the community.

Business development boards carry the work of chambers of commerce further. They are often the official economic development agency of regional governmental organizations. Their economic development plans include strategies for the expansion of their elements and relocation of productive businesses from other places, with a focus on strengthening buyer/supplier networks and developing resources to meet industry-specific workforce and infrastructure needs. Tourism is a principal asset to be developed. These boards build the critical mass of the industry and establish linkages among tourism-producing and -serving businesses.

Destination Level

A tourism destination is smaller than a region. However, it could be as small as a resort complex or as large as one or more local communities with many tourist facility and attraction complexes linked to one another. Tourism destinations conjure sometimes glorious images in the minds of tourists. They are the areas where recreational and utilitarian activities are the targets of their interest. Tourism destinations could be highly urbanized areas with a large mix of attractions and facilities. Or, they could be environmentally sensitive undeveloped areas where tourist attractions consisting of natural features dominate the landscape.

At the lowest level of planning, tourism deals with individual projects forming the mosaic of a destination. Projects are planned, designed, financed, owned, and operated independently. If they are owned by the government, projects are funded through a public budgeting process involving capital and annual budgeting. If they are owned by the private sector, projects are scheduled according to the rising demand for and profitability of the venture. Site planning, landscape design, civil engineering, architectural design of buildings, and engineering design of related facilities like marinas, airports, and piers are examples of planning and design at this level. Each project is subject to local regulations and receives appropriate hearings and permits before it can be started and completed.

5.5 DECIDING TO ENTER THE INTERNATIONAL TOURISM MARKET

The decision by governments and private sector businesses to start developing tourism can be easy or difficult. The decision is often based on tempting but uncertain premises. Several hypothetical scenarios may emerge. In one scenario, a foreign private sector business approaches the national government to discuss building and operating a profitable tourism project, perhaps the first international hotel in the country.

In this scenario, the entrepreneur selects a remote virgin location, or seashore, as the site for the hotel project. Next, the entrepreneur presents a series of facts demonstrating the benefits of the project to the country's national, regional, or local economy. If the project is interesting, intense negotiations follow between the entrepreneur and the government. The entrepreneur may request special privileges and demand certain conditions. These may include acquiring the rights to build on the land, which may be based on a ninety-nine-year lease; duty-free importation of building materials and equipment; a tax-free holiday for ten or more years of operation; reimbursement of certain expenses; repatriation of untaxed profits from the operation; a limit on what other kinds of establishments can be built in the area; and, most important of all, extending the runway at the local airport for landing jets and building a road at government expense from the airport to the remote site of the hotel.

If the conditions are acceptable to the government, the decision on whether the country will enter the international tourism market is quickly made and the project proceeds. However, difficulties may soon arise. There may not be detailed benefit-cost and feasibility analyses among the information submitted by the entrepreneur. The government may be at a disadvantage because it may be short on technical expertise to evaluate such a project. In this scenario, the potential for making a hasty and ill-considered decision is very high.

The scenario is different when the decision to enter the international tourism market is based on careful study of national, regional, and local priorities. The experience of other countries in entering the international tourism market is helpful in setting up precedents. Their case scenarios are educational and informative in identifying pitfalls. This is where international tourism organizations can provide guidance. The UNWTO and the United Nations Conference on Trade and Development (UNCTAD) are two major sources for such technical assistance.

When national governments make a request for international technical assistance, a team of experts arrives to determine the wisdom of joining the world of international tourism. The team, joined by local staff assigned by the national government, evaluates the tourism potential of the country in terms of attractions, facilities and destination regions, relative costs, and comparative advantage. Then the government determines whether tourism could be a leading sector of the national economy, possibly the only leading sector. The benefits and costs of establishing linkages with other economic sectors of the economy are then evaluated. If the government accepts the results of the evaluation, a national tourism policy will be drafted. The government then commits resources for planning and developing tourism at all of its levels with the participation of private sector and international assistance.

5.6 RELATIONSHIP BETWEEN INTERNATIONAL AND DOMESTIC TOURISM

Once the decision to develop tourism is made, national priorities may require careful evaluation of the balance to be maintained between international and domestic tourism. International tourism may point at a **leading destination region** for international tourists where the benefits will be greatest and the standards will be highest. By contrast, depending on the disposable income and preferences of the domestic population, domestic tourism may require an entirely different set of standards and destinations. If one assumes that tourists from wealthier countries come to destinations in a country where incomes are considerably lower, the facilities created for international tourists may not be affordable by the majority of domestic tourists. Domestic tourists will want facilities and services they can afford. This type of demand is particularly valid for young couples and families with children. Package tours for domestic groups is the partial answer to accommodating this particular domestic tourism market without developing a duplicate set of facilities for domestic tourists.

Until the 1990s, countries in Eastern European—Russia, for example—had developed a domestic tourism industry based on separate destinations for the *nomenklatura* (elite or privileged people) and for the rest of their population. There was no international tourism, except from countries with similar planned economic systems aimed at their *nomenklatura*. Exclusivity was intentional despite claims for a classless society. After making changes in their economic systems, these countries are now receiving international tourism from the entire world. Until economic equality is achieved, two separate forms of tourism will continue to exist. Major Western hotel chains are now building five-star hotels in cities like Moscow, St. Petersburg, Prague, Warsaw, and Kiev. Massive hotels inherited from former regimes are being upgraded to meet international standards. Older and affordable facilities serving domestic tourists are still in demand and will remain so for the near future. Their facilities may be upgraded. International special interest tourism, like adventure tourism, will continue to use existing simple facilities in remote areas like Kamchatka and Siberia.

In countries with capitalistic market systems, domestic and international tourism overlap. Facilities serve them both. Without creating a class-conscious social order, tourism development must create a proper mix of attractions and provide multiple levels of service for both international and domestic tourists. From five-star hotels to simple but well-kept motels and bed and breakfast lodgings, attractions, facilities, and services must offer a quality but diverse tourism product. When the proper mix is attained, symbiosis between international and domestic tourism will be achieved.

5.7 ECONOMIC LINKAGE AND LEAKAGE

One justification for developing tourism is to benefit from its spending multiplier effects. The effects are diffused by creating linkages among the elements of the economy. These linkages are horizontal, between supplier establishments at the local level, and vertical, between national and local supplier establishments. Several research models can be calibrated and used to quantify and demonstrate the dimensions of these economic linkages. An input-output model including the tourism sector, or a simpler linear multivariate regression model, can illustrate the basics of these economic linkages. Developing these specialized computer models should be a priority.

As an example, one can consider a tourist destination with many attractions of international, national, regional, and destination-level significance. Using the NAICS, horizontal and vertical linkages between Subsector 721 Accommodation establishments and their suppliers at local and national levels can be as follows:

- The three-digit level **Subsector 721 Accommodation** industry is part of the two-digit upper-level **Sector 72 Accommodation and Food Services** and has four-digit, five-digit, and six-digit lower-level industries:
  - **Subsector 721 Accommodation**
    - 7211 Traveler Accommodation
      72111 Hotels (except Casino Hotels) and Motels
      72112 Casino Hotels
      72119 Other Traveler Accommodation
      721191 Bed-and-Breakfast Inns

721199 All other traveler Accommodations
- 7212 Recreational Vehicle Parks and Recreational Camps
72121 Recreational Vehicle Parks and Recreational Camps
721211 RV Parks and Camp Grounds
721214 Recreational and Vacation Camps
- 7213 Rooming and Boarding Houses
72131 Rooming and Boarding Houses

Assuming a developed economy, Subsector 721 Accommodation could be horizontally linked to a variety of establishments with two-digit and three-digit industries:

Sector 22 Utilities
- Subsector 221 Utilities

Sector 23 Construction
- Subsector 233 Building, Developing, and General Contracting
- Subsector 235 Special Trade Contractors

Sector 44-45 Retail Trade
- Subsector 442 Furniture and Home Furnishings Stores
- Subsector 444 Building Material and Garden Equipment and Supplies Dealers
- Subsector 445 Food and Beverage Stores
- Subsector 453 Miscellaneous Store Retailers

Sector 48-49 Transportation and Warehousing
- Subsector 481 Air Transportation
- Subsector 482 Rail Transportation
- Subsector 484 Truck Transportation
- Subsector 487 Scenic and Sightseeing
- Subsector 491 Postal Service

Sector 51 Information
- Subsector 511 Publishing Industries
- Subsector 514 Information Services and Data Processing Services

Sector 52 Finance and Insurance
- Subsector 524 Insurance Carriers and Related Activities
- Subsector 525 Funds, Trusts, and other Financial Vehicles

Sector 53 Real Estate and Rental and Leasing
- Subsector 531 Real Estate
- Subsector 532 Rental and Leasing Services

Sector 55 Management of Companies and Enterprises
- Subsector 551 Management of Companies and Enterprises

Sector 81 Other Services (except Public Administration)
- Subsector 811 Repair and Maintenance
- Subsector 812 Personal and Laundry Services

The U.S. Census of Business defines an **establishment** as "a single physical location where business is conducted or where services or industrial operations are performed," whereas a **firm** is defined as "a business organization consisting of one or more domestic establishments in the same state and industry that were specified under common ownership or control." The firm and the establishment are the same for single-establishment firms. For each multiestablishment firm, establishments in the same industry within a state are counted as one firm. Single tourism facilities and attractions are counted as establishments. Out-of-state parent companies of establishments, like the Disney theme parks, are recorded but not used for calculating spending impacts and their multipliers for in-state or in-region tourism potential analysis and planning (except where the attraction and supporting facilities are located in the same state as the home corporate offices, like Disneyland in Anaheim, California, and the Disney Corporate Headquarters in Burbank, California).

Since the tourism sector includes many types of subsectors and establishments, the impact of linkages can be very large. When all subsectors and establishments are horizontally and vertically connected, a complex network of economic relations emerges. These relations can create thousands of jobs, bring large amounts of foreign currency to the country, and produce income from sales of goods and services.

One might argue that the impact created by economic linkages is really all that matters. In fact, there are follow-up questions. The most important question is the extent of **economic leakage** from tourism. These questions include:

- How many jobs are created for citizens and residents of the country or region?
- How many foreign workers are employed in the industry?
- How much of their wage income is transferred to other countries or regions?
- What is the import content of the tourism product and services?
- How much gross income earned, and foreign currency received, stay in the country or region?
- How much of the income is transferred to other countries or regions as payments for imports and services?

The answers to these and other questions help determine the extent and nature of the economic leakage from the country or region.

For example, when most capital for a new hotel is imported from outside the country or region in the form of a long-term loan from a foreign source, many conditions can be attached to the deal. In addition to principal and interest payments on the loan, profits from the operations could be repatriated without paying taxes for a number of years. This would leave only the return on local investment in the hotel to remain in the economy of the country or region. The return, in the form of a share of net profits, could be reinvested in the local economy. However, if local participation in the hotel involves only the land, the cash value of the land would be frozen and could not be used, other than as collateral, until the property is sold and the proceeds are reinvested. The following questions are then asked:

- What is the multiplier of local investment in the hotel?
- How often is this money recycled in the national or regional economy?
- Who benefits most from the hotel project?

The problem of import content is also an important aspect of economic leakage. In building luxury hotels, for example, this content can be very high. Except for land and basic construction (foundations and building frames, for example), the rest of the hotel may require imported materials. This could include a large variety of imported construction elements, finished walls and exterior coverings, furniture, fixtures, equipment, and salaries of foreign contractors and management staff. When this import content is low, benefits from investment and operation of the hotel are higher for the destination country. Initially, an LDC may be forced to make economic sacrifices by importing materials and equipment for its luxury hotel. However, as the economy of the country improves, many materials and equipment can be supplied by local emerging import substitution industries, and by architectural and engineering designs that use locally available materials.

It is difficult to prescribe one simple, all-encompassing remedy for all the problems caused by defective linkages and leakages. Certainly, following the tourism planning process will eventually lead the planners to the root causes of these problems. Solutions may include:

- Improving the tourism multiplier by eliminating inefficiencies in interindustry linkages of the tourism sector
- Substituting for imported goods and services their equivalents produced by local industries and designing facilities that require minimum imported goods
- Encouraging and creating opportunities for the reinvestment of capital by providing financial incentives to investors
- Closing legal loopholes for unauthorized use of labor and transfer of funds to other countries

Chapter Highlights

- Private initiative, risk taking, and entrepreneurship drive the market economic system. Government plays a supporting role.
- In market systems, comprehensive planning for tourism development applies only weakly. The push and pull effects of the economy regulate the market, and investors respond accordingly.
- In command and mixed economies, there is more reliance on governmental comprehensive planning and analysis to guide tourism-related investments.
- Social entrepreneurship is emerging as an important factor in tourism planning, especially in LDCs.

- The tourism economy evolves according to these effects.
- Trickle-down and multiplier mechanisms distribute some of the costs and benefits of tourism.
- Government incentives include providing funding and loan guarantees for private sector projects.
- Additional issues like import content, profit repatriation, and needed tax incentives and public infrastructure investments must be resolved in advance of project development.

6

Practicing Sustainable Tourism Development

This chapter describes what sustainable development is, how it is applied to regional and national tourism development, and how it should be related to issues and procedures to be followed to achieve it. Sustainable development scenarios are analyzed by giving examples of their economic, social, and environmental impacts.

- Sustainable development ensures continuity of environmental and cultural treasures from the present to future generations. However, in LDCs, the current problems of economic survival may necessitate urgent solutions in which sustainability may not be given the highest priority.
- Social, cultural, and environmental impacts of tourism should be monitored closely.
- Substituting duplicates for authentic attractions saves the original treasures from damage or destruction and promotes cultural conservation.
- Regional economic integration and alleviation of poverty can be achieved at the same time by adopting sustainable policies. Tourism is part of this process.
- Crime and terrorism can derail all efforts to develop tourism.

6.1 DEFINING SUSTAINABLE DEVELOPMENT

Sustainable development conserves environmental, cultural, and other economic resources for future generations while still bringing benefits to the present generation. This act of balancing resource use for economic growth requires the implementation of selective development policies. An initial definition provided by the World Commission on Environment and Development in 1987 explained the concept in general terms: "Sustainable development is progress that meets the needs of the present without compromising the ability of future generations to meet their own needs."

In September 2002, the World Summit on Sustainable Development was held in Johannesburg, South Africa. It was decided that a program for sustainable development and for reducing poverty would be initiated by participating countries. The organization phase of the program was completed in 2003, and work has begun on several subject areas. The current UNWTO definition of sustainable tourism is given in Section 1.3 of Chapter 1 of this book.

In recent years, the definition of sustainability has been broadened to include not only economic and environmental assets, but social assets as well. Understanding social sustainability, however, has not progressed to the level of understanding of economic and environmental sustainability. The cause is cultural diffusion. Societies evolve over time. Social stress breaks down the norms, values, standards, and accepted behaviors of a society. It jeopardizes intergenerational well-being. These events are not understood fully today.

The concept of sustainable development for tourism has been known since the 1980s. It had, however, been used under different names long before. It took only common sense to realize the importance of conserving the very resources that made tourism possible. In due time, the concept was given its current name. Definitions and discussion about sustainable tourism appear on the following Wikipedia Web site: http://en.wikipedia.org/wiki/Sustainable_tourism.

Tourism is an integral part of the sustainability of a national economy. Sustainable tourism conserves nonrenewable and fragile resources and dictates a balance between economic and social responsibility. This realization changed the approach to developing tourism, particularly in LDCs, over the past thirty years. It raised the questions of how to coordinate economic, social, and environmental sustainability at all levels of development.

Sustainable development is about ensuring the future well-being of people. The concept of **well-being,** however, is highly subjective. It varies for individuals, societies, and generations. All, however, agree that it includes the ability to shape one's life. This ability is acquired by better education, better health, material comfort, self-respect, inclusiveness, physical security, basic civil and political liberties, and human rights. These needs are a tall order for anyone, but they are even more so for an individual in a country emerging from deprivation and poverty.

Enjoying fresh air and clean water, as well as living among an abundance of plant and animal species, is taken for granted by most persons. The ability to shape one's life and achieve satisfaction and happiness starts with these basic needs. Society's ability to improve individual satisfaction also depends on choices made by firms, communities, and governments interacting with one another. Cutting down forests, clearing mangroves, filling wetlands, polluting the air, poisoning the water, eroding the soil, dumping waste, propagating visual ugliness, destroying historical relics and monuments, and causing the extinction of living species are issues at the core of sustainability. Improving human well-being on a sustained basis requires that society manage the natural and human-made assets of the world wisely. What, then, are the indicators of sustainability and alternative development paths that a country can pursue to achieve that sustainability, and what role can tourism play in this effort?

6.2   INDICATORS OF SUSTAINABLE TOURISM

The largest challenge in ensuring sustainability of development involves measuring the current condition of assets and preparing methods for evaluating their change. Since the 1980s, much of the work done in devising indicators for measuring sustainability has been in the economic and environmental fields. They include extended national accounts, biophysical accounts, equally weighted indices, unequally weighted indices, eco-efficiency measures, and other measures prepared under the auspices of the United Nations Commission for Sustainable Development. Social indicators are less developed and need more research to be useful for measuring sustainability.

Some of the principal indicators of environmental sustainability are:

- **Extended national accounts**

  Green accounts system of environmental and economic accounts

  By the United Nations—A framework for environmental accounting

  Adjusted net saving

  By the World Bank—Change in total wealth, accounting for resource depletion and environmental damage

  Genuine progress indicator, redefining progress, and index of sustainable economic welfare

  By the United Kingdom and other countries—An adjusted GDP figure reflecting welfare losses from environmental damage

- **Biophysical accounts**

  Ecological footprints (i.e., carbon footprints), redefining progress

  By the World Wildlife Fund and others—Measures of the productive land and sea area required to produce food and fiber, as well as the energy (renewable and nonrenewable) consumed by different lifestyles within and among countries

- **Equally weighted indices**

  Living planet index

  By the World Wildlife Fund—An assessment of the populations of animal species in forest, freshwater, and marine environments

  Environmental sustainability index

  By the World Economic Forum—An aggregate index spanning twenty-two major factors that contribute to environmental sustainability

- **Unequally weighted indices**

  Environmental pressure indices

  By the Netherlands—A set of aggregate indices for specific environmental pressures, such as acidification or emission of greenhouse gases

  Well-being of nations

  By Prescott-Allen—A set of indices that capture elements of human well-being and ecosystem well-being and combines them to construct barometers of sustainability

- **Eco-efficiency**

  Resource flows

  By the World Resources Institute—Total material flows underpinning economic processes

- **Indicator sets**

  United Nations Commission for Sustainable Development and many countries

  Source: *Sustainable Development in a Dynamic Economy—World Development Report 2003;* http://www.dynamicsustainabledevelopment.org (accessed April 27, 2011).

Here, equally weighted indices are those whose components are equally weighted and then aggregated, while unequally weighted indices give some components greater weight than others. Weights are determined in each application by local or national priorities and conditions.

6.3 GROWTH POLICIES FOR SUSTAINABLE DEVELOPMENT

It is necessary to remember that transformation toward sustainability is taking place throughout the world. The most important social and economic changes, such as transformation from traditional rural to modern urban life, occur spatially. Economic and social sector planning for sustainable development ties in with spatial physical planning at the national, regional, and local levels.

Sustainable development is sensitive to environmental change. Problems appear soon after humans subject the environment to uncontrolled stresses. Territories of plants and animals shrink or expand. Destruction of species multiplies. Invasive species are introduced. Food chains are interrupted. Flora and fauna may gradually adapt to these changes over a very long time or are irretrievably lost.

It takes centuries to grow mature forests but only a few decades to cut down the trees and turn their areas into wastelands. Historically, it took one hundred acres of forest to generate enough quality timber to build one sailing-era warship. Starting from the time of the Roman Empire two thousand years ago, thousands of acres of forest have disappeared from the mountains and valleys in Spain, France, Italy, Greece, Turkey, Syria, and Lebanon. The trees were cut indiscriminately, ignoring the fact that it would take centuries to replace them. The wood was used for building thousands of triremes, galleys, carracks, caravels, and galleons in order to fight for supremacy in the Black and Mediterranean seas and their related waters.

Human well-being calls for more than material comfort. The distinction is important for preparing a policy of sustainable development. The policy of "develop now, clean up later" is costing the present generation around the world less than it will cost future generations. Reducing poverty requires lasting economic growth. Growth interrupted by setbacks in resource preservation is not conducive to sustained development.

Developing countries do not have to follow the path used since industrialization began three hundred years ago. The successes and mistakes of past generations are well known. More of the same is not the prescription for the development maladies of our age. Because of technological and scientific progress, it is now possible to avoid the mistakes of countries that developed earlier. Economic growth will not be sustainable unless environmental assets are protected and social change is sustainable. Attention must be focused on priorities that will balance economic, environmental, and social factors of development in the short and long run. This balancing act suggests three alternative growth policies:

- Simultaneously addressing environmental, social, and economic issues of growth on equal terms
- Placing higher priority on economic growth while giving less emphasis to environmental and social issues
- Placing higher priority on restoring the environment and accelerating social change over economic issues

Sustainable tourism development plays a variable role in each of these growth policy approaches. Alleviating poverty and promoting tourism are among concerns that influence the selection of the particular approach. The national political process determines the choice. Although there are exceptions, international pressure and bilateral and multilateral treaties can influence the outcome. A good example is the Kyoto Protocol, an international agreement linked to the United Nations Framework Convention on Climate Change. The major feature of the

Kyoto Protocol is that it sets binding targets for thirty-seven industrialized countries for reducing greenhouse gas emissions. These targets amount to an average reduction of 5% of the 1990 levels over the five-year period 2008–2012.

6.4   SOCIAL CHANGE AND THE IMPACT OF TOURISM

Tourism is an agent of social change. The volume of visitors, cross-cultural exchanges, and commercial opportunities created has impacts on the well-being of communities. Positive impacts include job and income generation, improved infrastructure, and increased government revenues. Standards of living are improved for people living in tourism destination areas. The role and social status of women are elevated. Local residents take pride in demonstrating their culture to visitors.

The beneficial things that happen to local people, however, come at a cost. Changes are inevitable, and turning the clock back is not possible. Changes result from the demonstration effect of tourism, that is, how host communities imitate and adopt the behavior and appearance of visitors. The intensity of social impacts depends on many factors, including the rate of tourism growth, the ratio between visitors and locals, seasonal trends, and the absorption rate of new sociocultural traits. The conflict of cultures is inevitable. Tourists bring expectations based on their culture. Locals, in turn, have their own expectations.

Concerns about social change caused by tourism grow over the years. It is difficult to differentiate social change owing to social evolution initiated by economic development from social change attributable to the demonstration effect of tourism. However, the baseline cultural and behavioral status of a particular social group has to be established before analyzing and measuring changes over time. Social scientists have developed survey techniques to establish this baseline. For example, scientists from MIT and Turkey developed and conducted one such survey in Turkey in 1960. The results were used to establish community development guidelines in connection with changes planned in the 1960–1965 First Five-Year National Development Plan in Turkey.

The 1997 Tourism Leaders' Meeting organized by the UNWTO summarized concerns about social change resulting from both economic development and tourism demonstration effects:

- *Image of the destination.* Marketing is a very important component of tourism. Image is such an important aspect of tourism development that government, as a public service, has to get involved in deciding how to portray and promote the country.
- *Exploitation.* The demonstration effect transfers to the host country examples of a different culture. This can create a sense of envy among local people about the appearance and lifestyles of foreigners. The gap between income levels could be such that local people, although they are the hosts, feel inferior if not respected by their guests.
- *Cultural deterioration.* It is a challenge for the host country to maintain its traditions and values when meeting the expectations of visitors. Cultural deterioration takes place when the challenge is not met and solutions are not channeled in productive directions.
- *Capacity consideration.* It is difficult for local people to understand and accept the priority of satisfying the needs of tourists at their expense. Increasing their capacity to accommodate their guests could lead to substantial lifestyle changes for natives.
- *Estrangement.* A feeling of estrangement may arise and lead to serious dissatisfaction, and even open hostility, toward tourists when luxury resorts and enclaves are created separating local populations from foreign visitors.

- *Host–guest relationships.* Most visitors have little or no appreciation of the local culture. Conversely, local communities may have little or no understanding of their visitors' cultures. These situations are further complicated when there is a language barrier.
- *Sharing benefits and costs.* Although tourism provides many positive impacts, host destinations absorb its negative impacts. Unless some, if not most, of the economic benefits accruing from local tourism remain in the host community, the cost of receiving and accommodating tourists could become too great to bear. Where this happens, resentment and hostility could arise.

In response to the Rio de Janeiro Earth Summit held on June 3 to 14, 1992 the UNWTO and the World Travel and Tourism Council (WTTC) responded to counteract these negative social impacts by establishing an agenda for the twenty-first century. The objective was to have governments make a collective effort to overcome the challenges posed by the social impacts of tourism. Taking into account the cultural, economic, and physical context of each case, the agenda included the following actions:

- Community participation in tourism development planning
- Community tourism awareness campaigns
- Human resource development
- Distribution of tourism benefits
- Entrepreneurial initiatives
- Image building
- Providing better legal frameworks for tourism
- Recognizing women's rights

The verdict on the efficacy of this campaign is still pending.

In an anthropological sense, **culture** is all of the beliefs, customs, and knowledge acquired, shared, and passed on by a social group. Culture lies not in arts, music, languages, and literature alone. It includes everything that defines a way of life. Culture is distinct from "cultured" in that the latter connotes well-educated individuals. But culture signifies a social invention. It is transmitted by learning, not by genetics. Consequently, culture is associated with the geographic space within which its common traits are transmitted from groups to individuals.

Cultural traits are highly diverse and complex. They include:

- Family structure and the hierarchy of its members
- Social structure, class distinction, and the distribution of power and influence
- Religion
- Group and public behaviors, including expressions of thought and emotion
- Lifestyle in work, in leisure, and at home
- Roles and status of members of a family and a society
- Holidays, ceremonies, and rituals
- Humor
- Language and modes of communication, including body language
- Education
- Traditions and customs regulating social behavior
- History and its roots in culture
- Food and eating behavior
- Attitudes toward work
- Ethnic identity
- Other appropriate local and national traits

Areas of common culture may overlap and form cultural regions and even continents. The boundaries defining these regions may include culturally homogeneous nations representing people who have shared cultures. Preserving the traits as well as artifacts of the local, regional, or national culture is an important subject for tourism planning.

6.5 PRESERVING THE CULTURAL HERITAGE

The 1999 seminar on tourism and culture organized by the UNWTO was held in Samarkand/Khiva, Republic of Uzbekistan, which is one of the earliest centers of culture in Asia. The conference addressed many issues and made many important resolutions. Among them were:

• Some values of tourism are found in authentic cultural resources.
• Landscape and cultural artifacts establish an identity for local populations.
• Conserving cultural relics has its own intrinsic value. These relics are more than subjects of interest for tourists alone. Culture belongs to everybody.
• Tourism contributes to the emergence of a new global culture.
• With rising levels of education, tourists have increased expectations.
• Broadening the cultural experience of tourists could increase mutual understanding and improve guests' relations with local populations.

As early as 1972, the Conference of the United Nations Educational, Scientific, and Cultural Organization (UNESCO) passed the World Heritage Convention for protecting the cultural and natural heritage of the world. There are about one hundred eighty cities on the list of World Heritage Cities and more than seven hundred sites. The World Heritage Cities organization has its headquarters in Quebec, Canada. Among its duties are developing a database of useful information for tourists and experts and promoting the protection of historical sites around the world, particularly in times of armed conflict. (See Appendix A.)

Tourism influences culture and environment in many ways. Native people at a destination area are drawn toward the culture and environment of visitors. This is the result of the demonstration effect. It begins with subtle changes in the local culture. A revealing example is found in Nepal, where trekkers and mountaineers who began to arrive numbered fewer than two thousand in 1972 and increased to more than twenty-five thousand in 2000. They are required to provide high-altitude climbing gear and clothing to their Sherpa guides, called *sirdar,* and their porters. The clothing and gear are part of the compensation package and have a resale value often higher than the cash compensation Sherpas receive. As a result, the imported clothing became a status symbol and is now accepted for everyday wear. Only women continue to wear their traditional clothing made of local fabrics. As the Sherpas prospered, they adopted other creations from the outside world. In certain areas electricity replaced oil lamps, two-story houses became a status symbol, schools were built, and students received an education and learned the ways of the outside world. Young men sought less dangerous work and better-paying jobs. They began to migrate from the region of the Sherpas, Khumbu and Pharak, to Nepal's capital city, Kathmandu, and set up trekking businesses. Old ways were replaced by new ways that offered more benefits to people.

Protecting, preserving, and enhancing environmental and cultural resources are essential for sustainable tourism development. However, some accommodations must be made for the wear and tear caused by local residents struggling to subsist. Almost all forms of tourism development depends on maintaining and, if necessary, improving the quality of the tourism product. The environmental and cultural resources of a developing country should not be allowed to degrade or be destroyed by irresponsible actions of both government and people. When the quality of the tourism product of a destination is compromised, the area declines as a desirable place to visit. Every attraction or facility that defaults on its maintenance draws fewer and fewer tourists and contributes to the decay of the destination area. The ultimate result is that tourists bypass the area that has lost its competitive advantage and move on to other emerging destination areas.

The most extreme method for preserving the quality of a pristine cultural and environmental resource is to bar it completely against any form of use. Wilderness areas are often treated this way. Exploitation of the Alaskan wilderness, involving drilling and transporting oil south by truck and pipeline from Prudhoe Bay, was controversial from the moment it was proposed. Proposals for expansion of these activities are blocked by concerns for the fragile nature of the area and its wildlife. These arguments have been occupying environmentalists and government alike for many decades. In the tropics, environmentalists argue that the exploitation of the Amazonian and Indonesian rain forests for logging and subsistence farming intensifies global climate change and destroys many species of life forever. It is also argued that carbon dioxide emissions from tens of thousands of cars in key tourism cities like Los Angeles, Delhi, and Beijing contribute to global warming and to the destruction of many cultural edifices.

Mountaineering and trekking groups in Nepal on their way to higher altitudes in the Himalayas are posing environmental threats by littering trails with rubbish and destroying the sanctity of a clean environment. The trails leading from Namche Bazaar (Nauje) to the highest peak in the world, Everest, are increasingly being strewn with empty oxygen tanks, plastic containers, and other debris. There are mixed opinions, however, about the extent of damage done to forests and shrubs by both resident Sherpas and tourists who are passing through in increasing numbers. Sherpas differ from outsiders on the environmental and cultural impacts of tourism. They state that since 1970, environmentalists and outsiders have exaggerated the negative consequences of tourism in the region of Nepal where Sagartmatha National Park is located. As a compromise, the government has allowed Sherpas to live in their settlements within the park, but has prevented them from clear-cutting the forest and using firewood excessively.

Some owners and managers of key historic buildings want to restrict access to credentialed researchers, and exclude the general public on the grounds that their use contributes to undue deterioration and the ultimate destruction of the buildings. This attitude is especially prevalent where funds for adequate maintenance and repairs are lacking.

The world's attention is also drawn to irreplaceable cultural resources of various kinds. It is argued that these resources should be closed to tourist traffic altogether. However, both overuse and no use of environmental and cultural resources are unacceptable options for tourism and national development. Selective and controlled use of both types of resources is the only option. In the process, however, not only the proponents and opponents from the rest of the world, but also the individuals who live and practice the tenets of their culture within their environment must be heard. Their opinions on whether environmental and cultural change is undesirable may not coincide with those of outsiders. Their opinions must be respected.

6.6 CONTROLLING NEGATIVE IMPACTS AND ENSURING SUSTAINABILITY

Controlling the negative impacts of tourism and encouraging the positive ones requires finding a balance between sometimes opposing positions. This balance is achieved by involving the communities that would be subjected to these impacts. Community participation is, therefore, essential for ensuring balanced tourism development. During the planning process, close attention must be paid to what local leaders have to say about the benefits and costs of tourism.

There are three basic subjects to be addressed:

- Conservation of important natural areas and ecosystems
- Conservation of archeological and historic sites
- Maintaining or improving environmental quality and preventing pollution

Particular environmental issues to be resolved include:

- Water pollution resulting from improper management of solid and sanitary wastes. Lakes, rivers, and coastal areas are particularly vulnerable. Pollution of aquifers for extracting drinking water is a critical problem. Pollution of marine habitats where fish and corals grow, and where scuba divers explore undersea wonders, is a serious ecological and tourism issue.
- Internal combustion engines cause air pollution. This pollution is aggravated by excessive burning of coal and wood in homes and by emission of sulfuric particles from industrial plants, causing acid rain. It is necessary to reduce this pollution.
- Uncontrolled disposal of solid and untreated sanitary waste, particularly in areas near tourism destinations, is a serious health hazard.
- **Deforestation** is defined as excessive tree cutting. Lumber and firewood should be harvested according to the rate of tree growth (using sustained yield practices). Substitution of other fuels for firewood in households is a priority issue.
- Noise pollution results from aircraft flying over resort and urban areas; excessive street noise generated by indiscriminate use of vehicular horns; and poor facility design in which noisy machines are located near guest rooms in hotels. Noise pollution is distracting and causes stress. It should be reduced.
- Vehicular and pedestrian traffic congestion at attraction sites causes delays, frustration, discomfort, and waste of time and fuel. Alternative forms of transportation can alleviate the problem. Some delays are unavoidable because of the "peaking" nature of travel and visitation, both in vehicles and on foot. Managers of some popular attractions have been able to mitigate the discomfort of waiting in lines by the use of electronic presentations, illustrations on walls, street performers (i.e., jugglers and mimes), and soothing music. Another widely used solution is to intercept automobiles in fringe parking areas and transport their passengers in shuttle buses and vans to the tourist destinations areas.
- Visual pollution of urban and natural landscapes caused by human neglect, poor taste, indiscriminate design, and poverty creates a vicious circle of decay and erosion of tourism.
- Haphazard destruction of the environment caused by poorly planned and improperly located infrastructure projects such as dams and roads, as well as earth-moving operations such as strip mines, leave indelible and sometimes irreversible marks on the environment.
- Ecological disasters caused by all of the above problems in the ecosystem of a region result in the destruction of the tourism potential.

Other issues to be addressed for conserving the cultural and human-made heritage include:

- Protecting visible and buried archeological sites and digs of cultural significance.
- Restoring historic buildings, structures, and neighborhoods depicting life in specific time periods.
- Preventing unauthorized exploration of sunken ships and other artifacts of marine archeology.
- Preventing congestion from diminishing visitors' experiences. At many attractions, visitors are divided into reasonably sized groups that are sent on designated tours through the

premises. This minimizes overcrowding and random pedestrian movements that may conflict with each other. This practice is more acceptable to visitors if a guide for each group is provided (often volunteers) to lead and enhance the visiting experience.
• Monitoring cultural change by observing the changing customs, behavior, and other elements of local culture and, if deemed desirable, modifying the exposure to outside influences.

It is important to address these issues before constructive tourism policies and practices are established. The opinions of the local population regarding each of these issues must be clearly understood and reconciled with the opinions of the authorities before any action is taken.

6.7 SUBSTITUTING HUMAN-MADE DUPLICATE ATTRACTIONS IN ORDER TO CONSERVE AUTHENTIC ATTRACTIONS

Excessive demand can be destructive. Tourist facilities and attractions can eventually suffer from too many visitors. The popularity of these places may exceed their capacity to absorb and accommodate the demand. The resulting crush could necessitate lowering service standards and end by eroding the quality of the tourism experience. It could also destroy the very attractions that bring tourists by altering environmental conditions.

It is time to change tourism practices when the threshold capacity of attractions and facilities is reached. One solution for conserving environmental and cultural attractions is to spread and limit the volume of visitors by allocating visiting hours to groups of ticket holders. Allowing visitation only to scholars and supervised groups, requiring visitation by appointment, and reducing the promotion of the destination are other options.

To meet the demand, building additional tourist facilities and attractions is another solution. When tourist site attractions that create great demand are unique and irreplaceable, excess demand could lead to irreversible damage. The quality of the environment suffers. Physical structures could deteriorate to the point where shutting down the unique attraction may become necessary. If rebuilding is chosen as an alternative, the attraction could lose its intimacy and originality due to ill-conceived improvements, and the tourism experience may suffer. Careful restoration must be used.

The other alternative is to build duplicate facilities and attractions that will preserve the original place and accommodate the demand.

Two prime examples from the distant and recent past illustrate the concept of duplicating attractions. The painted grottoes in the Vallee de la Vezere, France, were discovered in 1940. Sliding down a path, the discoverers found the large grotto known today as the Great Hall of the Bulls. The rock paintings on the walls and ceiling of the hall are among the best examples of paleolithic art in the world. Dating back to 18,000 BC, these paintings of horses, bulls, and deer were created by early humans by using pigments extracted from eight minerals. Their discovery created great excitement, and tourists arrived by the thousands. By 1955, the first traces of deterioration in the paintings began to appear due to the excessive carbon dioxide in the air. A few years later, green stains produced by algae and mosses became visible. This was followed by colonies of bacteria and fungi. Emergency measures were taken and environmental contamination was eliminated, but the grotto remained closed to the public. In 1980, the authorities decided to replicate the grotto, down to the smallest detail, and open it to the public. Colors, incisions, and even the granular quality of the original rock were reproduced. The replicated grotto opened to the public in 1983 to great acclaim.

The Upper Paleolithic paintings in the Altamira caves in Spain were found in 1880. They consist of a large collection of horse, boar, deer, and bison paintings. Carbon-14 dating placed the creation of these paintings between 18,000 and 10,000 BC. Although they lasted for thousands of years in complete darkness, the paintings were susceptible to deterioration by changing environmental conditions. Even the breath of thousands of visitors who came to admire the paintings began to cause damage. Visits to the caves were limited to one hundred fifty scholars per week. A duplicate cave with copies of the paintings on the walls and an attached paleo-anthropological museum was built nearby and opened to the public in 2001. The duplicate attraction is now receiving more than one million visitors a year.

A duplicated attraction is planned to protect the original attraction and to accommodate larger crowds by providing preplanned facilities and better access. The appearance of the original is duplicated closely. The theme park concept originates from this objective. To give a general idea of a real attraction, the duplicate acts as a surrogate. For mass tourism, this solution is ideal. The duplicate brings the experience offered by the original attraction closer to the visitor and makes it more affordable.

Authenticity of the building materials and the layout, however, is not an issue. Desired visual effects are achieved by using new technology and new materials. Certain liberties are taken with the layout and dimensions of the original attraction to ensure better crowd control. The key is to duplicate the tourism experience of the original without claiming authenticity. The duplicate is allowed to compromise with the real thing in the interest of conservation, education, entertainment, and affordability.

For example, zoological gardens duplicate the ecosystem of animal species by creating substitute environments that approximate their real environment. But they offer healthier living conditions for the animals by keeping them under proper care. They also give visitors a better feel for and understanding of the ecosystem with which the animals interact. Another example is the Alamo in San Antonio, Texas, where a handful of Americans defended their independence. The original building is an historic site and a big draw for tourists. In Bracketville, only one hundred miles southwest of the original, however, stands the duplicate Alamo built as the movie set for shooting the film *The Alamo*. For some tourists, the duplicate offers experiences that are more educational than those provided by the original building.

The duplicate attraction has a theme and a message to convey to tourists. At its largest, a theme park is planned and built around one major theme, and the educational and entertainment messages it conveys. Disney World near Orlando, Florida, with its various theme parks, is a prime example of duplicate attractions where multiple themes with numerous messages are planned as one international site attraction.

Event attractions are also duplicated for prominent historic events. They are staged as reenactments with real persons for the entertainment and education of visitors. Reenactments of the Civil War battle at Gettysburg, Pennsylvania, and the annual Battle of Lexington Green in Lexington, Massachusetts, from the Revolutionary War are examples. Many staged acts in front of prominent hotels in Las Vegas, Nevada, like reenactment of Caribbean pirates in battle every four hours, are duplicate event attractions representing the real thing for the entertainment of visitors.

Duplications could be multiple. For example, a cultural center is a combination of a duplicated site and event attraction depicting the culture of a particular Native American tribe in New Mexico. It may contain exhibits, a gift shop, and a performance stage where tribal dancers and musicians perform for the visitors. The history and culture of more than six hundred native tribes are preserved at the American Indian Museum in Washington, D.C., where the artifacts are authentic but the building is not. In Cozumel, Mexico, local artists, musicians, and dancers welcome visitors arriving from cruise ships. They display their native arts, play their native music, or perform their spectacular act of hanging from their ankles and rotating around a tall pole until they reach the ground. These duplicated and staged site and event attractions have their origins in the Mexican culture. Hula dancing and luau feasts at Hawaiian themed attractions serve the same purpose. The theme and messages attempt to educate and entertain visitors. They duplicate the original event and site attraction to bring tourists closer to the native culture.

Another form of duplicate attraction has been evolving during the past several decades. With advances made in computer technology, virtual reality and video productions are gaining importance as more entertaining, and sometimes more educational, substitutes for real event or site attractions. Television is the primary conveyor of this medium. Documentaries made on adventure, nature, and historical subjects are expressions of duplicated attractions acting as surrogates for the real thing. Also, commercially available rental videos on all travel subjects play important roles in duplicating real attractions as virtual experiences.

Virtual reality is an example of advanced computer technology and a giant step forward in duplicating site and event attractions. Amusement parks and theme parks offer rides for thrill seekers. They provide total experiences in theaters depicting virtual reality or fantasy, where all six senses of visitors are engaged. Simulated environments surround the individual with sight, sound, motion, touch, smell and sometimes even taste. A flight simulator duplicates real conditions of flying an airplane as small as a single-engine Beechcraft and as large as a giant four-engine Boeing 747. The flying experience is duplicated in all its perils and pleasures in the simulator. Other experiences are created by imagineers who can duplicate an earthquake, flood, fire, or some other natural disaster for thrill seekers in a simulated environment.

This trend started several decades ago when three-dimensional movies became fashionable. By wearing special glasses that created the perception of depth, a completely new visual experience was created. More recently, 360-degree round screens with multiple projectors have carried that virtual reality experience further.

Damage to authentic historic and archeological sites could be irreversible. Without proper policing, tourists and vendors may find artifacts that may have eluded local authorities. Burial grounds and archeological sites are particularly vulnerable to pilfering of antique coins, statues, and other historic specimens. To protect these irreplaceable national resources, governments may declare such places off-limits and direct the tourist traffic to museums and theme parks where duplicated event and site attractions can be visited in comfort and safety.

6.8   TOURIST SATISFACTION AND CULTURAL CONFLICT

Planning and providing satisfying experiences to tourists is essential for successful tourism development. Colorful brochures, advertising, and promotion bring tourists to their destination. This is only the beginning of the tourism experience. When they reach their destination, tourists finally come face-to-face with the reality of the place. If the perception conveyed by promotional media does not match the reality at the destination, disappointment sets in. An urge to forgo the experience and return home may engulf the visitor even before the experience begins. As a result, visitors are predisposed to criticize. By comparing the destination with their homeland, they tend to find something wrong with the place they are visiting. This scenario is played out often when a tourist has little knowledge of or interest in other cultures. When this negative attitude is combined with resentment about wasting vacation time and spending a considerable amount of money in the process, tourists can become demanding and insensitive. Locals can then take the attitude that "one cannot please everyone" and develop immunity to criticism. Or, realizing the need for adjustment, they may seriously consider ways of minimizing the criticism.

Intolerance for imperfections, particularly in LDC regions, is a trait of visitors coming from different cultural and economic backgrounds. Differences in values, in the sense of what is right or wrong, and in religion, race, and ethnicity play roles in this scenario. Overstepping the threshold of acceptable personal behavior or norms of hospitality may lead to conflicts with locals. Initially, host–guest relations observed by tourists and residents are based on mutual respect. Once the threshold of acceptability is crossed, however, relationships could sour and enter the realm of mutual bias. Tourism begins to suffer. The hostility of locals begins to threaten the personal security of tourists, and tourism development becomes difficult or impossible. Several examples are pointed out and discussed on the following Web site: http://antropologia.umh.es/ GIA/Index_revista/Num_01/Boissevain_english.PDF.

The perception works both ways. Tourists may offend their hosts from ignorance of local etiquette and values and insensitivity to their beliefs. They may provide unwelcome examples, introducing practices and ideas that are seen by residents as culturally and socially offensive. They may take cultural offense at local beliefs and customs. By expressing disapproval of local practices and values, they may embarrass and anger local people. These feelings are reinforced by the realization that the economic survival of locals depends on their being pleasant to tourists.

Conversely, some aspects of local culture, such as wearing native dress and ornaments, may facilitate change in the opposite direction. Locals take pride in wearing their traditional colorful garments. Visitors can be enchanted by the grace, appearance, and demeanor of local people. Certain segments of the local population, however, may find it prestigious to wear foreign clothing, use foreign words, and even become conversant in a foreign language. They may educate their children differently by adopting the traits of another culture. The demonstration effect of tourism may begin to affect the local culture. Purists may complain that the local culture has been compromised for the sake of meeting the expectations of tourists. They may interpret wearing traditional dresses, performing traditional dances, and playing traditional music as contrived and corrupt forms of local culture. If these practices are carried further, they say, an entirely new local culture can be created for tourist consumption.

From a positive viewpoint, officials may see these practices not as a corruption of local culture, but as distilling of it to provide an economic opportunity for local artisans and artists. They may encourage them to interpret native arts and crafts, albeit often poorly, in order to sustain the economic livelihood of their community and the souvenir trade. These inexpensive souvenirs are provided for mass consumption by tourists. But a few enterprising local merchants could start a very lucrative trade in authentic artifacts for collectors, sometimes against the export restrictions imposed by their national government, like carving elephant tusks.

Provided that the fake culture is not considered offensive, local people may adopt it as a venue for artistic expression and for tourist consumption. They will tolerate this commercialized culture and use it to their advantage for alleviating poverty. Their tolerance limit is reached, however, when tourists invade their temples and festivities, jostle their people, take pictures, make noise, or otherwise disrupt their revered cultural ceremonies.

What specifically can a tourist do to minimize cultural conflict?

- Respect the cultural diversity expressed in attitudes, customs, values, arts, and places.
- Wear clothes considered modest by local standards.
- Attempt to have conversations or exchange a few words with natives in their language.

- Follow native customs as signs of respect, but refrain from acting and looking like a native.
- Be prepared to expect the unexpected at all times and act reasonably if it happens.
- Be flexible and ready to improvise when things do not work out.
- Enjoy the tourism experience.
- Recognize that haggling is a way of life in some parts of the world. Accept and practice it.
- Contribute to alleviating poverty in locally accepted ways. Respect the dignity of people who are trapped in that poverty and the conscience of local residents and officials who deal with it on a daily basis.

6.9   INCREASING TOURIST SPENDING

Tourism income comes to a region from various sources. One source is package tours, in which participants make all payments for the trip in advance to the tour organizer and, through him or her, to the service providers. The tour organizer promotes the destination and channels income to the region. For example, no cash changes hand aboard the ship during a cruise (except for extra tips). The cruise is prepaid on shore, and discretionary expenses including nominal tips are charged to the room at sea. They are collected at the end of the cruise by the bursar before the travelers disembark. All supplies, including fuel, are loaded on board the cruise ship at the port of embarkation. Payments go to suppliers and service providers at this port.

Ports of call receive income from various fees, taxes, bus tours, taxis, restaurants, gift shops, and other venues of discretionary spending by tourists. Additional out-of-pocket expenses incurred by the visitors in hunting for souvenirs or visiting nightclubs that are not on the travel plan create direct revenues for the local and regional economies. Home ports, where passengers start and end their cruise, include spending on hotels, local tours, restaurants, transportation, and other related items. Spending in home ports and ports of call is quite large. *Business Research and Economic Advisors,* in a June 2009 study of the economic impacts of cruise ships in North America done for the Cruise Lines International Association, reported that in 2008, $1.72 billion was spent by passengers and ship crews in the ports of origin and ports visited. An additional $2.04 billion was spent on air travel, and $3.11 billion was spent on other transportation services in getting passengers to and from cruise ships from their home cities.

Room services, tips, and other discretionary expenses at destination hotels are charged to the room and are paid by the visitors according to American, European, or Full Plans in cash, or by checks or credit cards, before they leave the hotel. Suppliers and service providers receive their income from the hotel management. This leaves air, bus, or taxi transportation fares, entertainment, and food charges to be paid by the visitor at the destination. If the travel agent has booked the hotel room according to a package plan, he or she may include specific out-of-pocket expenses in the price of the package. Since visitors make most of their payments at the beginning of their travel, service providers and suppliers at the destination have to wait for their payments to filter down through the supplier chain.

An executive traveling alone to a destination as a tourist makes payments as he or she travels. After arriving at the destination, one of the tourist's first acts is to search for a money changer or a bank performing the same service. Usually, the most favorable exchange rates are found at the point of entry to the country, often at the airport concourse. Exchange rates offered by hotels, shops, or other service providers are less favorable. Commissions earned from exchanging the money stay with the establishment and the destination economy.

Determining who gets paid for what is generally determined by the marketplace. Aside from custom, visa, and port/entrance fees, government stays out of the workings of the market system. Taxation works at the local level directly in the form of room taxes for overnight accommodations and meals taxes in restaurants, and indirectly through real estate taxes, income taxes (if any at the local level), and if any, infrastructure use taxes and fees. Tourists usually pay a minimum charge for gaining entrance to government-owned and -operated national parks and historic places. Revenues usually go directly to the national agency that administers such places. Local government treasuries do not see much, if any, of the income from admissions.

On balance, revenues from tourism flow directly from the tourist through travel agents or other service providers to the local, regional, and national economies at the destination. After the costs of services and suppliers from outside the destination are paid, and after taxes and fees are paid, the residual income stays in the local/regional economy. It changes hands several times through the income multiplier process. When more money stays and circulates, more jobs are created and more incomes are earned in the destination economy. Finally, the savings of workers provide some of the needed capital for potential investments in building and operating additional tourist facilities and for generating more income.

The objectives of this process are to generate income and employment for local people, encourage savings, invest in economically productive activities including additional tourism-related ventures, and channel funds for local needs. This simple tourism development plan originates from the tourism product that happens to be marketable for international, national, and regional tourism. As the tourism economy grows, the mix of attractions and facilities grows with it. The circle of economic impact gets larger and includes new service providers and suppliers. In an emerging complex and diversified tourism economy, tourists find more attractions to visit, more facilities to patronize, and more activities to experience. Consequently, this expansion encourages tourists to stay longer and spend more money at the destination. Tourism, like other industries, grows more quickly from economies of agglomeration.

Training, entrepreneurship, capital formation, development regulations, investment in infrastructure, conservation, and distribution of income are among the issues to be considered in planning and developing sustainable tourism. It can be said that even the residents of remote areas of the world, like the plains of Patagonia in South America and the Gobi Desert in Central Asia, have the potential to benefit from tourism when they follow the model.

6.10   GEOGRAPHIC DISTRIBUTION OF BENEFITS FROM TOURISM

Regional development broadens the sphere of influence that the tourist destination has over its trade area. Spreading the benefits in proportion to the revenues generated by tourism depends on the national policy followed for sustainable development. The options are:

- Simultaneously addressing environmental concerns along with economic growth, even in the short run
- Placing higher priority on economic growth while addressing environmental concerns that can be dealt with at relatively low cost in the short run
- Placing higher priority on maintaining or restoring the environment in the short run

It is important to keep in mind the advantages tourism development has for reducing poverty in a region. By following the second of the above options, the principal goal of tourism development is not to provide entertainment for those who can afford to travel to distant lands. The principal goal of tourism development is to reduce poverty in the host areas, creating jobs and raising income by using sustainable tourism as a means to achieve it.

To spread the benefits of tourism for poverty reduction and income distribution, it is necessary to consider the following:

- Tourism is an export industry. It has direct linkages with other local businesses. Tourists must travel to a destination to consume the tourism product locally. The benefits are immediate. Other businesses may sell other products by exporting to distant lands, but they do not require the buyers to travel to the destination.
- Employment in tourism is relatively low-wage and labor-intensive, and tourism employs a high proportion of women. As a service industry, tourism demands long hours but offers less backbreaking working conditions than may be found in agriculture and other extractive industries common in LDCs.
- Tourism has the best potential for poverty alleviation in regions where there are few other job and income opportunities. Unlike other exports, tourism does not face tariff and non-tariff barriers in the countries of origin of most international tourists.
- Tourism may use assets that have limited economic value for other types of business pursuits. Culture, archeological and historical sites, mountains, and scenic views are assets that make the tourism product unique but seldom find other uses beyond the (nontourist) enjoyment of them by local residents.
- Tourism has a wide variety of contributing businesses that create a broad resource base from which many new businesses may emerge.
- International tourism is often the primary focus of tourism development. It can stimulate domestic tourism by bringing in and recycling economic benefits in the national economy.

Location of high-value attractions is the primary concern of tourism potential analysis. The location pattern of attractions determines where transportation corridors are needed for connecting regional destinations and forming a tourism network. This regional pattern, superimposed on an existing pattern of urban centers like villages, towns, and cities, forms a network that indicates where and how tourism development activities could take place.

Laborers employed in tourism-related businesses largely reside in support centers, like villages or towns located in the vicinity of destinations. Small arts and crafts and other cottage industries sometimes flourish in these settlements and bring in much-needed income. Employees engaged in supplementary services like house cleaning, automobile maintenance, gardening, landscape maintenance, and construction commute from these settlements to attractions and facilities within the tourism destination. Supplementary agricultural activities, like growing fresh vegetables, fruits, and perhaps poultry products, as well as fishing from the ocean or lakes and rivers, are also cultivated (most desirably) under strict public health controls.

The geographic distribution of the tourism product indicates what needs to be planned and developed in specific locations within the region. Destinations with high tourism potential for growth are planned and built first. These growth centers are connected to dependent satellite attractions and facilities. Proximity to transportation connections with major urban centers of the country is the primary reason for targeting these destinations. When these growth centers are reachable by ground and air transportation over international borders, tourism gains international market dimensions at these destinations.

Diversifying the tourism product induces tourists to lengthen their stay and spend more money. Diversification is faster and requires minimum investment for tourism infrastructure when it focuses on event attractions of the local culture. Drum beating, local dances, hair braiding, village tours, storytelling, handcrafts, botanical tours, local cooking classes, local fashions, and demonstrations of local social customs and etiquette are examples of such events.

Tourists are willing to stay longer in the destination region when there is more to do and see. They modify their schedule and visit other attractions in the vicinity. This leads to tours and more tourist spending. When new attractions are discovered or developed, the tourism product is further diversified. More tourists, longer stays, and more spending have the economic impact of demanding more labor, more goods, and more services from regional sources. The ultimate economic impact comes from replacing imported goods and services with domestic ones. Economic leakage is reduced and multiplier effects are improved. The trickling of economic benefits turns into a stream.

Once destination areas are selected, infrastructure facilities like roads, sewer and water systems, telecommunications, and power and transmission systems are planned and scheduled for development by the government. International technical and financial aid could expedite these projects. With more tourist money coming in, tax revenues improve. The benefits from government improvements are spread over the entire population of the region. Linkages between businesses and urban settlements are diffused from growth centers of tourism toward the periphery and eventually cover the entire region. Community participation and government leadership result in starting new businesses. When economic and spatial integration is achieved, poverty will be reduced and income distribution will be improved in the region. Poverty reduction will likely occur more rapidly if specific pro-poor policies and practices are adopted.

It is important to emphasize that this simple scenario will take years, perhaps decades, of planned development to complete. The scenario assumes that political and social stability of growth centers and region are established, and that poverty-caused afflictions like antisocial behavior, drug and alcohol addictions, and crime are controlled and are not impediments to tourism development. When social problems are extensive, they overwhelm social and political stability. Enthusiasm for self-betterment, escape from poverty, and the model for planned tourism development suffer. When social and political problems grow, only the social cohesion and determination of the community and government will overcome them and open the way to sustained tourism development.

The *sustainable implementation* of these policy principles is similar in large and small, rich and poor tourism destination regions; only the scale is different. A recent example from one of the world's most favored tourism destination regions is enlightening. Paris is considered the world's tourism capital. Tourism is the single most important industry in a region of ten million people. Its tourism economy generates more than $10 billion income annually and creates one hundred fifty thousand jobs. Too much of a good thing also brings problems, however. By some estimates, Paris will attract 75% more visitors annually during the next twenty years. This is where the capacity to absorb this extra influx of tourists becomes an issue. Tourists converge on the center of the city, where major attractions are located. Congestion is inescapable. But the center of the city is controlled by strict zoning regulations and expansion is not possible. What can be done? The government and tourism authorities have adopted a policy of developing **satellite tourism destinations** around Paris to reduce and disperse the impact of tourism on the region. St. Dennis, La Defense, Clichy, and Pantin were chosen for redevelopment as new satellite destinations. In La Defense, for example, high-rise office buildings are rising; old neglected historic monuments like the Basilica de St. Dennis, where ancient royalty was buried, is being restored; and a gigantic gateway, La Grande Arche de la Defense, welcomes visitors with its grandiose architecture. Open markets, shops, cultural events, and creative artists add to the vibrant atmosphere. New site and event attractions are created. Duplicate attractions are used where necessary. The result of this redevelopment policy is that tourists are induced to stay longer in the Paris metropolitan region and spend their money at these new destinations. Congestion at the center of the city is relieved. The tourism product is further diversified and distributed in new satellite destinations. Many new infrastructure projects are planned to implement this policy in the next twenty years (*source: Time* magazine, March 9, 2009).

6.11 REGIONAL ECONOMIC INTEGRATION BY TOURISM

Tourism is a complex industry. Its composition is seldom the same from one destination to another, or from one region or country to another. This complexity results in its uniqueness. Planning tourism requires selection of specific economic elements of the region where industries and businesses contributing to tourism economy are identified.

In substantially undeveloped areas where subsistence activities, herding animals, agriculture, and resource extraction industries prevail, the tourism industry consists of only the essentials. Camping at the outback for overnight accommodation; water and canned food brought from outside the region; walking, trekking, horses, or mules for land transportation; canoes or boats with outboard engines for water transportation; and guides for information services pretty much complete the industry mix of tourism.

Trekking in the Namcha Bazaar region of the Himalayas in Nepal and canoeing and boating down the Amazon River basin in Brazil are such examples. All tourism-related industries are located at the starting point of these expeditions. Supplies are brought in, transportation is secured, and a guide is found at the base location. As tourism grows, fresh food is brought to local markets, where local growers substitute it for imported dry food. At the base village, outdoor camps are replaced with lodges and restaurants with sanitary facilities built and operated by former guides who have now become entrepreneurs by pooling and investing the revenues of villagers obtained from tourism. When the government opens an unpaved, stabilized road by widening foot trails to the base location, four-wheel-drive vehicles take the place of mules and horses. Gradually, with the coming of the road, auto service facilities are developed to stand side by side with barns where pack mules are waiting to take expeditions into the interior. Now that major accessibility and service problems at the base have been solved, scenic trails are extended to ecologically sensitive areas where tourists engage in adventure tourism under close government supervision.

Development of tourism continues to evolve in the destination region. When natives give permission, tourists begin to attend cultural events and visit sacred site attractions. Respecting rituals and cultural sensitivities, guides advise tourists to stand clear, observe the ceremonies from a distance, and refrain from taking pictures if asked. When exposed to local culture, tourists begin to appreciate the specimens of that culture. Art dealers begin to visit to purchase, sometimes illegally, original specimens for their clients abroad. Arts, crafts, and souvenir cottage industries may prosper. When demand increases, suppliers for cottage industries broaden their search for material in the countryside. Although they appreciate their newfound prosperity, villagers recognize that cutting rare species of trees to supply wood carvers would soon deplete these species. Knowing that the sustainability of their tourism economy depends on replenishing and protecting their environment, village elders establish and enforce protective measures.

At the entrance to the destination village, construction of the lodge and restaurant progresses. Local people pool their collective labor and construction abilities and turn them into a viable construction contracting business. With increasing prosperity, a school, a clinic, and even a government office come into existence. Prominent visitors, like Sir Edmund Hillary, the first person who climbed Mount Everest with the Sherpa guide Tenzing Norgay, offer help and contribute money for building and operating needed facilities. The trade area of the village widens to include distant settlements, and the village becomes the service center of the region. When recip-rocal spatial and economic integration between center and hinterland is established, tourism has done its job and has helped to remove the region from its cycle of poverty.

6.12 ENCOURAGING COMMUNITY PARTICIPATION AND ENTREPRENEURSHIP

Local leaders play a critical role in interpreting tribal laws and cultural taboos. When community participation and entrepreneurship are needed for building a tourism project, leaders make it possible. The tribal chief, *damyo, sirdar,* or *imam* and, further up the ladder of political influence, the mayor, governor, and minister, have wisdom and influence over their people. They are in a position to understand the intent and consequences of tourism projects proposed in their community, region, or country. If the project is desirable, they rally their people and mobilize the resources of the community.

Endorsement of leadership is essential for raising awareness and motivating entrepreneurship. The measure of success is the ability to lift the community out of poverty and dependence on government handouts. Economic survival and prosperity from tourism demand communication and education as prerequisites. Demonstration effects combined with formal education and effective community leadership open the doors to creativity, risk taking, and entrepreneurship. They change the traditional society that tries to avoid risk taking by adhering to tested and tried customs, traditions, and collective decision making for ensuring their survival. Change, however, does not come easily. When positive results are shown, a new way of life with increased benefits is gradually accepted.

Authorities give destination communities a voice in deciding on tourism development strategies and projects. Community leaders discuss the proposed development guidelines and projects in their traditional community meetings with sheiks, emirs, and other higher authorities. If these guidelines and projects are accepted by consensus, they are implemented with community participation. Initially, government authorities persuade local leaders to invest community labor and material resources in essential tourism infrastructure projects. Government provides technical and financial assistance and invests in major portions of these projects.

In most cultures, negotiations with local leaders are preceded by the courtesy presentation of appropriate gifts. These are not bribes. The importance of this courtesy cannot be overemphasized. The outsider offering only inexpensive beads in exchange for asking community leaders to help create a prime location for a planned resort will be shunted aside politely. Someone who is so ignorant of local values and gestures of courtesy has no place doing business in that community. Learning at least a few words of the local language will go a long way toward bridging the cultural gap and gaining acceptance. But the entrepreneur offering to build a road, drill a well for water, generate electricity, or bring some other substantial benefit to the community will be rewarded handsomely by the community as a result of the goodwill built. The local government will assign an official, or a young intern or two, to the developer of the tourism project for on-the-job training and for learning the technical and business aspects of the project.

Follow-up is natural. One exceptionally successful project begets another. The hold of the demonstration effect on the locals will stimulate further pooling of community resources. Entire families will participate in the venture. They will be eager to contribute their labor, knowledge, and money to the cooperative effort. The profit motive and individualism, the two basic tenets of market system economics, are learned with practice. The influence of community leadership over the individual will be gradual. Traditional values, customs, and practices will not, and should not, be erased in one bold stroke. It will take time and effort to make the transition from a traditional to a market economy. Conditions for a dual economy and parallel cultures may persist and continue to coexist for decades.

This model is also applicable, with modification, in more advanced economies. The town hall is where negotiations with local authorities take place. The feasibility of the project, and its concurrence with local land use laws and building regulations, are evaluated. The developer comes to these meetings fully cognizant of the sustainability of the project in view of what is permissible and what is not. The developer often brings his or her consultants along to reinforce the credibility of the team that will undertake the project.

6.13   OPPORTUNITIES FOR WOMEN

Tourism is a service industry. It requires courtesy and a gentle disposition for serving the needs of tourists. Employment opportunities in all businesses associated with tourism are greatest for women in countries where women are emancipated and their rights are equal to those of men. Travel agents, airline clerks, flight attendants, pilots, housekeepers, cooks, front desk clerks, decorators, tour guides, servers, bartenders, hostesses, writers, and farmers have job opportunities for women.

In countries where the role of women is traditionally at home or in tending the fields, or limited to face-to-face contacts only with other women or with male family members, employment in tourism will push the limits of social acceptability. The cultural dimensions of employing women in the tourism industry are becoming increasingly important and relevant. Justification for keeping women at home is counterproductive when applied to tourism. All male service personnel employed at hotels and other tourism establishments in Saudi Arabia, Dubai, and some other Middle Eastern countries are guest workers from the Philippines, Pakistan, and other Southeast Asian and Middle Eastern countries. These host countries deprive one-half of their population of productive pursuits outside the house by importing this labor. In these cultures, women can own property, but they have no way of owning and running a business without the help of a family member.

Unequal educational opportunities compound the lack of job opportunities for women. In traditional societies, the formal education of a woman often stops when she reaches the marriageable age of twelve. Few women reach the educational level for employment as a teacher, nurse, or other occupations where necessary education exceeds the primary school level. When this bias is overcome, tourism, because of its close affinity to hospitality and home occupation, provides culturally acceptable employment alternatives for women.

The Charter of Human Rights adopted by the United Nations endorses the right of women to work in tourism and in other occupations. On December 10, 1948, the General Assembly of the United Nations adopted and proclaimed the Universal Declaration of Human Rights for everyone. The charter reaffirmed fundamental human rights, the dignity and worth of the human person, and equal rights of men and women. The charter promotes social progress and better standards of life with greater freedom.

The thirty articles of the Universal Declaration include the following:

Article 2.   Everyone is entitled to all rights and freedoms set forth in this Declaration, without distinction of any kind, such as, race, colour, sex, language, religion, political or other opinion, national or social origin, property, birth or other status. Furthermore, no distinction shall be made on the basis of the political, jurisdictional or international

Article 16.
status of the country or territory to which a person belongs, whether it be independent, trust, non-self governing or under any other limitation of sovereignty.

Article 16. (1) Men and women of full age, without any limitation due to race, nationality or religion, have the right to marry and to found a family. They are entitled to equal rights as to marriage, during marriage and at its dissolution.

(2) Marriage shall be entered into only with the free and full consent of the intending spouses.

(3) The family is the natural and fundamental group unit of society and is entitled to protection by society and the State.

Article 23. (1) Everyone has the right to work, to free choice of employment, to just and favorable conditions of work and to protection against unemployment.

(2) Everyone, without any discrimination, has the right to equal pay for equal work.

(3) Everyone who works has the right to just and favourable remuneration ensuring himself and his family an existence worthy of human dignity, and supplemented, if necessary, by other means of social protection.

Specifically, the United Nations Division for the Advancement of Women (UNDAW) is grounded on the vision of equality prescribed by the Charter of Human Rights. It advocates the improvement of the status of women throughout the world and the achievement of their equality with men. It promotes women as equal participants in and beneficiaries of sustainable development, peace and security, governance, and human rights. As part of its mandate, the UNDAW strives to stimulate the mainstreaming of gender perspectives both within and outside the United Nations system. It is a catalyst for advancing the global agenda on women's issues and gender equality. It conducts research, develops policy options, provides advisory services, and gives technical assistance. It promotes global standards and norms, shares best practices, and raises awareness on women's issues.

Sometimes appearances are deceptive and common knowledge is misleading. According to surveys conducted in 2003 by the *Chicago Sun-Times, New York Times, USA Today,* and the *New York Post,* as well as the Associated Press and Reuters and reported in *Time* magazine (April 11, 2005), average salary differentials of working women of different racial backgrounds in the United States indicate that women's progress has been remarkable. The surveys revealed that the average salary of college-educated Asian-American women was $43,656; that of college-educated African-American women was $41,066; and that of college-educated white American women was $37,761. The reason for this differential was education. Asian-American and African-American women got better educations.

6.14   CRIME AND TERRORISM

All good things that tourism development can bring crime can take away. Some crimes are universal. Others are imported. When traveling in a strange land, tourists have to use their best judgment to avoid situations that can harm them physically and, reciprocally, can harm the local population and culture.

Drug trafficking is one of the worst things that can happen to tourism and tourists. Local laws may allow or simply ignore the growing of opium poppies and coca (from which cocaine is made) as cash crops. In places of extreme poverty like rural Columbia and Afghanistan, drugs are a way of life. In places where opium is part of the local culture, as in China decades ago, it was considered medicinal. Raising narcotic crops, however, is a poor excuse for curing poverty, because it is a universally accepted crime. For ill-advised tourists participating in their trade or use, drugs spell disaster. The penalty for purchasing a gram of hashish could be years in a local prison. Drug trafficking could also discourage many tourists from traveling to these destinations because of its associated violence.

Theft of cultural artifacts is different from collecting and dealing. Legitimate collectors and dealers visit their contacts in local cultures often. They are businesspeople participating in an honorable profession. Cultural artifacts are not permitted to leave their country of origin because of their cultural value. When tourists buy and carry these artifacts without declaring them to the customs agent upon leaving, they become participants in the illicit trade. The wise thing to do is to refuse to buy artifacts authenticated for their originality by the authorities but not cleared for taking abroad. However, tourists should be encouraged to buy good specimens of duplicated artifacts in order to help local arts and crafts and cottage industries. Protecting the cultural heritage of the country, or what is left of it after years of pilferage and uncontrolled exports, is a priority for ensuring sustainable tourism.

Some tourists turn to local black markets for exchanging currency and selling certain questionable goods, like pornographic material, that are prohibited by local laws. Exchanging money on the black market is widely accepted because of the favorable rates of exchange given for the foreign currency. However, the practice has its drawbacks. The helpful concierge who volunteers to act as a go-between for the black market money changer and the tourist may conveniently fail to show up on time with the money before the tourist is due to depart from the hotel for the airport. Only the tourist can decide whether to bypass authorized money changers like banks and resort to using shady operators for gaining a slight edge in exchanging money.

The word **bribery** has different meanings in different contexts. In most countries, bribery means offering something, generally money, in exchange for an illicit favor or influence. In some parts of the world, bribery is considered a legitimate gratuity given in exchange for a service rendered. In the latter context, the word *baksheesh,* generally associated with Arabic-speaking countries, is a legitimate supplementary income for service providers. This form of soliciting is not to be confused with the bribery associated with corruption in any language.

Scams and setups to extort money from visitors under one pretense or another are to be avoided by tourists. Traveling with a group helps. In turn, tourists should not create a situation in which a bribe will corrupt an otherwise honest official and will demean the tourist in the process. After giving a bribe, one should reflect on the ill-advised example the tourist has provided and the poor image of the foreigner conveyed to the members of another culture.

Prostitution is the world's oldest profession for profit. The service is offered by high-priced professionals operating in luxury hotels with or without the consent of the hotel management in poor and rich destination countries alike. At the other end of the social spectrum, poor families in villages sell their twelve-year-old daughters to servitude in local seedy brothels often frequented by foreign visitors, including visiting military personnel. The consequences of such transactions are well documented. With the rising problem of AIDS in certain parts of the world, however, the probable contribution of tourism to the spread of this deadly disease cannot be overemphasized.

Among the lesser vices aggravated, but not necessarily caused, by tourism is begging on the streets and other small crimes in the world of the local marketplace. Begging is the act of soliciting money by asking for personal sympathy. Images from Charles Dickens' classic novel *Oliver Twist* are a common occurrence in the streets of the developing world. The character of Fagin, who maintains a stable of young boys in his attic for soliciting and stealing money from wealthy pedestrians, is found 170 years later in many cities. To get more money from their sympathetic victims, these unsavory violators of public decency search the countryside to find crippled children, a grotesquely disfigured man, or women with an infant who has various medical afflictions, including leprosy.

Begging at street corners near hotels is among the techniques used by these professional beggars. Municipal police periodically sweep these professionals from the streets and attempt to prevent them from hassling tourists. For the tourist, differentiating between the genuinely poor person who begs for survival and the professional is a difficult task. There are two schools of thought about expressing compassion for those who are really in need. One is to avoid giving any money to any beggar on the street but donating a sum to a legitimate local charity. The other approach is to give selectively in situations where giving is a form of social security payment approved by the local culture, particularly in a religious setting. The choice is for the tourist to make.

Trademark and copyright infractions are common in some parts of the world. Pirated music or movie videos and CDs find their way to legitimate stores or to stands that are set up by hawkers at street corners when the municipal police are not looking. Pirated material often looks identical to its original, and is sold at a fraction of its original price and without any obligation to pay royalties. Occasionally, third-rate copies are sold with amusing titles like *The Best Hits of Beethoven*. Tourists, and sometimes military personnel from foreign countries, sell a copy of a recently issued original CD at a high price to pirates and, by doing so willingly, contribute to the act of piracy.

Any form of violence is abhorrent to tourism. Political challenges to the government of the country and peaceful marches that turn into violent confrontations repel and frighten tourists. Where insurrection takes the form of armed civil war, tourism ceases to exist for the duration of the disturbance. It is not safe for tourists to visit many parts of the world, including the Middle East, as well as some countries in Latin America, where being caught in the conflict between the authorities and drug lords is a continuous hazard. World events that promote regional political divisions and polarize the affected population also limit international tourism in those geographic regions.

Problems of personal security also exist in some parts of the world where criminals often subject tourists to robberies and attacks with lethal weapons. Certain areas of the countryside and particular urban areas are not safe at any hour of the day. The presence of law enforcement officers will reinforce the sense of personal safety for tourists.

Finally, terrorism has become an international deterrent to the growth of tourism since the September 11, 2001, terrorist event that destroyed the two towers of the World Trade Center in New York City and caused the death of approximately three thousand victims from many countries. Since that date, the extra security measures taken by the authorities at strategic locations and facilities, particularly airports, have had a dampening effect on tourism in most countries. It is hoped that some day, terrorism around the world will cease to be a public safety issue for tourists.

The issues related to promoting and practicing sustainable tourism do not end with the few examples given in this chapter. Tourism development planners from both private and public sectors will have to consider all of the opportunities and impediments to the planning and growth of sustainable tourism in their respective areas. Nothing short of comprehensive review, analysis, and positive actions to solve existing problems will ensure the beneficial growth of tourism and its enjoyment by visitors and hosts alike.

Chapter Highlights

- Sustainable development conserves the environment, cultural, and other resources for future generations while still bringing benefits to the present generation.
- Indicators of sustainable tourism are based on quantifiable indices. These include extended national accounts, biophysical accounts, equally weighted indexes, unequally weighted indexes, eco-efficiency, and indicator sets.
- Tourism policies represent a balancing act among environmental, social, and economic variables.
- Three types of sustainable tourism policies may be possible: (1) simultaneously addressing environmental, social, and economic issues of growth on equal terms; (2) placing higher priority on economic growth, while giving less emphasis to environmental and social issues; or (3) placing higher priority on restoring the environment and accelerating social change over economic issues.
- The planning principles are the same in rich and poor regions; only the scale is different.
- Creating satellite (outlying) tourism destinations is one prescription for relieving congestion and overcrowding in highly popular and overused tourism regions.
- The value of tourism is found in conserving the authentic tourism resources. Their preservation is paramount for sustainable tourism.
- Substituting human-made duplicate attractions in order to conserve authentic attractions is a well-accepted and successful policy. This practice also enables the grouping of attractions in one place to increase the draw of a destination.
- Tourism is a service industry. There are many job opportunities for women.
- Crime and terrorism in many forms are impediments to drawing tourists and sustaining tourism's growth.

Planning Processes for Tourism Development

Part III introduces tourism planning and development steps followed by governments and the private sector in market, government-assisted mixed, and central planned command economic systems. It gives examples of model legislation and regulations for promoting and developing tourism. It also presents international, private, and government funding sources for financing tourism businesses and projects. Finally, it describes tourism organizations operating at national, regional, and destination levels for informing tourists and for promoting and managing the tourism industry.

7

Planning Cycles in Government-Assisted Tourism Development

This chapter discusses the steps involved in planning and developing tourism when the government takes the initiative; sets the policies, guidelines, and procedures; and encourages the private sector to implement the majority of tourism development projects.

- Planning and developing tourism is shared by the private sector and government.
- Planning is done at national, regional, and local levels.
- Methods of planning are applicable to all three economic systems, but the roles played by government and the private sector are different.

7.1 SECURING COMMUNITY PARTICIPATION AT NATIONAL, REGIONAL, AND LOCAL LEVELS

As noted in Chapter 5, tourism development is initiated by the government when it plays the central role in transforming a centrally planned economy into a mixed economy. This requires planning and building the tourism industry from top to bottom. Tourism potential studies and national development policies determine whether tourism can be a sustainable growth industry with the potential to have a significant impact on the economic development of the country. Government policies and planning will assign targets for tourism development. Generally, these policies will instruct the government to build the tourism infrastructure. In turn, the private sector will get assistance from the central government for starting individual projects at specified scales and selected destinations.

This planning and development scenario demands close cooperation between government and the private sector. Reaching private entrepreneurs and securing the cooperation of the public is the first step in this process. Starting sustainable and environmentally sensitive tourism development demands a meeting of minds and mutual education. Local culture, customs, and ways of doing business become considerations when authorities explore the feasibility of tourism.

Developing positive attitudes and an attitude of hospitality toward visitors, particularly foreigners, requires time and education of local people. This could be an ongoing process lasting many years.

The government takes the second step by demonstrating and publicizing what tourism can do for the country, region, and local communities. Initially, an agency of national government is assigned this role. In a simple government organization, the ministry of the interior or the home office could be the agency to get things started. With the cooperation of local authorities, representatives of the national government arrange a series of meetings with local tribal or ethnic leaders, if any, as well as prominent landowners, respected village elders, and emerging entrepreneurs. Roundtable discussions continue while the national government undertakes a national study of tourism potential.

7.2 DECIDING ON PLANNING STEPS

The government takes the lead in preparing the terms of reference for the tourism potential study of the country and for the tourism planning for sustainable development and possible poverty reduction that will follow. Preparation for the study involves community participation to ensure ongoing and ultimate agreement, consent, and compliance; establishing a vision for the program; setting study goals and objectives; selecting a study steering committee; determining the scope of services and activities to be undertaken by the contractor and/or the study team; determining a schedule and a time frame for the study; and determining the area or location the study will cover, the types of study results, the types of policy recommendations, and the proposed study budget.

In exploring the sustainability of tourism and its development potential, the initial study may be constrained by a shortage of funds and technical resources. In undertaking the study, the government could apply to international tourism organizations like the UNWTO, the United Nations Development Program (UNDP), and the World Bank for technical assistance and for funding the study.

The study will be an interdisciplinary effort. A typical approach will be to invite a team of technical experts from around the world, recommended and paid for by the organization that funds the project. Foreign experts often make up the majority of the team. They are joined by selected officials and technical personnel assigned by the government. These officials will play major roles in planning and developing tourism in the country. They are paired with their counterparts on the foreign expert team. Generally, the foreign expert team includes a tourism economist, a sociologist or social scientist, a regional and urban development planner, a historian, and an architect. Their respective areas of expertise cover the following aspects of the tourism potential analysis:

- *A tourism economist* collects and analyzes data concerning population counts, demographic characteristics, transportation and traffic movement, employment, the economic base, and the impact of the tourism sector. He or she estimates possible tourist expenditures, probable tax revenues, and the jobs and income generated by tourism. Given resource limitations, the economist estimates the economic sustainability of tourism. He or she calculates the overnight facilities necessary for accommodating tourists.
- *A sociologist* evaluates the characteristics of the local culture, customs, hierarchy, and structure of social organizations, social values, religion, attitudes, political stability of the country, and ethnicity in different regions. He or she determines whether tourism would be accepted by the locals and the extent to which they would be willing to maintain it.
- *A regional and urban planner* concentrates on the physical and spatial characteristics of the country, including topography, climate, location pattern of urban centers, their

hierarchy, linkages, potential site and event attractions, urban and rural activity possibilities, agriculture, forestry, wildlife, and conservation requirements. He or she also determines the tourism infrastructure requirements and prepares estimates of their costs.

- *A historian* researches the history of the country and identifies historically significant events and places that would be attractions. He or she evaluates the archeological sites and determines their tourism attraction values. The historian also proposes conservation measures.
- *An architect* makes a geographic and pictorial survey of the study area to identify locations for potential tourism destinations, facilities, and attractions. He or she evaluates the urban design, building design, and landscape design features of sites and structures. The architect creates schematic master plans for villages, towns, and destinations. He or she recommends where and what types of resorts and tourist facilities can be built and estimates the approximate cost of developing these sites.

The government provides and organizes logistical support for the international study team with funds allocated by the funding source. Transportation, camping facilities, food, beverages, accommodations, and local support personnel are obtained for the project. A visit or trek will be taken to the sites. The study team prepares and presents its combined report with recommendations to the government and to the sponsoring international agency. The report recommends basic steps for planning and developing tourism. These steps include:

- **Surveying potential attractions and facilities** that would be the tourism **product mix** of the country
- Analyzing the **distribution, quality,** and **activity potential** of the tourism product
- Deciding on the **comparative advantages** of developing international and domestic tourism
- Establishing **development goals and policies** at the national, regional, and local levels
- **Translating policies into development objectives** by subject area and level of government
- Preparing national, regional, and local tourism development **master plans**
- Establishing linkages and **integration** with other economic sectors and areas
- **Selecting projects** and **site-specific action measures** to achieve the objectives
- **Assigning projects and specific measures** to government agencies
- Including appropriate **capital and operating budget** items in the ongoing national budgeting process
- **Funding** and **implementing** projects and specific measures
- **Coordinating** the implementation of projects and specific measures
- **Evaluating the results** of implemented projects and specific measures
- **Redefining goals, policies, plans, and specific measures** after one cycle
- **Restarting the planning and development cycle** in specified years

The recommendations eventually lead to coordinated actions by the government, the private sector, and the international agency. Technical assistance my be a one-time affair or may last until local agencies take over. Policies are formulated and tourism development gets underway. (See Chapter 13 for the methodology used in planning sustainable tourism.)

7.3 SURVEYING THE TOURISM PRODUCT

The first step in the long process of developing tourism is to survey what is available that could be a *tourism product* at the given location. What would interest tourists is the first question answered—whether a fishing village on the shores of the finest beach in Polynesia or a Mayan ruin waiting for the archeologists to arrive. The simplest survey will include pooling the knowledge of local people and arriving at a consensus and a list of things for tourists to see and do. The list may include the obvious physical features like beaches, ruins, mountains, forests, and waterfalls that lie unused and with very limited current economic value, as well as Manuel's food shack, Jorge's outboard fishing boat, and Mama Leona's straw baskets, mats, and hats that local people use every day. Most important, despite their humble origins and modest means, is to determine whether local people are hospitable toward the strangers who would pass through. These elements of the potential tourism product are parts of the everyday life and culture of the local population. What locals have to offer includes a few possessions, what they can extract from the land and sea, rituals they observe for communal living, traditional handicrafts, and cottage occupations like carpet weaving and native food preparation. An example of the coverage of a tourism development survey for two cities in Jordan is given on the following Web site: http://ideas.repec.org/p/wiw/wiwrsa/ersa06p79.html.

As the scale of tourism increases from local to regional levels, the region of impact enlarges and the variety of tourism resources multiplies. In addition to simple natural exotica, human-made features found in urbanized areas gain importance. Examples of local architecture, historic remnants of past rulers, botanical gardens, and just about any curious or interesting artifact could qualify as a tourism product. However, the organizers of the emerging tourism industry must be aware of the sleaze factor and make sure that the good is separated from the bad and the ugly. Obviously, unsightly, noisy, dirty, and unsafe experiences and artifacts should be avoided. But the kitsch, the curio, and the unusual could find interested parties willing to spend time and money for the privilege of having the experience. After the survey is completed, local authorities will get together and, in concert with private organizations, create a database using the principles and possibly the techniques of the BIK System (see Chapters 2 and 11). The location of each *attraction* and *facility* surveyed is plotted on a map. The emerging tourism product is analyzed for the dispersion of its tourism attractions and facilities, as well as their corresponding activity, seasonality, and quality characteristics. The local authorities begin to create a visual image of the tourism geography. Today, this can be done electronically using computers and various software. In simplified surveys involving small databases, manual methods can be used.

At the national level, surveying the tourism product is simpler. Only major and nationally significant attractions and facilities are inventoried and plotted. The national database for tourism products is used for preparing government policies. Tourism infrastructure, laws and regulations necessary for sustainable tourism, training the labor force, and marketing the tourism product are among these policies.

For international promotion, a few internationally significant attractions in the country are selected from the tourism product and promoted as locations for glorious vacations, preferably at affordable prices. Human imagination does the rest and enhances reality by making the tourism product interesting for the visitors.

7.4   ANALYZING THE TOURISM PRODUCT

The methods for analyzing the tourism product are discussed elsewhere in this book (Chapters 2, 12, and 13). The purpose of the analysis is to identify the quantity and quality of tourism elements; their geographic location pattern; their weaknesses and strengths as attractions and facilities; their economic viability; their market potential; their human resource characteristics; their conceptual regions of influence and draw; and their potential for development.

Suffice it to say here that tourism resource analysis leads to recommendations for the government to develop tourism as a sustainable growth sector of the economy or to have it develop at its own pace without government intervention. The analysis points to policies that will support the orderly and expeditious growth of tourism.

7.5   DECIDING ON COMPARATIVE ADVANTAGES

International tourism relies on foreign visitors for growth and development, and on planning the industry according to internationally accepted standards. It is selective about where and how tourism development should take place to meet these standards. It is a direct source of foreign exchange. *Domestic tourism* focuses on accommodating domestic travelers. It does not earn foreign exchange directly. It induces domestic travelers to stay and forgo traveling to another country, thus preventing domestic currency from leaving the country to become foreign exchange.

In recent years, economic integration has begun to eliminate the inflow and outflow of foreign currency in tourism. The European Union and the creation of the euro as the official currency of the Union have eased travel restrictions among member countries. When the economies of countries are integrated, common characteristics of international and domestic tourism are the similar activities that bring both types of tourists to the same attractions and facilities. The development of similar activities that abide by the same standards merges two sets of development into one and, by doing so, reinforces the pull of the destination where these two sets meet. This meeting creates an undeniable advantage for selecting such regions and destinations as priority locations for both domestic and international tourism marketing.

When two or more countries compete for the same international tourism market, their respective comparative advantage is considered. A potential international tourist has to choose among these countries when he or she has the option to do so. The tourist will evaluate the comparative advantages that one or the other country is offering for his or her time, money, and personal interest. Once the choice is made and the journey is taken, a tourist becomes a statistic and a target for repeat marketing for that destination. For example, for many years, European tourists from northern cold-water countries compared the prices of holiday travel and accommodations in warm-water countries on the Balkan, Italian, and Iberian peninsulas and made annual vacation choices based on this information. The prices included currency exchange rates, a variable that has now been eliminated in most cases.

7.6   SELECTING TOURISM DEVELOPMENT GOALS AND POLICIES

The goals and policies for tourism development, at any level, are not decided in an information vacuum. The time for making critical decisions before committing the resources of the nation, region, or local community is reached when preparatory studies and consultations with all parties are completed. In government-dictated, top-down, command economic planning and development systems, this process is often ignored. The "central government knows best" process used in these countries will usually be missing the basic ingredients for making correct policies. In these systems, and in mixed economies with strong central command tendencies, this would be a grave mistake. Tourism, unlike other economic sectors, is largely focused on inanimate cultural and natural resources. These resources are fragile and often irreplaceable. By risking their sustainability, hastily prepared development goals and policies could be counterproductive and may result in destroying the very product on which the tourism industry depends. Centrally dictated decisions on tourism made without adequate consultation also risk alienating local groups whose acceptance and hospitality are critical to successful and sustainable tourism.

Formulating government policies is distinct from formulating and implementing the means of achieving these policies. These means consist of induced responsive actions by the private sector, guided by and responding to policy and program directives and infrastructure investments of the central government. Policymaking is a process in which the roles of the central government and the private sector are defined and balanced according to their respective strengths and weaknesses and evaluated by the extent of their effectiveness. When the private sector is in the early stages of emergence, policies will rely primarily on government actions. As the private sector matures and gains financial and managerial strength, the implementation role of the central government will diminish slowly. Because the processes of democratization, broader participation in government by the general public, and greater reliance on market signals could be slow in developing, central governments may not be willing to transfer economic decision making for program and project implementation to the private sector. The process and the degree of democratic rule achieved differ substantially from one country to another. Accordingly, the involvement and leadership of government in tourism development vary greatly.

There is no one ideal set of goals and policies. The goals and policies of the government in planning and developing tourism could be more or less than suggested below. The *goals* are summarized as follows:

- Optimizing the economic and social benefits from tourism for the country
- Spreading the benefits from tourism to all economic sectors and regions with possible pro-poor impacts
- Pursuing sustainable tourism development and protecting resources
- Creating a strong tourism sector capable of competing with other destination countries
- Balancing the needs and interests of international and domestic tourists

The following government *policies* are derived from these targets:

- Facilitating planning and developing tourism
- Promoting tourism and building a favorable image of the country
- Preparing national tourism development plans
- Preparing regional and local tourism development plans with municipalities
- Dedicating government-owned land for tourist infrastructure development
- Creating financial and other incentives for the private sector to pursue tourism development
- Encouraging international capital investment in tourism facilities
- Training the labor force and educating the public for tourism development
- Giving preference to low-income or very-low-income people in tourism jobs and secondary economic activities

7.7   TRANSLATING POLICIES INTO MULTILEVEL GOVERNMENT ACTIONS

The government translates its policies into actions in several stages. The *first stage* is the formation and consolidation stage, which could take ten or more years. During this period, government takes the following action steps:

- Builds demonstration tourism projects, like resorts and hotels that meet international standards and sets examples for the private sector
- Builds tourism infrastructure projects like roads, utilities, ports, and airports in selected destination regions

- Markets the attractions and facilities of the country in target countries abroad
- Builds a tourism information system
- Establishes a permanent government agency in charge of tourism development
- Adopts tourism development laws and regulations for land development in selected tourism destination regions
- Adopts tourist facility design, licensing, operation, and pricing standards for hotels, restaurants, marinas, and other facilities

The *second stage* involves liberalization in which the government transfers the responsibilities for tourism development to increasingly efficient private sector and market system operations. This stage can take another ten or more years. During this period, government takes the following action steps:

- Measures the effectiveness of past government actions and adjusts policies
- Revises national, regional, and local tourism development master plans
- Continues international marketing and improves market share
- Encourages multinational private investment in tourism projects

The government continuously monitors the changes taking place in the tourism industry by collecting and analyzing reliable and standardized statistical tourism information. The database is updated by collecting data directly from foreign tourists arriving in the country by air, land, and sea. Hotel owners are required to submit hotel occupancy and visitor profile information. Chambers of commerce, as well as hotel, motel, restaurant, and similar trade organizations, collect additional information for and from their memberships. Major attractions conduct periodic surveys of their attendees and keep records of attendance.

7.8   PREPARING NATIONAL, REGIONAL, AND LOCAL TOURISM DEVELOPMENT PLANS

At the national level, the country evolving into a mixed economic system starts by establishing certain planning goals and objectives for the national economy. Tourism enters into this process. Government decides on the general aims of economic policy and the measures to be taken. The planning group reconciles discrepancies among the measures, if any, and government enacts revisions as needed.

One of the initial targets to be established is the annual growth rate of the national economy. This goal depends on the realistic expectations of the economy. In certain countries, like Turkey and Egypt, the annual growth rate target for their national economies was set at 7% a year. This ambitious target was later adjusted to match the performance of their economies.

The next step brings the economic sectors and development regions into the planning process. It usually takes the form of consultations between government and private sector committees at the national, regional, and local levels. In France and Turkey, for example, a large number of permanent and ad hoc committees exist. Each of these committees is responsible for one industry. Each maintains a review function over the development of the industry along the lines established by the planning agency. In the Netherlands and Germany, organizations composed of both employers and workers advise the government.

Consultations with organizations at the regional and local levels are particularly necessary when the administrative organization of the country is based on autonomous districts or on ethnic and tribal domains. The British Commonwealth of Nations and the member countries of CARICOM in the Caribbean are examples of such political organizations.

When the national development plan is more or less ready, a council composed of leading government officials, ministers, and other representatives reviews and approves the plan. Procedures for approval are different. Some countries give the national development plan legal force and pass appropriate legislative measures for adopting it as the law of the land. In others, the government simply gives its consent to the plan. In these cases, the plans are for consultation only.

The main problem with this procedure is the order in which the consultative organizations are heard. Their recommendations may lose their effectiveness or be ignored if they are consulted late in the planning process. The second problem is the choice of representative groups. A list of interested parties is prepared. The list reflects the cross section of economic, social, and geographical regions of the country. It includes not only large but also smaller representative groups that will be playing roles in the implementation of the national development plan. When the list is long, decisions become difficult.

The solution to the problems lies in altering the methodology used for preparing the national development plan. When subjective decisions are minimized, econometric and other models can reduce the need for lengthy negotiations among participating groups. Conversely, if econometric models are used and conflict arises, negotiations are imperative. These models describe the economy in terms of a large number of simultaneous mathematical equations. These equations show:

- Resources and limitations of the economy
- Elements of the economy
- Monetary flows among the elements of the economy
- Goals and conditions set for attaining desired outputs
- Optimum performance of the elements necessary to attain a desired level of prosperity

The method of calculation differs according to the structure of the mathematical equations. In each equation, a certain type of information is needed at certain stages of the process. This information is obtained from its source at each prescribed stage. In addition to determining the number of contacts at the required time, this approach uses various techniques to define the shortest or optimum time period it will take for to prepare the national development plan.

In preparing the plan for the national economy, only a manageable number of *economic sectors* and *regions* are considered. Proportionate to the population, the complexity of the economy, and the geographic size of the country, the number may vary from two to twenty sectors and possibly from two to several regions. The actual numbers depend on many factors, including whether the country's population is relatively homogeneous or whether cultural differences such as language, religion, ethnic, and racial divisions are markedly pronounced. Another concern is the geographical characteristics of the country. Again, geographic homogeneity or differences play roles. Coastal areas, forested areas, plains, mountains, and islands help determine the sectors and regions.

Regional boundaries are determined partly by the transportation barriers between regions. Regions are formed by grouping administrative units. In Turkey, for example, sixty-seven provinces, where governors are chosen by local elections, are divided into ten development regions. In India, each state is considered a separate region. In other countries where development has been concentrated in certain areas, the country is divided into developed and less developed regions or into one dominant growth center and its service area.

Eliminating the income differential between developed and less developed regions is a principal goal of development planning. Tourism can play a major role in this process. The most direct answer to the problem of eliminating regional income differentials is migration. People in poorer regions migrate to richer regions in search of jobs and higher incomes. Massive internal migration, however, eventually creates massive urban problems in the dominant growth centers. Squatter housing, unhealthy living conditions, education needs for children, inadequate transportation, and other problems of rapid urbanization overwhelm available public services and infrastructure.

Regions differentiated by income require separate regional development goals. The goals in less developed regions often aim at creating an economic specialty to lead development. Goals for developed growth regions intend to use their resource base on mutual advantage and to diversify economically. Less developed regions may suffer from difficult environmental conditions. Erosion, mountains, or climate may adversely affect economic activity. When the tourism potential analysis indicates that those unfavorable conditions can be transformed into productive tourism resources, a new income-producing regional specialty is created. The Himalayan mountains in Nepal, the Grand Canyon in Arizona, beaches on Caribbean islands, and Mayan monuments in Mexico, combined with the climate, lifestyle, and cultures of their regions, can contribute to better equalization of incomes among regions through tourism.

Once regions are defined and regional boundaries are drawn, the spatial dimensions of regional development plans emerge. The rest follows. The composition of regional tourism industries is determined. Specific master plans for destination areas are prepared. Action measures by national, regional, and local governments are prepared and approved. Site-specific infrastructure projects are selected, funded, and scheduled for implementation. Regulations like those covering land use zoning for enforcing the provisions of regional and local master plans, design and development guidelines, and building and environmental standards are prepared and made available for private sector use. Therefore, the process from national to regional and local tourism development planning devolves from national policies down to site-specific local projects. Public agencies and private groups become the executors of these multilevel simultaneous actions. An example of a regional tourism development plan for the Babia Gora, Poland region is given at the following Web site: http://www.oete.de/tourism4nature/results/bg_pictures/bg2_TMP%5BEN%5D.pdf.

In planning *regional* development, basic or **export sector** industries take precedence over **nonbasic service industries**. At the *national* level, this is also true. National development plans usually focus on achieving export-oriented international and national goals. Regional goals are secondary and are subsidiary to the achievement of national goals. This makes tourism particularly sensitive to government actions because tourism activities fluctuate at all levels. Drawing international tourists to the country and sending them to destination regions is the responsibility of the national government. If international tourism marketing fails to achieve its objectives, the tourism economy at destination regions fails with it.

Chapter Highlights

- Securing community participation at the national, regional, and local levels is essential in preparing tourism policies.
- The first step in planning tourism development is to determine the tourism potential. This involves a systematic survey and evaluation of the tourism product.

- Regional and local boundaries are determined for each tourism area.
- Goals lead to policies. The policies, in turn, are translated into plans, specific programs, projects, and measures. Destinations are selected.
- Government measures and private sector actions are balanced and determined.

8

Tourism Development in Market Economic Systems

This chapter discusses tourism development initiated by largely spontaneous and interactive actions of the private sector and government in market economic systems and makes comparisons with government-assisted mixed and centrally planned economies.

- Trickle-down and multiplier mechanisms distribute the benefits of tourism.
- Private initiative and entrepreneurship drive the tourism market economy.
- Government plays the major role in planning and developing tourism in mixed economies with participation from the private sector.
- Centrally planned command economies rely on government for planning and developing tourism.
- Market economic systems rely on privately prepared and independent business and marketing plans for selecting tourism projects.

8.1 THE TRICKLE-DOWN AND MULTIPLIER CONCEPTS

Compared to mixed economic systems, market economies operate on the initiatives of the private sector. Government plays a supporting role that is limited to establishing and applying the laws and prescribing the regulations and standards related to these laws. On occasion, government may sell government-owned land to the private sector for development. In advanced market economies, tourism development does not appear to be a primary focus of national governments. These economies are complex, and industries are highly diversified. As an overlapping economic sector, tourism plays an important role. In comparison with other growth sectors, however, it may not be a major contributor to the GDP of the economy. For example, in the United States, international tourism accounts for about 1% of GDP, while in France, which leads the world in international tourism, it accounts for only about 2% of GDP. For some regions of developed countries, however, tourism may be a major contributor to local economies. For some small island nations, tourism may account for almost all of GDP. In Palau, an island nation in the western Pacific Ocean, tourism accounts for 73% of GDP (as reported in the economic statistics of Nation Master.Com).

In a market economic system, government enacts and executes measures that embrace all aspects of life, and protects and enhances the safety, security, education, and health of its citizens and national treasures. These include infrastructure like roads, airports, seaports, and rail systems, as well as national parks, museums, and other structures that benefit the entire population. The performance of the economy, however, is left to the invisible hand of the market system and to the laws and regulations governing it.

Without enacting special measures for inducing tourism activities, government relies on the market system to find business opportunities and turn these opportunities into profitable business ventures. The benefits to the national economy depend on the success of entrepreneurs in developing tourism opportunities. These benefits include jobs created, taxes collected, gross income generated, foreign exchange earned, cultural exchange, and labor training. The benefits achieved by tourism development are felt at all levels, ranging from the national, regional, and local levels down to the firm and individual levels through what might be called the **trickle-down** process. Benefits from the trickle-down process follow the money trail. Money left behind by tourists filters up and down from the point where it is spent through economic transactions conducted with and between primary, secondary, and tertiary industries and establishments working in the tourism industry. In economic base theory, these are know as **multiplier effects**, which are jobs created and resulting government revenues collected by repeated spending of the initial money spent in the economy.

Trickle-down refers to the phenomenon of money amounts and profits getting smaller and smaller as transactions occur between richer, well-established, and favored organizations at the top of a money trail and smaller organizations at the bottom of a trail of transactions. The problem is that at each stage or level, those with the ability to do so deduct profits, fees, commissions, and so on until there is very little left for those at the bottom of the money trail. The reverse process is no better for those at the bottom. The prices of goods produced and services provided by them are added to with commissions, fees, and profits by those acting in the middle, and in fact getting the lion's share of the transaction, before it reaches those at the top.

Jobs created follow the same money trail. Additional labor is recruited by tourism establishments and their suppliers when the demand for goods and services increases. Employers of primary establishments create job opportunities in secondary and tertiary establishments that supply them with goods and services. For example, money spent by tourists in a lodging facility creates a second round of expenditures by the employees of the facility. In addition, the establishment has payroll taxes, real estate taxes, and fees to pay. Payments are also made for amortizing the construction loan and preopening expenses, administrative and operating expenditures for food and beverage supplies, telephones, electricity, water, and laundry. Going down the line, additional third-, fourth-, and fifth-round expenditures create income and jobs for accountants, attorneys, bankers, dairies, farmers, fishermen, porters, taxi drivers, bus drivers, travel agents, carpenters, painters, repairmen, wholesale suppliers, manufacturers, and members of other trades.

Prior to opening for business, new tourist-serving establishments contribute heavily to the local economy. These preopening expenditures include the cost of purchasing land, design fees of architects and engineers, construction material, furniture, fixture and equipment costs, construction contracting and labor costs, finance charges, license and permit fees, and local impact fees. Investment capital for covering these preopening and postoperating expenses comes from entrepreneurs within the country, sometimes in joint ventures with international investors.

8.2 THE PUSH AND PULL EFFECTS

In market systems, a push-pull effect of tourism occurs between institutions, their constituent members, and government. In developed economies, these institutions have diverse functional specializations. They include membership organizations like chambers of commerce, hotel/motel associations, restaurant owners' associations, travel agency associations, workers' unions, airline associations, marketing and advertising associations, convention and tourism associations, media associations, and others. The lobbying branches of these institutions exercise a degree of influence over government policy decisions about tourism. They lobby to promote their members' interests. The push-pull effect among the three parties—institutions, their constituents, and government— is the essence of how the market system works.

Collectively, the tourism marketing strategies used by national, regional, and local institutions for promoting and developing tourism can result in the government's finding itself compelled to support the growth and well-being of the industry. This push-pull process is known as the **politics of tourism,** in which the political influence exercised by one or another group is likely to achieve its intended result.

8.3 PRICING THE TOURISM PRODUCT

In market economic systems, pricing the tourism product is no different than pricing other products of the economy. Each line of business acts on its own in setting the price of its product or service based on its own operational performance and the prices of its competitors. One factor determined by the government may influence pricing. Business establishments must abide by operational and quality standards that government sets for preserving the health and comfort of the traveling public. For example, these standards establish the quality levels of services provided by five-star, four-star, and three-star hotels, restaurants, and other establishments. Unlike government-assisted economies, however, government in market systems does not set prices for these services. Airlines may offer seats in first-class, coach, and business sections at different prices. Cruise ships may offer package deals that might have different prices according to the location or amenities of cabins and suites. All tourist facilities may charge prices that may fluctuate according to the seasonal demand for their businesses and the current state of the overall economy. In market system economies, competition rules the market and sets prices.

8.4 GOVERNMENT INCENTIVES

Government may still offer incentives for developing tourism. These incentives may take the form of sponsoring special events; giving technical assistance grants to local public agencies for analyzing tourism potential and planning tourism development strategies; joint ventures with private sector organizations in funding major tourism facilities like convention centers; and granting tax and fee concessions for a period of time. Private entrepreneurs enhance their chances of securing loans by having the government back them. To minimize the risk to the lender, government acts as a guarantor and provides the security necessary for the lender to advance construction and other types of loans to the entrepreneur.

To encourage foreign ventures, the U.S. Government has established various funds for several developing regions of the world. The Russian-American Enterprise Fund and the Central Asian-American Enterprise Fund are two U.S. Government–sponsored funds that provide loans and incentives. To qualify, American entrepreneurs present information about their projects in detail and if the projects are accepted, they receive funding. American companies are encouraged to buy political risk insurance from government or private insurance companies to protect their investment against seizure, blockage, internal insecurity, or similar actions of the foreign government. More information about the Central Asian-American Enterprise can be found on the following Web site: http://www.caaef.com/. Western European countries like the United Kingdom, Germany, and France have their own incentive funds for foreign projects. In recent years, these incentive programs have been increasingly underfunded.

8.5 PRIVATE INITIATIVE, ENTREPRENEURSHIP, AND SMALL AND MEDIUM-SIZED TOURISM ENTERPRISES

Private initiative and entrepreneurship are at the foundation of market system economies. Individuals willing to assume financial risk and effort make the system work. Entrepreneurship is an acquired skill requiring gradual development of business acumen and building a track record to gain acceptance in the business community. Not everyone has the aptitude to become an entrepreneur and be successful at it. A large majority of business ventures fail soon after they start. It takes more than money and skill to succeed in business. Tourism development requires certain specialized factors beyond basic entrepreneurial skills.

A self-administered test of key personality traits for entrepreneurship includes:

- I am persistent, with a great deal of drive and stamina. I see problems as opportunities. I have good intuitive sense and thrive on new ideas.
- I tend to push back against authority. I want to be my own boss.
- I am positive, communicate well, and enjoy working with people.
- I have a strong need to succeed, financially and otherwise.
- I am not afraid to make mistakes, and I learn from them.

It is wise to talk to experienced entrepreneurs who know the business subject intimately. It is safest to start a new business after conducting extensive research and making calculations based on that research. Who are the customers, investors, promoters, and suppliers? How much money is necessary for setting up the business? Where one can find the start-up capital?

A great idea may not be sufficient. The performance of a competitor is a good indication of whether the product or service will be of value to customers. Knowing the competitor's strengths and weaknesses indicates how much better or worse one's product or service will be. Having a good business plan allows the emerging entrepreneur to recognize the problems that may be encountered and prepare for corrective actions. The plan should be flexible. It may need to be adjusted to meet new circumstances and updated as the business evolves. The ability to change direction, find alternative ways of solving problems, and take advantage of opportunities are keys to success.

Promoting the business is important for gaining customer acceptance and for broadening the client base. It also helps to get the attention of investors and potential partners. Success comes to those who have the ability to network with potential customers, suppliers, and investors. It does not hurt to know government officials who would be instrumental in controlling various aspects of the business. Market research identifies what business opportunities exist. A marketing plan shows who the buyers are, and where and how they will be induced to buy the product or service.

The ability of the entrepreneur to manage budgets, business operations, and employees is critical. Anticipating future needs and providing for them in a timely fashion is a learned skill. However, avoiding excess is based on innate common sense. Spending lavishly for entertaining customers or decorating one's office with museum-quality antiques every six months are not wise moves for an emerging entrepreneur. Appearances are superficial. They must be backed by substance.

In starting a tourism business, there are several common mistakes that must be avoided:

- Starting the business as an equal partnership could lead to conflicts that may be difficult to resolve. Starting the business by having a controlling interest minimizes such conflicts.
- Beginning entrepreneurs may not have the managerial skills to cope with personality differences. Personality problems require gentle persuasion and reasonable compromise.
- Businesses may be started without adequate business planning and research. This could be an invitation to failure.
- Relying on a few customers could make the business vulnerable. When their businesses fail, one's business may fail with them.
- It is better to overestimate the required start-up capital than underestimate it. Cost control is helpful. When sales projections are not met, it is better to have reserve capital.
- Failure to admit mistakes could lead to losing the business altogether. One should admit the mistake, make adjustments, and move on. Underestimating the competition could lead to being overtaken by it. Good market research will help keep the business ahead of the competitors. The chances for business success improve when these common mistakes are avoided.

Government provides the effort and resources for improving private initiative and entrepreneurship. These two factors of sustainable development largely entail learned behaviors. For those who display key personality traits for entrepreneurship, the passage to a productive life in the tourism industry is easier. For others, help is necessary. In LDCs, government provides this assistance in the form of support for small and medium-sized tourism enterprises. This support involves providing the missing competitive advantage. Government contracts offer preferential treatment to small and medium-sized businesses by giving them grants, exempting them from fees, deferring taxes, and so on. Government assistance results in wider dissemination of the benefits from tourism in terms of jobs and income created. Against this positive impact, government assistance could generate a sense of entitlement among the receiving businesses and stifle the initiative for self-betterment.

8.6   SELECTING AND EVALUATING A TOURISM PROJECT

Selecting tourism projects for development in market economic systems calls for creative thinking, as well as knowledge of the market. Creative thinking is somewhat innate. It is not necessarily a learned trait. Innate intelligence allows the entrepreneur to determine how to use this largely natural gift productively. Knowledge of the market, however, comes only with experience, research, and development of the ability to read market signals.

Tourism development projects are grouped into two major categories: action measures and construction projects. Government and entrepreneurs initiate action measures for preparing the groundwork for construction projects. Action measures initiated by entrepreneurs include market research, feasibility studies, lobbying, financing, negotiation, acquisition, and permit application. Governments prepare laws, regulations, and incentives, give technical assistance when needed, and issue permits.

There are two kinds of tourism development projects involving construction: **attractions** and **facilities.** As explained in Chapter 3, attractions draw tourists by offering them a variety of recreational activities. The variety of activities and attractions around the world is enormous.

However, physical factors such as climate and environment, as well as cultural interests, limit the variety of a particular location. Facilities are primarily utilitarian.

For the entrepreneur, the motivation for selecting a project is the desire to make a profit. To determine the potential profit, the revenues and costs to the entrepreneur are compared with the capital invested. If government funds are needed for a project or some parts of it, the government will evaluate a project by analyzing its benefits and costs to the country. When projects are identified with positive benefit-cost analyses, including sufficient profits to assure continuation into the future, the project is deemed favorable. However, tourism projects compete with other types of projects for government funds. Tourism projects that require government funds must rate high enough among competing nontourism projects in benefit-cost analyses to be included in government budgets. If government funds are not required, then only the financial evaluation of the entrepreneur is the determinant.

The method of estimating the benefits, costs, and influence of a project on the economy includes both its construction and operation periods. The influence of the project may be direct or indirect. The direct effects consist of immediate contributions to production in the tourism sector, in particular where there is underused capacity. The indirect effects are those accruing to the economic sectors having vertical or horizontal connections with the tourism sector. As mentioned, tourism investment projects are evaluated in combination with the benefits and costs of other projects in the same area.

Assuming that an enterprise specializes in one type of business where its experience and its chances for making sizable profits are greatest, projects will be concentrated in that line of work. Market research narrows the options for project location and competition. It provides initial information necessary for preparing more in-depth studies. To illustrate, a company specializing in a certain type and quality of overnight accommodation initiates a hotel project. Its market research gives the company the information it needs for expanding its operations. Confirmation comes from the feasibility study that verifies the financial desirability of opening another hotel at a location where the competition, market share, and other factors indicate that the venture will be profitable.

Governments also own and operate attraction projects. National parks and historic sites are prime examples. Market considerations are sometimes not as important in government projects. Government is not in the business of making profits. But operating losses are not welcome either if they can be avoided. Government-owned attractions provide services considered to be in the best interests of the public, including preserving the heritage of the country and showcasing its natural features. Different criteria are used for selecting government projects where social benefits override financial benefits in importance.

Government-owned and -operated tourist facilities are primarily utilitarian. They include infrastructure projects that serve not only the tourism industry but also national and regional economies. From dams, power plants, highways, and rail lines to port facilities, national, regional, and local priorities determine the need for such multipurpose facilities. If developing tourism is one of these priorities, the facility is justified on its merits. For example, surface water resource projects that are undertaken primarily to generate electricity, improve navigation, and control floods usually have considerable recreational benefits and can be counted as tourist attractions.

It is appropriate to conclude this section on selecting tourism development projects with an anecdote that illustrates the importance of project selection. The anecdote was presented in an American television program and pertains to a country in central Africa where many tributary rivers are the breeding grounds for the famous Nile crocodile. In the recent past, an entrepreneur from a country in Western Europe visited the minister of the country who was in charge of national parks and tourism and offered to capture and display a very large crocodile that was terrorizing several villages. He had in mind a zoological tourist attraction for drawing tourists to that economically poor region of the country.

Reportedly, the crocodile mauled eighteen anglers on the shores of the river. The minister set a deadline of one month, and made available the services and resources of the government and villagers in the area. The entrepreneur scouted the beast, named Gustave, and found it enjoying its dominance over other living creatures on the river. It was about twenty feet (six meters) long and was estimated to be about sixty years old. It was the heaviest and longest crocodile ever encountered in the country. Having seen the beast, the entrepreneur decided that a special cage and a protected retaining pond would have to be built. He proceeded to build a steel cage more than twenty feet long with the help of a village metalsmith from scrap metals that the villagers foraged from various sources. In the meantime, villagers dug a well to fill the retaining pond with water. Bringing water from the river was not an option. The retaining pond measured approximately fifty by fifty feet (fifteen by fifteen meters).Villagers built a wall with stones quarried and carried manually to contain the pond. They paved the bottom of the pond with cement hauled manually from the city. When the cage was ready, it was carried manually about a mile along the shore of the river to the place where Gustave was last seen. The entrepreneur having provided technical know-how and villagers having contributed labor and material to the venture, the trap was ready for capturing the beast and turning it into a major tourist attraction and an economic asset.

The plan, however, had one major flaw. No one had informed the crocodile that it was supposed to enter the cage and be captured. With the cage door open on the riverbank, several days and nights passed. Time was running short; a month elapsed; desperate measures were needed. First, a live chicken placed in the cage was offered as bait to a monstrous animal that devoured humans and cows for lunch! The bait was upgraded to a live goat the next night. Again, there was no taker. The third night, a monsoon-sized storm hit the area; the river rose on its banks and carried away everything in its path, including the cage. It was found empty and half buried in the mud 1 mile downstream. The entire project had to be abandoned.

The moral of this true story is that foreign entrepreneurs and government officials should be very careful about gauging the success of a proposed tourism venture and not waste meager and scarce resources, energy, and the goodwill of the local population by pursuing ill-conceived projects. The common wisdom of the local population dictated that they obey government officials and the village elders by dedicating their collective labor and hoping for a flourishing tourism economy in their area. But a poorly chosen and executed tourism project dashed their hope and set back the economy of their village.

The follow-up to the story is that the villagers found other uses for the pond and the cage and salvaged, at least partly, their investment. At the last report (July 2009), Gustave was still at large and was sixty-five years old, with three bullet holes in his body.

8.7 MARKET RESEARCH, FEASIBILITY STUDY, AND BUSINESS PLAN

Conducting market research and preparing a feasibility study are two initial steps in the process of preparing a business plan. The techniques may differ from one type of business or project to another. In the context of tourism, the nature and location of the business or project determine the information to be collected and researched. The distinction lies in whether the venture is a new start-up tourism business or a new project to be built and operated by an existing tourism business at a specific site. The content of the document also depends on who the sponsor and beneficiary of the research is. If the document is for the exclusive use of the entrepreneur who commissioned it, the content will focus on the factors that will most likely make or break the proposed venture. If the document is for raising funds, it will follow the format demanded by financial institutions and will focus on the financial profitability and security of the investment. Preferably, a third-party consultant who has a track record and credibility in the opinion of the lender or investor should prepare the business plan.

For example, a typical international hotel project proposed for development by a multinational hotel development and management company in a joint venture with local investors may contain the following market, building, and financial feasibility information. This information is contained in the **Financial Feasibility Plan:**

- **Background and Objectives of the Owner**
- **Market characteristics**
  - Location and site of the proposed hotel
  - Tourism market demand, volume, and probable market share
  - Existing competition
  - Recommended size and type of the hotel
  - Marketing and pricing of the hotel
- **Preliminary architectural and site development plans**
  - Proposed building program, and applicable zoning and building regulations
  - Proposed site plan and parking
  - Proposed architectural and interior design of the building
  - Furniture, fixtures and equipment
  - Government incentives, if any
- **Operations plan and schedule**
  - Project design and construction team
  - Project management team
  - Hotel franchising company, if any
  - Project organization for design, construction, and management
  - Staffing and training
  - Schedule of financing, permitting, franchising, design, and construction
- **Critical risk analysis**
  - Cycles in tourism emphasizing possible downturns
  - Price cutting by competition
  - Delays in financing, permitting, design, and construction
  - Political liability and expropriation risks
- **Financial plan and feasibility**
  - Operational assumptions and ratios
  - Development and construction cost estimates
  - Pro forma financial analysis for five and ten years
    - Room occupancy projections
    - Operating revenue projections
    - Operating expense projections
    - Cash flow projections
  - Equity and debt financing assumptions
  - Incentives, loan origination fees, and other closing costs
  - Strategy for repayment of the construction loan and the permanent loan
  - Return on equity investment
- **Attachments:** Exhibits, photographs, maps, preliminary architectural and site plans

Concurrently, the **Business Plan,** which presents operational information that describes the implementation aspects of the project, begins to emerge. It is prepared in support of the Financial Feasibility Plan for seeking financing and for measuring the proposed progress made in reaching the plan's aims. The Business Plan normally consists of three parts:

- The operations plan shows the technology to be used, production process to be followed, materials to be purchased, and their delivery dates.
- The marketing plan shows how the market demand will be satisfied.
- The financial plan, which provides more detail than the initial Financial Feasibility Plan, estimates the fixed and variable costs of production and operation, pricing, revenues, gross and net profits, equity and debt financing.

The advantages of having a Business Plan are many:

- It helps measure performance.
- It gives guidance and direction to managers.
- It helps attract investors and secure financing.

There could be disadvantages if the study is not done properly:

- It has to be honest and realistic.
- It has to be written for the reader, not for the writer, avoiding overly technical language and incomplete explanations.
- It has to be flexible and adjusted to new circumstances.

8.8   MARKETING PLAN AND PROJECT PROMOTION

In competitive free-market economic systems, organizations that make and sell products are hard at work to prove the superiority of their product over those of others. Their financial success depends largely on their success in marketing and promoting their product.

Promoting a particular tourism product, whether it is a single attraction or facility or the combined tourism product of a city, region, or country, requires meticulous preparation. All organizations operating in a complex market environment must consider all external and internal factors that may affect the achievement of their marketing objectives.

Marketing planning produces two types of **marketing plans**. As a managerial process, it is a succession of steps leading to the setting and achievement of marketing objectives. The process includes two phases: the **Strategic Marketing Plan** and the **Tactical Marketing Plan**.

The Strategic Marketing Plan

The Strategic Marketing Plan is prepared for three or more years. It is prepared for the owner for the purpose of comparing the market position of the owner's product with its competition. The document defines the competitive advantage of the product, the strategy to be followed for achieving market superiority, and resources necessary for it.

The contents of the Strategic Marketing Plan include:

- *Mission statement.* It describes the subject, its future, and the purpose of marketing.
- *Financial summary.* It summarizes the financial profile of the marketing plan.
- *Market overview.* It describes market characteristics, trends, and structure.
- *Strengths, Weaknesses, Opportunities, and Threats (SWOT) analysis.* It describes strengths, weaknesses, organization, and threats that may characterize or be related to a

tourism project. It is a common business analysis procedure and is described on the following two Web sites: http://marketingteacher.com/Lessons/lesson_swot.htm and http://en.wikipedia.org/wiki/Swot_analysis.

- *Issues.* It describes the issues to be addressed derived from a SWOT analysis.
- *Portfolio summary.* It presents in graphic matrix form the strengths and weaknesses of a tourism project.
- *Assumptions.* It lists the standards and accepted norms for the marketing strategy.
- *Marketing objectives.* It states the quantified financial objectives to be achieved.
- *Marketing strategies.* It states how the objectives are to be achieved.
- *Resources needed.* It lists the resources (money, personnel, etc.) needed.

The Tactical Marketing Plan

The Tactical Marketing Plan is concerned with the marketing activities of all parties during the first year of operation. The plan is revised in the second and third years based on feedback information received at the end of previous periods. The activities are detailed and scheduled. A budget is prepared for money committed to various marketing activities.

The Tactical Marketing Plan does not repeat the information contained in the Strategic Marketing Plan. The mission statement, market overview, and SWOT analysis are not included. Other sections present detailed and specific marketing information for achieving the stated objectives for the first year. In larger organizations, the process of marketing is well structured and formalized. In smaller organizations, it is less formal. But the basic marketing steps remain the same in both.

The government plays an important role in marketing the tourism product. It prepares and implements its own marketing strategy and Tactical Marketing Plan for promoting the tourism products of the country, their various destination regions, and major public tourist attractions. The private sector does the rest. Marketing tools include advertising on television, radio, documentaries, and, increasingly, the Internet. The national agency in charge of tourism development, often at the ministerial level, may open tourism promotion and information offices in their target market countries abroad. These offices are closer to the traveling public and travel agencies that organize their tours. They distribute many kinds of promotional literature and assist potential tourists with their travel plans. They also engage in direct marketing by using mailing companies for promoting specialized tourism for targeted travelers. They distribute brochures and pamphlets to hotels, bus and rail terminals, airports, marinas, and chambers of commerce. They locate computer-operated tourism information equipment at high-traffic locations. They act as liaison between market and host countries.

8.9   BUILDING, MAINTAINING, AND OPERATING TOURISM INFRASTRUCTURE

By definition, tourism infrastructure facilitates tourism. Infrastructure is primarily utilitarian. It constitutes the basic facilities that must be present to have a functioning tourism industry. It provides basic services that any national, regional, and local government strives to provide for its citizens for their everyday needs. Both international and domestic tourists use these services.

Tourism infrastructure facilities and services include:

- *Transportation system.* Commercial seaports and terminals; airports; airlines; trains; railroad systems and terminals; marinas; local roads; arterial highways, parking facilities, bridges; tunnels; bus lines; and streetcar lines.

- *Power system.* Power generation plants and their power distribution systems.
- *Utility system.* Sewer and water treatment, storage, distribution, and collection systems.
- *Communication system.* Landline and cable telephone systems; cellular telephone systems; television and radio systems; e-mail; airmail and ground mail facilities and services; parcel post delivery services; and the Internet.
- *Banking system.* Commercial banks and investment banks.
- *Health system.* Hospitals, emergency clinics; pharmacies; physicians; dentists and nurses.
- *Security system.* Police; private security services; national guard and other military services.

Depending on the complexity of the economic system in which the tourism sector operates, these infrastructure systems and their facilities are built, owned, and operated by national, regional, or local governments. Alternatively, they may be largely privatized and operated by the private sector. In either case, their availability provides the level of comfort, convenience, and security necessary for a functioning tourism economy.

At a minimum, the traveling public must feel secure in the knowledge that these basic services are available when they are needed. Often, perception rather than reality may raise an issue. Hazardous locations and remote areas always cause concern. Tourists acknowledge and accept these concerns as safety challenges when engaging in risky adventure tourism.

8.10 WHO ESTABLISHES THE GROUND RULES FOR TOURISM DEVELOPMENT?

In complex market economic systems, the invisible hand of the market is largely responsible for determining where the demand is, or can be created, and how to act in order to satisfy that demand profitably. In developing tourism, market economic systems do not rely on comprehensive tourism plans at national or lower levels. Local convention and tourism bureaus establish policies and strategies for marketing, advertising, and promoting the tourism product. These policies and strategies are the primary mechanisms for reaching the goals of local tourism development. Occasionally, the lobbying arm of the tourism industry asks the national government to consider new legislation, or enact an executive order or administrative regulation, to resolve a problem that might have industrywide implications.

By comparison, centrally planned economies rely on government action to formulate and execute all national, regional, and local policies, programs, plans, projects, and measures for developing tourism. Because the centrally planned economy is a command system, the powers of central government originate from the top echelon of the administration. All ideas and actions, for better or worse, come from high-level authorities. They filter down through the command system, and as they do, their effectiveness diminishes. When a rare entrepreneur from a foreign country is interested in developing a tourism project, or organizing an educational conference for example, he or she has to go through the bureaucracy of the command system at every level, from top to bottom, to receive permission. In these situations, the entrepreneur is well advised to study closely the laws and regulations of the land before engaging in the venture.

Between market and centrally planned systems are mixed economic systems. In these systems, the government and the private sector engage in mutually supportive actions in developing tourism. The national government makes national policies, sets budgets, establishes marketing strategies, passes laws and makes regulations, and builds and operates basic infrastructure. As the economy develops, the private sector takes an increasingly active role and assumes many functions traditionally assumed by the government. Through this evolution, gradual privatization brings efficiency to operations and improves services to tourists.

Excesses are not uncommon in all three types of economic systems. Overbuilding tourism facilities intended to maximize profit, building unwanted facilities, and building facilities at the wrong locations degrade the environmental quality of tourism destinations, and as a result, tourism suffers. Sustainability is a goal common to all three systems for avoiding excesses.

8.11   IMPORT CONTENT

In open economies where market systems are not constrained by restrictive laws and practices, tourism could become a stellar growth sector and a pass-through channel for economic benefits and costs. The tourism sector may receive very large revenues from international and domestic tourists. The sector may multiply these revenues several times over by creating additional revenues in sectors connected with tourism. On the expenditures side of national accounts, imports of material, equipment, and foreign labor used in the tourism sector can be extensive. Repatriation of profits, interest payments to foreign lenders, payments to foreign suppliers and contractors, and finally, repatriation of investment principal can diminish the luster of the tourism sector. In the final analysis, residual benefits, after all foreign payments and transfers are made, may turn out to be negligible. Negotiations at the beginning of such ventures are key to preventing such an outcome.

The import content of the tourism sector, and its projects, is critical in appraising the contribution of tourism to the economy of the country and its regions. Various economic research techniques are available for this purpose. The input-output study is one of them. The technique is presented in Chapter 16 of this book. Economic leakage is a major negative factor if the import content of the tourism sector is high. The impact of this negative factor is compounded if the country or region does not have a plan for import substitution. Building materials, hotel equipment, and furniture are among the items substituted first with comparable items produced locally. New jobs thus created in the local economy help reduce the capital outflow caused by payments for imported items. However, the jobs created locally may not be of the quantity and quality sufficient for offsetting the losses caused by excessive capital outflow. Again, early negotiations are critical.

One way of compensating the local economy for economic leakage is lending or reinvesting the money generated in the community back into the community. The role of commercial financial institutions in compensating for economic leakage is important. In the United States, a federal law called the Community Reinvestment Act (CRA) requires each federal financial supervisory agency to use its authority to review the records of its member banks and lending institutions in meeting the credit needs, and reinvestment of its deposits, in the community. The review procedure includes three **performance tests:**

- Lending test
- Investment test
- Service test

The review also determines five **performance levels**:

- Outstanding
- High satisfactory
- Low satisfactory
- Needs to improve
- Substantial noncompliance

The types of loans and reinvestment made include:

- One- to four-family residential unit loans
- Five-family or more residential unit loans
- Nonresidential mortgages
- Land loans
- Commercial loans
- Consumer loans
- Investments
- U.S. Government and agency securities
- Mortgage-backed securities
- Mortgage derivative securities
- Other securities

The supervisory agency reviews all branch offices of banks, and other financial institutions, owned and operated by the same organization located within a definable area. In this case, counties of a state are the smallest geographic areas used. While the CRA has broader aims than reducing economic leakage caused by tourism development, its principles can be used to reduce leakage from local economies by creating reinvestment opportunities in the region.

Note: The shrinkage of the world economy in late 2008 has caused a review of all these and other practices and standards. The world's financial leaders have proposed many initiatives to restore economic order. Some of the basic conditions for market economies, especially those involving lending, may be substantially altered. This may change somewhat the way tourist attractions and facilities are financed in the future. In the short term, worsened economic conditions have reduced the demand for tourism, a situation that is expected to be corrected when economic conditions are normalized.

Chapter Highlights

- The tourism market is subjected to the same trickle-down, multiplier, and push-pull effects as the economy in free-market systems. Tourism is most sensitive to these effects. It is one of the early indicators of an economic downturn because it involves discretionary spending.
- Starting a new tourism business is subject to all the ups and downs of any business in market-driven economies.

- A Financial Feasibility Plan and a Marketing Plan must be used to determine the feasibility of tourism projects. Business Plans, Strategic Plans and Tactical Plans elaborate on the Marketing Plan.

9

Government Policies and Legislation for Tourism Development

This chapter describes the types of policies adopted and legislation enacted by governments for encouraging and guiding tourism development in mixed economic systems.

- Governments enact laws and regulations to prepare the groundwork for growth.
- Foreign investment is encouraged by giving incentives in selected regions.
- Procedures for investing in tourism projects apply to both government and the private sector.
- Certain important government and privately owned lands are protected in perpetuity. They include waterfront, military, and historic properties.
- Regulations concerning building and operating tourist facilities are extensive.
- Legal actions taken by governments for tourism are available from the UNWTO. The system is called LEXTOUR.
- Security and terrorism are two principal issues in tourism development regulations.

9.1 THE ROLES OF GOVERNMENT AND THE PRIVATE SECTOR

Many issues demand resolution and guidance from the government in mixed economic systems for developing tourism. The instruments necessary for the growth of the tourism industry are largely controlled by the government. This role grows in importance where the economy is simple and where a private sector for tourism is newly emerging.

Linkages among the industries that supply tourism with basic products and services can be established with government assistance. Most needed products and services are initially imported to meet international hospitality standards. As a nation's tourism economy grows, government supports the substitution of imported materials and equipment by those produced by domestic industries. To achieve it, government sometimes raises trade barriers to foreign competition and creates competitive advantages for local industries. Gradually, government ends this preferential treatment and encourages competition with international markets. During these later stages, linkages between primary, secondary, and tertiary industries grow stronger and tourism becomes a larger, more complex economic sector.

In the absence of technical capabilities at the local level, the central government in mixed economic systems assumes the responsibility for estimating the potential benefits and costs of developing tourism and determining its sustainability. This exercise may even require technical help from international organizations. Among the issues to be resolved are where and how to develop tourism in the regions of the country and how to establish targets against which the performance of an emerging tourism sector can be measured. Among these targets, gross foreign exchange earnings from international tourism is key for the national economy. Based on the draw and the competitive position of the country, government estimates the market share and foreign exchange earnings from tourism.

Foreign exchange earnings invested in tourism may help governments increase revenues from taxation and fees charged to tourism establishments. Property taxes paid at the municipal level, and state and federal corporate income taxes paid at the state and national levels by tourism businesses, are substantial. In the United States, hotel room taxes and fees paid to municipal governments could average around 5% of gross hotel revenues. Corporate taxes paid by tourism establishments to state governments could exceed 10% of their net taxable income, and corporate taxes paid to the federal government could exceed 30% of their net taxable income. Tax rates vary from state to state and from country to country.

The performance of a country's economy, measured in terms of GDP or GNP, helps its government determine a target share and productivity goals for its tourism sector. Depending on the complexity of a national economy, the anticipated share of the tourism sector could be large or small. In developing economies, tourism could be the most productive growth sector and have a large share. In geographically isolated countries where environmental conditions are favorable but other industries are not promising, tourism may remain the only growth sector for decades. Island countries are particularly sensitive. Their environment, culture, and way of life may be their only resource, and hope, for maintaining reasonable living standards. Developing tourism may be their only path to consequential economic growth. Examples are Palau in the western Pacific Ocean, where tourism accounts for 73% of GDP; Macao, a special administrative region of China, located on a peninsula and islands off the coast of China (67%); Aruba in the Caribbean (43%); the Seychelles in the Indian Ocean (39%); the Cayman Islands in the Caribbean (36%); and the Bahamas in the Atlantic Ocean (32%).

9.2 GOVERNMENT INCENTIVES FOR DEVELOPING TOURISM

Governments may enact new laws for encouraging tourism development. Legislation that encourages foreign investment is particularly important. This legislation gives foreign investors and lenders the guarantees they need for investing in tourism projects. The purpose of tourism incentive legislation is to create the conditions necessary for organizing, developing, and operating a successful tourism sector. An example from Barbados is given on the following Web site: http://www.barbadostourisminvestment.com/legislation_and_incentives.cfm.

Various laws have different conditions and characteristics for creating favorable impacts at the national, regional, and destination levels. They include the following principles:

- Investments must be beneficial to the development of the country.
- Investments are possible in any business sector. Foreign investors can share ownership with local partners, except where monopoly rights prohibit majority ownership for foreign investors.

- Foreign-sourced investment can take several forms:
  - Initial cash investment
  - Machinery, equipment, and other hardware
  - The cash values of licenses, copyrights, patents, and other intellectual properties
- Investment capital can be reinvested or repatriated.
  - Profits from previous operations can be reinvested in existing or new projects.
  - Profits in foreign currency can be repatriated based on current exchange rates.
  - The initial cash investment and interest can be repatriated after the sale of a business.
- Foreign ownership shares are guaranteed, transferable, and negotiable in world markets.
- Foreign personnel necessary for planning, constructing, and operating projects can be contracted with for a specific period. They can transfer their earnings to other countries.
- All civil and commercial laws, regulations, and rights applicable to native citizens are applicable on an equal basis to foreign businesses and citizens employed in projects.

In general, governments have multiple economic development objectives in promoting foreign investment in tourism projects. They want to reduce the differences in the economic welfare of regions, improve their competitive strength, create jobs, and invest in high-value-added projects consistent with national development goals. Foreign investment may be the best alternative for achieving all of these objectives.

Orderly growth of tourism depends on productive investment and operations at locations with the potential to attract large numbers of tourists. This calls for selective planning and development. Government selects the areas where tourism potentials exist and where government incentives will be productive. These areas represent five levels of economic activity:

- *Tourism establishment:* A commercial attraction or facility at one location owned and operated by an individual owner or a corporation
- *Tourism destination:* One or more tourism establishments within a tourism area
- *Tourism area:* One or more tourism destinations within a tourism region
- *Tourism region:* A distinct social-economic-geographic area of the country selected for tourism development
- *The nation:* All areas within the national borders harboring the national tourism product

Tourism regions, areas, and destinations are selected for their environmental, historical, archeological, sociocultural, and other tourism characteristics. Establishments are the smallest units and are at the base of this hierarchy. To benefit from the incentive laws, an establishment must qualify for an investment license and an operating license. These licenses are renewable at the end of their license period. Governments can extend the license period several times.

The highest tourism authority of the country coordinates the implementation of tourism incentive legislation. Government investment goes first to tourism areas, second to tourism destinations, third to tourism regions, and fourth to projects approved by the government for development outside tourism regions.

Government-funded tourism projects are scheduled by program and budget years according to their order of priority. Governments can apply for and receive loans on credit from foreign sources. These foreign-sourced loans are subject to the same terms specified by regulations governing loan requests by governments for other projects.

Government-owned land may be extensive in designated areas, regions, and destinations. Tourism-related projects proposed on these lands are eligible to receive an investment license when they are beneficial to the public. They should conform to the provisions of regional and local land use plans, zoning regulations, and building regulations. Sustainable tourism development protects natural and human-made environments. It gives highest priority to tourism projects planned on government land. In particular, it protects seashores, lakes, and riverfronts from indiscriminate and inappropriate development as well as overdevelopment. For example, government regulations often prohibit sand, gravel, and stone from being removed from these areas and used as building materials.

Private developers submit their plans to appropriate government agencies for all projects located within designated tourism destinations for review, revision, or denial. Outside of designated destination areas, private developers apply for a special permit when their proposed projects qualify for government incentives. These projects are evaluated independently.

Government agencies at local, regional, and national levels coordinate, review, and approve all tourism development projects. National tourism development authorities determine all the financial arrangements necessary for leasing, assigning, and permitting the use of government-owned land by foreign and domestic private developers. They include fees, a schedule of rental payments, rights and obligations of parties, conditions, and access to government infrastructure.

Government is responsible for expediting financing, planning, and constructing infrastructure, like roads and water, sewer, electricity, and telecommunication systems, in designated tourism areas and destinations. No funds allocated to building priority infrastructure projects can be diverted to other uses without the consent of national tourism development authorities. This provision of the law provides assurance to private developers that government will be held accountable for meeting public infrastructure construction schedules.

9.3 LEGISLATION AND REGULATIONS FOR LICENSING TOURISM PROJECTS

Except in market economies, government sets prices for certain elements of the tourism product. Every tourism establishment given a license to operate a tourist facility submits a price list to the government every year. When an establishment overcharges customers, penalties are levied. In practice, this provision of the law is often ignored or updated frequently because of changing economic conditions and inflation.

Transferring the rights to operate a licensed tourism establishment, or to sublease a facility to a third party, is subject to the approval of the licensing authority. All licensed tourism establishments are required to report their performance during the past six months to the authorities. This includes room occupancy ratios, average tourist expenditures, nationality of visitors, and length of stay. Governments use this information for compiling tourism statistics.

Government-owned utilities like water, sewer, gas, and telecommunication systems are extended to service licensed tourism projects. A special fee is charged for these services.

Under certain conditions, licensed tourism establishments can employ essential foreign staff and entertainers. Foreign personnel can earn and transfer their earnings freely to other countries after converting local money into the foreign currency of their choice. However, the ratio of foreign personnel to native-born personnel cannot exceed certain limits. Usually, a range of 10–20% is the norm. Employment of underage personnel in licensed establishments is generally prohibited by child labor laws.

Selling alcoholic beverages could be a major issue in Islamic countries, where cultural prohibitions forbid consumption of alcohol. Special regulations may apply in major tourist hotels, where selling such beverages to foreign visitors who consume them on the premises is usually permitted. Liquor stores do not exist in these countries. Other retail outlets, including supermarkets and restaurants, are forbidden to sell alcoholic beverages. The strictness of the laws and the degree of enforcement vary among Islamic countries. Such prohibitions do not apply in the rest of the world. However, drinking alcoholic beverages by underage customers is not allowed anywhere. All countries require a license for liquor stores, restaurants, and bars. Consuming alcoholic beverages and intoxication in public areas are not generally tolerated anywhere.

Under the provisions of tourism development laws, governments may exercise their right to identify and control strategic real properties in tourism development zones. These properties include those that are both privately owned and government owned. Historic sites, ruins, scenic areas, beaches, forests, and environmentally sensitive areas are among those properties. They are identified and surveyed. Their ownership is verified, and legally acceptable maps are prepared and recorded at the registry of deeds office. Henceforth, these properties are under government protection. Governments accept applications for licensing tourism operations in these protected areas. Proposed uses must be consistent with the intent of master development plans prepared by the tourism development authority. Sometimes the military owns large chunks of land in strategic areas. These areas are off limits.

Government tourism development authorities periodically review requests for assigning various jurisdictions and regulations to land, and for deciding which properties will be protected and designated for various regulations. Governments also periodically review applications of various organizations to use government land. In evaluating these applications, governments give preference to organizations that have international experience and the capacity for building, marketing, and operating projects on protected land. Adaptive reuse and recycling of protected historic buildings and archeological areas are subject to other special regulations.

Both private investors and government institutions may apply for building tourist-serving facilities and tourism infrastructure, like roads and utilities, on protected land. Allocation takes the form of leases as long as forty-nine years. The terms of these leases include the condition that the value of proposed projects shall not be less than a fixed percentage of the value of the government property. This proportion could vary between 10% and 20%. The amount of the annual lease could be as low as 5% of the value of assigned property. But the lease may have an annual escalation clause. Other fees can be deferred. In cases where the lessee is unable or unwilling to continue with the proposed improvement, the government is empowered to cancel the lease and reclaim the property. It can also ask for restitution. At the end of the lease period, the government generally can extend the lease or reassign the property to others.

Gambling is subject to strict regulations. In well-known international tourism destinations like Macao, Las Vegas, and Monte Carlo, where all forms of gambling thrive, local gaming commissions regulate the licensing and operations of these establishments. Gambling is allowed on cruise ships when they are sailing in international waters. Ships are required to close their casinos when they enter the territorial waters of countries where gambling establishments are forbidden. Sovereignty is an issue in permitting gambling licenses. In the United States, federal laws allow sovereign Native American tribes to open and operate gambling casinos. Many of them have thriving gambling establishments. In some countries, only visitors carrying foreign passports are permitted to enter licensed gambling establishments.

Regulations for yachting include provisions for encouraging the orderly growth of yachting tourism. Yachts are classified as sailing yachts, motor yachts, and mixed-power yachts. Provisions include approved locations for marinas; designing, building, and operating yacht ports, or marinas; and regulations governing yachts carrying foreign flags—their sailing, docking, and length of stay at ports.

Yacht-related regulations also include detailed physical requirements for designing and building port facilities, marine infrastructure, and marine superstructure. They specify the responsibilities of the harbormaster. They cover licensing requirements for operating facilities, yacht ownership, and bareboat or crewed boat leasing for recreational and tourism purposes.

They allow boats carrying foreign flags to be leased, operated, and moored at licensed ports for several years. If a native yachting establishment is operating with foreign-owned yachts, the yachts are allowed to hoist the flag of the host country. Yachting establishments are required to report their foreign exchange earnings from their yachting business to the government annually.

Foreign-owned yachts may be subject to additional conditions. In some situations, yachts cannot be leased for less than two months. Foreign yacht owners must guarantee that the foreign exchange collected will be a government-established multiple of the owner's net transferable earnings. The owner can contribute to a Tourism Development Fund, if it exists, when his or her yacht is wintering in port. The fund usually accepts only voluntary donations.

Yachts are leased with or without a crew. According to international maritime laws, yachts weighing less than one hundred gross tons and accommodating fewer than twelve passengers can be leased without a crew. Larger yachts with accommodations for more than twelve passengers must carry a crew. These regulations apply equally to foreign-owned and locally owned yachts. Nations have different requirements for operating yachts. For example, in the United States, the Coast Guard issues captain's and other seaman's licenses and certifications by examination, and with a review of a number of conditions including size of vessel, number of paying passengers to be carried, waters to be navigated and length of experience at sea.

Waterfronts are major draws for tourism. Seashores, lake fronts, and riverbeds are attractions that need protection. Regulations controlling waterfronts are strict to ensure sustainability of the natural environment and tourism. In general, governments control the uses of waterfronts. They specify permissible public uses and often give the highest priority to recreational use, although conflicts often arise when the waterfront is needed for commercial and transportation uses. Such conflicts usually occur in established port cities, although they can develop where new commercial ports are proposed in previously undeveloped waterfronts.

Protected waterfront consists of a shore ribbon that can be more than one hundred fifty feet wide between the setback line and the high-tide waterline. This is the minimum setback enforced for all structures and buildings. Walls, fences, pilings, and similar structures are not allowed in this ribbon, except by special permission. Waterfronts cannot be used for extracting sand, gravel, coral, and stone. The contours of the waterfront cannot be changed by grading, building ditches, or the like. Dumping building materials, garbage, and fill is not allowed. Coastal zone management provisions in some countries are quite strict.

Provided that the proposed use is consistent with the intent of the law and the owner secures appropriate permits, water-oriented structures may be permitted on the waterfront. They include piers, marinas, bridges, boathouses, pump houses, and boat landing and camp facilities for tourists. Major industrial facilities like shipyards, oceanographic institutions, and aquaculture facilities are subject to special permits. Filling or draining waterfronts can be permitted for government public purpose projects that meet the provisions of approved regional development plans. As mentioned, the use of waterfront property can be very controversial, especially where recreational or residential uses threaten to displace traditional port or industrial and commercial uses. Governments often prepare plans and adopt policies that allocate scarce waterfront land to each competing use. Tourism development is usually part of such plans and policies.

9.4   GUIDELINES FOR SECURITY AND ANTITERRORISM

September 11, 2001, entered the history books as a date of carnage and assault on civilization, and on the people of New York City and the Washington, D.C. area. Prior to that date, many acts of violence had taken place in airplanes, ships, trains, and other modes of transportation. Hotels, restaurants, nightclubs, and airports where tourists congregated were particularly vulnerable.

Every country affected by international terrorism has taken extensive legal and security actions to counteract terrorism. Since 1997, the United Nations has passed many resolutions dealing with terrorism. The international community has condemned all acts, methods, and practices of terrorism as criminal and unjustifiable, regardless of the motivation. Terrorism has been recognized as a blatant human rights violation.

Condemnation led to action. The international community made full use of the means already in place and bolstered them further by establishing an effective system that will deny terrorists their objectives. Resolution 1373 of the United Nations Security Council adopted on September 28, 2001, was hailed as a major step toward fighting terrorism. Its objective was to find the sources that financed terrorism and to eliminate all direct and indirect support for it.

The agenda included the following measures:

- All countries will become party to conventions and protocols for combating terrorism.
- A comprehensive report will identify the causes of terrorism.
- Bilateral, regional, and multilateral antiterrorism laws, agreements, and practices will be enforced.
- Safe havens will be denied to terrorists and their supporters.
- Perpetrators will be apprehended, prosecuted, condemned to the extent of local laws, or extradited to countries having a claim to prosecute terrorists and their supporters.
- Political motivation will be repudiated as grounds for terrorism.
- Terrorism will be recognized as contrary to the principles of the United Nations.
- An International Criminal Court will be set up to adjudicate serious terrorism crimes.

In addition to international organizations, certain countries, including the United States, took strict antiterrorism measures to protect their citizens. They recommended certain measures for traveling individuals.

- **Guard information about yourself.**
  - After needed use, destroy all items that show your name, occupation, residence, contact information, or other personal identification.
  - Instruct your family and associates not to provide strangers with information about the family.
  - Be cautious about giving out information regarding family travel plans, security measures, and procedures.
  - If it is allowed, consider removing your name, title, and occupation on your IDs.
  - Avoid using your name, citizenship, other personal information, and occupation on answering machines.
- **Establish telephone security.**
  - If you receive a threatening phone call or bomb threat, call the authorities.
  - If possible, have the call traced and report it to the authorities.
- **Guard information about yourself and your activities**.
  - Limit discussion and accessibility of any information that may provide terrorists with insights for targeting.
  - Always use secure means when passing sensitive information.
  - After use, destroy identifiable information.
- **Recognize and report unusual or suspicious behavior.**
  - Be aware of your surroundings.
  - Write down the license plate numbers of suspicious vehicles and note their occupants.
  - Report anything unusual to the authorities.

- **Be prepared for the unexpected.**
  - Plan for the range of threat possibilities and avoid established patterns.
  - Avoid opening or processing mail in close proximity to others.
  - Check mail and packages for suspicious items.
  - Clear the area immediately when the presence of a bomb is suspected.
  - Look for signs of tampering around your automobile.
  - Keep the doors of your automobile locked and the windows closed.
  - Alter your driving route and parking space frequently.
  - Report suspicious occurrences to the authorities.
- **Maintain a low profile while traveling.**
  - Wear simple clothing when using public transportation.
  - If you work for the government, avoid car markings identifying you as government personnel.
  - Remove old pass and parking stickers from the windows and other outside surfaces of your car.
  - Refuse to meet with strangers outside of secure places.
  - Select an inside hotel room, one with no street-side windows on the fourth to tenth floors.
  - Do not open the door of your hotel room to anyone until you know who the person is.
  - Advise associates or family members of your destination and time of arrival.
  - Inform family members and associates of a "duress word" to be used in times of crisis or terrorism.

9.5 UNWTO TOURISM LEGISLATION AND INFORMATION SERVICES

Among its many program activities, two services of the UNWTO are particularly important for establishing tourism policy planning, legislating, programming, regulating, and implementing guidelines in member states. These are LEXTOUR, designed to access a tourism legislative referral system, and the Tourism Satellite Account (TSA), a unifying framework for most components of the System of Tourism Statistics (STS).

The UNWTO has a branch organization that functions as a depository of worldwide legislation and regulations pertaining to tourism. Its Documentation Centre aims to promote and facilitate access to tourism information for UNWTO members and other institutional partners through information support services in three main subject areas:

- **Provision of information support services**
  - The objective is to provide permanent information services concerning legislative, administrative, and policy measures about the tourism sector.
  - The Documentation Centre operates an online access system for information on tourism legislation worldwide. The system is known as LEXTOUR.
- **Linking of networks between the Documentation Centre and its partners**
  - The objective is to provide a permanent tourism information referral service and a standardized tool for tourism information transfer and exchange.
  - The Documentation Centre operates a Tourism Information and Documentation Resource Centre Database (INFODOCTOUR), which provides online access to libraries, documentation services, information brokers, and databases related to tourism worldwide.
  - The Documentation Centre also operates the UNWTO Thesaurus on Tourism and Leisure Activities, which provides online access to a multilingual instrument for facilitating tourism information indexing and retrieval.

- **Promotion of tourism information networking**
  - The objective is to provide direct support to UNWTO members, especially to national tourism administration organizations in member states, and permit them to participate in tourism information networking development.
  - For technical assistance to member countries and political subunits, UNWTO provides guidelines for establishing and managing a Tourism Information and Documentation Resource Centre (TIDRC).

A legislative reference source was needed to initiate a dialogue between UNWTO and its members concerning a database of legislation for tourism development. LEXTOUR was the result. The UNWTO Documentation Centre set up the computer-based information system for tourism legislation in 2002. More introductory information on the LEXTOUR system can be found on the following Web site: http://www.unwto.org/doc/E/lextour.htm.

LEXTOUR is designed to access the referral system. It facilitates direct access through links to external web sites, databases, and information servers on tourism legislative data. Authoritative government agencies produce the data and distribute it to parliaments and other legislative bodies. These external information systems supply references, as well as the full text of national legislative and regulatory instruments governing the main aspects of social, economic, and tourism activities. Only one-third of the three hundred systems currently identified in some one hundred thirty countries focus exclusively on tourism legislation. LEXTOUR will encourage the creation of online tourism-related legislative information systems under the auspices of the national tourism administration in those countries where such databases are not yet available.

The Tourism Satellite Account (TSA) is the unifying framework for most components of the System of Tourism Statistics (STS). The UNWTO developed the TSA for analyzing the economic impacts of tourism and prepared two documents explaining its content. *Basic Concepts of the TSA* provides a broad overview of the TSA. *TSA in Depth: Analyzing Tourism as an Economic Sector* explains the process in detail. The UNWTO has decided to work actively with the United Nations Statistical Commission to refine the International Standard Industrial Classification of Economic Activities (ISIC) and the Central Product Classification (CPC), both of which are important for economic development planning including the tourism sector.

Chapter Highlights

- Many issues demand resolution and guidance from the government for developing tourism.
- Governments may enact new legislation to encourage tourism development.
- Every tourism establishment is given a license to operate. The license is renewable.
- Each type of establishment, including those for gambling, has its own sets of standards.

- Governments issue strict regulations and guidance for antiterrorism.
- The UNWTO has developed a system called LEXTOUR that provides many information services concerning tourism legislation around the world. The UNWTO's INFODOCTOUR system provides linkages with other sources of information for networking.

10

Financing Government and Private Sector Tourism Projects

This chapter discusses one of the most critical resources for developing tourism—finding capital. Capital is usually in short supply. Finding it is difficult, qualifying for it is at times discriminatory, and using it is full of potential hazards.

- Capital for financing tourism businesses and related real estate projects is available from private, commercial, government, and multinational lending institutions.
- Mortgage lending sources include savings and loan associations, mutual savings banks, commercial banks, and life insurance companies.
- Private sources of financing include investors, limited partnerships, real estate investment trusts, and venture capitalists.
- International sources of financing include the World Bank Group, Overseas Private Investment Corporation, United Nations Development Programme, regional development banks, bilateral agreements, and the EX-IM Bank.
- Other sources include government grants and loans, volunteering (substituting volunteer labor for paid labor, which requires capital), the Small Business Administration (SBA) in the United States (or other similar government organizations in other countries), finance companies, revolving funds, factoring, and personal means.

10.1 SEARCHING FOR MONEY FOR TOURISM PROJECTS

Where will the money come from for financing a tourism project? This is the question most often asked by an entrepreneur. There is no short and fast answer to the question. Money is usually in short supply, no matter what, in any economic system, anywhere. Finding the source is like finding a treasure, rare and precious. One has to know how and where to find it.

Finding money for starting a tourism business or developing a tourism project is not a simple process. If it were easy, many people would have done it. Projects involving real estate investment have slow capital turnover. Many years are required before the annual gross income derived from a property returns the total capital investment. For many types of residential, commercial, and recreational properties, it takes ten or more years to double the investment. Apart from the necessity of borrowing money for investment, the justification for acquiring debt is in the principle of trading on owned equity. It is economically advisable to borrow money when the use of that money brings a higher rate of return than the cost of borrowing. Trading on owned equity is sound, provided that the amount borrowed is reasonably proportionate to the amount invested and the debtor has the ability to meet the long-term obligations of the debt.

The primary source of all investment capital is the savings of individuals and corporations. The volume of savings depends on factors such as the economic health of the nation, prospects for stable business conditions, and stable prices and inflation. Different demands for investment funds are made on this pool of capital. Except in an economic downturn, a substantial share of the investment pool is in real estate mortgages. In turn, government fiscal policies can strongly affect the supply of credit, particularly for real estate lending.

10.2   SOURCES OF MORTGAGE LENDING IN THE UNITED STATES

Examples from the United States are presented as types of mortgage financing available in developed nations. The instruments used for real estate mortgage debt financing are of two kinds: **term** and **amortization** mortgages. The repayment terms differentiate the two types of mortgages. (1) Whenever a mortgage debt agreement calls for the repayment of the *principal* sum in full at the end of the lending period, the unamortized debt, or compounded interest, remains outstanding for a *term* of months or years. (2) The mortgage *amortization*, in turn, offers advantages by allowing periodic reduction of the mortgage over a longer period of time, lower interest rates, and monthly payments of interest and principal in equal installment amounts. There are also variations—for example, **balloon** mortgages, which have a larger payment at the end of the mortgage period (based partly on the assumption that the borrower's income will increase over time), and **adjustable rate** mortgages, whose rates vary with the cost of borrowing of the financial institution issuing the mortgage.

Mortgage companies provide mortgages not for their own portfolios, but for other financial institutions with funds to invest. The mortgage company needs only a relatively small amount of capital. It turns this capital over frequently during the course of making and selling mortgage securities. In addition to making and selling mortgages, the mortgage company serves as a loan correspondent for one or more life insurance companies or other financial organizations, such as pension funds, and may act as a loan broker.

Saving and loan associations are the descendants of cooperative associations, in which the members were both savers and borrowers. Today, they operate like savings banks, with depository and lending functions separated. The savers and borrowers are different. The savers are shareholders and receive dividends on their deposits. They may withdraw their deposits by giving notice or on demand. The associations are nonprofit institutions.

Saving and loan associations specialize in local mortgage investment. The law limits them to buying and selling mortgages and government securities. When authorized, they may also buy property contracts. The loans may be for up to 70% or more of the property's value and for terms of twenty to twenty-five years. The associations use the investment capital assembled from local savers, but they also act as channels for bringing mortgage money from outside sources.

Mutual savings banks are generally found in the northeastern states of the United States. To a large extent, they depend on local sources of investment funds. They are nonprofit institutions.

Depositors receive dividends rather than interest. Large portions of their assets are in mortgages. Traditionally, their loan terms are conservative.

Mutual savings banks derive their capital for lending from deposits made by corporations, individuals, correspondent banks, government agencies, nonprofit organizations, and many others. These deposits are in checking, time deposit, and certificate of deposit accounts. In the United States, the federal government charters some of the commercial banks. They have the word *national* in their names. They make commercial loans for tourism projects based on their merits, as they do for other projects. For projects ranging from building cruise ships to developing resorts and retirement golf communities, financing still depends on the track record, that is, experience, and financial solvency of the venture entrepreneur.

Commercial banks invest a relatively small proportion of their total assets in mortgages. They are, nevertheless, one of the more important sources of mortgages because of their very large resources. They prefer to make real estate loans on multifamily structures and commercial properties. Liquidity is important for commercial banks. That makes short-term construction loans a preferred form of investment.

Commercial banks give business loans to most small businesses secured with company or personal assets. Personal guarantees and collateral may be required from anyone who owns more than 20% of a venture. When the venture goes bad, the bank can call for full repayment of the loan before the end of its term.

Commercial banks also give consumer loans. They include home equity loans, second mortgages, mortgage refinancing, and personal loans. If one has a good credit history, consumer loans are easier to obtain than business loans. The loan must be used for the purpose for which it was declared. It is unlikely that a consumer loan would be called for full repayment before its term expires.

In addition to their role as insurers of lives, **life insurance companies** have become an important source of capital for world capital markets. They are a major force in real estate ownership and development, both as lenders and owners. They are the most important source of large loans on multifamily and commercial properties. Their loans are made on terms somewhat less liberal in value-loan ratio and maturity than those of saving and loan associations but somewhat more liberal than those of banks. They prefer quality loans on more expensive properties. Multifamily structures and commercial properties are their favored investments.

The proportion of its funds that a life insurance company makes available for real estate lending is largely a matter of corporate investment policy. The policy may reflect yields on alternative investments and considerations of portfolio diversification. It may also reflect expectations concerning current business conditions and interest rates.

10.3 A NOTE ON MORTGAGES

Other financial institutions have gotten into mortgage and mortgage-related businesses. New financial instruments such as subprime mortgages, mortgage-backed securities, and collateralized debt obligations have been created by financial institutions, which has led to real estate being overvalued through easy credit. Several years ago, the volume of money in real estate investments increased enormously. For example, the value of subprime mortgages rose from $50 billion to over $600 billion in the United States from 2001 to 2005, as reported by the *New York Times*. These easy money practices in real estate finance were major contributors to the severe economic downturn of 2008–2009. When lenders lost confidence that borrowers could repay their debts, the credit markets, on which virtually all businesses depend, dried up. Many countries besides the

United States were affected. Measures have since been taken by many countries to restore the needed confidence in credit markets and to better regulate the entire mortgage and real estate finance industry. The entire episode demonstrates the extent of the interconnections in the global economy and the very important role that real estate finance plays in that economy.

10.4 PRIVATE FUNDING SOURCES

The market system relies on private initiative and largely on private funds. Tourism development projects do not receive special consideration from all commercial and personal funding sources. If the project is profitable and the loan will be repaid on time with interest, due diligence will reveal the feasibility of the project. Then investors, mortgage brokers, and various commercial lenders will have an interest in funding the project. A special edge that tourism projects may have over other commercial ventures, for a lender, may be discounted prices or some other form of favorable treatment for the lender at the facility or attraction.

Angels are persons with money who are looking for an investment that will give them a better return than traditional investments. These are persons who inherited or accumulated their wealth by various means and from different sources. They may not know much about starting a tourism business or developing a tourism project. Their interest is in earning a handsome return for their money that would be higher than the return provided by other forms of investment at that particular time. By agreeing to finance a new tourism venture, they could be acting only as passive participants and would not be involved in the day-to-day operation of the business. They tend to invest in their home state or region, generally within fifty miles of their home or office. They expect approximately a 25% or better annual return on their investment. They turn down most investment offers due to insufficient growth potential, overpriced equity, poor management, and insufficient background information about the entrepreneur. First-time entrepreneurs need not apply.

The venture partner who brought the project to the investor may assume the majority share of the ownership. Presumably, he or she is the expert on the team. Some investors may agree to participate for a period of time, until they learn the business themselves and move on to a similar project. Or, they may be altogether removed from the venture but maintain a controlling interest by having their money work for them under very stringent conditions. They may turn over the job of overseer to their trusted salaried managers, who would act as their agents. Negotiations between the investor and the venture or project partner will determine the conditions of the financial agreement.

This provider of capital has several options. If the project is financially very promising, investors may be numerous and willing to invest heavily. However, things could change when the feasibility of the venture or project appears to be risky for one reason or another. Investors will be less inclined to participate. Alternatively, they will ask for stronger guarantees, buy risk insurance to cover possible losses, and raise their share of the ownership to ensure a higher return on the investment against the risk they are taking.

In selecting an investor or a financial partner, the entrepreneur/developer will have to look everywhere and try many venues. These venues include personal contacts, agents, licensed or unlicensed mortgage brokers, investment houses, construction companies, and other developers. It is advisable to verify the legitimacy and reputation of each of these sources before engaging in serious negotiations. In particular, the question of who would pay the due diligence investigation costs up front may create a stumbling block in negotiations. On occasion, these costs could be substantial, large enough to become a source of income without obligations for the intermediary. If the investor, his or her mortgage broker, or the agent insists on a venture partner's paying these costs, without giving any guarantee that they will be deducted from the loan later, caution must be exercised. After collecting this up-front money, the intermediary and his or her investor may declare that the project or venture is not worth pursuing and remove themselves from further consideration.

A **limited partnership** is an organization made up of a general partner with unlimited liability, who sponsors the partnership and manages its activities, and limited partners who put up most of the money but have limited liability and little or no say in the day-to-day management. Most limited partnerships are established for a specific period, usually seven to ten years, at the end of which the proceeds from the sale of the venture or project are distributed to the shareholders and the partnership is dissolved.

In the United States, limited partnerships may be private or public. Private partnerships are composed of as many as thirty-five limited partners who could invest a minimum of $20,000 each. A variation of the partnership occurs when accredited investors contribute additional capital. Private partnerships are not required to register with the federal or state securities and exchange commissions in the United States. As a result, limited partners need to carefully evaluate the qualifications of the general partner and the partnership before investing.

Public partnerships do not limit the number of investors and limited partners. The purpose of the partnership is to collect small amounts, about $5,000 or less, from as many investors as possible. It is required, however, that a prospectus is prepared and the partnership is registered with federal and/or state securities and exchange commissions. Other requirements may also apply.

From the viewpoint of the investors and limited partners, limited partnerships have certain unique characteristics. Tax and other obligations flow directly from the partnership to the individual investor. These obligations include income, capital gains, and tax benefits involving various types of businesses in which an individual investor is engaged. In the United States, these businesses often finance real estate and mortgage loans, oil and gas exploration and production, leasing, film production, research and development, and others.

Limited public and private partnerships aim to maximize income and capital gains. They provide tax benefits in the form of a tax shelter. They are used for leveraging assets with more than 50% borrowed money. With larger assets, they qualify for higher depreciation and are able to deduct interest charges on loans. One drawback of a limited partnership is its lack of liquidity. During the life of the partnership, it is difficult to sell shares on a secondary market, if it exists, and get out. To overcome the lack of liquidity problem, new programs were devised during the 1980s. The master limited partnership is one such program.

A **joint venture**—or, for some, "joint adventure"—is a business association distinguishable from a partnership only by the narrowness of its purpose and scope. It has been defined as an association of parties intending to engage in and carry out, for joint profit, a single business venture in which they combine their knowledge, skill, funds, efforts, and property, pursuant to an agreement for a community of interest among them, related to the undertaking's purpose.

A joint venture partnership may be formed for a single undertaking, but it is usually intended to encompass an indefinite number of transactions within a relatively broad line of business for an indefinite period. Typically, some or all of the partners devote their full time to the business. A joint venture is commonly a single undertaking or a series of related undertakings, not requiring the full attention of the participants, and having a short duration. A wide variety of formal and informal financial and business arrangements may be joint ventures, whether or not they use the term. In real estate, joint ventures are commonly used to carry out a single transaction or to develop and lease or sell a particular property. The participants may number in the dozens or hundreds when they are mainly suppliers of capital, or they may be as few as two.

The U.S. Congress authorized **real estate investment trusts (REITs)** to give small investors an opportunity to invest in large-scale real estate projects and benefit from their tax benefits. Shares of REITs trade publicly. The money is invested in a variety of real estate assets to minimize exposure and risk. Some REITs take equity ownership positions in real estate. Shareholders receive rental income and benefit from capital gains when the property is sold. Both rental income and the rise in property values provide protection against inflation.

Some REITs specialize in lending money to real estate developers. They are called **mortgage REITs.** Interest income received from loans is distributed among the shareholders. Other REITs do both. They lend money to developers and own equity properties. By U.S. law, REITs must derive 90% of their income from rents, dividends, interest, and gains from the sale of real estate properties. They must pay 95% of the proceeds to the shareholders. When they meet these requirements, REITs are exempt from federal taxes at the corporate level. Dividends are taxable at the shareholder level. The following Web site provides more introductory information about mortgage REITs: http://www.answers.com/topic/mortgage-reit.

For the investor, the advantages of investing through REITs are several. It provides limited liability, income, and tax benefits. It avoids double taxation and offers liquidity because shares are marketable. The down side of investing through REITs is that the values of shares are susceptible to change as much, and as often, as shares of stocks. Losses cannot be passed on to shareholders.

A variation of the REIT is the **finite life real estate investment trust (FREIT)**. FREITs are intended to sell or finance their holdings after a predetermined period and distribute the proceeds to the shareholders for realizing capital gains. But FREITs are subject to the same disadvantages as REITs.

10.5 VENTURE CAPITAL

Venture capitalists have large amounts of capital available for starting and expanding all kinds of businesses. Occasionally, tourism businesses are among them. Most venture capitalists set limits—minimum and maximum amounts they are willing to invest—and some specialize in certain regions of the country or certain industries. Most, invest exclusively in the United States. Some consider other countries. Biotechnology and high-technology businesses are currently favored by venture capitalists. However, services businesses, retail companies, and consumer companies could also be of interest if they have high expansion potential.

Experienced entrepreneurs exhaust cheaper sources of capital before turning to venture capital. They search for funds in banks for a line of credit, ask friends and relatives to invest, contact the Small Business Association, and, contrary to business wisdom, they invest much of their own money in the business. Most venture capital firms expect the entrepreneur to invest his or her own money before lending. It is important to understand that in venture capital lending, one gets an equity partner who may have his or her own ideas about how to use the venture capital invested. Most of all, a venture capital investor wants to see an exit strategy whereby he or she can "harvest" his or her investment after a few years. In some cases, that could mean making the venture public or, worse, selling the business altogether.

In general, venture capitalists are looking for extraordinary growth potential, management talent with a track record of successful ventures, and proprietary products or services like patents, copyrights, trademarks, or other rights to a product, or a valued service like government incentives given for developing a tourism project.

The entrepreneur should never give up-front fees or deposits to a person or firm that promises to give a loan or invest venture capital. Disreputable people posing as venture capitalists have defrauded thousands of entrepreneurs by asking for "good faith deposits." The excuses they use to collect these funds include legal fees, accounting reviews, travel expenses, research fees, communications expenses, document review fees, and others.

The legitimate venture capitalist requires from the entrepreneur an executive summary of the business plan. The complete business plan is not required initially. Following the first review, the venture capitalist may request additional information and the entire business plan. If the venture is promising, a venture capitalist will provide a *letter of interest* for funding the business or project. This letter will be used for creating interest from other lending institutions and, if applicable, as a *letter of guarantee*. Detailed negotiations normally follow.

10.6   INTERNATIONAL FUNDING SOURCES

The World Bank, formally named the International Bank for Reconstruction and Development and its affiliate, the International Development Association, are important sources of funding in developing countries. There are two other affiliates, the International Finance Corporation and the Multilateral Investment Guarantee Agency. Together, these affiliates and the IBRD are known as the **World Bank Group**. The common objective of these institutions is to help raise the standard of living in developing countries by channeling financial resources to them from developed countries.

The **International Bank for Reconstruction and Development** (IBRD) was founded in the wake of World War II's destruction in 1945. The bank is owned by more than one hundred sixty countries, which provide its capital. The capital is raised by borrowing from the world capital markets. A substantial portion of the IBRD's resources comes from its retained earnings and the flow of repayments on its loans. IBRD loans generally have a grace period of five years and are repayable over fifteen to twenty years. The loans are directed to developing countries at more advanced stages of economic and social growth. The interest rate that the IBRD charges on its loans is calculated according to a guideline related to its cost of borrowing.

The IBRD's charter spells out certain basic rules that govern its operations. It must lend funds only for productive purposes. The funds are to be used for stimulating economic growth in developing countries. Tourism development is one such productive purpose. Each loan is made to a government. The receiving country must ensure repayment of the loan. The IBRD's decisions to lend are based solely on economic considerations.

The IBRD's lending process goes through several steps. Initially, the applicant country prepares a funding application for a project following the format requested by the bank. A reconnaissance team composed of staff and experts from the IBRD visits the country and prepares a due diligence report on the merits of the proposed project. Preparing a due diligence report is a standard procedure for all banks and lending institutions around the world. Depending on the recommendations of the report, the loan committee of the IBRD allocates funds and determines a payment schedule starting at a certain fiscal year of the IBRD. The projects funded by the IBRD are published in the annual statements of the bank by regions and countries of the world. Technical assistance for preparing plans and designs for infrastructure projects are included in funding.

The **International Development Association** (IDA) was established in 1960 to provide assistance for the same purposes as the IBRD, but primarily in poorer developing countries and on terms that would bear less heavily on their balance of payments than would IBRD loans. The

IDA's assistance is concentrated in very poor countries—those with an annual per capita GNP of $610 or less (in 1990 US$). More than forty countries are eligible under this criterion.

Membership in the IDA is open to all members of the IBRD, and one hundred forty-two of them have joined to date. The funds used by the IDA, called *credits*, to distinguish them from IBRD *loans*, come mostly in the form of subscriptions, general replenishments from the IDA's more industrialized and developed members, and transfers from the net earnings of the IBRD. The credits are traditionally made only to governments. The terms of IDA credits include a ten-year grace period, thirty-five- or forty-year maturities, and no interest.

The **International Finance Corporation (IFC)** was established in 1956. Its function is to assist the economic development of LDCs by promoting growth in the private sector of their economies and by helping to mobilize domestic and foreign capital for this purpose. Membership in the IBRD is a prerequisite for membership in the IFC. There are forty-six member countries to date. Legally and financially, the IFC and the IBRD are separate entities. The IFC has its own operating and legal staff but draws upon the IBRD for administration and other services.

The **Multilateral Investment Guarantee Agency (MIGA)** was established in 1988. Its specialized function is to encourage equity investment and other direct investment flows to developing countries through the mitigation of noncommercial investment barriers. To carry out this mandate, MIGA offers investors guarantees against noncommercial risks; advises developing member governments on the design and implementation of policies, programs, and procedures related to foreign investments; and sponsors a dialogue between the international business community and host governments on investment issues.

The **World Bank** has traditionally financed all kinds of capital infrastructure, such as roads and railways, telecommunications, and port and power facilities. The centerpiece of its development strategy emphasizes investments that can directly affect the well-being of the masses of poorer people of developing countries by making them more productive and by integrating them as active partners in the development process. The bank's efforts to reduce poverty cut across sectoral lines and include investments to improve education, ensure environmental sustainability, expand economic opportunities for women, strengthen population planning, provide health and nutrition services, encourage tourism, and develop the private sector. The bank often requires positive economic restructuring in many of its borrowing member countries, including tax and land reform and changes in business regulations.

The mission of the **Overseas Private Investment Corporation (OPIC)** is to mobilize and facilitate the participation of private capital and skills from the United States in the economic and social development of LDCs and developing areas in transition from central planned to market economies, thereby complementing the development assistance objectives of the U.S. government.

OPIC accomplishes this mission by assisting U.S. investors through four principal activities designed to promote overseas investments and reduce the associated risks:

- Insuring overseas investments against a broad range of political risks
- Financing businesses overseas through loans and loan guarantees
- Financing private investment funds that provide equity to businesses overseas
- Advocating the interests of the American business community overseas

OPIC is a self-sustaining agency. It operates at no net cost to the U.S. taxpayer. Currently, OPIC programs are available for new and expanding business enterprises in approximately one hundred forty countries and areas worldwide. All of OPIC's guaranty and insurance obligations are backed by the full faith and credit of the United States.

OPIC supports, insures, and finances investment projects, including tourism projects, with substantial financial participation by U.S. companies or individuals ranging from 25% minimum to 40% of the project cost. Most project funding comes from other sources, and the projects must be financially sound, promise significant benefits to the social and economic development of the host country, and foster private initiative and competition. OPIC will not support projects that could result in the loss of U.S. jobs, or adversely affect the U.S. economy or the host country's development or environment. OPIC will not accept any proposed venture that would contribute to violations of internationally recognized workers' rights.

OPIC financial support is available for new investment projects, privatization, and expansion and modernization of existing plants. Tourism-related projects like hotels and privately owned tourist facilities and attractions are eligible. OPIC can generally insure the acquisition of self-sustaining enterprises. Neither financing nor insurance will be available, however, for projects with majority ownership by a foreign government. OPIC's financial support is intended to build up private sector activities. OPIC does not participate in projects subject to performance standards that would substantially reduce the potential for U.S. trade benefits of the investment. Performance requirements include that host government incentives are designed to result in a project operating in a way that is more beneficial to the local economy than would otherwise be the case. Of particular concern are trade-related performance requirements covering *local content, maximum import,* and *minimum export* levels, where the effect is to reduce U.S. trade benefits that would otherwise accrue.

The **United Nations Development Programme (UNDP)** is the technical division of the United Nations. Its primary function is to give technical assistance to governments. Governments requesting assistance are sent technical assistance teams. The teams are composed of experts chosen from academic institutions, consulting firms, and government agencies for studying particular tourism or other development problems or potentials. These teams define the purpose of the mission, analyze the subject, and make recommendations to the management of the UNDP. In turn, the UNDP activates its system and refers the project to the appropriate United Nations agency, one of which is the UNWTO, for funding and execution.

The UNDP can designate its own funding division, the **United Nations Capital Development Fund (UNCDF),** for funding a tourism project and assign its execution to the UNWTO. The UNCDF can fund small-scale capital assistance in the form of grants or long-term loans for social development projects that may include training workers for managing tourism projects.

Another agency of the United Nations, the **United Nations Center on Transnational Corporations (UNCTC),** offers technical assistance and finance to tourism-related companies for building international hotels and assists in negotiating hotel management contracts.

There are many regional (multination) banks that offer financial services to their member countries on several continents. They include the **European Development Bank**, the **Asian Development Bank**, the **African Development Bank**, and the **Inter-American Development Bank (IDB).** They can finance tourism projects that would assist the economic development of their member countries.

Bilateral funding is the result of government-to-government agreements for undertaking trade and development projects. Provided that the government receiving the loan abides by the terms of the agreement, many types of projects, including tourism projects, can be financed through these arrangements. However, there is no recourse for the lending government if the receiving government defaults.

The **EX-IM Bank** is an independent agency of the U.S. government. Its mission is to create jobs for U.S. citizens directly in the United States or indirectly in foreign countries by financing new ventures. The EX-IM Bank provides financing to U.S. companies exporting goods and services from the United States. In tourism businesses, The EX-IM Bank could finance hotel development projects that will employ American citizens in their management and use equipment and technical assistance coming from the United States. The EX-IM Bank accepts the risk that other financial institutions will not accept in their provision of loans and loan guarantees.

Export credit insurance policies of the EX-IM Bank protect the investor against both the political and commercial risks of a foreign buyer defaulting on payment. Short-term policies generally cover 100% of the principal for political risks and 90–95% for commercial risks, as well as a specified amount of interest. They are used to support the sale of consumer goods, raw materials, and spare parts, for example for refurbishing a hotel, on terms up to one hundred eighty days.

Guarantees of commercial loans to foreign buyers of U.S. goods or services cover 100% of principal and interest against both political and commercial risks of nonpayment. Medium-term guarantees cover the sale of goods and project-related services including architectural and engineering services. The EX-IM Bank also gives direct loans to foreign buyers with competitive fixed-rate financing for their purchases from the United States. The loans cover up to 85% of the project price. Exporters can obtain an EX-IM Bank Letter of Interest to assist in negotiations with a potential foreign buyer.

Where applicable in or adjacent to the European Union (EU), one source of international funding is the **European Bank for Reconstruction and Development (EBRD),** which provides funding for agrotourism projects, support for small and medium-sized tourism enterprises, tourism infrastructure, personnel training, and the like. The geographic scope of the bank's activities has grown over the years. Funding is not limited to EU members. It now includes some countries formed after the breakup of the former Yugoslavia and the Soviet Union, as well as LDCs.

10.7 OTHER FUNDING SOURCES

Government grants may be available most frequently to nonprofit companies or to government agencies at the local level, like those of municipalities. Some grants exist for for-profit companies, although start-up companies are exempted. Most grants are made for technical assistance, including tourism development planning, and for the development of a product or service that will benefit the public. Some state and local governments, in turn, grant money of their own or act as clearinghouses and conduits for the central government.

In the United States, the federal government publishes the *Catalog of Federal Domestic Assistance,* where grant information is available. Also, the *Federal Register,* published on weekdays by the government, has grant announcements.

State, provincial, and municipal governments offer economic development loans through their economic development offices. These offices provide financing and information on finding other sources of capital for business ventures. The criteria for a business loan may change from one location to another and from one year to another, depending on local economic and political conditions. Priority for lending is generally given to businesses that would improve existing economic conditions in areas of high unemployment or low per capita income.

Microfinance, including microcredit, consists of funds established to provide small amounts of capital to very small, sometimes one-person, businesses. Very small loans or credit advances are not adequate to fund tourism projects, but they can be used to fund very small (micro) businesses related to tourism (e.g., people making and selling handicraft items in bazaars and on streets). The funds are intended to provide capital to people who do not qualify for normal financing. Microfinance and microcredit are intended to pull people out of abject poverty into subsistence levels of living. The funds, which have social as well as economic objectives, are created by national and regional development banks, aid agencies, international NGOs, nonprofit corporations, charitable trusts, or funds held by donor and development agencies. Microfinancing, in which nominal interest rates are charged, can be used in any sector of an economy, including activities related to tourism.

Volunteering and **social entrepreneurship** are growing movements around the world. These movements were mentioned in Chapter 5. In cash-poor countries, volunteering takes the form of substituting labor for capital. Other terms for this phenomenon are **sweat equity** and **in-kind contributions**. Entire villages contribute their labor to build a community building or some other community-serving facility. Many organizations with social-cultural-religious affiliations send teams of volunteers to developing countries for organizing programs and building facilities. They secure building materials from donor companies and build infrastructure and housing at various locations, including privately owned land. Habitat for Humanity and Doctors without Borders are two such organizations.

Social entrepreneurship has existed throughout history. New citizen organizations now number in the millions around the world. Historically, these organizations were defined as nonprofit organizations or NGOs. Today, they represent a new sector of the local economy. In some developing countries, employment in this sector grew two and a half times faster than the overall economy. This growth is occurring on a scale never seen before. Organizations are globally more dispersed and diverse than in the past. They are moving from providing temporary solutions for short-term economic and social problems to solutions that are more systemic and long-term. These organizations are increasingly independent of religious or government institutions. They are forging partnerships with businesses, academic institutions, and even governments. Because of their increasing numbers, social enterprises are experiencing the results of competition. Further definition of them can be found on the following Wikipedia Web site: http://en.wikipedia.org/wiki/Social_entrepreneurship.

The **Small Business Administration (SBA)** is an agency of the U.S. government. It provides guarantees on loans given by commercial banks to small businesses. It is also a lender. Funds guaranteed by the SBA are used to start or expand businesses. However, they cannot be used to pay off creditors, to cash out investors, or for investment in real estate, including hotels.

Qualifications for an SBA loan depend on the nature of the business. There are limits to business size by type of business, and businesses must be for-profit entities. They must not have a monopoly position in their specific line of business and must be independently owned and operated.

Commercial finance companies make small business loans, including car loans. These companies finance riskier commercial loans than banks can handle. They accept higher ceilings for loans. High-growth businesses seeking higher loan ceilings, businesses with a questionable credit history, and businesses with a high debt-to-worth ratio but strong cash flow are target candidates for finance companies. High risk calls for higher costs. Finance companies charge fees and rates 2–10% higher than those of banks.

Governments may establish revolving funds for sponsoring incentives. Licensed tourist facilities in designated tourism areas and tourism destinations could be eligible for low-interest twenty-year loans for up to 15–20% of their total investment. These loans can be used for building a tourism facility and for international tourism promotion. The revenues supplying the funds come from various sources. They include appropriations of the government from national budgets, shares of profits from certain tourism operations owned by the government, interest received from previous loans, fees charged to visitors, and penalties collected from tourist establishments. In the event of transfer of ownership, loans and their terms remain in force. When these establishments cease to operate, however, their loans become due. An exception is made for establishments that close owing natural disasters and military conflict. Political risk insurance is available on international markets for these establishments owned by foreign investors.

Depending on the importance of a proposed project, like building a convention and exhibit facility, the government may offer cash assistance in the form of capital raised from the sale of government-backed long-term bonds. This assistance may include other incentives, like giving land in lieu of cash and using expedited special permit procedures. Fee and tax relief can also be part of a financial package. In turn, the applicant submits a permanent letter of credit or a guarantee from an internationally recognized bank amounting to as much as 5% of the project cost.

Some small businesses that need cash quickly turn to receivables financing as a fast, reliable source of capital. Commonly known as **factoring**, receivables financing is used to increase cash flow without increasing business debt. To use this financing method, a small tourism business sells its accounts receivable to a third party called a **factor.** The factor advances to the business the value of the receivables, less a fee, and then acts as a collection agent and assumes the responsibility and risk for collecting the money.

Factoring is not for all kinds of businesses. It requires a sizable volume of receivables to get the factor interested. It is not a long-term cash source. It is short-term financing. The age and quality of the receivables are important. Lenders will examine the credit history of the business and the risk associated with factoring very closely.

Factoring can help cash-needy businesses by providing a rapid cash infusion of 50–90% of the receivables, eliminating debt, and simplifying the collection of receivables. But it also has disadvantages. Factoring can be costly. Only a fraction of the receivables may be collected, and the factor's fee could be as high as 5–10% of the value of the receivables. Generally, ninety-day or older or long-term receivables may not be accepted by the factor.

Other, less favored sources of funding tourism businesses involve **raising cash through personal means.** They include selling personal assets like cars, houses, land, jewelry, antiques, and other valuables, as well as cashing certificates of deposits, mutual funds, stocks, and bonds. This may be the only way for a business to raise cash quickly.

Another method of raising quick cash is borrowing against one's **whole life insurance policy**. If the policy is three years old or more, it may have cash value. The insurance company may pay up to 90% of the value of the policy at that time. As long as the premiums are paid, the policy will remain active. The money borrowed against the cash value of the policy is subject to interest payments. The rate of this interest is generally lower than the interest charged for cash advances made by credit card companies. The principal and interest on the loan will be payable to the insurance company in installments.

A combination of sources is also possible for funding tourism projects. **Joint ventures, consortia**, and **leveraging private funding with public funding** are among methods that can be used, legal guidelines permitting. LDCs may have variations of these internationally accepted methods. As noted at the beginning of this book, finance is a field that can change rapidly. New financial instruments and regulations of finance are almost always being developed and refined. This chapter has given an overview of conventional financing methods. These methods are subject to alteration and vary from country to country. It is important for those interested in tourism development to research current financial institutions, regulations, and conditions applicable to their own situations before venturing into projects.

Chapter Highlights

- There are numerous national and international sources for raising capital for tourism projects and activities related to tourism. The timing and terms of the loans vary widely.
- Governments back many of these loans.
- Tourism projects located overseas have their own international lending sources. These include many regional foreign banks.
- The U.S. government has its own foreign lending sources. Objectives of these banks include promoting jobs and business opportunities for Americans.
- As a last resort, capital for a tourism project can be raised by selling personal assets.
- Tourism projects have substantial real estate components, which are subject to the same market variations, competitive circumstances, risks, and financing conditions that characterize all real estate.

PART

IV

Techniques for Planning and Developing Tourism

Part IV introduces information collected, techniques used, and procedures followed in consecutive or parallel phases of planning and developing tourism. It describes research methods used for surveying and analyzing tourism information. It describes tourism planning processes at national, regional, and destination levels. It examines the project design, permit, and construction steps. It describes methods for preparing and presenting financial information used for funding projects. It presents techniques for marketing and promoting tourism. In addition, it reviews specialized computer applications for simulation, design, and information processing.

11

Surveying the Tourism Product

This chapter presents the information to be collected and prepared for tourism development planning. In particular, electronic data processing and computer mapping as survey aids are reviewed. Statistical and descriptive techniques are presented for building the database.

- The tourism sector is defined in terms of industries classified by the NAICS.
- In its most complex (disaggregate) form, there are 232 types of establishments in the tourism sector.
- Tourist attractions and facilities, or establishments, are coded according to the BIK System using seventeen or more groups of data.
- Computer, graphic, and manual applications of the BIK System are possible.
- Economic, demographic, environmental, legal, and regulatory information are among the data surveyed.

11.1 DEFINING TOURISM AS AN ECONOMIC SECTOR

The North American Industrial Classification System (NAICS) is a production classification system that divides the economy into twenty sectors. Five sectors are largely goods-producing and fifteen are entirely service-producing industries. Tourism is not one of these sectors. The reason is that tourism is an *overlapping sector* (as discussed in Chapter 1). It is not classified by itself. It includes types of establishments belonging to several major and minor categories of NAICS industries. Currently, the UNWTO has an ongoing long-term process of defining variants of the tourism sector in economies that are in different stages of development around the world. Further information about the NAICS can be found on the following Web site: http://www.census.gov/eos/www/naics/.

We should remind ourselves that the BIK System used in this procedure was tested in 1970 in developing and applying the system in Massachusetts using the SYMAP computer program. SYMAP is no longer available. It has been superseded by more advanced mapping and related information processing and tabulation software. But the thirty-two maps and extensive data tabulations produced in the 1970 Massachusetts application can be duplicated by newer programs. For now, the BIK System can be used to process data manually.

Pending possible UNWTO resolution, using the BIK System, the author has selected his own tourism sector industries from NAICS to illustrate the wide spectrum of tourist site and event attractions and facilities owned and operated by establishments listed in selected subsectors of NAICS that make up the tourism sector. Site attractions have fixed locations and are classified readily using the NAICS. More often than not, they are located where the establishment that owns and operates them is located. Event attractions are more difficult to classify. They are temporary, do not always occur at the same location over time, and may not have easily identifiable sponsors or organizers. They are also more problematic to classify within the NAICS system. When these surveying difficulties are resolved, the BIK System includes event attractions together with site attractions in the survey. Otherwise, a separate survey not using the NAICS method may be necessary for surveying event attractions.

In NAICS, industry categories are listed at *two-digit sector* and *three-digit subsector* levels and are further detailed as *six-digit establishments*. The composition of the tourism sector selected for this book is subject to change, depending on the complexity of a particular tourism economy. Fewer types of establishments mean a smaller tourism sector for that particular location.

The U.S. Census of Business defines an **establishment** as a "single physical location where business is conducted or where services or industrial operations are performed." A **firm** is defined as a "business organization consisting of one or more domestic establishments in the same state and industry that are specified under common ownership or control." The firm and the establishment are the same for single-establishment firms. For each multiestablishment firm, establishments in the same industry and in the same state are counted as one firm.

The stage of its economic development and the characteristics of the country influence the selection of the tourism sector industries and the types of establishments that make up the *attraction mix* and *facility mix* of the country. The content of the selected sector may range from a simple mix at the local destination level to a highly diverse and complex mix at the regional and national levels.

The sample tourism sector used in this book presupposes the following:

- Establishments that represent tourism site and event attractions and tourism facilities are located in a hypothetical country having a temperate climate and a rich mix of geographic, environmental, social, and cultural characteristics.
- The country has a well-developed market economy that is supported by the government to the extent of providing essential public services and operating public attractions and facilities.
- Private entrepreneurs, nonprofit institutions, and government own all establishments that operate all tourist attractions and facilities.
- Establishments that own and operate attractions and facilities are the **primary,** or first-tier, industries of the tourism sector.
- Tourists use all products and services of attractions and facilities in the tourism sector directly and personally.
- Establishments that serve tourists indirectly by supplying goods and services to primary, or first-tier, industries are **secondary**, or second-tier, and **tertiary,** or third-tier, industries.
- Secondary and tertiary industries are not included in the tourism sector presented. However, their economic multiplier effects would be included in the impact of the sector.

The primary, or first-tier, establishments are chosen from six-digit establishments listed in the following three-digit NAICS subsectors. The complete list of 232 types of establishments is presented in Appendix B. The seventeen NAICS sectors and fifty-three subsectors that comprise the tourism overlay economic sector are as follows:

SECTOR 11 Agriculture, Forestry, Fishing and Hunting

- Subsector 113 Forestry and Logging
- Subsector 114 Fishing, Hunting and Trapping

SECTOR 22 Utilities

- Subsector 221 Utilities

SECTOR 23 Construction

- Subsector 233 Building, Developing, and General Contracting

SECTOR 31-33 Manufacturing

- Subsector 312 Beverage Product Manufacturing
- Subsector 336 Transportation Equipment Manufacturing

SECTOR 44-45 – Retail Trade

- Subsector 443 Electronics and Appliance Stores
- Subsector 444 Building Material and Garden Equipment and Supplies Dealers
- Subsector 445 Food and Beverage Stores
- Subsector 446 Health and Personal Care Stores
- Subsector 447 Gasoline Stations
- Subsector 448 Clothing and Clothing Accessories Stores
- Subsector 451 Sporting Goods, Hobby, Book, and Music Stores
- Subsector 452 General Merchandise Stores
- Subsector 453 Miscellaneous Store Retailers
- Subsector 454 Non-Store Retailers

SECTOR 48-49 Transportation and Warehousing

- Subsector 481 Air Transportation
- Subsector 482 Rail Transportation
- Subsector 483 Water Transportation
- Subsector 484 Truck Transportation
- Subsector 485 Transit and Ground Passenger Transportation
- Subsector 487 Scenic and Sightseeing Transportation
- Subsector 488 Support Activities for Transportation
- Subsector 491 Postal Service
- Subsector 492 Couriers and Messengers

SECTOR 51 Information

- Subsector 512 Motion Picture and Sound Recording Industries
- Subsector 513 Broadcasting and Telecommunications
- Subsector 514 Information Services and Data Processing Services

SECTOR 52 Finance and Insurance

- Subsector 522 Credit Intermediation and Related Activities
- Subsector 523 Securities, Commodity Contracts and Other Financial Investments and Related Activities

- Subsector 524 Insurance Carriers and Related Activities
- Subsector 525 Funds, Trusts, and Other Financial Vehicles

SECTOR 53 Real Estate, Rental and Leasing

- Subsector 531 Real Estate
- Subsector 532 Rental and Leasing Services

SECTOR 54 Professional, Scientific, and Technical Services

- Subsector 541 Professional, Scientific, and Technical Services

SECTOR 56 Administrative and Support and Waste Management and Remediation Services

- Subsector 561 Administrative and Support Services
- Subsector 562 Waste Management and Remediation Services

SECTOR 61 Educational Services

- Subsector 611 Educational Services

SECTOR 62 Health Care and Social Assistance

- Subsector 621 Ambulatory Health Care Services
- Subsector 622 Hospitals

SECTOR 71 Arts, Entertainment, and Recreation

- Subsector 711 Performing Arts, Spectator Sports, and Related Industries Subsector
- Subsector 712 Museums, Historical Sites, and Similar Institutions
- Subsector 713 Amusement, Gambling, and Recreation Services

SECTOR 72 Accommodation and Food Services

- Subsector 721 Accommodations Subsector 722 Food Services and Drinking Places

SECTOR 81 Other Services (Except Public Administration)

- Subsector 811 Repair and Maintenance
- Subsector 812 Personal and Laundry Services
- Subsector 813 Religious, Grant Making, Civic, Professional and Similar Organizations
- Subsector 814 Private Households

SECTOR 92 Public Administration

- Subsector 922 Justice, Order, and Safety Activities
- Subsector 924 Administration of Environmental Quality Programs
- Subsector 925 Administration of Housing Programs, Urban Planning and Community Development
- Subsector 926 Administration of Economic Programs
- Subsector 928 National Security and International Affairs
- **TOTALS   17 Sectors (Industries) at the two-digit NAICS level**
  53 Subsectors at the three-digit NAICS level
  232 Establishment types at the six-digit NAICS level

The ultimate list of primary, or first-tier, establishments, and by association, attraction, and facility types, chosen by the author number 232. These establishments constitute the ultimate tourism sector. (See Appendix B for the complete list of establishments.)

As mentioned, the secondary, or second-tier, and tertiary, or third-tier, establishments chosen from among other three-digit industries serve or supply the primary tourism sector industries. Tourists do not come face-to-face with these establishments. Therefore, for tourism planning purposes, the BIK System does not include these second- and third-tier establishments and the industry categories they represent as part of the tourism sector. These are establishments that generally serve/supply more than tourism sector businesses.

Depending on the complexity of the economy, second- and third-tier establishments and industries would greatly enlarge the composition of the tourism sector. If desirable, these establishments could be surveyed, and their multiplier effect on the tourism economy could be included in the study of the impacts of tourism spending. The choice of this advanced and intensive analysis depends on the practical limitations of data, staff, budget, and computer resources available. Complex input/output economic studies can be done, usually with preexisting, precalibrated models, tracing the spending impacts of tourism sector activities through second- and third-tier establishments—indeed, throughout an economy. This could be done as a supplement to application of the BIK System for analyzing tourism attraction and facility mixes for the purposes of tourism development planning.

Import substitution also affects the composition of the tourism sector. Typically, an expanding national economy includes many emerging tourism sector establishments that will substitute local products and services for imported ones. Import substitution enhances the growth and competitiveness of local industries. It affects the composition of the tourism sector by adding new industries as the economy is growing. As the import content of the tourism industry gets smaller, substitution industries emerge in ever-larger numbers.

Selecting facility types and a highly favorable facility mix depends on the country, region, location, environment, culture, and people, as well as the goals of tourism development. The UNWTO is still refining its definition of the tourism sector in terms of the establishments that comprise it. Currently, the best alternative source for defining the tourism sector and the establishments owning and operating tourist attractions and facilities is the NAICS. The BIK System uses the NAICS as a source for selecting appropriate tourist facility types for continental North American locations. Elsewhere in the world, the selection is based on local choices following NAICS guidelines as much as possible. The tourism sector defined here can be used in all economic and geographic regions of the world with appropriate modifications to suit local circumstances.

It may not be possible, or necessary, to rate all tourist facilities existing in a tourism destination area. Some facilities may be below the standards set by the government for licensed tourist establishments. Some restaurants and overnight accommodations fall into this group. The important fact is that, to have complete service capability, the tourist facility mix of a destination must include at least one tourist facility for each six-digit establishment type of the tourism sector.

The survey of tourist attractions and facilities should then be computerized. However, the survey could be done manually using the BIK System when circumstances warrant it. In either case, the cost effectiveness of the survey method must be considered before deciding. Besides convenience, using readily available printed information may have advantages. Some information may be plentiful, (e.g., directories, guides, web pages, and ratings of hotels and restaurants). Other types of information may require special surveys.

The Internet is the primary source for electronically generated and stored tourist facility information. Other sources, like Mobil, the American Automobile Association, and the Fodor, Frommer, or Michelin guides, print a large variety of tourism information, including rated tourist facilities. Many cities have independent facility listings on web pages that describe, rate, and provide current reviews of local accommodations and eating and drinking establishments.

One or more of these sources can be used for the facility survey, provided that their quality ratings are comparable. The tourist facility mix survey procedure includes the following steps:

Step 1   Identifying information sources

Step 2   Extracting the information from sources, including follow-up calls and interviews

Step 3   Coding the information by NAICS categories

Step 4   Verifying the accuracy of the coded information by sampling

Step 5   Preparing a facility-by-area matrix by columns and rows

Step 6   Identifying missing establishment types in the mix

Step 7   Adding totals by columns and rows

The resulting matrix shows existing types of facilities at a given location. By comparing with a referenced tourism sector selected for the area, it also identifies how many more facilities are needed to provide a more favorable mix for the area.

As noted earlier, the BIK System operated on a computer mapping program called SYMAP. The program is no longer available. Several newer, more comprehensive, and powerful computer geographic information systems are available in which the BIK System could be applied to replace SYMAP. In the absence of a computer program, manual tabulation still works with the BIK System.

11.2   SURVEYING TOURIST ATTRACTIONS AND FACILITIES

The details of coding the attractions and facilities using the BIK System are explained in Section 11.3. Surveying tourist attractions and facilities using the BIK System is described here. The process involves the following steps:

- The tourism sector of a particular country, region, or local destination is selected from the three-digit, 53-subsector industries and the six-digit, 232 types of establishments of the BIK System.
- After the tourism sector is selected, tourist attractions and facilities in the locality are surveyed using conventional or customized surveying methods and are coded. The first level of data gathering employs printed brochures, books, and magazines supplemented by telephone and personal interviews. The second level employs customized door-to-door surveys conducted by enumerators trained for the job, similar to the way some travel guides are prepared with personal visits.
- In both methods, data are entered in the database using the BIK coding system. Commercially available spreadsheet software can be used or data can be tabulated manually and entered on individual index cards.
- The data for each presumed attraction and facility are coded according to the coding system of the BIK System.
- Selected attractions and facilities are rated from 1 to 10 to determine their dual characteristics, differentiating them as attractions if they are rated from 1 to 5 or as facilities if rated from 6 to 10.
- Differentiated attractions and facilities are then matched with the list of establishments of the tourism sector and are coded by the corresponding six-digit establishment numbers.
- Other characteristics of attractions and facilities are entered in the database and are coded similarly.

This process is repeated for all selected attractions and facilities until all elements of tourism products have been surveyed for the area.

11.3   CODING TOURIST ATTRACTIONS AND FACILITIES USING THE BIK SYSTEM

Traditionally, the methods used for surveying the tourism product—tourist attractions and facilities, their varieties, characteristics, and functions—were left to the subjective judgment of the surveyor. The tourism industry was not particular about collecting data that could be used for systematically analyzing tourism attractions and facilities. Information was prepared and published in some form to describe and promote attractions and facilities. The methods used were simplistic and diverse, often resulting in noncomparable data. Without technical definitions, mere lists of attractions and facilities,were available, leaving the user to interpret the limited data in order to reach personal conclusions. A better method for tourism resource analysis was needed.

In the modern information age, the data storage and processing capacities of computers have increased dramatically and the costs of hardware and software have decreased substantially. Although the rationale of the BIK System remains the same, the scope and format of the 1970 survey have been expanded over the following decades. Using the BIK System, a typical attraction and facility survey now includes a dozen or more characteristics. Each characteristic is assigned a particular digital code for computer processing. The attraction or facility is identified by a six-digit establishment category selected from the two-digit subsector of the tourism sector chosen for the region surveyed. In addition, each attraction and facility is tagged with a serial identification number.

In the twenty-first century, high-speed computers and advanced software not only enable the BIK System to compile and process much larger databases, and code more characteristics, but also allow a variety of simulation scenarios for tourism planning. Index cards are now eliminated, except when the manual method is used. Data for each attraction and facility are entered into a computer directly. The database is updated periodically when new attractions and facilities are built or created. The number of administrative jurisdictions is now greatly increased. The variety of attraction and facility characteristics total eighteen and could be more. Administrative jurisdictions are different for each survey and destination.

The sample digital coding system for recording tourist attractions and facilities, used manually or electronically by the BIK System, contains the following:

Group 1   **Attraction or Facility ID:** Indicates the attraction/facility *identification number*. The *name* of the establishment is cross-referenced from the *Directory of Establishments* separately. This number is assigned in numerical order by subareas. Additions and subtractions are possible. The upper limit is 9,999. Thus, *four* digits are allocated.

Group 2   **Address:** Indicates the tourism *region, state or province, county,* and *municipality* in which the tourist attraction/facility is located. Ordinarily, there will not be more than ninety-nine regions. Two digits are allocated. States or provinces are allocated two digits. Counties are allocated three digits. Municipalities are allocated three digits. Altogether, *nine* digits are allocated.

Group 3   **Location Coordinates:** Indicates the location in terms of the *Global Positioning System (GPS)*. A map locates the attraction/facility. Thus, four digits for longitude and four digits for latitude, or *eight* digits, are allocated.

Group 4   **Type of Attraction:** Indicates whether the attraction is a *site* or *event attraction*. Thus, *one* digit is allocated.

Group 5   **Attraction-Facility Duality Index:** Indicates the attraction/facility duality, ranging from 1 to 5 and 6 to 10. Thus, *two* digits are allocated.

Group 6   **Attraction or Facility Type:** Indicates the *six-digit NAICS establishment type* selected and assigned from the list of two-digit subsector industries making up the tourism sector. The subsector is shown as the first two digits from the left. Establishments are identified as the following four digits to the right. Thus, *six* digits are allocated.

Group 7   **Accessibility:** Indicates accessibility of the attraction/facility establishment from the nearest urban place in a tourism region, from the entry port to the country, or from the international place of origin. It is measured in miles/kilometers between two end coordinates of a link in a network of urban places. Accessibility is calculated in terms of the shortest distance by adding the distances of links between two chosen urban places. Thus, *four* digits are allocated.

Group 8   **Owner or Operator Number:** Indicates the person or company that owns and operates the establishment. The number is cross referenced to the *Directory of Establishments*. Thus, *four* digits are allocated.

Group 9   **User Fee:** Indicates *average (median) entrance ticket prices* for attendees/visitors in the local currency. Thus, *four* digits are allocated.

Group 10   **Estimated Spending** per visitor or attendee at the attraction or event. *Five* digits are allocated. (*Note*: For both Groups 9 and 10, more digits may have to be allocated in the case of very low value units of local currencies.)

Group 11   **Assigned Activities:** Indicates specific *activities* that tourists could perform at the attraction/facility. The activities are selected and assigned from the *List of Activities* compiled for the region. Thus, *two* digits are allocated.

Group 12   **Seasonality:** Indicates seasonal availability of the attraction/facility establishment, depending on whether the particular activity or activities are suitable at a particular season, or seasons, of the year at that particular location or remain open by the owner's choice. Thus, *one* digit is allocated.

Group 13   **Attendance:** Indicates the actual or estimated number of users compiled at the gate or reception area by season or year. Thus, *six* digits are allocated.

Group 14   **Quality Rating:** Indicates the quality rating of the attraction/facility in terms of its *significance* and *level of interest* for the tourist. Four levels of interest are defined, corresponding to the hierarchy of four concentric market areas. The rating also represents the comparative cost, measured as the distance tourists are willing to travel, and how much money they are willing to spend, in order to reach the attraction/facility and use the tourism service/product it offers. The levels of significance are:
- Attraction of *international* significance
- Attraction of *national* significance
- Attraction of *regional* significance
- Attraction of *local* significance

Thus, *one* digit is allocated.

Group 15   **Total Number of Paid Employees:** Indicates the maximum number of employees working at the attraction/facility establishment during the peak season of the year. Thus, *three* digits are allocated.

Group 16 **Number of Low-Wage, Nonprofessional, Minimum Training Requirements Paid Employees:** A measure of the potential of the facility/attraction to alleviate poverty. Peak season employment in this subcategory of total employment should be measured. *Three* digits are allocated. (Care must be exercised in measuring this number since some employees are paid low base wages but make considerably more in tips and gratuities.)

Group 17 **Promotion Budget:** Indicates the annual *advertising budget. Seven* digits are allocated.

Group 18 **Other:** *Six* digits are allocated.

A total of *seventy-six digits* are allocated for eighteen groups. More digits can be allocated when the number of characteristics surveyed exceeds eighteen or, attractions and facilities are exceptionally large, or, as noted, when very-low-value local currencies are involved. The eighteen groups are summarized in Figure 11.1.

A word of caution is in order. Rating the attractions and facilities by four levels of significance is based on the level of interest each attraction or facility creates in the minds of tourists. The governing principle of rating is to appraise the tourism value perceived by the tourist based on the recreational or utilitarian characteristics of the attraction and facility, not on other purposes they may serve. In turn, the tourism value corresponds to the level of interest and comparative cost expressed in terms of the size of the market area. The market area shrinks in size for that attraction or facility when the tourism value and level of interest go down. Major attractions and facilities draw tourists from longer distances and larger market areas.

11.4 SURVEYING TRAVEL STATISTICS FOR INTERNATIONAL AND DOMESTIC TOURISTS

Moving people around the globe by air, sea, and land is the first order of business for tourism. The origins of tourists, where they are going, for what purpose, for how long, and when they will get there are all information that is relevant for tourism planning.

The process of collecting travel statistics can be daunting. The sheer number of tourists and their particular characteristics may pose several challenges. They include:

- *Why conduct the survey?* The most important purpose of the survey is to understand the motivation of individual travelers as potential consumers of tourism products. Their behavioral preferences, activity choices, timing, expenditures, and length of stay are useful information for defining tourism market characteristics.
- *What to survey?* International travel statistics are primarily concerned with the origin of travelers, their nationality, the purpose of their visit, their modes of transportation, the length of their stay, and the amount of money they plan to spend during their visit. Additional questions may include the destination(s) they will be visiting, their age, income, marital status, and preferred activities. The date of the survey answers the seasonality question. Sensitive questions like age and income are often asked by establishing categories to allow respondents some sense of privacy. Names or precise addresses are not usually asked.
- *Where to conduct the survey?* The survey is conducted at entry points to a country, region, destination, attraction, and facility where the traveler comes face-to-face with survey takers, survey agents, or recording equipment. The nature of the information collected and the response vary, depending on the information needs of the place and on the willingness of the tourist to participate in the survey. Surveys are often conducted at locations where

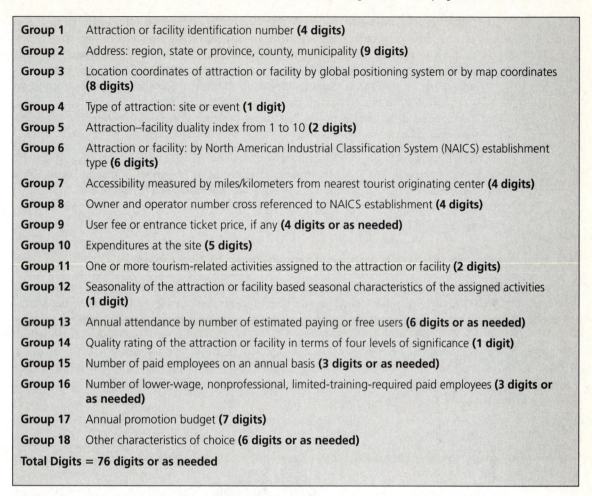

Group 1	Attraction or facility identification number **(4 digits)**
Group 2	Address: region, state or province, county, municipality **(9 digits)**
Group 3	Location coordinates of attraction or facility by global positioning system or by map coordinates **(8 digits)**
Group 4	Type of attraction: site or event **(1 digit)**
Group 5	Attraction–facility duality index from 1 to 10 **(2 digits)**
Group 6	Attraction or facility: by North American Industrial Classification System (NAICS) establishment type **(6 digits)**
Group 7	Accessibility measured by miles/kilometers from nearest tourist originating center **(4 digits)**
Group 8	Owner and operator number cross referenced to NAICS establishment **(4 digits)**
Group 9	User fee or entrance ticket price, if any **(4 digits or as needed)**
Group 10	Expenditures at the site **(5 digits)**
Group 11	One or more tourism-related activities assigned to the attraction or facility **(2 digits)**
Group 12	Seasonality of the attraction or facility based seasonal characteristics of the assigned activities **(1 digit)**
Group 13	Annual attendance by number of estimated paying or free users **(6 digits or as needed)**
Group 14	Quality rating of the attraction or facility in terms of four levels of significance **(1 digit)**
Group 15	Number of paid employees on an annual basis **(3 digits or as needed)**
Group 16	Number of lower-wage, nonprofessional, limited-training-required paid employees **(3 digits or as needed)**
Group 17	Annual promotion budget **(7 digits)**
Group 18	Other characteristics of choice **(6 digits or as needed)**
Total Digits = 76 digits or as needed	

FIGURE 11.1 Digital Computer or Manual Coding System for Surveying and Recording Tourist Attractions and Facilities Using the BIK System.
Source: Bulent I. Kastarlak

travelers have some time between travel activities, such as airport lounges and train and bus stations while passengers are sitting and waiting to board.

- *When to conduct the survey?* Depending on the nature of the tourism products offered and the vacation or business habits of the traveling public, dates of travel surveys are variable. It is important to collect information that is consistent by tourism seasons for ensuring seasonal and annual comparisons.
- *Who conducts the survey?* Generally, the organization that will process and analyze the data is the entity that conducts the international and domestic travel surveys. This could be an international organization like the UNWTO or the country's bureau of the census or department of statistics. Chambers of commerce, hotel, motel, and restaurant associations, or other private or government organizations conduct special-purpose surveys for the benefit of their membership and the public. Surveys conducted at the borders and by airlines are also primary sources information.

- ***What level of statistical reliability to accept?*** There are various statistical tests that can be applied to ensure that the inferences drawn from the survey data are reliable enough to provide useful answers for the various questions surveys are designed to answer. Care should be taken to ensure that tests of randomness, confidence levels, and margins of error are met in the survey design and execution. Surveys often are designed to achieve a ±3% error rate with a 95% confidence level. This generally means taking a random sample producing about twelve hundred usable responses for each question asked.

The UNWTO compiles and distributes international travel statistics. Each member government surveys and collects the data as time series according to its own set of standards and procedures. Currently, these international statistics are not comparable and are not internally consistent because of their multiple sources. These quality and compatibility problems remain to be resolved.

11.5   COMPUTER APPLICATION OF THE BIK SYSTEM

The BIK System of surveying data for tourism planning was first developed and introduced in 1970. The basic principles underlying the technique are discussed in Chapter 2. The fundamentals of these principles remain the same today. The electronic data processing technology, however, has improved exponentially. To take advantage of these new computer capabilities, refined survey and mapping techniques should be applied. (For the details of how the BIK System was conceived, see Appendices C and D.) An example of one of the original oblique-view topological maps of tourism destinations in the state of Massachusetts, using the SYMAP program, is shown in Figure 11.2.

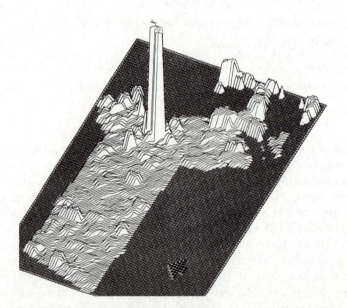

FIGURE 11.2   SYMAP Graphic Depicting Total Tourist Attractions by Municipality from the 1970 Tourism Development Report on Massachusetts.
Source: Bulent I. Kastarlak

The BIK System coding procedure has been updated to benefit from the advances in computer technology. Existing spreadsheet or database software programs for surveying and analyzing the tourism potential at national, regional, and local destination levels can be used based on this expanded coding procedure. The chosen software should allow for interactive use, tailoring the tourism information output to the specifications of the user—for example, optimizing the choice of activities, interest level, travel time, cost, season, and other preferences. The location of each activity point, attraction, or facility could be derived from the coordinates obtained through the GPS. The BIK System coding and software application could be used in concert with a geographic information system (GIS) for tourism planning. Display features of the software, such as charts, tables, maps, and graphs, could be incorporated into an overall software package. The software package, when developed with a database, could be available on the Internet or could be acquired by individual tourism analysts, travel planners and agents, students, tourism development planners, government planners, and others. Initially, databases for the BIK System could be developed selectively for priority tourism destinations, regions, and countries and could be applied to each separately. The software package could be broken into its component subprograms and also applied separately. These subprograms could be customized to the specifications of user markets like students, travel agencies, professional planners, and travelers.

11.6 MANUAL APPLICATION OF THE BIK SYSTEM

In some cases, electronic data processing and mapping may not be cost effective or may be unavailable. A comprehensive tourism resource survey covering all regional, state, and local municipalities will probably justify electronic data processing and mapping. However, smaller areas, like individual local destinations, may achieve very good results by building the database and generating maps manually. The BIK System, and its basic principles and procedures, are suitable for surveying both large areas with attractions and facilities having a large number of characteristics and small areas with many fewer characteristics. The system provides cumulative quantities by adding values from smaller to larger market areas.

Surveying individual tourist attractions and recording the information on standard index cards (or their equivalent) can be done manually if the attractions and facilities to be surveyed do not exceed about fifteen hundred items. This will correspond to approximately one hundred site and event attractions and facilities found in the given area. Municipal and regional planning agencies can undertake such surveys in a matter of weeks with three full-time staff. This staff should be composed of one professional planner, who also acts as the project manager and analyst, one graphic artist for mapping, and one clerical person for entering the information in the database. Searching data sources, tabulating, mapping, analyzing, and planning may take longer.

11.7 BUILDING THE ATTRACTION AND FACILITY DATABASE FOR THE BIK SYSTEM

There are many products of a tourist attraction and facility survey. To perform a tourism sector analysis and make statistical calculations, certain minimum data are required. If the data are not sufficient, supplementary surveys may be necessary.

A minimum database for analyzing attractions consists of:

- Total tourist attractions by six-digit NAICS categories and municipalities
- Total tourist site attractions by destination municipalities and region

- Total tourist event attractions by destination municipalities and region
- Total tourist site attractions of national significance by municipalities
  (Attractions of lesser significance are optional.)
- Total tourist event attractions of national significance by municipalities
  (Events of lesser significance are optional.)
- Winter and summer tourist site and event attractions by municipalities
  (Year-round attractions are desirable.)
- Tourist site and event attractions by activities and municipalities
  (Type of activity assigned by type of attraction)

A minimum database for facilities consists of:

- Total tourist facilities by six-digit NAICS categories by municipalities and region
- Tourist facility mixes by destination municipalities and region
- Most common facility types in the facility mix by region
- Comparisons between attraction mix rank and facility mix rank by municipalities
- Comparisons between facility mix and population density by municipalities
- Comparisons between facility mix and seasonality by municipalities
- Comparisons between facility mix and attraction mix by activity types
- Total number of establishments owning and operating all attractions and facilities

11.8   SOURCES OF ECONOMIC AND DEMOGRAPHIC DATA

The economic impact of daily excursionists can be substantial but difficult to estimate accurately because of their lack of travel records. Tourists, on the other hand, leave records in overnight accommodation establishments on their way to distant destinations. Their economic impact can be calculated from these records. Additional information, like expenditures on maintenance and construction of seasonal homes, and on sporting and recreational equipment, is desirable. However, data are often not available or usable. In the United States, economic data on recreational facilities operated by many government agencies and on private nonprofit recreational operations like membership golf, yachting, and riding clubs are generally not available. Some data for the economic analysis of the tourism sector can be drawn from the Censuses of Retail Trade and Services.

Another source is the United States Department of Labor, Bureau of Labor Statistics, Office of Survey Methods Research, which works with each state in compiling statistics, where information on employment, wages, and unemployment in industries covered by employment securities laws are collected. The details of these data and their method of collection may vary from one state to another. But employment and wage data for lodging places, eating and drinking places, amusement and recreation places and receipts, and receipts per capita from these places are available. The Bureau of Labor Statistics collects employment and earning statistics for the United States. National Income and Product Accounts of the United States are collected by the United States Office of Business Economics. Finally, the United States Census of Housing may be useful for estimating the number of seasonal homes.

The data collected in the United States are not perfect, but they can be used for calculating several indicators of the tourism economy. For international tourism information, the UNWTO is the best source for economic and demographic data collected by and for member countries.

11.9 SURVEYING THE GEOGRAPHIC AND ENVIRONMENTAL DETERMINANTS OF TOURISM

Mobility is the first and foremost environmental determinant of tourism. Tourism relies on the ability of consumers to move from their permanent place of residence to the location where the tourism product is consumed by performing certain activities. These activities are located at activity points of attractions and facilities. For spatial analysis, several vectors are given to each activity point for indicating the geographic directions of incoming tourists.

The mobility of tourists depends on many natural and human-made factors. Climate is by and large given. It is not controllable. It changes according to its natural rhythm. Topography, however, is partially controllable. For tourists to reach their destinations, the destinations have to be accessible. This accessibility is made possible by transportation facilities operating by air, sea, and land. Road, highway, tunnel, and bridge systems that accommodate private cars and public buses; railroads and train stations that accommodate trains; rails that carry streetcars; airlines and private airplanes operating from airports; cruise ships, private or chartered yachts, and marinas are used to access destinations. These are human-made and controllable factors.

Tourism development, like any other human activity, affects the elements of the natural environment in some ways. No other creatures in the history of the world ever affected their environment as strongly as humans have. Alteration of the ecosystem cannot be attributed to tourism alone, however. In fact, the opposite is true. Preservation of the environment is a top priority for tourism development. Damage to the environment includes environmental stresses in water and the atmosphere, including climate change, acid rain, desertification, deforestation, soil erosion, waste disposal, and biological diversity. All these considerations enter into the process of surveying and selecting tourist facilities and attractions. Strip mines left in their despoiled state without landscaping and other site-restoring improvements, destroyed forests, polluted rivers, floating dead fish, and garbage substantially negate tourism potentials.

11.10 HIERARCHY OF URBAN PLACES AND RANK SIZE OF TOURISM DESTINATIONS

The geography of tourism is closely tied to the past and present geography of urban development. Urban places increase progressively in size from a hamlet, village, town, and city to megacities or metropolitan (conurbation) areas. One or more of its functions determine the location of an urban place. Not only their proximity to water and farmland, but historically, their defensibility against enemies, convergence of trade routes on land or sea, and heads of navigation on rivers played roles in the choice of location for urban places. When these functions became obsolete or unnecessary, or when natural disasters like silting of a port, earthquakes, flooding, or changing travel patterns occurred, they caused cities to decline and in some cases to cease to exist as human habitats. Today, some of these once thriving urban places are relics. Ancient cities like Troy, Pompei, and Sardis in Europe and the Middle East; the lost cities of Mayan and Aztec civilizations in Central America; and, more recently, abandoned mining and cattle towns in the United States are tourist attractions and the focus of new tourist destinations nearby. The World Heritage Sites listed by UNESCO are the primary source for learning about these destinations of international value. (See Appendix A.)

In most geographic regions there is one dominant urban place or metropolis, but there are many large cities and even more towns and numerous villages. When their locations are marked on a map, urban places exhibit a distinct a pattern. The pattern shows a hierarchy of urban places, a system of urban settlements that is not a product of random selection. This pattern and hierarchy have led urban geographers and city planners to devise the Rank-Size Rule and central place theory.

The Rank-Size Rule and the pattern of hierarchy of urban places found interesting parallels with the rank size of tourist destinations and their geographic distribution. These relations are analyzed in Kastarlak's 1970 study *Tourism and Its Development Potential in Massachusetts* (see the Bibliography). The geographic pattern of tourism destinations gives important clues about the functional specialization of these destinations. Rank-size analysis assists in locating and developing new tourism destinations. It is an important indicator used for understanding the characteristics of the tourism product and determining whether a destination is of local, regional. or national significance

11.11   IDENTIFYING NATURAL ATTRACTIONS

Sightseeing to appreciate the beauty of land and sea, witnessing creatures frolicking on land and under the water, has been of great interest to tourists everywhere. Finding specimens that would have the highest tourism value is an exercise in the search for excellence. The breathtaking beauty of high mountains and the rustic beauty of the valleys between them; the lure of the ocean for sailing, cruising, and diving; or the rolling dunes of the desert for camel riding, as well as for holding rallies for high-performance specially adapted vehicles, have created specialized forms of tourism. Mountain climbing and skiing have been joined by rock climbing; cruising the seven seas; and visiting exotic ports of call, now including the crumbling glaciers of Alaska and Antarctica and the stepped Mayan temples. In pursuit of adventure, the forces of nature in raging rivers are not only admired, but also challenged by rafters.

The process of identifying natural attractions starts with reading the geography of the land, mountains, coastal areas, and seas belonging to the country or region where tourism may have potential. In reading the geography, the surveyor intuitively matches the visual qualities he or she is observing with recreational activities that would qualify the place as an attraction. Visual images are observed and interpreted intuitively or according to certain visual imageability guidelines that were proposed by Kevin Lynch during the 1960s. (See Chapter 2.)

Selecting scenic views from among the best viewing sites begins as an exercise in cartography. The conventional method of identifying natural attractions is walking or conducting a windshield survey (from a slowly moving car). In addition, the past experiences of explorers and published material on history and archeology are valuable sources. Flying over an area in a helicopter, or in an airplane equipped with special cameras and high-technology sensors, yields a photo mosaic that can be interpreted by specialist photo interpreters. Potential natural and human-made attractions can be identified even when they are buried and forgotten in a jungle or underground. Using new technology, it is now possible to read natural and human-made features buried under the Sahara, for example. When aerial photography is done scientifically, photogrammetry and photo interpretation can translate this information into tourism maps. Orbiting satellites can pinpoint relatively small structures on Earth from space and produce photographs of exquisite detail. The lost city of Ubar, known only in legends, was discovered in the sands of southern Oman by satellite imagery. GPSs can establish the coordinates of important natural and human-made attractions with great accuracy.

After assigning outdoor activities to all identifiable natural attractions, the surveyor can then superimpose these activities to identify an emerging destination and to demonstrate the strength of its attraction mix. Yellowstone National Park is a typical example of a place where the above-described method yielded multiple attractions suitable for sightseeing, camping, trekking, picnicking, animal studies, climbing, and rafting activities.

11.12   IDENTIFYING HUMAN-MADE ATTRACTIONS

Tourism is not limited to experiencing the marvels of nature. A protected environment can coexist with the marvels that human intelligence has created for thousands of years. There is something for every tourist's taste, preference, and interest to enjoy in the world. A rich, high-quality mix of natural and human-made attractions is a sure bet for a successful tourism destination.

Historically, human-made attractions, as opposed to natural attractions, are not the products of mindless human actions. They were created to serve purposes and functions that were needed during their time in history. These places were abandoned after having served the purposes and functions for which they were intended. However, their physical forms survive and are being turned into productive economic resource once again. Pyramids in Egypt, Mayan temples in Central America, the cliff palace at Mesa Verde National Park in Colorado, forgotten cities like Petra in Jordan, and medieval fortifications like Carcassonne in France are examples. Many more recent human-made marvels continue to attract a healthy volume of tourism. The Eiffel Tower in France, the Empire State Building and the Statue of Liberty in the United States, and Disney World in Orlando, Paris, and Tokyo draw thousands of visitors every day.

History, archeology, science, and human emotions like fear and joy are used by tourism developers with fertile imaginations as themes to create human-made attractions. In particular, unused, forgotten, or obsolete creations are recycled into new attractions. Supercomputers and other highly complex technology are now transforming these relics into mega attractions. Records and tales left behind by explorers are rich sources for finding and creating new human-made attractions.

The story of human kind from its early days is one of continuous adaptation in dealing with environmental conditions. Natural disasters, changes in the Earth's climate, and the exhaustion of game compelled hunter-gatherers to migrate and discover new areas and sources for their sustenance. About fifty thousand years ago they created their first weapons and tools, which increased their efficiency in the search for prey and in cultivating land. Their artifacts are now surfacing around the world and are becoming inspirations for the creation of new forms of tourist attractions and destinations.

During the past two millennia, important discoveries were made by roaming explorers in search of gold, trade, and knowledge. When Marco Polo traveled from his native Italy to Khan-Balek, the present site of Beijing, China, he opened the Silk Road. Today, this road is a major tourist attraction. When Pizzaro set out to conquer the Inca city of Cuzco in search of gold, he traveled inland from the coast with his small band of Spaniards on horses that terrified the natives. Today, tourist trekkers travel over the same trail and are captivated by breathtaking views as much as they are amazed by the audacity of the Spaniards.

More recently, the story of Petra, the lost and rediscovered city in Jordan first occupied by the Nabateans around 100 BC, is fascinating. Literally carved into the rocks of the valley and entered only through a very narrow slit between two rocks, Petra is an attraction of international status. Over the centuries, the place was occupied by many powers including the Greeks, Romans, and Byzantines. The last occupiers were the Crusaders, who abandoned their fortification in AD 1189. Over the span of many centuries since then, the Bedouins grazed their animals over the terrain of Petra, but in the Western world, it was completely erased from human memory and from the maps of the area. Only a few scholars remembered it. In 1812, a young Swiss explorer, Johann Ludwig Burckhardt, rediscovered Petra. British artist-explorer David Roberts immortalized the place in 1839 by producing four volumes of exquisite lithographs about the region and Petra. Today Petra is a major tourism destination. The nearby town of Wadi Mousa (Valley of Moses), where Moses preached, is prospering by providing the necessary tourism services.

Inspired by their great potential for drawing tourists, these and thousands of other natural and human-made attractions can create a rich mix of activity points. The objective of conducting surveys is to discover these thousands of natural and human-made attractions that potentially offer a future of sustainable tourism growth for their countries.

11.13   SURVEYING LAWS, REGULATIONS, AND GUIDELINES

The action programs, laws, and regulations that govern the day-to-day practices of tourism are derived from government tourism development policies. They include certification standards for public accommodations and restaurants, as well as special area regulations for seashores, yachting, national forests, and archeological treasures. Health codes protect the public from contamination and health hazards. At the local level, building codes, zoning ordinances, subdivision regulations, and historic preservation and environmental regulations protect the use of land and the safety, integrity, and longevity of structures. Urban development programs, laws, and regulations guide the preservation and growth of the built environment.

The depository of this information varies from one country to another. These documents are usually available from private publishers and from local and national agencies. The ultimate source of tourism-related legislation is the international depository at the UNWTO. The information can be found on the following Web site of the UNWTO: http://www.unwto.org/index.php.

A summary list of the laws and regulations pertaining to tourism development includes:

- Tourism laws governing the organization and practice of the ministry of tourism (or its equivalent)
- Typical municipal urban development laws and regulations
- Regulations governing planning and implementation in incorporated and unincorporated areas of municipalities, counties, and states
- Regulations governing the organization of development planning agencies
- Regulations for tourism-related facilities and areas
- Typical building codes
- Typical historic preservation regulations
- Typical antiquities and archeological protection regulations
- Typical land use zoning laws
- Typical environmental protection laws
- Typical property ownership laws
- Regulations governing licensing and practices of professionals
- Regulations governing the licensing of retail establishments such as liquor stores, bars, and restaurants

11.14   SURVEYING ENVIRONMENTAL, ECONOMIC, SOCIAL, AND CULTURAL IMPACTS OF TOURISM

Because of the enormity of the task, surveying the economic, social, and cultural impacts of tourism is a collective effort of universities, academicians, consultants, and government and international organizations. The costs of these surveys are usually paid by grants given by a coalition of governments and international organizations like UNWTO, UNESCO, and UNDP. Occasionally, cultural foundations like the Ford Foundation or the National Geographic Society, and tourism associations like convention bureaus and chambers of commerce, participate in funding these surveys.

The process starts with the tourism or academic organization preparing a survey proposal asking for a grant. The grant-giving source reviews the proposal. Depending on its merit, funds are authorized, an agreement is drafted and signed, a project manager is appointed, and technical staff is assigned and starts working. Sometimes outside experts are brought in for their specialized knowledge. Periodic progress reports are submitted. Payments or advance draws from the grant are received and disbursed. At the end, a final draft and then a final report are submitted, presented, and evaluated. If approved, the information is ready for use by many beneficiary organizations.

One particular aspect of these surveys merits further examination: how to prepare a field survey for collecting raw data directly from the subject population. For statistical accuracy, personal interviews are conducted with a random sample of individuals. A questionnaire is carefully prepared, taking into account the cultural sensitivities of the individual interviewees. A typical cultural attitudinal survey of a remote village in an area designated for tourism, for example, may result in the following information after processing the questions and answers of the field survey:

- Social structure, village organization, and village solidarity
- The village economy
- The household economy
- Household and family structure
- The domestic cycle
- Kinship
- Marriage
- Social rank
- Groups, feuds, and power
- The village and the world
  - Government in the village
  - Attitudes toward foreign visitors
  - Host–guest relationships
  - Pressures for social change
  - The demonstration effect
- Conclusions and recommendations

11.15 SURVEYING COMMUNITY PARTICIPATION

Community participation is a critical element in tourism planning. A sensitive approach is required to ensure the participation of the community. Strict and inflexible planning dictated from the top is a recipe for failure. Local movers and shakers, property owners, spiritual and cultural leaders, advocates, professionals, and business leaders are all part of the local decision-making process that could make or break a tourism development plan. The intensity of the dialogue, local protocol, attitudes toward foreigners, particularly tourists, and anticipated revenues and costs to the community from tourism are among the factors that enter into community deliberations.

One way to make it easier to obtain community support for a tourism project is to invite the community to participate in the deliberations of a public hearing. To ensure the participation of the community, property rights must be protected and the projected positive environmental, economic, social, and cultural impacts of the project must be convincing. Tourism policies must be deliberated by the national assembly of the country before becoming law, and must have input from the community and other interested parties. The future of tourism depends on this collaboration.

11.16 WHY USE THE BIK SYSTEM?

One might ask, why would one use the BIK System for analyzing in detail the potential of tourism at any given location? The answer to that question is the same today as it was when first given in 1970, when the method was developed and used in connection with Kastarlak's *Tourism and Its Development Potential in Massachusetts* (see the Bibliography). *At that time, and in many ways still today, there was (is) no objective, comprehensive planning method derived from a well-articulated set of basic principles available for understanding the complexities of the tourism industry.* What was available then, and to a large extent still is today, was a compilation of all kinds of narrative printed information from the media that could not be compared, evaluated, quantified, and analyzed systematically for identifying the composition of the tourism industry and the strengths and weaknesses of the tourism product. Subjectivity and inconsistency characterized the process, resulting in highly generalized opinions that could be interpreted in a number of ways. Traditionally, these opinions were judged sufficient before the researcher's attention turned to the two subjects that were considered more important—economics and marketing. The entire process of tourism planning revolved around these two subjects. Not surprisingly, most tourism researchers came, and continue to come, from these two professional disciplines.

The BIK System offered then, and forty years later is offering still, an alternative method that can put the tourism product, as it were, under a microscope. The internal structure, organization, and chemistry of the product are now visible to the naked eye. One can manipulate the quantified data in many ways to investigate the inner workings of the tourism industry objectively. It is now possible to explore the spatial dimensions and distribution of the product over the economic geography of subject areas. Another discipline is now emphasized in the process—regional development planning. Computer technology aids in making this detailed analysis possible at a scale to be useful for large cities, regions, and nations. However, when used as a manual method, with reduced data inputs and for smaller geographic areas, the BIK System still produces superior results and lends itself to planning and developing a viable and sustainable tourism industry.

Chapter Highlights

- Tourism planning starts by defining tourism as an economic sector. For this purpose, the NAICS classification system is used. Other comparable systems can also be used.
- Surveying and coding the tourism product uses the coding system proposed.
- Surveying natural attractions opens the possibility of creating many human-made attractions.
- Surveying travel statistics for domestic and international visitors is a separate operation generally undertaken by government departments.
- In the absence of computer technology, manual application of the BIK System is also possible, producing useful results.

- Classifying the hierarchy of urban tourism destinations determines the dominant center and its service area.
- Surveying the various impacts of tourism should be done methodically.
- The survey of government regulations covering various functions of the tourism industry should be consistent with the government's tourism policies and its multilevel plans.
- Community participation is essential for helping to determine and better articulate policies, plans, and regulations.
- Indices of sustainability and contributions to reducing poverty should be included in the tourism database and the analysis process.

12

Analyzing Tourism Economies and Tourism Products

This chapter presents analytical procedures used in establishing the potential of tourism and calculating various indicators that describe the characteristics and dimensions of the industry. The chapter discusses cause–effect relations among the production factors of tourism and techniques for quantifying some of the indicators using information published by the government or other sources.

- Tourism market demand is analyzed at the national, regional, and local destination levels.
- Analyzing tourism products can be done reasonably, accurately, and efficiently using the BIK System developed for surveying and analyzing attractions, facilities, and their characteristics.
- Tourism regions and their comparative advantages for attracting tourists depend on their pull effect, which can be measured by the Gravity Model.
- Tourism multipliers measure the jobs and income created by tourist expenditures traced through spending in secondary and tertiary tourism-related industries.
- Other analytical techniques for evaluating tourism projects include collecting data on tourists' expenditures, room occupancy, and carrying capacity, as well as using the Critical Path Method.

12.1 CONDUCTING MARKET DEMAND STUDIES

Tourism markets are demand pulled or supply pushed. In market economies, when demand is high for a product or service, the supply will try to catch up by producing more products or services. When the supply is excessive, demand is induced by promoting the product or service and/or lowering the price for the excess product or service. Several pieces of critical information are needed to analyze supply and demand to arrive at their equilibrium price. They include the volume and composition of market demand for the tourism product and services in the particular country, region, or local destination, and the quality and capacity of the tourism product and services, or supply, offered. These two groups of data-gathering exercises—on supply and demand—are undertaken separately, but are timed concurrently and ultimately brought together for economic analysis.

For estimating the market demand for international and domestic tourism at all three levels, the government of the country, region, or local destination compiles several types of information from various sources. At the national level, the government surveys incoming visitors at entry points. Also, as a member of UNWTO, the country may request data from that organization. Then the government processes the survey information for conducting the following analyses:

- Data and analysis of demand at the national level include:
  - Estimated number of international tourists traveling abroad from target countries
  - Estimated market share of international tourists coming to the destination country from target countries
  - Actual number of tourists entering the destination country from target countries, counted at air, land, and seaports of entry
  - Actual number of tourists entering the destination country from target countries, counted by length of stay and purpose of visit
  - Difference between assumed and actual market share
  - Seasonal change in the number of international tourists entering at ports of entry
  - Sex, age, and purpose of visit of incoming tourists surveyed at ports of entry
  - Estimated tourist expenditures by country of origin
- Data and analysis of demand at the regional level include:
  - Actual number of international tourists staying at regional overnight accommodations by country of origin, length of stay, and purpose of visit, enumerated as the sum total of local counts
  - Actual number of domestic tourists staying at regional overnight accommodations by place of residence in the country and length of stay, enumerated as the total of local counts
  - Seasonal change in the number of tourists staying at regional overnight accommodations, enumerated as the total of local counts
  - Estimated number of domestic and international tourists staying with friends and family relatives, enumerated as the total of local counts
  - Total number of domestic and international tourists and local excursionists attending various tourist attractions, enumerated as the total of local counts
  - Estimated tourist expenditures by country of origin and regional destination
- Data and analysis of demand at the local level include:
  - Actual number of international tourists staying at local overnight accommodations by nationality, length of stay, and purpose of visit, counted as the total of individual establishments
  - Actual number of domestic tourists staying at local overnight accommodations by place of residence in the country and length of stay, counted as the total of individual establishments
  - Seasonal change in the number of tourists staying at local overnight accommodations, counted as the total of individual establishments

- Estimated number of domestic and international tourists staying with friends and relatives
- Total number of domestic and international tourists and local excursionists attending various tourist attractions, counted as the total attendances at all local establishments
- Estimated tourist expenditures by country of origin and local destinations

The results of these analyses give planners the data needed for calculating the differences between supply and demand for the tourism product in terms of international and domestic tourists arriving at national, regional, and local levels.

12.2 ANALYZING THE SUPPLY, QUALITY, AND QUANTITY OF THE TOURISM PRODUCT

The computer-aided and manual methods used by the BIK System for surveying attractions and facilities are described in detail in Chapters 2 and 11. Here, the procedure applicable to both computer-aided and manual methods of analyzing the tourism product is presented. It is important that the procedure be followed as described. The choice of method depends on the volume of data to be analyzed and the complexity of the tourism economy of the country, region, or local destination. It also depends on the cost effectiveness and availability of the methods and the project time available.

The BIK System analyzes the tourism product in terms of attractions and facilities at four levels of planning: international, national, regional, and local destination. In addition, the tourism product is analyzed in terms of site and event attractions. The method and data requirements are different for each level.

- Data and analysis of attractions at the international level are confined to a few chosen attractions selected from among attractions at the national level. These attractions are used primarily for international marketing of the destination country.
- Data and analysis of attractions at the national level include:
  - National total tourist site attractions of national significance as the total of all regional tourist site attractions of national significance
  - National total tourist event attractions of national significance as the total of all regional tourist event attractions of national significance
  - National total tourist site and event attractions by types of activity as the total of all regional tourist site and event attractions by types of activity
  - Seasonality of national tourist attraction mixes based on seasonal activity characteristics
  - National tourist attraction mix of national significance by types of activity
  - Other supplementary analyses of the tourism product if appropriate
- Data and analysis of facilities at the national level include:
  - Scheduled international airlines serving the country, their schedules and total carrying capacity
  - Scheduled international cruise ships serving the country, their schedules and total carrying capacity
  - Scheduled and chartered international buses serving the country, their schedules and total carrying capacity
  - Accessibility of regional destinations from national ports of entry by air, land, and sea, by seasons of the year
  - Scheduled interregional airlines serving the regional airports of the country, their schedules and total carrying capacity
  - International and interregional highways and their carrying capacity

- International and interregional railways and their passenger-carrying capacity
- National total of selected tourist facilities, and their capacities, as the total of all regional tourist facilities and their capacities
- National comparison of selected regional facility mixes
- Other specialized analyses, including those of hotels, convention centers, communication systems, airports, their capacities and ratings
- Data and analysis of attractions at the regional level are optional but desirable for regional development planning purposes. They include:
  - Regional totals of tourist site attractions of regional significance as the total of all local site attractions of regional significance
  - Regional totals of tourist event attractions of regional significance as the total of all local event attractions of local significance
  - Regional totals of tourists site and event attractions by types of activity
  - Seasonality of regional facility mixes based on activity characteristics
- Data and analysis of facilities at the regional level include:
  - Regional totals of tourist facilities, and their capacities, as the total of all local tourist facilities and their capacities
  - Regional totals of tourist facilities by types of activity
  - Regional comparison of selected local facility mixes
  - Other specialized analyses of facilities
- Data and analysis of attractions at the local destination level include:
  - Local totals of tourist site attractions of national significance
  - Local totals of tourist event attractions of national significance
  - Local totals of tourist site attractions of regional significance
  - Local totals of tourist event attractions of regional significance
  - Local totals of tourist site attractions of local significance
  - Local totals of tourist event attractions of local significance
- Data and analysis of facilities at the local destination level include:
  - Local totals of tourist facilities and their capacities
  - Local facility mixes
  - Local totals of tourist facilities by types of activity

12.3 CORRELATION BETWEEN TOURISM PRODUCT AND TOURISM POTENTIAL AT LOCAL DESTINATIONS

Patterns are clues to underlying causes. When a sufficient number of attractions and facilities are correlated, their characteristics can help to explain the causes that made some destinations successful and others less successful or unsuccessful. Four correlations in particular have given significant clues. They are:

- Correlation between common facility types and the number of local destinations
- Correlation between the rank of attraction mix and the rank of facility mix
- Correlation between the facility mix and the population density of local destinations
- Correlation between the facility mix, attraction mix, and seasonality

Other correlations drawn from characteristic patterns of the tourism product are possible. The findings of Kastarlak's *Tourism and Its Development Potential in Massachusetts* study, completed in 1970 (see the Bibliography), are presented here as illustrations.

In facility mixes of 351 cities and towns of Massachusetts, the following ten most common facility types were found:

Number of Municipalities	Facility type	Rank	NAICS number
307	Drinking Places	1	722410
291	Auto Service Stations	2	447410–447190
198	Public Parks	3	712190
196	Hotels, Motels, Tourist Courts	4	721110–721120
			721191–721199
194	Gift Shops	5	453220
184	Eating Places	6	722110–722211
			722212–722213
179	Antique Stores	7	453220
174	Intercity Bus Lines	8	485210
155	Bowling Lanes	9	713950
144	Golf Courses	10	713910

The ranking of tourist facility types by municipalities identified the ten most common tourist facilities in Massachusetts. These facilities served all residents, excursionists (day trippers), and tourists. Their analysis revealed that only the facility mixes of 26 municipalities out of 351 had the ten most common facilities. Facility mixes grew in diversity in proportion to the growth of their population. The municipality with the largest population and the largest facility mix was Boston. At the bottom of the mix rank, only one town, with the smallest population, had one type of facility. This correlation confirmed the supposition that the rank order of the population size of a municipality was equal to the rank order of its tourist facility mix in a region.

This ranking exercise showed other possibilities. The next correlation was between rankings of tourist attraction mixes and facility mixes. A correlation was made between the rankings of thirty-three municipalities with the highest attraction mixes and the rankings of their facility mixes. The findings demonstrated the veracity of the central place theory and Christaller's pattern of urban places. Boston was the largest urban place in Massachusetts. It ranked first in the ordering of both attraction mixes and facility mixes. It provided specialized services to residents, excursionists, and tourists in its hinterland in Massachusetts, but also in southern New Hampshire to the north, Rhode Island to the southwest, and Connecticut to the southwest. Concord, New Hampshire, Providence, Rhode Island, and Hartford, Connecticut, were secondary urban centers with their own hinterlands. Boston, however, was the dominant central place of the New England region that included all three secondary hinterlands. The attraction mix–facility mix correlation indicated that seventeen of the thirty-three municipalities with the highest-ranking attraction mixes also had the highest-ranking facility mixes. This finding suggested that municipalities with the largest number of tourist attractions had more than a 50% probability of having the largest number of tourist facilities. This finding raised the question of why the remaining 50% of municipalities did not have more tourist facilities.

The three-way correlation among facility mix, attraction mix, and population density of tourist destination municipalities provided the answer. Municipalities with fifty facility types in their facility mix and population densities ranging from zero to fifteen thousand people per square mile were selected. The selection revealed that fifteen of the forty-five municipalities at the top of the attraction mix ranking had larger facility mixes than other municipalities with comparable population densities. This finding suggested that tourist destination municipalities needed the extra facility types in their facility mix to serve excursionists and tourists visiting their communities. Conversely, compared to other municipalities, those where facility mixes were more diverse than their resident population need were also major tourist destinations and had more diverse attraction mixes. The clue lay in the diversity and complexity of the economic base of the communities. This finding was consistent with the *basic* versus *nonbasic* classification of establishments used by planners and analysts for studying the economic base of areas. The concept is briefly explained in the following Wikipedia Web site: http://en.wikipedia.org/wiki/Economic_base_analysis.

Why did some urban centers with high attraction mix ratings have low facility mix ratings? The answer lay in the degree to which these municipalities had controlled their commercial development. These communities in Massachusetts had strict land use standards and zoning law enforcement. Towns like Lexington, Concord, Salem, and Greenfield, with important historic attractions and beach resort communities like Chatham, Wellfleet, and Sandwich in Cape Cod had particularly strict comprehensive planning and zoning enforcement practices. This finding suggested that destinations with highly ranked attraction mixes discouraged some commercial development in their communities. However, communities around them formed rings of highly diverse facility mixes to take advantage of the economic opportunities generated by these highly ranked tourist destinations in their center.

It is often stated that one of the major problems in developing tourism is solving the problem of seasonality. Wide fluctuations in the number of tourists arriving at different months of the year, combined with traditional vacation seasons, have exerted strong influences on the economy of many destinations. While certain fixed costs of operating tourism establishments are spread over a twelve-month period, revenues are confined to the months when the establishments remain in operation. In cases where profit objectives are attained during these few months, and for other personal reasons, the seasonality of the businesses is acceptable. However, in most commercial operations, year-round, well-balanced business operations are considered essential for growth and better return on investment. Thus, seasonality could cost the community dearly in terms of reduced employment, payrolls, and wholesale and retail sales by underutilizing the tourism potential of the destination.

Businesses of tourist establishments, both attractions and facilities, are improved by using two types of growth scenarios. One growth scenario is to extend the tourist season at both ends by adding more attractions and activities to the mix. This would increase the revenues somewhat, but fixed costs would increase. The second growth scenario is to expand the capacity of the establishment where the length of the season is the same. Here, fixed costs would remain basically the same, but revenues would expand according to the anticipated increase in the market share of the establishment. A third option exists for those activities that are essentially mobile. They can move from one peak season tourist area to another area with a different peak season. For example, excursion ships, airplanes, and some land vehicles can migrate from northern areas to southern areas, and vice versa, following peak tourist seasons. Some indoor and outdoor vendors (e.g., those with food and gift shops, carts and stalls) can also move. Entertainment venues such as circuses and stage shows can also migrate; in fact, many prosper by going on tours.

Several conclusions can be drawn from the correlations stated above:

• Destinations with the largest tourist attraction mixes have more than a 50% probability of having the largest tourist facility mixes.
• In municipalities where the diversity of the tourist facility mix is greater than their resident population may demand, the local economy is engaged in the export activities of tourism

and, compared to other municipalities with less diverse facility mixes, has more diverse attraction mixes.

- Destinations with highly diverse attraction mixes but limited facility mixes discourage commercial development in their communities. But the ring of communities around them often offers larger and more diverse facility mixes to satisfy the demands of residents and tourists.
- The seasonality of tourism could cause diminished employment, payrolls, and wholesale and retail sales. Extending the tourism season at both ends or expanding the tourist facility without extending the season are two possible scenarios that can be used to overcome the effects of seasonality. Both scenarios will be more effective if the attraction mix expands concurrently.

Comparative analyses of the tourism product of a country at the national, regional, and local destination levels show the strengths and weaknesses of the attraction and facility mixes at each level. A study of the geography and spatial distribution of attractions and facilities and their relation to the urban system identifies the locations where tourism development can be concentrated. The study is also helpful in preparing a marketing strategy for maximizing the national, regional, and local benefits of tourism development.

12.4 DEFINING TOURISM DEVELOPMENT REGIONS

Tourism regions and local destinations are created where concentrations of high-quality tourist attractions are found. The boundaries of regions are drawn around areas occupied by attractions, and facilities serving them, by following municipal boundaries or other government jurisdictions as much as possible. Tourism development regions are overlay regions. Their boundaries may not coincide with the jurisdictional boundaries set by the government. Although an overlay region is useful for geographic precision, it can present many survey and analytical problems. The data collected may be limited to statistical and administrative units of the government. Surveying tourism regions with free-form boundaries can be expensive. Therefore, the smallest common administrative unit for which statistical information is collected by the government is the building block for delineating tourism regions for development planning. Depending on the country's system of government, these smallest units could be the village, municipality, county, state, department, canton, prefect, province, *ilçe, il, opanchayat*, and the like. Statistical consistency is ensured by grouping these smallest government units together. Care must be taken to ensure that each tourism destination region includes at least one administrative and distribution center with ties to the regional and national transportation networks.

There are different guidelines for drawing the boundaries of economic development regions. It is likely that the boundaries of tourism regions will match the boundaries of some, if not all, economic regions. If statistical data are available for both, the more tourism regions match a few, or all, economic regions, the better. The actual number of economic regions into which the country is divided depends on the natural terrain of the country, its size, and whether or not it has homogeneous characteristics. Large countries are divided into greater numbers of regions than smaller countries. If there are clear language, religious, ethnic, or racial differences, the basis for defining the regions will be cultural. Generally, the differentiation is based on natural factors of the land, economic specialization, and the transportation system. The physiographic and environmental characteristics of the area, like topography, geology, climate, and accessibility of urban centers, play roles in delineating the boundaries of economic regions.

Administrative units are best for defining tourism and economic development regions. For example, the United States has forty-eight contiguous states in North America. They are combined into regions such as the Northeast, Northwest, Southeast, Southwest, South Central, and North Central. The states are divided into counties and their municipal jurisdictions. Turkey has sixty-seven provinces composed of municipalities that are combined into ten economic development regions. About four of these regions coincide with high-priority tourism regions. Holland has two regions, eastern and western.

12.5   COMPARATIVE ADVANTAGE OF TOURISM DEVELOPMENT REGIONS

Tourism development policy is based on creating advantages among competing tourism destination regions for attracting visitors. In market economies, the policy attempts to establish equilibrium prices in one region that will be lower than those of other regions in order to create a comparative advantage. Other than in perfect competition, however, equilibrium may not be attainable, particularly in developing economies where prices are controlled artificially by the government. In these situations, government, not the market system, determines where capital for tourism development is allocated. Government encourages economic activities in leading sectors to obtain a pattern of production and trade that will maximize income and employment in the regions. If tourism is one, or the only, leading economic sector, the government will favor concentrated and sequential growth strategies to achieve economies of scale that will induce further development in the leading sector and in other sectors to which tourism is linked. This kind of policy has broad applications in making investment decisions for tourism-related projects.

12.6   TOURISM AS AN EXPORT SECTOR

Classical growth theory holds that one of the major reasons a region expands its economy is increased demand for its exportable commodities and services, whether due to an increase in income or a change in taste in its market area. Reduction of the processing or transportation costs of the export region will likewise promote growth. Historically, in a growth region, the creation of a new export industry results in the influx of capital investment for both the export industry and its related supporting industries. Investment leads to growth of exports. Calculating the volume of these exports leads to the calculation of the optimum size and sustainability of the growth industry.

By its very nature, tourism is an export industry. Its entire product is exported to visitors from other lands. The distinction from the products of other export industries lies in the fact that the consumer—the tourist—consumes the tourism product at the place of its production, which is in the tourism region. To the extent that the export is profitable, investment capital will flow in and some of the profits will be reinvested. Both indigenous savings and reinvested capital will go to the growth industry until returns begin to diminish. Then savings and reinvestment capital will tend to flow to other economic sectors and possibly to other regions with higher rates of return.

A regional tourism economy operating under the conditions of a fully developed market system need not pass through the classical stages of economic growth. Florida, in the United States, for example, substantially expanded its tourism growth in the tertiary stage of its economic development (when service industries were predominant in the economy). Given sufficient resources, the ability of a region to start or substantially expand a tourism industry depends on two conditions. First, the regional economy is open (no trade barriers) and government plays a supportive role. Second, other regions of the country, and perhaps even other countries, are able to supply the supporting products and services the region needs for tourism development. When these conditions are present, a tourism economy can start to develop at any stage of overall national economic development.

12.7   TOURISM MULTIPLIERS

Multipliers are measures of increased economic activity created throughout an economy by activity in its basic or export-oriented sectors. One kind of multiplier is the employment multiplier of tourism. An employment multiplier can be applied to employees working in establishments constituting the first-tier or tourism sector of a tourism region. The multiplier estimates the number of employees needed to work in the second- and third-tier establishments elsewhere servicing and supplying the first-tier establishments. Additionally, as wages are spent in the regional economy by employees of the first-, second-, and third-tier establishments, a need is created for even more employees. An overall employment multiplier should account for both types of growth stimuli. A flow diagram of tourist investment expenditures moving through an economy, creating a multiplier effect, is shown on the following animated Web site: http://www.geographyfieldwork.com/TouristMultiplier.htm.

Another indicator is the income multiplier of tourism. This multiplier compares every unit of money spent by tourists in a tourism region for buying the services and products of first-tier establishments with the units of money earned by second- and third-tier establishments elsewhere servicing and supplying the first-tier establishments. For both types of multipliers, the indicator is a ratio. Employment multipliers can range from a low of 1:1 to a high of 3:1. Income multipliers could range even higher, depending on other factors, like the import content of the tourism product and services. Income and employment multipliers measure the same phenomenon: money circulating through a regional economy. Both are calculated and used because planners and policymakers are interested in reporting both employment and income impacts.

Economic base studies use multiplier analysis. These studies distinguish between basic and nonbasic industries. Their analysis accepts the principle that a region grows by producing goods and services locally and by selling them beyond its borders. These basic or export activities not only pay for any raw materials that the region cannot produce itself, but also provide means for supporting nonbasic service activities that supply local industries.

When applied to tourism, the classic basic and nonbasic multiplier concept needs further interpretation. Tourism functions as an export or basic industry. But the majority of tourism industry establishments belong in the nonbasic, or service, category. The anomaly is that although they are service establishments, they behave as if they are basic industries exporting their products and services.

The explanation for this contradiction lies first in the fact that the tourism product is never shipped out from its place of production and is not exported in the conventional sense. It is consumed at the place of production, therefore making tourism both a basic and a nonbasic industry at the same time. Second, service industries serve local residents regularly. When tourists demand services, their demands are added to those of residents. As a result, establishments in attraction and facility mixes of tourist destinations are more diverse and larger in number than in other communities. Tourism expands the business of local service establishments beyond that of serving residents. Although it is largely a service industry, tourism behaves like a basic industry, and when it grows owing to nonresident expenditures, related or supplier industries grow with it.

The 1970 tourism survey conducted in tourism destination cities and towns of Massachusetts revealed that the variety and number of tourism sector establishments were significantly above those necessary to sustain the resident population. This was the result of the export and multiplier effects of tourism. Michael Peters, in his book *International Tourism* (1969), was among the first researchers to make a detailed investigation of tourism multipliers. His multipliers were aggregate multipliers of expenditures in the regional tourism economy. An **aggregate multiplier** proposes that any increase in tourism demand will have the same multiplier effects throughout other sectors of the economy. The concept led John M. Bryden to propose the following income multiplier formula:

$$Kt = \frac{\Delta Y}{\Delta T}$$

where Kt is the income multiplier of tourism, ΔT is the change in expenditures attributable to receipts from tourism exports, and ΔY is the consequential change in domestic incomes resulting from the change in tourist receipts.

The classic Keynesian multiplier for the tourism economy, on the other hand, is a weighted average of the individual sector multipliers comprising the tourism economy. Tourism sector establishments collect tourist receipts, and the tourism income multiplier becomes the average of multipliers for each group of establishments comprising the tourism overlay sector. In turn, the income multiplier of each group is weighted by its share of total tourist receipts.

There is disagreement about the validity and usefulness of tourism multipliers. Tourism multipliers are conceived as a method to measure either the benefit or the potential benefit of tourism to the economy as a whole. But any attempt to measure the benefits from a particular economic activity requires some assessment of the real cost to society for devoting resources to that activity (the opportunity cost of not devoting the resources to other activities) and a comparison with the benefits to be obtained from the allocation of these resources to other activities. Tourism multipliers do not make these comparisons. Because of this shortcoming, the critics believe that benefit/cost analysis is a better method to assess the overall benefits of tourism.

Another criticism is that the magnitude of multipliers decreases as full employment is achieved in an economy, and this is rarely accounted for overtly in multiplier analyses. If there are no or few people to take the new jobs created by more tourism expenditures circulating through the economy the employment multiplier will be small, becoming zero if there are no new job seekers. This is a somewhat hypothetical criticism because full employment is rarely achieved and because labor is quite mobile, being attracted to new jobs, especially in developing economies. Despite their criticisms, tourism multipliers remain accepted indicators used in the absence of better ones.

12.8 EVALUATING TOURISM INVESTMENT PROJECTS

Appraising the multiple impacts of proposed tourism projects is a complex but necessary process. Available technical procedures may not always be useful in exploring and measuring all variants and dimensions of proposed tourism projects. Often, the process is more subjective and descriptive than quantitative.

The following information is needed for reviewing and appraising investment projects in general and tourism projects in particular:

- A description of the technical and economic characteristics of the project. These include location, site analysis, building program, market analysis, and demographic, social, and cultural traits.

- Estimates of the project's impact on the economy during both the construction and operation periods. The influence of the project may be both direct and indirect. The direct effects consist of direct contribution to employment, income, taxes, and production within the sector. The indirect effects are those on second- and third-tier establishments of the sector.
- Use of financial criteria for selecting projects including cash flow projections, profitability, repayment terms, and foreign exchange earnings.

The traditional investment criterion is the profitability of the project. Annual profits are calculated as monetary revenues minus costs to the entrepreneur and are related to the capital invested. However, benefit/cost analysis is a more appropriate method when the investment is evaluated from a national or public policy point of view. Tourism investment projects are particularly well suited for this method. Benefit/cost analysis includes as benefits not only the monetary benefits but also imputed monetary returns. The benefits are not compared with the capital invested, but with the annual total costs, including capital, operating, environmental, and social costs. There is no easy way to choose between the two methods. For some, profitability and benefit/cost objectives have the same effects. They believe that profit maximization leads to optimum welfare for the community as a whole, accepting the classic assumptions of general economic analysis (e.g., perfect competition, inability of one producer or a group of producers to affect market prices, perfect ease of entry into markets, perfect market information, and perfect access to capital and labor markets).

In developing countries with mixed economic systems, profit maximization leading to community welfare is usually far from realized. Scarcity of capital and foreign exchange is combined with large unemployment to distort the basis of the benefit/cost analysis. In these economies, market prices of products and factors of production are not a correct expression of costs. For the appraisal of investment projects in developing countries, it is necessary to have a benefit/cost method that takes into account the specific circumstances of their economies. In its adaptation to developing economies, the benefit/cost analysis may include the following factors:

- Investment projects are not considered individually, but as a combination or as a program of projects. The projects to be included in the program need not be of the same kind. For example, in appraising a mixed-use resort destination, it is preferable to consider the hotel, golf club, and residential and commercial facilities as a complex, rather than appraising the hotel and other facilities individually.
- The benefits are measured as additions to the national product induced by the investment program. The values of scarce factors used are counted as negative benefits and are subtracted from the positive benefits. Land is one such scarce factor, particularly when agriculture is the main source of employment and subsistence in traditionally agrarian countries or regions. The loss of the arable land in perpetuity for developing tourism facilities and attractions could be a serious blow to the economic stability of the region.
- If the tourism facility is poorly designed, built, and operated, it will fail. The failure of the facility will cause a sizable amount of capital to be frozen in an unused facility, and possible environmental damage as well.
- Poverty alleviation is a factor of major importance in evaluating the merits of a tourism investment project. The issue is not academic or even entirely financial. It has human and cultural dimensions. It concerns whether the project will cause dislocations in the social fabric of the region and whether it will improve the lives of the native population by reducing poverty.

- The extent to which the local economy will benefit from the investment project depends on the integration of the project into the everyday life of the destination population and on the linkages it has with regional and national economies. Factors like the import content of the project have important implications for import substitution potential.

12.9   CRITICAL PATH METHOD FOR SCHEDULING TOURISM PLANNING AND PROJECT ACTIVITIES

Planning and developing tourism is a complex process. Since its inception during the 1970s, the number and sequence of individual planning tasks identified by the BIK System have grown and now include a great many considerations. This is a welcome change. Tourism planning is progressively becoming a multidisciplinary vocation requiring more than descriptive and narrative deliberation and simple concepts. The process now requires computational capabilities, quantifiable factors, formulas, statistically sound procedures, and three-dimensional spatial thinking. The Critical Path Method (CPM) is one tool that could be used to make planning and developing tourism a more orderly process.

With the evolution and broadening of tourism development planning, new tools for survey, analysis, and plan making became necessary. As the capabilities of computer technology increased over the past four decades, new technology found new applications. Tourism development planning is one of these new applications. It is now possible to apply many planning methods, and computational and graphic techniques used in economics, real estate, geography, urban and regional planning, and business management to tourism development planning. This makes tourism planning an interdisciplinary and better-unified decision-making process that can be used to understand and organize the future of the tourism sector. The invisible hand of market economics is paired with the knowledge acquired from tested and tried past experience to guide the future of tourism. The Gantt Chart and CPM are two methods that have found new use in tourism development planning.

In the late 1930s, military project managers needed a method for planning and controlling their projects. They needed to visualize the sequence of tasks, or schedule, of their project work over time. This need became imperative during World War II. A new method conceived by Henry Gantt found wide application. This method involved the use of the **Gantt Chart**, which shows graphically the beginning and end of each task in parallel horizontal bars over time, displaying the tasks and their scheduled starting and completion dates in terms of calendar days, months, and years. Gantt Charts that are more complex show the progress of the work in terms of who is doing what. In addition, the S curve indicating the cash disbursements made from start to finish is superimposed on the Gantt Chart. Another superimposed normal bell curve indicates the man-hours spent on the project.

The Gantt Chart is simple to construct and easy to interpret. It is widely used in many lines of work and many types of project. However, it has its shortcomings. Interrelationships and interdependencies between tasks are not shown. There is no contingency time. It is not possible to know which task is critical and could hold back the progress of the project. The chart cannot be used for analyzing the impacts of tasks performed. It gets cumbersome when there are too many tasks and many persons or companies working on these tasks. Consequently, Gantt Charts are used when smaller amounts of information are necessary and the project is relatively simple.

CPM is a business management technique that has found practical application in tourism surveys, analysis, and planning. It originated from a need, as most inventions do. In the late 1950s, the Dupont Company was engaged in a project for renovating its petrochemical refineries.

The managers of the project needed a project planning and control technique, particularly for reducing the amount of time necessary for phasing a refinery out of service for repairs. At about the same time, the U.S. Navy's Fleet Ballistic Missile division was engaged in designing and building the Polaris nuclear submarine. The Navy needed a better technique for predicting the impact of delays caused by its many subcontractors on the project.

CPM is a major improvement over the Gantt Chart and some other more advanced techniques like matrices and curves. CPM has three major elements: activities, activity durations, and linkages or interrelationships. These elements are organized into a network of project activities showing their planned progression in a specified direction. The duration of each activity is also given. Cumulatively, the path and the length of the project are shown graphically by following the path of activities and indicating their combined duration. As a refinement, high, medium, and low estimated durations for each activity can be incorporated, yielding overall alternative total project durations, which can be used to reallocate project resources to specific activities to minimize the total time for project completion.

There are several subsidiary methods derived from CPM. They include the Arrow Diagram Method (ADM), the Precedence Diagram Method (PDM), and the Program Evaluation and Review Technique (PERT). These derivative methods are not described here. The reader should consult sources containing in-depth explanations of CPM.

The smallest elements of CPM are three subelements—node, activity, and arrow—that, when connected to other subelements, form the network. The network is represented graphically in two ways. In PDM, the node defines the work activity and the line with the arrow shows the direction and the relation of that activity to the next node of specified activity. In ADM, the opposite happens. The line with the arrow shows the activity between two consecutive nodes or the beginning and the end of the activity.

CPM is used for planning and scheduling tasks to ensure control of the project. During the planning stage, the project is broken down into specific activities; the amount of time required to complete each activity is estimated; the total duration is calculated by adding individual activity durations; and the network of relations is selected and tested for its logical sequence. During the scheduling stage, the limitations of time and resources are determined; a work calendar is established; and the critical paths are determined. Float activities (those off the critical paths) are also identified.

In choosing activities, it is important to estimate the probability of a particular activity's contributing to the completion of the project. In determining the path to project completion, it is important to determine the sequence of activities and whether one activity can be ongoing while other activities are still being completed or just starting. The technicalities of CPM call for defining other terms, like **forward pass–backward pass**, **total float**, and **free float**.

Two critical paths are defined: first, as the sequence of activities and relationships of the project network from beginning to end with the longest cumulative duration and, second, as the total of all activity durations on another path equal to the shortest project duration. If the project completion date is set for the earliest possible project completion, the shortest path is selected. If project objectives include more even distribution of resources, the longest path may be selected.

CPM has multiple advantages:

- It gives a clear idea of the project's activity sequence and network of relationships.
- It shows the project's phases and forecasts their completion dates.
- It enables project planners and managers to analyze the timing and sequence of phases before committing further time and money to the project.

- It identifies problems and omissions in advance.
- It gives a total overview of the project to the project team.
- It indicates critical activities and assists in making decisions about allocating resources to them.

Nevertheless, CPM has certain shortcomings:

- It could become overly complex.
- Detailed information may not be available.
- It requires thorough knowledge of the project.
- Monitoring and reporting the work could become time-consuming.
- Full-time, specialized staff may be required to manage CPM.

In planning and developing tourism, CPM can be invaluable at all three levels: national, regional, and local. The tasks or activities of projects are different at each level. At the macro or national level, activities consist primarily of studies and reports that are statistical and computational in nature. At the regional and local destination levels, activities consist of managing construction projects associated with new attractions and facilities of the tourism product. CPM is useful in conducting all of these activities.

12.10   GRAVITATIONAL PULL OF TOURIST ATTRACTIONS AND DESTINATIONS

For many decades, urban planners, social scientists, traffic engineers, and economists have been using a modified version of one of Isaac Newton's laws of gravitation for estimating the flow of people, automobiles, and trade between geographic points of origin and destination. Like the gravitational pull between stars, planets, and any other objects with mass, the gravitational pull of tourism between origins and destinations is measured for areas like zip code areas, traffic zones, census tracts, cities, countries, and even continents.

The gravitational pull (mass) of each tourist destination is measured in terms of the competitive advantage of one destination over another (expressed as the size and mix of attractions and facilities). In turn, the competitive advantage of a destination depends on the comparative cost of experiencing the tourism product at that destination. Accordingly, the Gravity Model can be used for estimating the gravitational pull of each destination. Another application of the Gravity Model is in examining consumer behavior in market areas. The model uses population and employment as measures of mass or size and distance or travel time as measures of separation between the masses. Social scientists use the population size of two places and their distance from one another for measuring the strength of the bond between two geographic locations. The relative bond between two locations is equal to the population of A multiplied by the population of B divided by the distance between A and B squared:

$$\frac{(\text{Population A} \times \text{Population B})}{(\text{Comparative Cost as Distance from A to B})^2} = \text{Gravitational Pull}$$

An attraction value, instead of population, can be estimated from surveying and coding of the attraction. It is multiplied by A, the population of the zone or area being evaluated. The product of A and B is divided by the comparative cost of reaching B from A squared. The result is the measure of the bond between the two points or the gravitational pull of the attraction or destination, A or B. The gravitational pull of destination B from origin A can also be expressed in terms of its competitive advantage over C and D or more destinations when similar gravitational pulls are calculated for C and D or more destinations with respect to A. The exponent 2 used in the denominator of the ratio is an approximation. In applications analyzing travel behavior, the exponent is calibrated from survey data.

12.11   CORE INFORMATION FOR PLANNING SUSTAINABLE TOURISM

Core indicators were developed by the UNWTO to provide assistance to tourism planning and development agencies. They represent the base-level prototype information necessary to manage sustainable tourism in most destinations. Core information covers a limited range of subjects and serves to monitor key elements of the human–environment interaction.

Core indicators are practical to obtain and are selected by the UNWTO for the broadest possible use by most nations, regions, and destinations around the world. Each indicator is connected to a set of conservation measures applicable to a particular area for protecting the environment. The core indicators are:

- Site protection
- Stress
- Use intensity
- Social impact
- Development control
- Waste management
- Planning process
- Critical ecosystems
- Consumer satisfaction
- Local satisfaction
- Tourism's contribution to the local economy
- Carrying capacity
- Attractiveness

This information can be collected, prepared, and posted in detail on their Internet Web site by the authorities of each nation or region. Public and local tourism establishments can use the information and adopt it to local conditions. It is possible to merge the UNWTO data with the database of the BIK System for local and regional tourism development planning.

Chapter Highlights

- For estimating the market demand for countries, regions, or local destinations, governments compile several types of information from various sources.
- The results of market analysis give planners the data needed for calculating the differences between the supply of and demand for the tourism product in terms of international and domestic tourists arriving at national, regional, and local levels.
- The BIK System has successfully analyzed the tourism product in terms of attractions and facilities at four levels of planning—international, national, regional, and local destination levels—analyzed separately. In addition, attractions are analyzed in terms of site and event

attractions. The method and data requirements are different for each level.

- Patterns are clues to underlying causes. When a sufficient number of attractions and facilities are correlated, their characteristics can help to explain the probable reasons that made some destinations successful and others less successful or unsuccessful.

- If tourism is one, or the only, leading economic sector, governments will favor concentrated and sequential growth strategies to achieve economies of scale that will induce further development in the leading sector, and in other sectors to which tourism has linkages. This policy has broad applications in making investment decisions for tourism-related projects.

- Various methods of analysis are used to evaluate tourism potentials and recommend tourist programs and projects. Among these are tourism multipliers of initial tourist spending, calculating rates of return on invested capital, benefit/cost analysis, PERT, CPM, gravitational attraction analysis, and use of core indicators.

Planning Tourism at National, Regional, and Local Destination Levels

This chapter presents the sequence of policies, goals, plans, programs, projects, and measures to be prepared at the national, regional, and local destination levels for planning and developing tourism. It presents the information collected and analyzed and the conclusions reached. It describes the regulations necessary for managing the tourism industry.

- The tourism planning process involves many decision-making steps for preparing policies, plans, programs, projects, and measures.
- Standards and regulations are derived from tourism development policies.
- There are two types of marketing plans. They serve to promote long-term and short-term tourism goals.
- Ideally, tourism planning regions coincide with economic development regions.
- Themes of new attractions are developed to carry cultural, entertainment, and educational messages through activities offered by sites or events.

13.1   THE TOURISM PLANNING PROCESS

Planning the growth of sustainable tourism follows the same rationale and decision-making process used in problem solving. Whether the process is used at the national, regional, local, or firm level, the following steps are common to all economic systems:

Step 1 Define the problem.

Step 2 Gather information relevant to the problem.

Step 3 Analyze the relevant information to find the causes of the problem.

Step 4 Establish goals that, when realized, could eliminate or mitigate the causes of the problem.

Step 5 Prepare alternative solutions that would possibly achieve the goals.

Step 6 Select one alternative solution for detailing action programs.

Step 7 Program the elements of the selected solution.

Step 8 Implement the elements of the selected solution.

Step 9 Verify the consequences of the selected solution after a period of time.

Step 10 Return to Step 1 through feedback and restart the process for another cycle of planning. The length of the cycle depends on the nature of the problem.

Before this decision-making procedure can be applied to sustainable tourism development, a basic question must be answered. At the national planning level, the government authorities must answer the fundamental question of whether the country has the potential to engage in sustainable tourism development. If the answer is *no*, because of a perceived poor competitive position, insufficient economic benefits, lack of quality attractions and facilities, or simply lack of interest in having tourists, tourism development ceases to be an issue. If the answer is *yes*, a series of decisions should be made to conduct various surveys and studies to verify the potential and commit government resources for developing tourism. If the answer is *maybe*, further deliberations and studies are needed to arrive at a definitive conclusion. Needed information is defined in the first three problem-solving steps outlined below.

In free-market economies, the decision to develop a tourism economy is made spontaneously by the elements of the private sector, which takes all the usual risks. The government trails rather than leads in the execution of this decision, although some government infrastructure, financing, and promotion programs may be undertaken to support tourism investments. In mixed economies where the government holds the power to make major economic decisions for the country, the decision to develop tourism, especially international tourism, is made at the national level. The decision is translated into a series of top-down policies from which plans, programs, projects, and measures are drawn.

It is important to distinguish development policies from plans. They are not the same. In fact, one follows the other. For some, a policy is an action identified as the means to accomplish a goal set by the plan. For others, policies are defined more broadly as statements that establish guidelines for plans, followed by implementation steps (actions) and regulations. Either way, guidelines precede actions.

It is important to clarify the meaning of several terms used in conjunction with the role of the government in planning consecutive and increasingly specific elements and subelements of sustainable tourism:

Policy:	A consistent set of principles considered expedient and advantageous for determining government decisions
Goal:	A statement of intent derived from a policy
Plan:	A detailed method worked out beforehand for the accomplishment of a goal established by a policy
Program:	A listing of the order of related actions, procedures, schedules, and projects used for implementing the elements of a plan
Project:	A specific action requiring concerted effort for accomplishing a particular element of a plan, generally involving physical construction
Measure:	A specific action taken to accomplish a particular element of a plan not involving physical construction

Taken together, decisions made in these six areas are the essence of sustainable tourism development planning. Applying the problem-solving method to planning at the *national level* involves the following steps:

Step 1 *Defining the problem:* Is tourism right for the country?
- Is there a potential for tourism?
- What are the issues associated with entering domestic tourism?
- What are the issues associated with entering international tourism?

Step 2 *Gathering information:* Supply and demand analyses
- Demand profiles of international and domestic tourism
  - International tourist arrivals
  - Countries and regions of origin
  - Purpose of travel
  - Duration of visits
  - Expenditures by tourists
- Supply profiles of tourism resources of the country
  - Attractions and facilities of international and national significance identified by NAICS (or similar classification system) establishment categories
  - Labor resources
  - Financial resources
  - Environmental resources
  - Cultural and social issues of tourism

Step 3 *Analysis of needs:* What is needed for starting a tourism economy?
- Defining tourism sector requirements of the country by NAICS (or similar) subsectors and establishments
- Determining the needed carrying capacity, distribution, and quality of attractions and facilities
- Analyzing the sustainability of tourism growth and its probable impacts
- Determining the views and demands of the private sector
- Evaluating entrepreneurship potentials
- Estimating labor force training requirements
- Evaluating the compatibility of cultural and social values with tourism
- Determining whether sustainable tourism can be developed? If the answer is yes, proceed to Step 4. If it is no, stop.

Step 4 *Further topics for government decision making on developing tourism and preparing policies*
- Macroeconomic goals and policies for alleviating poverty
- Macrosocial and cultural goals and policies for alleviating poverty
- Defining a macro-level developmental role for the tourism sector
- Defining the terms of sustainability
- Legislative goals and policies
- Regional goals and policies
- Environmental goals and policies
- Labor force training policies
- Financial goals and policies
- Marketing goals and policies
- Organizational goals and policies associated with cooperation of the private sector and government

Step 5 *Alternative national tourism development plans*
- Alternative Plan A: minimum plan
- Alternative Plan B: maximum plan
- Alternative Plan C: optimum plan
- Select and adopt a preferred national tourism development plan. It is common in planning practice, including tourism planning, to select a preferred plan that combines elements of alternative plans. It is unlikely that alternatives A, B, or C will be selected in their entirety. It is more likely that elements of two or more will be synthesized into a preferred plan.

Step 6 *Illustrative contents of an adopted national tourism development plan*
- Economic measures and investment projects
- Social and cultural measures and investment projects
- Legislative measures
- Tourism regions for priority development
- Environmental measures and conservation projects
- Labor force training measures
- Marketing measures
- Organizational measures
- Roles assigned to the private sector and resources allocated to it

Step 7 *Programming the elements of the selected development plan*
- Preparing specific project packages for investment projects
- Preparing specific packages for legislative and regulatory measures
- Scheduling specific projects and measures by annual programs
- Legislating management and coordinating organizations/agencies for scheduled projects and measures, and establishing channels of authority and responsibility

Step 8 *Implementing the projects and measures of the development plan*
- Investing in government infrastructure projects
- Preparing a labor force training strategy and programs
- Investing in government labor force training projects
- Financing investment projects from public funds
- Developing marketing and promotion strategies
- Legislating tourism incentives for development
- Legislating tourism development regulations

Step 9 *Evaluating the results of projects and measures implemented after a plan period of several years*
- Reporting the results of actions taken to the national government
- Resolving issues and deciding on corrective actions

Step 10 *Repeating Step 1 through feedback and restarting the planning cycle*
- Revise the goals as needed.
- Revise the policies as needed.
- Revise the tourism development plan as needed.
- Program and schedule new projects and measures.

The culmination of government actions at the national level results in concerted actions of the public and private sectors toward a mutually agreed-upon tourism growth strategy. These actions can be further replicated at the regional level of tourism planning where appropriate (where regions are large enough and strong enough economically to merit separate tourism development plans to be integrated with national tourism development plans).

13.2 NATIONAL TOURISM POLICIES AND MULTISECTORAL DEVELOPMENT PLANNING

In free-market systems, tourism policies, if they exist at all, are largely left to the private sector. The process is bottom-up. The national government enters the process only for facilitating the growth of the tourism industry by taking measures that the private sector needs and for building multipurpose infrastructure projects. One of its principal functions is marketing the destinations of the country abroad. For this purpose, the government may use the commercial media and government-owned and -operated tourism information offices opened at major target countries around the world. Other policy measures may concern government investments in major infrastructure projects, particularly in transportation; foreign policy relations of the country; issuing travel advisories for outgoing tourists; issuing visas to foreign visitors; ensuring the health, and safety of international and domestic travelers; preventing terrorism; and adjusting monetary policy for exchanging currencies.

In mixed-economy systems, the government is more involved in developing tourism, particularly when poverty alleviation is a major goal. The process is top-down. The initiative clearly belongs to the government. The private sector plays a supporting role. Macro-level national planning includes the elements of tourism development and articulates tourism policies and programs for the country. Projects, measures, and their implementations are articulated in annual programs and capital improvement budgets. Otherwise, the process follows the steps used for articulating policies, plans, programs, and projects in other macroeconomic sectors of the country.

Government investment in major infrastructure projects serves both the nation and tourists. Power plants, interstate highways, dams, water and sewer treatment plants, airports, seaports, and communication and electrification systems are among the investment projects undertaken by the government to provide benefits to the nation. Policies identify the priorities in selecting and building these infrastructure facilities.

The government may choose to discourage its citizens from visiting certain countries where travel is considered dangerous or that may have some affiliation with terrorist organizations. Travel advisories and passport issuance are two methods used to implement such a policy. If they are suspected of some malfeasance, incoming foreign tourists from these countries may be closely scrutinized.

The twenty-first century has created new impediments to free and safe travel. Terrorism and AIDS are the two new curses challenging world civilization and endangering the welfare of millions. These challenges are larger than one country can handle. They require the concerted efforts of many countries and international organizations.

Money changing is a routine transaction in tourism. Every international traveler has to carry or have access to the currencies of the countries he or she is visiting. Government policy regarding the setting of exchange rates, when the rates are not free-floating in the currency market, is critical to attracting international tourists. When the government establishes the exchange rates of the local currency with the currencies of other countries, the monetary policy artificially dictates the rates. Sometimes the local currency is overvalued in comparison with benchmark currencies like the U.S. dollar, British pound, euro, and Japanese yen. When foreign currency can be exchanged only in the central bank of a country, considerable inconvenience to tourists results.

When the currency of the country is allowed to float freely according to the fluctuations of the financial market, exchanging money becomes easier. Exchanging currencies becomes a business. One can still find traditional money changers in the old bazaar in some countries, where a stool and a stack of money on a table constitutes the open-air office of the money changer. The whole transaction is based on trust. But newer exchange offices can be found at central locations frequented by tourists, including commercial banks, airport and train terminals, and even hotel front desks. The exchange rates are usually better at the airport and train terminals than in the hotels.

In mixed economies, the role of the government is central to preparing and implementing the economic policies of the country. Policies for tourism development are derived from macroeconomic development policies and plans prepared by the national government. Various methods for preparing national accounts or conducting an econometric simulation of the economy were discussed in Chapter 12 and are discussed again in Chapter 16. Government can determine the effectiveness of the goals assigned to a tourism sector by using computer simulation and econometric and other modeling.

Public investment is an important development policy in every country. The government makes substantial investments in projects relevant to the public sector of the economy. These investments are intended to stimulate private investments that will follow. Public infrastructure and superstructures are among the most expensive and prominent government investments. Long-term policies guide in determining where and when these investments will be made. Highways, power plants, ports, airports, and most utilities are among the public investments that not only serve the public but also benefit tourists and the tourism industry.

Other macroeconomic government policies include education; taxation and subsidies; market regulation; foreign trade; construction industries regulation; wages; and price, financial, and monetary policies, all of which influence the conduct of a country's tourism industry. These policies are revised periodically as they affect the tourism industry when tourism is an important growth industry of a country. Educating the public about tourism and its social impact is particularly important. Traditional host–guest relations inevitably change in character when tourism becomes an important business. Internationally accepted codes of behavior and standards replace traditional ones. The demonstration effects of tourism serve as a precursor for social change.

Taxation and subsidy policies of the government are essential for starting or substantially expanding a vibrant tourism economy. When taxes are low and capital is available, inducement for investing in tourism establishments is greatest. In some situations, private equity, government subsidies, and financial guarantees for commercial loans are protected with political risk insurance.

Privatization is a major government function. Privatization of state-owned enterprises is an established movement that received increased attention in the early 1990s during the transition from centralized planned economies to market economies in Eastern European countries. This transition is continuing. The original policy viewed privatization as a way to raise cash for reducing government debt, to curb public spending, to increase output, to improve the quality of goods and services, and to broaden the base of ownership and participation in the economy. Many developing countries considered private entrepreneurs and market economies as providing salvation from the inefficiencies of centralized planning. They were only partially right. The sudden shift from centralized planning to market-driven economies caused many hardships, particularly for the elderly, pensioners, and children, and met resistance from entrenched interest groups like political parties, private groups enjoying special privileges, powerful government and military officials, and labor unions. In countries where some private investors are politically unacceptable and are discriminated against by the government, similar feelings of suspicion are often expressed toward foreign investors.

In countries partway between privatization and a market economy, government policies toward tourism development may suffer from the same maladies of transition. In overcoming these difficulties and ensuring a productive private sector, the government needs to form solid alliances with reform-minded elements in the private sector. These alliances diligently pursue the institution of democratic principles and the rule of law as a way to do business in the country. Divestiture of state-owned enterprises, including tourist facilities for mass recreation and holidays, includes stock offerings to employees for creating broader equity ownership and public support. Deregulation and tax reductions follow in due time when the transition to a mixed economy and ultimately to a more complete market system is appropriate. A tourism economy ultimately benefits from privatization when opportunities for development can no longer be ignored and foreign investors are welcome.

13.3 NATIONAL REGULATIONS AND STANDARDS FOR TOURISM PLANNING

Tourism policies do not establish operational guidelines for government agencies and the public to follow. For this purpose, national policies are translated into operational guidelines that include regulations and standards in all areas pertaining to organizing and implementing the orderly growth of tourism. Tourism planning uses these specific interpretations in planning at the national, regional, and local levels. Government agencies, as well as private sector businesses and the tourism establishments they own and operate, are compelled to operate by these regulations and standards.

A tourism establishment must adhere to a complex regulatory procedure when starting a new business. Many regulations established at the national level are also applicable at the regional and local levels. The establishment is required to present its qualifications to authorities and solicit certification from the government, possibly at all three levels. Health codes, building codes, environmental protection codes, and industry codes of one kind or another usually dictate the tourism facility standards that the establishment must meet. Foremost among them are hotel and restaurant quality certifications.

Hotels and restaurants are rated by the "star" system. In some developed regions, the star is assigned not by the government but by the relevant industry association using industry standards. To qualify for a star, the establishment must meet certain location, building, and service standards. One, two, three, four, five, and even six star designations reflect the quality and pricing of the services offered. The higher the designation, the more personal and pricier the service becomes. Prices fluctuate according to the business climate and season. In some developing regions of the world where central government has a lot to say about the desirability of tourism development and services, standards and tariffs are set for each service and accommodation. Municipal authorities enforce these standards and tariffs by periodic inspections. However, they do not frequently update the prices for hotel and restaurant services. As a result, approved tariffs are often ignored by the management and are left hanging on the wall of the establishment as a decoration.

Accommodations and other facilities that do not meet the standards are often left to their own means to survive, deteriorate, or disappear. This Darwinian process of natural selection is one of the realities of the free-market system. In developing regions where tourism is encouraged as a major source of employment and income, defects are corrected by training and providing government-backed subsidies. The owners and staff of substandard facilities receive special training in tourism development and management and benefit from financial incentives. Through these programs, national tourism policies encourage entrepreneurship and cooperative enterprises where limited capital and labor force resources can be pooled to organize new business enterprises. Cooperative government programs can be particularly useful in traditional societies where tribal and cultural customs favor cooperation instead of competition among their members.

13.4 PLANNING, PROGRAMMING, BUDGETING, AND SCHEDULING NATIONAL TOURISM DEVELOPMENT MEASURES AND PROJECTS

The process of planning, programming, budgeting, and scheduling measures and projects for national economic development is different in each country and economic system. The large majority of central economic planning around the world now takes place in mixed economies where government and the private sector share responsibilities. A model for such collaboration can be suggested only in general terms. Each country has its own version of the model.

In general, government spending for economic planning and development involves three types of budgets:

- The general budget of a nation, state, or province
- A budget for independent state economic enterprises
- Budgets of mixed corporations consisting of joint ventures of government and the private sector

The expenditures of each entity are divided into two major sections, current expenditures and investments. Once a year, the budgeting office of each government agency is instructed to prepare its budget proposal for the coming year. Proposed budgets are supposed to be in line with the proclaimed expenditures or general development policies of the government. Each department of the agency prepares and submits its budget proposal to the departmental directorate of accounting. When there are discrepancies, the directorate of accounting reconciles the differences and submits the agency budget to the head of the agency for his or her review and approval.

A typical routing is as follows: The directorate of the budget and financial control collects the agency budgets. The directorate reviews the proposed budgets and submits its recommendations to the council of ministers. The council of ministers decides on the final shape and size of the government budget and gives instructions to the ministry of finance concerning reductions or additions to be made in each ministry budget. The budgetary proposals are then returned to the respective ministries for revisions. The revised budget estimates are again returned to each agency's directorate of the budget and financial control for final packaging. After the annual government budget is given its final form, it is submitted by the council of ministers and the grand national assembly of the country for approval.

Mixed public/private corporations play an important role in the transition from centrally planned to mixed economies. When the government decides that a new business venture might prove attractive and profitable for private investment, it encourages the organization of mixed public/private corporations in which the relevant state economic enterprise participates in providing the capital. In most cases, the controlling interest in the mixed corporation is owned by the public economic entity.

Strictly speaking, private investment enterprises follow their own internal procedures for preparing their annual budgets. When they need capital for investment, they apply for funds to the country's industrial development bank. The bank applies a criterion of social marginal productivity in screening the applications for long-term credit. When approved, the loan is included in the annual budget of the private enterprise. The bank most often cooperates with the World Bank.

In considering their investment projects, agencies will also recommend an allocation mechanism for foreign exchange reserves that will be used for purchasing materials and equipment from abroad. In some cases, inflationary tendencies in the national economy could warrant a stabilization program and perhaps devaluation of the currency. To oversee these activities, an economic coordination board composed of the ministers of foreign affairs, coordination, finance, commerce, industry, and construction are often given the authority to make major policy decisions in line with government policies.

After their budgets are reviewed, the agencies program and schedule their investment projects over future years. Every year a segment of each project is budgeted and scheduled together with action measures to be executed during that year. The project sponsor and coordinator are accountable for the project's execution. Finally, the entire annual package of investment projects and measures is usually submitted to the council of ministers and the grand national assembly for their approval as the annual development program of the country.

13.5   SELECTING TOURISM REGIONS AND DESTINATIONS FOR INVESTMENT

Making the tourism product interesting and accessible is key to developing it effectively. Identifying regions and destinations where the best mixes of attractions and facilities are located is the first step toward shaping the development strategy. The second step consists of superimposing the overlay tourism regions on the economic development regions and seeking a match that will identify investment projects common to both. An example is shown for the country of Romania on the following Web site: http://www.mdrl.ro/index.php?p=171&lang=en

Using the analytical methods explained earlier, spatial concentrations of internationally and nationally significant attractions are combined with resident population data to yield a tourism density for the particular destination areas of a region. The density indicates where tourists are most likely to go and where growth will take place. In addition, activity mixes and seasonality characteristics of the destinations are shown. These characteristics yield other layers of boundaries. The superimposed concentration of attractions, facilities, activities, and seasonal characteristics finally suggests where tourism investments should be made and where a priori conservation measures should be taken. All these layers suggest an enveloping boundary for the tourism region. To ensure data availability, the regional boundary is drawn to coincide with the outer boundaries enveloping the municipalities in the region.

A parallel exercise involves the process of defining economic development regions for government and private sector investment based on macro-level economic planning. Extensive research involving regional input-output studies, comparative advantage, and growth center strategies suggest other regional development priorities. The objective is not to equalize growth rates in all regions and in all economic sectors. Rather, the objective is to gauge a "critical size" for a few urban regions where economies of scale, internal and external economies, multiplier effects, and manpower training potentials suggest certain a priori regions.

The final reconciliation takes place when economic development regions and tourism development regions are superimposed. When the boundaries of the two types of regions have a close match, the result will be conclusive. If this happens, tourism regions will become integral parts of the economic development regions. This will simplify and reinforce regional tourism and economic development planning significantly. This will also ensure that public infrastructure and private investment projects will be complementary and will serve multiple purposes. When the two types of boundaries do not match closely, a best-case scenario will help define a compromise boundary for the tourism region, usually by following municipal or some other administrative boundaries.

13.6 PROMOTING ENTREPRENEURSHIP

In developing tourism, particularly in traditional societies where social values regarding ways of doing business have been established for many centuries, entrepreneurial challenges require social acceptance to succeed. Creating and expanding a new industry that will bring in a large number of total strangers to one's territory and comfort zone could pose serious questions of social and economic dislocation, but also of opportunities. The answer lies in management, leadership, and risk taking—in a word, entrepreneurship.

Balancing established social values, customs, and decision-making processes with the norms and practices accepted by the rest of the world for tourism development is a management as well as a leadership issue. It is, however, important to differentiate between the two. Leadership and management are two distinct and complementary systems of action. One does not substitute for the other. **Managing** involves coping with complexity; its essence is problem solving. Good management brings a degree of order and consistency to key decisions that ensure the success of the organization. The whole purpose of good management is to complete routine and repetitive tasks successfully by following a process that is as fail-safe and risk-free as possible.

Leadership, by contrast, is about coping with change. Change replaces the customary values and processes that govern traditional business and social relationships with new ones. Exploring the new is risky. A traditional social and economic order established after centuries of trial and error is reluctant to upset the equilibrium that ensures its stability and survival. A departure from the traditional is fraught with danger. When a suggestion is made to change one's ways, the tradition-bound individual reacts defensively by saying "We have always done it this way."

Within the context of tourism, planning is a management process. It is deductive in nature and is concerned with arriving at results through an orderly process. Direction-giving leadership, on the other hand, is inductive. It does not produce plans. It energizes people and creates vision and strategies. It motivates and steers actions toward more risk taking, exploring the unknown and trying the new. Successful motivation ensures that the individual has what it takes to overcome obstacles for reaching goals.

Management and planning work best not as a substitute for direction-setting leadership, but as a complement to it. Working together, they balance each other. Competent management and planning serve as a reality check on direction-setting leadership. Conversely, competent direction-setting leadership provides the focus for management and planning. It helps clarify what kinds of planning and management are essential and what kinds are irrelevant.

Leadership is a quality that some believe is inherent in certain individuals. The people who possess this quality are considered natural leaders. Others believe that leaders rise spontaneously from the masses when the situation demands it. In both types of leadership, a leader leads willing followers. A leader leads in a situation created by external events. A leader can only lead by being "out in front" of the followers. The leader provides the vision, the goals, and the direction that followers follow willingly. He or she is trained to take some carefully considered risks in order to achieve goals. He or she tries to change established values, norms, and processes to improve the chances for success.

The personal traits and qualities found in a leader include:

- They like to have authority and enjoy influencing others.
- They do not have a strong need to be liked by others.
- They are emotionally mature and not self-centered or aggressive.
- They do not need to be at center stage.
- They do not seek all the credit for their group's accomplishments.
- They do not frequently lose their temper or sulk when things go wrong.
- They enjoy using their authority to build a better organization.
- They help subordinates grow and develop.

In planning and developing tourism, these qualities become necessary at all levels of government and private sector actions. Management, leadership, and risk taking open the doors to creative solutions and better ensure a thriving tourism industry.

13.7 LABOR FORCE TRAINING AND SKILL DEVELOPMENT

Tourism is a service industry. It is labor intensive and creates largely lower-income jobs. It is susceptible to large fluctuations in income and employment during economic downturns. Tourism businesses and employment suffer first when disposable income is scarce. Tourists stop coming when there is a political upheaval or war. Job tenure and security are not widespread. Pensions are rare. Most of the income earned by many employees is from tips, not salaries. Nevertheless, by comparison with some other economic sectors, tourism offers the best opportunity for more rapid growth in regions where economic growth is lagging and where there is no practical use for certain historical and natural assets.

Tourism establishments require mostly employees with lower levels of skill. They employ many unskilled women. By and large, tourism provides cleaner and healthier working environments than many other economic sectors. It often creates temporary or part-time employment opportunities for those, like students, who need supplementary income. It is a large and immediate source of foreign exchange revenue for the nation without the need to sell any goods or services abroad. In the case of cruise ship tourism, it allows the transfer of wages directly to the families of the crews in their homeland while providing generous time off for the crews (up to three months a year). Similar opportunities are found in other types of tourism employment.

In tourism growth regions, labor force training covers most subsector industries and establishments. On-the-job training is largely the norm. Specialized jobs, however, require structured training. They include skills in hospitality, hotel, and restaurant management and operations. Travel agents and airline employees, among others, go through extensive training and licensing.

Depending on its complexity, a country's tourism economy may employ three workers in related second- or third-tier supplier industries for every one worker directly serving tourists in first-tier or frontline occupations. Initially, workers in traditional occupations like agriculture, arts, and crafts can continue without major changes in their methods of operation. Eventually, however, they may need to be introduced to more efficient methods to increase their productivity and keep up with the demand for their products. These new methods may require certain attitudinal and value changes toward work. Ideas like punctuality, efficiency, and commitment may have to be presented to and accepted by the workers.

New occupations, starting with serving visitors in restaurants, hotels, travel agencies, and transportation facilities, call for meticulous personal grooming, hygiene, attention to detail, courtesy, and a sense of commitment and responsibility for getting the job done. Some of these traits may be widely accepted by local culture and customs. Others may need to be introduced. Labor force training addresses these traits from fundamental elements through advanced technical requirements.

Universal education and economic well-being, which often go together, have a great deal to do with the scope and intensity of labor force training. With the possible exception of some menial jobs, the tourism industry will not have much use for a large proportion of the population who cannot read or write. In dealing with tourists, in most countries minimum conversational proficiency in one or more foreign languages is a must. Specialized training like front desk management, housekeeping management, and maintenance at hotels is provided by the employer or by community colleges and trade schools that award certificates of completion.

Employing foreign-trained labor in critical service positions is a short-term solution for the shortages in skilled labor categories. Most hotel franchises, for example, require that foreign-trained and certified managers be employed in their hotels. All parties concerned must understand that after a certain period, locally trained personnel will replace the foreign personnel.

13.8 PREPARING PHYSICAL MASTER TOURISM DEVELOPMENT PLANS

The physical component of tourism development planning involves studying the spatial distribution of assets and activities over the horizontal and vertical planes of the national, regional, and local topography. The location of these assets and activities, the distances and landforms separating them, and the climate enter into the preparation of the physical master tourism development plans at the national, regional, and local levels. An example of a final summary update of a national master tourism plan for Tanzania in Africa is shown on the following Web site: http://www.docstoc.com/docs/39980802/Tourism-Master-Plan-Presentation—PowerPoint-Presentation.

The information that goes into these physical master development plans is different at all three levels. The differences lie in the level of detail and in their relevance for a particular study. Plans at the largest scale carry general information and give a global view of the asset and activity distributions. Both potentials and problems are identified graphically and in text. As the scale gets smaller, more information is presented for an increasingly small area. Using the metric system, the scale of maps and drawings could range from 1:3,500,000 for international and national planning, to 1:500,000 for regional planning, to 1:1,000 for local-level planning. At the project level, map and drawing scales could be 1:100 or less. All this information can be presented on manually drawn maps or in digitized computer mapping form.

Using appropriate icons, the following information is superimposed on a background of national borders and is pinpointed on national development plans:

- Major urban centers, from metropolitan areas to principal cities of the country
- Populations of major urban centers shown in increasingly large circles and pie charts
- Major topographic features like major mountains, rivers, wetlands, seas, and lakes
- Provincial, state, county, and municipal administrative boundaries
- Major infrastructure assets like interstate highways, dams, ports, railroads, and airports
- Overlay of national tourism development concepts showing major destinations and tourism development regions

- Maps of attraction concentrations in tourism regions
- Overlays of various attraction and facility characteristics
- Overlay of international and domestic tourist flows and major originating urban centers
- Overlay of travel times among major tourism regions and destinations
- Overlay of economic and tourism development regions and major destinations
- Overlay of proposed major interregional infrastructure improvement projects
- Overlay of national tourist attraction and facility mix ratings
- Overlay of climatic information and seasonality rating of tourism attraction-facility mixes

Using appropriate icons superimposed on a background for each tourism development region, the following information is placed on plans at the regional level:

- Urban centers from provincial capitals to cities, towns, and villages
- Detailed topographic features like major mountains, rivers, wetlands, seas, and lakes
- Provincial, state, county, municipal, and other administrative boundaries
- Detailed infrastructure assets like highways, dams, ports, railroads, and airports
- Overlay of the regional development concepts showing planned growth centers, growth axes, and linkages between the growth centers within regions
- Overlay of tourist attractions of national, regional, and local significance
- Overlay of the seasonality of the attraction-facility mix
- Overlays of tourist facilities for specific type of establishments like hotels, marinas, and historic sites chosen from regional attraction-facility mixes
- Overlays of specific tourism activities chosen from regional attraction-facility mixes
- Overlay of major regional land uses like agriculture, forestry, and conservation areas
- Overlay of tourism destinations of national, regional, and local significance
- Overlay of proposed destinations and their accessibility from one to another
- Overlay of proposed land uses, including recreation and conservation areas
- Overlay of proposed regional infrastructure improvement projects
- Overlay of proposed land development control areas and zoning
- Overlay of traffic and circulation impacts of proposed improvements

Again using appropriate icons superimposed on a background delineating the boundaries of each tourism destination, the following information is located on plans at the local (destination) level:

- Detailed topographic features like mountains, rivers, wetlands, seas, and lakes
- Detailed infrastructure assets like highways, dams, ports, railroads, and airports
- Land use plan of the administrative units like city, town, and village
- Zoning plan of the administrative unit
- Designated tourism development incentive areas
- Overlay of proposed tourism destination development areas
- Overlay of proposed tourism development projects
- Overlay of the conceptual urban design plans of proposed development projects
- Overlay of the proposed local transportation plan

The information graphically shown on the maps is collected and processed during the survey and analysis stages of the tourism development planning process. The data are stored in the Geographic Information System (GIS) using the coding method employed by the BIK System and are processed by computers. However, the same information can be compiled manually using the BIK system where computer mapping and data processing are not available or cost effective.

Aerial photographs taken from satellites can enhance the master development plans. Preferably, these photographs are three-dimensional and have the same scale as the maps for easy referral. Both base maps and aerial photographs are often available commercially.

These series of maps and photographs are visual graphic aids to tourism planning. But they are not substitutes for other research techniques presented in this book. The graphic approach to planning is useful when knowledge of locations, spatial relations, patterns, and distances among various assets is necessary for the tourism planning process. Descriptive and statistical information obtained by other techniques is equally important to complete the information base for tourism planning.

It is important to note that as the focus of attention changes from planning at the national level to regional and local levels, a fundamental change also occurs in the nature of the information and its presentation. At the national level, and decreasingly at the regional and local levels, economic, demographic, and financial data give way to two- and three-dimensional area planning, site planning, and architectural design. The ultimate concern at the local destination level is how human-made and natural assets complement and enrich one another. Harmony between nature and humans is essential for attracting tourists and providing them with quality experiences.

13.9   THE LOCAL COMPREHENSIVE PLAN AND ITS ASSOCIATED PLANS AND REGULATIONS

The comprehensive plan is an official public document adopted by local governments as a policy guide for organizing the development of the community. It is a general plan having a long-range horizon of ten to twenty years. Because it is general, it is used as a reference guide. It generally does not prescribe exact locations for activities or have the specificity of enforceable regulations. The plan encompasses the territory of the community and its functional elements. Three major subjects are covered in some detail: land use, community facilities, and circulation. Other subjects covered usually include housing, economic development, utilities, civic design, natural resources, cultural resources, historic preservation, open space, and recreation and tourism as functional specializations of the community. Some states in the United States have an even longer list of required elements.

Comprehensive plans are prepared to ensure the welfare, public health, aesthetic environment, and safety of the resident population and property owners. Within the limits of its consideration, visitors (nonresidents) are also covered. Their needs are an extension of the needs of the resident population. Where needed, additional services for visitors are shown on an overlay tourism development plan for the community. Regulations associated with the comprehensive plan include land development regulations covering land use, zoning, and subdivision regulations and some other specific regulations for protecting seashores (coastal zones), providing parking facilities, and prescribing and enforcing building codes, health codes, and the like. Local comprehensive plans include demographic and economic analyses and forecasts, often coordinated with, and sometimes prepared by, regional planning and analysis agencies.

The tourism dimension of the comprehensive plan addresses policies followed by local administrative units for planning and developing tourism. These policies reflect the hierarchical version of the guidelines laid out by the national and regional tourism policies. Higher-level tourism development policies are translated into community-specific actions and are treated as an overlay set of actions incorporated into a local comprehensive plan. Regulations made for ensuring the welfare and safety of resident population are also made for satisfying the needs of visitors.

13.10   LAND DEVELOPMENT REGULATIONS

Subdividing and developing land are the subjects of land development regulations. Before developing the land, the owner is obligated to have the land surveyed, markers placed, and boundaries defined. He or she submits to permit authorities a plat plan showing the layout of the proposed subdivision of land. When land improvements are made in accordance with sub-division plans and expenditures are made to provide essential site facilities, these field actions are called **land development**. Effective and proper planning and execution of land develop-ment requires detailed study and application of the combined skills of urban planners, envi-ronmental specialists, architects, landscape architects, civil engineers, real estate consultants, and financiers.

Subdividing is motivated by the application of the real estate industry's concept of "high-est and best use" to the area as a whole and to the site under development. Environmental and conservation concerns play a large role in tempering the highest and best use. Economic con-cerns are not the sole criteria used in this process. Market studies, fiscal impact studies, traffic analysis, and other studies are considered in approving and supporting the subdivision design of the land.

Land development regulations include those that govern the implementation of policies stated in the comprehensive plan. These regulations have legal standing. They guide and encour-age the orderly development of future growth; provide adequate light, air, and privacy; prevent overcrowding; protect and enhance the visual character of community; minimize conflicts between uses; conserve the value of the land, buildings, and improvements; divide the commu-nity into districts, each having its own subset of standards that reflect the underlying land uses; establish standards for building heights, floor-area ratios, and building setbacks; protect open spaces and environmentally sensitive areas; and provide for a smooth flow of traffic. The general provisions of land development regulations state where the review and decision-making author-ity lies and how the review procedures are carried out. A sample section in land development reg-ulations include:

- *The zoning ordinance* is the principal implementation tool of the land use plan. It covers an entire municipal jurisdiction and defines zoning districts in which specified land uses are permitted, not permitted, or permitted only with special permits or exceptions obtained after review by planning authorities. A zoning ordinance is adopted as a legal document. If it is not based on a land use plan, it is technically inaccurate. It may have serious negative consequences in managing the growth of the community. When the two plans are not consistent with each other, they represent contradictory urban planning principles. States in the United States increasingly require consistency between land use planning and zoning.

   A typical zoning ordinance for a low-density, medium-sized community (population forty thousand) may include the following sections:
   - Zoning districts and their designations on the official zoning map
   - Definitions of terms used in the ordinance
   - Identification of the types of land use permitted in each district
   - Minimum lot size requirements
   - Building setback requirements (from lot boundaries)
   - Building height restrictions and maximum building coverage of lots
   - Standards for utility easements, trash storage/removal, and illumination
   - Standards for signs, art for public view, retained open space, and landscaping

- Standards for the protection of environmentally significant features
- Standards for protecting public water supplies and waste water disposal
- Standards for on- and off-street parking and loading of vehicles
- Standards for drinking establishments
- Standards for adult entertainment establishments
- Standards for keeping animals
- Standards for noise, odor, and smoke emissions
- Restrictions of home occupations
- Various overlays governing land uses in floodplains, near water bodies, over aquifers, and for the purpose of promoting economic development
- Code administration and enforcement

- *Subdivision regulations* are the set of design standards and procedures used for converting raw land into building sites. This is accomplished through plat approval procedures. Approvals are contingent on compliance of the proposed plat with the development standards. Compliance allows lots to be sold, streets and sidewalks to be used, and building permits to be issued.

  A typical set of subdivision regulations may include, among others, the following sections:
  - Design requirements for street and sidewalk improvements, utilities, lights and bridges
  - Drainage and storm water management
  - Floodplains
  - Potable water supply
  - Wastewater treatment
  - Easements
  - Public uses
  - Natural resources, features and amenities
  - Land readjustments

- *Traffic performance standards* pertain to the safe, convenient, and orderly flow of vehicular traffic for ensuring the health, safety, welfare, and convenience of the public. The intent of these standards is to ensure that roadways are in place and adequate to provide the level of service mandated.

  A typical section may include the following:
  - Applicability of the standards
  - Level, link, intersection, radius, and phasing standards
  - Traffic impact studies
  - Parking and vehicle loading areas
  - Levels of service to be achieved concerning traffic flow and roadway capacity

- *Open space standards* are enforced to ensure that open spaces are provided within all approved developments. Open space standards come in a variety of shapes and forms. They include standards for:
  - Recreational facilities
  - Water bodies
  - Environmentally sensitive lands, including wetlands
  - Pedestrian areas
  - Public parks
  - Private lands
  - Historical and archeological sites

13.11 BUILDING CODE

The building code is an official local enforcement document for the building industry. Its intent is to ensure public safety, health, and welfare as they are affected by building construction through structural strength, adequate egress facilities, sanitary conditions, equipment, light, heat, ventilation, and fire safety, and in general to ensure the safety of life and property. The building code controls:

- Construction, reconstruction, alteration, repair, demolition, removal, inspection, issuance, or revocation of permits or licenses, installation of equipment, classification and definition of any building or structure, and use or occupancy of all buildings and structures
- Rehabilitation, alteration, and maintenance of existing buildings
- Standards or requirements for materials to be used in connection with the provisions for safety, ingress and egress, energy conservation, and sanitary conditions
- Establishment of reasonable fees for the issuance of licenses and permits

The procedures and standards of a typical building code are grouped in several sections:

- Administration and enforcement of the building code
- Definitions and classifications
- General building limitations
- Special use and occupancy requirements
- Light, ventilation, and sound transmission control
- Means of egress
- Structural and foundation loads and stresses
- Materials and tests
- Steel, masonry, concrete, gypsum, and lumber construction
- Building enclosures, walls, and wall thicknesses
- Fire-resistive construction requirements
- Chimneys, flues, and vent pipes
- Mechanical equipment and systems
- Fire protection systems
- Precautions during building construction and operations
- Signs
- Electrical wiring and equipment
- Elevator, dumbwaiter, and conveyor equipment, installation, and maintenance
- Plumbing and gas fitting
- Manufactured buildings, building components, and mobile homes
- Light-transmitting plastic construction
- Energy conservation
- Special building code provisions for one- and two-family buildings
- Special provisions for repair, alteration, addition, and change of use in existing buildings
- Special provisions for earthquakes, landslides, hurricanes, and flooding in areas susceptible to natural disasters

Cities, towns, provinces, and states adopt building codes. State building codes apply to all municipalities in a state. Because of its uniformity, scope, and high standards, the **International Building Code** has been adopted by many states and nations. Many municipalities simply adopt their state building codes to assure conformity with it. It should be noted that some of the same subjects or topics appear in several of the land development regulations. For example, the uses of land in floodplains are controlled by zoning regulations, while the design of civil engineering features in floodplains is controlled by subdivision regulations. Modern land development regulations have become rather complex, given the increased public sensitivity to environmental degradation, the effects of natural disasters, and the increasingly accepted need for energy conservation and sustainable building practices. It is becoming imperative for a variety of professional services beyond site planning, architecture, and engineering to be involved in land development plans and projects.

13.12   SELECTING THEMES FOR SITE AND EVENT ATTRACTIONS

Destinations aspiring to augment their tourism product mix and improve their competitive position sometimes resort to creative solutions. Developing high volumes of domestic and international tourism depends partly on climatic conditions and the natural environment, but also on human-made attractions and facilities. According to the principles of the BIK System discussed in earlier chapters, attractions draw tourists and facilities serve them. Increasing the quantity, quality, and diversity of attractions results in drawing more visitors for longer periods. To maximize their satisfaction, visitors select destinations where the attractions match their interests, offer activities they favor, and have the quality that meets their expectations. To meet this demand, destinations have to evaluate their tourism product and create new attractions and facilities.

The process starts by searching for underused or unknown places or sites where certain types of tourism activities are possible for creating new sites or event attractions. These activities deliver messages that are inspired by themes. The process is sometimes reversed by first selecting a theme and a message for creating an event or a site attraction and then searching for sites that can be transformed into venues for performing the activities. Cultural forms like history, music, adventure, literature, arts, science, sports, entertainment, education, politics, business, fantasy, gambling, and piracy are interesting themes for creating new site and event attractions and tourism activities.

A tourism destination is not limited to what nature, past history, and culture have provided. It is possible that exciting new ideas, new applications, and new uses for long-established places can transform forgotten, undervalued, misunderstood, staid, and plain ugly places into exciting new site and event attractions and facilities for delivering high-quality, rewarding experiences.

Tourism messages are extracted from themes and are delivered to tourists by promoting activities that express these messages. Theme parks are prime examples. The entire attraction and its many activities are built around a theme and its messages. Disneyland in Anaheim, California, and Disney World in Orlando, Florida, Tokyo, and Paris convey many messages from themes of culture, nature, entertainment, and science selected from around the world. Other examples are found in Las Vegas. Hotels designed like a fortress (e.g., Excalibur), like a circus (e.g., Circus Circus), like an Italian palace (e.g., Bellagio), like the New York City skyline (e.g., New York New York), like the location of pirates of the Caribbean (e.g., Pleasure Island), or like the Eiffel Tower (e.g., Paris) are all theme attractions. Their architectural style is their message. Some of the activities and products they offer reflect their theme.

At the opposite end of the continental United States, one can find successful examples in Boston, where the old Market Place at Faneuil Hall and Quincy Markets have been converted into a wide variety of food stands. That success has been repeated on the waterfront of Baltimore, Maryland, and other places as festival marketplaces. The Baths of Caracalla in Rome now serve as a backdrop for orchestral concerts with world-class artists. The ancient Himeji Castle in Japan has served as a movie set for the James Bond movie *You Only Live Twice* and has become a favorite tourist stop. Many old caravan stops on the ancient Silk Road from Turkey to China are now much-sought-after theme hotels. The pyramids in Egypt and the Blue Mosque in Istanbul serve as stages for historic reenactments and sound and light shows.

The strategy used to create a new site and event attraction in the Magic Kingdom of Disney World, for example, started by adopting the world of fantasy as the theme. The next step was to develop messages based on notions like innocence, kindness, and wickedness. The third step was to plan and design the physical venue and media to convey these messages to the visitors. The result was the Castle of the Magic Kingdom and every object and event in it. The last step was to market the attraction for drawing visitors by packaging, pricing, and promoting it.

Another Disney creation is the Animal Kingdom Theme Park. In 1989, the corporate office decided to build a park for animals as its theme. The Disney Corporation was first built around the adventures of a likable rodent. Zoos did not make money. The theme park had to be something more. The imagineering designers developed a concept and presented it to the board. The park was to consist of three equal parts. A traditional theme park, a pavilion, and a nontraditional zoo were the chosen physical venues and media. Love for animals was the message. This message was tailored to three stages of human growth. The psychology behind the message was that in childhood, love of animals comes from fantasy, myth, and stories; in adolescence, love of animals is expressed by a longing for adventure; for adults, love of animals is more intellectual. It is manifested as appreciation, understanding, and protection.

Being an animal was central to the theme concept from the beginning. Live animals were to be presented as naturally and as close to visitors as possible, with no visible barriers between them. The sense of adventure emanated everywhere. Realism was paramount to creating the impression of excitement. All sets were "aged" and sheltered in foliage. As plans for the theme park progressed, the sense of sharing the space with animals grew in importance. It was said that proximity equals excitement. At one meeting, a live four-hundred-pound female Bengal tiger restrained only by a slender chain was brought into the Disney boardroom. The experiment succeeded in creating a sense of danger among the executives sitting around the table. This illusion of danger had to be present in park exhibits. In designing the master plan of the physical venue or media, care was taken to block all peripheral buildings from view. A central symbol in the shape of an artificial one-hundred-forty-foot-tall Tree of Life with one hundred thousand leaves occupied the middle of the park. The village, the river ride, the safari ride, collapsing bridge, whitewater thrills, poachers, and wetlands with Nile crocodiles all concealed the working part of the park with its miles of utility pipes and animal habitats. The animals and the environment were the true masters of the park.

Creating a duplicate site attraction thousands of miles away from its original site has important educational and conservation implications. The original attraction may be fragile and located far away. It may be time-consuming and expensive for the average tourist to visit. The duplicate attraction can serve as a convenient surrogate and can accommodate many more tourists. They can approximate the educational experience in a theme park nearby for the price of a ticket.

Another application of the theme concept involves finding a new use for a long-abandoned structure or site. Recycled derelict sites add value to the tourism product and serve as convenient surrogates for the real thing. The seasonality factor adds another dimension to planning new theme attractions by recycling old venues. When indoor themes are chosen, recycled venues are transformed into year-round attractions, facilities, events, and activities. The result is a tourism season extended at both ends.

13.13   TARGETING ATTRACTION-FACILITY-ACTIVITY MIXES

Achieving greater returns from tourism is an important goal of tourism planning. This goal is achieved by improving the attraction-facility-activity mix of a destination. Survey and analysis of the tourism product provide many of the answers. Other answers come from capacity analysis of the destination. Capacity studies concerning beaches, hotel beds, hotel rooms, utilities, and traffic and road systems indicate how many more tourists can be accommodated at the destination. Various tourism development scenarios are developed, ranging from expansion in all categories of the mix to no expansion in any category. Basically, there is no single ideal mix. Minimum, maximum, and optimum mixes of establishments making up the tourism sector are scenarios evaluated for development. Each destination considers its own set of circumstances before deciding which mix conforms to its sustainable tourism development plan. The benefits of a tourism product mix compared to the cost of realizing it determine the economic sustainability of the tourism industry. To the extent that other noneconomic factors and impacts, such as energy conservation and environmental degradation, can be included in the benefit/cost analysis, a broader definition of sustainable tourism can be achieved.

13.14   ANALYZING SOCIAL, CULTURAL, AND ENVIRONMENTAL IMPACTS OF TOURISM

To the extent that important noneconomic dimensions cannot be included in a comprehensive benefit/cost analysis, it is important to consider them in supplementary studies. Social, cultural, and environmental dimensions of tourism are discussed in Chapter 6. Experts are needed to conduct in-depth social, cultural, and environmental studies that will cover the entire social structure, cultural background, and ecosystems of regions and countries. Their recommendations are evaluated against the goals and guidelines of the tourism development plan. The evaluation leads to measurement of probable impacts in all three subject areas and focuses on mitigation measures that would make it possible to reduce or eliminate any unfavorable impacts. The requirements for impact analysis and the approval of reports on impacts are often spelled out in separate national or state legislation.

Chapter Highlights

- At the national planning level, government authorities must answer the fundamental question of whether the country has the potential to engage in sustainable tourism development.
- A ten-step process can be followed for planning the growth of sustainable tourism using the same rationale and decision-making process employed in problem solving.
- It is important to distinguish development policies from plans. They are not the same. Policymaking precedes and becomes an important input for planning and the actions that are defined by planning.

- Policies are consistent sets of principles considered realistic and advantageous for determining government decisions.
- Plans are detailed methods worked out for the accomplishment of goals derived from policies.
- Programs are listings of the order of related actions, procedures, schedules, and projects used for implementing the elements of a plan.
- Projects are specific actions requiring concerted efforts for accomplishing a particular element of a plan generally involving physical construction.
- Measures are specific actions taken to achieve a particular element of a plan not involving physical construction.

- In free-market systems, tourism policies, if they exist at all, are largely left to the private sector.
- In mixed-economy systems, the government is more involved in developing tourism, particularly when poverty alleviation is a major goal.
- In situations partway between privatization and a market economy, government policies toward tourism development may suffer from the problems of transition.
- Tourism establishments are subject to complex regulatory procedures when starting new businesses. Some of this complexity also governs substantial expansion of existing tourism businesses.

- Tourism development plans and projects need to be coordinated with local comprehensive master plans for overall development of a municipality.
- Consideration of the major plan implementation regulations for local plans is essential for tourism development plans and projects. Among these regulations are zoning regulations, subdivision regulations, traffic performance standards, open space and conservation standards, affordable housing requirements, and building and occupancy codes.
- Themes for site and event attractions are important in creating and expanding tourism destinations and extending their seasons.

14

Project Design, Permit, and Construction

This chapter introduces the specific steps for designing, permitting, and building tourist attractions and facilities at the destination or local level of tourism development planning. It focuses on project planning and development for building attractions and facilities that will draw and accommodate tourists. It defines the roles played by design professionals, owners/developers, and permit-granting authorities. It summarizes regulations that must be followed for developing land. It presents project management procedures and tools:

- From idea to realization, every tourism project has to go through a permit process administered by local government authorities.
- Many factors and professionals play roles in preparing permit documents and receiving and reviewing site and building plan approvals.
- Public participation in the local permit process is welcome. Among other issues, the law commonly protects the rights of property abutters.
- Government-funded rebuilding projects like waterfront rehabilitation and urban redevelopment projects serve as economic generators and follow a similar permit process, although certain military and other government projects and properties are exempted from regulations imposed on the private sector, but often have their own sets of regulations governing rehabilitation, redevelopment, and conversion to other uses.
- The project's chief architect plays a coordinating role in managing the project team and supervising the completion of the project following receipt of permit documents.
- There are several methods for undertaking, guiding, and facilitating project management.

14.1 THE IDEA, DUE DILIGENCE, MARKET STUDY, AND GENERAL FEASIBILITY STUDY

The process of developing a tourist attraction or facility starts with an idea. The entrepreneur, or government, may arrive at an idea intuitively or use the theme-message-medium correlation. Translating the idea into a project requires professional help. The professional tourism planner develops the idea further and gives it shape. Sketches, photographs, and computer imaging all contribute to the creative process of conceptualizing the idea and transforming it into a physical project. Using an industry expression, this is the imagineering process.

It is important to note that when the process of planning tourism development has reached the level of projects, national, regional, and even local-level issues have been reviewed, discussed, and resolved by the government by making policies and taking action measures. Macroeconomic issues, pertinent national laws and local regulations, and so on have already been addressed by others. They are not issues to be considered and resolved at the project level. At this point in the process, the project has the sole purpose of achieving the specific targeted objective for which it is conceived.

When the project idea is developed into a unique concept with physical dimensions, market and feasibility studies are done. Tourism development planners prepare an initial market analysis to make a preliminary determination of whether there will be a demand for the emerging project or, alternatively, whether a demand can be created by marketing the unique features of the project. The study determines whether there is enough evidence and justification for committing time, money, and talent to the project. The demand is measured in terms of the potential number of visitors drawn to the region, the potential revenues, and the market share of the project vis-à-vis other competing attractions and destinations.

At this stage, the search for a site starts with the assistance of real estate professionals. A real estate attorney is engaged to look into legal matters related to the project. The task includes collecting legal information, like proof of ownership of the land, a perimeter plan, a "metes and bounds" description of the properties, liens, easements, outstanding mortgages, taxes and charges, and so on, information that in legal parlance is collectively called the **due diligence** process.

Project financial feasibility analysis follows market assumptions and projections. The number of visitors to the project, tourists and excursionists alike, is estimated for various seasons of the year. Probable construction costs and revenue and operating expense projections lead to a cash flow analysis. Acquisition as well as soft and hard construction cost estimates, lead to calculations of investment/equity requirements. After determining the profitability of the venture, the entrepreneur negotiates with the government and determines whether the project is eligible for government incentives in the form of a long-term lease for the public land, exemptions from zoning regulations, cash investment in public infrastructure, or tax deferment. With this information, a refined estimate of the project's profitability can be made. The market analysis, legal due diligence analysis, and financial feasibility analysis are of prime importance to lending institutions that may be involved in the project.

14.2 ACQUIRING THE LAND

With the project idea verified, and with the market demand analysis and financial analysis complete, acquisition, or control, of the land becomes the next priority. The results of the legal due diligence work are now important before making an offer to purchase or lease the land. Once the offer is made and accepted, the land is under contract for a specified period for securing debt financing from commercial and international lenders. The equity investor/project owner/developer of the project prepares an application to qualify for the loan. Once the terms of the application are accepted by the lender and borrower, the land deal is closed between the owner/developer of the project and the owner of the property in the presence of the lender and legal counsels. Legal counsels make sure that the property is registered legally with the authorities and that there are no encroachments, no warranty, and no other objections to ownership or lease. Title insurance is secured, and the deed or lease is drafted and signed. The title to the property is transferred to the new owner/developer at the closing, and the owner/developer becomes eligible for drawing from the construction loan approved.

A variation of this scenario occurs when a local investor interested in developing a tourism project searches for an international partner. In this situation, the international investor acts as a financial partner and provides the needed equity, the debt capital, and possibly the proficiency and management expertise needed. An investment in a five-star hotel project, for example, may include in the business agreement with the international partner provisions for supplying specialized equipment, training and managing the hotel staff, and securing a well-known hotel franchise. The international investor may recover its investment in a few years and sell its share of the project to the owner at a predetermined date and price. This "exit" provision is negotiated during initial business discussions.

14.3   PROJECT MANAGEMENT

The project starts with the owner/developer securing assistance from a real estate broker, mortgage banker, legal counsel, accountant, and tourism development planner. The project team is later expanded to include the architect and the electrical, structural, civil, mechanical, landscape, and HVAC (heating, ventilation, and air conditioning) consultants. Finally, the construction contractor is selected and joins the project team. This team divides the acquisition, financing, planning, design, and construction duties among its members under the leadership of the owner/developer. Alternatively, the owner/developer may choose to appoint a professional project manager for coordinating and managing the project and the project team.

The project team prepares a plan of action and assigns tasks. A CPM or at least a bar chart (or Gantt Chart) is prepared (as described in Chapter 12) to show the tasks, responsible individuals, beginning and ending dates, and connecting tasks. The responsibilities are clearly spelled out in mutual agreements. A simple critical path diagram is shown on the following Web site: http://www.mycoted.com/Critical_Path_Diagrams.

14.4   SITE ANALYSIS

Each tourism attraction or facility project built from the ground up is subject to extensive analysis to determine its physical and financial feasibility. The results of the analysis must conform to the requirements of local and national standards and state and local regulations. A work plan and a checklist are prepared for this analysis.

The owner/developer provides information and business objectives for the project to land planning and architectural consultants. Civil and environmental engineers conduct the physiographic survey of the site, showing its dimensions, topography, surface vegetation, wetlands, and human-made structures. A geotechnical survey, test borings, landforms, surface features, and shape of the parcel determine whether the land is suitable for building the subject attraction or facility. Negative results in these tests and analyses could cancel or alter the project, including a search for an alternative site.

Working with project designers, other consultants on the project team conduct a traffic impact and circulation study showing the accessibility of the site; required environmental studies, sometimes done in two or three stages; a community impact study showing the effect of the project on local utility, school, police, and fire protection systems and capacities; and an analysis of issues concerning zoning ordinance, land use, and neighborhood character. Again, negative implications of these studies could result in alteration of the project, including the introduction of more stringent impact mitigation features.

14.5 BUILDING PROGRAM, PRELIMINARY SITE PLAN, AND ARCHITECTURAL PLAN

The owner/developer and the architect translate the information into a building program, that is, preliminary site and building plans that show the elements and floor areas of the building and site. The architect prepares a "bubble diagram" showing functional relationships and circulation among various building areas, site areas, and parking areas. He or she designs preliminary site and architectural plans of the building. Internal and external relationships of the building are shown within the perimeter of the area determined by setbacks, or building envelopes, prescribed by the zoning ordinance. The site plan shows all buildings, structures, site engineering, parking, and landscaping information.

The architect also prepares a preliminary construction cost estimate based on the previously estimated floor area and type of structure. Construction costs are estimated by using industry unit prices for square meters or square feet of construction by each building trade. Governments usually publish these unit prices for estimating official government projects. Alternatively, unit prices are estimated by private industry organizations based on permitted projects completed in various regions of the country. The owner/developer verifies that the preliminary construction costs are acceptable and authorizes the design team to proceed.

14.6 PROJECT PLANNING

Equity investments committed by the owner/developer and by other investors, if any, are confirmed in writing. Letters of interest are secured from all participants specifying the services they have agreed to perform. These letters are submitted to the lender. With project planning well underway, the project team, now including the owner/developer, his or her partners, other investors, and the lender, meet and agree on a written work plan to complete the project on schedule and within budget. The contributions, roles, and responsibilities of the team members to complete the project are plotted on a critical path diagram. Often special computer programs are used for managing the project. The team acts according to tasks prescribed by the program.

14.7 LOCAL GOVERNMENT PERMIT PROCESS

Getting a permit for building a tourist attraction or facility can be a difficult experience. Certain rules and regulations that are supposed to clarify the steps of the permit process may not be clear to the applicant and, sometimes to the permit-issuing agency as well. The confusion is understandable but not acceptable. Clarity is required in dealings between the public and the government.

An answer lies in mapping the permit process by using a critical path diagram showing the permit steps taken and timelines along the path of the project from beginning to end.

The building permit and construction process involves four groups of activities:

- Review and approval of the site plan
- Agreement between the owner/developer and public authorities
- Review and approval of building plans
- Construction supervision and occupancy permit

The first phase, the site plan review process, starts with the owner/developer of the project requesting a pre-application conference with planning and zoning officials for reviewing the rules and regulations that would apply to the project. In addition, the steps of the permit process, and the amount of time it might take to complete the review and approval process, are discussed. The critical path through the four phases of the permit and approval process is explained. This initial briefing is critical in setting the project on a proper course. Zoning issues, development conditions, and the appropriateness of the project vis-à-vis the provisions of the local comprehensive plan and the master tourism development overlay plan are reviewed during the conference. When applicable, related studies are requested or required by the authorities. Traffic and circulation issues, the environmental impact of the project, and concurrency terms regarding public facility improvements are discussed. When regional and national government actions are needed, appropriate applications to other authorities are required.

In phase two, professional staff of the government permit-granting authority reviews the site plan and prepares a report showing the compliance of the plan with local land development regulations. Then elected or appointed officials of the planning and zoning board, in meetings usually open to the public, hear and review the project's site plan. Site plan review and approval activities may require one or more public hearings where the owners of abutting properties, community representatives, and other interested individuals have the opportunity to study and comment on the possible impacts of the proposed project.

Abutters to the subject property receive a notice from the authorities about the hearing. Citizens' comments made at the hearing are noted. The hearing may result in modifying the proposed site plan. At the end of the hearing process, the planning board reviews the preliminary site plan submitted by the owner/developer and sends it with its recommendations to the local municipal council. Final site plan approval is granted after the council reviews the plan in a session open to the public. Once approval is given by the council, the site plan may still have to be approved by regional and national authorities as required. In many jurisdictions, especially in the United States, the planning board has the authority to approve or deny a site plan (with provisions for an appeal to another board in the event of a denial).

With the site plan approved by local as well as possibly regional and national permit authorities, the owner/developer authorizes the professional team to proceed and prepare construction drawings and specifications for the site and building. When these plans are completed, the entire package of construction documents, including specifications, plans, quantities, and engineering calculations, are submitted to the authorities for a building permit. Required fees are paid, the project is thoroughly reviewed, and changes are made if necessary on the plans to conform to the building code. Finally, the permit-granting officer of the agency issues a building permit. The review process may get complicated when zoning variances are required. An appeal process could result in extensive changes to the plans. These changes are stated in the "Development Order," an agreement used in some jurisdictions between the owner/developer and the authority.

In phase three, the owner/developer agrees to any changes and enters into an agreement with the authorities. The latter may stipulate several financial conditions, like community impact or mitigation fees, and concurrency for approving the plans. In turn, the owner/developer may negotiate terms for community incentives, involving financial and other concessions, if the community is expected to receive major benefits from the project.

A word of caution is appropriate here. Even the best tourism project cannot be realized unless public opinion favors it and the community supports it. Community support is sometimes hard to obtain. Elected or appointed community leaders, for reasons of their own, may block the project. Pleadings of the owner/developer through news media may not be sufficient to mobilize public opinion in support of the project. At this point, the opinions of professionals favoring the project may become less influential than political considerations. Serious disputes can arise. The owner/developer may have to do crucial soul searching before proceeding or dropping out. At this stage, community political action groups, like local condominium associations that may have the power to influence public opinion, could help his or her cause. If these citizen groups cooperate and invite the owner/developer to air his or her grievances and demonstrate the benefits of the project to the community, indirect pressure could secure community support and modify the position of elected or appointed community leaders.

The fourth phase of the permit process involves construction. Adhering to local building codes, several inspections during the construction are required for the foundations, the structural system, the electrical, HVAC, sanitary, sign, and other systems of the building, and the landscaping plans. When the final inspection is completed, a compliance certificate is issued and an occupancy permit is given to the owner. Depending on the complexity of the project, the design, permit, and construction process may take months or years.

14.8 DETAILED PROJECT FEASIBILITY STUDIES

Private sector tourism projects that do not require government incentives or financing follow a somewhat different planning and review process. Funding and building a commercial hotel project, for example, may involve a cumbersome funding and permit process. The scenario begins to take shape with the emergence of an idea to build a hotel at a particular site in a tourism destination area. Then other steps follow:

- The owner/developer of the project commissions a feasibility study to describe the dimensions and financial projections of the proposed hotel.
- The feasibility study verifies the zoning and tourism overlay requirements of the destination area, and the owner/developer conducts a market analysis, includes a site and architectural design concept, and presents a financial and business plan.
- The owner/developer solicits interest from reputable hotel management companies for operating the hotel and entering into a franchise agreement.
- The owner/developer presents the site and architectural design concept to local permit authorities for a pre-permit conference and receives initial instructions and comments.
- The owner/developer approves the findings and recommendations of the feasibility study and proceeds to implement the recommendations.
- The owner/developer presents the feasibility study to private investors and commercial banks and applies for an acquisition and/or construction loan.
- The owner/developer commissions the architectural and engineering team to prepare the required presentations for the site plan permit.

- After a review process, the authorities approve the site plan and the architectural concept of the hotel.
- The owner/developer signs a letter of intent with the hotel management and franchise company.
- The owner/developer closes the acquisition and/or construction loan.
- The owner/developer authorizes the architectural and engineering team to prepare a full set of construction drawings and specifications.
- The owner/developer submits the construction drawings and specifications to the authorities and applies for a building permit.
- After the review process and development conditions are completed, the building permit is granted.
- Construction starts and various inspections are done during the course of construction.
- At completion, a postconstruction final inspection is done and an occupancy permit is granted. Often, an "as-built" set of construction drawings are prepared and submitted to public authorities to recognize any design changes than may have been made in the construction process.

The feasibility study may have several dimensions. It may be limited to a financial analysis verifying the development costs, operational expenses and revenues, and profitability of the proposed venture. Or it may be expanded into a business plan covering the market analysis, corporate objectives, and participants and their shares. It may also include a set of conceptual architectural and site plans for providing more specific information about the physical aspects of the project. If it is an adaptive reuse project of an existing structure(s), the feasibility of using structural, decorative, and historically significant elements of the structure(s) in the proposed project may be included in the feasibility study.

A typical feasibility study for a resort hotel contains the following:

- Introduction of the project and its participants
- Objectives and scope of the feasibility study
- Description of the land and its location
- Market characteristics of the attraction-facility mix and the destination region
- Existing and projected domestic and international visitors
- The master tourism development plan of the region and its requirements
- The place of the proposed hotel in the regional and/or local master plan
- Selected themes and attraction-facility characteristics
- Proposed design and development plans of the resort hotel
- Furniture, fixtures, and equipment schedule
- Possible government incentives
- Operations plan, management team, and schedule
- Critical risks and potential problems
- Financial assumptions
- Building program and development costs
- Revenue, expense, occupancy, and cash flow projections
- Projected financial pro forma for expected operating results of the resort hotel
- Exit or repayment strategy for the loan

It is important to note that creating a new and interesting destination is a matter of good business judgment, but also of inspiration and creative talent. The feasibility study does not provide the inspirational dimension. Successful developers of many destination resort hotels and casinos appreciate this important dimension and encourage their creative teams to conceive imaginative, one-of-a-kind, and highly successful projects.

14.9 ARCHITECT–OWNER/DEVELOPER RELATIONSHIPS AND RESPONSIBILITIES

A large tourism resort community, for example, requires extensive advance preparation before permits can be obtained. These preparations include feasibility, market, financial, traffic, zoning, and environmental studies. The owner/developer retains the services of an architect for coordinating most of these studies and developing a design concept. The role of the architect, his or her responsibilities, and procedures for preparing the documents and executing the construction of buildings are described in the *Architect's Professional Book of Practice* adopted by the American Institute of Architects (AIA).

Over the years, the board of the AIA has approved a series of policies that are structured as part of a policy framework that addresses fundamental aspects of the profession. The policy framework is derived from the conviction that architecture profoundly affects people. The work of architects is essential to human well-being, and architects must embrace the ethical obligation to uphold the public trust inherent in their profession.

As members of their communities, architects are professionally obligated to use their knowledge, skill, and experience to engage in civic life. Design, construction, and society are constantly changing. To serve society, architects must commit to achieve continual professional growth through learning, innovation, and exploration. The AIA maintains that the practice of architecture should be regulated. The privileges and responsibilities of professional practice should be extended only to those architects who demonstrate through education, experience, and examination that they are ethically and technically prepared.

With an obligation to the future of their profession, architects must encourage, recruit, and inspire those who would become architects. Regulation of the construction industry shapes the built environment. As stakeholders, architects must participate in the development and application of appropriate regulations and standards. The financial health of architectural businesses is essential to the future of the profession. Architects should advocate within the law for sound business practices and methods of compensation reflecting the architect's value to society.

The AIA policy further stipulates that leadership in design and construction requires collaboration. Architects must encourage and celebrate the contributions of those who bring diverse experiences, views, and needs to the design process. Architecture expresses the values of society and has the power to enhance the quality of life of present and future generations. Architects must advocate for responsible design that results in beautiful and healthy places that respect and accommodate society's diverse cultures and needs. The creation and operation of the built environment requires an investment of the earth's resources. Architects must be environmentally responsible and advocate for sustainable use of those resources.

The architect is primarily the owner/developer's professional adviser for providing basic design services, preparing a report of the probable cost of the project, and selecting systems and materials of construction. In this capacity, he or she proposes the best design solution for the project. The architect may assume larger responsibilities, including client representation, and provide additional services. Assuming larger responsibilities makes the architect an impartial arbitrator between the owner/developer and the construction contractor of record for the project.

In turn, the owner/developer has a series of obligations. He or she agrees to pay the architect full and fair compensation for services rendered. He or she is required to furnish the architect with full legal and physical information about the project site and establish a budget for the project. But the architect is not obligated to commit him- or herself to this budget. The architect will make every legitimate effort to deliver the project within the stated budget. The owner/developer is obligated to give prompt consideration to the architect's drawings and specifications and to cooperate with him or her in achieving the project objectives. The owner/developer must understand that drawings and specifications are the architect's way of communicating with the responsible parties. The architect has ownership rights of the drawings and specifications.

The architect's project team consists of an office staff that may include other professional associates, as well as engineering and other consultants who may be needed for their specialized expertise. The overall responsibility for the management of the project rests with the architect, who puts his or her signature and registration stamp on all design documents leaving his or her office. The authorized signature and stamp authenticate the legitimacy of the construction documents.

The owner/developer and the architect jointly prepare a realistic timetable for executing various phases of the project. Construction scheduling is not a part of this timetable, because the architect has no control over the circumstances of the construction contractor. The schedule is updated as the project progresses.

The most common method of compensating the architect for services rendered involves comparing the phases of the project with the services of the architect in terms of the percentage of the work completed. Usually, the owner/developer makes monthly payments in proportion to the percentage of the basic fee for services performed by the architect and his or her consultant team. By one convention, the following payments are made in proportion to basic fees for completing consecutive phases of the project:

- Schematic design phase   15%
- Design development phase   20%
- Construction documents phase   40%
- Bidding or negotiating phase   5%
- Construction phase   20%

                          Total   100%

By mutual agreement, the owner/developer makes these payments to the architect and includes payments to consultants serving the architect. The combined compensation of the architect and his or her consultants during the **construction document phase** generally covers 40% of the architect's basic fee for the project. This 40% portion is often divided among the members of the project team as follows:

- Architect's compensation for construction drawings   18%
- Engineer's compensation for structural drawings   6%
- Engineer's compensation for electrical and mechanical drawings   12%
- Architect's compensation for specifications   4%

                                 Total   40%

The balance of the architect's fee is paid in monthly installments when a particular phase is completed.

14.10   PHASES OF THE ARCHITECT'S DESIGN SERVICES

The objectives of the **schematic design phase** are to assist the client in understanding the project program, to illustrate possible solutions that will take the shortest possible time and the least expense, and to assist in determining the feasibility of the project.

The schematic design phase includes:

- Site plan, with diagrammatic drawings showing the relationships of project parts
- Vertical sections through the site if the topography requires such studies
- Small-scale line drawings of principal floor plans
- General description of the project
- Statement of the probable project construction cost

The objectives of the **design development phase** are to fix and describe the size and character of the project and other essentials. The design development documents are based on schematic design studies approved by the owner/developer. The documents include:

- Site plan indicating the general location and nature of site improvements
- Plans, elevations, sections, and schedules for fixing the architectural, structural, mechanical, and electrical systems
- Outline of specifications
- Updated statement of probable construction costs

The objectives of the **construction documents phase** are to depict graphically the characteristics and extent of the project when it is ready for construction. The documents consist of drawings and specifications. They show concisely the information required by the contractor for making a bid proposal to construct the project. The construction documents are based on design development documents approved by the owner/developer. Together, the documents show the following information:

- Drawings arranged in a logical sequence
- Plans, elevations, sections, and details that are free of superfluous information
- Drawings drawn to scale and dimensioned accurately
- Drawings and specifications that describe, locate, dimension, and identify physical properties, performance characteristics, and sources of supply

In short, the documents show *what* is involved, *where* it is located, *what* the physical dimensions and materials are, *where* they can be obtained, and *how* they are to function. Drawings and specifications are instruments of service. They are the property of the architect whether the project for which they were prepared is executed or not. The owner/developer has the obligation to pay the architect his or her basic fee and has no rights of ownership over the construction documents. The documents are not to be used by the owner/developer on other projects, except by agreement with the architect and for additional compensation.

14.11   SELECTION OF CONTRACTORS AND CONSTRUCTION ADMINISTRATION

The objective of contractor selection for building construction is to procure the building materials, skilled labor, and management necessary to complete the project on schedule and for the agreed-upon price. The parties to the contract for construction are the owner/developer and the contractor. The contractor is responsible for performing the work, and the owner/developer is responsible for paying the contractor for his or her performance.

The award of the construction contract involves the following steps:

- Determination of the awarding system

  Direct selection

  Negotiation

  Competitive bidding

- Determination of the contract system

  Single contract

  Separate contracts

- Determination of the suitable type of contract

  Stipulated sum

  Cost plus fee

- Examination of the prequalification of bidders
- Preparation, assembly, and distribution of bidding documents
- Preparation, receipt, and tabulation of bids
- Recommendations and award of contracts
- Execution of contracts

The architect is responsible for the administration of the contract between the owner/developer and the contractor. The architect, or his or her representative as agents of the owner/developer, discharges this responsibility by:

- Interpreting the contract documents and their changes
- Establishing the standards of acceptability
- Judging the performance of the contractor by his or her conformity to the plans
- Issuing certificates authorizing payments to the contractor on work completed
- Making a special inspection to determine the date of substantial completion of the work
- Informing the owner/developer about the progress and status of the project

The architect protects the owner/developer against defects and deficiencies in the contractor's work. If the architect finds defects and deficiencies, he or she can reject the contractor's work. The right to reject work is not intended as a safety precaution or to determine the adequacy of construction means, methods, techniques, sequences, or procedures. The contractor is solely responsible for these issues.

The architect is also not responsible for the contractor's failure to carry out the work according to the construction documents. The contractor is responsible for all aspects of the work specified. But the architect is responsible for exercising due care and skill to determine whether the project is progressing according to the construction documents. Failing to do so, he or she could be held liable by the owner/developer for negligence.

The contractor, or his or her representative, has responsibility for the supervision required to assemble materials and perform labor to complete the construction of the project. The contractor discharges this duty by:

- Studying, comparing, and following the contract documents, laws, and regulations affecting construction, and cooperating with the architect and other contractors and subcontractors

- Directing the construction of the work with the best skill, attention, and urgency
- Constructing and completing the project in accordance with the requirements of the contract documents

If consultants are employed to design structural, mechanical, electrical, landscaping, or similar systems, their services are usually continued in the contract administration phase for the work they have designed.

While attentive in performing his or her professional function, the architect must consult a lawyer when legal issues arise. Under some circumstances, the architect may relay the advice of his or her lawyer to the owner/developer for the purposes of clarifications and/or negotiation.

14.12   PROJECT PLANNING AND CONTROL SYSTEMS

Project planning and control systems (PP&CSs) are used by government agencies and private developers for tracking the planning and execution of tourism and other development projects at the local level. These systems can be quite detailed, depending on the size, duration, and complexity of plans and projects. The objectives of the PP&CS are to:

- Establish for the executing agency a master business plan for executing projects and updating them
- Provide the executing agency with a work breakdown for following the progress of its projects
- Provide the executing agency with periodic appraisals of project performance against the formal plan concerning scope, schedule, and costs
- Provide a common database of planning and control information ensuring consistent understanding and communication concerning the projects

The principal features of the PP&CS are:

- It uses proven project management techniques in a coordinated, systematic manner.
- It provides a coding structure that facilitates comparison of scope and cost relationships within the plan.
- It contains systematic summaries making the proper degree of detail available to the executing agency.

The PP&CS tries to accomplish the following:

- Facilitate the planning and control functions in a disciplined, consistent, and orderly manner
- Provide the means to track the costs and performance of any element of the work breakdown
- Provide the executing agency an early warning system for identifying potential problems before they become serious
- Provide the executing agency the flexibility for making planning and control adjustments and taking corrective actions as needed

The basic elements of the PP&CS are:

- A work breakdown structure (WBS) used to display the project's scope, schedule, costs, and responsibilities within its larger program context

    The WBS subdivides work into elements at various levels for planning, budgeting, and controlling the project. It has an end-item orientation rather than a functional department-oriented work organization. As such, it has four levels: (1) The program level subdivides the work into construction, operations, and services. (2) The project level identifies the three types of work involved in each individual project. (3) The facility level is a further subdivision of the project work identified by geographic area. (4) The contract level is the smallest component of the facility level. Within the WBS, it covers cost estimations, schedules, and contract language.

• A coding structure integrating the planning information flow from all functional sources involved in each element of the WBS

The coding structure has the ability to trace all resources and summarize the work element for the next level of the WBS. Through the coding structure, all resources budgeted, committed, and expended can be traced to a specific WBS element. In the work schedule, the coding structure also makes it possible to combine data for all elements at one level and pass them to the next level for reporting purposes. The coding structure employs a nine-character alphanumeric code unique to each contract that identifies the individual elements at each of the four levels of work breakdown. This facilitates preparation of plans and budgets and the continuous monitoring of actual performance.

• A work plan describing the project and facility scope, schedule, cost, functional responsibilities, project procedures, and subsequent budgets

The work plan is further detailed by incorporating policies, assumptions, organization, staff, supply and demand data, commitments, and revenues, if any. The project and facility scope statements contain the basic information used for planning and describing the major physical components of the project, including sizing and quantities. The schedules present the long-term continuous supply of elements necessary to meet the demands of projects and facilities. The staffing estimates for the scheduled work are prepared by evaluating the schedules of contract packages. The supply and demand data are complied for all work items and for each executing agency. Commitments, expenditures, and revenues are tallied for each work item for the current fiscal year and forecasts for the near term.

• A monitoring system measuring performance against the plan and budgets through trends and forecasts

The monitoring system is set in place when the work plan and schedule are prepared and approved by the agency administration. The administration defines the responsibilities, timing, and inputs of various departments of the agency, as well as the reviews and approvals necessary for implementation of the monitoring system. By measuring performance with the quantities and schedules prescribed by the work plan, the dates and quantities are periodically reviewed and changed as needed.

• A reporting system enabling the agency administration to stay current on the progress of its projects

Reporting is done electronically or by distributing printed documents. These documents are prepared as automatic by-products of the work plan. They cover all aspects of the work in progress and show thousands of pieces of information.

Management reports are prepared monthly for active contracts, completed contracts, targets and accomplishments, contract change orders, and subcontract vendor data.

Planning and control reports include the work plan and the approved work plan changes.

Planning and scheduling reports include the master staging schedule, summary schedules, project logic schedules, contract package schedules, supply-demand data, late events, contract formulation, contract administration, node count, bidders list control, and milestone status.

Cost engineering reports include commitments and expenditures, the budget status report, overtime reports, and monthly forecasts.

Graphic material accompanies the reports. The results are such that the project management function is better structured and performed in an orderly way. The technical management team of the agency administration at all levels is more aware of current and anticipated problems and can act accordingly.

The planning and control mechanism does not stop at the agency or private business level. It also incorporates reviews by the public. Progress hearings for the public are scheduled for receiving feedback about the progress and emerging environmental, social, and economic impacts of projects. Tourism projects in particular are susceptible to these periodic reviews and information meetings with the government. When they are multipurpose projects serving the community in many ways, their effectiveness in attracting and serving tourists is closely monitored.

- The benefits should include not only the direct, but also the indirect effects made possible by the existence of unused capacity.
- Secondary or multiplier effects should be considered and accounted for.
- When market prices are not a correct expression of equilibrium prices, accounting or shadow prices have to be used for evaluating the effects of the projects on the economy.
- The costs should include the value of all scarce factors used in the investment program.
- It is not sufficient to determine the influence of an investment program on the national economy for one year. The delayed effects of savings, for example, require longer periods for accurate evaluation of the program.
- The influence of the investment program on other objectives of national economic policies, such as employment, balance of payments, and regional income distribution should also be measured. Monetary values are given to each of these elements in order to reduce several aspects of the program to a single unit of measure by adding the values.

The above material outlines and lists major components of project planning and control systems. For more details, see *Application of Integrative and Predictive Project Planning and Control Systems*, by Russell D. Archibald, in *Max's Musings,* August 2001, published on the Internet by R. Max Wideman, Vancouver, British Columbia, Canada at http://www.maxwideman.com/guests/ceo/planning.htm.

Chapter Highlights

- The process of developing a tourist attraction or facility starts with an idea. Translating the idea into a project requires professional help.
- When the project idea is professionally developed into a unique concept with physical dimensions, market and feasibility studies are done.
- With the project idea verified, and with the market demand and financial analysis complete, acquisition or control of the land becomes the next priority.
- Detailed planning, design, engineering, and construction of a project involve complex processes. Topics to be covered in these processes include performing a site analysis, preparing a building program, obtaining necessary permits, managing a multidisciplinary team of professionals, and overseeing construction.

- The architectural design process is subject to a well-understood relationship between the architect and the owner/developer of a project and covers the following phases: schematic design, design development, preparation of construction documents, bidding/negotiating by construction firms, and construction with oversight by the architect.
- Project planning and control systems are normally used by government agencies and private developers for tracking the planning and execution of tourism and other development projects and for assuring the accountability of the various organizations involved in project implementation. These systems can be quite detailed, depending on the size, duration, and complexity of the plans and projects.

15

Project Financing, Agreements, and Ownership

This chapter reviews the process of preparing information packages necessary for raising capital in planning and developing private and government-owned tourism projects involving construction. The package includes various financial calculations for determining the feasibility of a project. It studies the role of franchising in facilitating fund-raising. It also outlines the steps and agreements in closing the purchase or sale of real property that will be part of a tourism project. Raising capital for tourism ventures not involving construction has similar, but not identical, procedures.

- Information packages are different for private and government projects.
- Many financial calculations accompany project descriptions and plans.
- Acquiring a reputable management franchise improves the possibility and terms of financing a project.
- The final act of closing a deal for purchasing and financing a tourism project is one of commitment by all parties concerned.

15.1 PREPARING PROJECT PACKAGES FOR TOURISM PROJECTS

In all business transactions, exchange of information precedes exchange of money. This is true for tourism planning and development. However, this basic fact of business is often ignored until the very end of lengthy discussions, when it is discovered that one party does not have a viable product to sell or the other party does not have the money to purchase it. Information packages minimize this potential misunderstanding and expedite early closings. Project packages contain vital information and present the facts of the project initially to prevent complications later. These packages are sometimes called "developer's kits." The following Web site contains rather lengthy investment information about a planned public/private tourist project in the Sindh Province in southern Pakistan: http://www.pppunitsindh.gov.pk/site/downloads/9.pdf.

The project package for a privately financed tourism project contains proprietary background information and graphics. The owner/developer or his or her consultant prepares the package. Its main purpose is to present information for securing a construction loan and permanent financing. The package may also be submitted to government authorities for securing a permit or receiving financial incentives. Project packages are prepared for typical privately owned and financed hotel, golf course, resort, and marina projects.

The package for a privately financed tourism project contains:

- *Legal definition* of the project, including ownership, site, applicable comprehensive plan, zoning, land development, building regulations, and related conditions of the tourism destination, due diligence, deed, survey of the land, and inspection report
- *Physical description* of the project, including location, accessibility, infrastructure, proposed building program, site and architectural development concept, and probable traffic and environmental impacts
- *Socioeconomic information* on the project, including demographic and economic information about the country, region, or destination, conformity with national and regional tourism development goals, employment created, economic multiplier effects, and probable social and cultural impacts
- *Financial information*, including estimated construction and development costs of the proposed project, projected operating expenses and revenues, operating profits, value-loan ratio, equity, return on investment at sellout, proposed sources and terms of financing, exit strategy, and repayment terms
- *Appraisal* of the property's value by a licensed/certified appraiser
- *Project team*, including the background of the owner, professional architects, engineers and consultants, attorney, management company, and franchisor
- *Project planning, management, control, and scheduling*, including the critical path diagram of project steps, phases, and schedules
- *Risk management plan*, including political risk insurance (if any)
- *Business plan*, including market analysis, competition, and a schedule of expected revenues and costs for a multiyear period
- *Graphics*, including site analysis, site plan, conceptual architectural plans, photographs, publicity and informational brochures, compact disks, illustrations of Web sites, and promotional videos
- *Copies of legal documents*, including the purchase-and-sale agreement, deed, mortgage application, survey, references, and other documents that may be required, such as easements on the property
- *Other*, including applicable special provisions if the project does not involve construction, such as the acquisition of a hotel or a travel agency business

Tourism development reaches its operational stage when national development policies are translated into a series of government infrastructure projects and measures. These are funded by program years and are implemented locally. Information packages for government infrastructure projects are prepared and presented by a sponsoring agency or a consulting firm working for the agency.

The project package for a government-financed project has a modified purpose and content. Depending on the scope and type of project, it is prepared by the relevant agency of the national, regional, or local government. Its purpose is to invite developers, contractors, or design-build teams to plan, design, and execute a tourism development project conceived by the government.

Packages for a highway, airport, power plant, city or national park, public beach facilities, and so on are examples. The project could have a lump sum award or it could be a build-operate-transfer (BOT) project. The package contains:

- Invitation letter to applicants
- Purpose and scope of the solicitation for services
- Project registration fee and general information
- Legal description, as above
- Physical description, as above
- Appraisal of the property by a licensed/certified appraiser
- If applicable, a general description of how the project would be planned, designed, built, operated, and transferred
- Contract documents, including form agreements, drawings, specifications, and bids
- Time of completion, including "substantial completion" and "completion" dates
- Insurance and bonds, royalties, patents, copyrights, and trademarks, if any
- Bidding documents, including list of bidders, forms, and their submission dates
- A request for qualifications of the bidder and its team
- Issuance of drawings and specifications
- Unit prices, if available
- Terms for selecting a chosen bidder
- Contract forms for the prime contractor and subcontractors

The project package is also submitted to a government or international funding agency for information, coordination, and release of the funds that were agreed upon earlier between the agencies. The funds are drawn according to the agreed-upon program schedule.

The capacity and other impact information that affects the expansion of the tourism destination are presented separately as an appendix to the project package. Depending on the nature of the project, the government package may also include:

- Information about the government agency that initiates the project and the ruling of the council of ministers authorizing the project
- Procedures to be followed for inviting bidders and evaluating bids
- The objectives of the infrastructure project (e.g., to produce the benefits of a new hydro-electric power plant, dam, and electrification system for a region)
- Technical specifications for each subsection of the project
- Applicable codes and regulations
- Expected economic impact of the project in terms of employment, business and public services, and tax revenues generated
- Financial pro forma information that could be used for financing the project
- Expected schedule of actions from the date of invitation to bid for the project to the date of project completion
- Bidding documents and fees submitted by the bidder on or before the date of the bid to the recipient authority
- Engineering drawings, photographs, critical path diagrams, and project management organizations

When the government project is slated for international financing by organizations like the World Bank and/or EX-IM Bank, the package includes detailed cost and revenue projections and repayment schedules for the construction loan.

15.2   PREPARING PROJECT PACKAGES FOR URBAN REDEVELOPMENT PROJECTS

When the project combines national and regional governments as funding sources and local government as the executor of a multipurpose urban renewal effort, the project package contains other background information separately identifying the legal obligations of all three governments. Local government procedures are followed for selecting the project developer. Aside from funding, regional and national governments enter the process only when the project has regional and national implications. Local government is the primary beneficiary of the project. (State, provincial, and national taxes go to these higher levels of government.) Judicial branches of federal, state, and local governments resolve conflicts jointly when they arise.

For example, a typical multigovernment and multipurpose project could be a waterfront urban renewal project having important tourism development implications. Decaying waterfronts often have the potential to become major tourist destinations and growth centers. The national government takes the initiative in redeveloping these once thriving and now derelict waterfronts. Changing economic priorities and technologies are among the reasons for the declining waterfront, shifting its functions inshore where alternative transportation and room for commercial expansion are available.

In relation to waterfront development, national governments have environmental concerns for water and air quality, wetlands protection, shoreline maintenance, storm and flood damage control, and allocation of funds for local infrastructure. State governments or provinces handle legal issues related to land assembly, reclamation or preservation, and issues of multilevel jurisdiction. Local governments resolve property and hotel and restaurant tax issues, zoning (including watersheet zoning) competition among land uses, waste disposal, permits for building and structures (including marinas), and construction processes.

The public is drawn to a waterfront for its variety of water-based recreational activities and attractions. In the United States, the urban renewal mechanism was used successfully for redeveloping many waterfronts in major cities. Since the 1960s, the Federal Urban Renewal Program redeveloped well over thirty coastal city waterfronts. Such waterfronts are considered integral parts of the urban and regional fabric and are prime economic assets. Some of the successful waterfront projects with multiple recreational, residential, and commercial uses completed in the United States since the early 1960s include:

- New York City, New York: South Street Seaport
- Boston, Massachusetts: Atlantic Avenue developments including Quincy Market and the Faneuil Hall Marketplace
- San Antonio, Texas: Riverwalk
- Baltimore, Maryland: Inner Harbor
- Portland, Oregon: River Place
- Newburyport, Massachusetts: The Harbor
- Portland, Maine: The Old Port

Project objectives of waterfront redevelopment include the following:

- Creating a safe and secure environment
- Mixing multiple uses of land and building areas
- Recycling deteriorating and abandoned areas and structures
- Overcoming isolating physical barriers such as freeways
- Providing visual access

- Creating open spaces, parks, plazas, artwork, and so on
- Introducing a focal point of interest such as a historic sailing ship
- Connecting the waterfront activity points with a shoreline pathway
- Creating marinas, ferry terminals, and boat charter and water sightseeing facilities
- Protecting commercial fishing fleets

The project package for a local urban development project includes all specialized information and supporting studies that help justify the project. Interested real estate developers are given copies of project information packages and are informed of the special conditions of the project specified in supporting studies.

The procedures for preparing and submitting project packages may differ widely from one country to another and from one funding or permitting institution to another. An example of a detailed project prospectus for a marina village in Fiji can be found on the following Web site: http://www.marinavillagefiji.com/PROSPECTUS.PDF.

15.3   SOLICITING INTEREST FROM FRANCHISORS

Most tourism projects depend on their own identity for marketing their product. The exception is when a particular operation becomes so successful that it lends its identity, management expertise, and proprietary knowledge to others in exchange for a fee. This is the essence of franchising.

In tourism-related businesses, fast food and brand name restaurants, gift shops, car rental agencies, and, in particular, hotel companies are prominent franchisors providing their names and operational knowledge to private investors/developers/owners. The case for high-quality hotels describes the advantages of franchising.

Soliciting and securing a franchise for a prospective hotel has many advantages. For one, sources for financing the hotel will be more inclined to think that the hotel has a high probability for success with the help of its well-known franchise. This would reduce the risk of failure and default. But getting a franchise is not simple. The process is lengthy, expensive, and highly selective.

The advantages of obtaining a hotel franchise include:

- Benefits from volume purchasing of food, beverages, furniture, fixtures and equipment from the franchisor's suppliers
- Use of the distribution services of the franchisor
- Use of the design and construction services of the franchisor
- Use of the franchisor's trademark and other visual images
- Use of the prototype architectural plans and specifications of the franchisor
- Use of the finely detailed and tested quality service experience and procedures of the franchisor
- Training of the hotel management team by the franchisor
- The franchisee's participation in and benefit from the marketing and promotional programs of the franchisor
- Use of the room reservation system and other communications systems of the franchisor

The franchise agreement includes compulsory training requirements for the management and staff of the hotel. Some of this training takes place initially; other training occurs continuously or at monthly intervals. It is provided in the classroom or on the job. It includes concierge, front desk, housekeeping, and maintenance services; revenue management; team building; managing guest relations and staff relations; and competitive procurement of needed goods and services.

The process starts with an application, requiring substantial fees. Other fees that are required later in the process include royalty, marketing, reservation system, property management system, training, design and construction assistance, procurement, and accounting fees. In addition, the franchisee invests in, and bears the cost of, land acquisition, the market study, building construction, furniture, fixtures and equipment, computer hardware and software, signs, supplies, telephone systems, opening inventory, and insurance.

The franchisor offers the franchisee the means to develop and operate a trademark hotel located at a specified site. However, it does not give the franchisee exclusive territorial and market protection, and it may not offer direct or indirect financing. Other obligations of the franchisor include:

- Approving the site selected by the owner
- Providing the owner with a set of prototype plans and specifications
- Reviewing the construction drawings for compliance with standards
- Inspecting the construction of the hotel periodically
- Inspecting the hotel when construction is completed
- Providing on-site training to hotel management and other staff
- Permitting the use of the franchisor's hotel operating manual
- Providing the connection with the hotel reservation system
- Performing quality assurance checks during the operation of the hotel
- Managing a marketing program for advertising and marketing the franchise hotels

In addition to paying its franchise fees on time, the principal obligations of the franchisee include:

- Site selection, lease, or acquisition
- Preopening leases or purchases
- Site development and other preopening requirements
- Initial and ongoing training
- Opening the hotel for business
- Compliance with standards, policies, and procedures
- Trademark and proprietary compliance
- Restrictions on products and services
- Warranty and customer service requirements
- Ongoing product and service purchases
- Maintenance, appearance, and remodeling requirements
- Insurance
- Supplemental advertising and promotion
- Indemnification
- Owner's participation, management, and staffing
- Records and reports
- Inspections and audits
- Transferring the franchise
- Renewal of the franchise
- Posttermination obligations
- Non competition covenants
- Guarantees
- Joining and participating in the franchisee association

Generally, the value of having a franchise far exceeds the expenses involved. With the franchise agreement in hand, the owner may have many possibilities for securing financing for the hotel from various sources, and may enjoy the name recognition and quality expectations of the franchisor.

15.4   PROJECT FEASIBILITY CALCULATIONS

The project package includes several calculations that demonstrate the financial feasibility of the project. The information is prepared by the seller, and sometimes by both the seller and buyer of the property or the participants in the project. For comparison, lending institutions prepare their own independent financial evaluations.

The project feasibility calculations for the tourism project are described in detail in Appendix J. They include:

- Estimating construction costs
- Calculating the debt-to-capital ratio
- Calculating the payback period
- Calculating the expected rate of return
- Calculating the return on investment
- Calculating the total return
- Preparing a profit and loss account
- Preparing a cash flow statement
- Calculating depreciation
- Appraising the real estate and other property value, such as equipment and furnishings

15.5   CONSTRUCTION AND PERMANENT FINANCING OF THE TOURISM PROJECT

The construction loan is secured from one of a series of sources discussed earlier. After construction is completed, the building goes through final inspection and the permitting agency issues the occupancy permit. With construction completed, the construction loan is converted into a permanent loan with different loan terms by the same or another lending institution. This procedure requires a detailed business plan and a list of operational assumptions for the facility from the borrower. Operating results and cash flow analysis showing the revenues, expenses, and other operational assumptions are projected for the duration of the permanent loan. Distribution of net income before taxes, during or at the end of the period, is calculated and the profitability of the venture is determined. Incentives, loan origination fees, and other closing costs are verified.

15.6   SECURING FINANCING

Lending sources and types of financing for tourism development projects were discussed in Chapter 10. Depending on the nature of the project, involving construction or otherwise, one or more sources could be used for financing a tourism project. Apart from the characteristics of a proposed tourism project, the ability of the host country, region, and locality to attract tourists, simply because of their favorable image and popularity, is a major factor in evaluating the financial prospects of the project.

The information package prepared by the owner for the proposed project contains the information that the source of financing will initially require. After preliminary evaluation of the data submitted by the owner, the source of financing will conduct its own due diligence to arrive at a clear and independent opinion about the project. This may take several steps and multiple fees. The lender will employ the services of a real estate attorney, title searcher, title insurance company, land surveyor, and several other specialists for examining the documents and the site of the project.

The process of due diligence by the lender and closing of the loan will generally include the following steps:

- The borrower prepares a "Loan Prequalifier Worksheet" or submits the project information package, including the business plan and executive summary.
- The lender or investor reviews, evaluates, and conducts the prequalification test, resulting in acceptance, proposed revision, or denial of the application.
- The lender or investor prepares a document indicating general interest, with lending terms, in the form of a proposal to the borrower.
- The lender or investor prepares a financing agreement. When it is approved and signed by the borrower, the lender or investor issues a "Letter of Interest."
- The lender requests additional data, if any.
- The lender examines all documents and conducts a due diligence examination.
- The board of the lender accepts the results of the due diligence examination and issues a loan commitment and terms to the borrower.
- The borrower accepts the terms of the loan and the agreement is signed by the parties, the loan is closed/completed, and the draw of payments schedule becomes effective.

Government and international lending sources like the World Bank, the Overseas Private Investment Corporation (OPIC), and others employ processes resembling the basic process described above.

15.7 TITLE TRANSFER

Once the money is secured, the property to be developed is ready to be sold if it is not already in the hands of the developer. Transferring title to real estate is a legal concept that gives the holder a lawful claim to all the requisites that constitute ownership, that is, the bundle of rights inherent in property ownership. Among these rights is the legal power to defend the title holdings. Historically, the method by which the title was transferred consisted simply of delivering the possession. A family who had been in possession of a property for generations was presumed to be the owner. The title was transferred verbally in the presence of a witness who knew both the buyer and the seller.

Many traditional societies still observe this practice. In remote parts of the world where pristine conditions of nature are an attraction, a tourist destination begins to emerge by first assembling land from those who may have owned it for generations. Observing local practices in securing legal ownership that can be defended in a court of law is in essence a cultural sensitivity test. Governments that fail to protect the generations' old ownership rights of their constituents and instead serve the interests of resort hotel developers destroy the trust of their people and greatly harm the cause of fair and profitable tourism development. Outsiders taking control of the land, sometimes by fraudulent means and at minimum cost, would set an unfavorable precedent.

15.8 CLOSING THE SALE

The agreement on the sale of the property generally provides information for title closing and the delivery of the deed at a particular date at a certain location and hour. The closing date usually gives the seller and buyer enough time to make their preparations stipulated in the agreement. Many steps are required before the closing, including a title search or its equivalent (some land is registered and does not require a title search every time it is sold). The buyer's attorney, or his or her assistant, carries out the research and prepares a report for the buyer. In addition, conducting a survey of the subject land to confirm its dimensions is advisable. A licensed surveyor or civil engineer verifies these dimensions and the layout. It is important to make sure that the surveying entity is acceptable to the lender and the title examining company. Another important step is conducting an inspection of the property. Professional building inspectors must be employed to verify the conditions of the building. Other inspectors verify that there are no hazardous wastes, residues of harmful substances, or injurious insects such as termites on the property. The report of the title, survey report, and inspections will adequately inform the buyer. All encumbrances shown on the title report, other than those waived by the buyer, are removed before the closing. The seller comes to the closing prepared to remove these encumbrances.

A number of individuals attend the closing. Both sides bring to the meeting their respective sets of documents. The seller is required to provide the following upon closing:

- Seller's copy of the agreement
- Latest tax, water, and assessment receipted bills
- Latest meter readings of water, gas, or electric utilities
- Receipts for the last payment of interest on any mortgages, if there are any
- Originals of all fire, liability, and other insurance policies
- Any subordination agreements
- Evidence of any easements on the property
- Any compliance receipts for liens, judgments, or mortgages
- List of tenants and their contracts
- Assignment of leases
- Affidavit of title
- Bill of sale for the building contents
- Seller's last deed and other instruments

Upon closing, the buyer is expected to do the following:

- Have the buyer's copy of the agreement
- Obtain a copy of the title
- Obtain the report of the title
- Examine the deed to verify its compliance with the agreement
- Ensure that the deed is properly executed and recorded
- Have payments ready as required in the agreement
- Verify that all liens are removed and disposed of
- Obtain assignment of unpaid rents and leases
- Obtain copies of notification letters to tenants
- Obtain the affidavit of the title
- Document the authority of the agent (if any) representing the seller
- Obtain the bill of sale of the building contents
- Examine the survey and inspection reports

- Verify any covenants, restrictions, and consents affecting the property
- Have bills for unpaid taxes, utilities, or assessments
- Have the interest on the mortgage(s) computed up to the date of closing
- Make adjustments as called for in the agreement
- Examine the new mortgage for purchasing the property and execute it
- Have damage awards for existing public improvements and assessments assigned to the buyer
- Obtain any unrecorded instrument affecting the title

After the closing is completed, the parties go their separate ways unless there is a remaining legal obligation between them. However, the parties maintain their right to legal recourse when and if needed.

Chapter Highlights

- Information packages minimize potential misunderstandings between the parties involved in developing tourism projects. Project packages contain vital information and present the facts of the project initially to prevent complications later. These packages are sometimes called developer's kits.
- The capacity and other impact information that affects the creation or expansion of a tourism project is usually presented separately, as an appendix to the project package, depending on the nature and complexity of the project.
- A government information package prepared for the purpose of interesting potential project developers in a government-defined and -sponsored project usually includes information about the government, agency procedures, objectives of the project, technical specifications, applicable codes and regulations, expected economic impacts, financial pro forma information, expected schedule of actions, and a request for the qualifications of potential proposers.
- Franchising is an important means of obtaining the mix of activities and expertise and corporate imagery useful for developing and operating tourist facilities, especially hotels.
- Due diligence by the lender and borrower in financing projects is required to meet the conditions of prudent business practice.
- Both the buyer and the seller have an extensive list of documents to prepare before a sale of property can be completed.

16

Computer Simulation, Computer-Aided Design, and Geographic Information Systems

This chapter presents computer applications for tourism development planning, including mathematical simulation and analytical models adapted from economic research, computer graphics, and computer data processing methods.

- Computer simulation and modeling, in its many forms, replicates the real world in its various economic, social, and physical development dimensions and scenarios.
- There are many promising analytical methods that could be adapted to and used for tourism planning. They include input-output methods, linear and nonlinear programming, econometric models, decision tree analysis, and industry complex methods. These methods need further applications and research.
- Computer-aided design facilitates the comprehension of social, economic, and physical data by translating them into visual images; conversely, it creates data by designing new images.
- The computerized Geographic Information System found a new application in 1970 when the BIK System used it to increase understanding of the tourism industry and for planning its development. Today GIS has many applications in tourism planning and can use widely available equipment capable of presenting data in a large variety of forms.

16.1   SIMULATION AND MODELING

Simulation is a tool for representing and understanding the structure and dynamics of a process or system. In dynamic terms, simulation is used for building a model that replicates the appearance of reality. It is the representation of a real set of objects or events and their interrelationships.

It is built at different scales, uses different media, and describes the behavior of the interacting elements. Simulation can be used to test alternative hypotheses and theories. Together, simulation and modeling constitute an applied methodology that can be used for several purposes:

- It describes the behavior of a system.
- It tests theories and hypotheses that would explain the observed behavior.
- It predicts future behavior based on past behavior and theories of behavior.
- It forecasts the consequences of alternative courses of action (by testing "what if?" scenarios).

A **system** is a group of interrelated or interdependent elements that forms a complete entity. The systems approach attempts to observe the performance of a system by studying its structure and behavior through simulation. Applied to tourism planning, simulation and modeling provide a tool necessary for taking a comprehensive look at the behavior of a tourism system and derive hypotheses and theories. The BIK System was conceived in this manner.

The relationship among the elements of the system determines how the overall system behaves. Both the elements and their interaction depend on the purpose for which they are designed. Therefore, the first step in building a model and undertaking simulation is to define the purpose of the model. The model focuses on essential elements and represents a real event or object in a simple or abstract form. As modeling becomes progressively more sophisticated, more elements are introduced, the elements become less abstract, and simulation gets closer to the complex reality it is intended to represent. Models and simulations are developed based on known past events and objects and their known consequences. Models often contain combinations of observed past events and theories or hypotheses that are assumed to be true. Once they are developed, calibrated, tested for reliability, and verified, models and simulation are ready to encapsulate perceived reality and explore the future.

Simulation models are classified in terms of whether they replicate the image of reality or an abstraction of it. The first type of model represents a copy of the reality in a different medium and scale. It is used in driving and flight simulators for training drivers and pilots. The second type of model describes the reality and the interaction among its elements in mathematical terms. An analogue computer that operates by manipulating controlled physical quantities is used for the simulation. A digital computer has much greater precision and range because it can calculate mathematical functions and follow logical procedures.

Provided that the system and its purpose are well defined, almost any kind of system can be simulated. A few examples of simulation applications include:

- *Economics:* Macro- and microeconomic planning and econometrics
- *Tourism:* National, regional, and local destination tourism development planning
- *Urban planning:* Land use, traffic and transportation, recreation and water and sewer systems planning
- *Information systems:* Database management and data processing
- *Business:* Management, stock analysis, pricing, cash flow, and forecasting
- *Manufacturing:* Material handling, inventory management, and operating production processes
- *Government:* Military tactics, health care delivery, and criminal justice
- *Environment:* Weather forecasting, ecology, and resource management
- *Demography:* Population analysis and forecasting
- *Sciences:* Biology, astronomy, biomedicine, and physics
- *Political science:* Voting behavior

Simulation models generally estimate the output of a system for given inputs. Simulation is a tool for pretesting proposed systems, theories, and strategies. Policies, plans, projects, and operating procedures are tested by simulation to verify whether they will achieve their intended purposes before they are implemented at great cost in real time. Economists have adopted the term **input/output** as a label for a specific type of model that traces flows of resources throughout an economy between sectors of an economy. This type of model can also be used to trace flows of resources between regions in an overall economy. This is discussed below in Section 16.5. The following Wikipedia Web site provides a definition and some discussion of input-output analysis: http://en.wikipedia.org/wiki/Input-output_model.

The greatest advantage of simulation is its ability to explore "what if" propositions. Customized tourism simulation models help users understand how the tourism system works and expedite decision making. But these models are not substitutes for effective tourism planning. Optimal answers to proposed problems still require repeated changes to inputs until the desired output is obtained. This trial-and-error process of building and operating a simulation model is educational but expensive. Special training is required for using a simulation model and interpreting its results. The expense of building the database and calibrating the variables of the model must be justified in view of the complexity of the tourism economy it represents. Simple tourism questions can be answered well by using manual tourism analytical and planning methods. For example, simple bivariate or multivariate statistical regression models can be used to describe relationships that are important for tourism development planning like predicting the number of international vacation trips taken per year by members of a given population. An example of an econometric multivariate regression model for evaluating the impacts of tourism (in this case casinos) on local government budgets is given in the following article published in 2009 in the journal Tourism Economics. http://mtre.asu.edu/publications/files/effects-of-tourism-on-municipal-revenues-and-expenditures.pdf.

16.2 NATIONAL AND REGIONAL INCOME ACCOUNTS AND THE GROSS TOURISM PRODUCT

Many new analytical models are available. However, older methods are presented here because of their simplicity and universal applications. One source is the work of Walter Isard. In his path-breaking book *Methods of Regional Analysis* (see the Bibliography), Isard emphasized the need to understand the national income accounts at the macro level before discussing regional income accounts. Macro-level and sector discussions of development planning, specifically tourism, are directly related to national accounts. The regional income account is often taken as a percentage breakdown of national income estimates. The method used for calculating regional accounts is an adaptation of the simulation method used for the national accounts. Although this approach had its critics, it gives a close approximation of the values necessary for calculating the gross national product (GNP), national income (NI), personal income (PI), and gross regional product (GRP). In the same manner, the gross tourism product (GTP), at national and regional levels, is defined in terms of percentages of national and regional income accounts. Accordingly, from GNP, the calculation steps are:

- **Gross National Product**
  - Less: Capital consumption allowances
  - Equals: **Net National Product**
  - Plus: Subsidies minus current surplus of government enterprises
  - Less: Indirect business tax and nontax liability
  - Business transfer payments
  - Statistical discrepancy

Equals: **National Income**
Less: Undistributed corporate profits
Corporate profits tax liability
Corporate inventory valuation adjustment
Contributions for social insurance
Excess of wage accruals over disbursements
Plus: Net interest paid by government
Government transfer payments
Business transfer payments
Equals: **Personal Income**
Less: Non corporate depletion charges
Net imputed rent of owner-occupied dwellings
Changes in farm inventories not held for sale
Employer contributions to private pension and welfare funds
Income in-kind to armed forces
Government military life insurance benefits
Business transfer payments
Noncorporate inventory valuation adjustment
Plus: Premiums to military life insurance funds
Private pension payments
Equals: **Income Payments to Individuals including**
Wages and salaries
Proprietors' income
Other income

Source: U.S. Department of Commerce, Bureau of Economic Analysis, *Guide to the National Income and Product Accounts of the United States,* undated

- **Gross Regional Product**
  Method 1) Value added in the production of goods for export
  Plus: Value added in the production of goods for:
  a) Local consumption
  b) Local capital formation
  Equals: **Gross Regional Product**
  The same result could be obtained for GRP by a second method.
  Method 2) Sales of goods to the rest of the world
  Less: Imports of final and intermediate goods for:
  a) Production of goods and services for export
  b) Local consumption
  c) Local capital formation
  Plus: Purchases of goods and services by local consumers
  Plus: Purchases of capital goods and services by local businesses
  Equals: **Gross Regional Product**

Source: Adapted from C. L. Leven, John Legler, and Perry Shapiro, *Analytical Framework for Regional Development Policy,* Regional Science Studies Series (Cambridge, MA: MIT Press, 1970).

GTP, in turn, is derived from GNP and GRP by using percentage shares of GDP representing the production of tourism sector industries. This percentage varies in every country and region and is calculated individually.

16.3   INTERREGIONAL AND REGIONAL INPUT-OUTPUT ANALYSIS

Input-output analysis describes the underlying processes that bind together sectors or an economy, or by extension, a system of regions in all major facets of their economies. The strength of the method lies in showing in great detail the production and distribution characteristics of individual industries of different regions and the nature of the interrelationships among these industries and among the industries of other economic sectors. It describes the basic fabric of an interindustry system as it exists not only within each region but also among regions. Delineating the similar relationships between the industries making up the tourism sector, as well as other regional and interregional industries, is essential for understanding the complexity of the tourism economy. (See Figure 16.1.)

Two scales of input-output studies are useful for tourism analysis. The more limited scale aggregates the activities that involve tourism-related businesses. This is shown in Figure 16.1. The broader scale disaggregates all sectors of an economy, which allows for a more complete tracing of the impacts of tourism expenditures. Economic input-output models have been constructed for many regions around the world, especially in developed complex economies. It is possible to use these models to input and trace the impacts of tourism spending. Existing input-output models are likely to disaggregate the seventeen economic sectors selected for tourism analysis into more detailed subsectors. If a more limited model, showing only the seventeen aggregated sectors, is desired, it would have to be developed from relevant data sources, including a more disaggregate model if available. Developing an economic input-output model at any scale is expensive and time-consuming.

The chief limitation of the local area and interregional input-output model is the scarcity of complete and current data even in the best circumstances. This weakness has led to the design of models requiring much less data. In one regional model, the region has a fixed number of municipalities and counties and no trade relationships with the rest of the world. It assumes that this isolated, self-sufficient region is stationary; no growth or change is taking place in its economy.

At its best, the input-output model exposes the structure of an economy. It is a general technique that shows the complex interdependence among diverse businesses, consumers, and political and cultural units of the society. A typical regional model shows what each industry has purchased (input) from other industries (columns of the table). Conversely, it shows how the production (output) of each industry was sold to every other industry (rows of the table). By using the BIK System and NAICS industries, a simpler seventeen-industry by seventeen-industry input-output table can be constructed for the tourism sector (see Figure 16.1). The matrix lists the industries vertically and horizontally. The intersection of each column with a row gives the value of the interindustry transaction. When data are plentiful, recent, and accurate, the model works well. But the model works best when used with other analytical techniques covering all aspects of the economy. Input-output models are often used to trace tourism spending impacts through a local or regional economy. An example of a regional input-output tourism impact study can be found on the following Web site. http://www.visitkissimmee.com/downloads/1309369865.30283300_fe62d19f7c/Economic%20Imp act%20-%20Osceola.

16.4   INDUSTRY COMPLEX ANALYSIS

Interregional and regional input-output models are generally unable to analyze adequately economies of scale, localization of economies, urbanization agglomeration, and regional price variations. These shortcomings of the model have led to the design of **industry complex analysis,** which includes these factors and is derived from input-output analysis.

An **industry complex** is defined as a set of economic activities occurring at a given location and belonging to a subgroup of activities, (e.g., tourism) that are subject to important production,

PURCHASING SECTORS

SELLING SECTORS	Agriculture, Forestry, Fishing and Hunting	Manufacturing	Information	Professional, Scientific and Technical Services	Arts, Entertainment and Recreation	Accommodation and Food Services	Retail Trade	Construction	Transportation and Warehousing	Educational Services	Other Services (Except Public Admin.)	Utilities	Finance and Insurance	Real Estate, Rental and Leasing	Waste Management and Remediation Services	Health Care and Social Assistance	Public Administration
Agriculture, Forestry, Fishing and Hunting																	
Manufacturing																	
Information																	
Professional, Scientific and Technical Services																	
Arts, Entertainment and Recreation																	
Accommodation and Food Services																	
Retail Trade																	
Construction																	
Transportation and Warehousing																	
Educational Services																	
Other Services (Except Public Administration)																	
Utilities																	
Finance and Insurance																	
Real Estate, Rental and Leasing																	
Waste Management and Remediation Services																	
Health Care and Social Assistance																	
Public Administration																	

FIGURE 16.1 Interregional Input-Output Table for Seventeen Sectors with Tourism Activities.

Source: Bulent I. Kastarlak.

marketing, or other interrelations. An industry complex of tourism is composed of more than a few industries. Using the BIK System, interactivity linkages among twenty-three sectors representing 232 establishments of the overall tourism industry constitute the industry complex for tourism (including six sectors that were not included in the illustrative input-output table in Figure 16.1 because they have only a few minor subcategories related to tourism). This is where the interregional or regional input-output model can be used in tandem with the industry complex method for tourism sector analysis. Such a study is likely to be complicated, expensive, and lengthy, depending on the available data. The existence of a useful, appropriately disaggregated, and current input-output model of a region will help shorten the study period.

16.5 LINEAR AND NONLINEAR PROGRAMMING

Linear programming and **nonlinear programming** are other mathematical modeling techniques that can be used for studying factors important to tourism. Linear and nonlinear programming are specific applications of a broader set of techniques called **mathematical programming** and are optimizing techniques. They seek to maximize or minimize some condition (called an **objective function**), subject to constraints. Linear programming uses only linear constraints, while nonlinear programming extends the analysis to the use of nonlinear constraints. Both types of programming have a wide variety of applications and are used extensively in determining the proportions of needed inputs in manufacturing processes—for example, in food processing and petroleum refining.

Linear programming is applied to problems in which the objective is to maximize or minimize some linear function, subject to related capacities or constraints. For example, given a set of limited resources and their prices, and given a technology, it calculates production activities in order to maximize profits, social gains, total income, employment, or some other factor. Linear programming shows considerable promise for studying aspects of tourism. For example, hotel chains or tourism agencies can use it to determine how best to spend their promotion budgets or where discounts in prices are likely to produce the most revenue. Other applications may include minimizing transportation costs or infrastructure investments to produce a given level of tourism visits. Linear programming is further defined and discussed in the following Wikipedia Web site: http://en.wikipedia.org/wiki/Linear_programming.

16.6 DECISION TREE ANALYSIS

Decision tree analysis has many applications and can be used in tourism planning and development in several ways. For example, it can be used to determine how tourism organizations can best spend their promotion budgets to determine target groups and topics that will most interest those target groups. It can also be used to determine the most favorable locations for tourism attractions and support facilities, and to determine the proper scale of investments in creating or altering attractions and facilities. Quantitative and qualitative analysis are used in preparing and evaluating decision tree diagrams. Preparing a decision tree diagram is a relatively straightforward exercise in which the major decision to be made is placed on the far left side of a piece of paper and factors that affect and lead to the decision are listed and displayed in a series of points and lines that connect to the decision, moving across the paper to the right. Setting up the decision tree is a matter of applying qualitative professional judgment. Filling in the diagram with data on probabilities of success and quantitative outcomes involves both qualitative judgment and quantitative information. The following Web site provides further information describing decision trees and how to prepare and use them: http://www.mindtools.com/dectree.html.

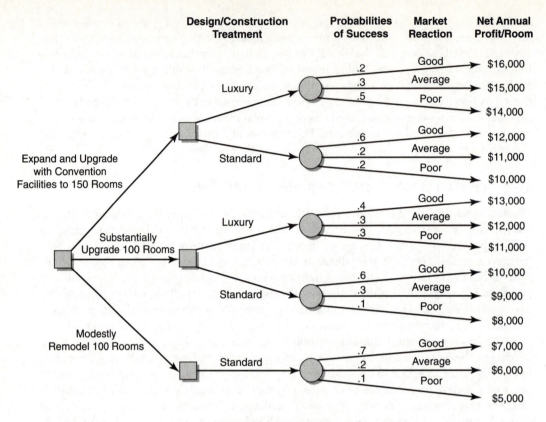

Design/Construction Treatment	Probabilities of Success	Market Reaction	Net Annual Profit/Room

Profitability Calculations

Treatment	Rooms	Probability	Market Reaction	Annual Net Profit per Room	Annual Profit
Luxury	150	0.2	Good	$16,000	$480,000
"	150	0.3	Average	$15,000	$675,000
"	150	0.5	Poor	$14,000	$1,050,000
Standard	150	0.6	Good	$12,000	$1,080,000
"	150	0.2	Average	$11,000	$330,000
"	150	0.2	Poor	$10,000	$300,000
Luxury	100	0.4	Good	$13,000	$520,000
"	100	0.3	Average	$12,000	$360,000
"	100	0.3	Poor	$11,000	$330,000
Standard	100	0.6	Good	$10,000	$600,000
"	100	0.3	Average	$9,000	$270,000
"	100	0.1	Poor	$8,000	$80,000
Standard	100	0.7	Good	$7,000	$490,000
"	100	0.2	Average	$6,000	$120,000
"	100	0.1	Poor	$5,000	$50,000

FIGURE 16.2 Decision Tree for Selecting Optimum Improvements for an Existing Older Hotel.
Source: Brian Barber

A very simple example of decision tree analysis is shown in Figure 16.2. The decision is whether to modestly renovate a one-hundred-room hotel; or to substantially upgrade it with either luxury or standard modernization features and design; or to add fifty more rooms and conference facilities, again, either with luxury or standard-quality construction. The result, expressed as total annual profit, is shown in the table in Figure 16.2. The simple analysis shows that the highest annual profits would result from adding fifty more rooms and conference facilities with standard-quality construction. Informed professional judgment is required to establish reasonable probabilities for three levels of market response. Data on past levels of annual net profits per room are required to compute estimated annual profits.

16.7 GRAVITY MODEL

Measuring the gravitational pull of tourism destinations was reviewed in earlier chapters. For tourism analysis purposes, **mass** is defined as an area where tourism destinations are concentrated or an area that is populated by people seeking tourism destinations and opportunities. The Gravity Model calculates the size of an attraction between two masses and can also be used to calculate the proportions of people from an originating area who are likely to visit the destination. Specifically, the product of the two masses is divided by the distance or travel time between them raised to some exponent. A starting analysis value for the exponent is commonly 2 (the distance or travel time squared), but it can be some other figure calibrated from data on existing trip volumes between the two masses. (See Figure 16.3.)

Most common applications of the Gravity Model are in transportation planning for estimating the trip volumes of people traveling between traffic analysis zones of a region. The model depicts the interaction of people within the region as a function of the populations of subareas (traffic analysis zones), employment or recreational opportunities, or other attractions such as shopping opportunities, and the variable distances or travel times among them. This interaction is described in terms of trips defined by purpose (work, school, recreational, shopping, etc.). Tourist trips can be defined as a trip purpose. The Gravity Model can be an aid in defining the market area of a tourist destination.

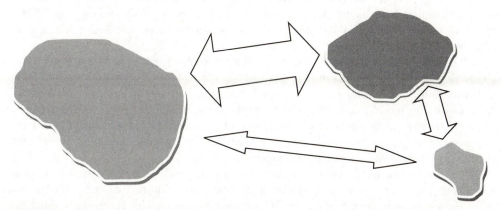

FIGURE 16.3 Representation of the Gravity Model. The arrow widths represent the strength of mutual attraction between objects.
Source: Brian Barber

16.8 GEOGRAPHIC INFORMATION SYSTEM

Geographic Information System (GIS) and many other related terms are becoming increasingly familiar to the public as the computer/information age evolves and expands in many directions. CAD and CADD, AM, and AM/LIS, defined and described below, have entered the everyday lexicon.

Since the 1970s, computer-based tools that manage geographic data have multiplied exponentially. The proliferation of terms was the result of this expansion. GIS and other methods have one characteristic in common: They all use geographic data for spatial analysis. It is important to distinguish between information stored in map form as opposed to text form. GIS uses both. It contains map information stored in a computer in digital form for producing maps and prints text material and reports related to it. Why are location and geography important for spatial analysis of tourism? The answer lies in the fact that natural features are widely located in many places, and humans make decisions based on *location*. Bringing the *where* to bear on the *what* is the essence of GIS analysis. Choosing a site for a tourist destination and finding ways to connect the attraction sites with the facility sites calls for an efficient arrangement of locational factors. GIS links the information to places. It is used for mapping and analyzing the geographical distribution of data. Spatially mapped data are linked directly to attributes of the areas mapped. Text and numeric information about these attributes can be shown on the output display along with the map. Presentation of graphics including maps, pictures, and text and numeric databases can be expanded to include animations, sound (voice and music and sound effects), and serial presentation of graphics screens, providing multimedia presentations. (See Figure 16.4.)

GIS is a computer technology that combines mapping and information stored as data to generate maps and reports for providing a planned and systematic method of collecting and managing location-based information. GIS is widely used for improving planning and decision making. A GIS can also link independent databases to perform additional functions. Among these functions, GIS is used for planning community development, environmental protection and engineering, public works engineering, integrated public safety systems, infrastructure management, transportation planning and modeling, property assessments, facility siting, vehicle routing, permitting and licensing, election management, real estate management, and many other applications. In 1970, the BIK System modeled and used one of the earliest GISs (SYMAP) for surveying, analyzing, and planning tourism development more than a decade before such applications were widely known and applied.

The generic GIS is a specialized spatial tool for data management. GIS implies not only an ability to map information and refer to features that can be located geographically, but also an ability to identify relationships among mapped features and process their geometric characteristics for spatial analysis. GIS map files can represent the entire world geography or any of its parts, in small or large scales, by any subdivisions, postal zones, or administrative or analysis areas, or by overlays depicting its lakes, seas, highways, and mountains. These databases are created from publicly and commercially available data sources.

GIS processes two different sets of data. One type defines the shape and location of places. It draws the map. This type of data is called **spatial data**. The other type describes what is inside those shapes and locations. It makes the data more meaningful. This is called **attribute data**. Although they are structurally different, the two types of data work together as a unit. Publicly and commercially available map files normally include both.

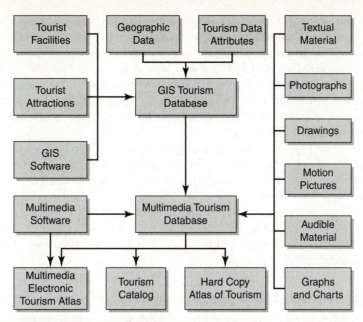

FIGURE 16.4 A Modern Multimedia GIS Database.
Source: Bulent I. Kastarlak

Spatial data are divided into three types. **Vector data** represent geographic features as points, lines, or polygons. **Raster data** divide geographic space into a matrix of identically sized cells. **Image data** include satellite and aerial photographs and optically scanned maps. Image data serve as background for vector data. They are used to create vector data through a digital tracing process called **remote sensing**. For example, the map of the United States is created with vector data. State capitals are represented as points, interstate highways as lines, and state boundaries as polygons.

Raster data are useful in the display and analysis of geographic phenomena that change gradually over a surface, like population density, topography, or the gravitational pull of a tourist destination. A three-dimensional relief map is generated by a digital elevation model from surveyed elevation points.

One common source of image data is digital pictures of the Earth's surface taken from Earth-orbiting satellites like the U.S. Landsat and the French SPOT. These high-resolution satellite images generally serve as visual backdrops for any vector data. The Earth's surface is completely photographed from space by these satellites, and the photographs are updated continuously. Aerial photographs are taken from a much lower altitude, usually from an airplane. Using the latest technology, satellite images can show many categories of information using the "signatures" obtained from those technologies (e.g., using infrared and ultraviolet sensors).

Attribute data shown within the vector data are drawn from a multitude of sources. Demographic, business, consumer, insurance, economic, health, and sports information are common uses of these data. For tourism planning, attribute data include attractions, facilities, and more than two hundred thirty establishment types; ratings of attractions and facilities in terms of their tourist gravitational pull potential and their international, national, regional, and local significance; more than one hundred tourist activity types; seasonality of attractions and facilities in terms of year-round, winter, spring, summer or fall seasons; travel times between activity points; preferred tours of attractions by activity types and seasons; best travel routes between destinations; economic data including population and employment; and projected number of tourists by nationality, by destination, and by many other data combinations that are useful for planning and developing tourism. GIS has the capability to record, organize, interrelate, and display this multitude of data.

There are several types of magnetic storage devices for GIS and other applications. Disk drives, flash drives, and tape drives are used for storing digital data and application programs for GIS. Workstations, desktop keyboards, and laptop keyboards provide access to the system by the user. They are equipped with devices to input, manipulate, edit, and display the data. Other equipment includes the graphic display screen, plotter, optical scanner, and computer output microfilm (COM) that can produce a map or drawing directly on microfilm. Users requiring contour lines for mapping elevations of the land often use stereo digitizing plotters as input devices to automated mapping systems.

16.9 OTHER COMPUTER PLANNING AND DESIGN APPLICATIONS

There are many other planning and design computer applications. Collectively, they are known as the **CAD (computer-aided design)** or **CADD (computer-aided design and drafting)** group of software. CADD is an electronic tool that replaces hand-drafted drawings. The place of hand-drafted drawings in architecture and engineering is secure, however. Hand drafting will continue to be useful in small, traditional projects where acceptable results can be obtained without resorting to high technology. The advantages of CADD become clear, however, when complex projects and tight schedules require advanced technology. CADD produces accurate, quick drawings that are neat, clean, and highly presentable. They are modified easily and can be presented in various formats.

Hundreds of CADD programs are available. Some are used for general drafting. Others are employed for specialized engineering applications. They include two-dimensional and three-dimensional drawings, renderings, shadings, and calculations for space planning, structural design, utility layouts, plant and building design, and project management. CADD provides single line drawings only. It has limited capabilities for creating art, except for the three-dimensional model of a building that can be viewed from all angles and rendered realistically.

The advantages of CAD and CADD include:

- Production of multicolor and multishaded presentation drawings
- Flexibility in editing for making quick changes to drawings
- Production of highly accurate geometric shapes, avoiding time-consuming calculations
- Allowing fast and convenient organizing of drawings in electronic storage media
- Sharing the same drawings among a number of users for better coordination
- Preparing project reports by linking data with graphic information
- Allowing for analysis of drawings from multiple disciplines

  CAD or CADD software is composed of the following:

- CAD systems store spatial data as graphic information. These systems enable users, primarily architects and engineers, to use the data for preparing building and civil engineering drawings.

- CADD systems are designed for drafting, designing, and modeling structures. The user interacts with a visual image on a computer screen, to create, change, and rotate three-dimensional drawings.
- **Automated mapping (AM)** is a graphic system used to create, edit, and manipulate cartographic data. The resulting image files are a compilation of simple drafted features with no information processing capabilities other than displays of different series of map data, views, and scales.
- **Automated mapping/facilities management (AM/FM)** systems combine a subset of the CAD system for interactive graphics, data entry, and data storage with database management capabilities. They are used for converting manual maps and records into a digital database for work-order processing, facilities modeling, and management. These systems often lack spatial analysis capabilities.
- **Automated mapping/land information systems (AM/LIS)** use computers to produce, edit, and analyze the pictorial aspect of the overall GIS system.

Most GIS software has applications in planning and developing tourism. These applications include planning and designing tourist attractions and facilities, finding the best routes to destinations, managing various tourism projects simultaneously, testing development scenarios, analyzing probable impacts, and others. A partial list of commercially available GIS programs and equipment includes:

- National Geographic Trip Planner
- Microsoft Automap Streets: Digital street maps
- Street Pilot: Portable GPS
- AAA Trip Planner: The ultimate road trip resource
- MapObjects: Embeddable GIS and mapping components for application developers
- Spatial Database Engine (SDE): The universal spatial server
- ArcView Business Analyst: Integrated business geographic solutions
- Mapquest: Driving map, providing directions, travel time, and the distance from the origin to the destination
- Primavera Project Planner: Manages multiple projects for multiple users
- AutoCad Map (Autodesk Inc.): Mapping and GIS
- ArcInfo: A general and very flexible set of software for mapping and computing data

Note: This list is by no means complete. New products and improvements to existing systems are being developed all the time.

16.10   THE BIK SYSTEM FOR BUILDING A GIS FOR TOURISM PLANNING

In concluding this chapter, a last word is appropriate about the BIK System. This system was conceived in 1970 because of the need to rationalize a general system for documenting and analyzing tourism development, and for proposing methods, a databank, and GIS to plan it. Only fragments of general principles and procedures for doing this existed at the time. Judgments were largely subjective and speculative. Few formulae other than simple calculations for occupancy, capacity, and financial analysis existed. Data limitations largely contributed to this state of affairs. Computer technology was in its adolescence, and GIS for tourism was not widely known for a decade or more. GIS maps for the project were produced by the Harvard Laboratory for

Computer Graphics and Spatial Analysis, which spawned other organizations in the GIS business, including ESRI, one of the largest.

Today computer technology has advanced to the point where equipment as small as a handheld calculator (palmtop) can store very large amounts of data that can be used for customizing travel plans or for planning the development of a tourism destination. It is now possible to develop a database for a region that would include the inventory of 232 types of tourism establishment from fifty-three economic subsectors and seventeen major sectors of the national economy. The data show the location and a variety of other characteristics of the tourism product. They can be cross-referenced for deriving verifiable tourism planning conclusions. The BIK System attempts to build a general system for comprehensive documentation and analysis, and provides the preliminary tools necessary to advance tourism development planning in that direction.

Chapter Highlights

- Simulation is a tool for representing and displaying the operations of complex processes or systems. In dynamic terms, simulation is used for building a model that replicates the appearance of reality. It is the representation of a real set of objects or events and their interrelationships.
- Gross tourism product (GTP), at national and regional levels, can be defined in terms of percentages of national and regional income accounts.
- Economic input-output analysis is a general technique that shows the complex interdependence among diverse businesses, consumers, and political and cultural units of an economy. A typical regional model shows what each industry has purchased (input) from other industries. Conversely, it shows how the production (output) of each industry was sold to every other industry. It has several applications in tourism development analysis and planning, most notably for tracing tourist spending and respending impacts through an economy.
- Industry complex analysis has been derived from input-output analysis. An industry complex is defined as a set of economic activities occurring at a given location and belonging to a subgroup of activities (e.g., tourism) that are subject to important production, marketing, or other interrelations.

- Linear and nonlinear programming are techniques that seek to maximize or minimize some condition, subject to constraints. Linear programming shows considerable promise for studying aspects of tourism.
- Decision tree analysis is a widely used business investment and management technique that can be applied to tourism planning and development. It is flexible enough to yield useful results at a simple level and at more complex disaggregated levels.
- The Gravity Model calculates the size of an attraction between two masses and can be used to estimate the proportions of people from an originating area who are likely to visit a given tourist destination.
- A geographic information system (GIS) is a widely used tool for improving planning and decision making. It can be used to display maps and related databases of tourism information. It can also be linked to other software to provide multimedia presentations that are useful for planning and promoting tourism.
- Computer-aided design and drafting (CADD) is an electronic tool that replaces hand-drafted drawings. CADD makes quick, accurate drawings that can be used for engineering tourist attractions and facilities and for displaying tourism plans.

17

Managing, Planning, and Marketing Tourism

This chapter presents the international, national, and regional organizations that manage, plan, develop, and market tourism. It presents their organizational structures and describes the multiple functions they serve. It discusses the traditional method of marketing the products and services of the tourism industry. It reviews the methods of preparing marketing plans. It presents emerging electronic technologies and describes their impact on the traditional methods of generating and distributing tourism information for marketing. It reflects on the future of the Internet as a source of information for tourism planning and marketing. The following topics are important in managing, planning, and marketing tourism:

- United Nations World Tourism Organization (UNWTO), its role and services
- National tourism organizations in market system countries
- National tourism organizations in countries with mixed economies
- Motivation, direct and strategic marketing
- E-marketing, the Internet, and traditional marketing

17.1 UNITED NATIONS WORLD TOURISM ORGANIZATION

The United Nations gave the World Tourism Organization (UNWTO) the central role of promoting the development of responsible, sustainable, and universally accessible tourism. The objective is to contribute to economic development, international understanding, peace, prosperity, and universal respect for human rights and fundamental freedoms. In pursuing this goal, UNWTO pays particular attention to sustaining the best interests of developing countries.

Acting as an umbrella organization for world tourism, UNWTO plays a catalytic role in promoting technology transfers and international cooperation, stimulating and developing public sector–private sector partnerships, and encouraging the implementation of the Global Code of Ethics for Tourism. UNWTO encourages member countries, tourist destinations, and businesses to maximize the positive economic, social, and cultural effects of tourism while minimizing its negative social and environmental impacts.

Through tourism, UNWTO works to stimulate economic growth and job creation, provide incentives for protecting the environment and the host country's cultural heritage, and promote peace, prosperity, and respect for human rights. UNWTO encourages governments, in partnership with the private sector, public authorities, and NGOs, to play a vital role in tourism.

UNWTO began when the International Congress of Official Tourism Associations was established in 1925 in The Hague in the Netherlands. It was renamed the International Union of Official Travel Organizations (IUOTO) after World War II and moved its headquarters to Geneva, Switzerland. IUOTO later became the UNWTO, and its first General Assembly was held in Madrid in May 1975. The Secretariat was installed in Madrid in 1976.

In 1976, UNWTO became an executing agency of the United Nations Development Programme (UNDP). In 2003, UNWTO was upgraded to an agency of the United Nations. Since its early years, UNWTO's membership and influence in world tourism have continued to grow. In 2009, its membership included 154 countries, 7 territories, and over 400 affiliate members in over 80 countries, representing the private sector, educational institutions, tourism associations, and local tourism authorities.

The General Assembly is the principal gathering of UNWTO. It meets regularly to approve the budget and program of work and to debate topics of vital importance to the tourism sector. Every four years it elects a secretary-general. The General Assembly is composed of members and associate members. Affiliate members and representatives of other international organizations participate as observers.

The Executive Council is UNWTO's governing board, responsible for ensuring that the organization carries out its work and adheres to its budget. It meets twice a year and is composed of twenty-seven members elected by the General Assembly, with one associate member for every five full members. As the host country of UNWTO's headquarters, Spain has a permanent seat on the Executive Council. Representatives of other countries participate as observers.

UNWTO has six regional commissions—for Africa, the Americas, East Asia, the Pacific region, South Asia, and Europe with the Middle East. Each commission meets at least once a year and is composed of all full members and associate members from that region. Representatives of other countries participate as observers.

Specialized committees of UNWTO advise members on management and program content. These are the Programme Committee, the Committee on Budget and Finance, the Committee on Statistics and Macroeconomic Analysis of Tourism, the Committee on Market Intelligence and Promotion, the Sustainable Development of Tourism Committee, the Quality Support Committee, the UNWTO Education Council, the UNWTO Business Council, and the World Committee on Tourism Ethics.

The secretary-general who supervises about one hundred full-time staff at UNWTO's Madrid headquarters leads the Secretariat. The deputy secretary-general is the second highest officer of the Secretariat. These officials are responsible for implementing UNWTO's program of work serving the needs of members. The Secretariat has a regional support office for the Asia-Pacific area in Osaka, Japan.

Full membership in UNWTO is open to all sovereign states. Associate membership is open to all territories not responsible for external relations. Affiliate membership comprises a wide range of organizations and companies working directly with the travel, tourism, and related sectors. These may include airlines, hotels, restaurants, tour operators, travel agents, banking institutions, insurance companies, publishing groups, and others. UNWTO is the only intergovernmental organization that offers a membership category to these operational sectors of tourism. It provides a unique contact point for discussion between government officials and industry leaders.

The UNWTO Business Council utilizes a partnership approach to tourism to promote cooperation and understanding between the public and private sectors. To achieve its objectives, the council aids members in expanding their tourism businesses through industry networking, forming contacts with necessary government officials, strengthening the industry–education relationship, and conducting special research projects on the private sector.

UNWTO provides leadership in the fields of information technology (IT) and tourism, as well as helping to bridge the digital division between the haves and have-nots among UNWTO's membership. UNWTO carries out new research and studies in IT in connection with the promotion and development of tourism. In addition, UNWTO considers tourism technology projects especially suited to cooperation between the public and private sectors.

The UNWTO Human Resource Development Department works to add value to the tourism sector of UNWTO member states by improving their capacity building and providing direct support for tourism education, training, and knowledge. The UNWTO Education Council is made up of leading tourism education, training, and research institutions as well as business schools worldwide.

The program on Quality in Tourism Development focuses on important issues in the perception and assurance of quality in tourism activities and experiences. They include regulatory trading frameworks, tourism's social impact, health, safety and security, and quality standards.

On trade issues, UNWTO works closely with the United Nations Conference on Trade and Development (UNCTAD) and is an observer with the World Trade Organization. The objective is to develop links between the rules and disciplines of the General Agreement on Trade in Services (GATS) and tourism liberalization measures.

The UNWTO General Assembly adopted the Global Code of Ethics for Tourism in 1999. This code was acknowledged by a special resolution of the United Nations General Assembly in 2001. It sets out a ten-point blueprint for safeguarding resources on which tourism depends. One of its objectives is to ensure that the economic benefits of tourism will be shared equitably. The code is founded on the principles of sustainability that underpin all of UNWTO's programs. It emphasizes involving local communities in planning, managing, and monitoring tourism development. It includes nine articles outlining policies for destinations, governments, tour operators, travel agents, tourism workers and developers, and travelers themselves.

Currently, UNWTO does not set international standards for tourism surveys, measurement, and reporting. Nevertheless, in 1993 the United Nations adopted UNWTO's recommendations on collecting and processing tourism statistics. These recommendations are intended to create a common language for tourism statistics and to allow destinations to compare their performance with that of their competitors. In 2000, the United Nations approved the standards and methodology, making tourism the world's first sector to have international standards for measuring its economic impact in a credible way. Now UNWTO is working to implement these standards and methodology and to provide the world with consistent and comprehensive tourism statistics.

One of UNWTO's most important functions is to serve as a permanent source of information. UNWTO has an extensive series of publications and electronic products. In 2011, their publications catalog lists 132 titles available in several languages. They have a system of seventy-eight cooperative depository libraries with tourism materials in countries on six continents. They also have an E-library on the Internet with over 900 tourism-related books in English, French, Spanish, Russian, and Arabic. UNWTO gives up-to-date quantitative and qualitative information on tourism activities in its periodically issued *Tourism Factbook* and *UNWTO News* (issued as an

E-magazine available at http://www.unwto.org/media/mag/en/mag.php?op=2). UNWTO also offers online access to a tourism legislation database (LEXTOUR) that provides bibliographic and textual data on laws and regulations. It is described on the following Web site: http://www.unwto.org/documentation/lextour/en/lextour.php?op=1&subop=2.

Tourism in the advanced market economies of North America and Western Europe occupies an important position in the hierarchy of their governmental organizations. However, considering the size of their economies, measured in GNP, the contribution of tourism is not as large as that of other major sectors. In some developing market economies with much smaller GNPs, however, tourism is vital and a key national government agency is dedicated to it. In these countries, there is likely to be a ministry of tourism answering directly to the president or prime minister. In the advanced market economy countries, governmental tourism agencies are likely to be part of other cabinet-level ministries or departments, such as a department of commerce. In both advanced and developing market economy countries, tourism is considered important and government tourism officials are likely to have access to the highest level of power if needed to pursue significant policy issues.

In advanced market economies, the invisible hand of the market system is the chief instrument for planning and developing tourism. A multitude of private companies and trade associations interact and essentially self-regulate the tourism industry. At the national level, a federal department may have a promotion-support role, usually provided by a bureau in the department or ministry of commerce. The bureau collects tourism statistics, promotes the country using various media, and stays current about domestic (and to some extent international) tourism developments and conditions. In the United States, coordination with other national agencies, like the Department of the Interior, State Department, Department of Homeland Security, Department of Labor, and Department of Transportation, is common.

At the state, regional, and provincial levels, advanced market economies have established large, relatively well-financed tourism promotion organizations. Convention bureaus, hotel and restaurant associations, regional tourism promotion organizations, and chambers of commerce all vie for tourist dollars and promote their areas and trades. State governments may have a tourism bureau attached to one of their departments. Provincial or state governments appropriate annual tourism promotion budgets. Some government agencies are financed by dedicated funds from a tourism revenue source such as a hotel tax. Some of the funds are channeled to regional and local tourism promotion groups in the form of grants. The primary function of these bureaus and groups is to distribute public information on tourism in their areas to the general traveling public. They may have official kiosks in central locations like airports and interstate highway stops for providing tourism information. Hotels, restaurants, and other tourist facilities visited by tourists distribute literature about attractions and facilities.

17.2   NATIONAL AGENCY FOR TOURISM PLANNING AND DEVELOPMENT

In countries with developing mixed economies and strong tourism potentials, the national agency for tourism planning and development can be an independent ministry represented at the council of ministers by a minister. The internal organization of the ministry can be simple or complex, depending on the demands of the tourism industry. It may consist of the offices of the minister, one or more deputy ministers, a research and planning division, a promotion division, a tourism investments division, and supporting administrative departments. In some cases, as in Turkey, where tourism, culture, and information functions are merged in one ministry, the national tourism organization may serve multiple purposes. Ministries of the interior, public works, transportation, and finance play important roles in supporting a ministry of tourism. This extended coverage of the tourism industry by the government puts the responsibility for sustainable tourism development squarely in the hands of the national government. The private sector plays the critical role of investing in maintaining and expanding the tourism economy.

In mixed economies, up and down the government echelon, the network of linkages among national, regional, and local tourism agencies may be extensive. These linkages are with the directorate of national museums, public relations office, copyright and trademark office, revolving tourism funds, national library, national theater, national symphony, and others. Municipal governments receive guidance from the national tourism agency and, if it exists, from the agency in charge of public sector planning and coordination. This agency is usually attached to the office of the prime minister.

Again, state, provincial, and municipal governments support the tourism industry with their infrastructure facilities and promotional efforts. Also, trade associations distribute tourism information to visitors through their member hotels, restaurants, and other tourism establishments.

17.3 MOTIVATION AND MASS-MARKETING TOURISM

The motivation to travel comes from the need to know, to experience and participate in the activities of tourism. This could be adventure, learning, entertainment, business, sports, and a multitude of other desired human experiences. (See the listing of twenty-seven types of tourism in Chapter 4.) The more these experiences satisfy tourists, the more the tourism industry's productivity, quality, and services will improve. Those who control the product and services make adjustments and improvements to meet the demands of tourists.

Motivating people to travel is key to traditional tourism mass marketing. Determining which factors are important and which ones are passing fads is vital in shaping the marketing strategy. When factors that impede the desire to travel are eliminated, motivation increases. When tourists are motivated to commit time and money to travel to a destination, this indicates that negative factors have become less important than positive factors, and the traditional mass-marketing strategy has worked.

Implementing a mass-marketing plan calls for persuasive communication with the target public. The methods used to address mass audiences are advertising, sales promotion, and publicity. Advertising uses paid mass media to communicate with the target public, sometimes without identifying the individual. Sales promotion is used to stimulate immediate purchase. Publicity includes paid and unpaid media coverage of an event or a product. On certain occasions, personal selling brings the mass audience as a group face-to-face with the marketer.

Tourism advertising, particularly for overnight accommodations, has two major objectives:

- Increase consumer awareness of the tourism product of a destination region.
- Improve consumer perception of particular tourism establishments in the destination region.

Tourism promotion stimulates primary and selective demand. Promotion for **primary demand** refers to encouraging the demand for the product itself, like choosing specific airlines and hotels. Promotion for **selective demand** is about differentiating the product from the competition. The response to these promotions by target audience follows three stages:

- *Cognitive stage:* Attention, awareness, perception
- *Affective stage:* Interest, liking, intention
- *Behavioral stage:* Action, purchase, trial, adoption

Publicity generally occurs through some third party, like a reporter, editor, or publicist. The conventional methods of publicity include advertisements, news releases, feature articles, speeches, parties and other gatherings, and news conferences. The marketer can increase the impact of the publicity by serving food and beverages at these gatherings. A new element added to existing tourism products or services could serve as the occasion for such publicity affairs. Combining publicity with merchandising a representative sample of the product or service could also enhance its impact on the target audience. Offering linked discounts for travel or accommodations when other goods and services are purchased is a common form of marketing.

17.4   DIRECT MARKETING

Direct marketing is targeted to the individual, not the masses. It is essentially a mix of traditional mail order selling and direct mailing. It involves more than making a one-on-one sale and uses all types of media. It is personal, focusing on individual messages. Each marketing message is coded; therefore, the result can be tallied. Compilation of individual results reveals the effectiveness of any direct marketing strategy. There are huge databases containing the characteristics of individuals, including age, gender, household size, life cycle status, income, shopping, and travel preferences, creditworthiness, residence history, and contact information (addresses and phone numbers). Some of these databases are publicly available; others are commercially available. These databases are used by marketing companies to classify individuals into market segments and target them with promotional material about products and services they have been known to consume and are therefore likely to consume in the future.

In tourism, direct marketing is growing in importance. It focuses on motivating the individual tourist rather than promoting the virtues of the tourism product or services. It is effective when applied in three distinct steps:

- Identifying the target audience and surveying its interests and preferences
- Staying close to identified target audiences (segments) and ensuring repeat visits
- Testing the results and making adjustments in the message and delivery

Direct marketing is ideal for complex products and services that require detailed explanations and leisurely study. Pressure tactics do not work in direct marketing. When distances for the delivery of the product and services are large, direct marketing is effective. In tourism, once motivation is achieved, it still takes a personal visit to consume the tourism product and use its services. Occasionally, personal face-to-face selling complements direct marketing. Direct response advertising, telephone marketing, e-mails, or direct mailings signed by a celebrity can be effective.

The critical factor in direct marketing is building the database that identifies each recipient by name, address, and other contact information, interests, preferences, and other individual characteristics. Details are added as they become available. The most interesting aspect of the strategy is providing incentives. This often means losing money at first and making it later. Ensuring repeat business will secure a larger return on invested capital.

Direct marketing is focused. Mass marketers concentrate on the most effective medium, whether it is radio, television, magazines, or newspapers, to reach the largest mass audience. Direct marketing tries to isolate the individual and make him or her the focus of attention. This is achieved by including the individual within a highly specialized market segment (niche). As mentioned, these segments include income, age, and interest groups. Segmentation is a major issue in tourism planning and marketing.

Customer value is an important issue in direct marketing. Generally, a small percentage of repeat customers buy most of the product and services offered by the tourist industry. Like banks, credit card companies, and automobile manufacturers, tourism-related businesses rely on long-term relationships with their customers. They keep sending direct mail to this selected groups of individuals with new information about the travel packages they offer for the next travel season. For example, advance sales and bookings of repeat customers account for a large portion of the cruise ship business.

Initially, the direct marketer tests the market on a small scale. Techniques, media, and groups are tested for their effectiveness. Applied in full scale after adjustments, the direct marketing process addresses the following issues:

- Identifying target groups, organizations, and individuals
- Strengthening relationships with repeat customers
- Reducing the marketing risk by repeated testing
- Complementing direct response advertising, telephone marketing, and e-mailing to high-value customers with personal-approach selling to lower-value customers
- Treating personalized letters as the most important element of direct mailing

17.5 NATIONAL TOURISM MARKETING PLANS

Marketing is fundamental to developing tourism. Unlike other products, tourism is consumed at the place of production, not at the place where tourists have their primary residence. As consumers, tourists have to be motivated to travel to the places where the tourism product, namely destinations, attractions, and facilities, are located. Creating that motivation is the art and science of tourism marketing.

Marketing involves commitment to detailed analysis of future opportunities to meet consumer preferences. Preparing marketing plans is the process by which the producer determines its own position in the marketplace and plans the budget and activities necessary to meet its objectives. The most effective tools for selling the product and services to well-defined tourism market segments are selected in the marketing plan. The marketing plan separates the long- and short-term sales objectives. It also prescribes the products that the producer must match with what the consumer wants.

There are two principal kinds of marketing plan:

- *The Strategic Marketing Plan.* This is a *long-term* marketing plan for three, four, or five years. It describes the marketer's perception of its own position in the market relative to its competitors, its competitive advantage, the objectives it wants to achieve, how to achieve them, the resources necessary to achieve them, and the results it expects.
- *The Tactical Marketing Plan.* This is a *short-term* marketing plan for scheduling and pricing the specific actions necessary for completing what needs to be done during the first year of the strategic marketing plan. Second-year actions specified by the Strategic Marketing Plan are modified with information from a feedback review of first-year experiences.

It is important to keep in mind that the Tactical Marketing Plan is derived from the Strategic Marketing Plan, not the reverse. Also, sales forecasting and budgeting must not be confused with strategic marketing planning. The marketing strategy is planned around the product, price, place, and promotion. Considering all the above factors, some national governments, especially those in countries with mixed economies, assume the responsibility for preparing the Strategic

Marketing Plan for the country's tourism development and implementing it by annual tactical marketing plans.

The Strategic Marketing Plan includes:

- *Mission statement of the organization, its products, and its services.* The national government, and the agency given the principal role of marketing tourism, state their mission and single out the target tourist markets and the number of tourists to be drawn from these markets. The targets are expressed in terms of tourist arrivals, mode of travel from the country of origin, purpose of travel, length of stay, and estimated expenditures.
- *Summary of financial implications over the period of the marketing plan.* The three or more years encompassing the marketing period include both revenues and expenditures by the government. These financial activities are specified in the form of a budget and a pro forma financial analysis.
- *Market overview of trends, key elements, and competitors.* The country's tourism sector performance is compared with target markets in terms of current and anticipated trends in tourist arrivals, length of stay, and other characteristics.
- *SWOT (strengths, weaknesses, opportunities, threats) analysis of the organization.* The country's strengths and weaknesses compared to those of its competitors are evaluated to show the superiority of the activities, attractions, facilities, and destinations in its tourism product and to identify the improvements necessary for increasing its competitive advantages.
- *Specific product issues to be addressed.* Tourism resources, consisting of labor, capital, entrepreneurship, attractions, and facilities, can raise many issues about their availability, quality, disposition, and carrying capacities. Policy decisions for resolving these issues should be reflected in the marketing plan.
- *Assumptions* critical to the planned marketing objectives.
- *Specific marketing objectives* stating what the organization wishes to achieve.
- *Specific marketing strategies* stating how the objectives are to be achieved through promotion measures.
- *Resources* to be allocated, including costs, revenues, and budget.

In preparing the Strategic Marketing Plan, a variety of factors must be considered. Motivating tourists to travel to prescribed destinations embraces social, behavioral, personal, and economic factors that influence the traveler. They include:

- *Social factors.* Cultural background, social class, and reference groups
- *Personal factors.* Age, family, lifestyle, life cycle, occupation, income, status, and interests
- *Behavioral factors.* Motivation, perception, learning, and personality
- *Economic factors.* Pricing, purchasing, and competition

The annual Tactical Marketing Plans are similar to Strategic Marketing Plans, except that they omit the mission statement, market overview, and SWOT analysis. The marketing objectives and marketing strategy are more detailed, specific, and quantified. The schedule of development projects and measures are tied to the marketing strategy. The end-of-year performance reviews are used to update next year's marketing objectives, if needed, to stay on course toward achieving the marketing goals of the Strategic Marketing Plan for the target year.

The operational uses of the two types of marketing plans are often misunderstood. In market system economies, the national tourism Strategic Marketing Plan of the country consists of broad strategic goals suggested by the responsible agency of the national government. The achievement of these goals, however, is largely left to the initiative of each tourism destination acting on its own and competitively. There is no central authority directing or coordinating this process. A regional Strategic Marketing Plan is bypassed in favor of whatever assistance the national and state governments or private sector organizations can provide to marketing organizations at local destinations.

In fact, the effectiveness of national tourism marketing depends on the effectiveness of the marketing done by organizations that represent tourism establishments. In the United States, for example, large hotel franchise companies, hotel associations, cruise ship lines, and world-class attractions like Disney World transcend the national borders and market their domestic and international assets separately. The American Automobile Association (AAA), with their membership covering the entire country, provides travelers with excellent regional directories of hotels, restaurants, attractions, and maps supplemented by insurance, road assistance, and similar support services. High-quality travel guidebooks by Michelin, Mobil, Frommer, Fodor, Baedeker, and other companies are regularly published and updated, and have earned the respect of the traveling public.

Another marketing tool used in tourism is certification of sites, programs, and tours. Certification is done in an attempt to ensure that minimum standards are met to protect the environment, local cultures, and the traveling public. Certification in tourism has been done for accommodations and restaurants for quite some time—for example, in travel guides. It is now being extended to complete tourism experiences, with particular attention to achieving sustainable tourism, as exemplified in the handbook covered in the following Web site: http://www.rainforest-alliance.org/tourism/documents/practical_steps.pdf.

In many mixed economic systems, national governments, regional organizations, and establishments at the local destination level work in concert with centrally prepared and coordinated tourism marketing plans. Marketing is an integral part of the national tourism development priorities. The national government markets the country abroad, often by opening tourism marketing information offices in target countries and cities around the world. Regional and local destinations market their respective assets by tying into the national marketing strategy. Here, a Strategic Marketing Plan for tourism is effective through vertical and horizontal coordination. Tactical Marketing Plans for tourism, by contrast, are subordinated to the national tourism Strategic Marketing Plan. They are prepared annually according to the priorities set by the Strategic Marketing Plan of the country.

Segmenting the tourism market is particularly important for overnight accommodations. Segmentation defines submarkets. This, in turn, allows the Strategic Marketing Plan to address several subgroups simultaneously and ties the tourism marketing operations closely to marketing to these specific submarkets. The characteristics of the market segment serve as a detailed benchmark for making marketing decisions for the duration of the plan. Segmentation allows the Strategic Marketing Plan to focus on the most profitable group at any given season of the year. It offers the opportunity to make more cost-effective use of direct marketing techniques. Segmentation is further discussed on the following Web site: http://www.taskbc.bc.ca/documents/SegmentationDiscussionPaper_000.pdf.

Marketing tourism involves many venues. In some developing countries, the national government has combined tourism, culture, and communication responsibilities, and has assigned them to the ministry of tourism, culture, and information or to an authority with an equivalent name. The ministry is empowered to monitor and guide the tourism development of the country. It is given the job of operating information and public relations offices in certain key countries, where they work in concert with cultural attachés assigned to their embassies and consulates.

Under the policy guidelines established by the ministry, each office prepares its own marketing strategy to suit the tourist characteristics of that particular country and the preferences of potential tourists for recreational activities. For example, tourists from colder northern countries in Europe prefer sun-sea-sand types of vacations in warmer southern countries. In contrast, tourists from Far Eastern warmer countries are primarily interested in cultural attractions in the West. The ministry reviews the strategy for each target country and funds it annually. The objectives of the strategy are to establish a positive and individual image for each regional destination, increase their market shares, and improve the flow of tourists and expenditures from that country. The strategy is coordinated with private sector tourism promotion efforts in the regional destinations.

Another important objective of the national tourism marketing policy is to extend the tourism season of the country by offering year-round or multiseason attraction and facility experiences. When high-quality attractions and facilities may be visited before and after the sun-sea-sand season (e.g., by scheduling special events such as fishing tournaments or harvest festivals), the tourism potential of the country and its various regions could benefit from this extension. Health tourism, adventure tourism, cultural tourism, special event attractions, and even pilgrimage tourism could increase the tourism industry by filling empty beds in hotels during the slower seasons.

Practical application of these marketing principles involves the following specific promotional actions:

- Identifying important primary (international), secondary (national), and tertiary (regional) markets from which tourists are drawn
- Deciding on the types of promotional techniques to be directed at tour operators, travel writers, hotel companies, and the public
- Scheduling the promotion to coincide with a major destination-opening event
- Creating a symbol and an image for positive recognition of the destination
- Using countermeasures to overcome market resistance and the impact of negative political or international events
- Selecting media outlets such as printed material, audiovisual material, and advertising on radio, TV, travel trade fairs, guidebooks, and the Internet

17.6   MARKETING TOURISM ON THE INTERNET

The Internet came onto the world scene only two and a half decades ago. During its relatively short life, its usage grew exponentially. According to the Travel Industry Association of America, in 1994, there were 25 million Internet users in the United States. This number increased to 40 million in 1997 and to 95 million in 2001. Abroad, more than 619 million people in the English-speaking and non-English-speaking worlds had access to the Internet in 2002. By 2009, the number had increased to 1.67 billion people. The ability to communicate almost instantaneously throughout the world, with simple, relatively user-friendly means, at any given time was the largest motivation for people everywhere to use the Internet. The production of an enormous amount of endlessly varied content placed on the Internet adds to its appeal and usefulness.

Tourism is an intense user of information. History shows that tourism was among the first industries to capitalize on new technologies. Tourism marketing depends heavily on finding new and more efficient means of collecting and distributing information. Information for making accommodation and transportation reservations, and for developing travel plans, are among applications intended to increase the satisfaction of the traveling public. In booking trips or rooms, the Internet is increasingly playing a pivotal role. The Travel Industry Association of America has estimated that about 64 million travelers used the Internet in 2002 to get information on destinations, prices, and schedules. The BIK System can eventually be tied to this network.

Statistics show that Internet users are a major target group for travel marketing. They are under the age of fifty-five, have an annual income above $75,000, are college educated, and have professional/managerial occupations. By one estimate, this group of users spent about $13 billion in 2000 for purchasing travel and related services on the Internet. Another target group is senior citizens (age sixty-five and over) who have incomes allowing discretionary travel and the time to travel because they are retired or semiretired. This group is likely to have Internet access because they were exposed to computer technology in the latter part of their careers.

An additional benefit of the Internet is the convenience it offers by allowing users to bypass travel agents and contact airlines, tourism offices, hotels, and car rental agencies directly. In addition, the Internet offers retail shopping and banking facilities that add considerably to the convenience of travelers by saving time and effort for routine transactions. The growing popularity of the Internet is attributed to several unique characteristics:

- Everyone on the Internet can communicate as an equal with anyone else. Every business in the tourism industry can market its products and services directly to customers. Anyone having an Internet Protocol (IP) address can host server functions.
- The Internet is an interactive system. It allows all users, including travelers, travel agents, airline clerks, and hotel managers, to have an online conference call. This has resulted in the development of real-time spontaneous reservation systems. These systems also allow tourism businesses to obtain feedback and to plan new products and services for test marketing.
- The Internet has hyperlink capability. By a simple click of the mouse, the user can reach the next level of information. This simplifies the research process and saves time.
- The Internet allows each user to choose his or her own network technology. This is called **open architecture networking**. It does not demand central control over the user requirements of that network.
- The Internet is platform independent, meaning that whatever operating system the user chooses for connecting to the Internet, he or she can still communicate through other types of operating systems.
- Internet access is affordable and requires only a simple procedure to register. Anyone with access to the Internet can compose his or her own Web page and publish it through the server.
- The Internet allows users to communicate in the comfort of their own home or office and eliminates the need to travel to make arrangements or get information.

These characteristics have inevitably led the Internet to become an important marketing tool for all businesses. The Internet has an increasingly important role to play in every aspect of the tourism industry. Information distribution, product and service purchases, and travel and tourism development planning are among these expanded uses. Tourism destination marketing is an area where dramatic changes are taking place.

In 2000, Zhou and Lin (see the Bibliography) conducted a survey on the use of the Internet and other media in marketing tourism. An important question was which information source was used in travel planning. About 34% of the travelers surveyed chose traditional printed brochures and the Internet combined. Printed brochures alone were chosen by 30% of respondents. Almost 12% of respondents relied on the Internet exclusively. By comparison, word of mouth was used by 19% of respondents. Somewhat surprisingly, only 6% of respondents received information from travel agents. When asked where they had access to the Internet, almost 35% of respondents said that they used the computer at their home, 34% at the library, and 31% at the office. It is apparent that this trend will continue. As personal computers become more affordable and portable, more individuals, homes, and workplaces will be equipped for access to the Internet in the future.

Many major corporations in the United States own travel Web sites. Expedia (http://www.expedia.com) is owned by the giant software company Microsoft. Travelocity (http://www.travelocity.com) is owned by Sabre, one of the major global distribution systems. Priceline (http://www.priceline.com) claims that consumers can name their own price for a travel reservation. Many hotels, airlines, rental car companies, and cruise lines offer online travel reservations and provide incentives and promotional devices. Additional services, including reservations in clubs, theaters, and restaurants, are also offered.

Travel agencies were seriously affected by the introduction of this new information technology. They are now going through restructuring and reorganization. Smaller agencies have closed. Others have merged with larger agencies. Still others are attempting to use the Internet to their advantage by offering specialized services.

17.7 DESTINATION MANAGEMENT

Destination management is a term that has come to be applied to the desirability of practicing sustainable tourism, especially in the context of avoiding overuse of a destination or attraction. Work continues, especially by the United Nations Environment Programme, on refining the concept and publicizing the need to practice sustainable tourism. Manuals for marketing and engaging in destination management have been prepared and disseminated. An example is contained on the following United Nations Environmental Programme Web site: http://www.unep.fr/shared/publications/pdf/WEBx0010xPA-MarketingTourism.pdf.

The needs, expectations, anticipated benefits, and possible harm of tourism vary greatly from one destination to the next, and there is certainly no "one size fits all" approach to destination management. One approach to encouraging more tourism destination operators to manage their attractions with sustainable practices is to establish local or regional destination management councils that issue "destination management certificates" after examining and approving the practices of local tourism operators.

17.8 EMERGING NEW TECHNOLOGY FOR DIRECT TOURISM MARKETING

The idea of accessing an electronic database for travel planning originated around 1970, when the first computerized tourism information kiosks were installed at airports, hotels, and government tourist information offices. These units were compact and convenient but had limited capacity. They were programmed to do simple travel planning. Few were equipped with a printer to print the information requested. Using different levels of information and a logic tree, the user was able to reach his or her particular data after several operations and observe them on the screen. With their introduction, these kiosks opened the doors to direct and unassisted tourism and trip planning through personal communications by electronic media. Before that time, electronic media for tourism purposes were restricted to travel agents and front desk agents of hotels, airlines, railroads and other facilities.

Around 1970, the advantages of a stationary electronic information unit were not much different from those of a printed directory. The unit presented limited lists of tourist attractions and facilities but did not allow quality comparison and activity evaluation for tourism development planning. It was not interactive with the user, and the information was not customized. The information in the database was not complete. Only those establishments that chose to pay for the service had their names, and little else, in the database. A comprehensive concept that explained tourism as an industry did not exist. The BIK System, conceived in 1970, had, among other objectives, overcoming the shortcomings of the early electronic information units.

Marketing is a function through which the marketer links the consumer with the producer. The Internet provides the link. At one end, the consumer knows the general product or service he or she wants. But he or she does not have enough details and does not know where to find it at an affordable price. At the other end, the producer has a specific product or service to sell at a price that will be profitable, but he or she does not know who will buy it. The Internet brings these two parties together and supplies the information that both of them need. Changes can be made over time to update prices and information about the products and services.

New technologies will bring new applications to tourism. Broadband communication, wireless application, and artificial intelligence will find new marketing outlets. For example, Datalex (http://www.datalex.com) will make live airline reservations using the Wireless Application Protocol (WAP) technology. Datalex technology will be provided to travel and cellular network companies to help them develop the global cell phone market. This technology is already making strong inroads in global cell phone networks. Using wireless technology, personal digital assistants (PDAs) and pocket and palm computers, users will be able to access market information just about anywhere at any time.

A subset of the Internet is known as **e-commerce** for the commercial purposes it serves. Internet services will be increasingly associated with travel marketing. Such services will carry the information on tourism products and services that is currently available in printed form. Tourist attractions, facilities, activities, and the services associated with them are now available. The BIK System database prepared for tourism development planning can be used for interactive travel planning on the Internet as well.

17.9   E-COMMERCE IN TOURISM

Travel agents, travel planners, tourism marketers, hotel reservationists, car rental agencies, advertisers, and airlines, among others, all use the Internet to reach their customers directly. E-commerce is one way to do this.

E-commerce involves a Web site where customers can find information on products and services and place an order using their e-mail address. The company's order-filling center then finds and ships the goods or provides the service. A customer service center assists the customer with answers to questions and the procedure for returning goods. The *Oxford Dictionary of Economics*, available on the Internet, defines e-commerce as "The practice of advertising and selling goods and services over the Internet." However, e-commerce is more than the act of buying and selling goods and services online. It encompasses all of the activities associated with buying and selling, financial transactions, business data exchange, and communication with customers and suppliers.

E-commerce can be based on two models. The first model of e-commerce business is organized by business operations. It includes businesses that operate only online and businesses that include both online and "bricks-and-clicks" operations. The second model of e-commerce business is organized by types of transactions. It includes both buyer and seller types of e-commerce. Almost 90% of e-commerce is conducted between businesses.

17.10 TYPES OF E-MAIL MARKETING

E-mail marketing has proven to be an inexpensive and effective way of marketing the tourism product of a country, region, destination, and establishment. This medium can be used on a broad front for getting the message across and informing the world about the best tourism opportunities a locality offers. E-mail marketing offers several advantages over other types of online media. First, the e-mail message can be personalized and the content customized. Personalization and customization are standard operations in e-mail marketing. Reaching the person by name and addressing the message to the person's specific travel interest helps to ensure that he or she will pursue the intent of the message. Both factors can increase the effectiveness of the message.

Second, e-mail can deliver up-to-date marketing information that can be revised and quickly resubmitted. This eliminates the problem of sending messages with obsolete information, a sure way of losing business. Third, e-mail messages can stay in the recipient's inbox until they are read, stored, or deleted. This ensures that the recipient will get the message sooner or later. Fourth, the effectiveness of an e-mail marketing message can be measured precisely and instantly. Through a built-in mechanism, the computer can tell the marketer how many targeted recipients have opened the e-mail. Other documentation is also possible. The effectiveness of e-mail marketing can be measured with precision and without delay, allowing immediate adjustments in the timing and content of messages.

The success of an e-mail marketing campaign depends largely on five factors:

- Correctly identifying the target audience
- Personalizing a greeting
- Customizing the message
- Delivering only the content that the recipient needs and wants
- Building consumer trust by ensuring privacy and preventing unwanted e-mail

An **e-newsletter** is a special e-mail marketing tool published and sent to a target audience on a regular basis. It has the convenience of e-mail plus the attractiveness of a printed newsletter with customized information. Most e-newsletters are sent to consumers on a personal permission basis. There are companies that specialize in developing e-newsletters. The message changes but the subject remains the same, in this case tourism.

There is also a service called the **Bulletin Board System (BBS)** where anyone can log in, post messages, and receive replies. Unlike e-mail and e-newsletters, BBS messages are not delivered to an e-mail box. The recipient has to log on to BBS to retrieve them. Marketing tourism can take into account all of these venues available via electronic media. The **chatroom** is an extension of this new technology. It is an interactive Internet communication tool whereby people with a common interest come together and discuss a subject. Exchanging information about the best places to visit or the best hotels in which to stay at a destination is an instant media event and an effective marketing tool.

Craigslist has become a very popular advertising site on the Internet, with a growing set of categories that include some topics of interest on tourism. There is also a growing number of large, interpersonal social networks (e.g., Facebook, LinkedIn, Google, YouTube, Twitter, Ning, Flickr, Digg, and MySpace) with millions of members exchanging billions of messages daily containing information, graphics, and opinions. Items of tourism interest are embedded in many of these messages. Moreover, the networks are supported by advertising, which provides an additional outlet for tourism ads.

A well-designed Web site is a powerful marketing tool. It is an important aspect of Internet marketing and the marketing plan. The marketing process is divided into three phases:

- Registering the Web site with the main Web search engines
- Making sure that online users can access the Web site with ease
- Making the Web site a portal for existing and potential customers

A **Web portal** is a Web site that offers a broad range of services, resources, and links for various interests or a specified area of interest. Some of the largest travel and tourism Web sites are portals with diverse functions. Sites such as http://www.expedia.com, http://www.travelocity.com, and http://www.orbitz.com provide a variety of information for travel and tourism planning. Some of the features and activities that can be included in a Web portal for tourism planning are:

- Planning trips to special interest attractions and destinations
- Maps and descriptive information about these destinations
- Links to user groups, chatrooms, discussion groups, e-newsletters, and e-mails
- Latest news about subjects of special interest
- Online subscription to e-newsletters and e-mailing lists
- Links to other online reservation and information Web sites
- Links to tourism databases

The primary objective of the Internet for planning and marketing tourism is to motivate potential tourists to make repeated use of the Web sites. The tourist should be able to easily find the information that addresses his or her special interest. The information should be accurate, up-to-date, and presented attractively.

17.11   E-MARKETING TECHNIQUES

Some traditional tourism marketing techniques have found new uses in electronic tourism marketing. Internet marketing uses several traditional tourism marketing techniques. For example, push marketing is widely used.

In **push marketing**, information is sent to the customer without his or her request. Traditional media, in particular broadcast media, almost exclusively use push marketing techniques. The Internet uses e-mail for pushing messages that no one really wants to receive because they can become a nuisance. The information is presented in an attractive form and is accessed easily. The idea is to entice the receiver to read it. Many tourism-related products and services are promoted in this manner.

Push marketing techniques use search engines. The consumer searches for a particular company or service on the Internet using key words or phrases. If the information does not appear, it is unlikely that the consumer will use the missing company's services or products. One should not confuse the quality of the Web page with the quality of the product or service offered by the company. The consequence of this initial selection is critical for the commercial success of the subject company. Companies listed in the database that the Internet uses have a distinct advantage in promoting their products or services over those that are not included.

The **search engine optimization (SEO)** criteria used for ranking the quality of Web pages consist of the following:

- Keywords in the title of the product or service
- Keywords near the top of the Web page

- Frequency of keywords
- Link popularity
- Penalty for repeat keywords
- Ability to obtain the target audience's e-mail addresses
- Provision of valuable information that the target audience requests
- Offers of incentives and benefits
- Provision of convenient ways for the audience to sign up
- Provision of an option for the audience to opt out of the program

Internet marketing should be used in the broad context of marketing the products and services of the tourism industry. Whether Internet marketing will be effective on its own, or will achieve greater results in combination with traditional means of marketing the tourism industry, is a determination that should be made individually at the national, regional, local, and establishment levels. The guiding principle of the master marketing plan should be to target an audience and use the appropriate channels of communication to achieve the best results.

17.12 CHOOSING BETWEEN E-MARKETING AND TRADITIONAL MARKETING

Printed brochures, displayed on the racks of travel agencies, picked up in hotel lobbies, restaurants, and tourism information offices, or sent by mail, were once the principal means of providing information to tourists. With the increasing popularity of the Internet, the use of printed brochures began to fade. The classic weakness of printed material has been that in locations where tourist attractions and facilities constitute a tourism product rich in variety and experience, no one rack or group of racks could possibly accommodate hundreds (sometimes thousands) of tourism opportunities. If their brochures are absent from the racks, many attractions and facilities are unable to catch the attention of their targeted audience. In addition, when they are available, filling a shopping bag with brochures and carrying them around is not the most effective way of collecting tourism information. Moreover, brochures were normally printed once a year and therefore were not updated more often than that. Web sites can be updated as often as needed, at any time, to reflect new information.

The survey conducted by Zhou and Lin in 2000 indicated that the majority of respondents had access to the Internet. About one-half of them used the Internet more than six hours a week. About 43% indicated that they used both printed brochures and the Internet for making their travel plans, whereas only 38% relied on printed brochures exclusively. That means that nearly 60% of respondents used the Internet exclusively or in combination with printed materials. This figure has undoubtedly increased in recent years as new Internet services have become available and computer use has become much more widespread.

The Zhou-Lin survey revealed that there is a very large market for tourism advertisers on the Internet. Convention and visitor bureaus and other destination promotion organizations have traditionally relied mostly on printed brochures for marketing their destinations. The Internet is now providing an excellent alternative. In the not too distant future, it may replace printed brochures, including maps, altogether.

Online brochures have several advantages over traditional printed brochures:

- As noted, internet brochures are more accurate since the information can be updated as it is received. Pricing, event dates, weather conditions, special promotions, and road maps change over time. This information can be quickly updated on the Internet.

- Internet brochures can be customized according to the interests and conditions of the individual tourist. (The BIK System has this capability.) Customization is key to the future development of destination information distribution and marketing.
- Internet information can be accessed anywhere in the world. In the near future, broadband wireless Web technology will carry this capability further. Travelers are now able to carry a mobile brochure via a Web-based wireless device wherever they travel. Using this device, travelers can access travel information in many locations, for a wide variety of purposes, anytime they desire. This technology consists of GPSs, Ipads, Kindles, Nooks, smart phones, and other products that are increasingly available and being produced in ever-greater numbers. Presently, geographic coverage is limited by the extent of communication transmission systems installed by various providing companies. Eventually, most of the settled world will have coverage.
- Internet information distribution reduces the capacity problems of a brochure, which can carry only a limited amount of information. With the Internet, limits are the Web server's storage space and the message capacity of the receiving device. Both are substantially larger than printed material on a typical brochure. Theoretically, destination marketers can place all the information they want on their own Web site. The database structure and software could be developed for customizing tourism planning information.
- Animation and sound can be included on Web pages, increasing their interest level.

Customized travel information can now be accessed away from home. It is possible to locate a tourism destination on a map screen on the dashboard while driving a car by establishing a link with the database through a GPS built into some cars and widely available as relatively inexpensive portable hardware. The future will bring additional conveniences. Cellular telecommunication equipment that fits in the palm of a hand is also providing access to tourism databases. The BIK System could be included on such interactive devices, which could also provide hard copies of the information scanned.

17.13 THE FUTURE OF E-MARKETING FOR TOURISM DEVELOPMENT

The Internet will continue to gain prominence, allowing tourism marketing to be increasingly customized to suit the interests of the traveling public. From national marketing to marketing at the local level, the Internet will play a major role. But with new technologies, it is likely that tourism marketing will continue to innovate. It will also experience changes in substance. New forms of tourism activity will be discovered and will be entered into the tourism planning lexicon. Additional changes that the future will bring to tourism might include the following:

- Electronic technology will not replace human services in marketing tourism. Rather, it will supplement these services and make marketing less dependent on human factors.
- Tourism information will be distributed increasingly by electronic means. New information delivery tools, like handheld cell smart phones and wireless systems, will be available for tourism marketing and planning in ever-growing numbers.
- Tourists will look for value, not quantity, in their search for customized, satisfaction-assured experiences. Electronic technology will make this search more cost effective.
- Changes will also affect those employed in the tourism information industry. Reservation services and marketing will continue to be electronically handled. Travel agents, airline and hotel reservationists, brochure printers and distributors, information officers, and tourism development planners at all levels will be affected by these changes.

Where these changes are taking tourism is hard to predict. The industry is expanding around the world, and together with that expansion, new technology and world events are influencing changes in lifestyles. As a result, the tourism product and services offered are evolving as well. It is important to monitor this evolution and plan a sustainable tourism economy that will primarily benefit host countries and will ensure that tourists return home fully satisfied with their unique experiences.

Chapter Highlights

- Acting as an umbrella organization for world tourism, UNWTO plays a catalytic role in promoting technology transfers and international cooperation, in stimulating and developing public sector–private sector partnerships, and in encouraging the implementation of the Global Code of Ethics for Tourism.
- Through various media UNWTO provides up-to-date qualitative information on tourism activities. UNTWO offers online access to a tourism legislation database (LEXTOUR) providing bibliographic and textual data on laws and regulations.
- State, provincial, and municipal governments support the tourism industry with their infrastructure facilities and promotional efforts. In addition, trade associations distribute tourism information to visitors through their member hotels, restaurants, and other tourism establishments.
- Implementing mass marketing in tourism calls for persuasive communication with the target public. The methods used to address mass audiences are advertising, sales promotion, and publicity.
- In tourism, direct marketing is growing in importance. Compared to mass marketing, direct marketing is focused. Its purpose is to motivate the individual tourist rather than to promote the virtues of the tourism product or services.
- Direct marketing intends to isolate the individual and make him or her the focus of attention. This is achieved by including the individual in a highly specialized market segment. Segmentation is a major issue in tourism planning and marketing.
- There are two principal kinds of marketing plans: the long-term Strategic Marketing Plan and the short-term Tactical Marketing Plan.
- The Internet, including e-marketing, has become an extremely important medium for marketing tourism and managing its operations, such as reservations and procurement.

The Technical Editor's Postscript: Progress in Recognizing the Importance of Reducing Poverty through Tourism

Chapter 1 briefly discussed the implications tourism development has for poverty reduction. The term **pro-poor tourism** was introduced. In its simplest and most general form, pro-poor tourism is defined as tourism strategies designed to alleviate poverty. This definition has been expanded and qualified in many ways since its introduction in 1999. It has become increasingly recognized both as an important objective and as an operating principle in tourism development, especially by governments and aid-dispensing organizations.

In an influential 1999 report titled *Sustainable Tourism and Poverty Elimination Study*, prepared by Oliver Bennett, Dilys Roe, and Carolyn Ashley, for the United Kingdom Department for International Development, six reasons for devoting greater attention to poverty reduction in tourism development were given. They were:

- Because of the size of the tourism industry, even small positive actions favoring poverty reduction could be very helpful in raising the incomes of poor people.
- Tourism has the potential to reduce poverty quickly because of the relative speed with which pro-poor policies and practices can be adopted, combined with the relatively short time periods needed to develop tourism projects.
- Even if the very poorest cannot be helped by tourism projects, the relatively poor can be. These include small-scale vendors, unskilled workers, and artisans.
- After direct means such as intervention investments in health, sanitation, education, and agriculture, tourism probably has the most potential for raising the incomes of poor people.
- Progress in recognizing environmental issues in tourism development plans and policies has demonstrated how targeted actions can be implemented relatively quickly. This can serve as a model for pro-poor tourism.
- Because there is not enough experience in implementing pro-poor tourism policies and practices, we do not know their potential in detail. We need to investigate further.

The report also covered the major means of promoting pro-poor tourism. These are:

- Create and use business partnerships including:
  - Partnerships between small businesses and larger tourism-involved businesses.
  - Improving information about opportunities for small businesses to become partners in the tourism industry.
  - Support for training in partnerships.
  - Support for government–business partnerships and institutions.
- Conduct proactive pilot programs to achieve greater involvement of companies that are in the chain of tourism-related activities and employ low-income people.
- Promote the principles of pro-poor tourism at the international level. Bring the levels of knowledge about, and sensitivity to and support for, pro-poor tourism up to the levels of community tourism, ecotourism, and sustainable tourism.
- Encourage collaboration between donor aid agencies to better coordinate pro-poor tourism policies and programs.

In 2008 a report titled *LDC Poverty Alleviation and the Doha Development Agenda: Is Tourism Being Neglected?* by Dale Honeck, for the World Trade Organization, two important aspects of tourism were identified as potentially contributing to poverty alleviation: the dual use of tourism infrastructure and the prospects for turning economic leakages into linkages. **Dual use** refers to opportunities to use services created for one use for additional uses. An example given in the report is the use of airline services for transporting tourists to and from Kenya for also transporting cut flowers from Kenya to Europe. **Turning leakages into linkages** refers to import substitution programs undertaken to provide locally produced goods and services used in tourism establishments in place of goods and services purchased from other countries. The report acknowledged that while import substitution was favorable from a host/destination country's point of view, perhaps too much was being made of it because of unreliable information about it and because of the continued need for tourism establishments to import goods and services of higher quality than those available locally. The report is available on the following Web site: http://www.wto.org/english/res_e/reser_e/ersd200803_e.pdf.

In a 2008 working paper titled *Reducing Poverty through Tourism,* by Dain Bolwell and Wolfgang Weinz of the International Labor Office, the authors argue for further measures to promote pro-poor tourism, including targeted interventions that would better enable poor people to become part of mainstream economic life and capture opportunities to improve their economic and social conditions. They also state that additional policies should be established to diminish and hopefully eliminate harassment of the poor, and to reduce and hopefully end restrictions on how they support themselves. The authors also advocate use of the concept of **decent** work in tourism, defined as productive employment in "conditions of freedom, equity, security and human dignity."

The authors note that these concepts and policies can be incorporated in poverty reduction strategy papers (PRSPs), which enumerate a country's economic, social, and political policies and programs for a three- to five-year period. The World Bank and the International Monetary Fund (IMF) have agreed that nationally prepared participatory poverty reduction strategies should be the basis for concessional lending and debt relief. PRSPs are comprehensive plans prepared by governments, with support from development partners, that identify the poor and include proposed strategies for overcoming poverty, including policy and expenditure targets. About fifty countries have prepared such documents.

Bolwell and Weinz also believe that pro-poor tourism should become an approach applied to all tourism development and operations, distinguishing it from niche activities like ecotourism and community-based tourism. They reiterate tourism's potential to contribute to United Nations Millennium Development Goals, consisting of eight goals, eighteen targets, and forty-eight indicators. Achievement of these objectives has a target year of 2015. The eight goals are presented in Chapter 1 of this book. The Bolwell-Weinz paper is available on the following Web site: http://www.ilo.org/public/english/dialogue/sector/papers/tourism/wp266.pdf.

Finally, in an opinion article titled *Pro-Poor Tourism: What's Gone Right and What's Gone Wrong?* published in 2007 by the Overseas Development Institute in London, Caroline Ashley and Harold Goodwin summarize the successes and shortcomings of the pro-poor approach to tourism development. Successes are seen in Africa and Asia. In Africa, recent poverty alleviation strategies increasingly utilize tourism, and new tourism policies are used to connect tourism to poverty reduction, not simply to generate foreign exchange. In Asia, the Asian Development Bank has been very receptive to adopting pro-poor tourism criteria in its aid programs. Also, the Stichting Nederlandse Vrijwilligers (SNV), a Netherlands development organization, has sent pro-poor sustainable tourism advisors to Asia, Africa, and Central and South America. The

UNWTO has established a trust fund and program titled "Sustainable Tourism—Eliminating Poverty." A 2007 meeting on tourism in developing countries preceding a United Nations Conference on Trade and Development highlighted the importance of pro-poor tourism for developing countries. A summary of its discussions can be found on the following Web site; http://www.unctad.org/en/docs/td427_en.pdf. Moreover, a number of conservation and development NGOs are assisting the poor to engage in tourism activities.

The shortcomings identified in advancing pro-poor tourism are its relatively narrow focus, its inattention to markets, and its limited documentation. Its narrow focus results from its being applied primarily at the micro level, such as community-based tourism projects, campsites, and trekking activities. If the principles of increasing involvement of the poor were applied to beach resorts, urban hotels, conferences, wilderness tours, and construction projects, poverty reduction would be realized on a larger scale.

Some tourism projects with pro-poor practices have failed because not enough attention has been given to analyzing the markets for the tourism products. It is essential that proper business expertise, market analysis, and private sector partners, where appropriate, be involved in tourism development projects with pro-poor practices. Having a correctly balanced and experienced team of professionals is essential to all tourism development projects, including those with explicit pro-poor policies and practices.

The final shortcoming identified in the Ashley-Goodwin article is one identified in other writings on pro-poor tourism: limited documentation. The authors do not know of any projects where the entire range of impacts of tourism development on poverty levels has been carefully assessed. They claim that very few rigorous before-and-after assessments are done and published. There is a substantial literature to guide the adoption of pro-poor strategies, but there is scant literature that properly assesses project- and program-level poverty reduction.

The authors conclude by recommending several means of increasing pro-poor tourism policies and practices. They observe that "Pro-poor impacts are likely to be higher in destinations where out-of-pocket spending is high, small and micro-enterprises have access to capital and business support, un-skilled and semi-skilled workers have access to training, small-scale infrastructure supports local business development, and tourism companies' demand for locally procured products is matched by adequate capacity for production and marketing on the supply side" (p. 2). This is a fairly extensive but attainable list of conditions to be met. Achieving these conditions will be facilitated by applying the planning principles proposed in this book.

Ashley and Goodwin claim that there is also enough experience to show some useful strategies for establishing these key conditions. "One is to make the business case for companies to invest in local linkages. Another is to bring together the formal private sector, the small and informal entrepreneurs, residents, and government within a country, or region or local destination and develop a multi-stakeholder partnership approach. A third is to combine pro-poor strategies with upgrading the product and the destination, rather than as a disconnected activity. A fourth is to adopt a 'market access' perspective, assessing any product development or regulation to consider how it expands or impedes market access for poor producers" (p. 2). This article is available on the following Web site: http://www.odi.org.uk/resources/download/526.pdf.

Pro-poor tourism policies and practices have been defined and applied, admittedly in a relatively modest way, for only ten years. Given the extent of tourism development activities, the size of the tourism industry, and its relative importance for many countries, it is likely that there will be many more opportunities for such policies and practices to be put into effect, especially since large international funding and sponsoring organizations are increasingly embracing the concept.

V

Histories and Case Studies of Tourism Planning

Case Study 1

Waterfront Tourism Destination and Redevelopment, Boynton Beach, Florida, United States

PROJECT BY: Bulent I. Kastarlak
YEAR: 2000

The Case

Boynton Beach stood on the threshold of a promising decade of redevelopment as South Florida entered the twenty-first century. The future of South Florida does not lie in expanding development toward the interior of the state. Ecological disaster courted by pushing "sprawl" farther inland toward environmentally sensitive wetlands of the Everglades, where wildlife thrives, is not consistent with sustainable development. Vacant land available for development is in short supply in most communities in South Florida. More than one hundred fifty golf courses consume more than two hundred acres of land each. Planned communities, built with one- or two-story houses, further contribute to the fast-disappearing vacant land. The retirement market demands these low-density housing and recreational lifestyles. The reality of the situation, however, demands a change.

The answer to the approaching urban and environmental crisis lies in selectively redeveloping long-established low-density older neighborhoods on the waterfront into higher-density neighborhoods. This calls for an urban planning strategy that will encourage replacement of substandard housing from the waterfront inland by accommodating high-rise and mixed-use redevelopment. This is a controversial and sometimes politically suicidal remedy requiring lifestyle changes unless the advantages of the strategy are demonstrated. Replacing older, less expensive, affordable housing with newer, more expensive housing requires concerted actions. One action is to have the higher property tax revenues from new construction allocated to the development of new, affordable housing elsewhere to serve the people who may be displaced by upscale waterfront redevelopment. This model is tested in the redevelopment of the Boynton Beach waterfront.

History and Location

Tourism is Florida's primary industry. The economy of the state depends on the expenditures of foreign and American tourists retiring to or vacationing in Florida. There is somewhere to visit and something to do for everyone. Orlando with its theme parks, Miami Beach with its beaches and nightlife, and Palm Beach with its social swirl and golf communities for retirees are magnets for millions of visitors and residents alike. Until recently, Boynton Beach remained on the fringes of these tourism destinations, with little to offer the visiting public. Policymakers reluctantly adopted the recommendations of the city's urban planners to upgrade and increase densities in the waterfront area when a few developers showed interest in redeveloping the waterfront and then selling hundreds of apartment units, sight unseen, almost overnight. Now planners are at work on preparing a Master Plan for the corridor defined by the Intracoastal Waterway and the I-95 interstate highway, a corridor varying from one to two miles in width. The area and the process of redeveloping it are called "eastward ho."

Boynton Beach has the potential to create a new growth center and tourism destination between Miami Beach to the south and West Palm Beach to the north. The redeveloped destination will be a candidate for receiving an ample market share of Florida's incoming two million new residents plus visitors during the next decade. When the market pull characteristics of Boynton Beach are translated into a rich mix of attractions and facilities, new residents and visitors alike will be drawn to the destination.

By redeveloping its waterfront with higher-density settlements, Boynton Beach offers the following advantages in its tourism product:

- A central location for the South Florida market of five million people
- Access from I-95 and US1 to the Intracoastal Waterway
- Access to the Atlantic Ocean from a nearby outlet
- Strong potential for creating new attractions
- Undervalued and obsolete real estate on the waterfront
- Major employment and shopping facilities like the BB Mall
- Pro-development citizenry and supportive local government
- A highly receptive business community willing to expand

To achieve its tourism destination potential, however, Boynton Beach needs to upgrade its public infrastructure, build high-end residential and commercial facilities, and develop the lifestyle that depends on recreational pursuits, all within the narrow coastal corridor. It has become clear that existing natural and human-made assets on the waterfront are not sufficient for that task; a highly integrated mix of new and existing attractions and facilities is needed. Planning and developing a destination area, and turning the waterfront of Boynton Beach into a growth center offering a unique tourism product, will take a decade or more.

The north–south US1 highway divides downtown Boynton Beach into waterfront on the east and commercial areas on the west. The downtown area has not seen growth for decades. The street connecting the City Hall and the waterfront goes through the commercial area. It consists of a few struggling stores and two restaurant/bars. On-street parking provides most parking places downtown. Currently, there are two restaurants on the waterfront. They occupy both ends of two piers separated by two canals fronting the Intracoastal Waterway. Two canals serve as locations for a marina for a small fishing fleet, for private boats, and for an excursion boat that takes scuba divers to a reef twice a day. A recently rebuilt bridge connects the mainland to the affluent Ocean Ridge community over the Intracoastal Waterway. There is a continuous parade of yachts and boats on the Intracoastal. The area between the waterfront and US1 is occupied by a condominium office building dating back to the 1950s, a bank building, and several small buildings and stores. The most interesting feature of the area is a city park dedicated to preserving the only untouched mangrove area on the Boynton Beach waterfront. A retention pond for collecting the surface drainage water from downtown completes the existing assets of the waterfront. Access to the waterfront is from north–south US1 and Interstate I-95 only half a mile away.

Project Description

The survey and analysis of Boynton Beach's waterfront area reveals that the existing tourism product is not competitive with other waterfront destinations in Miami Beach, Fort Lauderdale, Boca Raton, and West Palm Beach in South Florida. But it has the potential to greatly expand and diversify its tourism product by building attractions and facilities that will encourage pedestrian traffic by connecting all recreational and commercial elements of the waterfront. When completed, the waterfront will encourage further development of the downtown inland region as a second ring of service areas. The development of the waterfront will have a multiplier effect and will create many other projects, jobs, income, and tax revenues for the city.

The concept for developing the waterfront is based on two planning objectives:

- Build new recreational attractions and improve existing ones to draw large numbers of tourists and excursionists from South Florida.
- Provide supporting facilities that will serve as attractions, draw additional residents and workers, and populate the downtown area by creating a larger market for businesses.

The first objective requires expanding and diversifying the tourism attraction mix. To achieve this objective, a string of continuous water-oriented attractions along the waterfront is being considered. The second objective is achieved by relocating all service and support facilities behind the attractions and providing maximum pedestrian and vehicular access to the waterfront. The following Web site shows features of the area. http://boyntonharbormarina. com/our-vision/.

Building Program

The Master Plan prepared for developing the waterfront includes the following attraction and facility projects:

Projects 1 and 2 (Marina Bay, Phases I and II): Lot Area 9.04 Acres

Retail	Buildings A+B (Level 1)
	Restaurants 1, 2, 3
	Outdoor cafes 1, 2
	Festivity Square and outdoor public area
	Music shell
	Thirty-three-boat-slip marina
	Carousel for children
	Sightseeing boat
	Fuel station

	Building C (Level 1)	
Office	Buildings A+B (Level 2)	
Garage	Building C, 800 parking spaces (Levels 1, 2, 3)	
Residential	Buildings C1, C2, C3, 180 condominium apartments (Levels 4, 5, 6)	
Common Areas	Pedestrian walkways	
	Two lobbies	
	Building C perimeter arcade	
	Roof garden, clubhouse, swimming, tennis	
	Other	
	Total building floor area	989,000 sf

Project 3 (Promenade): Lot Area 2.75 Acres

Retail	Building A	
Service	Building B (toilets, storage)	
Common Areas	Pedestrian mall, fountain, street lighting	
	Portable cubicles for art and green market events	
	Total building floor area	14,000 sf

Project 4 (Retention Pond and Park)

Retention pond
Kiosk and boardwalk
Rowboats

Project 5 (Commercial Block): Lot Area 2.9 Acres

Retail	Building D (Level 1)	
Office	Tower 1	
	Tower 2	
Garage	Building D, 662 parking spaces (Levels 1, 2, 3)	
Common Areas	Building C, perimeter arcade	
	Two lobbies, roof garden	
	Total building floor area	606,000 sf

Project 6 (Residential Boutique Hotel)

Hotel	100 suites	
Retail	Stores	
Garage	120 parking spaces	
CommonAreas		
	Total building floor area	179,000 sf

Projects 7+8 (Restaurant)

Retail	Restaurant and deck	
	Scuba diving, charter boat dock	
	Total building floor area	27,000 sf

Project 9 (Restaurant)

Retail	Restaurant and deck	
	Stores	
	Total building floor area	**27,000 sf**

Project 10 (Museum + Police Station + Information Center)

Retail	Museum and gift shop	
	Police station and information center	
	Total building floor areas	**3,000 sf**

Project 11 (Theme Lake Village Motel)

Motel	30 cabins on stilts	
	Building total floor areas	**13,000 sf**
	Gross Building Floor Area for the Destination	**1,858,000 sf**
	Total Parking Spaces Provided	**1,952**

Master Plan

The positioning of the building program over the area of the waterfront destination has three main objectives:

- Provide maximum pedestrian access to waterfront recreational activities from parking areas behind the waterfront.
- Connect all waterfront attractions into one continuous chain of tourism experiences for pedestrians.
- Provide convenient service facilities for resident and working populations.

The central theme and spine holding all attractions and facilities together is **Project 3**, the **Promenade**. This project is conceived as a pedestrian extension of the main thoroughfare, Boynton Beach Boulevard, bringing tourists from the north–south I-95 highway one mile away. This paved half-mile-long pedestrian mall starts with a highly visible entrance with flags, a drop-off zone, a welcome area, comfort facilities, gift shops, and a taxi stand, and continues from east to west with a succession of activity points. First, a round fountain serves as a rotary for pedestrians entering the Promenade from four directions and as a focal point with its 100-foot-high multicolored jet water display. The jet is visible from I-95 one mile away. It changes color and pattern. The mall continues toward the east and accesses **Project 4**, the **Retention Pond and Park**. In addition to its drainage function, the park is planned to provide water-related entertainment. Rowboats are available. The kiosk will serve as a platform for band concerts, with audiences sitting around the pond on portable folding chairs. Opposite the pond, pedestrian traffic going and coming from **Projects 1 and 2**— the **Marina Bay, Phases I** and **II**—connects to the mall. Farther to the east, the mall gets a splendid view of Mangrove Park on one side and the marina, with its many activities drawing the attention of visitors, on the other. The Promenade terminates at the Intracoastal Waterway with a turnaround and a beacon that flashes at night. The entire length of the mall is public property. Underneath lays the easement for the treated drainage water outfall to the Intracoastal Waterway.

The Promenade will serve as the site for celebrations, art festivals, a farmer's market, and multiple other special events that will attract large numbers of visitors to downtown and the waterfront of Boynton Beach. Once tourists get there, other attractions will draw them. Among them, the most prominent are Projects 1 and 2—the Marina Bay, Phases I and II. The important feature of the project is its central parking facility. The Master Plan calls for the Marina Bay to dedicate its waterfront to the free circulation of pedestrians, allowing them to experience a large variety of activities. One can walk from the Promenade to Festivity Square in Phase I, where many recreational events and attractions are planned. They include dancing, music, pushcart vendors, street performers, a video projection, light and sound shows, a juice bar, sightseeing boats, and a sampling of many retail stores. Two two-story theme restaurants with outdoor cafes will frame the square. A colorful carousel will bring joy to children and adults alike.

The pedestrian shore walk continues along the marina and provides access to many retail stores along the way. It ends with a third restaurant when it reaches the Intracoastal Waterway. **Phase II of Marina Bay** constitutes the service areas. An entire city block is planned for a large public/private garage. An arcade of stores front and disguise the garage on three sides. Behind the stores, the three-level garage can accommodate 800 parking spaces. The lower two levels are dedicated to 502 public parking places for visitors to all three restaurants, cafes, stores, and other activities on the waterfront. When they leave the garage, pedestrians have the freedom to walk anywhere and experience everything without their cars. All long-term parking spaces are removed from the waterfront and contained in the garage. *Cars do not compete for precious ground space with recreational and commercial activities on the waterfront.*

The third level of the garage supports 298 parking spaces and 180 condominium apartments in two or three towers sitting on top of the garage block. These luxury apartments will have a 360-degree view of all activities on the waterfront and the ocean beyond. Separated from the ground by three levels of garage, they will be isolated from the humming festivities below. Limited access will provide complete privacy to the apartments. The remaining areas of the garage roof above the third level will be used for a swimming pool, clubhouse, tennis courts, and private gardens for the apartment units. Thus, with residents assured of direct access to the waterfront, luxurious accommodations, and privacy, the apartments will fetch high prices. In one proposed apartment building, the developer received deposits toward the sale of 75% of the 338 planned units at the end of the first day of preconstruction sale promotion.

Other projects will provide additional diversification for the tourism product of the destination. **Project 6**, the **Boutique Hotel**, will bring South Florida hospitality and services to visitors in luxurious comfort in its custom-decorated rooms overlooking the waterfront. **Project 5**, the **Commercial Block**, with its own multilevel garage, will bring downtown many businesses whose employees and patrons alike will want to be close to the attractions and facilities of the waterfront. **Projects 7+8** and **Project 9** are two existing restaurants that will be totally rebuilt. **Project 10**, the **Museum**, **Police Station**, **and Information Center**, will provide guidance to tourists and ensure the security of waterfront establishments. Finally, **Project 11**, the **Theme Lake Village Motel**, will be inspired by the architecture of the native Seminole Indians who built villages on stilts for protection from wild animals on the vast wetlands of the Everglades hundreds of years ago. This replica motel will have access through the Mangrove Park. Car parking will be at the central parking garage, and the boats of guests will be moored at the marina.

This highly integrated destination and its interdependent multiple-use projects will create the anchors for the growth and rebirth of Boynton Beach downtown and will rejuvenate its sagging economy through tourism development.

Tourism Activity Mix and Seasonality

The eleven-project destination area of downtown Boynton Beach combines a rich variety of recreational and business opportunities in its attractions and facilities. The activities planned for these tourism assets include *attending outdoor concerts, informing the public, using the comfort station, eating, drinking, exploring nature, sport fishing, observing art shows, partying, picnicking, playing tennis, vacationing, riding bicycles, riding the carousel, riding in cars, shopping, sightseeing, sailing, scuba diving, snorkeling, sleeping, swimming, sunning, surfing, visiting, watching tournaments, water skiing, walking, yachting, and many more . In fact, of the over 300 recreational and utilitarian activities* identified for 232 types of NAICS establishments constituting the tourism sector, more than 100 activities are accommodated in the tourism attraction-facility mix of the proposed waterfront tourism destination. Given Florida's warm climate, a large majority of the activities and establishments are suitable for year-round operations (see Figure 2.6 in Chapter 2). This will enable a consistent, year-round tourism industry for Boynton Beach.

The attractions, however, are primarily of regional significance. There are no nationally or internationally significant attractions, past or planned, in the destination. This was intended. The objective of the planned destination is to stimulate redevelopment of the downtown area and growth of the Boynton Beach tourism economy. In the interest of the public, protecting the fragile waterfront ecosystem and the intimate urban character of the waterfront precluded very high-density attractions and very high-rise development. It remains to be seen, however, how future events will influence the application of this planning principle prescribed by the Master Plan. Financial gain undreamed of only six years ago and political expediency may eventually distort the intent of the Master Plan by leading to the development of nationally significant attractions.

Financial Analysis

Projects 1 and 2, Marina Bay (Phases I and II), are the first projects to be developed. They are the initial magnets of the destination area. Financial analyses for other projects will be prepared later. A simplified financial analysis for the subject projects is presented here.

A) Cost Analysis

Phase I Hard and Soft Construction Costs—Marina, Retail Stores, Restaurants, Offices
Demolition, seawall, street widening, paving, drainage, sewer, water systems
Fixed piers for thirty-three marina slips.
Landscaping.
Restaurants 1, 2, 3
Retail and office space (A)

	Total	$5,572,000

Contingency @ 5%
Architectural, engineering, landscaping, signage fees @ 3.3%

	Total	$488,000
	Grand Total Hard and Soft Costs	**$6,060,000**

Phase II Hard and Soft Construction Costs—180 Apartment Units, 800-Car Garage, Retail Stores
Demolition, site work, drainage, sewer, water systems,

Landscaping.
Apartments
Roof clubhouse, recreational amenities, tennis courts
Garage 3 levels.
Retail and office space (B), arcade

	Total	**$28,653,000**
Contingency @ 5%		
Architectural, engineering, landscaping, signage fees @ 3.88%		**$2,593,000**
	Grand Total Hard and Soft Costs	**$31,246,000**
	GRAND TOTAL PHASES I AND II	**$37,306,000**

Other Soft Costs

Cost of land, finder's fee, closing costs, real estate broker commission, project management fee, construction management fee, appraisal fee, impact and permit fees, legal fees, insurance premium	**$13,665,000**
Mortgage brokerage fee, interest for three years, taxes during construction	**$5,604,000**
Project planning and development fee @ 3%	**$1,287,000**
PROJECT DEVELOPMENT COST	**$57,862,000**

B) Revenue Analysis

Total revenues at sellout	**$75,901,000**
Less selling expenses @ 4%	**($3,036,000)**
Net revenues before debt service charges	**$72,865,000**

C) Return on Investment

Equity investment on land only @ 24%	**$13,665,000**
Debt financing @ 76%	**$44,197,000**
Interest on 4 year loan @ 8%	**$ 7,071,000**
Total Debt Financing	**$51,268,000**
Total Equity and Debt Financing	**$64,933,000**
Profit Before Distribution	**$ 7,782,000**

D) **Internal Rate of Return (IRR) on Investment in Four Years 57%**

Evaluation

The proposed tourism destination for the waterfront of Boynton Beach will be the spark necessary for interesting developers in redeveloping the downtown area. It will also demonstrate the way to prevent further sprawl to the west. The technical and financial aspects of the proposal have already found acceptance, albeit reluctantly, and the Boynton Beach waterfront has become a hot property. Several projects are in their implementation stage.

The conception and planning of the destination has a political dimension that merits a case study of its own. The process has gone through several stages:

- The city's urban planning staff evaluated the economy and physical characteristics of the city and decided that the waterfront has great potential. Contrary to accepted practice, the staff decided that remaining passive was not in the city's best interest for developing that potential; the city would have to play a proactive role. This proposed change rankled many local politicians, and resistance to changing the "business as usual" attitude became great. After a key proactive professional was dismissed, a turnaround occurred and local leaders and politicians warmly adopted the Master Plan concept, with certain exceptions.

- When the staff presented the proposed Master Plan to the city administration, they received a negative response. *The city leaders stated that they should not be in the business of telling property owners what to do with their real estate.* By adopting this attitude, they denied the very essence of urban planning as a profession dedicated to protecting the public interest. The Master Plan was put on hold for reasons of political expediency. No further action was taken for many months.
- A major real estate developer became aware of the Master Plan and its key Marina Bay Phase I (Project 1) concept. He declined to purchase the land for Phase II (Project 2). He objected to the key planning principle of the Master Plan, which is to pull back development from the shoreline and provide free circulation and recreational activities for pedestrian visitors. Instead, he insisted on placing his buildings directly on the shoreline and reserving the waterfront for the exclusive use of its residents, thus interrupting free pedestrian circulation and eliminating an open space for public recreational activities. By not buying the land for Phase II, he declined to provide a central parking facility on his property for those who were not residents or tenants of his building. Thus, visitors to several restaurants (Projects 7+8 and 9) and other waterfront attractions were forced to continue parking their cars on valuable waterfront land, causing traffic congestion that will eventually impede the orderly growth of the waterfront.
- The developer won. The city allowed him to build where he wanted and set the stage for a parking-pedestrian nightmare along the waterfront. Other projects, including the Promenade, are now underway. It is not known how the development of downtown will proceed without the benefit of a central parking facility near the waterfront and without continuous, easy pedestrian access along the waterfront. The conflict between the rights of private property ownership and the public interest of the community at large remains unresolved.

The political history of the Boynton Beach waterfront tourism destination has not been repeated in other downtowns with waterfronts in the United States. Well-planned and well-executed downtown waterfront festival marketplace destinations, like Faneuil Hall Marketplace and Harborwalk in Boston; Bayside in Miami, Florida; the Inner Harbor in Baltimore, Maryland; Riverwalk in San Antonio, Texas; and Kemah Boardwalk in Kemah, Texas, are among the examples of excellent public sector–private sector collaboration giving priority to the public interest, providing opportunities for successful economic revival, and maintaining continuous public access to waterfronts.

Conclusions and Lessons Learned

- Tourism potential at the destination level can be translated into productive businesses and public recreational opportunities by conducting a thorough analysis of the potential and preparing a visionary tourism development plan. The tourism destination Master Plan must close the gap between public interest and private entrepreneurship.
- Government taking a proactive posture in developing tourism is consistent with sustainable future development in market economic systems. By contrast, a passive posture prevents the city from taking an objective look at its tourism potential and guiding its growth in the best interests of the people.
- Detailing an attraction-facility-activity mix is a very good planning as well as promotion tool. The proposed Master Plan for the destination illustrates the preferences of the

government consistent with the approved Comprehensive Development and Zoning Plan of the City. Prospective developers receive a full briefing from city staff before planning their projects.

- The destination Master Plan and its Financial Feasibility Plan give developers and city administrators representing the public interest justification for collaborating and for estimating their mutual benefits from that collaboration. The issue is not who wins and who loses, but how both can win by reconciling public and private interests. In this endeavor, the city administration must stand firm.

Study Questions

- What was done to identify the tourism potential of the Boynton Beach waterfront?
- How was the attraction-facility-activity mix for the waterfront destination determined?
- How were functionally complementary projects connected on the proposed Master Plan?
- How was the building program for the Marina Bay project determined?
- What was the role of the city government in preparing and executing the proposed Master Plan for the waterfront destination?
- How were the public interest and private property rights reconciled by the city government?

Suite Hotel and Resort (Apart-Hotel), Marmaris, Turkey

PROJECT BY: Bulent I. Kastarlak
YEAR: 2000–2002

The Case

The parcel of land is located on the shores of the Mediterranean Sea in Marmaris, Turkey. The owner is interested in finding a strategy to sell or develop his land. Both alternatives call for rezoning the land from its present national park use to some other financially and economically productive use permissible under the provisions of the local Master Land Use Plan and the zoning regulations. Since it already controls the use of the privately owned land within its national park borders, the National Park Service of Turkey has no incentive to buy the parcel at this time. The owner prefers not to engage in a lengthy lawsuit against the National Park Service that would allow him to rezone, sell, or develop his land. Instead, he is interested in proving to the authorities that productive use of the parcel, rather than leaving it for open, undeveloped national park use, will better serve the conservation objectives of National Park Service and the regional tourism development strategy and will allow him to sell or develop his land at the same time. The case is built on demonstrating to the authorities that the tourism potential and sustainable tourism impact of the subject parcel justify rezoning the land from national park to preferred residential use.

History and Location

Two thousand five hundred years ago, the Greek raconteur and historian Heredot described Marmaris as the pearl of the Mediterranean. The city's history dates back to 3400 BC, when it was established by Karians. The civilizations of Rhodes, the Assyrians, Ionians, Persians, Macedonians, Syrians, Romans, Byzantines, Selchukids, and Ottoman Turks left their marks on the city and its environ. Today, the city's many environmental and historic tourist attractions continue to draw thousands of visitors every year.

Marmaris is located in Mugla province of the Republic of Turkey. Its place is on the shores of the Mediterranean, where it meets the Aegean Sea. It is accessible from the island of Rhodes, only forty-five minutes away, by hydrofoil boat. Marmaris is one of the primary tourism destinations planned and encouraged by the government of Turkey. Its mild climate, many beaches, pine forests, historic sites, and access from the sea, land, and air make this city one of the favored destinations for foreign and domestic tourists. Dalaman Airport is one hour's driving time away. The Marmaris harbor and its modern marina accommodate more than eight hundred yachts from around the world. The atmosphere is relaxed, people are friendly, and service is meticulous. Four-star hotels line the beach, fronted by open-air restaurants and nightclubs. Nightlife goes on until the wee hours of the morning. Shopping at the town center and sightseeing at the cultural attractions are among the favorite activities.

In 2000, more than 1.5 million foreign tourists entered Mugla province. Approximately 40% of these tourists were from Germany, and 3% were from the United States. Over 109,000 visitors entered from the port of Marmaris. Not surprisingly, more than 4,200 yachts of foreign registry visited Marmaris during the year. Another 2,600 yachts of Turkish registry arrived at the harbor, testifying to the popularity of Marmaris as one of the preferred yachting destinations around the Mediterranean. The peak tourism season of May through August, coinciding with summer school vacation, brings families to Marmaris. Per capita tourist expenditures by foreign visitors using the U.S. dollar as currency is in excess of $450 per capita for an average five-day stay. A substantial number of wealthy retired couples, both domestic and foreign, stay as long as six months and spend far more. Hotel occupancies range from 80% to 94% during the season. Features of the area are shown on the following Web site. http://www.marmarisland.com/Turkey-guide/Marmaris/Fun-and-sun.htm.

Project Description

Suite hotels are not new in Turkey. Condominium ownership is known and has existed there for many decades. Law No. 634, passed by the government in 1965, regulates this form of real estate ownership. For most Turkish people, real estate ownership represents the preferred method of achieving financial security and providing a bulwark against inflation. *Apart-hotel* is the name given to suite hotels in Turkey. The concept works like time-sharing. Individuals or corporations own one or more apartment units of the resort facility. These units are fully furnished. In addition, the facilities normally found in hotels serve residential units. They include a restaurant/nightclub, food and beverages, administration, recreational facilities, parking, security, maintenance, and housekeeping. Apartment units are rented by the day or for a longer period by a professional team that manages the apart-hotel. The owner of each unit designates the periods of the year when he or she plans to occupy the unit and frees up the rest of the calendar year for paying guests.

The subject apart-hotel project is planned on an 18 acre (70,700 m^2) waterfront parcel on the outskirts of Marmaris. An individual owns it fee simple, the highest level of private ownership, superseded only by the right of the government to take the land for public purposes with just compensation to the owner. The parcel is located at the terminal point of waterfront development extending from Marmaris. It is within the boundaries of the government-owned national park but outside the Master Land Use Plan and tourism destination area over which the Marmaris Municipality has jurisdiction. The park and parcel share a common boundary with the area of municipal jurisdiction. The owner wants to sell or develop his land but is unable to do either. Given the environmental characteristics, location, and tourism potential of the parcel, the owner believes that the national park use designation is not "the highest and best use" for his land. If the community and economic impact of the rezoned parcel in the Marmaris tourism region is consistent with the objectives of the land use and tourism development Master Plan of the region, the owner contends that rezoning the parcel will be the preferred option.

The topography of the parcel extends from the waterfront to the interior approximately 400 feet (120 meters), with a slope of 10–30%. The area is covered with minimum vegetation, making 50% of the land buildable. The balance of the land has steeper slopes and is covered with a pine forest. The natural character of the landscape can be preserved by developing the area closer to the waterfront and leaving higher elevations in their natural state, thus creating a transition or buffer zone to the national park area beyond. The waterfront has a narrow beach suitable for sunning and swimming. It is the last stretch of natural beach area on the bay. The national park has no other sandy beachfront that would interest private developers. A concrete pier extends into the bay. It can accommodate several yachts. It is owned by the stand-alone rural restaurant next to the subject parcel. The restaurant is in the municipal area of jurisdiction. There are several private residences nearby. The remains of the well-known thousand-year-old Amos Castle overlook the bay.

Alternative Scenarios

There are two possible scenarios for the owner to choose:

Sale of the Parcel

Given the present national park zoning status of the parcel, the most likely potential buyer of the land is the National Park Service. Since the land is already under its control, the National Park Service has no incentive to buy it at this time. This scenario offers no advantage for the tourism region and does not solve the owner's problem.

Developing the Parcel as an Apart-Hotel

Demonstrating the advantages of rezoning the parcel is the only course of action the owner can take. The demonstration relies on showing the sustainability of environmental and economic benefits. If it is approved, rezoning will take the parcel out of the National Park Service Plan and include it in the local Master Land Use Plan, thereby assigning it a new use: **preferred residential** land use. According to the provisions of this new use, zoning allows construction and operation of a residential facility, which can also be used as a tourist facility. Specifically, the second-use facility will be an apart-hotel. Tourist facilities require a Tourism Investment License from the national government. By having the license, the facility will be designated a priority development project by the Marmaris Municipality, and municipal services like road, water, sewer, electricity, and trash collection will be extended to the site on a priority basis. The designation will facilitate the development or sale of the parcel.

Building Program

Zoning allows 1,970 sf (600 m^2) of floor area per residential unit for preferred residential use. Accordingly, 118 apartment units will be permitted on the 17.47 acre (70,700 m^2) area of the parcel. Zoning also allows a cluster design that would permit grouping allowable units on only 50% of the parcel area. This would help conserve more than 75% of the existing pine trees and preserve the character of the site.

Based on the tourism statistics available for Marmaris, the average stay of longer-staying tourists in apart-hotels is one month. This lengthy stay generates more per capita expenditures from tourists than from tourists staying in conventional hotels. Units in apart-hotels are leased for one month or more to families, small groups, and wealthy individuals. They can accommodate up to six guests in relatively luxurious comfort. Retired wealthy couples and celebrities favor apart-hotels because of their combination of comfort, service, convenience, security, and privacy.

The building program for the planned apart-hotel includes 118 residential units and at least three typical floor plans, which are combined into two-story and three-story attached duplexes. In addition, the resort will have a heated swimming pool, juice bar and buffet, dressing rooms, tent cottages, tennis court, restaurant and bar, function room, business center, kitchen, housekeeping facilities, toilets, laundry, employee locker rooms, toilets and showers, administration and reception areas, maintenance and storage, a gatehouse, and security. Parking will be grouped outdoors.

All suites will be equipped with automatic telephone lines and connected to the reception, service, and housekeeping areas and will have long-distance access. All suites, the clubhouse, and the reception area will be air-conditioned. A dish antenna will provide television access to Turkish, European, and American channels from all suites. The clubhouse and the pool area will be suitable for leisurely pursuits and live entertainment on weekends. Local delicacies will be prepared and served from the resort's kitchen. Guests will be able to tour the attractions in the region and will take a water taxi to Marmaris for shopping and dining at local restaurants. Private yachts will be berthed on the pier of the resort. In addition to having room, housekeeping, and gardening services, guests can employ private maids and cooks. Limousines with drivers will be available.

The resort will have its own water purification and waste treatment unit. Rainwater will be stored in catchments and used for irrigation. Access to the parcel will be achieved by extending the paved road already approved by the municipal plan. The road will lead to two parking lots and the reception building of the resort. There will not be individual driveways to residential duplex units. Cars will be left at the parking lot. This will minimize the cutting of the pine trees and will preserve the environmental character of the resort.

Master Plan

The 118 residential units will be sited as four-unit, two- and three-story duplexes on 26 ft (8 m) × 39 ft (12 m) or 52.5 ft (16 m) × 39 ft (12 m) pads terraced from the ledge. Stone excavated from terraces will be used for building walls, patios, pathways, and decorative areas. Other clustering arrangements of units are possible. The natural slope of the land will allow most units to have a view of the sea. Pedestrian walkways will connect residential units with the reception-administration building and recreational amenities. Zoning requires residential units to have a 164 ft (50 m) setback from the waterline. All units will be sited behind the setback line. Service and recreation areas are exempted from the setback.

The swimming pool area, tennis court, and clubhouse building will be located within the setback zone. The security gate, gatehouse, and reception building will ensure privacy to all guests. Valet parking will be provided for arriving visitors.

Architectural Plans

Three residential luxury models, A, B, and C, have been designed. Two more models are possible by combining models A and B. The units can stand alone as two-story duplexes and as three-story quadriplexes. All models are based on a 13.12 × 13.12 ft (4 × 4 m) module. Model A is a three- or four-bedroom unit and includes 1,960 sf (184 m^2) of air-conditioned space. Model B consists of 1,100 sf (104 m^2) of air-conditioned space with one or two bedrooms. Both models have bedrooms with a walk-in closet and bath, a living area with a double high ceiling and fireplace, an eating area with a bar, a kitchen, and a 172 sf (16 m^2) terrace with a jacuzzi. Model C has 860 sf (80 m^2) of air-conditioned space with one bedroom and bath with a walk-in closet, a kitchen, a dining area, a living area with a fireplace, and a patio. Access to floors will be by outdoor and indoor stairs, depending on the floor plans.

The design of the residential buildings is inspired by indigenous architectural elements, such as stone walls, stucco finish, barrel clay tile roofing, tile floors, rustic wood finish in trims, and exposed beams, doors, and windows. The owners will decorate the interior of their units according to certain guidelines. Each unit will be decorated differently. Furniture and fixtures will be installed according to agreed-upon guidelines. Traditional Turkish carpets, divans, antique copper and brass artifacts, hand-painted glazed tiles, and Turkish porcelain will adorn the suites. A bathroom and kitchen with modern appliances will complete the interiors.

Tourism Activity Mix and Seasonality of the Project

The following activities are planned and will be provided for guests at the resort: residing, vacationing, walking, hiking, swimming, sightseeing, sleeping, eating, drinking, dining, driving, boating, sailing, yachting, sunning, playing tennis, and partying.

A more detailed activity mix can be selected from more than 300 activities listed for 232 types of tourism establishments identified on the attraction/facility-activity-seasonality list for tourism (see the Correlation list in Appendix K).

Based on the types of activities planned for the resort, seasonality of the attractions and facilities in the Marmaris region will be year round, allowing the resort to operate during all four seasons of the year. This maximum operational capability will be reflected in the financial analysis of the project.

Financial Analysis

The financial feasibility of the project is critical to rezoning the parcel. The financial analysis is conducted in three steps. Unit prices for construction in Turkish lira (TL) are taken from the *2002 Official Gazette* of the government and converted to U.S. dollars.

Summary of Estimated Development Cost and Financing

19 three- and four-bedroom units	
50 one- and two-bedroom units	
49 one-bedroom units	
Club building	
Club outdoor facilities	
Reception and administration	
Total construction cost of buildings	$6,554,000 (1)
Site work	
Forest conservation	
Infrastructure	
Total construction cost of site and infrastructure	$2,991,000 (2)
Total construction cost	**$9,545,000 (3)**
Contingency @ 5% (3)	$ 477,000
Furniture, fixtures, and equipment @ 10% (1)	$ 655,000
Engineering, architecture, legal, other costs @ 5% (3)	$ 477,000
Project management and brokerage fees @ 5% (3)	$ 477,000
Total development cost	**$ 11,631,000 (4)**
Interest for 70% (4) loan and 8% (4) during two years of construction	$ 641,000
Grand Total Development Cost	**$ 12,272,000 (5)**
Equity investment @ 30% (5) for construction	**$ 3,682,000 (6)**
Construction loan @ 70% (5)	**$ 8,590,000 (7)**

Summary of Revenues at Sellout

Grand Total Development Cost (5) at 70% of sellout value	$12,272,000
Value of unimproved land @ 10% of sellout value	$ 1,753,000
Profit @ 20% of sellout value	$ 3,506,000

Revenues from sellout	$17,531,000 (8)
Average sellout price of a residential unit (8)/118	$ 149,000

Summary of Operating Income

Gross Operating Income (Year 1)	$7,013,000
Operating Expenses (Year 1)	$4,825,000
Net Operating Income (Year 1)	$2,728,000
Cumulative Net Operating income (Year 4)	**$ 15,716,000 (9)**
Principal of a 30-year permanent mortgage (7)	$ 8,590,000
Cumulative interest on principal @ 7%/Year for 4 Years	$ 2,670,000
Balloon payment at the end of 4th year of operations	**$ 11,260,000 (10)**
Net Operating Income After Amortization @ 4th Year	**$ 4,456,000 (11)**
Net Profits from Sellout of Resort @ 4th year (8) + (11)	**$ 21,987,000**

- Both operating and selling the resort will be profitable options for the owner/investor.
- Asking price for the raw land will be @ $97,200/acre × 18   **$ 1,750,000**

Evaluation

This case is remarkable not only for its project planning process for tourism development, but also for the context in which government plays a critical role and tourism planning helps to correct a legal problem concerning property rights that has been left unattended for decades.

The following objectives will be achieved by having the National Park Service and the Municipality of Marmaris approve the owner's application for rezoning the subject land from national park use to preferred residential use:

- After rezoning, the owner of the parcel will be able to sell his property at a commercial market price. Based on the income and replacement cost methods, the value of the parcel is appraised at around $1,750,000 or $97,200 per acre. A sales tax will be levied at the closing.
- The buyer will guarantee to protect the environment of this strategic parcel and will invest in excess of $14,000,000 for developing the resort. Some, if not most, of this investment could come from foreign sources.
- In case of court challenges, the government will not be forced to resort to eminent-domain procedures and pay sizable compensation. If the price determined by the court is below the market value, the owner can appeal the ruling to the higher court.
- After rezoning, the terminal point of the Marmaris area waterfront will gain a high-value anchor and become a magnet for regional tourism.
- High-income tourists will be drawn from foreign countries for long-term stays in relatively luxurious as well as culturally and environmentally interesting surroundings.
- The facility mix of Marmaris will be further diversified, and the tourism product of Marmaris and its region will be improved.
- The revenues of the Municipality of Marmaris will increase proportionately.
- The economic impact and multiplier effect of the resort will be felt in all tourism sector establishments in the region and beyond.
- The hotel suites to jobs ratio will be about 1:2. For every suite, approximately 2 jobs, or a total of about 236 jobs, will be created by the resort. Outside the resort, the employment multiplier could be as high as 1:3.

- The income multiplier is estimated as 3.0. For every dollar spent by tourists, three dollars will be spent for supplying services and materials in the tourism sector of the region.
- Under private ownership, the park and the environment on the parcel will be better protected from pestilence and fire.

Conclusions and Lessons Learned

- The strategy will enable the owner to rezone and sell his parcel at a considerable profit.
- The land will be worth $1,750,000, or $97,200 per acre, after rezoning.
- Foreign investors are likely to invest a large share of the capital for developing the land as an apart-hotel.
- The National Park Service will benefit by ensuring conservation and maintenance of environmental assets under private ownership.
- The municipality will benefit from a major anchor attraction, jobs, income, and tax revenues created.
- The regional economy will benefit from a large investment and its multiplier effects.
- If he or she chooses, the owner/developer will benefit by paying off investors and the construction loan in four years and having debt-free operations after the fifth year.
- Investors will benefit by operating the apart-hotel, profitably with a high rate of return on investment.
- Alternatively, investors will benefit by selling all apartment units of the resort at a profit within five years of their completion.

In summary the proposed strategy will be beneficial to government and all parties concerned.

Study Questions

- Why is tourism the preferred use for the subject land?
- Why hasn't the National Park Service purchased the subject land?
- Why is a detailed strategy necessary for rezoning the subject land?

Wadi Mousa Golf Resort, Petra, Jordan

PROJECT BY: **Bulent I. Kastarlak**
YEAR: **2000**

Notice: This summary is extracted from a report authored by Bulent I. Kastarlak in 2000 while working as a member of the team of experts appointed by Abt Associates under contract with United States Agency for International Development (USAID). By special permission of Abt Associates and USAID, the information contained in this case study alone is in the public domain and is exempted from copyright coverage. The information can be reprinted without permission by acknowledging its source.

The Case

Jordan's arid climate poses a chronic condition of water scarcity. It creates a challenge to the country's economic growth and self-sufficiency. An important sewer and water project is located in and around Petra, one of the world's great archeological sites, also listed among UNESCO's World Heritage Sites. The area holds an ancient hidden city, wholly carved out of pink sandstone by the Nabataean people 2,000 years ago. Two millennia ago, an arch-supported aqueduct brought water to the city. Today the Water Authority of Jordan (WAJ) is working on a project to provide towns in the area with a modern water supply and wastewater system. By reclaiming wastewater for reuse, the project will ensure that valuable water resources are not wasted.

The report for the **Wadi Mousa Wastewater Treatment Project**, **Analysis of Effluent Reuse Options**, was prepared by a group of experts retained by Abt Associates for the Ministry of Water and Irrigation. The final report was submitted to the Ministry in December 2000. The report was prepared to assist the Ministry to understand the most feasible options available for the commercial reuse of treated effluent at the new wastewater treatment plan. Two options were considered: **agricultural reuse**, including tree or wheat farming, and **recreational** reuse, including a golf course and resort hotel. Only the recreational reuse option is presented here.

Two contiguous sites were identified as wastewater reuse sites for the project. Within the wastewater treatment plant boundary, approximately 69 dunum (17 acres), and adjacent to the wastewater treatment plant, approximately 1,000 dunum (247 acres) that fall within the Petra National Park borders will be available for using the treated effluent. The Government of Jordan wishes to lease the 1,069 dunum (264 acres) of land as a wastewater reuse site and charge a fee for the land and irrigation water provided.

The wastewater treatment facility initially treated 1,000–1,500 m^3/day from the four towns served in the Wadi Mousa (Valley of Moses) region. The average flow will reach 3,400 m^3/day by 2010. With regard to recreational reuse of wastewater for irrigation, a **golf course and resort** hotel seemed to be the option that would best use the effluent and . . . the land profitably. Depending on the amount of land ultimately available, if such a golf course and resort is developed, treated effluent will be used also to irrigate agricultural crops that will support the resort and surrounding market.

History and Location

The Kingdom of Jordan is a constitutional monarchy. It is rich in historic sites. Parts of the Jordan Valley are irrigated, making arable farming possible on 20% of Jordan's land. The remaining 80% of the land area is desert. About 85% of the 4.5 million inhabitants of the country are educated. Life expectancy is 73 years. Jordan has poor water, oil, and coal supplies. About 64% of the labor force is in the service sector, including tourism. The average per capita income is only $1,510 a year.

The historic lost city of Petra is located 260 kilometers (km) south of Amman, the capital city of Jordan. The lost city is accessible by car and bus over the Desert Highway, or for more scenic travel, over the King's Highway through Madaba. Most references made to the inhabitants of biblical Wadi Mousa come from the Old Testament. The Edomites occupied the area east of Wadi Mousa. According to Genesis, Moses reached the southern borders of Edom with his Israelite followers but was forced to deviate by a local king. Around 668 BC, Nabataeans emerged from obscure origins. By one account they were nomads, brigands and pirates. But they were also very successful traders. They became prosperous and took control of Wadi Mousa. Petra became famous for its culture, massive architecture, complex water channels and dams. At the height of its power, the Nabataean Kingdom stretched to Damascus and the Negev and Sinai Deserts. Over the centuries, the Nabataeans built Petra as their capital. Alexander the Great, Romans, Byzantines, and Crusaders took turns controlling the Nabataeans' land. After 1189 AD, when the last stronghold of Crusaders was abandoned, the Nabataeans and Petra receded into oblivion. Petra all but disappeared from maps and minds alike, and was known only to scholars from a few references by Greek, Roman, Byzantine and Crusader authors. A Swiss explorer, Johann L. Burckhardt, rediscovered Petra in 1812 AD. Others followed. Among them were the British artist David Roberts, who came to Petra in 1839 AD and captured the scenes with his artistry. He produced four volumes of lithographs of the Middle East, including many scenes of Petra drawn in exquisite detail.

What has captured the imagination of explorers, artists, historians and tourists since is the uniqueness and mystery of Petra. Much of Petra's appeal comes from its spectacular setting, accessible only by a deep, narrow gorge, the al-Siq, one mile walking distance from the commercial center of Wadi Mousa, with many modern hotels and facilities. The gorge is 1.2 km long, barely 6 m (20 ft) wide in places, and is hemmed in by 120 m (400 ft) high cliffs. Petra's most famous monument, the Treasury (al-Khazne), appears dramatically at the end of al-Siq. The monument was used in the final sequence of the film *Indiana Jones and the Last Crusade*. After the al-Siq, the valley widens and reveals hundreds of buildings, facades, tombs, baths and rock drawings carved into the rose-colored stone walls of the valley. A 7,000-seat theater, several Royal Tombs, the Colonnaded Avenue, the Byzantine Church, the Nabataean Temple (Qasr al-Bint), and after an arduous climb, the Monastery (al-Deir), line the path of visitors. Today, though carvings are eroded in places, the flowers, fruits and leaves on the friezes, pediments, and capitals still look crisp. Human figures, however, have been largely vandalized and subjected to target practice by Muslim Arab residents over the centuries. Lastly, Aaron's Mountain (Jabal Haroun) is a place of great sanctity to the people of Israel because it is the place where Moses's brother, Aaron, is believed to have died and been buried. The shrine is located on top of the mountain, rising 1,350 m from the sea level. It has spectacular views of the mountains and valleys surrounding Wadi Mousa. General features of the area are shown on the following Web site. http://www.visitjordan.com/default.aspx?tabid=63.

Project Site Description

The wastewater reuse project consists of exploring the feasibility of using the proposed 1,069 dunum site allocated by the government and treated effluent from the Wadi Mousa Wastewater Treatment Plant for recreational development, specifically for a golf course with a resort hotel. The scenario is based on a building program that includes an *18-hole golf course with clubhouse, a 100-suite resort hotel with amenities, a conference center, a casino with restricted access, private villas and an adjoining agricultural area for growing vegetables, fruits, a plant nursery and a retention pond for excess treated irrigation water*. The characteristics of the project site show advantages and disadvantages for the proposed use.

- *Accessibility.* Getting to the project site is difficult and time- consuming. From Amman, it takes four hours by car, and from Aqaba, about three hours. There is no airport serving Wadi Mousa. The latter is needed for the reuse project to succeed. It is unlikely that tourists representing the target markets for the golf resort will endure arduous travel by car from entry points of the country in Amman and Aqaba.
- *Utilities.* The wastewater treatment plant has already received the utility infrastructure necessary for its operations. Connections to this infrastructure will be relatively easy. Irrigating the course turf grass is feasible. The large root system of the grass has the potential of removing pollutants from the treated water further. Fertilizer will not be needed in large quantities.
- *Topography.* The site has a bowl shape. There are three entrances to the bowl cut through by nature from 120 m high cliffs. The bottom of the valley is relatively flat, with a 4% incline to one side allowing good drainage. Three streams drain the rainwater during the rainy season. This configuration is consistent with golfing greens that can be oriented in the North–South direction. Watching the sunset will be an experience to remember. A perfectly conical hill rising 120 m from the valley floor makes a perfect landmark and an observation point.
- *Mapping.* The Royal Geographic Center in Amman provides topographic maps at 1:25,000 and 1:50,000 scales and aerial photographs of the site with special government permission. There is no perimeter, ground survey, or legal description of the site in existence. Recently, a 2 km long easement has been established for the main underground irrigation line that originates from the wastewater treatment plant and divides the site into two segments. Buildings are not allowed over the easement, but a golf course can be built over it.
- *Orientation.* A big plus for any golf course site is a predominantly North–South orientation. Holes that run East–West present annoying sun glare problems for golfers in early morning and late afternoon hours. Holes that run West–Northwest are particularly undesirable. The project site offers possibilities for avoiding these orientations.
- *Privacy.* The relative isolation of the project site is a distinct advantage for the proposed golf resort. The site is accessible over a paved road from the commercial district of Wadi Mousa (Beida) 12 km away. The target tourist market cherishes its privacy and is willing to pay the price for it. They, the tourists, enjoy each other's company and wish to be free of intruding bus-loads of non-guest visitors.
- *Surface vegetation.* The arid environment allows scarce vegetation only at low points where moisture is available. Typical desert scrub covers the site. An occasional tree dots the landscape. Through irrigation, the golf course and selective areas can grow vegetation. The beautiful texture and colors of the valley walls, however, make up for the lack of vegetation over the surrounding terrain.

- *Climate.* The area tends to be exceptionally dry for most of the year. Winter and spring are cooler. Much of the rainfall occurs between December and March, causing severe, short-lived but destructive flooding. The hottest months of the year are June to September, when temperatures rise to 32°C (90°F). The period between December and February is the coolest, when temperatures stay around 15°C (59°F) during the day but can fall below freezing at night. Prevailing winds sweep in from the North; during winter they come in from the South.
- *Soil.* In designing a golf course, the most important factors are soil and drainage conditions. Good drainage is essential for growing healthy turf. Deep sandy loam is the best base for the course. According to the soil map of the area, the site consists of fine sandy soils more than 2 m deep deposited by floods occurring over thousands of years. No core samples were taken.
- *Drainage.* Three small streams drain the site. The depth of the water table is not known. There are no wells on the site. The treatment plant has its fresh water supply coming from the groundwater system of Wadi Mousa fed by wells.
- *Irrigation.* An 18-hole golf course will consume about 5 m^3/day/dunum of effluent during the summer months and about 2 m^3/day/dunum during the winter months. Thus, for a 648 dunum (160 acre) typical golf course, a minimum of 1,296 m^3/day and a maximum of 3,240 m^3/day is consumed. At its peak in 2020, the wastewater treatment plant will be treating 4,947 m^3/day effluent. The chemical quality of the irrigation water will be acceptable for unrestricted irrigation, including parks and a golf course. For health and cultural reasons, the effluent will be used only for restricted irrigation. The effluent will not irrigate vegetables, like tomatoes and leafy greens, which may be eaten raw. Other crops like stone fruits, apples, grapes, alfalfa and barley for fodder, and olives can be irrigated. Under a mixed-use alternative, combining a golf resort and agriculture, effluent consumption will have different ratios of consumption.
- *Public services.* Schools, housing, police, fire and ambulance services are available in Wadi Mousa.
- *Land use.* Other than occasional grazing of goats and light planting by Bedouins, the project land is vacant and unused. The government will settle with the Bedouins for their limited planting and grazing rights. No documentation was found about remnants of historical significance on the site. An archeological survey may be conducted prior to construction of the golf course. But whatever 2000 year old remains may exist below the ground will not be disturbed by the layer of golf course landscaping above.
- *Regulations.* The government controls all land within the National Park of which the site is a part. Policy differences among various Ministries and claims of individuals, if any, will be resolved during the due diligence phase. The land of the project site will not be sold. A long-term land lease with the government will allow its development.
- *Trained labor.* This is in short supply in the project area. Some positions at the resort will be filled by unskilled and semi-skilled personnel recruited from nearby villages in al-Beida, B'doul, and al-Hai and trained in Wadi Mousa. Most skilled labor in golf course and resort management will be hired from Amman, where trained Jordanian and Palestinian labor exists.

Public Infrastructure

To be made habitable, an isolated site requires an assortment of public infrastructure. In the case of a tourist destination, the requirements are even more stringent. The proposed Wadi

Mousa Golf Resort will benefit from many infrastructure facilities that are already in operation or planned for implementation during the next two decades.

Drinking water for domestic use will come from the Qa'a Ma'an water supply system. The plans for expanding the system significantly to meet the water needs of the area by year 2020 are in preparation. The existing seven wells serving the Qa'a pump station supply an average flow of 6,700 m³/day and a seasonal peak flow of 10,700 m³/day. By 2020, the seven wells will have the capacity to supply 13,800 m³/day. In addition, new well fields in Wadi Jiththa now provide an average yield of 4,000 m³/day and a seasonal peak flow of 6,400 m³/day. Four additional wells at Wadi al-Ain al-Beida will provide an additional 3,100 m³/day on average and a seasonal peak flow of about 5,000 m³/day by 2010. These flows will be pumped via a 350 mm transmission main to the ground storage reservoir of 4,500 m³ capacity at the al-Ail pump station. Currently, the wastewater treatment plant is served by a 100 mm water line coming from al-Beida.

Any extension of the water line from the wastewater treatment plant to the site of the golf resort will require recalculation of the water supply. A 100-suite resort hotel will require approximately 60 m³/day (130 gal/day/suite) for all guest suites at peak flow and another 20 m³/day for miscellaneous uses, excluding irrigation of raw eaten vegetables. It is anticipated that this supply will be made available from the existing distribution system without additional capacity expansion. It is assumed from the records available that the aquifer and well fields are adequate to supply all additional needs and that excessive well drawdown or depletion of the aquifer will not occur.

Improved road access to the resort site and an airport/landing strip for short take-off and landing propeller airplanes and air taxis will require early consideration. A helicopter landing-pad will be available at the resort. The road from Wadi Mousa and the proposed site will be upgraded to a minimum of a 2-lane, hard bituminous road with a posted speed limit of 40 km/hour. This distance is approximately 12 km. The road will be connected at its midpoint to the proposed airport/landing strip and bring the arriving guests from the airport to the resort in less than 5 minutes. An improved road will take guests from the resort to the commercial district of Wadi Mousa in al-Beida in less than 15 minutes.

To minimize travel time from Amman and other places and preserve the privacy of guests, private propeller airplanes, helicopters and air taxis will be used to reach the resort. The airport/landing strip will be located between the resort and al-Beida for serving both destinations. The facility could be owned and operated by the resort under a management contract with an operator. Or the Government of Jordan could be responsible for building and operating the airport. Initially, commercial flights are not necessary and may not be feasible. Airport services will be initially limited to passengers arriving and departing in small propeller planes because of the short length of the landing strip. The airport will have minimum navigational aids and may not have refueling and repair facilities. It will provide connection by air taxis to and from Amman, Beirut, Tel-Aviv, Kuwait, Damascus, Jeddah, Riyadh, UAE (the United Arab Emirates), Bahrein, Cairo, Cyprus, Antalya and Athens.

For energy, the resort will connect to the existing grid in Wadi Mousa. The transformer in Wadi Mousa supplies 630 KVA to the pump station. A similar transformer supplies 630 KVA to the wastewater treatment plant. Currently there are no plans to expand the service. The proposed golf course and resort will probably need 500 KVA service.

Pending the extension of sewer collection services to the entire service area, wastewater will continue to flow into cesspits in Wadi Mousa. This practice will end when all wastewater is collected at the new wastewater treatment plant, which will not be until 2020. The new wastewater treatment plant will be located about 1 km from the proposed golf resort. Due to the intervening topography, the plant will be only partially visible from the resort. This visibility can be further diminished by transposing real or artificial rock formations between the plant and the resort. Also, the required lime silo can be painted camouflage colors to blend in with the background. A potential olfactory problem will be resolved by selecting a treatment process that will eliminate odor. Approximately 80 m^3/minute of odorous air will be withdrawn and conveyed through buried PVC ducts to a biofilter for treatment. The biofilters provide reliable and low-cost treatment of gas.

The treatment plant will generate effluent that will be safe and suitable for disposal by discharge to various users as irrigation water. The proposed golf course, resort, associated landscaping and agricultural areas will be the designated users. A desert type 18-hole golf course will consume about 5 m^3/day/dunum of effluent during summer months and about 2 m^3/day/dunum in the winter months. Thus, for the proposed 648 dunum (160 acre) course, a minimum of 1,296 m^3/day and a maximum of 3,240 m^3/day irrigation water will be needed. By calculation, it is estimated that the irrigation water demand of the golf resort complex will be met entirely by the effluent from the treatment plant. The date and timing of the golf resort project are realistic because of the lead time necessary for planning, designing, permitting and construction. If a retention pond is provided, the demand for irrigation water could be met earlier. The sludge produced from the wastewater treatment plant will be well stabilized by anaerobic digestion wherein the solids' retention time can be measured in months. This sludge will drain and dry readily when drawn to the drying beds to a depth of 200 to 300 mm. The sludge will be used as fertilizer in agriculture and horticulture areas of the project.

Demand for a Golf Resort in Jordan

Wadi Mousa and Petra are internationally significant tourism destinations. Demand for general and historic sightseeing is proven and growing. But demand for golfing tourism has never been researched as a tourism marketing issue. In Jordan golfing, as a form of recreational pursuit, is not pursued with the same ardor as in countries where it has been historically one of the most popular sports, in fact, in some cases an all-consuming obsession. There may be cultural and climatic as well as financial reasons for such lack of reception. The fact remains that demand for golfing will have to be created in Jordan, rather than tapping existing possible nearby markets. Since there are no statistics on the subject and since the demand for golfing has not been measured in the past, a method had to be devised to show the magnitude of demand for golfing that needs to be created in order to justify the proposed golf resort project in Wadi Mousa. *The availability of effluent irrigation water is not, by itself, a justification for the resort.* The resort, primarily a tourist facility, will depend on the attraction value of golfing and other attractions in the Wadi Mousa region to generate demand and justify developing a new destination.

The method of analyzing the demand that can be created for golfing is based on the following assumptions:

- That the *nationality* of the tourist is the best indicator of his/her propensity to play golf while visiting Jordan.
- That *tourists arriving by air* are the most likely visitors to play golf and bring along their personal golfing equipment.

- That the number of golfers arriving in Wadi Mousa changes, depending on the *season.*
- That hotel occupancies in Wadi Mousa will not change appreciably, because their target markets are different from those of the resort.

All four assumptions are verifiable. After making the necessary calculations, it appears that only the "maximum daily golfers" estimate of *52 golfers a day* will be approaching the range necessary for supporting the golf course. There are limiting factors, however. It is highly unrealistic that every potential golfer will play. Furthermore, golf tourists staying one extra day to play golf will not have an appreciable effect on the room occupancy rates of hotels in Wadi Mousa. Two or more extra days of golfing will achieve better results both in terms of sustaining the golf course and . . . increasing discretionary tourist expenditures in the region. But this extended stay may not be realistic for most visitors staying in Wadi Mousa. They are traveling on relatively fixed budgets and have set schedules. The current tourism market will not do. A new market is needed.

This analysis points at the necessity of creating an entirely new market for Wadi Mousa and the proposed golf resort. Whether they stay in Wadi Mousa hotels or at the golf resort, the tourists in this new market will play golf and will spend extra money. This market is composed primarily of *wealthy, famous, celebrated, powerful individuals, and corporate and political leaders of the world.* They are distinguished from other types of tourists by their expectations for superior personal service, excellent but casual facilities, privacy and security, flexibility and a money-is-no-object attitude. This market segment demands nothing less than a full-service five-star resort hotel and a championship golf course. These persons are likely to spend the money necessary to sustain both.

According to calculations, a high occupancy rate (65–70%) of the hotel portion of the resort will compensate for the probable losses incurred at the golfing portion. Even if it cannot sustain itself financially, the golf course will be an important draw with the social "ambiance" it will help create. It is anticipated that the resort will draw about 5,000–6,000 guests a year who will stay on . . . average 5–7 days and spend about 5,000 Jordanian dinars (JD) per guest ($7,060), including, room, food, drinks, shopping, entertainment and golfing. The resort hotel, golf course, and clubhouse will have gross annual revenue of 14,285,000 JD–28,490,000 JD ($20,178,000– $40,228,000). Gross revenue could go higher when special event attractions, like tournaments and conferences, are included. These special events could raise the room occupancy rate well above 70%. If permitted by the authorities in a predominantly Muslim country, a casino could bring additional revenues and raise the occupancy even higher. These higher expectations are not calculated in the report.

In creating the demand, the marketing strategy of the golf resort is aimed at two types of tourists.

- The **Free Independent Traveler (FIT)** market segment consists of destination tourists who represent visitors who have selected a resort market area as their primary vacation destination and have arranged their accommodations either directly with the hotel or through a travel agent. When individuals book their reservations, they do not receive discounts. Typically, the FIT segment is not price sensitive. Peak seasons and weekends account for significant FIT demand. Singles, couples, and families with children are attracted to this type of resort because of its understated elegance and suite accommodations. The jet set of the world—film stars, artists, fashion designers, famous models, or simply very important persons (VIPs)— . . . make up this group.

- The **Group Market** segment generally includes three primary sub-segments: corporate groups, association groups, and special interest groups. Although a limited number of resort hotels rely almost entirely on occupancy by FITs, many have mounted major efforts to attract conference and business meetings. The **corporate** group sub-segment consists of individual companies and professional membership organizations that select a resort as a meeting location where golfing and other recreational activities, combined with an agreeable climate, create a major draw. The **association** group sub-segment is defined as professional or service or fraternal/sororital membership organizations that meet to discuss new development or issues affecting their area of expertise or concern. Some political groups or national and international leaders would seek the privacy, security and amenities of the resort to review and discuss issues of national, international and worldwide importance without the glare of constant media attention.
- **Special Interest** groups are made up of individuals who travel to a resort to partake of a specific activity. The category includes social organizations and/or individuals who share a common set of interests, goals and/or objectives. The activities include professional seminars designed primarily for presenting and discussing specialized information. These groups are often smaller and more focused than association gatherings.

The FITs, including the jet set, and the group markets will make up the overall target market for the proposed golf resort. They are distinct from the markets currently serving the tourism industry in Wadi Mousa and Jordan in general. They are magnets and trendsetters for attracting other types of tourist sub-markets. Their needs are different, as are their economic, financial and social impacts.

The essence of tourism is to motivate and transport the tourist from his/her primary residence to a destination where the tourism product is consumed. Tourist attractions, tourist facilities and activities associated with both constitute the tourism product. A preliminary survey and analysis of the tourism product in Wadi Mousa revealed a rich variety of attractions and a growing number of facilities.

- The attraction mix of Wadi Mousa is focused on a large variety of historical monuments found in Petra. They number about 36 major monuments that were excavated and are being gradually restored. In addition, the geology and topography of the ancient city are very dramatic in their scale and visual impact. This is a high-quality product for international tourism markets.
- It takes about one full day for an average tourist to absorb the visual images and get an impression of Petra. It could take, however, much longer for a tourist having a special interest in antiquities. Currently, there are no exhibits, reenactments, or audio-visual presentations explaining how life was lived in Petra 2,000 years ago.
- The sole museum open to visitors is modest in its content. An attendant on duty compensates for this shortcoming by his warm hospitality and verbal narrative of the events that took place two millennia ago. All monuments and graves were robbed centuries ago. They are empty of artifacts. The tourist is left . . . to imagine the life and economy of the Nabataeans. Questions like how the Nabataeans carved these monuments on the walls of the canyon and established an ingenious water storage and distribution system are left unanswered.
- The historic Petra is open to visitors during the daylight hours between 6 A.M. and 6 P.M. These hours could be extended during the summer months if certain monuments are

illuminated. Special live shows, reenactments, and light and sound presentations could be held during summer evenings at the open-air Nabataean theater.

- Rock formations surrounding Petra and the project site are dramatic. They could be challenging for walking, hiking, trekking, horseback riding and supervised rock climbing. Ecotourism could blend historic and natural attractions and create numerous new activities for tourists, thereby motivating them to extend their stay in Wadi Mousa.
- All artifacts have been removed from the historic sites and most of them have been taken from the country. Remaining artifacts lay buried under the soil. Protection of what remains is a priority concern of the government.

The tourist facility mix of Wadi Mousa is growing. Several three- and four-star hotels exist. About 1,600 hotel rooms in a dozen hotels are available for occupancy. Some of these hotels have their architecture inspired by local traditions, materials, handicrafts and spectacular views of the valleys. The service and attitude toward tourists are excellent.

Master Plan

The proposed site development scenario is contingent upon the following goals and conditions:

- The use of the wastewater effluent will be limited to golf course, clubhouse, hotel, and associated agricultural and service facilities.
- The project will be subject to the policies, rules and regulations of the Kingdom of Jordan governing the exploration, protection and restoration of antiquities that might exist underground at the site. These antiquities will be protected under the site or removed to other locations before proceeding.
- The proposed project will be consistent with and will support the goals and objectives of the Government, the Petra Regional Planning Council, and the Petra National Trust in, respectively, increasing net jobs and revenues from tourism, creating a regional growth center, and preserving the unique combination of antiquities, natural environment, and culture of Wadi Mousa.
- Although financial feasibility will be critical, subjective factors like national prestige may play a role in deciding on the implementation of the project. Income from reuse of wastewater for irrigation and lease of the land are important targets for the government. But creating a self-sustaining tourism destination of international significance is equally important.
- Financial participation by the government will be minimized. The government with the backing of international bilateral funds can guarantee debt financing. The great majority of investment capital will be secured from private sources, most likely in the form of joint ventures or a partnership between Jordanian and foreign investors.
- The resolution of intergovernmental issues resulting from the project will be the responsibility of the government. Investors will receive government support and fair treatment according to international guidelines governing such projects.

Golf courses are built by various organizations. They include municipal agencies, real estate developers, private clubs, municipal daily fee courses, corporations, and golf resorts. By matching the goals and requirements of the project site with the realities of golf course development, the following process of elimination resulted in the preferred market choice:

- The municipal agency in Wadi Mousa is not experienced in building and operating a public golf course.

- Citizens of Wadi Mousa have not been introduced to golfing and the local population of potential golfers is not sufficient to sustain a public golf course.
- There is no market for a privately developed residential golf community of hundreds of houses wrapped around a centerpiece golf course.
- Private membership golf club will require a large number of members—1,000 or more. There are not enough potential members in Wadi Mousa to sustain the club.
- A Jordanian corporation large enough for building the golf course for the exclusive use of its employees was not found.

The decision was to analyze the *golf course, clubhouse and resort hotel* alternative.

A complete regulation course includes 18 holes, with play to a "par" of between 69 and 73 strokes, and is at least 6,000 yards (5,486 m) long from its middle tees. A par of 72 strokes is considered ideal. A length of 6,500 yards (5,944 m) is considered a good median. Provision may be made for front and back tees to give the course an effective range of 5,200 yards (4,755 m) to 7,200 yards (6,584 m). The United States Golf Association defines **par** as the number of strokes an expert golfer would take in errorless play of a hole, always allowing the player two putts after his/her ball is on the green. Thus a par-3 hole is one in which the green is to be reached in one shot. To achieve a par 72, the course should contain 10 par-4 holes, 4 par-3 holes, 4 par-5 holes, or 5 par-4, 2 par-3 holes, and par-5 nine holes. These holes should be distributed evenly between two circuits of nine holes.

A regulation 6,500 yard course, situated on gently rolling land, complete with clubhouse, parking, practice and related facilities, will require 648 dunum (160 acres) to 728 dunum (180 acres) of land. Steep topography, irregular parcel configuration or rocky sections may increase the needed area by 200 dunum (49 acres) or more. Courses laid out on less than 607 dunum (150 acres), however, are apt to be crowded and cause unsafe conditions for golfers. For attracting international golfers and tournaments, a regulation golf course is preferred.

Golf is one of the few sports in which the configuration of the playing field is not standardized. Golf courses may be classified according to their general layouts on the ground. The two basic categories are the **core** golf course and the **loop** golf course. Either layout can have fingers with single or double fairway loops and both can have returning or non-returning nines. Courses with non-returning nines that leave the clubhouse on the 1st tee and return at the 18th green are called **links**, which are common in England and Scotland.

In the United States, most traditional courses, whether private, municipal or daily fee, are core courses contained on a single, consolidated piece of land. In many courses, finger and loop layouts are associated with housing development with golf course frontages. A core golf course with fingers is a self-contained unit. The holes are designed in groups of two, three, or four to radiate out and back from the clubhouse area. Maintenance and control problems are reduced on such compact, self-contained courses. Single and double fairway loop courses require the most acreage but also provide the largest number of frontages for home lots. A core golf course is the best choice for playability and operations.

No golf course is truly popular unless it includes some basic support facilities.

- *Clubhouse.* There should be at least limited food and beverage service for golfers who stop for lunch between nines or after a round. Food service ranges from vending machines to elaborate dining facilities. Most clubhouses include a golf shop, men's and women's lockers, and a golf cart storage shed.
- *Parking.* Separate parking for daily fee and resort guests is preferable. A combined parking area is acceptable after careful land planning.

- *Practice range.* Golfers need a place to loosen up and get warm before engaging holes. A professional golf instructor uses the range when giving lessons. A putting green is desirable at one corner of the range.
- *Additional recreational facilities.* Standalone golf courses need additional recreational facilities like tennis courts, saunas, swimming pools, cabanas, etc. A golf resort accommodates most of these facilities.

The proposed golf resort is planned in terms of three basic components:

- An 18-hole golf course, clubhouse, and maintenance facilities.
- A 100-suite hotel, its associated service areas, conference centers, casino (if approved), shopping, and recreational facilities.
- Acreage for agricultural and horticultural production for cultivating fresh vegetables, flowers, turf building, a barn for riding horses and camels, and forage.

Other characteristics of the self-contained resort hotel for Free Independent Traveler (FIT) and Group markets include:

- A lobby which is expandable to accommodate live entertainment, retail space, and gathering spaces.
- Outdoor yards which are large enough to include water features.
- Guest rooms which are large and can be combined into suites.
- Food and beverage operations which have additional variety for captive resort guests.
- A swimming pool and deck that can be expanded and have more features for adults and children.
- Recreational activities that are diverse.

The hotel must be positioned at a superior location with views of the golf course and the spectacular surrounding environment. This unique setting will give the hotel a superb reputation in the world market. The architecture of the hotel must meet the expectations of guests with its own unique design. Today's resort guests demand many of the comforts they enjoy at home. Smoke-free suites, handicapped access, a children's playroom, a wives' secluded area, and business equipment in suites are standard, and a health club is a must.

For the "rich and famous" to mingle with their own kind, an understated atmosphere of "barefoot elegance," conducive to privacy and community at the same time, is an essential requirement. On the operations and management side, a resort hotel involves creating a finely tuned marketing strategy. The first and most important element of that strategy is to invest in revenue-producing facilities that add permanent long-term value to the development and ensure its sustainability. In resort marketing, excellent public relations, quality of personalized service and word-of-mouth communication are critical. In fact, a high-quality resort does not need to devote a large portion of its operating budget to advertising and promotion after the initial years because its reputation is its main selling factor.

Ultimately, the primary task of developing a successful resort is to plan the right facility at the right place at the right price and at the right time. This task is particularly applicable to the proposed Wadi Mousa Golf Resort and Petra. The region appears to be ready for a destination resort several levels above the quality standards established by four-star hotels in the area.

A detailed building program precedes the design of the golf resort and layout of the golf course. This program for the project was derived from the best comparable resorts around the world. It was based on two- or three-bedroom suites, and a wide array of service facilities were included.

The design theme was selected from the historical context of Petra and Wadi Mousa. Understanding the history and culture of the region is the first step toward interpreting the past and deriving design elements from it. The process is sensitive to the past as well as the present.

The functions of many monuments carved into rocks of Petra are not wholly understood. This does not distract from the impressive imagery and symbolism they convey to the visitor. Carved with rudimentary tools, the sculptured surfaces of canyons, or the colonnaded avenue facing the "agora," or public square, were inspired by precedents set earlier in Greece, Macedonia, and Rome. For example, tombs carved by Lycians in Caunos, near Koycegiz, and Telmessos near Fethiye in Southern Turkey date back to the fourth century BC. These tombs must have inspired Nabataeans when they traveled to these lands in search of trade.

To this day, the artistry of the tomb carvings and their scale are symbolic of the civilization and times of the Nabataean nation. The linear colonnaded avenue with its triple arched gate and the massive ashlar stone construction of the great Nabataean temple, today known as Qasr al-Bint, form contrasts in geometry with the massive rocky bowl formed by surrounding hills. Another inspiration comes from the symbolism of Bab al-Siq as the main entry passageway to Petra. The deep and narrow slit on the ground, claimed to be a miracle of Moses, is majestic. But the Nabataeans also used it to bring water to their community. Channels carved into the walls of the canyon carried water from an ingenious water collection and storage system, which has not been surveyed entirely. These symbols and others are considered and used in the architecture of the resort hotel and layout of the golf course. Collectively, they form the **Petra theme** for the design of the project to achieve a world-class tourist attraction and destination.

Golf Course Design

The proposed golf course and resort has a compact 1,000 dunum (247 acre) site. Due to the challenging configuration of the site, the golf course covers 900 dunum (222 acres). The remaining 100 dunum (25 acres) has been set aside for the resort hotel and occupies the high North-East corner of the site. The 18-hole core type golf course wraps around the resort hotel. The sole access road entering the valley from the South connects to the trail that leads to the Northern territory. Two connecting roads lead to the main and service entrances of the hotel, respectively. The easement for the irrigation line crosses the site under the golf course. All historic artifacts that might exist underneath are protected.

The access road to the hotel divides the golf course into two 9-hole segments. Three underpasses connect the two segments for cart crossing. A utility easement follows the access road. The layout of the golf course is inspired by championship courses in warm and arid climates of the United States. The landscape of the golf course should be dotted with replicated historic theme artifacts chosen for their visual effects. Simulated piles of architectural remains and archeological ruins will be built to orient golfers and inspire them with the historical significance of the area. Artificial materials will be used to imitate real stone. The rest of the landscape outside fairways will be treated with desert planting.

A 2 km long irrigation line, together with distribution boxes, has already been installed from the future wastewater treatment plant to the golf course and beyond. The location and design of pump stations and other elements of the irrigation system have not been completed. At the lowest Western end of the site, a 10 dunum (2.5 acre) retention pond is planned for collecting storm water during the rainy season. The water will be used for fire protection, irrigation and emergency supply.

Walking and riding trails fan out from the resort hotel to various points of interest. Two of these points of interest are a 300-seat amphitheater to be built in a narrow gorge for holding special events. The other is the conical hill immediately to the north of the resort hotel for rock climbing and scenic sightseeing.

Other elements of the site include land for planting feed and fodder for animals; a garden for growing fresh flowers; a tree nursery; a storage shed for hay; a vehicle and equipment maintenance shop; a carpenter shop; a blacksmith shop; and housing for resident employees. These elements are located outside the perimeter of the golf resort to the north. The resort will draw most of its semi-skilled and unskilled employees from Wadi Mousa. They will commute to the resort by a company shuttle bus around the clock. The manager and higher ranking staff will be given their own independent housing accommodations in the project area.

Resort Hotel Design

It is particularly important to keep in mind the purpose of the proposed golf course when designing the resort hotel. The major reason for proposing the luxury hotel is to justify the golf course, which, in turn, will justify a higher and better use for the irrigation water generated by the wastewater treatment plant. Demand for the golf course and resort hotel will be created, and the design of the destination will play an important role in creating that demand. The architecture of the resort, in particular, will have to be highly creative and rich in exceptional recreational experiences for guests. The following design concept is preliminary. It is proposed for the purpose of illustration and for quantifying certain elements.

The proposed design concept is based on creating a hotel in the form of a village inspired by the Petra theme. An atmosphere of "barefoot elegance" in a historic setting will prevail. All 100 suites hotel are arranged on one level along two intersecting axes. This gives all suites a frontage either on the golf course or toward the dramatic rocky surroundings. The east–west axis provides a favorable orientation to a maximum number of suites during the hot hours of the day. Both axes act as open alleyways simulating the meandering streets of Wadi Mousa, from which access is gained to suites. Their intersection forms a village square where multiple events and interaction among guests take place under the cool and dry night sky of Wadi Mousa.

Surrounding rock walls will be lighted in a display of color and shadow to dramatize the setting. During the day, shaded sitting areas and a coffee/tea shop under a vine trellis on the square are possibilities. Arts and crafts and fashion shows, antique sales, live music and dancing could take place under the stars during summer months. The two wings of suites form two quadrangles with their own swimming pools and spas for promoting privacy. The spas are designed separately for men and women where various health-enhancing therapeutic and cosmetic services are offered. Outdoor swimming pools will be inspired by Roman baths.

The western end of the east–west axis is for public areas of the hotel, including reception, shops, two or more restaurants, a clubhouse and other elements in the building program. Arriving guests enter the lobby and reception from a *porte-cochere*. The latter will be weaved by Bedouin women from goat hair simulating their nomadic tents. The 1st and 18th holes will start and end at the nearby clubhouse. A third swimming pool will serve golfers.

Panoramic views of the surrounding hills will make the clubhouse and pool area favorite meeting places for guests.

The exterior architecture of the hotel will be inspired by the frontal elevations of monuments in Petra. Greek and Roman pediments, columns with Doric and Corinthian or Ionic capitals, urns and sculptures will adorn the facades. Stone or stucco finishes are "distressed" to reflect archeological remains. Various shades of earth colors are borrowed from the palette of rock formations around Petra. They will blend the structure of the hotel into its environment. From a distance, the profile of the resort hotel will be one of an ancient settlement that has survived for two thousand years. Close up, the hotel will emerge as a unique combination of up-to-date technology, luxury and elegance.

Various expressions, like "barefoot elegance" or "understated opulence," could best describe these informal but luxurious accommodations. Highly trained staff will provide personalized service to individual guests. Providing privacy, comfort and security will be the primary objectives of the hotel management. The hotel is designed to satisfy the needs and whims of the target market. The hotel will serve almost exclusively the Free Independent Traveler (FIT) and members of the corporate, association and special interest groups. Packaged tours for groups, if or when found to meet the standards of the hotel, will be the exception rather than the rule. Package tours will be received during the slow season. World leaders in arts, entertainment, sports, politics, finance, corporate entities and royalty, alone or with their families, will find the resort as a retreat, ideal for their discreet recreational respite or business dealings.

The core of the hotel is the guest suite. The design of the suite reflects the hotel theme, lifestyle of its guests, and the purpose of their visit, whether it is for business or recreation. The composition, dimensions, space, furniture, equipment and décor in each suite will be selected to match the individual preferences of guests from around the world. Based on time tested standards, the conventional 4 m $\times$ 12 m = 48 m^2 module for guest suites will be modified for the resort project.

- For fifty 2-room suites, 1.5 modules or 6 m $\times$ 12 m = 72 m^2 (775 sf)
- For fifty 3-room suites, 2.5 modules or 10 m $\times$ 12 m = 120 m^2 (1,292 sf)
- For four 4-room guest villas, 3.5 modules or 14 m $\times$ 12 m = 168 m^2 (1,808 sf)
- For one 6-room Royal/Presidential Suite, 5.0 modules or 20, m $\times$ 12, m = 240 m^2 (2,584 sf)

The typical 2-room suite combines four different living zones into one integrated unit: living-dining, atrium-pool, bedroom-bath and patio. Depending on the mood and time of the day, one or the other living zones becomes the focus of guest activities. In particular, the atrium-pool area, open to the sky, will provide a very private inner space separated from adjoining suites by high walls on both sides. If requested by a guest, two adjoining 2-room suites can be combined into one 4-room suite through a two-way connecting door in the living-dining room. This arrangement is particularly suitable for families with children, providing separate but connecting living spaces for parents and children.

The 3-room suite will create the larger accommodation without combining adjoining suites. Again, the unit will have four different living zones: two larger bedrooms with private baths and separate patios, a larger living-dining-study space, and a larger central atrium-pool area, where small private parties can be held.

Efforts will be made to individualize each suite, particularly at the request of regular guests. This might include business oriented suites, recreation oriented suites, or suites decorated in a particular style. This eclectic diversity, both decorative and functional, will be one aspect of the resort hotel which will distinguish it from other world-class resorts. Details like complimentary monogrammed towels and robes, stationary and flower arrangements will be standard items for each suite.

The four guest villas will occupy the two ends of the north and south wings. They will have individualized decors. The Royal/Presidential Suite will be positioned away from the rest of the resort for maximum privacy and security at the end of the east wing. It will have its own private pool. It will not be for the exclusive use of the Royal/Presidential *entourage*, however.

All suites, guest villas, and the Royal/Presidential suite will have individual climate equipment and controls, electrical, sanitary, and communication/TV/entertainment systems. Outside the suites, however, guests will wander through the street/corridor and village square open to the sky to reach the lobby and other public areas. Many interesting details will be built into these areas. The common areas include one or more restaurants specializing in different cuisines. The *ambiance* is uniformly elegant, although the styles are different. One has an outdoor terrace tied to the clubhouse swimming pool patio to be used for private parties. A billiard room, young people's room, and arcade of small shops complete the common areas. Reception, administration, laundry, housekeeping, and employee lockers and showers are behind the walls from common areas. An enclosed service yard and a loading dock will be provided. Two lighted tennis courts with their lights shielded will be available for night tennis. A social director will be responsible for organizing social activities of the resort.

Activity Mix and Seasonality

The golf resort will focus on recreational activities associated with golfing. For golfing purists, the course will provide a challenging golfing experience. Facilities for playing tennis, swimming, horseback riding, rock climbing, hiking and an assortment of other physical activities will be available. Business related activities like attending conferences, meetings and seminars will be possible in elegant surroundings. Families with children will have access to separate activity points like sunning, receiving health care, and playing billiards or computer games. Nights will allow attending concerts, shows, and dining. Sightseeing historic places will be followed by shopping. In short, close to 100 activities in and around the proposed resort will be possible.

Correlation of these activities with four seasons indicates that a year-round resort with very strong attraction qualities is merited. Seasonal variations in use are minimal, suggesting strong demand for all seasons.

Financial Analysis

For basic financial analysis, a simple model driven by comparable hotel suite rates, occupancy, rounds of golf, expenses reflecting the initial cost of constructing the golf course and the hotel, and operating costs, including land lease, irrigation, water costs and landscaping, was used. The analysis is for the first 10 years of operation, excluding 2 years of planning, designing, permitting and construction. Construction cost estimates are based on "unit prices" supplied by the United Enterprise Company, General Contractor, Amman, Jordan, and on "quantities" supplied by the Golf Course Builders Association of America, Jupiter, Florida, United States. The costs, revenues and expenses are shown in Jordanian Dinars, which at the current (year 2000) exchange rate is **1 JD = \$1.41**. (This rate was still 1 JD = \$1.41 in May 2011.)

The cost of the land lease will be set inversely by the cost of irrigation water. The lower the cost of irrigation water, the higher the land lease will be. The land will be leased on a long term basis from the government, and the **lease fee** will be an operating expense for the resort. Topsoil is scarce for growing grass on fairways. It will be brought in. Certain golf course costs like soft costs for design, planning and legal work are not specified at this time but are included in construction costs. The design of the golf course will conform to the standards and design guidelines for a high-end **desert** type course seen in arid parts of the world.

Resort Hotel Construction Cost Estimate in JD

Guest suites and villas	$10,512 \text{ m}^2 \times 1,300 \text{ JD/m}^2 =$	13,665,600 JD
Common areas and areas		
behind homes	$7,008 \text{ m}^2 \times 1,000 \text{ JD/m}^2 =$	7,008,000 JD
Outdoor facilities	$34,480 \text{ m}^2 \times 100 \text{ JD/m}^2 =$	3,448,000 JD
Total hard construction costs		24,121,600 JD
Total soft costs at 10% of hard construction costs (HCC)		2,412,160 JD
Hotel furniture, fixtures and equipment (FF&E) at 15% of HCC		3,618,240 JD
Contingency at 5% of HCC		1,206,080 JD
Total Construction Cost for the Hotel		**31,358,080 JD**

Golf Course Construction Cost Estimate in JD

This figure includes, mobilization, layout, erosion control, land clearing, other selective clearing, on-site topsoil, off-site topsoil, excavation, rough shaping, storm drainage, golf drainage, an irrigation pump station, greens, tees, bunkers, bridges/underpasses, bulkhead, cart paths, fine grading, seedbed preparation, grassing and seed-sprigs-sod.

Hard and soft construction costs	3,925,986 JD
Bonding at 1%	39,260 JD
Total Construction Cost for the Golf Course	**3,965,246 JD**

Golf Clubhouse Construction Cost Estimate in JD

This figure includes men's lockers, toilets, and showers, women's lockers, toilets, and showers, lounge, guests' informal bar and dining roominformal food and beverage dispensing, pro shop, equipment repair space, office and golf cart storage shed.

Total hard construction costs (HCC)	$600 \text{ m}^2 \times 1,000 \text{ JD} =$	600,000 JD
Total soft costs at 20% of HCC		120,000 JD
Furniture, fixture and equipment (FF&E) at 15% of HCC		90,000 JD
Total Construction Cost for the Clubhouse		**810,000 JD**
Grand Total Construction Cost		**36,943,326 JD**
(In U.S. dollars $52,163,976)		

The **revenue assumptions** are:

- Hotel room-suite rates are based on the target market of wealthy, Free Independent Travelers (FIT) and the Group Market, including corporate, association, and special interest groups.
- Hotel occupancy starts low (conservative scenario), based on occupancy rates in the surrounding Petra area, but increases gradually at its own pace as the resort creates its own market.
- Other revenues associated with the resort include food, beverage, telephone, services, etc.

- Golf course and clubhouse revenues include guest/membership dues, greens fees, daily fees for guests, cart fees, food, beverage, merchandise purchases and the driving range.

The **expense assumptions** are:

- Hotel expense assumptions include departmental expenses for rooms, food, beverage, telephone, services, etc. as percentages of line item revenues, undistributed operating expenses for G&A, management, marketing, property operations/maintenance, utilities, insurance, and fixed charges as percentages of general operating revenues.
- Golf clubhouse expense assumptions include the cost of goods sold for food and beverages, merchandise and rental expenses as percentages of line item sales and operating expenses, undistributed expenses, marketing, general and administrative expenses (G&A), and a replacement reserve.
- Golf course expense assumptions include course maintenance, golf operations, carts, pro shop and driving range costs, undistributed expenses, marketing, general and administrative, and irrigation water expenses and the land lease. Marketing expenses will gradually decrease by relying on word-of-mouth.
- Irrigation water will be tied to a long term contract, with the Wastewater Management Authority freezing the price of irrigation water for many years. The same arrangement will be made for the land lease once the appropriate relation between the two is established . Water and land lease prices will be determined by assuming a rate of return acceptable for investors (Minimum: 20%).

The Hotel, Golf Course, and Clubhouse Annual Operating Statement

Revenues	Year 1	Year 10
Hotel operating revenues	13,757,142	26,833,760
Golf course and clubhouse revenues	528,776	1,656,495
Gross operating revenues	14,285,918 JD	28,490,255 JD
Expenses		
Hotel departmental expenses	4,720,960	8,925,509
Hotel undistributed operating expenses	3,439,286	6,708,440
Hotel fixed charges	412,714	805,013
Golf cost of goods sold	76,317	235,016
Golf operating expenses (excluding irrigation)	1,275,444	1,267,309
Irrigation of the golf course	38,880	38,880
Gross operating expenses	9,983,601 JD	18,000,168 JD
Net operating income	**4,302,317 JD**	**10,490,087 JD**

According to the Winter 1999/2000 issue of an annual investor return survey focusing on luxury resorts published by Cushman & Wakefield, an average 13.6% discount rate and an average terminal value multiplier of 9.9 were considered. Taking into account additional capital risks associated with investing in Jordan, the discount rate is adjusted higher, but the terminal value multiplier is kept the same.

Two financial scenarios are prepared. With a *conservative* scenario of lower occupancy rates and fewer golf members, the golf resort can attain an internal rate of return (IRR) between *18%* and *19%*. Using a more *optimistic* scenario with higher occupancy rates and more golf members, the internal rate of return (IRR) can be raised to *22%* or *23%*. Using the conservative scenario of 18% IRR and irrigation water cost of 20 fils/m^3, the income for the government from the land lease will be only 3 JD per dunum. *However, under the less than optimistic scenario for 20% IRR and an irrigation water cost of 20 fils/m^3, the land lease will generate an income of approximately 747 JD per dunum to the government.* As a result, this middle scenario is preferred as the most realistic answer to the question posed by the project. A slight decrease in capital expenditures could markedly increase the IRR. Investors will consider that possibility. From a management viewpoint, higher operating costs for the hotel and the golf course are believed to be controllable and are not likely to increase the risk factor for investors.

Conclusions and Lessons Learned

- Effluents need not be wasted. Water of any kind is precious in dry desert climates. Finding a good use for treated wastewater is an objective of the proposed project. For an internationally acclaimed tourism destination like Petra, it is natural that first priority is given to tourism as a possible user of reclaimed wastewater.
- Creating a new tourism magnet in Petra starts with the reverse process of creating an attraction for a use. Treated wastewater is the use, and the attraction created for it is the golf resort.
- Demand for the new attraction is also created by meeting its conditions. To attract the FIT and Group Market, a very luxurious golf resort and a championship golf course must be created.
- The ultimate pricing of the tourism product and the prices of treated wastewater and the land lease are a function of arriving at a balance between the two prices and ensuring an IRR of 20% acceptable to investors.
- The golf resort will be possible under stable political conditions in Jordan.

Study Questions

- What were the dual objectives and justifications for the project?
- What role does the ancient city of Petra play in creating a destination?
- How will the proposed golf resort satisfy the objectives of the project?
- What will be the components of the regional multiplier effects of the proposed golf resort?

Case Examples 4

Military Sites, Battlefields, and Museums as Historic Tourist Attractions

YEAR:　　　　**From Antiquity to Our Time**

Background

Human conflict seems to be eternal. Resolving conflict by using force has been part of the human species since prehistoric times and does not seem to be fading away. Organized violence, nations fighting for supremacy over one another on land, at sea, or in the air has left behind a multitude of relics, implements, weapons, structures, and lasting memories in all corners of the world. Over time, each nation chose or developed its own means of conquering or defending itself from its enemies. Armed conflict was often central to the "charter events" that many nations use to help legitimize themselves and continue to use to encourage and energize patriotism. Armies, navies, and, more recently, air forces have used changing tactics, weapons, and places of conflict to their advantage. Poor and rich countries alike engaged in these conflicts. Often, innocent third parties took the brunt of the violence. This book is not the place to analyze the causes and consequences of human conflict. However, it is appropriate to note the sacrifices of millions of men and women who found themselves on all sides of these conflicts, lost their property, and at worst lost their lives and the lives of loved ones.

War is intense drama and commands attention. Fascination with human conflict is a major form of tourism around the world. Entire industries have developed around making war. One of these has emerged as a branch of tourism. In addition to military history depicted in films and on television, tour operators, hoteliers, retail and service businesses, publications, souvenir stores, transportation systems, parades, reenactments, commemorations, and museums draw millions of visitors. Weapons of all kinds used in these battles reflect the applications of scientific discoveries on battlefields for achieving military supremacy. A few airworthy World War II airplanes—the B-17 Flying Fortress, B-24 Liberator, Mk II Spitfire, F-51 Mustang, Messerschmitt-109, Nakajima-B5N2 (Kate), and Mitsubishi A6M2 (Zeke) among them—still fly at air shows and fascinate the young and old alike. Remnants of 3,000 behemoths like the Panzer Tiger and Russian T-34 tanks that fought the largest tank battle in history on the plains of Ukraine at Kursk still dot the landscape. Retired and restored galleons, battleships, aircraft carriers, submarines, and aircraft that fought in these battles are preserved as tourist attractions and monuments. Dioramas re-create the battle scenes in miniature. Cannons create key points of interest on pubic property, like memorial sites and city and town halls. Films, and now computer games, simulate the action in these battles in detail. Toy soldiers dressed in period uniforms bring to life in children's mind imaginary battlefields.

Replicas of historic oared ships like the trireme, galley, and bireme rest in the museums of old Mediterranean ports. The Viking ship *Osberg* is located in the Oslo Museum in Norway. The two oldest existing commissioned warships, Admiral Nelson's flagship at Trafalgar, *Victory*, rests on dry dock in Portsmouth, England, and the *USS Constitution* is docked in the water at a pier in Boston. They are the scenes of many sea battles that draw thousands of visitors. The human-powered *Turtle*, dating back to the American Revolution in 1776, was one of the precursors of modern submarines. Replicas of it can be found in museums in Groton and Essex, Connecticut, in the United States and in Gosport in England. The first nuclear submarine, the *USS Nautilus*, is on display in Groton, Connecticut. The last of the commissioned battleships, the *USS Missouri*, the Big Mo, is tied at Pearl Harbor near the *USS Arizona* Memorial. The *USS Massachusetts* is docked in Fall River, Massachusetts, and the *USS Alabama* rests in Mobile, Alabama. They are the centerpieces of war memorials, with many other types of vessels around them. The captured German submarine U-505 is a major attraction at the Museum of Science and Technology in Chicago. Many losing and winning warships rest on the bottom of oceans around the world where they sank and became permanent tombs to thousands of brave sailors. The *HMS Hood* lies in the North Sea, the *USS Yorktown* at Midway, and the *Bismarck* in the East Atlantic; the mighty *Yamato,* one of the two largest battleships ever built, rests off Kyushu, Japan. They are visited by boatloads of visitors on the anniversary of their demise.

Famous battles on land and sea are remembered by visiting their battlegrounds. Carthage, Thermopylae, Kosovo, the conquest of Constantinople, Preveza, the Spanish Armada, Trafalgar, Navarino Bay, Lexington/Concord, Wounded Knee, Shiloh, Bull Run, the Alamo, Gettysburg, Waterloo, Austerlitz, Gallipoli, Jutland, Sakarya, Blitzkrieg, the Battle of Britain, Stalingrad, Battle of the Atlantic, Kursk, Battle of the Bulge, Pearl Harbor, Coral Sea, Midway, Guadalcanal, Iwo Jima, Okinawa, Al-Alamein, Normandy, Pusan Perimeter, Inchon, and the Tet Offensive are only a very small sample of human conflict where valor and ultimate sacrifice were the norm.

Often, these conflicts are remembered by the military leaders who fought them. Hannibal in Carthage; the Spartans in Thermopylae; Sultan Murad I and King Lazar in Kosova; Fatih Sultan Mehmet in Constantinople; Admiral Barbaros Hayreddin and Andrea Doria in Preveza; Admiral Nelson in Aboukir Bay and Trafalgar; Admiral Drake against the Spanish Armada; Wellington in Waterloo; Napoleon in Austerlitz; David Crockett, James Bowie, William Travis, and Santa Ana at the Alamo; General Custer and Native American Sioux and Cheyenne Chiefs Sitting Bull and Crazy Horse in the Battle of Little Big Horn; Generals Grant and Lee in the American Civil War; Mustafa Kemal (Ataturk) in Gallipoli and Sakarya; Admirals Jellicoe and Scheer in Jutland; General Von Runstedt in Blitzkrieg; Air Marshall Dowding at the Battle of Britain; Marshal Zhukov and Marshal Von Paulus in Stalingrad; Admiral Donitz in the Battle of the Atlantic; General Hoth and General Vatutin in the Kursk tank battle; Admiral Yamamoto at Pearl Harbor and Midway; Admiral Halsey in the Coral Sea; Admiral Nimitz and General MacArthur in all Pacific battles during World War II; Generals, Eisenhower, Bradley, and Patton on the European Front of World War II; Field Marshal Montgomery and Marshal Rommel in Al-Alamein and the European Front; and General Westmoreland and General Giap in Vietnam are names of military leaders who served their countries in many military conflicts.

Collections of weapons used in these battles are widely scattered around the world. Countries that excelled in military technology and conquest have by far the most extensive collections. From armors for men and beasts, shields, bows and arrows, clubs, catapults, knives and swords to rifles, cannons, bombs, grenades, tanks, aircraft, rockets, and other weapons and implements of destruction are on display in armories and military museums. Live demonstrations depict important military routines like changing of the guards, display of uniforms, bands, and music daily. Lectures by scholars analyze historic military events.

Over a thousand years ago, the Chinese discovered the black powder that we know today as gunpowder. They used it for entertainment in pyrotechnic displays. The Western world used it for changing the concept of warfare. Gunpowder found its application in large cast bronze cannons that knocked holes in perimeter walls surrounding cities under siege. Until gunpowder arrived, infantries and cavalries armed with shields, clubs, swords, axes, spears, and bows and arrows walked and rode to a plain nearby and confronted each other at a throwing distance. They hacked, slashed, whacked, stabbed, and clubbed each other until no adversary was left standing. Some of their infantry tactics are still being taught in military schools today. Gunpowder gradually changed the warfare from an offensive to a defensive action. Defense against cannons and bullets consisted of building fortifications. The defenders hid behind high walls, ditches, moats, and towers, and in tunnels and caves, storing enough food and water to outlast their determined attackers. In modern times, this defensive mode resulted in sophisticated but still fixed defenses. More recently, World War II brought mobile warfare to battlefields and advanced the concept that "the best defense is a good offense."

Thousands of stone fortifications survived the ravages of time. Wood fortifications rarely did. One of the oldest and largest fortifications is the Great Wall of China. It protected the Chinese dynasties from the onslaught of Mongol hordes attacking from the north. Its building started in the fifth century BC. It has many branches more than 6,000 km (3,700 miles) long. Today, crumbling in most places but restored in a few, the Great Wall is accessible from Beijing after a short ride. It attracts large crowds of visitors and has helped reintroduce the world to ancient Chinese civilization.

Other prominent military fortifications include the walls around the Old City of Jerusalem. They were built by the Ottoman Sultan Suleyman the Magnificent between 1536 and 1541. Carcasson and Mount St. Michel in France are unique examples of advanced fortifications. In more recent times, the trenches of the Western Front stretched for many miles during World War I. They were replaced by more permanent fortifications in World War II. The Maginot Line in France and the Sigfried Line in Germany had underground tunnels and living quarters, fortified and fixed gun emplacements, and tank barriers. They were unable to stop invasions from both sides. Similar Normandy fortifications faced the English Channel to prevent the amphibious invasion of Europe by Allied forces in World War II. They were unable to stop the Allied landings, albeit at great cost of human life to both sides. The U-boat pens in Brest, Saint Nazaire, and La Rochelle in France and Trondheim in Norway protected the German submarines when they were in port inside thick concrete bunkers. But in the later years of the war, the submarines were decimated by the Allied navies once they ventured into the Atlantic Ocean. On the Pacific front of World War II, the fortifications at Corregidor Island in the Philippines gave American forces time to organize and retaliate against the Japanese. The caves, tunnels, and gun emplacements dug into the volcanic rocks of Iwo Jima were effective in defending the island against American marines when the tide turned. The bloody battle that ensued was costly in human lives to both sides.

Today, monuments, cemeteries, landmarks, historic sites, national parks, museums, battle reenactments, and many anniversaries and ceremonies honor the memories of those who died in these conflicts. The fortifications are protected as lasting examples of humanity's ability to ensure that following generations comprehend the ferocity of wars fought. These military sites and event attractions draw visitors by the millions throughout the year from distant lands and from among former foes and friends alike. Only a sample of selected military attractions and facilities that have been left behind for tourists are described here to illustrate how they were turned into assets for tourism development. Some military grounds and battlefields are sites for major works of art that are attractions in their own right. For example, the Gettysburg battlefield is a national military park with a number of statues of generals on their horses that are excellent examples of late-nineteenth- and early-twentieth-century heroic sculpture created by well-known sculptors.

Examples of Military Site and Event Attractions

The Conquest of Constantinople and the Istanbul Military Museum

The Byzantine land walls surrounding ancient Constantinople (Istanbul), originally the seat of the Eastern Roman Empire, extend from the Sea of Marmara to the Golden Horn isolating the peninsula from mainland Europe. These walls are about 6.5 km (4 mi) long. They protected Byzantium from its enemies for a thousand years and greatly influenced the history of medieval Europe. The land walls were mostly constructed during the reign of Byzantine Emperor Theodosius II in the first half of the fifth century AD. Constantinople withstood twenty-nine sieges conducted by a multitude of Christian and Muslim armies including Crusaders and Arabs. After a siege lasting for fifty-three days, the young Ottoman Sultan Mehmed II breached the western walls, with large cannons cast by a Hungarian named Urban, and took the city from its defender, the last emperor of Byzantium, Constantine Dragozes Paleolog, on Tuesday, May 29, 1453. The military strategy used by Mehmed II was unique in its creativity and daring. He surrounded the city from land and sea. He had the largest bronze cannons cast to that date. Their diameter was 24 inches. They were capable of throwing a projectile weighing one ton a distance of one mile. Mehmed battered the walls of Constantinople from land and sea. He made the first use of mortars to demolish the Byzantine navy hiding behind the heavy chain stretched across the Golden Horn. His ships could not break through the chain and encircle the city from the sea. He decided to transport about seventy of his oared and sailing ships overland from the Bosphorus to the Golden Horn. During the night of April 21–22, 1453, thousands of soldiers and sailors, with the help of unfurled sails and cattle, pulled the ships over wood planks lubricated by olive oil and slid the vessels into the Golden Horn. When the defenders of Constantinople woke the next morning, they saw the Ottoman fleet behind their defenses with their guns aimed at their walls. The encirclement of the city and the destruction of the Byzantine fleet were complete. It took another month to break through the walls from all sides. Hand-to-hand combat ensued. The Byzantine emperor died fighting for his city. Three days after its capture, Sultan Mehmed II granted amnesty to all surviving residents and defenders of the city and gave them their freedom. On Friday, June 1, 1453, he went to the magnificent Saint Sophia Church—converted to a mosque after the fall of the city—and prayed for the fallen Muslim and Christian soldiers.

The artifacts, uniforms, and weapons of the Battle of Constantinople are now preserved among the extensive collection of the Istanbul Military Museum. The origins of the museum date back to 1726, when the military collection accumulating since the conquest of Istanbul by the Ottoman Turks was first gathered at an old Byzantine church. The most recent museum building was completed in 1993. Its content exceeds nine thousand items carefully selected from a collection of fifty thousand. The museum is more than a depository. It incorporates all the elements of modern museums and serves as a center for cultural displays, research, military technology, and education. The galleries displaying rare military artifacts used by the Ottoman army and its adversaries since 1453 include bows and arrows, cavalry scimitars and other swords and knives, armory, artillery, and uniforms. The museum also covers the First World War, Gallipoli, the War of Turkish Independence, establishment of the Republic of Turkey, the Korean War, ethnography, military tents, flags, uniforms, paintings, General and President Kemal Ataturk, presidents of the republic, chiefs of staff, and heroes of the republic. For centuries, military operations were accompanied by military music. In boosting the morale of Turkish warriors and spreading fear among their adversaries, the

Mehter was most effective. The military band dates back to the Selchuk Turks of the early twelfth century AD. The authentic musical instruments used by the *Mehter* include a variety of wind and percussion instruments, among them cymbals and *Kös,* the large drum that can be heard from miles away. The *Mehter* band is composed of up to forty-eight musicians wearing their traditional Ottoman uniforms and standing in a half-circle around the *Kös* and the conductor. The elaborate traditional ceremony and concert are presented during the visiting hours of the museum by the *Mehter,* which is composed of musicians in active Turkish military service.

The Tower of London, England

(Attracted 2,161,095 visitors in 2008, up 9.6% from 2007)

The Tower of London was built by William the Conqueror (AD 1066–1100) for the purpose of protecting and controlling the city. London lays within the old Roman city walls. After many expansions over the centuries, it now covers an area of 18 acres. Of the present buildings, only the White Tower is of the Norman period. The other buildings, structures, and fortifications represent an array of architectural styles. The Tower has in the past been a fortress, a palace, and a prison and has housed the Royal Mint, the Public Records, and the Royal Observatory. It was for centuries the arsenal for small arms and guarded the crown jewels of England.

The oldest and most important building is the Great Tower or Keep, also called the White Tower. The Inner Ward is defended by a wall containing thirteen towers. The only surviving original entrance is under the Bloody Tower. The Outer Ward is defended by a second wall flanked by six towers facing the River Thames, where access to the Tower was gained from the river through Traitor's Gate under the St. Thomas Tower. A ditch or moat, now dry, encircles the whole complex. It is crossed by a drawbridge that leads to the Byward Tower.

The Tower of London has always contained an armory. The present collection took its shape in the reign of Henry VIII (1509–1547). The enormous body armors of Henry VIII and his horse are displayed in the Tudor Gallery in the White Tower. After the restoration of 1660, when body armor had fallen largely into disuse, Charles II concentrated the collection of small arms and armor at the Tower. The historical Line of Kings was set up during his reign. At various times, additions and alterations were made to increase the exhibit areas for, among others, displaying the body armor worn throughout Europe. The Royal Exhibits remain and tie the armories to the history of England. After the introduction of gunpowder, for nearly two centuries weapons of offense were supreme. Helmets and body armor returned to the battlefield in World War I (1914–1918) and have been widely used by military and police forces around the world ever since.

Various galleries in the White Tower contain weapons dating back to the Middle Ages that were used for sport and battle. There is a fine collection of crossbows for the hunt and for target shooting, elegant silver-mounted hunting swords, and a great variety of firearms, from massive elephant guns to richly decorated fowling pieces. Different types of armor developed for jousting are on display. Scales models demonstrate the evolution of medieval armor. The "giant" armor for a man about 6 ft 10 in. (2.08 m) in height is a centerpiece in one gallery. The Mortar Room and the Cannon Room contain a variety of bronze mortars, cannons, and other ordinance, some dredged from the bottom of the sea. The nefarious Bowyer Tower now houses a collection of instruments of torture and punishment, including the block and axe that were used to behead Queen Ann Boleyn and many others.

The Imperial War Museum, London, England

(Attracted 833,893 visitors in 2008, up 11% from 2007)

The history of war and weapons reached its climax with World War I. In 1917, the English government decided that a national war museum should be set up to collect and display weapons and artifacts relating to the war. The interest expressed by the then colonies led to the museum's being called the Imperial War Museum.

The museum was opened in the Crystal Palace by King George V on June 9, 1920. From 1924 to 1935 it was housed in two galleries adjoining the former Imperial Institute in South Kensington. On July 7, 1936, the Duke of York, shortly to become King George VI, reopened the museum in its present location, the former Bethlem Royal Hospital building. The east and west wings were demolished in the early 1930s to make room for the park that now surrounds the museum.

The Imperial War Museum is an unusual place in many ways. Poignantly, it is a museum devoted to modern war housed in an ancient mental hospital. The collections range from tanks and guns to works of art and films, but their focus is human behavior. The museum deals with many controversial and often unpleasant topics. It also reflects the exceptional qualities of courage and self-sacrifice that are brought out by war. Conscientious objectors as well as military heroes are represented. The stories of the front line and the home front are equally present.

The diversity of interest and the all-embracing nature of modern war make the museum perhaps the most comprehensive war museum of the twentieth century. Its primary role is educational. The museum achieves this goal by blending the facts with hundreds of interesting exhibits. The ground floor has a large atrium opening to the sky. Large exhibits, including tanks, cannons, airplanes, and temporary exhibits, a cinema, a gift shop, a cafe, and a reception and information areas are contained here. The same exhibits can be observed from the first-floor viewing gallery. The top floor is reserved for art galleries and administration. The below-ground level is reserved for World War I (1914–1918) exhibits including full-scale replicas of living and fighting in the trenches, war in the air, war at sea, the Gallipoli episode, and the home front. World War II (1939–1945) exhibits include the decades leading to war, the Blitzkrieg, the Battle of Britain, the home front, war at sea, the Mediterranean and Middle East fronts, the Eastern Front, Europe under the Nazis, concentration camps, the bomber offensive, North and West Europe, the war in the Far East, and Victoria Cross medal recipients.

The museum's administration includes a Department of Documents, a Department of Printed Books, a Department of Art, a Department of Sound Records, a Department of Film, and a Department of Photographs. Other related exhibits and museums include the Cabinet War Rooms of Winston Churchill reinforced against bombs under a government building, the Duxford Airfield displaying one hundred twenty aircraft and many exhibits, and the *HMS Belfast,* the last surviving big gun ship of the Royal Navy, which is permanently moored opposite the Tower of London on the River Thames as a floating naval museum.

United States Naval Memorials

The United States has been the world's dominant naval military power since World War II. The mighty fleet that won the Pacific and Atlantic Ocean wars was composed of untold numbers of small and large vessels at the end of the war. These vessels witnessed many acts of human courage and heroism. As the years went by, they were retired in increasing numbers and were replaced by more modern ships. Some were upgraded and had a second life in the

Korean War and the Gulf War. Many ships, commemorated in glorious written and verbal histories, were retired into mothball fleets. Many were towed to scrap yards and lost forever. A few, however, survived through the loving care and persistent efforts of their former crews. Energetic fund-raising saved some of the ships that played major roles in, and were the focus of, many naval victories. The authorities transferred their ownership to nonprofit corporations for operating them as naval memorials. Many U.S. naval memorials are members of an international organization, the Historic Naval Ships Association, with more than one hundred organizations in thirteen countries, and a total of more than ten million visitors per year at all the organization's sites.

The *USS Arizona* is the most revered ship in the U.S. Navy. It lies under the waters of Pearl Harbor Battleship Row. It is the final resting place of one thousand sailors who died during the December 7, 1941, attack by Japanese warplanes. The memorial structure crosses over the beam of the sunken ship. Visitors are ferried to the memorial from the mainland by boat. An estimated one to one and a half million people visit it each year. The names of the military personnel who lost their lives during the attack on the ship are carved permanently into the marble walls of the memorial. It is a National Historic Landmark. The battleship *USS Missouri*, which hosted the formal surrender of the Japanese Empire at the end of World War II on its deck while anchored on that memorable day, September 2, 1945, in Tokyo Bay now is permanently docked as a museum nearby.

Courage comes alive at the 175-acre **Battleship Memorial Park**, located along the shores of Mobile Bay, Alabama. The visitor experiences heroism spanning more than seven decades from World War II to Desert Storm. The mighty battleship *USS Alabama* is the recipient of nine Battle Stars in World War II. The valiant warship served as home to two thousand five hundred Navy seamen and marines. The Mighty A first saw action in the Atlantic. Then in mid-1943, it joined the Pacific Fleet and fought heroically at Leyte, the Gilbert Islands, and Okinawa. At the end of the war, in September 1945, it proudly led the American Fleet into Tokyo Bay. The exhibits include a video presentation on the main deck and living and working quarters on the decks below. Nearby stands the submarine *USS Drum*, hero of America's silent service. It earned twelve Battle Stars for valor in World War II. An exhibit shows how modern-day engineering helped to rescue the aging submarine from the ravages of time. Many of these ships have been declared National Historic Landmarks. Other exhibits in the park include an Iraq War tank, a Vietnam PBR river patrol boat, and an aircraft pavilion dedicated to the twenty-eight Medal of Honor recipients from Alabama, displaying the Corsair, P51-D Mustang Redtail (the kind flown by the Tuskagee Airmen, America's first African-American military aviators), the B-52 Stratofortress, and the super-secret A-12 Blackbird spyplane aircraft.

A similar array of ships is on display at **Battleship Cove** in Fall River, Massachusetts. It contains the world's largest collection of twentieth-century U.S. naval warships. These include the famed battleship *USS Massachusetts*, the submarine *USS Lionfish*, the destroyer *USS Joseph P. Kennedy, Jr.*, the cruiser *USS Fall River*, and Elco-Class and Higgins-Class patrol torpedo (PT) boats. It also includes the *Hiddensee*, a Soviet-built missile corvette formerly in service in the East German Navy. Next to Battleship Cove is the Fall River Heritage State Park, which has a waterfront esplanade, harbor boardwalk, visitor center, and boathouse. Also nearby is a Marine Museum, containing a collection of model ships and a large exhibit of *HMS Titanic* memorabilia, including a 28-foot model of the passenger ship. These ships and the museum, along with an old-fashioned working carousel on the property, form a large enough attraction to draw hundreds of thousands of visitors each year. A number of memorial services are held on the properties, which increases the overall annual attendance.

The **National Museum of the Pacific War**, formerly known as the Nimitz Museum, honoring the five-star Fleet Admiral Chester Nimitz, is located in his birthplace in Fredericksburg, Texas. The main structure of the museum, now restored, was once a hotel and belonged to Admiral Nimitz's grandfather. The personal life of the admiral is presented in a separate room. At the peak of his naval career, Admiral Nimitz held awesome power, comparable to that of all admirals preceding him combined. The large Japanese vice admiral's flag was taken from the battleship *Nagato*, which had been Admiral Yamamoto's flagship. Interesting episodes of the war in the Pacific are depicted in separate exhibits. They include the role of submarines, the Doolittle-Halsey Tokyo raid, Bataan and Corregidor, the Battle of the Coral Sea, Codebreakers and the Battle of Midway, Bloody Bunya, Guadalcanal, the Yamamoto Incident, the Naval Battles of the Solomons, islands and atolls, island hopping, Turn on the Lights for night landings, Coastwatchers, Codetalkers, the story of the B-29, the Battle for Leyte Gulf, Bloody Iwo Jima, and dropping of the atomic bomb. The name of Admiral Nimitz was commemorated with the naming in 1975 of the nuclear-powered aircraft carrier *USS Nimitz*.

The expanded galleries of the museum now include the Admiral Nimitz Museum depicting Admiral Nimitz's life and career; the George H. Bush Gallery describing the beginning of the Pacific War; the Center for Pacific War Studies consisting of the research library and collections; the Pacific Combat Zone presenting samples of tanks, planes, and living history; the Memorial Wall dedicated to the participants of the war; the Plaza of the Presidents, including ten national leaders from all nations who had a hand in World War II; and the Garden of Peace, a gift from the people of Japan. A nine-member commission appointed by the Texas state legislature oversees the operations of the museum. The Admiral Nimitz Foundation provides financial assistance and raises funds for the maintenance and expansion of the museum.

The Japanese Garden of Peace was a gift from the Japanese nation to the people of the United States after World War II ended. The symbols used in the design of the landscape and water pond are typical Shinto Japanese. The small stream represents the River of Life, and the expanse of white gravel is the Endless Sea. Carefully raked stones represents waves; larger rocks represent islands. The exact replica of Admiral Togo's study cottage was made and assembled in Japan, and was taken apart and reassembled in Fredricksburg without using any nails. It is intended to invite meditation. On the way out from the garden, the History Walk of the Pacific War depicts famous ships and events of the war. The stone memorial at the entrance to the garden summarizes the lessons learned from the conflict between the two nations. It reads: "The Garden of Peace is a gift to the people of the United States from the people of Japan with prayers for everlasting world peace through the goodwill of our two nations symbolized by the friendship and respect that existed between Admiral Togo and Admiral Nimitz."

The Alamo

(Attracts over 2.5 million visitors each year)

To Americans, the Alamo is the symbol for which the United States stands. Pursuit of freedom, self-sacrifice for the good of the nation, courage in the face of seemingly superior forces, and ordinary men doing extraordinary feats describe the American spirit. All of these themes came together in March 6, 1836, at an abandoned mission, the Alamo, located on a dusty plain in Texas. Together with the name of the mission, the names of David Crockett, William Travis, James Bowie, and Antonio Lopez de Santa Ana were forever entered into the annals of American and Mexican history.

In 1820, a Connecticut native, Moses Austin, agreed to bring three hundred settlers to Spanish Texas and secured a land grant. His son, Stephen Austin, and the settlers were attracted to Texas by promises of deferred taxation and land. In exchange, they declared their loyalty to their adopted country. Nevertheless, deep-rooted American independence and republicanism prevented genuine loyalty and acceptance of Spanish religious and political institutions. Austin discovered that there was more to Spanish Texas then met the eye. Mexicans were ready to declare their independence from Spain. Their new constitution was patterned after the U.S. Constitution. Two factions competed for power. The conservative *centralistas* were against American settlers. The liberal *federalistas* supported the settlers for bringing economic growth to the region.

Corruption, graft, and oppression of the weak were rampant. Finally, in 1834, Santa Ana took control of the government, abolished the 1825 Mexican Constitution, and dismissed the congress. American settlers named themselves Texians and opposed Santa Ana. Texas was populated at the time by Indian tribes and by Tejano, Anglo, and African settlers. The largest community was San Antonio de Bexar. The Anglo settlers had fought and defeated England twice. They were not going to submit to the rule of dictator Santa Ana. A few skirmishes followed. The settlers talked about setting up a provisional government independent of Mexico. As dictator, Santa Ana would not tolerate insurrection and separatism in his domain. He moved his army toward the seat of the rebels in San Antonio de Bexar.

Young American men eager to follow in their settler fathers' footsteps left for the new frontier in Texas to help those they believed to be their fellow citizens. They came from all areas of the country. Groups known as the New Orleans Greys, the Alabama Red Rovers, the Kentucky Mustangs, and the Tennessee Mounted Volunteers joined their countrymen. Their desire to be free of oppression united them against Santa Ana. In December 1835, about three hundred Texians led by Colonel Ben Milam attacked the Mexican garrison at San Antonio. The Mexicans retreated to the abandoned Mission Alamo within shouting distance of the San Fernando church, the seat of the Mexican garrison. They fortified the mission compound with guns and other defensive improvements. The following attack by the Texians ended with the surrender of the Mexican garrison at the Alamo. The Mexican soldiers under the command of General Martin Perfecto de Cos were allowed to leave and head south. Texians under the command of Colonel James C. Neill took control of the Alamo compound. A large booty of gunpowder, muskets, and other weapons, clothing, blankets, field kitchens, wagons, beds, horses, donkeys, and oxen were captured.

In the days that followed, many Texians thought the war was over and went back home. About 120 men were left in the Alamo with Colonel Neill. James Bowie, a well-known Indian fighter and famous for his use of the "Bowie knife," arrived on January 19, 1836, with 30 men. The work of transforming the mission into a fort continued. On February 3, William B. Travis, a young lawyer who practiced in San Felipe, arrived with about 30 men. On February 8, the legendary hunter, adventurer, fighter, and later twice Tennessee legislator and three times U.S. congressman David Crockett arrived with his Tennessee Mounted Volunteers. He was a natural leader. Not anticipating immediate danger from Santa Ana, more local militia men left the compound to tend their affairs at home. By February 10, 1836, the Texian garrison at the Alamo numbered only 142 men and a few women with children. Colonel Neill left the Alamo for unknown reasons. Travis and Bowie shared the command of the fort. Soon afterward, Bowie was incapacitated by a serious illness and was confined to the barracks. Travis took full command. The advanced guard of Santa Ana's army was sighted on February 23 on the outskirts of San Antonio. The Texians were ordered to regroup at the Alamo.

The former mission and chapel, now fortified and converted into a defensive fortification, became the home of its Texian defenders. Since its beginning as a collection of crude huts on San Pedro Creek in 1718, San Antonio's first mission, San Antonio de Valero, seemed destined for oblivion rather than immortality. Its construction on a two-story stone structure was completed in 1727. Containing living quarters, offices, a dining hall, and kitchens, it was to become as famous as the Long Barrack during the Alamo siege. The present stone church of the mission was begun in 1758. However, it was never completed during the mission days. A series of epidemics depopulated most of the Texas missions, and the Alamo was abandoned. Spanish cavalry moved into the abandoned mission and occupied it until Mexican troops took over in 1821.

The mission complex consisted of modest accommodations. When the defenders took the Alamo from Santa Ana's General Cos, the complex included the chapel, a horse corral, a cattle corral, and a large courtyard surrounded by high walls and several barracks. A gap existed between the chapel and the nearest barrack. Water was taken from the nearby San Antonio River. The defense of the complex was fortified with 3-, 8-, 12-, and 18-pound cannons. The gap between the chapel and barrack was closed with a stockade. The Alamo garrison consisted of 189 to 257 men. The men of the Alamo used everything they could find to defend the Alamo. Cut-up chains, horseshoes, and scrap iron transformed 3-pound cannons into giant shotguns. These men were not professional soldiers, but they knew how to use long rifles, shotguns, muskets, pistols, and cannons.

The Mexican assault force of Santa Ana, dressed in their Napoleonic uniforms, consisted of about six thousand five hundred soldiers, including about five hundred reserves. William B. Travis answered Santa Ana's surrender ultimatum with a cannon shot. For twelve days, the defenders of the Alamo withstood the bombardment and attacks of the Mexican Army. With their ammunition and supplies all but exhausted, they awaited the inevitable. On the morning of March 6, 1836, at about 5:30 A.M., Santa Ana gave the signal to attack. With bugles sounding the dreaded "Deguello"—no quarters to the defenders—Mexican soldiers attacked the walls from the east, west, south, and north. Total confusion ensued. Men, cannons, and anything handy were thrown into the melee. Unsheathing his sword during a lull, William B. Travis drew a line on the ground before his battle-weary men. He described the hopelessness of their plight and said, "Those prepared to give their lives in freedom's cause, come over to me." Without hesitation, every man but one crossed the line. James Bowie, stricken with pneumonia, asked that his cot be carried over the line.

Finally, Mexican soldiers climbed the 12-foot walls. Hand-to-hand combat left dead and dying men by the dozens. The first to get hit was William B. Travis. After unloading both barrels of his shotgun, he received a mortal bullet wound on his head and died on the north wall he was defending. Mexican soldiers fought their way to the Long Barrack and blasted its massive doors open with a cannon shot. Its defenders, asking no quarter and receiving none, were put to death with grapeshot, musket fire, and bayonets. The delirious James Bowie was too sick to leave his bed. He rose and sat there with his gun and his famous Bowie knife in his hands. His pistol emptied and knife bloodied, his body riddled with a volley from Mexican soldiers, he died on his cot. Greatly outnumbered, about seventy-five defenders attempted to escape from the Alamo and jumped over the wall. The Mexicans were ordered not to take prisoners. All of the escaping Texians were killed by Mexican lancers. The defenders made a final stand inside the chapel. David Crockett, who was in charge of defending it, retreated with his men inside the church. By one account, he was killed fighting outside the chapel while using his empty rifle as a club. By another account, Mexican soldiers blasted the doors of the chapel down and overwhelmed the surviving Texians.

General Manuel Fernandez Castrillon spared the lives of six men and David Crockett. He presented the prisoners to Santa Ana, who ordered their immediate execution. Many other surviving defenders were slashed to death with swords. The official death toll among the defenders was 189, but unofficially as many as 257 Texans may have died. The Mexicans may have suffered as many as 600 deaths. Santa Ana minimized the importance of his losses, but his aide declared that one more victory with similar losses would be the end of the Mexican Army.

The defenders were not zealots bent on ritual suicide. They fervently hoped that their ultimate sacrifice would prove unnecessary. They were citizen soldiers defending their next of kin. The slaughter at the Alamo awakened the Texians to the fact that the war with Mexico was not over. It forcefully drove home the reality that they had to come together and fight the enemy or lose their independence. The defenders of the Alamo quickly became legends for books and, later, films. The three famous defenders became role models for their bravery. Ironically, if Santa Ana had been willing to take prisoners, he would have deprived the battle of its moral power. The fall of Travis, Bowie, Crockett, and the other brave men provided a potent rallying symbol, filling Texians with righteous anger. Forty-six days after the fall of the Alamo, Santa Ana met his own destiny at the battle of Jacinto, northeast of present-day Houston. Less than eight hundred angry Texans and volunteers led by General Sam Huston launched a furious attack, shouting "Remember the Alamo!" They completely routed the remaining Mexican army of fifteen hundred in a matter of minutes. Santa Ana was captured. The Alamo became a very important icon in the annals of American history.

Time and winds have changed the surface of the Alamo battlefield. In 1836, the main plaza of the fort contained almost three acres, making the defensive perimeter approximately a quarter of a mile long. Most of the perimeter buildings and barracks were destroyed. Battered during the battle, the mission buildings remained untouched until 1849, when they were repaired by the U.S. Army. The church, in use as a warehouse, was purchased by the State of Texas in 1883. In 1876, a frame roof was erected over the walls of the Long Barrack. Offered for sale as a hotel site in 1903, it was purchased by a benefactor, Clara Driscoll, a member of the Daughters of the Republic of Texas, a civic organization. In 1905, the state repaid the benefactor for the Long Barrack property and placed the entire property in the custody of the Daughters of the Republic of Texas "to be maintained in good order and repair," without financial assistance from the state. To this day, the Daughters of the Republic of Texas take care of the historic site without accepting city, state, or federal funding and without charging an admission fee, relying solely on generous donations and proceeds made from their sales at the gift shop.

Today, the Alamo no longer resembles a makeshift fort. The site is surrounded by the growing city of San Antonio. The facade of the church, now a famous landmark, opens to a plaza and a park cleared from the urban debris of years of neglect. Luxury hotels, shopping malls, and the well-known Riverwalk have been built nearby. A new museum and gift shop building stands in the interior courtyard. Inside and outside yards have been landscaped to accommodate large crowds of visitors. The Long Barrack has been converted into the Republic of Texas Museum. The chapel is now called the Shrine in honor of the men who died there. The interior of the Shrine has been rebuilt, and the wood frame roof has been replaced by a concrete vault enclosure. The earth ramp built by the defenders during the siege to place a cannon at the level of the high window on the wall has been removed. Artifacts pertaining to the Alamo's heroes who died in the battle of 1836 are also exhibited in the former church. The famous Bowie knife is among them. Pictures of the existing site are contained on the following Web site. http://thealamo.org/.

It is interesting to note that many tourists want to visit a battleground. Instead, they find a shrine at the site of the original battle. One of the most famous battlegrounds of early American history is now a monument, a tranquil haven amid a bustling city. Nevertheless, those old stones retain their ability to awe and inspire. Tourists find the excitement of the battle in the movie set of film star John Wayne's 1960 epic *The Alamo* in Bracketville, a small town 100 miles southwest of San Antonio. The movie set is located on a remote plain of Texas where the original 1836 battle scene is replicated to close specifications. Having seen that film, tourists have an increased appreciation of the reconstruction of the battle scene. Many say that they learned more about the battle from walking around this replica Alamo than they gleaned from the real one. Children especially enjoy the Alamo Village, where they can give their imagination free rein without being overwhelmed by the atmosphere of solemnity found in the original structure.

Evaluation

Military attractions and facilities are major tourist draws. Patriotism, defense of freedom, founding of countries, territorial expansion or conflict, and the ambitions of a malevolent monarch, dictator, or political regime were among the factors that caused conflicts among nations and have resulted in the loss of millions of lives over many centuries. Advancing technology enabled the creation and use of ever-deadlier weapons of war and destruction. Participants in some recent conflicts find solace in visiting their fallen comrades buried in military cemeteries in distant lands. Preserving the artifacts and facts of history left behind by the participants of these conflicts has become a large industry. A whole service industry evolved around these attractions. Hotels, gift shops, and museums surround restored castles and preserved battlefields. As a whole, these historic sites serve to immortalize the heroism of the few, the sacrifices of the many, and the inhumanity of humans to fellow humans.

Fascination with military history and conflict of any description seems to endure. War is high drama. Depending on their size, brutality, heroism, and importance in changing the course of history, military attractions will continue to draw visitors. Old combatants will come from around the world to relive the memories of international conflicts fought, from participating nations to honor the fallen soldiers sailors and airmen who died in defense of their nation, and even from communities where local heroes are remembered.

Governments and civic organizations work together closely to preserve the past and honor the dead. Special events are organized around them regularly. A large majority of the military sites are owned and maintained by governments as national historic landmarks, cemeteries, monuments, battlefields, and museums. The ownership of the military sites discussed here varies. The Istanbul Military Museum is owned and operated by the Turkish government through its Military Museum and Site Command; the Tower of London is owned and maintained by the Department of the Environment of Her Majesty's government; the Imperial War Museum in London is in the custody of the Imperial War Museum Trust; The National Museum of the Pacific War in Fredericksburg was authorized and funded by the Texas state legislature and is maintained by the Texas Parks and Wildlife Department; and the Alamo is maintained by the volunteer civic organization Daughters of the Republic of Texas. Many of these sites depend on public funding supplemented by individual and corporate donations.

The activities performed by tourists on these military attractions are primarily educational. Sightseeing, moving around, reading inscriptions, remembering, researching, meeting friendly and adversarial former combatants, narrating the personal history of the conflict to members of the family or to school groups, and reliving the horrors of concentration camps are among the activities contemplated and performed by tourists. Military attractions have an exceptional ability to induce repeat visits, a quality that many attractions lack.

Conclusions and Lessons Learned

- Military attractions often have international tourism significance. Their purpose is to preserve the heritage of a nation or nations. They are educational assets and important generators of tourism throughout the year. National tourism promotion campaigns use these sites as primary destinations.
- Military artifacts and weapons are preserved in national military museums. Large specimens like battleships and castles actually house their own museums.
- Battlefields and structures are protected under special legislation or by outright acquisition from private owners. State and federal agencies for parks and many civic organizations are entrusted with the operation and maintenance of these sites.
- Special fund-raising campaigns augment the revenues of civic organizations from the proceeds of their gift shop sales and gate receipts. These additional funding sources enable military sites to sustain their operations with minimal government funding.
- The location of battlefields is determined by historical events. They cannot be changed. They may be in remote areas (New Guinea), urban areas (Stalingrad), islands (Iwo Jima), plains (Kursk), shorelines (Normandy), or mountains (the Alps).
- The implements of war can be moved to locations where they can be displayed in military museums built where they are accessible by visitors. Alternatively, the implements themselves (warships) can be moved to locations where they can be the main attraction and house a museum.
- Almost any relic or site of military conflict can serve to promote tourism. Their level of historic significance determines their market area for promotion.
- Duplicating original military sites at other nearby locations serves to preserve the original site and helps to depict contemporary characteristics on the date of the events that made them historic places. Visitors must know that they are visiting the replica of the original.
- Historical facts should not be compromised when promoting military destinations. Credibility should be the governing principle for ensuring the draw and preserving the authenticity of the place. Tourists should be prepared to respect the memory and heroism of fallen soldiers, sailors, and airmen and the emotions of those to whom the memorials mean so much.

Study Questions

- What makes a military site or event a historic tourist attraction?
- Can historic military attractions be duplicated and relocated?
- What is the significance of historic authenticity in creating a military attraction?
- What is the educational value of military attractions in preventing international armed conflicts?

Case Study 5

Early Tourism Development in Nepal—A Historical Review

PROJECT BY: Bulent I. Kastarlak
YEARS: 1950–1972

The Case

The Regional Context

Toni Hagen set foot on Nepalese soil for the first time in 1950 shortly after the country opened to foreign visitors. He was a Swiss geologist visiting the "forbidden country" in connection with the bilateral program of Swiss Technical Assistance. He covered on foot a total distance of 14,000 km (8,700 miles) in eight years, crisscrossing the country from one end to the other by walking through virtually all of its valleys. He was fascinated with the geographic resemblance of Nepal to Switzerland. However, the resemblance ended there. Although Switzerland presented itself as a development model for Nepal, the economies and cultures of the two countries were directly opposite. Hagen's impressions of Nepal were revealing in their detail and their prognosis for the future. They set the frame of reference for what was to follow in the name of national development and the role tourism played in it.

In the book he wrote in 1961(see the Bibliography), Hagen exudes awe and admiration: "If the expression Wonderland has any justification outside the fairy tale, then it is here: the Wonderland of Nepal! The traveler discovers marvel upon marvel, and there are probably few countries in the world where so many monuments of art may be found within such a small compass as in the Kathmandu Valley. If one asks a foreign tourist for what purpose he wants to travel and see other countries, he will say that he is attracted by anything unusual. Nepal has many unusual things to offer—the Himalayas, a rich and ancient culture, beautiful temples, ethnologic and cultural diversity, the beautiful old Newar towns which are masterpieces of architecture, the jungle, the wildlife, and the amiable people."

Hagen's earlier impressions were replaced by alarm and despair after his next visit to Nepal in 1968: As reported in his updated book on Nepal published in 1971, "Shangri La in Katmandu is vanishing fast. A real concrete mania has overtaken the city and its beautiful parks . . . are bare of trees, and fenced with ugly concrete constructions. Apartment houses of the most tasteless style have mushroomed; and last but not least, the streets are strewn with hippies and hashish addicts which in this form hardly fit into the ancient culture."

The realization that Nepal was fast losing its heritage led its government to seek international assistance for taking corrective and preventive measures. His Majesty King Mahendra affirmed that the primary goal of developing his country and preserving its heritage should be to plan for the overall development of Nepal, and that the plan should be implemented only after a careful examination of the resources, their proper utilization and their impact on the national economy The first step was to find a sponsor for preparing these plans. The United Nations came through with funds and technical assistance. The result was *The Physical Development Plan for the Kathmandu Valley*, which was adopted in August 1972.

The objectives of the plan were:

- To preserve the historic and present image of the valley
- To preserve valuable agricultural land as much as possible
- To develop an efficient transportation system for the valley

- To reduce the density of congested areas in the cities
- To try to provide more efficient densities for the low-density city areas
- To propose an effective urban renewal program
- To formulate programs for the development of the villages in the valley
- To prepare a land use map that would be useful for the next twenty years

The plan represented the first regional approach to development in Nepal. Owing to lack of ample funds, earlier aerial photographs taken by Toni Hagen were used for preparing the initial base maps.

By 1972, His Majesty's government had adopted and implemented three consecutive national plans. These plans were prepared by sectors of the economy, and their implementation was assigned to departments of the government. Each department was given the task of preparing action programs for its economic sector. These programs, individually or in relation to one another, had seldom been the product of systematic planning. Central government expenditures and programs lacked coordination at the regional and local levels. The local plans prepared by *Panchayats* (groups of village elders who led their local governments) were relevant for their intended objectives but were often in conflict with the implementation programs of sectoral plans.

The government instituted a top-down central planning process and ordered the central planning agency to overcome the coordination problems. The central planning agency needed more than budgetary control, which was traditionally left to the Ministry of Finance. The task of the central planning agency was to prepare a comprehensive plan based on the total available resources of the country, expressed in financial terms and weighted according to national priorities defining the most urgent needs by sectors of the economy. Regional plans evolved from the national plan.

Regional plans were considered "horizontal" in the sense that they combined various elements of sectoral plans for a particular region. It is at the level of regional planning that the physical plan worked. Within a regional context, physical planning sought a comprehensive analysis of existing and potential activities and resources for formulating a spatially relevant physical development plan. The process required identification of indigenous human and natural elements and their interrelations for directing future development within the regional space.

In Nepal, regional physical planning, economic planning, and social planning were adopted as the three parts of the same comprehensive development planning process. Economic planning was concerned with the maximum use of scarce resources and the development of their production potential. Physical planning addressed location and land use issues and coordinated the sectoral plans and projects spatially. Social planning included improving education and delivery of health services. These plans and projects were intended to facilitate economic and social development.

The planners chose several regions with urban growth centers for development. The principal region was the Kathmandu Valley. The Pokhara Valley and the Gandaki-Lumbini Valley were next. Migration of people from the villages on the mountains to these emerging regional urban growth centers in search of jobs necessitated the creation of economically viable settlements on high hills. Thus, the basic plan for the concept of urban-centered growth regions was to anticipate population movements, provide the infrastructure necessary to link these centers, and improve the subsistence economies on the hills to minimize outmigration by inducing regionally balanced socioeconomic development. Tourism was given a major role in this process.

Comprehensive regional development plans included the three broad groups of survey, analysis, and recommendations. Topics included were:

- Economic aspects of regional agriculture, industry, trade and service sectors, including tourism
- Infrastructure aspects including interregional roads, ropeways, bridges, air transport, electricity, water supply, and sanitation facilities
- Social service aspects concerning housing, schools, medical facilities, and tourism facilities

How was tourism made part of the development of growth regions? Until the revolution of 1951, Nepal was inaccessible to foreigners. Even after the country and Kathmandu were opened, very limited air transport and few hotel facilities kept the annual number of visitors in the years immediately following 1951 very low. Eventually, the development and expansion of transport and communication links with India to the south led to a sharp increase in tourist traffic. The establishment of regular airline service between Kathmandu and Patna, New Delhi, Dacca, and Calcutta has been primarily responsible for the influx of tourists, as more than 90% of Nepal's foreign visitors, with the exception of Indian citizens, enter the country by air. It is worth noting that the government of India financed and undertook the construction of the two-lane stabilized road from the border with India to Kathmandu. It is reported that before the construction of this road, the first automobile entering Nepal was carried from India on human backs piece by piece and assembled in Kathmandu. Quickly, the government of China followed by building a road from the border with now Chinese Tibet to Kathmandu.

Tourism Statistics

Nepal is among the poorest countries in the world. In this country of mighty mountains, sweet climate, and genuinely friendly people where all major religions and cultures coexist peacefully, life is difficult. According to the *World Bank Annual Report* (*2008*), the gross national income (GNI) per capita is only $400 per year. It is no wonder that poverty in South Asia, and its measurement, are being debated energetically. Poverty continued to decline from over 40% in the mid-1980s to around 25% in India and to slightly more than 30% in Bangladesh, Nepal, and Pakistan. However, there are indications that poverty might have stayed at this level or even risen in Nepal and Pakistan during the 1990s. Among other concerns, building a climate for investment and implementing programs for controlling communicable diseases, particularly AIDS, are lagging. Economic leakage is worrisome. It is difficult to measure how much or how little tourism has helped to improve Nepal's living conditions since the opening of the country to foreign visitors in 1951.

Tourism statistics for 1957, the first year for which they are available, show that a total of 1,987 foreign tourists visited the country. By 1960 this number had risen to 3,971, and the income from tourism has increased substantially since that time. It is important to note, however, how these tourist statistics were collected. For statistical purposes, Nepal defined tourists as citizens of all foreign countries, except India (and persons of Nepalese origin), visiting the Kingdom of Nepal and staying at least 24 hours and at most six months for various purposes, like recreation, health, study, religious pilgrimage, business, sightseeing, attending conferences, and mountaineering. Representatives or staff of organizations permanently stationed in Nepal, and not required to fill out the disembarkation cards, are not included in tourist statistics. Visitors are required to fill out the cards at Tribhuvan Airport in Kathmandu or at the Birgunj Checkpost at the border with India. Visitors entering at other points of the country, including pilgrims who journey to the holy site of Lumbini near Bhairawa on the Terai, and then coming to Kathmandu and leaving the country from there are excluded because they are not required to fill out disembarkation cards.

These early statistics were used randomly. Starting in 1962, they were used in formulating the tourism development policies of Nepal. During the eight-year period 1962–1970, the first *Nepal Tourism Master Plan* was prepared and adopted in 1972. The statistics collected during this period show a sharp increase in tourist arrivals every year. The number of tourists increased from 6,179 in 1962 to 45,970 in 1970. The rates of annual increases were consistently between 30% and 40% except during 1965, when a conflict between India and Pakistan arose over border issues. Among the major factors for the increase in tourism were intensive international promotion of the country, improved transportation facilities, expansion of hotel facilities, establishment of modern banking facilities, and the growing number of travel agencies in Nepal.

According to Wikipedia, in 2007 the number of international tourists visiting Nepal was 526,705, an increase of 37.2% compared to the previous year. In 2008, the number of tourists decreased by 5% to 500,277. In 2008, 55.9% of the foreign visitors came from Asia (18.2% from India), while Western Europeans accounted for 27.5%, 7.6% were from North America, 3.2% from Australia and the Pacific region, 2.6% from Eastern Europe, 1.5% from Central and South America, 0.3% from Africa, and 1.4% from other countries.

Foreign tourists visiting Nepal in 2008 stayed in the country for an average of 11.78 days. About 79% of the tourists arrived in Kathmandu by air and 21% by land. The national airline of Nepal (RNAC) and seven foreign airlines were responsible for the influx. Most tourists came for sightseeing. Among other purposes of visits, mountaineering became increasingly popular after Mount Everest (Sagarmatha to the Nepalese—elevation 29,028 ft) was reached by Sir Edmund Hillary and Tenzing Norgay on May 29, 1953. Because of the mild climate of Kathmandu, tourist arrivals were spread evenly over the twelve months of the year. The arrivals peaked in October, November, and December, when the dry season began and mountaineering conditions were the best. Further tourism information is contained on the following Web site. http://www.tourism.gov.np/.

Tourism Potential

The *Physical Development Plan for Kathmandu Valley* began to analyze the tourism potential systematically. At the same time, the *Nepal Tourism Master Plan* was in preparation. The two planning teams coordinated their work. The tourism plan emphasized the foreign exchange earnings from tourism. One way to increase these earnings was to extend the average stay of foreign visitors from three to four days. It was calculated that the existing three first-class hotels, several second-class hotels, and numerous third-class hotels had the capacity to accommodate this increase in average stay. In 1972, the five-star Soaltee Oberoi Hotel, with 220 beds, was favored by sightseeing tourists. It charged $20 for double occupancy and $14 for single occupancy. The four-star Hotel Annapurna, with 180 beds, was the hotel of choice of foreign mountaineers and official visitors. It cost $20 for double occupancy and $14 for single occupancy, including breakfast. The three-star Shanker Hotel, with 112 beds, was a former royal palace converted into a hotel. There was no central heating in the rooms. Electric heaters were used to ward off the night chill. It cost $15 for double occupancy and $9 for single occupancy. All three meals were included in the rate. About half a dozen restaurants provided food and drinks to foreign visitors. They were mostly owned and operated by the members of the royal family. A foreigner owned the famous hangout Yak and Yeti, where foreign adventurers, among others, exchanged tall tales about trekking and mountaineering in Nepal. As mentioned, by 2008 the average stay for foreign tourists was 11.78 days, quite an increase from the 1970s.

The Kathmandu Valley offers tourists the creations of a unique civilization. Its towns and settlements, with their multitude of cultural and historic sites and special events, are located in picturesque settings on terraced fields blooming with yellow mustard plants and rice paddies. The peaks of the majestic Himalayan Mountains form an impressive background. Within the valley, there are numerous sites of prime archeological, historic, and religious value. Concentrations of these temples and monuments are found in the *darbar* (gathering place or reception area) squares of Kathmandu, Patan, and Bhadgaon.

Kathmandu is the seat of the kingdom that was united by King Prithvi Narayan Shah. The major historic, cultural, and archeological attractions in Kathmandu include:

- **Machhendra Nath Temple** is located at Machhendra Bahal. It is dedicated to the God of Rain and Mercy.
- **Hanuman Dhoka** is the historic palace of the ancient kings of Nepal. The complex includes Taleju Temple, built by King Mahendra Malla in 1549; the gigantic figure Kal Bhairav, God of Terror; and Basantpur Darbar, with its coronation platform and many pagoda-style temples.
- **Swayambhunath** is a Buddhist stupa (a mound-like structure containing religious relics) more than two thousand five hundred years old.
- **Pashupatinath** stands on the banks of the sacred Batmati River. This structure, with its two-tier golden roof and silver doors, is famous for its architecture. Entrance is restricted to Hindus.
- **Budhanath Stupa** is the largest stupa in the world, built more than two thousand five hundred years ago. Four pairs of eyes of Buddha keep eternal watch over the people in all four directions.
- **Budhanilkantha** is the stone image of Vishnu sleeping on a bed of snakes. It is a fine example of the art of stone sculpture of Nepal.

Bhadgaon (Bhaktapur) is the home of medieval art and architecture, containing immortal creations of anonymous masters. It is a city where stone and wood have a story to tell. The towering temples combine massive bulk with delicate ornaments. Every piece of art has religious significance, and every human action has its roots in ancient culture. The culture exudes tolerance and acceptance of diversity. Unlike other countries, in Nepal Buddhists, Hindus, and Muslims live in complete harmony. Everyday life on the streets is carried out with delicate courtesy and without a trace of malevolence toward others. To Western tourists, this is a very striking feature of the local culture. The major attractions include:

- **Darbar Square** includes temples built in the Pagoda and Shikhara styles. Ancient brick buildings with exquisitely carved wood windows and doors surround the square. Golden statues of kings are perched on top of stone columns. Guardian deities look out from their sanctuaries.
- The **Lion Gate** is guarded by two huge statues of lions dating back to AD 1696.
- The **Golden Gate** is the richest specimen of its kind in the world. It is embellished with figures of mythical creatures.
- The **Palace of Fifty-Five Windows** was built by King Yakshya Malla in AD 1427. It was the residence of the Malla kings of Bhadgaon. It is remarkable for its carved balcony and the row of fifty-five windows projecting out.

- The **Pashupati Temple** is the replica of the famous temple by the Bagmati River in Kathmandu. It was built in AD 1682 and is noted for the erotic carvings on its struts holding the roof.
- **Nyatapola**, meaning "five-storied," is the tallest pagoda temple in Kathmandu Valley. The flight of stairs leading to the sanctum has stone statues of wrestlers, elephants, lions, and tigers faced by mythical figures on both sides.
- **Changu Narayan**, dating from the Lichhavian era, is a temple generally acknowledged as the most artistic pagoda in Nepal.

The ancient name of **Patan** is **Lalitpur**, meaning "the city of beauty." The four corners of the compass around the town are marked by Buddhist stupas. The town is full of temples, palaces of other kings, and monuments.

- **Darbar Square** is the city's focal point. The ancient palace of the Malla kings and the marketplace are surrounded by a stone temple of Lord Krishna and the Royal Bath.
- **Hiranya Varna Mahavihar** is the three-story pagoda-style golden temple of Buddha built in the twelfth century AD by King Bhaskar Varma.
- **Kumbheshwar** is the five-story pagoda-style temple of Lord Shiva. Ritual bathing takes place here every year in August and September.
- **Mahabuddha Temple** is a fourteenth-century masterpiece of terra-cotta architecture. Every one of its nine thousand bricks contains a figure of the Buddha. It was destroyed by an earthquake in 1935 and was rebuilt soon afterward to the original specifications.
- **Ashoka stupas** occupy the four corners of Patan. All of these Buddhist stupas were built in AD 250 at the time when Buddhism was making its headway in Kathmandu Valley.
- **Godavari** is situated at lower elevations of the Phulchoki Peak about six miles outside of Patan. It is a popular picnic spot for vacationers. It has a highly prized butterfly population. There is a fish hatchery amid the dense woodland. The Royal Botanical Garden has a wide-ranging collection of high-altitude orchids and cacti. Every twelve years, a great religious fair lasting for a whole month brings thousands of pilgrims for ritual bathing in the holy pond.

The holidays and festivals of Nepal number in the hundreds, suggesting to some tourists that the Nepalese find an occasion to celebrate some event every day of the year. Although this is an exaggeration, the many colorful parades and festivals never cease to amaze visitors with their spectacular displays of local culture. Fortunately, it has been the welcome practice of visitors coming to Nepal to maintain a low profile and remain respectful of the people and their customs.

Nepal is called the "land of festivals." Not a week passes without some festival taking place in some part of the country, which is observed either locally or nationally. Whether the events are of local or national significance, most festivals are associated with some divinity sacred to Hindu or Buddhist theology or mythology. It should be noted that regardless of whether a given festival is of Hindu or Buddhist origin, the Nepalese people celebrate it as a festival common to all and with the same solemnity or gaiety, as the case may be. The extreme degrees of religious tolerance and acceptance have been the major social traits of Nepal, and were first recorded by the Chinese explorer Huen-Tsang in AD 700. If not then, certainly today, the rigidity and orthodoxy of religious belief have completely died out. Consequently, all religions animate and give meaning to almost all festivals and have come to be a force of national solidarity rather than sectarian division. This trait is unique in the world. Religious intolerance and even hatred still permeate all levels of social strata in the developed countries of Western Europe and the Americas.

Unfortunately, many of the festival sites and routes have been increasingly encroached upon by vehicular traffic, utilities installations, and unsightly new construction. In 1970, many of the temples and monuments were in advanced stages of deterioration, which was often aggravated by the effects of modern environmental intrusions. Vibrations from heavy trucks and equipment, unsightly concrete structures destroying the beauty of traditional design, installation of power and telecommunication lines and transformer stations at historic sites, and theft of artifacts removed from ancient buildings contributed heavily to this accelerated destruction. The Department of Archeology, with a very limited budget, attempted to restore selected monuments but was unable to carry out this work on the scale required. Foreign assistance was needed. UNESCO responded, and the restoration of Hanuman Dhoka, the historic palace of the kings of Nepal in Kathmandu, was undertaken.

Kathmandu is the point of entry for the majority of tourists to Nepal. It is also the base of activities for organizing, supplying, recruiting porters, and starting groups on trips to other parts of the country. These groups head west to Pokhara and east to the Base Camp near the Khumbu Icefall for climbing Mount Everest.

The **Himalayas** provide the main attraction outside Kathmandu Valley. Himalaya means "the home of snow," and true to their name, the mountain peaks are permanently covered with snow. The Himalayan range extends along the entire northern border of Nepal with Tibet-China. It features the highest peaks in the world, enormous glaciers, yawning ravines, and deep gorges. Beneath their shadows at the bottom of valleys lie fertile lands, meadows, and raging rivers. Annual monsoons produce lush vegetation up to the snow line at 16,000 feet. The valleys are dotted with picturesque villages amid pine and rhododendron groves. The Nepal Himalayas are divided into four zones from north to south: the Trans-Himalayas, or the Border Ranges; the Greater Himalayas; the Lesser Himalayas, or the Mahabharat Lekh; and the Outer Himalayas, or the Churia Range. The Nepal Himalayas constitute the central portion of the Himalayas. They stretch from the Mahakali River in the west to the Sikkim border in the east. There are 240 peaks ranging from 20,000 to 29,028 feet, the highest being Mount Everest. As a footnote, the height of the highest peak in the world was increased by 7 feet to 29,035 feet in 1998 when GPS equipment was installed at the summit. As a further footnote, the entire Himalayan Range is increasing in height by 2.4 inches every year.

Nepal's Himalayas are of exceptional interest for mountaineers and have the most impressive scenic views anywhere. The first attempt to climb Mount Everest was made in 1922. Sir Edmund Hillary and the Sherpa guide Tenzing Norgay climbed to the top in 1953. Since that date, twelve hundred men and women from sixty-three nations have reached the summit. "Well George, we knocked the bastard off!" (as reported in the *National Geographic* article of July 1, 1954, "Ascent of Mount Everest" by John Hunt and Edmund Hillary) Hillary boasted to his teammate George Lowe as he and Tenzing descended from the peak. The occasion is reported in this article as a humbling affair. Neither Hillary, nor Tenzing, nor the expedition leader, John Hunt, had come to the mountain expecting personal fame. "It was not glory we sought," wrote Hunt in that article, "unless it be the common glory of man's glory over Nature—and over his limitations." Tenzing's son Jambling followed his father to the top of Mount Everest in 1996. He wrote in his 2001 book *Touching My Father's Soul: A Sherpa's Journey to the Top of Everest*, "Humans are granted no more than an audience with Everest's summit, and then only rarely and for brief moment." These men succeeded with luck, skill, and endurance.

A record number of 89 climbers made it to the summit of Everest on a single day in 2001. A total of 175 foolish, careless, unskilled, or just unlucky climbers have perished on its slopes since 1922. Many more lost their toes to frostbite or suffered from high-altitude sickness or cerebral and pulmonary edema. The summit was climbed from both sides of the border between Nepal and Tibet-China. Various expeditions discovered fifteen routes to the top. These feats would not have been possible without extensive organization, preparation, trekking over Khumbu Glacier, acclimatization at the Base Camp, courage, and the skills of hundreds of Sherpa porters and guides who respected the challenges posed by Sagarmatha, the Nepalese name for Mount Everest

Two other mountain ranges are important for mountain climbing in Nepal. The Annapurna Himal, lying south of the Marshyangdi River, stretches to the Kali Gandaki River to the west. The principal peaks in the Annapurna Himal group include Annapurna South (23,683 feet), Annapurna I, II, III, and IV, and the picturesque Machhapuchhare or Fish Tail (22,942 feet) overlooking the second largest town of Nepal, Pokhara. The second mountain range, Dhaulagiri Himal, extends from the Kali Gandaki River Valley in the east to Thuli Bheri in the west. The prominent peaks in the Dhaulagiri Himal include Dhaulagiri I (26,795 feet), Dhaulagiri II, III, IV, V, and VI, and Tukche (22,430 feet). Dhaulagiri I sharply drops almost 19,000 feet to the valley floor of the Kali Gandaki River to an elevation of 8,000 feet. This is the longest uninterrupted drop of elevation in the Nepal mountains. The green and unspoiled Kali Gandaki Valley and its tributaries are dotted with many villages. Working from south to north, they include Ghasa, Lete, Sirkung, Larjung, Marpha, Shyang, and Jomosom. The next stop is Mustang, close to the border with the Tibet region of China.

Trekking, as opposed to **climbing**, is also popular and growing in Nepal. Climbing the two hundred forty Himalayan peaks of Nepal involves serious mountaineering skills and preparation, whereas trekking stays close to level ground and rarely exceeds the snowline at 16,000 feet. The trails are established by yak caravans and by the movement of native people over many centuries. Carved from the side of the mountain, they often narrow to 2 feet in width. The side of the mountain often drops 1,000 feet into the raging river below. The trails traverse gorges over flimsy rope bridges and, if the bridges are swept away, over a wooden log. Only the steady bare feet of the young Nepalese porter, loaded with eighty pounds of supplies, and yaks are accustomed to these conditions. For the trekkers, the exhilaration that comes from observing the spectacular scenery and experiencing the dangers of a long trail is worth the hardship.

A growing number of local travel agencies in Kathmandu organize the treks. The best season for trekking is from February through April, and again in October and November. During other months of the year, snowfall, rock slides, and rain make trekking difficult and sometimes treacherous. Wooden and rope bridges over raging rivers and streams are impassible in some places, and the areas become inaccessible for months.

When all the members of the group are accounted for, the trekkers are assembled in the early morning in front of the hotel. They are outfitted with their own personal gear. The best clothing for trekking is a thick flannel shirt, a cotton undershirt, and a warm parka jacket. The climate can change from tropical to winter as trekkers move from lower to higher elevations. Trekking footwear must be broken in and worn with two types of socks—wool over silk. Getting blisters by wearing new boots is the best way to spoil a trek. Other equipment includes a backpack to carry personal effects, first aid equipment, water purifier tablets, still and video cameras, and a down sleeping bag. Cellular phones may not always work. Trekkers often sleep in individual tents under clear skies. Porters carry the tents and set them up every night. The trek organizer provides several porters, a cook, and a multilingual Nepalese Sirdar who acts as the guide and crew chief. The policy is to carry everything in and everything out, most importantly the rubbish. This includes all provisions, drinking water, the cooking stove, fuel, and tents. Nothing is left behind when decamping every morning. The load is divided among the porters and carried in wicker baskets held with a strap passing over the porter's forehead. This is a time-tested, efficient way to distribute the load from head to toe. Porters prefer their traditional way to backpacks carried on shoulders.

Transportation is provided from the city to the beginning of the trail. On the trail, trekkers eat dinner and breakfast around the campfire. Lunch is taken on the run. Occasionally, simple overnight accommodations, and even a basic restaurant, can be found at some villages, like Namche Bazaar and Khumjung, on a trek to the Everest Base Camp. As the first order of business each day, the Nepalese cook brings a hot cup of tea (a sign of hospitality) to the tent and announces the weather forecast. Personal grooming and comfort are left to the discretion of the trekker. On the trek, toilet facilities and running water are not available. The day goes by rapidly. The muscle stiffness of the first few days gives way to acclimatization to the high elevation and to the sheer joy of experiencing the environment. Daily treks usually take six to ten hours between stops.

There are several well-traveled trek trails.

- The **Everest Trek** is between Kathmandu and the Khumbu Glacier. It takes fifteen days to complete the trek one way. It passes through some well-known Sherpa villages, like Khumjung and Namche Bazar. The villages are spaced a one-day trek apart. The return (downhill) trek usually takes fewer days. The trail rises from an elevation of 5,200 feet in Kathmandu to 16,400 feet at Khumbu Galcier. The Base Camp for Everest climbers is located at 17,600 feet. In village markets, the trekker can find local products, poor-quality cigarettes, kerosene, coarse clothes, and foodstuffs like maize, rice, ghee (refined yak butter), vegetable oils, chicken, and eggs. Fresh vegetables are not available everywhere. In case of a medical evacuation to Kathmandu, the short take-off airstrip at Lukla is used. Helicopter evacuations are seldom attempted because of the thin air at these higher elevations. There is a modern school for Sherpa children at Khumjung built by Sir Edmund Hillary. At Banepa, there is a mission hospital.

- The **Kathmandu to Pokhara Trek** starts at Trisuli after a forty-five-minute ride from Kathmandu with a motorcar. The round trip takes about fifteen days and covers 140 miles. The trek goes through a dozen villages, among which Gorkha is famous for its military tradition and for its units serving with the armed forces of the United Kingdom. For more than a hundred years, Gorkha units were sent to many parts of the British Empire and were renowned for their discipline and combat acumen. Trekkers can find local foodstuffs like sugar, rice, flour, eggs, potatoes, maize, chicken, and salt at local markets.

- The **Annapurna and Dhaulagiri Trek** starts from Pokhara in central Nepal. A forty-five-minute flight from Kathmandu brings the trekkers to this beautiful town. The lush green Pokhara Valley has many lakes (*Tals*), and is situated at an elevation of 2,900 feet. The Annapurna range, rising to 26,000 feet, provides the spectacular background image of the valley. It is only twenty-four miles from the town. Machhapuchhre (Fishtail), which looks down on the town, reflects its image in the tranquil waters of Phewa Tal. The mountain takes its name from its unique shape, with two peaks resembling the tail of a fish. The trekking trail starts at the valley and loops over the ridge between the

Mardi and Seti rivers. It goes through several Gurung villages, like Ghachok and Hengjachaur. It takes about two days to complete the loop and return to Pokhara.

- The **Jomosom Trek** is known as the "hot springs holiday" trek. It starts from Pokhara and goes through nine villages. Among them, Tatopani and Dana are renowned for their hot springs, although modern facilities do not exist. The warm spring water is known to contain sulfur, iron, and rock salt. The trail between Pokhara and Jomosom is approximately sixty-eight miles and can be covered in six days one way. The elevation of Jomosom is 12,000 feet. After leaving Pokhara, the trail reaches Kusma, enters the majestic Kali Gandaki Valley, and heads north between the Dhaulaghiri and Annapurna massifs. The valley had been the traditional trade route between China and India until it was closed to traffic at the Chinese border in the 1950s. Yak caravans carried salt, spices, food, and other goods up and down from India to China. Now Mustang stands as the isolated terminal point of the trek close to the border. Trekkers can find roofs over their heads at night stops in villages. Larger villages like Dana, Tatapani, Marpha, Tukche, and Jomosom have local markets. The scenery all along the trail is very impressive. The Kali Gandaki Valley reaches the lowlands in the Terai region, where entirely different scenery and culture await.
- The **Gosaikunda Trek** is a sacred pilgrimage trek for Hindus. The trek starts by motor car from Kathmandu and reaches Trisuli forty-four miles away. It continues on foot over the Helambu pass and reaches Gosaikunda, approximately thirty-one miles away, at an altitude of 16,000 feet. The return trip is from Sundarijal. The scenery is spectacular all along the trail. Colorful floral displays, yaks grazing, mountain peaks, and many lakes are the backdrop for several monasteries. The trek takes twelve days to complete.
- The **Helambu Trek** is best known for its scenic beauty, mild climate, and short duration. The trek takes four days and forty-five miles to complete at an average altitude of 8,000 feet. Helambu is famous as a health resort. It is a typical Nepalese highland village of the Sherpas. Trekkers have a chance to stay and study Sherpa households and customs. By tradition, Sherpas are very hospitable people. They welcome their guests to their homes. In addition to Sherpa hospitality, there are seven monasteries to visit and experience in the region.

The Nepal Tourism Master Plan

Nearly two decades after his country opened to the outside world, His Majesty King Mahendra Bir Bikram Shah gave directives to prepare a master plan for developing tourism in Nepal. In 1970, the government of the Federal Republic of Germany provided the funds for technical assistance and a study team. The work was completed with the cooperation of the Nepal Tourism Development Committee and His Majesty's government. The project was assigned to a group of experts from Bundesstelle für Entwick-Lungshilfe, a branch of the German Ministry of Economic Cooperation. The plan was approved by His Majesty's government in August 1972 and printed for distribution in December 1972.

Over a period of ten months the study team, comprising experts in such fields as tourism economy, tourism industry, geography, and regional planning, collected and analyzed data and information in their relevant fields. A comprehensive long-term plan and an action-oriented implementation program were completed for the 1970–1980 period.

The plan was intended to provide a basis for integrated growth in the tourism sector in concert with other sectoral plans of the economy. It was prepared on the basis of extensive field surveys, evaluation of the existing conditions of tourism, and analysis of the impact of tourism on the overall economy of Nepal. The *objectives* of the plan included the following:

- To provide growth of international tourism to and within Nepal in an optimum manner that would help attain the aims of the country's social and economic policies and create sustained economic benefits for Nepal
- To provide planned development of the tourism sector that best utilized the resources and potentials of Nepal with regard to international travel
- To induce economic activities and to assist in the development of agriculture, industries, and infrastructure through the establishment of employment opportunities, the increase of foreign exchange, and the creation of economic incentives in depressed areas
- To develop tourism in a manner that would preserve and enhance the social, cultural, and historic values of Nepal

The plan was intended for the following *uses:*

- To assist His Majesty's government of Nepal in deciding on measures to be taken in the tourism sector and the passage of legislation, and to create integrated policies for the development of tourism and supporting sectors
- To guide private sector activities in tourism in order to promote initiatives and investment both locally and internationally
- To provide for coordination of private and public activities in tourism development, promotion, and marketing
- To attract international financial and technical assistance to preserve Nepal's natural and cultural resources for the country and for world tourism
- To attract visitors to the country; to inform the international travel markets that Nepal was preparing a long-range development program in tourism; and to develop awareness of Nepal's tourism potential both in the country and abroad

The German team of experts made one exceptionally farsighted observation for its time and perhaps for all time. Contrary to the conventional wisdom in 1970, the team did not base its plan on a basic planning concept generally adopted in Western European and North American countries with developed economies. The prevalent method was to make demand projections and meet the requirements of the demand by planning the supply side of tourism. The team questioned the wisdom of using this planning concept because meeting the projected demand could be very costly for the economy of a poor country like Nepal. The **demand-pushed** approach would also require a pace of development that would be beyond the capacity of the country to sustain, even with external assistance. The objective was to increase the inflow of tourists by building more hotels, importing all kinds of material and equipment to build and operate these hotels, and paying for them with foreign exchange previously earned from tourism. Because of excessive economic leakage, the country had a hard time accumulating foreign exchange from tourism for developing other sectors of its economy. The economy leaked from all sides. Tourism development failed to bring sustained benefits. The real beneficiaries of this laissez-faire economics were foreign investors and operators.

The German team considered the low volume of tourism in 1970 and decided that Nepal should not rush into rapid tourism development. They stated that moderate, sustained development that aimed at removing obstacles that prevented Nepal from receiving a greater share of international tourism, and from ensuring the sound growth of the tourism industry, was the best strategy. The plan concentrated on eliminating critical bottlenecks and determining the maximum tourism demand that could be accommodated without creating environmental, social, and economic dislocations in the country. This **supply-pulled** tourism planning was new for its time and was also the basis of the tourism planning advocated by Bulent Kastarlak in 1970 in other tourism development projects. The Tourism Master Plan for Nepal:

- Reviewed the general background of the country, its geography, and other characteristics
- Studied the socioeconomic conditions and regional economies and their problems based on available data
- Studied external and internal transportation issues and accessibility problems, owing to their importance for Nepal
- Conducted a comprehensive survey of Nepal's tourist attractions and facilities, including regional natural, scenic, recreational, cultural, and historic potentials
- Collected and analyzed statistical data collected since 1962
- Analyzed specific problems and potentials of the service industry, including quantitative and qualitative analysis of the problems associated with overnight accommodations, banking, and government institutions
- Estimated a comparative market demand for the tourism regions of Nepal based on similarities of the motivation to travel to India
- Recommended policies for managing the economic and social impacts of tourism
- Set economic and social objectives for the country based on sustainable growth and development principles for tourism
- Prepared a long-term strategy (for ten years) to reach immediate and mid-term targets

The basic idea behind the tourism development concept was to expand sightseeing tourism in the short run by promoting round-trip tours and treks that would take tourists to various regions outside Kathmandu and lengthen their stay in the country. Basic features of the plan were as follows:

- It was important to lengthen visitors' stays and increase regional dispersion to achieve sustained and balanced growth of tourism throughout the country, resulting in unique Nepalese-style tourism.
- The development concept was translated into annual implementation programs for ten years for each priority region.
- The program recommended expanding the stock of overnight accommodations only to meet targeted, sustainable demand in terms of total numbers of tourists and length of stay.
- Separate improvements were proposed for recreational and pilgrimage tourism from India.
- Reflecting the development concept and the volume of tourists targeted, the plan defined a public works program of public facility and infrastructure projects.
- The plan recommended the future organization of tourism authorities, including their scope of activities, functions, and capacity for implementing the programs.
- The plan also identified supporting programs for tourism development, including marketing and sales promotion, internal publicity, personnel training, and parallel measures and policies for industrial and agricultural improvements.
- The plan further recommended a financial program that included sources and phasing of public expenditures and projections of anticipated public revenues.
- Finally, the plan set forth guidelines for creating a central agency responsible for tourism affairs and for the role the government was to play.

The writers of the Nepal Tourism Master Plan employed many superlatives to reflect Nepal's wealth of natural and scenic attractions, human-made treasures, very hospitable people, and the cultural heritage, which was relatively all-embracing. They appreciated the fact that the kingdom holds within a comparatively small area a wealth of tourist attractions that probably has no parallel in the world. The urgent necessity of preserving the cultural and environmental heritage of Nepal and ensuring the self-sustaining growth of tourism prompted the preparation of the Nepal Tourism Master Plan. This initial ten-year plan focused on sustainability and on the role of government. The importance of the private sector was not denied. But **supply-oriented** planning was favored over **demand-oriented** planning, and maximizing profits for tourism businesses was to be guided by the principle of achieving optimum benefits from tourism for the country.

Pokhara–Jomosom–Lumbini: Account of a Personal and Professional Journey of Bulent Kastarlak Written by Him

One early morning in the summer of 1972, I received a call from the United Nations Technical Assistance Office in New York. The office was organizing a technical assistance mission to Nepal in October of that year. Was I available to participate in the mission as the expert in tourism and urban planning? The mission involved a resource survey and analysis for the region of Kali Gandaki Valley, which extended from Pokhara to Jomosom in the north and Lumbini and Terai in the south. The mission was led by a project manager from the United Nations Development Programme (UNDP) and included other international experts from the fields of hydrology, community development, and agriculture. The objective of the mission was to evaluate the resource potential of the region for cash crop agriculture and horticulture, hydroelectric power, water and power distribution systems, preservation of cultural values and social organization, and tourism development and urban redevelopment sensitive to cultural preservation. This was a prelude to preparing a regional development plan for the Kali Gandaki Valley similar to the regional master development plan completed the same year for the Kathmandu Valley.

Travel to Kathmandu was uneventful. I was met at the Tribhuvan Airport by an official from the Ministry and, after reciprocal pleasantries, taken to the four-star Hotel Annapurna near the royal palace. Accommodations and reception were most agreeable. The team finally got together the next day, and the UNDP and ministry officials briefed us. We were to depart for Pokhara with a caravan of motor cars the next morning. Taking advantage of the few hours left, I took a stroll in the commercial district of Kathmandu, where I purchased a wide-brimmed Gurkha soldier hat as headgear and a *kukri*, the traditional sword of Nepalese soldiers, as souvenirs from Nepal. I still have them.

The team gathered in front of the Hotel Annapurna early the next morning dressed for the mission. The fruit bats that were returning from their nightly search for food were settling noisily on the branches of the three tall trees across the street. Their cacophony was a reminder that we were in a very different country. The ministry provided each expert with a counterpart official for training purposes. The director of physical planning and the UNDP official jointly headed the team. In addition to the Nepalese staff, the team included porters, a cook, and a Sirdar (mountain and trek guide). All supplies and personal equipment were loaded on several Land Rovers. My equipment included a backpack containing my personal effects and camera equipment. I was prepared to carry my backpack personally during the trip. Our hosts gently reminded me that a porter was already assigned to carry my personal effects and tent and that I should not deprive him of his job for the three weeks that we would be trekking on the countryside. I hastily obliged. The porter loaded my backpack into his wicker basket and then secured it on top of the car.

The caravan wandered through the charming countryside over a recently graded road between Kathmandu and Pokhara. Cultivated terraces were ablaze with yellow mustard flowers and rhododendrons. Picturesque villages dotted the hills. Every piece of level land was cultivated. That left only the hillsides for compact housing for villagers. We arrived in Pokhara in late afternoon and set camp on the shores of Phewa Tal. One of the largest lakes in the region, Phewa Tal was a favored recreation spot for royalty; a royal cottage adorned the edge of the lake. The 23,000 foot high peak of Machhapuchhare (Fish Tail) overlooked the Pokhara plateau and reflected its image on the lake. In the background, the peaks of the Annapurna and Dhaulagiri ranges were visible from our campsite. We turned in early after consuming a hearty dinner while sitting around the fire.

Our trek got underway early the next morning. We continued toward our destination at Jomosom at a steady pace. We swung around the Annapurna massif and headed down to the Kali Gandaki valley. The enormous spectacle of the Dhaulagiri massif grew before our eyes. We camped overnight under clear skies. When we arrived in Kusma, our advance party had already secured accommodations in several houses. I began my survey of the tourism potential and urban conditions of the village, sketching its layout from personal observation. There were no base maps. This practice was repeated in every village we visited. Only an overlay topographic map of the region drawn from old British military maps was made available to us. I photographed clusters of buildings, interesting building details, and culturally significant aspects of village life. Craftsmen practicing their trades, customers having haircuts on the street, and women and children waiting and gossiping in the village square, waiting to fill their jugs from the only running water in the village, were my subjects. The serenity of the village life was evident. Although poor by world economic standards, none of the villagers looked destitute or miserable. They carried themselves with dignity, and were courteous and charming to us and to each other on every occasion. I classified and coded each item of possible interest to tourists and located possible service facilities and project sites. My colleagues in the mission performed their own sets of surveys.

Our trail followed the river as we traveled north. It was getting gradually colder at night as we trekked to an ever-higher altitude. We passed through Baglung, where we observed the most colorful sunset reflected from the Annapurna massif. Beni, Dana, and Tatopani were our next stops. Their hot springs were known for centuries to have medicinal qualities. It felt good to take our first bath since we left Pokhara. I visited a typical multistory house clinging to the hill behind. The bottom level served as shelter for the animals. Hay for the yak, horse, or goat was stacked in the corner. The second level was set aside for living quarters. The third level was the roof. It was accessible by a ladder and served several purposes. Its flat surface was ideal for drying grain under the sun. It also served as sleeping quarters during the hot season.

The precious firewood was stacked all around the edges of the roof. A prayer flag flapped from its pole. The walls of the house were built of stone. The ceilings and roof were made of compacted mud and straw over a wicker mat resting on rough-hewn wood joists. The house did not have running water and sanitary facilities. Women carried water from the river in brass and copper jugs. There was no electrical power service to the village. Aside from a few cooking and serving utensils and a kerosene burner, there was no furniture. Sleeping quilts were rolled in the corner of the room. All cooking, eating, and socializing were done on the floor. Since there were no roads, there was no need for wheels. Every item was carried on human backs, by horses, or by yaks. Both men and beasts had to be sure-footed on the narrow trails.

As we climbed to 16,000 feet, the valley got wider and Kali Gandaki became tamer. Jomosom appeared after a turn of the trail. Trees and vegetation disappeared at this elevation. The alluvial flat at the bottom of the valley next to the river was cultivated. A narrow shoulder was scraped by hand to create a landing strip for short take-off airplanes and helicopters. The remains of a crashed Twin Otter airplane rested at the end of the strip as a reminder of the hazardous flying conditions in the valley. In fact, Jomosom was accessible by air only in early morning and late afternoon hours, when the wind constantly blowing through the valley calmed down.

Our group passed by a stand of prayer wheels and flags and reached the first indoor accommodation since we left Pokhara. The "hotel" consisted of a one-story mud-plastered structure with a sign on the front wall proudly displaying its name. It had several large rooms opening to an interior courtyard. Each room accommodated groups of five or six travelers. There was no furniture. A plastic sheet covered the only room with a window where our host and his family lived. There was no electricity or generator, sanitary facilities, or running water in the building. The young proprietor and his wife greeted us warmly on our arrival and served hot tea with yak milk. Our cook prepared our dinners from our own supplies. Later, I learned that the proprietor served as Sirdar in several expeditions, and having seen the hotels in Kathmandu, he returned home and used his meager savings to build his Hotel Jomosom. He was an astute entrepreneur.

After surveying the area for a day, we departed Jomosom in two groups. One group took an early morning helicopter flight to the end of the trail at Mustang, now located in a military zone at the border with Tibet, and returned to Beni. The adventurous expatriate British helicopter pilot showed his skills by avoiding being slammed by shifting winds against the walls of the valley. The second group returned on horseback and on foot and rejoined the first group in Beni three days later. Together, we continued on our trek, surveying the valley toward Tansen and Butwal. The elevation and vegetation changed around us. A lush tropical environment met us in Terai. Our last destination was the border town with India, Bhairawa. We arrived at a very busy urban center where the urban character of Nepal was replaced by the urban character of India.

The sacred pilgrimage site of all Buddhists is Lumbini. It lies about fifteen miles southwest of Bhairawa. It is the birthplace of Lord Buddha. According to historical sources, King Suddhodhana, the father of Lord Buddha, was the supreme head of the tiny republic in Terai with Kapilavastu as its capital. According to the legend, Maya Devi, the queen of King Suddhodhana, was traveling from Kapilavastu to the home of her parents when she gave birth to a child, a boy, in Lumbini Garden while taking a rest under the big sal tree on the full moon day of May, 563 BC. The boy was named Siddhartha Gautam. When he reached the age of twenty-nine, he left Kapilavastu and attained enlightenment at the age of thirty-five. He died in 483 BC at the age of eighty. During his reign, Emperor Ashoka of India came to Lumbini on a pilgrimage in 244 BC and erected a stone pillar at the site. The inscriptions on the pillar confirmed the site as the birthplace of Lord Buddha. At its side, he built a stupa. The stone pillar was discovered in 1836. It was found broken and now measures 20 feet high and 8 feet in diameter. To the east of the pillar stands the Rummindeyi Temple, where the image of Maya Devi standing under the sal tree is located. The image is carved in high relief on a large slab of sandstone. Over the years, the blind faith and superstition of pilgrims caused the image to be covered with a thick coat of vermillion and oil. The people of Lumbini strongly believed that drinking the water after rubbing the image assured fertility in women. This left the image totally eroded.

Our last item of business was to visit the famous tiger park, where beautiful Bengal tigers and majestic elephants roamed the grassy fields and thick jungle. A short survey enabled me to confirm the obvious value of the park as a major tourist attraction and conservation area. Our mission completed, and loaded with survey and potential project information, we flew from Bhairawa to Kathmandu. I spent one more week writing my findings and recommendations. I submitted my mission report to His Majesty's Ministry and UNDP. The bond that formed between us experts and our Nepalese counterparts was memorable for years to come. In fact, I returned to Nepal two years later for another assignment.

Evaluation

The early tourism development of Nepal exhibits all the symptoms that most LDCs display when they first undertake the development of their tourism potential. They are economically poor but rich in ancient culture or have exceptional environmental assets to offer visitors. They also need technical assistance, at least initially. The cycle of poverty has to be broken at some level to get the country moving in the direction of sustainable growth. Mistakes are made, and Nepal has made its share of them.

After the country opened to the outside world in 1952, the first decade of development was chaotic. Laissez-faire development was the norm. Opportunistic foreign elements took advantage of the receptiveness of the country and introduced unchecked initiatives. The physical effect of these initiatives on the environment in which tourism was to take place bordered on the disastrous. In a few short years, Kathmandu was overcome by rapid urbanization creating ugly intrusions into the fabric of the country's cultural heritage. Incongruous concrete jungles surrounded temples already suffering from neglect. The government came to realize that something had to be done to establish order. Government agencies were given authority to prepare their own remedial programs. These turned out to be ineffective, partly because they were not coordinated and often were in direct conflict with each other. The government sought and received technical and financial assistance from abroad. A multisectoral macro-plan was prepared, and a central planning agency was established to oversee its implementation.

The multisectoral macro-plan prescribed regional development plans based on identifiable urban growth centers. Kathmandu Valley, with Kathmandu as its growth center, was the logical first region. Again, an international team of experts was recruited. The *Physical Development Plan for the Kathmandu Valley* used the conventional planning approach of survey-analysis-recommendation-implementation steps and focused on physical features, and on some economic and social features, of the valley. Tourism received its first consideration within the regional context of the capital city. Next came the more focused and action-oriented *Nepal Tourism Master Plan*, which expanded the scope of tourism planning to the entire country. The team of experts exhibited an early appreciation of sustainability and properly managed growth in this plan. They established guidelines for the country's capacity to absorb tourism growth and to protect its assets. In particular, cultural tourism, trekking, and mountaineering were given detailed prescriptions.

At the time of my arrival in Nepal in 1972, the *Nepal Tourism Master Plan* and the *Physical Development Plan for the Kathmandu Valley* were entering their implementation phase. The Kali Gandaki Valley region, with the Pokhara-Jomosom-Lumbini urban growth axis, was the next priority region for comprehensive evaluation and planning for tourism development. My survey and analysis of the tourism potential of the Kali Gandaki Valley included the following observations:

- The valley had the only centuries'-old land access over the Himalayas between India and China through Tibet. The valley served as a traditional trade route. Over the centuries, many urban settlements were established as stopovers for yak caravans, which passed through regularly during the trade season. This trade route was an excellent theme for tourism planning, development, and marketing.
- Pokhara served as the *Panchayat,* or seat of government, for the region. In the context of tourism, it could also be the service and growth center of the region. This role required land and air access from Kathmandu and appropriate infrastructure facilities to accommodate groups of tourists. This measure had already been taken.
- The potential for organizing treks originating from and returning to Pokhara and Bhairawa at the southern border with India was excellent. At least three major trekking loops were possible. The scenic beauty and physically challenging landscape, combined with the cultural attractions, made the region ideal for adventure tourism.
- Mountaineering expeditions to Dhaulagiri (26,975 feet) and Annapurna (26,146 feet) also started and ended in Pokhara. Next to the Everest group of peaks, these two mountain groups had the most popular and challenging peaks. This potential, combined with the relative proximity of Pokhara as a service center, made the Kali Gandaki Valley the second most important destination in Nepal.
- Pokhara's rural character blended well with the trade route theme of the valley. The historic settlements in the valley were to be protected from the intrusion of ugly and irresponsible new construction. This required careful destination planning emphasizing small bed and breakfast and supply facilities for trekkers and mountaineers. It was essential that these settlements preserve their original urban character while improving their local economies.
- Compared to other settlements in the valley, pilgrimage tourism to Lumbini and thermal springs tourism to Beni, Tatopani, and Dana required special infrastructure and accommodations. These two types of tourism, combined with trekking and mountaineering, had good potential for diversifying the regional tourism economy and extending its season at both ends.
- Pilgrimage necessitated simpler accommodations. However, in improving the facility mix of the region, it was desirable to merge the two types of tourism rather then develop two superimposed tourism patterns and facilities—one for Nepalese and Indians and one for foreigners.
- Festivals deserved particular attention for their tourism as well as religious values. They were not to be allowed to turn into staged events for the benefit of tourists.
- At the level of the development plan for the Kali Gandaki Valley region, sustainability of tourism development was to be the primary test for evaluating tourism development projects and related actions.

Conclusions and Lessons Learned

- The conclusions and lessons learned from the early tourism development in Nepal are significant for their application to other LDCs that exhibit tourism potential. Except for agriculture and some service industries, these countries may not have complex economies. As a result, they are vulnerable to fluctuations caused by internal and external events. Internal conflicts like sectarian wars that have been going on for decades (e.g., in Ethiopia), as well as external conflicts and despotism (e.g., in Iraq), can prevent the growth of tourism in these countries. Nepal was particularly fortunate in having a stable government and welcoming people in the early stages of its tourism development.

- Self-motivation is generally not enough to plan and develop tourism in LDCs. External technical and financial assistance—preferably without political strings attached—is necessary. At the outset of the survey and evaluation of the tourism potential, the team of experts had to agree on the planning philosophy and methodology of building a reliable and comparative database. The choice of planning procedures in a mixed economy like Nepal's was different from those in a market economy.

- Soon after Nepal opened to the outside world, ideas, people, and money poured in. The government was most accommodating. Laissez-faire prevailed for one decade. The excesses of this policy became visible, however, and corrective actions were taken to bring order out of chaos. This was accomplished by tourism development planning at the national level, but particularly at the regional and local levels.

- **Sustainability** and **regionalism** entered the lexicon of tourism planning several decades ago. However, market-oriented consultants and other experts largely ignored these concepts and prevailed in imposing what they knew best: the primacy of private sector initiative and minimum public planning as their prescription for mixed or even centrally planned economic systems. Nepal was fortunate in that both its *Nepal Tourism Master Plan* and *The Physical Development Plan for the Kathmandu Valley* were prepared by technical assistance teams who subscribed to the sustainability and regionalism principles of tourism planning.

- Today, Nepal is continuing to fascinate the world of tourism. However, the country is not the same as it was thirty years ago. Ultimately, the successes and failures of the country in planning and developing its tourism will be measured by the advances made in alleviating its poverty. The full social, cultural, and environmental costs of tourism remain to be seen. It is hoped that observers will not fall into despair, as Toni Hagen did more than fifty years ago.

Study Questions

- Why did Nepal choose tourism for its national development?
- Why was international technical assistance used for preparing the tourism development plans?
- What was the basic principle of sustainability used in the *Nepal Tourism Master Plan*?
- How was a regional approach to tourism development planning used in connection with sectoral economic plans?
- How did the initial demonstration effect of tourism influence social change and encourage entrepreneurship in selected destination areas of Nepal?

APPENDIX A

Selected World Heritage Sites

Designated by the
United Nations Educational, Scientific, and Cultural
Organization (UNESCO), 2004

The **General Conference of the United Nations Educational, Scientific, and Cultural Organization** (UNESCO) took place in Paris from October 17 to November 21, 1972, for the purpose of deliberating about the protection of the world's cultural and natural heritage. The **World Heritage List** was adopted by UNESCO on December 17, 1975. The objective was to identify, study, and protect the monuments, complexes, and natural and human-made sites that have **"outstanding universal value"** from a historical, artistic, scientific, naturalistic, archeological, or anthropological standpoint.

The 1972 convention defined **cultural heritage** and **natural heritage** as follows:

For the purposes of this Convention, the following shall be considered as **"cultural heritage:"**

–*Monuments:* architectural works, works of monumental sculpture and painting, elements of structures of an archeological nature, inscriptions, cave dwellings, and combinations of features which are of outstanding universal value from the point of view of history, art, or science;

–*Groups of buildings:* groups of separate or connected buildings which, because of their architecture, their homogeneity or their place in the landscape, are of outstanding universal value from the view point of history, art or science;

–*Sites:* works of humans or the combined works of nature and humans, and areas including archeological sites which are of outstanding universal value from the historical, aesthetic, ethnological or anthropological point of view.

For the purpose of this Convention, the following shall be considered as **"natural heritage:"**

–*Natural features* consisting of physical and biological formations or groups of such formations which are of outstanding universal value from the aesthetic or scientific point of view;

–*Geological and physiographical* formations and precisely delineated areas which constitute the habitat of threatened species of animals and plants of outstanding universal value from the viewpoint of science or conservation;

–*Natural sites* or precisely delineated natural areas of outstanding universal value from the point of view of science, conservation or natural beauty.

Each State party to this convention agreed to identify, protect, conserve, present, and transmit to future generations the cultural and natural heritage referred to by the convention. To achieve this goal, each State agreed:

–to adopt a general policy which aims to give the cultural and natural heritage a function in the life of the community and to integrate the protection of that heritage into comprehensive planning programmes;

–to set up within its territories, where such services do not exist, one or more services for the protection, conservation, and presentation of the cultural and natural heritage with an appropriate staff and possessing the means to discharge their functions;

–to develop scientific and technical studies and research and to work out such operating methods as will make the State capable of counteracting the dangers that threaten its cultural or natural heritage;

–to take the appropriate legal, scientific, technical, administrative, and financial measures necessary for the identification, protection, conservation, presentation and rehabilitation of this entire heritage; and

–to foster the establishment or development of national or regional centres for training in the protection, conservation and presentation of the cultural and natural heritage and to encourage scientific research in the field.

The convention fully respected, without prejudice, the property rights and sovereignty of the states on whose territory the cultural and natural heritage are situated. But it required States that were parties to the convention:

–to recognize that such heritage constitutes a world heritage for whose protection it is the duty of the international community as a whole to co-operate;

–to give help in the identification, protection, conservation and presentation of the cultural and natural heritage . . . if the States on whose territory they are situated so request;

–to undertake not to take any deliberate measures which might damage directly or indirectly the cultural and natural heritage. . . .

For the purpose of the convention, international protection of the world's cultural and natural heritage is understood to mean the establishment of a system of international cooperation and assistance designed to support States that are parties to the convention in their efforts to conserve and identify that heritage. As of 2011, forty-two additional sites in forty countries are being considered for designation as world heritage sites under various categories.

THE TREASURES OF ART

To merit listing in the World Heritage List as **cultural** property, a monument, a complex, or a site, at least one of the following criteria must be met:

1) Represent a masterpiece of human creative genius; or
2) Exhibit an important interchange of human values over a span of time or within a cultural area of the world, involving developments in architecture or technology, monumental arts, town planning, or landscape design; or

3) Bear a unique or at least exceptional testimony to a cultural tradition or to a civilization that is living or has disappeared; or

4) Be an outstanding example of a type of building, or an architectural or technological ensemble, or a landscape that illustrates a significant stage in human history; or

5) Be an outstanding example of a traditional human settlement or land use that is representative of a culture, especially when it has become vulnerable or is under the effects of irreversible change; or

6) Be directly or tangibly associated with events or living traditions, with ideas or beliefs, or with artistic and literary works of outstanding universal significance.

The following 100 sites in fifty-five countries were selected by Marco Cattaneo and Jasmina Trifoni for their publication *World Heritage Sites—The Treasures of Art* from among 400 sites listed by UNESCO.

The Americas

United States—New York	United States—Taos	Mexico—Guanajuato
Mexico—Oaxaca	Cuba—Havana	Guatemala—Antigua
Columbia—Cartagena	Peru—Arequipa	Brazil—Salvador de Bahia
Brazil—Brazilia	Bolivia—Sucre	Argentina—Cordoba

Europe

Portugal—Tomar	Portugal—Sintra	Spain—Barcelona
Spain—Alcala	Spain—Granada	Spain—Cordoba
Spain—Siviglia	France—Rheims	France—Paris
France—Versaille	France—Mont Saint Michel	France—Chartres
France—Loire Valley	France—Arc Et Senans	France—Avignon
Great Britain—Ironbridge Gorge	Great Britain—Westminster	Great Britain—Canterbury
Belgium—Brugge	Belgium—Brussels	Netherlands—K. Ellshouy
Germany—Potsdam	Germany—Aachen	Germany —Würzburg
Germany—Völklingen	Germany—Maulbronn	Denmark—Kronborg
Sweden—Drottninghom	Norway—Urness	Norway—Bergen
Finland—Verla	Estonia—Tallinn	Latvia—Riga
Russia—Kizhi Pogost	Russia—Saint Petersburg	Russia—Moscow
Poland—Krakow	Czech Republic—Lednice	Austria—Schönbrunn
Italy—Milan	Italy—Vicenza	Italy—Venice
Italy—Ravenna	Italy—Pizza	Italy—Florence
Italy—Assisi	Italy—Vatican City	Italy—Caserta
Croatia—Dubrovnik	Hungary—Budapest	Bulgaria—Ivanovo
Greece—Mount Athos	Greece—Meteora	Turkey—Istanbul
Turkey—Safranbolu	Cyprus—Troodos	

Africa

Morocco—Fez	Mauratania—Quadane	Mali—Bandiagara
Mali—Djienne	Libya—Ghadames	Egypt—Cairo
Ethiopia—Gondar	Tanzania—Zanzibar	

Asia

Syria—Damascus	Israel—Jerusalem	Yemen—Sana'a
Iran—Isfahan	Uzbekistan—Khiva	Uzbekistan—Samarkand
Pakistan—Lahore	India—Delhi	India—Agra
Sri Lanka—Galle	Nepal—Kathmandu	China—The Great Wall
China—Beijing	China—Taishan	China—Lhasa
Laos—Luang Parabang	Vietnam—Hue	Korea—Haeinsa
Japan—Kyoto	Japan—Himeji Jo	Japan—Itsukushima

NATURE SANCTUARIES

To be registered on the World Heritage List as a **natural site,** a geographical area has to meet at least one of the following criteria:

1) Be outstanding examples of major stages of human history, including the record of life, significant ongoing geological processes in the development of landforms, or significant geomorphic or physiographic features; or

2) Be outstanding examples of significant ongoing ecological and biological processes in the evolution and development of terrestrial, freshwater, coastal, and marine ecosystems and communities of plants and animals; or

3) Contain superlative natural phenomena or areas of exceptional beauty and aesthetic importance; or

4) Contain the most important and significant natural habitats for in-situ conservation of biological diversity, including those containing threatened species of outstanding universal value from the point of view of science or conservation.

The following 100 sites in fifty-seven countries were selected by Marco Cattaneo and Jasmina Trifoni for their publication *World Heritage Sites—Nature Sanctuaries* from among 167 sites listed by UNESCO.

The Americas

United States/Canada—Kluane/Wrangell, St Elias, Glacier Bay, and Tatshenshini Alsek Parks

Canada—Wood Buffalo National Park

Canada—Canadian Rocky Mountains Parks

Canada—Dinosaur Provincial Park

Canada—Gross Morne National Park

Canada/United States—Waterton Glacier International Peace Park

United States—Yellowstone National Park

United States—Redwood National Park

United States—Yosemite National Park

United States—Grand Canyon National Park

United States—Great Smoky Mountains National Park

United States—Everglades National Park

United States—Hawaii Volcanoes National Park

Mexico—Whale Sanctuary of El Vizcaino

Belize—Belize Barrier Reef

Costa Rica—Isla De Cocos

Costa Rica—Guanacaste Conservation Area

Panama—Parque Nacional Darien

Venezuela—Parque Nacional Canaima

Ecuador—The Galapagos Islands

Peru—Parque Nacional Huascaran

Peru—Parque Nacional Manu

Bolivia—Parque Nacional Noel Kempff Mercado

Brazil—Pantanal Conservation Area

Brazil—Atlantic Forest South-East
  Reserves
Brazil—Fernando De Noronha and Atol
  Das Rocas Reserves

Argentina/Brazil—Iguazu Falls
Argentina—Parque Nacional Los
  Glaciares
Argentina—Peninsula Valdes

Europe

Sweden—Lapland
Belarus/Poland—Bialowieza Forest
Great Britain—Giant's Causeway
Great Britain—The Coast of Dorset and
  E. Devon
France (Corsica)—Cap Girolata, Cap Porto,
  Scandola Nature Reserve, and Piana
  Calanches
France/Spain—Pyrenees, Mont Perdu
Spain—Parque Nacional De Coto Donana
Portugal—The Laurisilva of Madeira

Switzerland—The Jungfrau, Aletshhorn,
  Bietchhorn
Italy—The Aeolian Islands
Slovenia—The Caves of Skocjan
Croatia—The Lakes of Plitvice
Yugoslavia—Durmitor National Park
Slovakia/Hungary—The Caves of Aggtelek
  Karst and Slovak Karst
Rumania—The Delta of the Danube
Russia—The Western Caucasus

Africa

Mauritania—Banc D'Arguin National Park
Niger—Air and Tenere Natural Reserve
Uganda—Bwindi Impenetrable National
  Park
Ethiopia—Simien National Park
Uganda—Rwenzori Mountains National
  Park
Kenya—Lake Turkana National Parks
Kenya—Mount Kenya National Park/
  Natural Forest
Congo—Virunga National Park
Tanzania—Serengeti National Park

Tanzania—Kilimanjaro National Park
Tanzania—Ngorongoro Conservation Area
Tanzania—Selous Game Preserve
Zambia/Zimbabwe—Mosi Oa Tunya,
  Victoria Falls
South Africa—Ukhahlamba/Drakensberg
  Park
South Africa—Greater St. Lucia Wetland
  Park
Seychelles—Aldabra Atoll
Madagascar—Tsingy De Mebaraha Strict
  Nature Preserve

Asia

Turkey—The Valley of Göreme
Turkey—Pamukkale
Russia—Lake Baikal
Russia —The Kamchatka Volcanoes
Russia—Central Sikhote Alin
Russia—The Golden Mountains of Altai
China—Huanglong and Jiuzhaigou
China—Huangshan
China—Wulingyuan
Japan—Shirakami Sanchi
Nepal—Royal Chitwan National Park
India—Nanda Devi National Park
India—Kaziranga National Park

India—Manas Wildlife Sanctuary
India—Keoladeo National Park
Sri Lanka—Sinharaja Forest Reserve
Bangladesh—Sundarbans
Thailand—Thung Yai and Huaki Kha
  Khaeng
Vietnam—Ha Long Bay
Philippines—Turbataha Reef Marine
  Park
Malaysia—Kinabalu National Park
Malaysia—Gunung Mulu National Park
Indonesia—Ujung Kulon National Park
Indonesia—Komodo National Park

Oceania

Australia—Kakadu National Park
Australia—The Wet Tropics in Queensland
Australia—The Great Barrier Reef
Australia—Fraser Island
Australia—Shark Bay
Australia—Uluru Kata Tjuta National Park
Australia—Central Eastern Rainforest
   Reserves

Australia—Greater Blue Mountains
Australia—Macquarie Island
Australia—The Parks of Tasmania
New Zealand—Te Wahipounamu
New Zealand—The Sub-Antarctic Islands
   of New Zealand

ANCIENT CIVILIZATIONS

To be included in the World Heritage List as an **ancient civilization,** the same criteria for cultural property must be met. The following 100 sites in forty-seven countries were selected by Marco Cattaneo and Jasmina Triffoni for their publication *World Heritage Sites—Ancient Civilizations* from among 188 properties of archeological interest listed by UNESCO.

The Americas

United States—Mesa Verde
Mexico—Teotihuacan
Mexico—Monte Alban
Mexico—Palenque
Mexico—Uxmal
Mexico—Chichen Itza
Guatemala—Tikal
Guatemala—The Archeological
   Park of Quirigua
Honduras—The Mayan Site
Peru—Chavin De Huantar of Copan

Peru—Chan Chan
Peru—Machu Picchu
Peru—Cuzco
Peru—The Lines and Geoglyphs of Nazca
   and the Pampas of Jumana
Bolivia—The Political and Spiritual Center
   of the Tiwanaku Culture
Brazil—The Serra De Capivara
Chile—Rapa Nui National Park
Argentina—The Cueva De Las Manos in
   the Rio Pinturas Valley

Europe

Sweden—The Rock Incisions at Tanum
Ireland—The Megalithic Monuments of
   the Boyne Valley
Great Britain—Hadrian's Wall
Great Britain—Stonehenge and Avebury
Germany—The Roman Monuments
   of Trier
France—The Painted Grottoes in the Vallee
   de la Vezere
France—The Pont du Gard
France—The Roman Theater and the
   Triumphal Arch of Orange
France—The Roman Monuments of Arles
Spain—The Cave at Altamira
Spain—The Aqueduct of Segovia
Spain—The Roman Monuments of Merida

Italy—Villa Adriana
Italy—Ancient Rome
Italy—Pompei, Herculanum, and Oplontis
Italy—Cilento and the Vallo di Diano with
   the Sites of Paestum and Velia
Italy—The Villa at Cassale
Italy—The Valley of the Temples in
   Agregento
Croatia—The Historic Center of Split and
   the Palace of Diocletian
Bulgaria—The Tracian Tomb of Kazanlak
Greece—Vergina
Greece—Delphi
Greece—The Acropolis in Athens
Greece—Olympia
Greece—Mycenea

Greece—Epidarus
Greece—Delos
Greece—Samos

Malta—The Megalithic Temples
   of Malta
Cyprus—Paphos

Africa

Morocco—Volubilis
Algeria—Timgad
Tunisia—Carthage
Tunisia—Dougga
Tunisia—The Amphitheater
Libya—Sabratha
Libya—Leptis Magna
Libya—The Tadrart Akakus
Libya—Cyrene

Egypt—Memphis and Its Necropolis
Egypt—The Pyramids from Giza to
   Danshur
Egypt—Ancient Thebes and Its
   Necropolis
Egypt—The Nubian Monuments from
   Abu Simbel to Philae
Ethiopia—Aksum
Zimbabwe—The Great Zimbabwe

Asia

Turkey—Nemrut Dagi
Turkey—Hierapolis-Pamukkale
Syria—Aleppo
Syria—Palmyra
Syria—Bosra
Lebanon—Baalbek
Lebanon—Tyre
Israel—Masada
Jordan—Qusayr ʻAmra
Jordan—Petra
Iraq—Hatra
Iran—Persopolis
Afghanistan—The Minaret of Jam
China—The Caves of Magao
China—The Tombs of the First Qin
   Emperor
China—The Longmen Grottoes
China—Mount Emei and the Leshan
   Giant Buddha
China—The Yungang Grottoes
South Korea—The Seokguram Grotto
   and Bulguksa Temple
Japan—The Monuments of Ancient Nara

Japan—The Buddhist Monuments in the
   Horyu-Ji Era
Pakistan—The Buddhist Monastery of
   Takht-I-Bahi and the Ruins of the City
   of Sahr-i-Bahlol
Nepal—Lumbini, the Birthplace of Buddha
India—Khajuraho
India—The Buddhist Monuments at Sanchi
India—The Caves at Ajanta
India—The Caves at Ellora
India—The Monuments of Hampi
India—The Monuments at
   Mahabalipuram
Sri Lanka—Sigiriya
Sri Lanka—The Sacred City of
   Anuradhapura
Sri Lanka—Polonnaruwa
Thailand—Ayutthaya
Cambodia—Angkor
Vietnam—The Sanctuary of My Son
Indonesia—The Temple of Borobudur
Indonesia—The Temple Complex of
   Prambanan

Oceania

Australia— Kakadu National Park

APPENDIX B

Tourism Sector Industries and Establishments

Representing Tourist Site and Event Attractions and Tourist Facilities Selected from the North American Industrial Classification System (NAICS)

SECTOR 11 Agriculture, Forestry, Fishing, and Hunting

Subsector 113 Forestry and Logging

113210 Forest Nurseries and Gathering of Forest Products

113310 Logging

Subsector 114 Fishing, Hunting, and Trapping

114111 Finfish Fishing

114112 Shellfish Fishing, Clam Digging, Crabbing, Lobstering

114210 Hunting, Trapping, Game Preserves

SECTOR 22 Utilities

Subsector 221 Utilities

221110 Electric Power Generation

221122 Electric Power Distribution

221210 Natural Gas Distribution

221310 Water Supply and Irrigation Systems

221320 Sewage Treatment Facilities

SECTOR 23 Construction

Subsector 233 Building, Developing, and General Contracting

233110 Land Subdivision and Land Development

233210 Single-Family Housing Construction, Alterations, Prefab Housing

233220 Multi-Family Housing Construction, Prefab Apartment

233320 Commercial and Institutional Building Construction, Alterations

SECTOR 31–33 Manufacturing

Subsector 312 Beverage Product Manufacturing

312120 Breweries

312130 Vineries

Subsector 336 Transportation Equipment Manufacturing

336612 Yachts Not Built in Shipyards

SECTOR 44–45 Retail Trade

Subsector 443 Electronics and Appliance Stores

443130 Camera and Photographic Supplies Store

443111 Appliance Store – Household

Subsector 444 Building Materials, Garden Equipment and Supplies Dealers

444110 Home Centers

444190 Building Materials Supply

Subsector 445 Food and Beverage Stores

445110 Supermarkets and Other Grocery Stores (Except Convenience)

445120 Convenience Stores

445210 Butcher Shops

445220 Seafood Markets

445230 Produce Markets

445310 Beer, Wine, Liquor, and Package Stores

Subsector 446 Health and Personal Care Stores

446110 Pharmacies, Drug Stores, Health and Beauty Aids Stores

446120 Cosmetics, Beauty Supplies, and Perfume Stores

446199 All Other Health and Personal Care Stores

Subsector 447 Gasoline Stations

447110 Gasoline Stations with Convenience Stores

447190 Other Gasoline Stations

Subsector 448 Clothing and Clothing Accessories Stories

448110 Men's Clothing Stores

448120 Women's Clothing Stores

448210 Athletic Shoe Stores

448130 Children's and Infants' Clothing Stores

448310 Jewelry Stores

448320 Luggage and Leather Goods Stores

Subsector 451 Sporting Goods, Hobby, Book, and Music Stores

451110 Sporting Goods Stores, Gun Shops, Fish Tackle Stores

451140 Music Stores

451211 Book Stores

451212 News Dealers and Newsstands

451220 Prerecorded Tape, Compact Disc, Record and Video Stores

Subsector 452 General Merchandise Stores

452110 Department Stores

452910 Warehouse Clubs and Superstores

452990 Variety Stores

Subsector 453 Miscellaneous Store Retailers

453110 Florist

453220 Gift, Novelty, and Souvenir Stores

453310 Antique Stores

453920 Art Dealers, Auctions

453930 Manufactured (Mobile) Home Dealers

Subsector 454 Non-Store Retailers

454110 Electronic Shopping and Mail Order Stores

454390 Flea Markets, Street Vendors

SECTOR 48–49 Transportation and Warehousing

Subsector 481 Air Transportation

481111 Scheduled Passenger and Commuter Air Transportation

481211 Nonscheduled Chartered Passenger Air Transportation, Helicopter

Subsector 482 Rail Transportation

482111 Line-Haul Railroads

482112 Short Line Railroads

Subsector 483 Water Transportation

483112 Deep Sea Passenger Transportation, Cruise Lines

483114 Coastal and Great Lakes Passenger Transportation, Chartering Ship with Crew

483212 Inland Water Transportation, River Passenger Transportation, Water Taxi

Subsector 484 Truck Transportation

484121 General Freight Trucking Long Distance

Subsector 485 Transit and Ground Passenger Transportation

485111 Mixed-Mode Transit Systems

485112 Commuter Rail Systems, Local Passenger Rail Systems

485113 Bus and Other Motor Vehicle Local Transit Systems

485119 Other Urban Transit Systems

485210 Interurban and Rural Bus Transportation

485310 Taxi Service

485320 Limousine Service

485510 Charter Bus Industry

485991 Handicapped Passenger Transportation

485999 Airport Limousine Services

Subsector 487 Scenic and Sightseeing Transportation

487110 Scenic and Sightseeing Transportation on Land, Cable Car, Monorail, Bus

487210 Scenic Sightseeing Transportation on Water, Boat Charter, Dinner Cruises

487990 Scenic Sightseeing Transportation, Airplane and Helicopter Rides

Subsector 488 Support Activities for Transportation

    488111 Air Traffic Control

    488119 Other Airport Operations, Rental Aircraft Hangar

    488190 Aircraft Maintenance and Repair Services

    488210 Support Activities for Rail Transportation, Terminals

    488310 Port and Harbor Operations, Docking Facilities

    488390 Drydocks

    488410 Motor Vehicle Towing, Emergency Road Service

    488490 Bridge, Tunnel, Highway Operations

Subsector 491 Postal Service

    491110 Postal Service

Subsector 492 Couriers and Messengers

    492110 Couriers, Local Letter and Parcel Delivery, Messenger Service

SECTOR 51 Information

Subsector 512 Motion Picture and Sound Recording Industries

    512131 Motion Picture Theaters

Subsector 513 Broadcasting and Telecommunications

    513112 Radio Stations

    513120 Television Broadcasting

    513210 Cable Networks

    513310 Wired Telecommunication Carriers

    513322 Cellular and Other Wireless Telecommunications

    513340 Satellite Telecommunications

Subsector 514 Information Services and Data Processing Services

    514110 News Syndicates

    514120 Libraries and Archives

    514191 On-Line Information Services

SECTOR 52 Finance and Insurance

Subsector 522 Credit Intermediation and Related Activities

    522110 Commercial Banking

    522120 Savings Institutions

    522130 Credit Unions

    522291 Consumer Lending

    522292 Real Estate Credit

    522310 Mortgage and Non-Mortgage Loan Brokers

Subsector 523 Securities, Commodity Contracts, and Other Financial Investments and Related Activities

    523130 Foreign Exchange Services, Commodity Contracts

Subsector 524 Insurance Carriers and Related Activities

    524126 Direct Property and Casualty Insurance Carriers

    524127 Direct Title Insurance Carriers

Subsector 525—Funds, Trusts, and Other Financial Vehicles

    525920 Private Estates Administration on Behalf of Beneficiaries

    525930 Real Estate Investment Trusts

SECTOR 53 Real Estate, and Rental and Leasing

Subsector 531 Real Estate

    531110 Lessors of Residential Buildings, Dwellings, Residential Hotels

    531120 Auditorium, Convention Center Rental or Leasing

    531190 Lessors of Other Real Estate Property, Mobile Home Rentals

    531210 Offices of Real Estate Agents and Brokers

    531311 Residential Property Managers

    531320 Offices of Real Estate Appraisers

Subsector 532 Rental and Leasing Services

    532111 Passenger Car, Van Rental

    532112 Automobile Leasing

    532220 Costume Rental

    532292 Recreational Goods, Bicycle, Pleasure Boat, Moped, Motorcycle, Row Boat, Ski Equipment Rental

    532310 General Rental Centers

    532411 Commercial Air, Rail, and Water Transportation Equipment Rental and Leasing

SECTOR 54 Professional, Scientific, and Technical Services

Subsector 541 Professional, Scientific, and Technical Services

    541110 Offices of Lawyers

    541199 All Other Legal Services

    541211 Offices of Certified Public Accountants

    541310 Architectural Services

    541320 Land Use Planning Services, Landscape Architects

    541330 Engineering Services

    541350 Building Inspection Services

    541370 Surveying and Mapping (Except Geophysical), GIS

    541410 Interior Design Services

    541430 Graphic Design Services

    541513 Facilities Support Services, Computer Systems, Data Processing

    541850 Advertising Services

    541921 Passport Photograph Services

    541940 Animal Hospitals

SECTOR 56 Administrative and Support and Waste Management and Remediation Services

Subsector 561 Administrative and Support Services

561421 Answering Services, Telephone

561422 Telephone Call Centers

561439 Copy Centers

561510 Travel Agencies

561520 Tour Operators

561591 Convention and Visitor Bureaus

561599 All Other Travel Arrangement and Reservation Services, Hotel and Time Share Reservations

561612 Security Guards and Patrol Services

561710 Exterminating and Pest Control Services

561730 Landscaping Services

561790 Other Services to Buildings and Dwellings

561920 Trade Show Promoters with Facilities

Subsector 562 Waste Management and Remediation Services

562111 Solid Waste Collection Services

562212 Solid Waste Landfill, Sanitary Landfills

562213 Solid Waste Combustors and Incinerators

562991 Septic Tank and Related Services

562998 All Other Miscellaneous Waste Management Services

SECTOR 61 Educational Services

Subsector 611 Educational Services

611310 Universities

611512 Flight Training

611620 Sports and Recreation Instruction

SECTOR 62 Health Care and Social Assistance

Subsector 621 Ambulatory Health Care Services

621111 Offices of Physicians

621210 Offices of Dentists

621399 Offices of All Other Miscellaneous Health Practitioners

621493 Freestanding Ambulatory Surgical and Emergency Services

621498 All Other Outpatient Care Centers

621512 Medical Laboratories, X-Ray, Radiology

621910 Ambulance Services, Air or Ground

Subsector 622 Hospitals

622110 General Medical and Surgical Hospitals

Subsector 623 Nursing and Residential Care Facilities

623312 Retirement Homes without Nursing Care

SECTOR 71 Arts, Entertainment, and Recreation

Subsector 711 Performing Arts, Spectator Sports, and Related Industries

711110 Theater Companies, Dinner Theaters, Burlesque, Comedy, Opera

711120 Dance Companies, Ballet Companies

711130 Musical Groups and Artists, Orchestras, Symphonic Orchestras

711190 Other Performing Arts Companies, Circuses, Ice Skating, Magic Shows

711211 Sports Teams and Clubs, Baseball, Basketball, Football, Hockey

711212 Racetracks for Automobiles, Dragstrips, Greyhound Dog Tracks, Horse Tracks, Motorcycle Tracks

711219 Other Spectator Sports

711310 Promoters of Performing Arts, Sports, Air Shows, and Similar Events with Facilities, Rodeos, Sports Arenas, Live Theaters

711320 Promoters of Performing Arts, Sports, and Similar Events without Facilities

711510 Independent Entertainers

Subsector 712 Museums, Historical Sites, and Similar Institutions

712110 Museums, Halls of Fame, Planetarium

712120 Historical and Archeological Sites, Battlefields, Heritage Villages, Forts, Ships

712130 Zoos, Aquariums, Arboreta, Safari Parks and Botanical Gardens

712190 Nature Parks and Other Similar Institutions, National Parks, Sanctuaries, Waterfalls

Subsector 713 Amusement, Gambling, and Recreation Services

713110 Amusement and Theme Parks, Piers, Summer Theaters, Water Parks

713120 Amusement Arcades, Pinball and Other Game Machines

713210 Casinos (Except Casino Hotels), Gambling Cruises, Riverboat

713290 Other Gambling Industries, Bingo Parlors, Bookies, Off-Track Betting Parlors

713910 Golf Courses and Country Clubs

713920 Skiing Facilities, Cross-Country, Downhill

713930 Marinas, Boating Clubs

713940 Fitness and Recreational Sports Centers, Ice Skating Rinks, Roller Skating, Swimming Pools

713950 Bowling Centers

713990 All Other Amusement and Recreation Industries, River Rafting, Sailing Clubs, Bathing Beaches, Adventure Operations, Nightclubs, Hunting Clubs, Driving Ranges, Dance Halls, Billiard Parlors, Bridge Clubs, Day Camps, Curling, Fishing Guide Services, Horse Rental, Mountain Climbing, Snowmobiling, Soccer Clubs, Riding Stables, White-Water Rafting

SECTOR 72 Accommodation and Food Services

Subsector 721 Accommodations

721110 Hotels (Except Casino Hotels), Motels, Skiing Resorts, Motor Inns, Motor Hotels, Health Spas with Accommodations, Hotels with Golf Courses

721120 Casino Hotels

721191 Bed-and-Breakfast Inns

721199 All Other Traveler Accommodation, Guest Houses, Hostels, Housekeeping Cottages

721211 RV (Recreational Vehicle) Parks and Camp Grounds

721214 Recreational and Vacation Camps (Except Camp Grounds), Dude Ranches

721310 Rooming and Boarding Houses

Subsector 722 Food Services and Drinking Places

722110 Full-Service Restaurants,

722211 Limited-Service Restaurants, Carry Out, Fast Food Restaurants, Bagel Shops, Doughnut Shops, Pizza Parlors

722212 Cafeterias

722213 Snack and Non-Alcoholic Beverage Bars, Coffee, Juice Bars

722320 Caterers, Banquet Halls

722330 Mobile Food Services, Beverages, Food Carts

722410 Drinking Places (Alcoholic Beverages), Bars, Taverns, Cocktail Lounges

SECTOR 81 Other Services (Except Public Administration)

Subsector 811 Repair and Maintenance

811111 General Automotive Repair

811118 Other Automotive Mechanical and Electrical Repair and Maintenance

811192 Car Washes

811490 Other Personal and Household Goods Repair and Maintenance, Boat Repair, Tailor Shops for Alterations

Subsector 812 Personal and Laundry Services

812111 Barber Shops

812112 Beauty Salons, Hair Stylists

812191 Diet and Weight Reducing Centers

812199 Saunas, Steam Baths, Tattoo Parlors, Turkish Baths

812210 Funeral Homes and Funeral Services

812211 Photographic Equipment Repair

812310 Coin-Operated Laundries and Drycleaners

812320 Dry Cleaning and Laundry Services (Except Drycleaners)

812910 Pet Care (Except Veterinary Services)

812922 One-Hour Photo Finishing

812930 Parking Lots and Garages

812990 Rest Room Operations

Subsector 813 Religious, Grant Making, Civic, Professional, and Similar Organizations

813110 Religious Organizations, Churches, Places of Worship, Shrines, Synagogues, Mosques

813312 Environment, Conservation, and Wildlife Organizations

813410 Automobile Clubs, Social Clubs

813910 Business Associations

Subsector 814 Private Households

814110 Private Households

SECTOR 92 Public Administration

Subsector 922 Justice, Order, and Safety Activities

922110 Courts

922120 Police Protection, Park Police, State Police

922130 Legal Counsel and Prosecution

922140 Prisons

922160 Fire Protection

Subsector 924 Administration of Environmental Quality Programs

924110 Administration of Air and Water Resource and Solid Waste Management Programs

924120 Administration of Conservation Programs, Fish and Wildlife Conservation

Subsector 925 Administration of Housing Programs, Urban Planning, and Community Development

925110 Administration of Housing Programs

925120 Administration of Urban Planning and Community and Rural Development

Subsector 926 Administration of Economic Programs

926110 Administration of General Economic Programs (Tourism)

926120 Coast Guard

926150 Regulation, Licensing, and Inspection of Miscellaneous Commercial Sectors

Subsector 928 National Security and International Affairs

928120 International Affairs, Embassies, Consulates, Peace Corps, United Nations, World Bank, Interpol

TOTALS **17 Sectors**

55 Subsectors

232 Establishment types at the six-digit NAICS level

APPENDIX C

History of the BIK System

It all started one warm summer day in 1968 when Commissioner Theodore S. Schulenberg of the Massachusetts Department of Commerce and Development (DCD) called Bulent I. Kastarlak into his office and informed him that Governor Francis W. Sargent had instructed the department and its Division of Tourism to look into the growth potential of tourism in the Commonwealth. The request was to produce a document for inspiring investors and tourism businesses to develop a "balanced," that is, sustainable, high-quality tourism industry with government assistance. Commissioner Schulenberg, Deputy Commissioner of Tourism Lawrence Flynn, and Assistant Commissioner Warren Dillon secured a grant from the New England Regional Commission and allocated state funds for a two-year study project.

The objective of the study was to evaluate the tourism potential in 351 cities and towns, 14 counties, and 12 tourism regions of Massachusetts and propose courses of action for forming a partnership between the private sector and government in planning and developing the tourism potential. Bulent Kastarlak was appointed principal author and project manager for the five-volume study. Carl Wendoloski was the collaborating economist. The Division of Tourism provided logistical support. The study results were made public two years later on December 9, 1970, in Boston.

As the principal author and project manager, Kastarlak immediately confronted serious theoretical and practical limitations. After a preliminary survey of the data sources and literature existing in early 1968, the study team decided that neither the data nor the methods of research available were satisfactory for a comprehensive tourism planning and development research project. An internally consistent database and new methods of analysis and planning had to be developed. A new set of fundamentals for tourism planning and development was conceived during these early months. Many existing economic and regional development theories and methods were tested. Some were adapted to tourism. Others had to be developed for the first time. Economics, geography, social and behavioral sciences, regional planning, community development, architecture, and engineering contributed to the development of these new analytical principles and methods for tourism development planning.

The sheer volume of data to be collected and analyzed, in addition to the rudimentary and highly subjective methodologies then existing in tourism research, necessitated a new and comprehensive analytical method. In inventorying the tourism product of Massachusetts, a mere listing of attractions and facilities seemed pointless in the age of emerging computer technology. Transforming raw survey data into useful planning information called for a new data processing approach that would transform the data into statistics and graphic images. The initial step in developing such a method was to understand the dynamics of the tourism industry. The outcome was an intensive six months of basic research in multiple disciplines that resulted in the **BIK System**, representing the initials of Bulent I. Kastarlak. The system consisted of a combination of interactive manual and electronic data processing methods based on selected tourism industry principles. A new vocabulary and a set of definitions were prepared to describe the system.

In 1968, computers were just coming of age, with more and more applications. Both computer hardware and software were evolving as research and planning aids. Among the leaders of this evolution was a new research laboratory founded at Harvard University, the Laboratory for Computer Graphics and Spatial Analysis (LCGSA), established by its cofounders, Prof. Howard T. Fisher and Allan H. Schmidt. The laboratory was one of the first academic institutions in the United States and the world to pioneer computer mapping science. The Harvard group was looking for a project to demonstrate the capabilities of a computer mapping technique called **SYMAP**. The Massachusetts tourism study was the ideal choice.

The collaboration of the two research groups was fortunate and timely. The result was the first GIS for tourism planning in the United States. The database for tourist attractions was translated into thirty-two computer-generated maps and three-dimensional oblique views by the laboratory. They were selected from among a possible one hundred forty graphic presentations. Computer maps and extensive tabulations made the analysis of tourist attractions spatially and statistically comparable for 351 cities and towns and helped to relate the data to tourist facilities serving them. Major conclusions emerged from the analysis of geographic distributions of tourist attractions and facilities for tourism development planning. In the context of tourism, the Massachusetts study defined an **attraction** as "possessing one thing of a quality or qualities that pulls another thing to it." A tourist **facility** was designed as an establishment "created to serve a particular function," in this case providing service for tourists.

The governor unveiled the five-volume set of reports, starting with Volume I , *Tourism and Its Development Potential in Massachusetts*, and made their conclusions public in Boston on December 9, 1970. Three Boston newspapers carried the results of the study. Four months earlier, in August of that year, Bulent Kastarlak presented the results of the study and methodology at the annual conference of the Travel Research Association held in Monterey, California, on August 10, 1970. Later, Prof. Helen Recknagel, editor of the *Cornell Hotel and Restaurant Administration Quarterly,* published the BIK System and the conclusions of the study in the February 1971 issue of the magazine with the title "Planning Tourism Growth." Bulent Kastarlak later used the system in many tourism planning projects around the world. Today, with advanced computer software and hardware available, the expanded BIK System is ready for wider applications. The complete five-volume set of *Tourism and Its Development Potential in Massachusetts* can be found (in the archives) at the Massachusetts State Library, the MIT Rotch Library, and the Harvard University libraries, among others.

In surveying tourist attractions and facilities according to the principles established by the BIK System, the conventional manual method was used. Surveying involved using a variety of information sources. Tourist pamphlets and brochures prepared by tourism promotion agencies and establishments were major sources of information. In addition, books, newspaper articles, and magazine articles on history, arts, sciences, and humanities were researched. Public information was supplemented by information collected from letters, personal interviews, windshield surveys (observations made from a moving vehicle), and telephone calls. Finally, all of this information on attractions and facilities was verified for location and reliability. The information was recorded and coded manually on thousands of 3x5 inch index cards, separately for attractions and facilities. About twenty-five thousand pieces of information were collected for five thousand tourist attractions and facilities. The facilities inventory was completed primarily for the tourism industry-mix analysis by tourism regions. As the main purpose and draw for tourism, attractions were surveyed in more detail. Inventorying and processing the data manually on index cards took several months. The survey and coding of attractions included the following information for each tourist attraction:

- Tourism region in which the attraction is located (twelve regions)
- City or town in which the attraction is located (351 cities and towns)

- Distinction as an "event" or "site" attraction (two types)
- Types of activities that could be performed at the attraction (fifty-eight activities)
- Identification number of the attraction (1–9,999)
- Quality rating of the attraction in terms of its drawing power (four levels):
  - Attraction of National significance
  - Attraction of New England–New York significance
  - Attraction of Massachusetts significance
  - Attraction of Local significance

Because of the budget and computer technology limitations in 1968, surveying and coding tourist facilities in Massachusetts was separated from surveying and coding tourist attractions. Again, a conventional manual method was used for processing tourist facility data and mapping the industry mix information. By the standards of the era, this low-technology, labor-intensive data processing and mapping method was acceptable when tourist facilities data, coded according to the BIK System, were manageable. In processing much larger amounts of tourist attractions data, however, the SYMAP computer mapping and tabulation method was employed. In addition to thirty-two computer-drawn maps, computer tabulations were made for each attraction map printed.

Manual processing fell short of providing acceptable results when large quantities of data needed to be processed. Today, the manual method still gives good results for smaller destination areas where fewer attractions and facilities exist. But data for larger and complex tourism product mixes must be processed by computers. Since 1970, major advances have been made in computer software and hardware. Particularly important for tourism development planning are the advances in mapping and GIS. The BIK System has now been expanded, and data for tourist facilities can be processed by computer hardware and software similar to those used to process data for tourist attractions. With increased capability came in-depth analysis. Data for the entire tourism sector, consisting of 232 types of NAICS establishments, representing all types of attractions and facilities and numbering in the hundreds of thousands, can be surveyed, coded, and processed by computer.

The BIK System used the SIC for tourism planning in 1969. The types of tourist attractions and facilities were selected from among establishments in each industry category that, collectively, formed the economic sector of tourism. Establishments were selected from fourth-level, four-digit SIC categories. Today, the NAICS gives a more detailed listing of establishments at the six-digit level. The criteria used for selecting tourism establishments divided the four-digit-level establishments into two major groups. Establishments that provide tourists with products or services directly were classified as primary tourism establishments. Establishments that provide tourists with products and services indirectly through primary establishments were classified as secondary tourism establishments. They supply goods and services to primary establishments. This classification can be further expanded for demonstrating the multiplier effect of tourism by classifying tertiary and lower-level tourism establishments.

In *Tourism and Its Development Potential in Massachusetts*, the BIK System selected sixty-one types of four-digit tourist establishments from fourteen industry groups at the two-digit level (Volume 1, Appendix Table V-4). These sixty-one types of establishments included both tourist attractions and facilities (Table V-1). They were all primary establishments. Secondary supplier establishments were not selected. At the time of the study's publication, software, hardware, and data were not available for analyzing and planning a large number of tourism industry variables. However, the potential of the BIK System was demonstrated.

After defining the tourism sector, the BIK System analyzed the economic impact of tourism in Massachusetts. Again, due to data limitations, only three major sector indicators were used: expenditures by tourists, payrolls generated by tourism, and employment. The following calculations and tabulations were made:

- Employment in eating and drinking, lodging, and amusement and recreation places covered by the U.S. Department of Labor (Tables I.1–I.13)
- Expenditures by overnight travelers at eating and drinking, lodging, and amusement and recreation places (Tables II.1–II.3, II.13, II.14, and Appendix Tables II.1–II.6)
- Location quotient index using employment and receipts as a measure of economic activity (Tables II.4, II.5, II.11, and II.12)
- Employment in eating and drinking, lodging, and amusement and recreation places (Tables II.6–II.10)
- Payroll data were limited to Massachusetts eating and drinking places.

Staff at the Harvard Laboratory for Computer Graphics and Spatial Analysis keypunched the attractions data from 3x5 inch index cards onto decks of six thousand computer cards. The data were later transferred to computer tapes and processed by the FORTRAN IV program. The individual inventory cards were stored in cardboard boxes in several steel file cabinets. The cabinets full of index cards were stored by the department in a state warehouse at the conclusion of the study. They were later misplaced and never found. The fate of the computer tapes generated is unknown.

After consultations, the study team and the laboratory decided to process the twenty-five thousand pieces of information in the form of thirty-two computer maps that were selected from a possible combination of one hundred forty maps. Data tabulations accompanied each map. Several oblique views were also made. By programming various permutations of the data, the thirty-two computer maps showed different patterns of attraction characteristics spread over the geography of Massachusetts. They include:

- Data shown by cities and towns of Massachusetts (351 municipalities)
- Data shown by two types of attractions (site and event attractions)
- Data shown in terms of four levels of attraction significance (national, regional, state, and local)
- Data shown by five levels of density or concentration of attractions (by municipality)
- Data shown by five seasons (four seasons plus year round)
- Data shown by selected tourist recreational activities (fifty-one types)
- Data shown by the permutations of the above characteristics

Computer maps and tabulations prepared using the BIK System were significant for their time in several respects:

- They established in 1970 for the first time in the United States, and possibly in the world, a consistent analytical method for evaluating the characteristics of the tourism product by communities, tourism regions, or counties and ascertaining their comparative advantages and disadvantages in drawing tourists.
- They provided the means necessary for conducting research on the social-economic-behavioral root causes of tourism by using tested research methods from various disciplines and by devising new methods, vocabulary, and definitions for tourism development planning.
- They established a scientific method of inquiry for tourism that can be duplicated by others, particularly development planners.

- They introduced tourism as a new field of application for emerging computer software and hardware technology.
- They demonstrated how many later commercial applications, like electronic travel planning, location finders, and customized one-step travel planning, could be done.
- They provided the framework for global understanding of tourism and demonstrated the existence of a wider group of players associated with the tourism industry.

The 1970 application of the BIK System to Massachusetts led to Bulent Kastarlak's appointment by the United Nations to prepare tourism development plans for a number of countries, and to prepare and deliver several papers for journals and conferences. It also led to his faculty appointment at the University of Nevada at Las Vegas.

The BIK System of 1970 has now been expanded and updated. There are many possible new applications. Data for both facilities and attractions and their attributes can be surveyed, coded, processed, and mapped by computers. The BIK System can be used interactively and personally on computer networks. The user can be connected to the Internet for customizing his or her travel plans. Tourism planning professionals now have a proven planning method and an operational system for tourism planning at the national, regional, and local levels. (See Chapter 17.)

The BIK System provides both detailed and generalized views of tourism resources and interrelationships. As indicated in Chapter 16, the database produced can be analyzed in a variety of accepted and useful applications, including statistical analysis, input-output analysis, industrial complex analysis, mathematical programming, decision tree analysis, and GIS. Having a tourism database of the scope and magnitude of the BIK System, and analyzing it with powerful tools, is like taking a fresh look at a familiar phenomenon. New patterns and interactions will be revealed.

APPENDIX D

Computer Mapping and Electronic Processing of Tourism Data Using the BIK System

In 1970, computer graphics was in its infancy. The Laboratory for Computer Graphics and Spatial Analysis at Harvard University was one of the pioneering academic organizations for this technology in the United States. They were ready to experiment with processing and mapping the data for Bulent I. Kastarnak's *Tourism and Its Development Potential in Massachusetts*. They had developed a software program suitable for the project.

The laboratory's original application of the computer program to surveying and analyzing tourist attractions and facilities of Massachusetts produced three products:

- Thirty-two computer maps showing the geographic distribution and concentration of total tourist attractions, and of site and event attractions, as well as season, quality rate, and activity characteristics of those attractions by municipalities in Massachusetts. Other characteristics could have generated up to one hundred forty maps, but this option was not used. The values were shown within the boundaries of each municipality. The concentration levels of characteristics were graphically represented in five tones, or density, of gray color that the plotter achieved by overprinting or underprinting predetermined letters of the alphabet.
- Four oblique views drawn by the plotter connected to the computer that showed the values of tourist attractions in terms of vertical heights or "hills" by municipalities. This topography showed the distribution of tourist attractions and their characteristics in three dimensions by angling the plane of projection.
- Thirty-two statistical data matrices were used that indicated the characteristics of tourist attractions shown on the computer maps and oblique views in numerical terms.

SYMAP, a program developed by Prof. Howard T. Fisher around 1970, was the mapping program used. SYMAP is a computer mapping program for graphically displaying spatially variable data through tonal inequalities by overprinting, or underprinting using a standard line printer.

Considering the state of computer technology at the time, the preparation of a SYMAP input deck was straightforward. The user provided approximately half a dozen introductory data cards followed by additional data cards in each of several **packages**. Three packages were used in the Massachusetts study:

- The **A-Conformoline** package contained the *x-y* coordinates in inches for each change in vertices on the outline of each municipality.
- The **E-Values** package called the appropriate data to be mapped from the databank.
- The **F-Map** package contained the title and all the specifications pertaining to the map, such as the size of the map to be made, the number of levels, the level breakdown, and the symbols to be used.

The input deck consisted of a few program cards that preceded the various packages. Three of these cards formed the skeletal framework of an optional subprogram known as SUBROUTINE FLEXIN. This framework of instructions was written in the FORTRAN IV computer language.

Considerable latitude and flexibility allowed large amounts and kinds of data to be extracted from the computer. Even if no data or program manipulation was desired, SUBROUTINE FLEXIN demanded a **dummy** form since it is an integral of the SYMAP deck. Such a dummy FLEXIN consisted of the three cards:

- SUBROUTINE FLEXINE (I, FORM, T, FIRST)
- RETURN
- END

This simple format told the computer that no special manipulations, such as databank retrieval, map axis rotation, card identification number for sequence, would take place for the computer to continue reading and executing the successive cards. In general, the databank consisted of more data than were applicable for any given map, so the necessary retrieval instructions to obtain the data pertinent to a single map were contained within the SUBROUTINE FLEXINE framework.

The instructions required to retrieve the data from the databank tape were placed in this subroutine. For this project, the term **databank** meant that each record contained several data values for a given municipality. Thus, the task of assembling six thousand cards into a databank of digestible form for computer input was facilitated by the thirteen-digit attraction classification code that was used on the tourist attraction index file cards. (The contemporary code classification uses seventy-six digits for eighteen groups.) The data from the original cards were stored on a tape, from which they were manipulated by a FORTRAN program. The resulting aggregate values for each city or town were written onto another tape, where they were then arrayed into a databank for easy retrieval. It was (1) this last tape, together with (2) the A-CONFORMO-LINES tape, (3) the SYMAP program source deck tape, and (4) the SYMAP control cards for the thirty-two maps of Massachusetts that produced the resultant maps.

Aside from the problem of getting an effective working databank on tape, the only other major task concerned the digitizing of the A-OUTLINE and B-DATA points packages. Later, it was decided that mapping of conformant zones would best suit the needs of the project because it called for municipal boundary delineation for purposes of comparison. In this type of mapping, all the x-y coordinates that defined the shape and location of each city or town went into the making of the A-CONFORMOLINES package. This package actually became 351 small packages, one for each city or town in Massachusetts. The order in which the data on cities and towns were fed into the computer had to be the same as the values pertaining to them. Thus, a direct 1:1 sequential relationship existed between the data files that described the location and values for each city or town. This package was generated by the dual independent mapping encoding (DIME) file program.

The base map from which the coordinates were taken had border dimensions of 30.2 by 47.6 inches. In order to reduce this scale to 13.0 by 20.5 inches, certain alterations had to be made so that a number of municipalities would not vanish in the reduction. It was therefore necessary to slightly exaggerate the size of such localities on the computer map.

An interesting capability of the SYMAP program and the C-OTOLEGENDS package was that they permitted the user to print and overprint legends within the map border. This was useful for preparation of the scale, name, study area, north arrow, notes, and other information. It must be kept in mind that when a multiple-map submission was made, the same legends had to appear on all maps. Thus, the title and textual explanations were specified by the user in the F-MAP package. They were purposely run separately in order to give the legends the option of their addition or deletion.

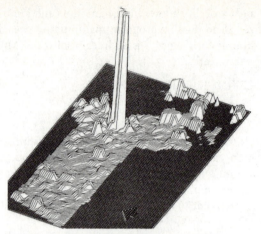

Total Tourist Attractions by Municipality

Tourist Event Attractions by Municipality

Tourist Site Attractions of National Significance by Municipality

FIGURE D.1 SYMAPs from the 1970 Tourism Development Report on Massachusetts

SYMVU was a second computer program that, when used with the SYMAP program, produced a three-dimensional angling (oblique views) representation of a statistical surface. The result was an oblique projection that looked much like the projection of a relief topographical model or an axonometric perspective. The great advantage of this program was that the user did not need to specify levels for the data. Given the state of computer mapping technology in 1970, the surface could be viewed from any vantage point and the result was a more aesthetic product than that produced directly by SYMAP. When option 21 was specified in SYMAP, the value of each character location on the SYMAP was written on tape. To produce an oblique view, all that was necessary was a few control cards and the tape with the coordinate values for each map desired. These cards contained the specifications for the title, viewing position, viewing height, height for the highest value, outside area tone, and others. The cards and the SYMAP tape produced yet another tape that was fed into a Cal-Comp plotter. The latter device was made to draw lines and symbols with a pen on a rolling sheet of paper to produce graphic results. The quality of these plots was high and the cost was exceptionally low.

The final stage of the project was the printing of a data matrix for each map. The data cards were read from tape and arrayed in tabular form in a regional and municipality breakdown by site and event attractions and activity code numbers. Totals for each map were also shown. The success of the project owed much to the enthusiasm, dedication, and hard work of the participants.

Examples of three SYMAPs are shown in Figure D-1.

APPENDIX E

Calculating Tourism Sector Indicators

This appendix presents several indicators for measuring the assets and performance of the tourism industry at the national, regional, and local destination levels of tourism development planning. These indicators were developed by many authors and have been tried and tested over the years. However, data are not always available for obtaining reliable results in all cases. The method of calculating each indicator is presented in four sections:

Source of data, Format, Calculation, Explanations

1. CALCULATING ESTIMATED ROOM RENT RECEIPTS FROM OVERNIGHT VISITORS (TOURISTS) BY ACCOMMODATION ESTABLISHMENTS WITH AND WITHOUT A PAYROLL

Source of data: U.S. Census of Business or equivalent

Format: Prepare a matrix table with types of accommodations listed in the left column, and by rows and method of calculation shown on the top row to the right.

Calculation:

Row (1) Year-round hotels with 25 or more rooms. Room rent receipts @ less than 100%

Row (2) Year-round hotels with less than 25 rooms. Room rent receipts @ less than 100%

Row (3) Seasonal hotels. Room rent receipts @ 100%

Row (4) Motels and tourists courts. Room rent receipts @ 100%

Row (5) Motor hotels. Room rent receipts @ 100%

Row (6) Camps and trailer parks. Room rent receipts @ 100%

Row (7) Total of rows 1–6

Row (8) Establishments without a payroll: Room rent receipts @ 100%

Row (9) Motel and tourist court adjustment

Row (10) Total estimated room rent receipts from overnight visitors

Total of Rows (7), (8), and (9)

Column (1) Total receipts from accommodations with payroll

Column (2) Proportion of receipts from overnight visitors. X% or less

Column (3) Receipts from overnight visitors = Col. (1) × Col. (2)

Column (4) Proportion of receipts from room rents. Y% or less

Column (5) Room rent receipts from overnight visitors = Col. (3) × Col. (4)

Explanation: Column (1) shows receipts of various accommodations with or without a payroll as reported in the U.S. Census of Business. It is assumed that all receipts from establishments without a payroll are room rent receipts. Thus, after calculating room rent receipts from establishments with a payroll, total receipts from establishments without payroll are added to arrive at the total in Column (5).

Column (2) shows room rent receipts from overnight visitors as percentages of total receipts from establishments with a payroll. These percentages are from overnight accommodation surveys conducted by industry sources for the particular location. For all types of establishments, all room rent receipts are from overnight visitors (100%). In year-round hotels, year-round residents are not counted as overnight visitors. The proportion of year-round residents, defined by the U.S. Census of Business as guests staying for one month or longer in year-round hotels, is estimated from the number of hotel rooms counted by the census. It is assumed that year-round residents pay reduced room rates. The figure thus obtained is the proportion of total receipts attributable to year-round residents. Subtracting it from 100% yields the proportions shown in Column (2) for receipts from overnight visitors. Application of these proportions to Column (1) yields the figures in Column (3) for receipts from overnight visitors for accommodations with a payroll. Column (4) shows, by type of establishment, the proportion of receipts obtained from room rents, as opposed to that obtained from meals, beverages, and other items. This proportion is obtained from surveys conducted by tourism industry sources. In Column (5), total room-rent receipts from overnight visitors are estimated by applying these proportions to the figures in Column (3). In Row (9), the figure designated as "motel-tourist court adjustment" is used to account for the possible omission of some establishments from the survey as being judged substandard and therefore not included in the data.

2. CALCULATING EXPENDITURES BY OVERNIGHT VISITORS (TOURISTS)

Source of data: U.S. Census of Business or equivalent.

Format: Prepare a table by rows showing calculations. From Table (1) above.

Calculation:

Row (1) Total expenditures of overnight visitors using commercial accommodations equals total estimated room rent from overnight visitors divided by lodging expenditure representing the percentage of total expenditures made by overnight visitors staying in commercial accommodations (less than 100%).

Row (2) Nonlodging expenditures of overnight visitors using commercial accommodations equals Row (1) less total estimated room rent receipts from overnight visitors.

Row (3) Total nonlodging expenditures of all overnight visitors equals Row (2) divided by the percentage of visitor nights used in commercial lodging.

Row (4) Total expenditures of overnight visitors equals Row (3) plus room rent receipts from overnight visitors.

Explanation: In Row (1), total estimated room rent from overnight visitors is taken from Table (1). The percentage figure is an assumption about the lodging expenditures representing a percentage of total expenditures made by overnight visitors using commercial accommodations. In Row (2), nonlodging expenditures of overnight visitors not staying in commercial accommodations are estimated. In Row (3), total nonlodging expenditures of all overnight visitors are estimated by dividing the figure in Row (2) by the percentage of visitor nights spent in commercial lodging. Finally, in Row (4), the total estimated room rent received from overnight visitors from Table (1) is added to total nonlodging expenditures of all overnight visitors to arrive at total expenditures made by overnight visitors.

3. CALCULATING ESTIMATED EXPENDITURES IN EATING AND DRINKING PLACES

Source of data: U.S. Census of Business or equivalent.

U.S. Survey of Consumer Expenditures, Bureau of Labor Statistics.

Format: Prepare a table by rows showing calculations.
- Receipts per capita, eating places ($a1$)
- Receipts per capita, drinking places ($a2$)
- Expenditures per family on food outside home and on alcoholic beverages within and outside Standard Metropolitan Statistical Areas (SMSAs)
- Expenditures per family inside SMSAs for food ($b1$) and alcoholic beverages ($b2$)
- Expenditures per family outside SMSAs for food ($b3$) and alcoholic beverages ($b4$)

Calculation:
- Income adjustment for expenditures per family in urban places outside SMSAs

    Percent income difference per family inside SMSAs and non-SMSAs = A
    - Food outside the home = $b3 + A(b3) = c$
    - Alcoholic beverages = $b4 + A(b4) = d$
- Income adjustment factors for urbanization.
    - Food outside the home = $b1/b3 = e$
    - Alcoholic beverages = $b2/b4 = f$
- Expenditure per capita in eating places inside and outside SMSAs
    - Percent of U.S. population living inside SMSAs = B
    - Percent of U.S. population living outside SMSAs = $100 - B = C$
    - Expenditures per capita in eating places outside SMSAs $D = a1/(A + B \cdot e)$
    - Expenditures per capita in eating places inside SMSAs $E = D \cdot e$
- Expenditures per capita in drinking places inside and outside SMSAs
    - Expenditures per capita in drinking places outside SMSAs $F = a2/(A + B \cdot f)$
    - Expenditures per capita in drinking places inside SMSAs $G = F \cdot f$

Explanation: The U.S. Census of Business provides receipts of eating and drinking places per person. In order to estimate for a region whether a net influx or outflux of expenditures for the services of these establishments is made, it is necessary to estimate expenditures per capita of residents and then compare this estimate with receipts of establishments located in the region. The comparison may lead to the conclusion that factors other than tourism cause differences in expenditures among regions. The calculations presented here attempt to estimate per capita expenditures starting with the national average. This figure is adjusted upward to reflect the fact that the region has a higher percentage of its population living in metropolitan areas than the nation. Next, the figure is adjusted upward (or downward) once again to reflect the fact that personal income per capita is higher (or lower) in the region than in the nation.

Calculation with data may show that the income elasticity of demand for food and for alcoholic beverages consumed outside the home may be close to 1. For example, a 1% increase in income produces about a 1% increase in expenditures on these items. Accordingly, expenditure figures for nonmetropolitan areas, or outside SMSAs, may have to be adjusted generally upward. The remaining difference between these figures and those for metropolitan areas, or inside SMSAs, reflects the difference in the degree of urbanization.

4. CALCULATING THE LOCATION QUOTIENT

Source of data: U.S. Census of Business or equivalent.

Format: Prepare a table by rows showing the calculations.

Calculation: The location quotient for industry *i*, tourism, in a given region is

$$LQi = \frac{Si/Ni}{S/N} \text{ or } \frac{Si/S}{Ni/N}$$

where:
- Si = number of wage earners in tourism industry *i* in a given region
- S = number of wage earners in all service industries in the same region
- Ni = number of wage earners in tourism industry *i* in the nation
- N = number of wage earners in all service industries in the nation

Explanation: A study of a region's export–import relations, of which tourism is a part, begins on a preliminary basis with a simple analysis employing the location quotient.

This quotient, or indicator, does not require extensive data collection and processing. It is a device for comparing a region's percentage share of a particular economic activity with its percentage share of the nation or some other aggregate.

Many economic activities other than wage earners can be used in computing the location quotient. Income, value added, population, or area, for example, can be substituted for wage earners in the industry. Because of its simplicity, the location quotient can be used as a benchmark in the analysis of a region's exports and imports. The indicator also has important use in conjunction with other techniques of analysis.

5. CALCULATING THE EMPLOYMENT MULTIPLIER FOR TOURISM

Source of data: U.S. Census of Population or equivalent.

Format: Prepare a table of rows and columns.

Calculation:

Total employment	$= A$
Local nonbasic service (tourism) employment	$= B$
Regional basic (export) employment	$= C$
Basic/nonbasic Ratio (*D*)	$D = \dfrac{C}{B}$
Regional employment multiplier (*E*)	$E = \dfrac{A}{C}$
Regional tourism employment multiplier (*F*)	$F = \dfrac{B}{C}$

Explanation: The interaction of the basic and nonbasic industries is the basis of this formula. It is a simple tool used for evaluating the benefits accruing in the form of employment and income generated by the tourism industry. There are other, more complex methods for estimating tourism multipliers.

6. CALCULATING TOTAL ROOM/NIGHTS OF INTERNATIONAL AND DOMESTIC TOURISTS STAYING AT COMMERCIAL OVERNIGHT ACCOMMODATIONS PER TOURISM REGION

Source of data: Incoming and outgoing international tourist statistics from national authorities. Estimated domestic tourist statistics from local and national authorities.

Format: Prepare a table of rows.

Calculation:

International tourists arriving by ports of entry per year = Ai

Estimated percent market share of the tourism region for international tourists = Bi

Percent of international tourists staying at commercial accommodations = Ci

Estimated room/nights per international tourist per visit = Di

Estimated number of international guests per accommodation room = Ei

Regional total room/nights for international tourists

$$RNi = \frac{Ai \times Bi \times Ci \times Di}{Ei}$$

Estimated number of domestic tourists traveling per year = Ad

Estimated percent market share of the tourism region for domestic tourists = Bd

Percent of domestic tourists staying at commercial overnight accommodations = Cd

Estimated room/nights per domestic tourist per visit = Dd

Estimated number of domestic guests per accommodation room = Ed

Regional total room/nights for domestic tourists

$$RNd = \frac{Ad \times Bd \times Cd \times Dd}{Ed}$$

Regional demand for total accommodation rooms

$$TAR = \frac{RNi + RNd}{365 \text{ (or less)}}$$

Explanation: The room/nights spent in the destination country differ for international and domestic tourists. The hard data collected by the authorities from the incoming tourists at ports of entry (Ai) are the most reliable source. The market share of incoming international tourists (Bi) is estimated. The next step is to make an assumption regarding international tourists staying at commercial accommodations (Ci). This could be close to 100%. For domestic tourists, however, staying with friends and relatives will reduce this percentage (Cd). Estimated room/nights that international tourists spend on vacation or business in the country depends on vacation or business habits. It could be one week or less

(*Di*). But domestic tourists (*Dd*) may make more frequent weekend trips, or may own a vacation house and stay less often at commercial accommodations. The number of visitors staying in each guest room may change for international and domestic tourists. International tourists come primarily as couples (*Ei*), whereas domestic tourists could bring their young families and stay in one or more rooms (*Ed*).

7. CALCULATING DEMAND FOR ROOMS AT COMMERCIAL OVERNIGHT ACCOMMODATIONS

Source of data: From calculation of room/nights.

Format: Prepare a table of rows.

Calculation:

Total estimated international and domestic room/nights

$$RN = RNi + RNd$$

Estimated room occupancy percent based on occupancy nights per year: *RO*

Rooms available for receiving guests during the year: *RA*

Total demand for rooms at commercial overnight accommodations: *R*

$$R = \frac{RN}{RA \times RO}$$

Explanation: This is a simple ratio. But arriving at the estimated percentage of average room occupancy that will be maintained (*RO*) over a period of twelve months could be an exercise in expectation rather than reality. Seasonal variations in room occupancy are common. Sometimes the accommodation is closed for the entire nonseason. Or, over the 365-day year, some of the rooms may be withdrawn from use. These withdrawn rooms may be reserved for long-term seasonal or annual resident guests. Other rooms may be withdrawn for repairs and remodeling. The remaining rooms available (*RA*) are used for calculating room demand (*R*). By dividing the estimated room/nights (*RN*) by rooms available (*RA*) and a realistic average annual room occupancy expected (*RO*), total demand for rooms (*R*) is estimated. If the number of beds needs to be calculated, an adjustment is made to the room demand. The standard double-occupancy, two-bed-per-room assumption made above is amended for (*Ei*) and (*Ed*). A third portable bed may be installed for the third person, usually a young child, in the room. Room occupancy remains the same. Only the assumption for bed occupancy changes.

There is a growing trend toward tourists preferring **suite** accommodations where the unit is a two- or three-bedroom suite with a kitchenette and living room. Accordingly, room and bed assumptions are again adjusted. Another adjustment is made when two thousand tourists arrive for a day-long visit with a luxury cruise ship at the port of entry. They stay overnight in their ship cabins. These tourists are left out of bed and room demand calculations. A different type of adjustment is needed when campers arrive. Tourists pitching their tents in the wilderness or at campgrounds, and those carrying their accommodation with them in recreational or camper vehicles, are also excluded from calculations. Further adjustments in room demand are made when students, elderly tourists, and special interest tourists stay in college dormitories or student apartments on campuses during semester breaks.

8. CALCULATING THE CARRYING CAPACITY OF A TOURISM ATTRACTION OR FACILITY (E.G., A BEACH)

Source of data: Various reliable sources.

Format: Prepare a table of rows.

Calculation:

Step 1 *Carrying capacity of a major attraction (beach) in the destination region*

(The capacity of indoor accommodations at a beach, not the number of people lying on the beach on blankets, on towels, or on beach chairs or swimming in the water)

- Estimated average density of beach area (A) in square meters (m²) or in square feet (sf) per tourist indoor bed based on seasonality of arrival of internationals interested in a sea-sand-sun vacation
- Total beach area (T) in m² (or in sf) = length of beach (L) in m (or in ft) × width of beach (W) in m (or in ft)
- Number of beds allowable (B) per linear m (or ft) of beach frontage = $\dfrac{T}{A} \times \dfrac{1}{W}$
- Total number of allowable beds (C), or tourists, for the beach = $B \times L$
- Total number of allowable rooms (D) for the beach = $\dfrac{C}{2 \text{ (or more beds/room)}}$
- Low-rated rooms located within walking distance inland (E) = $D \times a\%$
- High-rated rooms located on the beach (F) = $D \times b\%$ = $D \times (100\% - a\%)$
- Beach frontage for other hotel rooms and the public = $L \times a\%$
- Exclusive beach frontage for high-rated hotel rooms = $L \times b\%$
- Optimum number of tourists (V) per season (c days) = $C \times c$

Step 2 *Employee demand for carrying capacity of the destination*

- Direct employee demand ($E1$) for low-rated hotels = 0.4 employee/room × E
- Direct employee demand ($E1$) for high-rated hotels = 1 employee/room × F
- Direct employee demand for other attractions and facilities = $E3$
- Total direct employee demand (E) = $E1 + E2 + E3$
- Employment multiplier (M) for other subsectors of the tourism sector of the destination
- Indirect employee demand ($E4$) = $E \times M$
- Total direct and indirect employment generated by tourism ($E5$) = $E + E4$
- Shortage, or surplus of employees (G), from labor force (H) = $H - TE$

Step 3 *Social impact of tourism at the destination on the peak day of the peak season*

- Ratio (R) of optimum number of tourists (C) and local population (P) = $\dfrac{C}{P}$
- Ratio (S) of international tourists (T) and domestic tourists (O) = $\dfrac{T}{O}$

Step 4 *Carrying capacity of tourism infrastructure*

- Water (W) consumption per tourist bed (C) per peak day = $XM3/\text{day} \times C$
- Sewer (S) treatment capacity per peak day = $XM3/\text{day} \times C \times Y\%$
- Highway capacity (H) per peak day = number of trips/road capacity = or less than 1
- Power (P) kw demand per peak day = kw/hour/day × tourist bed (C)

Explanation: Calculating the carrying capacity of a particular tourism destination region is critical for preserving many environmental and social assets and preventing shortages and surpluses of service capabilities. The volume of tourists exceeding this carrying capacity will cause harm to the environment; overcrowding in major attractions; shortages of available room and beds in accommodations; excessive demand for power, water, and sewer services; and traffic jams on the roads. The opposite problem—a lower than expected volume of tourists—will cause underuse of tourism assets, excess capital investment, and a decline in employment and income. Calculating the carrying capacities of other utilities and infrastructure follows a similar rationale, starting with peak day usage per tourist bed, assuming 100% occupancy or less, and arriving at a ratio of total usage over total capacity not exceeding 1.

9. CALCULATING APPRAISED VALUE OF REAL ESTATE

There are three methods for calculating appraised value of real estate: the **development cost,** **market comparison,** and **discounted future income** methods. These methods are used individually and together. When they are used together, their results are averaged or reconciled to arrive at a final value.

The discounted (to present value) future income method is used primarily for appraising **income** and **investment** real estate. This method is not reliable for appraising owner-occupied residential properties. The income method uses three residual methods of capitalization. The following demonstrates their application:

	Subtotals	Totals
A) **Assumptions**		
1. Net income before interest and amortization		a
2. Anticipated economic life of the structure (years)		b
3. Rate of capitalization (%)		c
4. Land value under highest and best use		d
5. Building value under highest and best use		e
B) **Value under the land residual method**		
6. Net operating income (1)		a
7. Income attributable to building		
8. Building value (cost/new) (5)	e	
9. Rate of return on the investment (3)	c	
10. Rate of return of the investment (amortization at c% sinking fund over remaining life of b years)	f	
11. Total percentage return to building	g	
12. Required building income = (5) × (11)		h
13. Income residual to land = (6) − (12)		i
14. Land income capitalized in perpetuity @ c% = (13) × (c%)	j	
15. Total value		
16. Building value (cost/new) (5)	e	
17. Land value (4)	d	
18. **Total value = (16) + (17)**	k	

C) **Value under the building residual method**

    19. Net operating income (1)   a

    20. Income attributable to land

    21. Land value under highest and best use = (4) × (3)   i

    22. Income residual to building = (19) − (21)   h

    23. Return on the investment (3)   c

    24. Return of the investment (10)

        (over b years @ c% sinking fund)   f

    25. Combined rate of capitalization = (23) + (24)   g

    26. Building value = (12)/(25)   e

    27. Land value (4)   d

    28. Building value (5)   e

    29. **Total value = (27) + (28)**   k

D) **Value under the property residual method**

    30. Net operating income (1)   a

    31. Economic life period of the building (years)   b

    32. Rate of capitalization

    33. Rate of return on the investment (3)   c

    34. Rate of return of the investment (10)

        (over b years @ c% sinking fund)   f

    35. Combined rate of capitalization = (33) + (34)   g

    36. Capitalized value of net income = (1)/(11)   l

    37. Reversionary (original) land value (4)   d

    38. Present worth of reversionary (original) land value

        in (b) years = (4) × (m) or present worth of money @6%   n

    39. Property value, land and building, over (b) years = (36)   l

    40. Present worth of land, discounted @ c% = (38)   n

    41. **Total value = (39) + (40)**   k

When assumptions of rate, asset life expectancy, and income are the same in all three methods, the total value derived by each of the three residual methods will be identical. In this situation, only one method is selected for calculating the total appraised value. When assumptions are different, the three total values are reconciled by approximation, which sometimes involves simple averaging of the three outcomes.

The development cost and market comparison methods are relatively simple in concept but can require considerable research and/or accounting to arrive at a final estimated value. Development cost is the sum of all costs incurred in improving real estate, including the costs of land, on-site utilities, professional services, construction materials and labor, and financing. Market comparison estimates of value are based on identifying enough comparable recent free-market sales of similar (hopefully identical) types of real estate to provide a reliable indicator of what a property is worth. For more information on these two methods see Appendix J.

APPENDIX F

Attraction/Facility–Activity–Season Correlation*

NAICS Number	Attraction/Facility (By Six-Digit NAICS Establishments)	Activity	Season
113210	Forest Nurseries and Gathering of Forest Products	Growing, forest	Year round
113310	Logging	Logging	Year round
114111	Finfish Fishing	Fishing, finfish	Year round
114112	Shellfish Fishing	Fishing, shellfish	Year round
	Clam Digging	Digging, clams	Year round
	Crabbing	Crabbing	Year round
	Lobstering	Lobstering	Year round
114210	Hunting,	Hunting,	Year round
	Trapping, Game Preserves	Trapping	Year round
221110	Electric Power Generation	Generating, electric power	Year round
221122	Electric Power Distribution	Distributing, electric power	Year round
221210	Natural Gas Distribution	Distributing, natural gas	Year round
221310	Water Supply and Irrigation Systems	Distributing, water	Year round
221320	Sewage Treatment Facilities	Treating, wastewater	Year round
233110	Land Subdivision and Land Development	Developing, land	Year round
233210	Single-Family Housing Construction, Alterations, Prefabricated Housing	Constructing, housing	Year round
233220	Multi-Family Housing Construction, Prefabricated Apartments	Constructing, apartments	Year round
233320	Commercial and Institutional Building Construction, Alterations	Constructing, commercial and institutional buildings	Year round
312120	Breweries	Brewing, beer Distilling, liquor	Year round Year round
312130	Wineries	Pressing and curing, wine	Year round
336612	Yachts Not Built in Shipyards	Building, yachts	Year round
443130	Camera and Photographic Supplies Store	Shopping, cameras and film	Year round
443111	Appliance Store—Household	Shopping, appliance	Year round
444110	Home Centers	Decorating, home	Year round
444190	Building Materials Supply	Repairing, home	Year round
445110	Supermarkets and Other Grocery Stores (Except Convenience)	Shopping, groceries	Year round
445120	Convenience Stores	Shopping, convenience	Year round
445210	Butcher Shops	Shopping, meat and poultry	Year round

*Based on the BIK System using NAICS establishments. Seasonal correlation may vary, depending on the location and climate.

445220	Seafood Markets	Shopping, finfish, shellfish, crab, lobster	Year round
445230	Produce Markets	Shopping, produce	Year round
445310	Beer, Wine, Liquor, and Package Stores	Shopping, alcoholic beverages	Year round
446110	Pharmacies, Drug, Health, and Beauty Aids Stores	Shopping, drug, health, beauty aids	Year round
446120	Cosmetics, Beauty Supplies, and Perfume Stores	Shopping, cosmetics, perfume, beauty supplies	Year round
446199	All Other Health and Personal Care Stores	Shopping, other health and personal care supplies	Year round
447110	Gasoline Stations with Convenience Stores	Pumping gasoline	Year round
		Shopping convenience goods	Year round
447190	Other Gasoline Stations	Pumping gasoline	Year round
448110	Men's Clothing Stores	Shopping, men's clothing	Year round
448120	Women's Clothing Stores	Shopping, women's clothing	Year round
448130	Children's and Infants' Clothing Stores	Shopping, children's clothing	Year round
448210	Athletic Shoe Stores	Shopping, athletic shoes	Year round
448310	Jewelry Stores	Shopping, jewelry	Year round
448320	Luggage and Leather Goods Stores	Shopping, leather goods	Year round
451110	Sporting Goods, Fish Tackle Stores, Gun Shops	Shopping, sporting goods	Year round
451140	Music Stores	Shopping, music goods	Year round
451211	Book Stores	Shopping, books	Year round
451212	News Dealers and News Stands	Shopping, newspapers	Year round
451220	Prerecorded Tape, Compact Disc, Record and Video Stores	Shopping, record, disc, video	Year round
452110	Department Stores	Shopping, department stores	Year round
452910	Warehouse Clubs and Superstores	Shopping, discount superstores	Year round
452990	Variety Stores	Shopping, variety goods	Year round
453110	Florist	Shopping, flowers	Year round
453220	Gift, Novelty, and Souvenir Stores	Shopping, gifts, novelties, souvenirs	Year round
453310	Antique Stores	Shopping, antiques	Year round
453920	Art Dealers, Auctions	Shopping, arts	Year round
453930	Manufactured (Mobile) Home Dealers	Shopping, mobile homes	Year round
454110	Electronic Shopping and Mail Order Stores	Shopping, all goods via electronic and mail order media	Year round
454390	Flea Markets, Street Vendors	Shopping, bargain goods	Year round
481111	Scheduled Passenger and Commuter Air Transport	Flying, as passenger	Year round
481211	Nonscheduled Chartered Passenger Air Transport	Flying, as passenger Helicopter	Year round
482111	Line-Haul Railroads on main rail lines	Riding, passengers	Year round
482112	Short-Line Railroads	Riding, passengers on short rail lines	Year round
483112	Deep Sea Passenger Transportation, Cruise Lines	Sailing, ship as passenger	Year round

483114	Coastal and Great Lakes Passenger Transportation, Chartering Ship with Crew	Sailing, ship as passenger	Year round
483212	Inland Water Transportation, River Passenger Transportation, Water Taxi	Sailing, ship as passenger	Year round
484121	General Freight Trucking Long Distance	Trucking, freight	Year round
485111	Mixed-Mode Transit Systems	Riding, mixed-mode transit	Year round
485112	Commuter Rail, Local Passenger Rail Systems	Riding, commuter train	Year round
485113	Bus and Other Motor Vehicle Local Transit Systems	Riding, local transit	Year round
485119	Other Urban Transit Systems	Riding, other urban transit	Year round
485210	Interurban and Rural Bus Transportation	Riding, interurban bus	Year round
485310	Taxi Service	Riding, taxi	Year round
485320	Limousine Service	Riding, limousine	Year round
485510	Charter Bus Industry	Riding, charter bus	Year round
485991	Handicapped Passenger Transportation	Riding, handicapped transport	Year round
485999	Airport Limousine Service	Riding, airport limousine	Year round
487110	Scenic Sightseeing Transportation on Land, Cable Car, Monorail, Bus	Riding, sightseeing vehicle	Year round
487210	Scenic Sightseeing Transportation on Water, Boat Charter, Dinner Cruises	Sailing, sightseeing vessel	Year round
487990	Scenic Sightseeing Transportation, Airplane and Helicopter Rides	Flying, sightseeing plane	Year round
488111	Air Traffic Control	Controlling, air traffic	Year round
488119	Other Airport Operations, Rental Aircraft Hangar	Renting, aircraft	Year round
488190	Aircraft Maintenance and Repair Services	Repairing, aircraft	Year round
488210	Support Activities for Rail Transportation, Terminals	Processing passengers, in terminals	Year round
488310	Port and Harbor Operations, Docking Facilities	Docking, ships, boats, and yachts	Year round
488390	Drydocks	Drydocking, ships, boats, and yachts	Year round
488410	Motor Vehicle Towing, Emergency Road Service	Towing and servicing, motor vehicles	Year round
488490	Bridge, Tunnel, Highway Operations	Maintaining and toll collecting	Year round
491110	Postal Service	Mailing, letters and parcels	Year round
492110	Couriers, Local Letter, and Parcel Delivery, Messenger Service	Delivering, parcels and messages	Year round
512131	Motion Picture Theaters	Viewing, motion pictures	Year round
513112	Radio Stations	Listening, radio	Year round
513120	Television Broadcasting	Viewing, television	Year round
513210	Cable Networks	Viewing, television	Year round
513310	Wired Communication Carriers	Calling, by telephone	Year round
513322	Cellular and Other Wireless Telecommunications	Calling, by cellular telephone	Year round

513340	Satellite Communications	Calling, by satellite	Year round
514110	News Syndicates	Reading, news	Year round
514120	Libraries and Archives	Reading, books and periodicals	Year round
514191	On-line Information Services	Reading, on-line information	Year round
522110	Commercial Banking	Banking, commercial	Year round
522120	Savings Institutions	Banking, savings	Year round
522130	Credit Unions	Banking, credit unions	Year round
522291	Consumer Lending	Banking, consumer lending	Year round
522292	Real Estate Credit	Banking, real estate lending	Year round
522310	Mortgage and Non-Mortgage Loan Brokers	Brokering, mortgage loan	Year round
523130	Foreign Exchange Services, Commodity Contracts	Exchanging, foreign currency	Year round
524126	Direct Property and Casualty Insurance Carriers	Insuring, property and casualty	Year round
524127	Direct Title Insurance Carriers	Insuring, property titles	Year round
525920	Private Estates Administration on Behalf of Beneficiaries	Administering, private estates	Year round
525930	Real Estate Investment Trusts	Administering, real estate trusts	Year round
531110	Lessors of Residential Buildings, Dwellings, Residential Hotels	Leasing, housing	Year round
531120	Auditorium, Convention Center Rental or Leasing	Leasing, auditoriums, convention centers	Year round
531190	Lessors of Other Real Estate Property, Mobile Homes	Leasing, other real estate	Year round
531210	Offices of Real Estate Agents and Brokers	Brokering, real estate	Year round
531311	Residential Property Managers	Managing property	Year round
531320	Offices of Real Estate Appraisers	Appraising property	Year round
532111	Passenger Car, Van Rental	Leasing, vehicles	Year round
532112	Automobile Leasing	Leasing, cars	Year round
532220	Costume Rental	Leasing, costumes	Year round
532292	Recreational Goods, Bicycle, Pleasure Boat, Moped Motorcycle, Row Boat, Ski Equipment Rental	Leasing, recreational goods	Year round
532310	General Rental Centers	Leasing, tools	Year round
532411	Commercial Air, Rail, and Water Transportation Equipment Rental and Leasing	Leasing, transportation equipment	Year round
541110	Offices of Lawyers	Consulting, legal services	Year round
541199	All Other Legal Services	Consulting, notary public	Year round
541211	Offices of Certified Public Accountants	Consulting, accountancy	Year round
541310	Architectural Services	Consulting, architecture	Year round
541320	Land Use Planning Services, Landscape Architects	Consulting, land use planning and landscape architecture	Year round
541330	Engineering Services	Consulting, engineering	Year round
541350	Building Inspection Services	Consulting, building inspection	Year round

541370	Surveying and Mapping (Except Geophysical), GIS	Consulting, surveying	Year round
541410	Interior Design Services	Consulting, interior designing	Year round
541430	Graphic Design Services	Consulting, graphic designing	Year round
541513	Facilities Support Services, Computer Systems, Data	Contracting, computing services	Year round
541850	Advertising Services	Contracting, advertising services	Year round
541921	Passport Photograph Services	Photographing, passports	Year round
541940	Animal Hospitals	Caring, animals	Year round
561421	Answering Services, Telephone	Answering, telephones	Year round
561422	Telephone Call Centers	Calling, telephones	Year round
561439	Copy Centers	Copying, documents	Year round
561510	Travel Agencies	Consulting, travel agency	Year round
561520	Tour Operators	Consulting, tour operating	Year round
561591	Convention and Visitor Bureaus	Informing, tourism data	Year round
561599	All Other Travel Arrangement and Reservations	Reserving, hotel, transportation Services, Hotel and Time Share Reservations	Year round
561612	Security Guards and Patrol Services	Securing, persons and properties	Year round
561710	Exterminating and Pest Control Services	Exterminating, pests	Year round
561730	Landscaping Services	Contracting, landscaping	Year round
561790	Other Services to Buildings and Dwellings	Contracting, maintenance	Year round
561920	Trade Show Promoters with Facilities	Attending, trade shows	Year round
562111	Solid Waste Collection Services	Collecting, solid waste	Year round
562212	Solid Waste Landfill, Sanitary Landfills	Operating, landfills	Year round
562213	Solid Waste Combustors and incinerators	Operating, incinerators	Year round
562991	Septic Tank and Related Services	Contracting, septic tank services	Year round
562998	All Other Miscellaneous Waste Management Services	Contracting, other waste services	Year round
611310	Universities	Educating, research, community service	Year round
611512	Flight Training	Learning, to fly airplanes	Year round
611620	Sports and Recreation Instruction	Learning, to play sports	Year round
621111	Offices of Physicians	Treating, by doctors	Year round
621210	Offices of Dentists	Treating, by dentists	Year round
621399	Offices of all Other Miscellaneous Health Practitioners	Treating, by health practitioners	Year round
621493	Freestanding Ambulatory Surgical and Emergency Services	Receiving, emergency services	Year round
621498	All Other Outpatient Care Centers	Receiving, outpatient care services	Year round
621512	Medical Laboratories, X-Ray, Radiology	Receiving, laboratory services	Year round
621910	Ambulance Services, Air or Ground	Receiving, ambulance services	Year round

622110	General Medical and Surgical Hospitals	Receiving, hospital services	Year round
623312	Retirement Homes without Nursing Care	Receiving, retirement home care	Year round
711110	Theater Companies	Attending, theater	Year round
	Dinner Theaters	Attending, dinner theater	Year round
	Burlesque	Attending, burlesque	Year round
	Comedy	Attending, comedy	Year round
	Opera	Attending, opera	Year round
711120	Dance Companies, Ballet Companies	Attending, ballet	Year round
711130	Musical Groups and Artists, Orchestras,	Attending, concerts	Year round
	Symphonic Orchestras	Attending, symphonic concerts	Year round
711190	Other Performing Arts Companies	Attending, live performances	Year round
	Circuses	Attending, circuses	Year round
	Ice Skating	Attending, ice skating shows	Year round
711211	Sports Teams and Clubs		
	Baseball	Attending, baseball	Spring, summer
	Basketball	Attending, basketball	Fall, winter, spring
	Football	Attending, football	Fall, winter
	Hockey	Attending, hockey	Fall, winter, spring
711212	Racetracks for Automobile	Attending, automobile races	Spring, summer
	Dragstrips	Attending, drag races	Spring, summer
	Greyhound Dog Tracks	Attending, greyhound races	Fall, winter, spring
	Horse Tracks	Attending, horse races	Spring, summer
	Motorcycle Tracks	Attending, motorcycle races	Spring, summer
711219	Other Spectator Sports	Attending, other spectator sports	Year round
711310	Promoters of Performing Arts with Facilities	Attending, performing art events	Year round
	Sports	Attending, sport events	Year round
	Air Shows	Attending, air shows	Summer
	Rodeos	Attending, rodeos	Spring, summer
	Sports Arenas	Attending, events at sports arena	Year round
	Live Theaters	Attending, live theater	Year round
711320	Promoters of Performing Arts without Facilities	Attending, performing art events	Year round
	Sports	Attending, sport events	Year round
711510	Independent Entertainers	Attending, entertainment shows	Year round
712110	Museums	Visiting, museums	Year round
	Halls of Fame	Visiting, halls of fame	Year round
	Planetarium	Visiting, planetariums	Year round
712120	Historical Sites	Visiting, historical sites	Year round
	Archeological Sites	Visiting, archeological sites	Year round
	Battlefields	Visiting, battlefields	Year round
	Heritage Villages	Visiting, heritage villages	Year round

	Forts	Visiting, forts	Year round
	Ships	Visiting, ships	Year round
712130	Zoos	Visiting, zoos	Year round
	Aquariums	Visiting, aquariums	Year round
	Arboreta	Visiting, arboretas	Year round
	Safari Parks	Visiting, safari parks	Year round
	Botanical Parks	Visiting, botanical parks	Year round
712190	Nature Parks and Other Similar Institutions	Visiting, nature parks	Year round
	National Parks	Visiting, national parks	Year round
	Sanctuaries	Visiting, sanctuaries	Year round
	Waterfalls	Visiting, waterfalls	Year round
713110	Amusement Parks	Visiting, amusement park	Spring, summer
	Theme Parks	Visiting, theme parks	Year round
	Piers	Visiting, piers	Year round
	Summer Theaters	Attending, summer theaters	Summer
	Water Parks	Visiting, water parks	Summer
713120	Amusement Arcades	Visiting, amusement arcades	Year round
	Pinballs	Visiting, pinball arcades	Year round
713210	Casinos (Except Casino Hotels)	Gambling, casinos	Year round
	Gambling Cruises	Gambling, cruiseships	Year round
	Riverboat	Gambling, riverboats	Year round
713290	Other Gambling Industries	Gambling, other	Year round
	Bingo Parlors	Gambling, bingo parlors	Year round
	Bookies	Gambling, bookies	Year round
	Off-Track Betting Parlors	Gambling, off track	Year round
713910	Golf Course	Golfing, public courses	Summer
	Country Clubs	Golfing, country clubs	Summer
713920	Skiing Facilities	Skiing, lodges and lifts	Winter
	Cross-Country	Skiing, cross country	Winter
	Downhill	Skiing, downhill	Winter
713930	Marinas	Boating, slips and storage	Spring, summer, fall
	Boating Clubs	Boating, clubs	Year round
713940	Fitness and Recreational Sports Centers	Exercising	Year round
	Ice Skating Rinks	Ice skating	Year round
	Roller Skating	Roller skating	Year round
	Swimming Pools	Swimming	Year round
713950	Bowling Centers	Bowling	Year round
713990	All Other Amusement and Recreation Industries	Recreating, general	Year round
	River Rafting	Rafting	Summer
	Sailing Clubs	Sailing	Spring, summer, fall
	Bathing Beaches	Sunning swimming	Summer
	Adventure Operations	Exploring, thrill seeking	Year round
	Nightclubs	Partying	Year round
	Hunting Clubs	Hunting	Year round

	Driving Ranges	Driving golf	Summer
	Dance Halls	Dancing	Year round
	Billard Parlors	Shooting pool	Year round
	Bridge Clubs	Playing bridge	Year round
	Day Camps	Camping, day	Summer
	Curling	Curling	Spring, summer, fall
	Fishing Guide	Fishing	Year round
	Horse Rental	Riding, horseback	Spring, summer, fall
	Mountain Climbing	Climbing, mountain	Summer
	Snowmobiling	Riding, snowmobiles	Winter
	Soccer Clubs,	Playing, soccer	Spring, summer, fall
	Riding Stables	Riding, horses	Year round
	Whitewater Rafting	Rafting, adventure	Summer
721110	Hotels (Except Casino Hotels)	Staying overnight	Year round
	Motels	Staying overnight	Year round
	Skiing Resorts	Staying overnight	Year round
	Motor Inns	Staying overnight	Year round
	Motor Hotels	Staying overnight	Year round
	Health Spas with Accommodations	Staying overnight	Year round
	Hotels with Golf Courses	Staying overnight	Year round
721120	Casino Hotels	Staying overnight	Year round
721191	Bed-and-Breakfast Inns	Staying overnight	Year round
721199	All Other Traveler Accommodations	Staying overnight	Year round
	Guest Houses	Staying overnight	Year round
	Hostels	Staying overnight	Year round
	Housekeeping Cottages	Staying overnight	Year round
721211	RV (Recreational) Vehicle Parks	Staying overnight	Year round
	Campgrounds	Staying overnight	Spring, summer, fall
721214	Recreational and Vacation Camps (Except Campgrounds)	Staying overnight	Year round
	Dude Ranches	Staying overnight	Year round
721310	Rooming and Boarding Houses	Staying overnight	Year round
722110	Full-Service Restaurants	Dining	Year round
722211	Limited-Service Restaurants	Dining	Year round
	Carryout	Dining	Year round
	Fast Food Restaurants	Dining	Year round
	Bagel Shops	Dining	Year round
	Doughnut Shops	Dining	Year round
	Pizza Parlors	Dining	Year round
722212	Cafeterias	Dining	Year round
722213	Snacks and Non-Alcoholic Beverage Bars	Dining	Year round
	Coffee	Dining	Year round
	Juice Bars	Dining	Year round

722320	Caterers	Catering	Year round
	Banquet Halls	Catering	Year round
722330	Mobile Food Services	Snacking	Year round
	Beverages	Snacking	Year round
	Food Carts	Snacking	Year round
722410	Drinking Place (Alcoholic Beverages)	Drinking	Year round
	Bars	Drinking	Year round
	Taverns	Drinking	Year round
	Cocktail Lounges	Drinking	Year round
811111	General Automotive Repair	Repairing, autos and trucks	Year round
811118	Other Automotive Mechanical and Electrical Repair and Maintenance	Maintenance, autos and trucks	Year round
811192	Car Washes	Washing, cars	Year round
811490	Other Personal and Household	Repairing, household	Year round
	Goods Repair and Maintenance	Maintenance, household	Year round
	Boat Repair	Repairing, boat	Year round
	Tailor Shops for Alterations	Tailoring, altering garments	Year round
812111	Barber Shops	Barbering	Year round
812112	Beauty Salons, Hair Stylists	Styling, hair	Year round
812191	Diet and Weight Reducing Centers	Dieting, weight loss	Year round
812199	Saunas, Steam Baths, Turkish Baths	Bathing, steam	Year round
	Tattoo Parlors	Tattooing	Year round
812210	Funeral Homes and Funeral Services	Processing, dead bodies	Year round
812211	Photographic Equipment Repair	Repairing, photograph	Year round
812310	Coin-Operated Laundries	Laundering	Year round
	Dry Cleaners	Dry cleaning	Year round
812910	Pet Care (Except Veterinary Services)	Grooming, pets	Year round
812922	One-Hour Photo Finishing	Finishing, photo	Year round
812930	Parking Lots and Garages	Parking, autos and trucks	Year round
812990	Rest Room Operations	Relieving	Year round
813110	Religious Organizations, Places of Worship		
	Churches	Worshiping, Christian	Year round
	Shrines and Temples	Worshiping, Eastern religions	Year round
	Synagogues	Worshiping, Jewish	Year round
	Mosques	Worshiping, Muslim	Year round
813312	Environment, Conservation, and Wildlife Organizations	Conserving	Year round
813410	Automobile Clubs, Social Clubs	Associating	Year round
813910	Business Associations	Associating	Year round
814110	Private Households	Living, as tourists	Year round
922110	Courts	Attending, court	Year round
922120	Police Protection, Park Police, State Police	Policing	Year round
922130	Legal Counsel and Prosecution	Defending, prosecuting	Year round
922140	Prisons	Imprisoning, correcting, visiting inmates	Year round

922160	Fire Protection	Protecting, fire	Year round
924110	Administration of Air and Water Resource and Solid Waste Management Programs	Protecting and conserving natural resources	Year round
924120	Administration of Conservation Fish and Wildlife Conservation	Protecting and conserving wild animals	Year round
925110	Administration of Housing Programs	Administering, housing	Year round
925120	Administration of Urban Planning, Community, and Rural Development Programs	Planning, urban areas Developing, community	Year round Year round
926110	Administration of General Economic Programs	Developing, economies	Year round
926120	Coast Guard	Guarding, coasts	Year round
926150	Regulation, Licensing, and Inspection of Miscellaneous Commercial Sectors	Licensing	Year round
928120	International Affairs, Embassies, Consulates, Peace Corps, United Nations, World Bank, Interpol	Communicating, aiding, coordinating, conducting diplomatic relations	Year round

APPENDIX G

Procedures for Investing in a Tourism Project in Countries Where Such Procedures Are Required

Step 1 *Make the decision to invest*
Apply criteria for deciding on the most profitable use of investment funds.

Step 2 *Decide whether the tourism sector is a good investment.*
The answer depends on the tourism potential of the country and region. Tourism can be a driving force of economic growth. It is a profitable business. If the answer is yes, the investors proceeds to Step 3.

Step 3 *Review government-related information.*
- *Tourism regions:* Selected by the council of ministers
- *Tourism areas (destinations):* Priority tourism development destinations
- *Tourism Centers (local sites):* Sites of tourism importance
- *Tourism Investment Certificate:* Issued to the tourism project investor
- *Tourism Establishment Certificate:* Issued to the tourism establishment
- *Incentive Certificate:* Indicates the equity/credit ratio and rate of interest of the loan
- *Land use plan:* Includes master land use, landscaping, and implementation

Step 4 *Consider the types of tourism investment (for example).*
- *Primary accommodation facilities:* Hotels, motels, guest houses, camping sites
- *Auxiliary accommodation facilities:* Apartment hotels, second homes, hostels, recreational vehicles (RVs)
- *Dining and entertainment facilities:* Restaurants, cafeterias, clubs
- *Auxiliary service facilities:* Health/thermal pools, theme parks, golf courses, convention centers
- *Tourism complexes:* Residential vacation communities
- *Personnel training facilities:* Schools
- *Yacht tourism facilities:* Marinas
- *Travel agencies:* Travel planning establishments

Step 5 *Choose the type of investment.*
Select a type of facility that meets the investment criteria.

Step 6 *Choose a location for the investment project.*
(A) Build on land already owned by the investor.
- Status of land from the municipality, provincial public works department, etc.
- If there is no land use plan for the area, one should be prepared by the relevant authority and approved by higher authorities.
- Confirmation by higher authorities that the proposed use of the land is approved.
- Site planning requirements and allowable dimensions.
- The investor is ready to apply for a Tourism Investment Certificate.

(B) Purchase a plot to build on.
- Verify that the proposed land use on the plot is approved for the project.
- Verify the physical characteristics of the plot.

- Consult the authorities.
- Purchase the land.
- Other procedures that are the same as those in (A).
- Investor is ready to apply for a Tourism Investment Certificate.

(C) Apply for allocation of public land in a tourism area or tourism center.
- Authorities owning or controlling public land located in a tourism area or tourism center advertise for interested investors and prepare project packages.
- The investor applies for the allocation of the land and provides authorities with investment information.
- Provided that the conditions stipulated in the regulations are satisfied, the land allocation is approved and finalized by the authorities. The land is leased, not sold.
- The investor is ready to apply for a Tourism Investment Certificate.

(D) Apply for allocation of public land outside tourism areas and tourism centers.
- The investor submits an application to the authorities who own or control public land outside tourism areas and tourism centers for allocating a plot of land.
- The investor is given preliminary authorization for a period of several months to satisfy the conditions stipulated in the regulations and to receive a Tourism Investment Certificate.
- Provided that the conditions are satisfied on time, the authorities allocate land for the proposed project.
- The investor is ready to apply for a Tourism Investment Certificate.

Step 7   *Apply for a Tourism Investment Certificate.*
- The investor's design team determines the type, class, and capacity requirements of the project from regulations.
- The investor's design team prepares preliminary plans.
- The investor seeks an opinion from the authorities about the project design.
- The investor completes the project design and the associated information package.
- The investor applies for a Tourism Investment Certificate with documents and explanatory information about the project.
- One or more relevant authorities reviews the design and associated information.
- The project is approved/not approved by the authorities for receiving a Tourism Investment Certificate.

Step 8   *Apply for a building permit.*
- The investor completes the construction documents and applies for a building permit.
- The building permit authority reviews the documents, hold hearings when necessary, and approves the permit (with conditions if appropriate).

Step 9   *Apply for government financial incentives.*
- The investor applies to the treasury authority for an Incentive Certificate (to benefit from financial incentives if available).
- The Incentive Certificate is approved/not approved by the treasury authority according to the provisions of incentive regulations.
- The investor is exempted from certain fees when he or she receives Tourism Investment and Incentive Certificates.
- The investor may seek a foreign investor as a limited partner or joint venture partner.

Step 10 *Start and complete construction.*
- The project is designed and built according to the prescribed regulations and incentives.
- Final inspection is completed and an occupancy permit is issued by the building authorities.

Step 11 *Apply for a Trial Operation Certificate and a Tourism Establishment Certificate.*
- Authorities determine an appropriate trial operation period.
- Authorities issue a Trial Operation Certificate.
- Inspections are conducted by the authorities during the period.
- At the end of the period, authorities carry out an assessment to determine whether the facility has been operated properly.
- Facility operations are approved and a Tourism Establishment Certificate is issued.

APPENDIX H

Law for the Encouragement of Tourism in Turkey
Law No. 2634 (Adopted March 12, 1982)

The English translation of this law is available from the Internet.

Using a search engine like Google or msn.com, type in: Republic of Turkey Ministry of Culture and Tourism; On the Web page, click on English, then click on Ministry; On the Ministry Web page, click on Laws; On the Laws Web page, click on Law for the Encouragement of Tourism.

APPENDIX I

Law for the Organization and Duties of the Ministry of Culture and Tourism of Turkey
Abstract of Law 4848 (Adopted April 16, 2003)

The law is composed of forty articles, three temporary articles, and various tables. An unofficial summary translation of the first twenty-one articles is presented here.

ARTICLE 1. The goal of the law is to preserve and develop cultural values; prevent destruction of historic assets; ensure productive contributions of tourism to economic development; take measures necessary for planning, developing, marketing, and encouraging tourism; organize and manage affiliated government organizations; and work with private sector and civil organizations.

ARTICLE 2. The duties of the Ministry of Culture and Tourism are:
a) To research, develop, protect, and inform the public about national, historic, moral, cultural, and tourism values of the country, to strengthen its solidarity and to contribute to its economic development.
b) To give guidance to organizations affiliated with tourism and culture; to coordinate joint ventures with the private sector.
c) To protect historic and cultural assets.
d) To take necessary measures to develop tourism as a productive industry.
e) To give guidance to all investment, development, coordination and marketing activities in the fields of tourism and culture.
f) To acquire in fee simple, or by eminent domain, real properties, and studies and plans, to invest in and construct tourism and cultural projects.
g) To inform and promote the tourism and cultural resources of Turkey.
h) To conduct other duties assigned by the government.

ARTICLE 3. The Ministry of Culture and Tourism consists of headquarters, provincial branches and foreign information offices.

ARTICLE 4. The headquarters of the Ministry consists of administrative offices, advisory, supervisory, and service departments.

ARTICLE 5. The Minister reports to the Prime Minister and occupies a seat in the cabinet. He is the highest official of the Ministry. He is responsible for conducting the business of the Ministry according to the policies of the government, the national development plan, annual programs and for coordinating the work of the Ministry with other Ministries. He is authorized to oversee the conduct of affiliated organizations.

ARTICLE 6. A Permanent Undersecretary is the principal advisor of the Minister. He executes the instructions of the Minister according to the policies, plans and programs of the Ministry.

ARTICLE 7.   The principal departments of the Ministry of Culture and Tourism are:

a) General Directorate of Fine Arts.
b) General Directorate of Cultural Assets and Museums.
c) General Directorate of Libraries and Publications.
d) General Directorate of Copyrights and Motion Pictures.
e) General Directorate of Investments and Operations.
f) General Directorate of Research and Education.
g) General Directorate of Information.
h) Directorate of National Library.
i) Directorate of Foreign Relations and Coordination with European Union.

ARTICLE 8.   The duties of General Directorate of Fine Arts are to:

a) Follow contemporary, classic, and traditional art trends and ensure the development of fine arts consistent with these trends.
b) Develop the arts of painting and sculpture consistent with the development of traditional Turkish decorative arts.
c) Ensure the development of fine arts consistent with social and cultural development of the country.
d) Propose and execute the formation of fine arts galleries, orchestras, choruses, music, folklore, and dance groups.
e) Promote all fine arts and handicrafts in the country.
f) Perform other duties assigned by the Minister.

ARTICLE 9.   The duties of the General Directorate of Cultural Assets and Museums are to:

a) Conserve, evaluate, and present to the public all artifacts and rare elements of nature discovered by archeological excavations.
b) Propose and execute the formation of new museums, research centers, and laboratories.
c) Identify cultural assets previously taken and transported to foreign countries. Arrange for their return to Turkey.
d) Take measures to preserve and restore cultural assets in museums.
e) Conduct various studies for the protection of cultural assets.
f) Coordinate the actions of various Ministry committees.
g) Propose new information offices in and out of the country.
h) Encourage and provide resources for improving the science of restoring historic buildings and artifacts.
i) Perform other duties assigned by the Minister.

ARTICLE 10. The duties of the General Directorate of Libraries and Publications are to:

a) Take measures to expand the use of libraries and propose new libraries.
b) Establish standards for libraries and their operations.
c) Enrich the collections of libraries by acquiring new publications from national and international publishers.
d) Restore and preserve antique manuscripts for the benefit of researchers and the public.
e) Ensure public use of all historic documents and publications.
f) Play a guiding and supporting role in preparing and conducting technical research programs for all public and private libraries.
g) Establish a documentation center for researchers.
h) Establish training facilities and resources for tourism professionals.

i) Publish scientific and literary literature for promoting the culture and tourism assets of the country.

j) Publish brochures for promoting museums.

k) Take measures to ensure the propagation of culture by encouraging new works of art.

l) Establish a publication advisory council.

m) Perform other duties assigned by the Minister.

ARTICLE 11. The Duties of the General Directorate of Copyrights and Motion Pictures include:

a) Carry on the duties specified by copyright laws.

b) Supervises the work and finances of various associations.

c) Coordinate the dialogue between the Ministry and authors.

d) Supervise copyrighting procedures.

e) Carry on the duties specified by the laws of motion pictures, video, and music productions.

f) Promote national treasures by organizing exhibits, conferences, and documentary motion pictures.

g) Establish motion picture and video archives.

h) Coordinate and work with international associations for protecting copyrights.

ARTICLE 12. The duties of the General Directorate of Investment and Operations are to:

a) Identify tourism resources of the country; establish their development priorities; conduct studies to determine measures needed to protect the environment for tourism; cooperate with other government agencies and private sector organizations.

b) Depending on changes in the volume and type of demand for tourism, conduct research, collect, evaluate, and distribute statistics and information for reviewing and implementing policies and directing investments.

c) According to the provisions of Law No. 2634 (Law for the Encouragement of Tourism), identify the tourism regions, areas and centers of the country, inform the public and exercise the powers given to the Ministry regarding their development.

d) Identify tourism, cultural development, and conservation regions to be approved by the Council of Ministers, prepare plans for their orderly growth, secure investment for developing their historical, cultural and tourism potential.

e) Manage the process of acquiring and selling real estate, by eminent domain if necessary, and assigning approved government property to private investors for development.

f) Advise native and international investors about cultural and tourism issues.

g) Direct government and private sector infrastructure and superstructure investments according to the provisions of tourism development plans; prepare annual implementation programs and execute their projects.

h) Establish documentation centers for expediting the evaluation and distribution of information to various organizations.

i) In view of the sector development priorities and needs, take advantage of all available means to facilitate efficient operation of tourism investment and management organizations and improve the quality of their operations.

j) Manage the licensing process for tourism establishments and investors.

k) Establish and implement price guidelines for tourism establishments in view of world tourism trends and Ministry policies.

l) Monitor the performance of professional tourism organizations, and determine appropriate awards and penalties.

m) Cooperate with other national, state and municipal government agencies, professional tourism organizations, universities, and government economic enterprises for implementing the provisions of the subject law.

n) Investigate cases, articulate measures and seek the cooperation of related organizations based on complaints lodged by tourists against unlicensed tourism establishments.

o) Execute construction, restoration, restitution, and major improvement activities related to project design, survey, bidding and supervision of tourism superstructure facilities approved by the Ministry for rendering its services.

p) According to the provisions of Law No. 2876, Article 104, take charge of government facilities and land assigned by law to the Ministry and use, operate, lease, or reassign them to others.

q) Organize meetings, exhibits, courses, events, competitions, conferences, open permanent offices and galleries, and coordinate and cooperate with action programs of recognized tourism organizations in the country and abroad.

r) Fund, build, open, maintain, and operate culture centers in provinces and municipalities.

s) Conduct audits, inspections and reviews to evaluate the performance of all operations under the jurisdiction of the Ministry. The qualifications and licensing of auditors, inspectors and reviewers are determined by appropriate regulations.

t) Perform other duties assigned by the Minister.

ARTICLE 13. The duties of the General Directorate of Research and Education are to:

a) Conduct research and development in the field of fine arts, and build archives, and publish literature.

b) Conduct research and development in folk culture, literature, theater, traditions, customs, folk music and dances, trades, cuisine, apparel, fashion, and decorative arts.

c) Build archives for collecting specimens of folk culture.

d) Conduct research on the cultures of populations of Turkish extraction around the world, arrange reciprocal educational programs, and publish results of research.

e) Conduct research in the Turkish language and dialects spoken in other countries, and establish language schools.

f) Estimate manpower needs of the culture and tourism industries, take measures to supply the trained manpower, organize training programs, establish training centers, open tourist guide schools, and cooperate with other government agencies and private businesses.

g) Secure technical assistance from foreign sources for improving culture and tourism training programs.

h) Improve the knowledge and understanding of culture and tourism by working with institutions of learning.

i) Plan and ensure the education and training of government personnel associated with culture and tourism.

j) Plan and implement the education and training of Ministry personnel inside and outside of the country.

k) Plan and implement pre-employment training programs and on-the-job training for Ministry personnel.

ARTICLE 14. The duties of the General Directorate of Information are:

a) Informing the public in and outside the country of the country's national, historical, cultural, artistic, and touristic heritage, promoting this heritage by organizing inside and outside the country seminars, symposia, congresses, fairs, exhibits, festivals, competitions, awards, and similar activities and cooperating with other government, private, and foreign institutions.

b) To cooperate with and organize joint projects for domestic and international organizations to attract foreign tourists to the country and give assistance as needed.

c) Invite and welcome representatives of, and maintain communication with, organizations that can assist in influencing the general population and achieving the purposes described above.

d) Prepare, purchase, and distribute all necessary material for promoting and informing domestic and foreign markets.

e) Conduct research and prepare reports for evaluating tourism demand, and prepare policies inside and outside of the country.

f) Purchase publications and other communication media outside the country for promoting and increasing tourism demand for the country.

g) Perform other duties assigned by the Minister.

ARTICLE 15. The duties of the Directorate of the National Library are:

a) The General Directorate of the National Library is the depository of national culture and knowledge and serves as a conduit for their distribution. It performs the duties specified in Law No. 5632 describing the organization and purposes of the Library.

b) Secure copies of cultural and historical programs produced by the Turkish Radio-Television Association at the National Library.

ARTICLE 16. The duties of the Directorate of Foreign Relations and Coordination with the European Union are:

a) Organize and develop cultural and tourism relations with various foreign countries and international organizations within the context of each country's foreign policies.

b) Organize and implement the provisions of bilateral cultural and tourism agreements signed by the government with other countries for exchanges and collaborations.

c) Arrange and coordinate relations with international culture and tourism organizations.

d) Implement and coordinate provisions of policies of the government regarding subjects related to the European Union.

e) Follow and act on the policies of the European Union regarding culture and tourism.

f) Perform other duties assigned by the Minister.

ARTICLE 17. The advisory, research, planning and inspection divisions of the Ministry of Culture and Tourism are:

a) Inspection Division.

b) Research, Planning and Coordination Division.

c) Legal Advisor.

d) Ministry Advisor.

e) Public Relations and Media Advisor.

ARTICLE 18. The duties of the Inspection Division are:

a) Conduct inspection and perform investigation of the Ministry operations, its branches and offices abroad.

b) Based on its inspections and investigations of Ministry operations, prepare and submit recommendations to the Minister for improving these operations.

c) Perform other duties assigned by law and the Minister.

ARTICLE 19. The duties of the Research, Planning and Coordination Division are:

a) Prepare a work plan for the Ministry and assist in preparing a service policy and plan according to the policies and guidelines established by the government, Ministry, national development plans, programs, decisions of Council of Ministers, and national security.

b) Following scientific research principles, prepare measures and services that will be included in long-term development plans and annual programs, receive the approval of the Minister and submit the information to the Permanent Secretary of the State Planning Organization.

c) Prepare a personnel, money, and material resource allocation plan and budget for the Ministry to ensure productive implementation of prescribed measures and services.

d) Prepare annual work plans of the Ministry, collect information and statistics related to the operations of the Ministry.

e) Identify issues and problems arising from the implementation of the Ministry's annual work plan and propose solutions and resolutions at Ministerial level to the Minister.

f) Undertake and follow through other coordination and planning assignments connected to annual work plans.

g) Collect, organize, publish and distribute all data related to the operations of the Ministry.

h) Document the history of the Ministry.

i) Organize and operate the database and computer systems of the Ministry.

j) Perform other research duties assigned by the Minister.

ARTICLE 20. The duties of the Legal Advisor include:

a) Express opinions on criminal, financial and civil issues arising from the activities of the Ministry.

b) Take legal measures to protect the interest of the Ministry, prevent legal conflict with adversary organizations, and assist in drafting legal agreements.

c) Prepare all necessary information and represent the Ministry in administrative litigations.

d) Prepare and submit legal proposals for accomplishing the objectives of the plans and programs implemented by the Ministry.

e) Evaluate proposed laws, regulations and guidelines prepared by the Divisions of the Ministry and submit opinions that express the position of the Ministry.

f) Perform other duties assigned by the Minister.

ARTICLE 21. The duties of the Ministry Advisor, Public Relations and Media Advisor.

a) The Ministry can appoint up to thirty advisors for providing legal services in subjects related to its operations. These advisors report to the Minister.

b) The Public Relations and Media Advisor plans and executes Ministry activities involving the participation of the public.

APPENDIX J

Calculating the Financial Feasibility of Projects

Chapter 15 presented typical business financial analyses done for tourism development projects. This appendix elaborates and provides more details about these analyses. These analyses are done before a project is constructed and in operation, and therefore necessarily use estimates of cost and other factors. After a project is completed and operating, more detailed business financial techniques are used for decision making, that make use of the actual more detailed data available from operations.

ESTIMATING CONSTRUCTION COSTS OF A TOURISM PROJECT

Typical financial analysis starts by preparing preliminary construction and development cost estimates and a probable schedule for development activities. The quantities prescribed by the building program are multiplied by current unit construction costs by building trade, published by a reliable and accepted industry source, a company or a government agency. These unit costs are estimated in the metric system, or in feet and inches, for the specific country. In calculating the construction costs, care is given to converting the unit from one system to another. The steps are:

Calculate building floor area (or volume)

Multiply the two or three dimensions of the building in square meters (m^2) or square feet (sf) (or cubic meters [m^3] or cubic feet [cf])

Calculate "hard" costs ($)
- Demolition: Multiply cf (m^3) units by unit cost ($)
- Site work, excavations, parking: Multiply units (m^3, cf, space) by unit cost ($)
- Building floor areas: Multiply m^2 by unit cost ($)
- Landscaping, other outdoor areas: Multiply m^2 or unit trees, shrubs, and so on by unit costs ($)
  - Total hard costs = Sum of the above ($)
- Contingency: As percentage of the hard costs (%$)
  - Total hard costs including contingency ($)
- Furniture, fixture, and equipment costs (if applicable) ($)
  - Total hard costs = Sum of the above ($)

Calculate "soft" costs ($)
- Land acquisition, brokerage, and closing costs ($)
- Land appraisal cost ($)
- Architectural, engineering, consulting fees as percentage of construction cost ($)
- Construction management fee ($)
- Pre-opening costs and training ($)
- Insurance premiums during construction ($)
- Legal fees ($)

- Interest on construction loan multiplied by construction months ($)
- Permit fees, taxes, and other related costs ($)
- Franchise fee (if applicable) ($)
  - Total soft costs = Sum of the above ($)

Grand total before finance charges ($) = Lender charges ($)

Grand total for the construction loan ($) = Sum of the above ($)

After the soft costs and hard costs are known, the combined project cost to the owner/developer is calculated by adding the lender finance charges. The sum determines the amount of capital needed for building the tourism project. Assuming, for simplicity's sake, 100% financing, the grand total for the construction loan is determined by adding the lender's finance charges to the combined total. In realistic terms, the amount of debt capital as opposed to the cash investment required from the owner/developer is seldom 100%. Depending on the nature, location, and many other risk factors associated with the project, commitment of cash plus other forms of equity assets demanded by a lender can vary from 10% to 50% or more.

CALCULATING THE DEBT-TO-CAPITAL RATIO

The debt-to-capital ratio represents the percentage of total funding that the owner/developer company has borrowed for its tourism and other investment projects. It shows the extent to which the company uses borrowed money for funding its operations. The ratio is also the indicator of the borrowing capacity of the company and its ability to pay its debts. The ratio is used by capital lending institutions for assessing creditworthiness. A low ratio is not necessarily the best. Some businesses may temporarily have high ratios when they are expanding. When the ratio is high, it is important that the company have positive earnings and steady cash flow to ensure security.

The most common method of calculating the ratio is by dividing total long-term debt by total assets, including the shareholders' funds and equity:

$$\frac{\text{Total liabilities}}{\text{Total assets}} = \text{Debt-to-capital ratio}$$

One rule of thumb is that a debt-to-capital ratio between 40% and 60% represents sound financial management. A high ratio means less security for shareholders, because debt holders are paid first in case of bankruptcy. Having a respectable ratio for the company makes it easier to borrow money for the tourism project.

CALCULATING THE PAYBACK PERIOD

The payback period formula indicates how long it will take to earn back the money invested in a project. Straight-line projection is the simplest way to show the investment potential of a project. The calculation shows how many months or years it will take to recover the original cash investment in the project. More elastic formulas use nonlinear projections.

The simple straight payback period formula is:

$$\text{Payback period} (C \text{ years}) = \frac{\text{Cost of project} (A)}{\text{Annual cash revenues} (B)}$$

When the revenues generated by the project are expected to vary from year to year or month to month, the payback period is calculated differently by adding each year's revenues

$(B = B1 + B2 + B3 + B4)$ until total revenues (B) exceed the cost of the project (A) after so many years $(B > A)$. The years and days it will take to exceed the total cost will yield the payback period:

$$\text{Payback period } (C \text{ years}) = \frac{\text{Cost of project } (A)}{\text{Annual cash revenues } [(B1 + B2 + B3 + B4) > (A)]}$$

The major drawback of the straight-line payback period method is that it ignores the time-value of money principle. It also ignores the benefits that may be generated after the payback period.

CALCULATING THE EXPECTED RATE OF RETURN

An investment decision made by an investor or a corporation without first having an idea about how successful the investment is likely to be is inviting business disaster. The expected rate of return shows the projected percentage return on an investment based on the weighted probability of all possible rates of return.

The formula for expected rate of return (ERR) is:

$$ERR \text{ or } E[r] = \text{sigma}(s)P(s)rs$$

where $E[r]$ is the expected return, $P(s)$ is the probability that the rate rs occurs, and rs is the return at level s. The following example illustrates how the formula is used.

An investment of $10 is projected to grow:

- 25% higher if economic growth exceeds expectations representing a probability of 30%
- 12% higher if economic growth equals expectations, representing a probability of 50%
- 5% lower if economic growth fails to meet expectations, representing a probability of 20%

To find the expected rate of return (ERR), the percentages are multiplied by their respective probabilities and added to their result.

$$ERR = (30\% \times 25\%) + (50\% \times 12\%) + (20\% \times -5\%) = 12.5\%$$

The probability totals must always equal 100% for the calculation to be correct. Unreasonable expectations will result in an unreasonable ERR.

CALCULATING THE RETURN ON INVESTMENT

The return on investment (ROI) represents the overall profit or loss on an investment made on a project expressed as a percentage of the total amount invested. The ROI measures the project's profitability and, indirectly, the ability of the project team to use the funds they are entrusted with wisely.

The rule of thumb is that if net earnings of the business cannot exceed the cost of borrowing funds from financial markets, the prospects for the project's success are highly questionable.

The formula for ROI as a percentage is:

$$ROI = \frac{\text{Net profit}}{\text{Total investment} \times 100}$$

The ROI is calculated by dividing the net earnings (profit) by the total investment (total debt plus total equity in the project) and multiplying the result by 100 to arrive at a percentage.

A clarifying alternative formula of ROI as a percentage is:

$$ROI = \frac{Net\ profit\ after\ taxes}{Total\ assets \times 100}$$

The formula clarifies the fact that the return is calculated after all taxes are paid.

CALCULATING THE TOTAL RETURN

The investor is also interested in finding out how his or her investment will perform after a specified period of time. This is represented by the percentage change in the value of the investment, including capital gains, dividends, and the investment's appreciation or depreciation. Total return (TR) also gives much valuable information about the returns on each component of the investment. Investment objectives may differ. Some investors want to maximize their income. In this case, dividends are important. For those who compound their income by reinvesting their capital gains distribution, dividends, and profits, long-term growth is the objective.

The total return (TR) formula as a percentage is:

$$TR\ (\%) = \frac{Dividends + capital\ gains\ distribution + change\ in\ NAV}{Beginning\ NAV \times 100}$$

The formula represents the ways in which an investment may earn or lose money, where dividends, capital gains distribution, and capital appreciation or depreciation in the investment's net asset value (NAV) are indicators. The formula assumes that the period is one year and that dividends are reinvested. Total return measures past performance only. It cannot predict future results.

PREPARING A PROFIT AND LOSS ACCOUNT

The profit and loss (P&L) account shows the project's revenues and expenses over a period of months and years. The account is also known as **current and projected operating results** of the business. P&L is based on a simple rule of thumb: revenue minus cost equals profit.

There are two P&L formats, multiple-step and single-step. Both follow the generally accepted accounting principles (GAAP). The multiple-step format is more common. It includes:

Multiple Step Profit and Loss Account

	Subtotals	Totals
Net Sales		a
Less cost of goods sold		b
Gross profit		c
Less Operating Costs		
Selling expenses		
Salaries and commissions	d	
Advertising	e	
Delivery/transportation	f	
Depreciation/store equipment	g	
Other selling expenses	h	
Total selling expenses		i

General and administrative expenses

Administrative/office salaries	j		
Utilities	k		
Depreciation/structure	l		
Miscellaneous other expenses	m		
Total general and administrative expenses		n	
Total operating expenses		o	

Operating Income   p

Less (or More) Nonoperating Items

Interest expenses	q	
Less interest income earned	r	
Income before taxes	s	
Income taxes	t	

Net Income   u

The P&L account does not show how the business earned or spent its money. The account shows a series of months, not just one-month results.

PREPARING A CASH FLOW STATEMENT

The cash flow statement of a real estate investment company shows the cash coming in and going out during a period, usually one year. Cash flow is a key indicator of the financial health of an organization. It demonstrates to investors and creditors the organization's ability to meet its obligations. It reports the money at hand at the beginning of a period, money received, money spent, and money remaining at the end of the period. Cash flows are from operations, cash investment activities, and cash financing activities. The format of cash flow and its steps are:

Cash Flow from Operations	Subtotals	Totals
Operating profit		a
Less adjustments to net earnings	b	
Less depreciation	c	
Plus accounts receivable		d
Less accounts payable	e	
Less inventory	f	
Net Cash Flow from Operations	g	
Cash Flows from Investment Activities		
Less purchases of marketable securities	h	
Plus receipts from sales of marketable securities		i
Less loans made to borrowers	j	
Plus collections on loans		k
Less purchases of plant and real estate assets	l	
Plus receipts from sales of plant and real estate assets		m
Net Cash Flow from Investment Activities	n	
Cash Flows from Financing Activities		
Proceeds from short-term borrowings		o
Less payments to settle short-term debts	p	
Plus proceeds from issuing bonds payable		q
Plus proceeds from issuing capital stock		r

Less dividends paid	s
Net Cash Flow from Financing Activities	t
Net Change in Cash during Period	
Cash and cash equivalents, beginning of year	u
Cash and cash equivalents, end of year	v
Net Change in Cash	x

A cash flow statement does not include outstanding accounts receivable, but it does include the past year's account receivable. It is possible to add to the cash inflow amounts charged to depletion, depreciation, and amortization.

CALCULATING DEPRECIATION

In simple terms, depreciation is the cost of doing business. It reduces a company's earnings while increasing its cash flow. Tax laws govern depreciation values and practices. Depreciation is an allocation of the cost of an asset over a period for accounting and tax purposes. Depreciation is charged against earnings. It is a noncash expense.

In order to determine the annual depreciation cost of assets, it is necessary to know the initial cost of these assets, plus how many years they will retain some value for the business and what value they will have at the end of their useful life. To qualify for depreciation, assets must be used in the business, be items that wear out, become obsolete, or lose value, and have a useful life beyond a single tax year.

Straight-line depreciation is the most often used method. It assumes that the net cost of an asset is written off in equal amounts over its life measured in years. The formula is:

$$\text{Annual depreciation} = \frac{\text{Original cost} - \text{scrap value}}{\text{Useful life in years}}$$

Depreciation becomes a cost and is reported in the year-end income statement under "operating expenses." For tax purposes, accelerating depreciating is often done to increase operating expenses. This way, the declining-balance method produces larger deductions in the first years and smaller deductions in the later years.

APPRAISING REAL ESTATE VALUE

Appraising the current value of a property is critical to securing a loan for construction or managing the operations of a building. A licensed professional should do the appraisal. He or she must be acceptable to the lender and must follow an orderly process. Data are collected from reliable sources and analyzed. The analysis entails applying one of the three methods of appraising value, sometimes all three for comparison. The methods are development cost, comparable market, and discounted future income.

Under the **development cost** method, the appraiser determines whether the improvements on the land constitute the highest and best use of the land. If the determination confirms this, then the appraiser proceeds to estimate the depreciated replacement cost of the existing improvements on the land. To calculate the replacement value, the appraiser multiplies the area or volume of the structure, either on a square feet or cubic feet basis, by the unit cost of the improvement. Local construction cost sources or trade publications like *Means Construction Costs* provide the unit construction cost figures. Some governments issue inflation-adjusted construction cost data for estimating and bidding on public works projects. The quality and type of construction, plus the geographic location of the project, play roles in determining the unit construction costs.

The **comparable market** method is used to appraise buildings and land of the type found in sufficient quantities for comparison within the general area of the subject property. The method is based on comparing the sales value of comparable properties. Transaction prices of these properties are adjusted to the unit measure on a per-square-foot or per-acre basis. The unit prices are adjusted to compare the properties on an equalized basis.

The **discounted future income** method involves discounting of future rights to income to a present sum or capital value. The application of the income method requires careful determination of several factors. They include:

- The net income of the property after deducting all operating expenses, but before interest and amortization payments
- If it is a building, the remaining economic life expectancy of the property
- The applicable risk rate of interest or rate of capitalization
- The value of the land after it is free and clear of the improvements
- The replacement cost of the improvements, provided that they are new and represent the highest and best use of the land

The discounted future income method is used primarily for income and investment properties. Further information on the discounted future income method is given in Appendix E. When all three methods of appraisal are employed, it becomes necessary to reconcile the differences among the three values and correlate them to attain a final estimated value. If the values are close together, a mathematical correlation is not required. In this case, the appraiser normally selects the result of the method believed to have the most reliable data inputs and uses the other two methods with almost the same results to further justify the selected result. But when significant differences exist among the three values, the appraiser normally resorts to compensatory measures and looks for possible errors of judgment or in data reliability.

The final step in the appraisal process is the preparation of the appraisal report. A narrative appraisal in which value findings are presented must be convincing. The report could be in the form of a letter to the buyer, seller, or lender as a minimum. At its best, the report should be a detailed multiple-page narrative supported by statistical and graphic information extracted from dependable sources.

APPENDIX K

Examples of Attraction/Facility–Activity–Season Correlation
(Based on the BIK System for Temperate Climate Zones)

This appendix relates seasonality of activities to attraction and facility types, in contrast to Appendix F, which relates seasonality and attractions/facilities to the NAICS coding system and sorts the data by that system. In this appendix, the data are sorted alphabetically by activity type. Both appendices are presented as an aid to anyone who wants to establish a BIK System tourism database.

Attraction or Facility (Site or Event)		Activity (By alphabetic order)	Season

Example reading of the first correlation:
Attending an outdoor drama at an amphitheater in the summer.

Drama	Amphitheater	Attending, outdoor	Summer
Movie	Movie Theater	Attending, indoor	Year round
Lecture	Lecture Hall	Attending, indoor	Year round
Ballet	Ballet Theater	Attending, indoor	Year round
Concert	Concert Hall	Attending, indoor	Year round
Concert	Amphitheater	Attending, outdoor	Summer
Basketball	Gymnasium/Arena	Attending, indoor	Winter, spring
Track and Field	Stadium	Attending, outdoor	Summer
Soccer	Stadium	Attending, outdoor	Fall, winter, spring
Football	Stadium	Attending, outdoor	Fall, winter, spring
Baseball	Ball Park	Attending, outdoor	Summer
Tennis Tournament	Tennis Court	Attending, outdoor	Summer
Auto Race	Auto Racing Track	Attending	Spring, summer, fall
Horses	Horse Racing Track	Betting, horses	Spring, summer, fall
Dogs	Dog Racing Track	Betting, dogs	Spring, summer, fall
Bowling	Bowling Alley	Bowling	Year round
Camping	Camp	Camping	Summer
Canoe	River/Stream/Lake	Canoeing	Summer
Anniversary	Home	Celebrating	Year round
Wedding	Function Hall	Celebrating	Year round
Mountain	Trail	Climbing/hiking	Spring, summer, fall
Cruise	Cruise Ship	Cruising	Spring, summer, fall
Drinks	Bar	Drinking	Year round
Destination	Road	Driving	Year round
Sightseeing	Car	Driving	Year round
Food	Restaurant	Eating	Year round
Workout	Gymnasium	Exercising	Year round

Ecosystem	Nature	Exploring	Year round
Adventure	World	Exploring	Year round
Fish	Sea/River/Lake	Fishing, sport	Spring, summer, fall
Destination	Airport	Flying	Year round
Sport	Airplane	Flying	Year round
Winning	Casino	Gambling	Year round
Flowers	Garden	Gardening	Year round
Golf	Golf Course	Golfing	Spring, summer, fall
Hike	Hiking Trail	Hiking	Spring, summer
Game	Game Preserve	Hunting	Spring, summer, fall
Information	Information Center	Informing	Year round
Knowledge	School	Learning	Year round
Knowledge	Museum	Learning	Year round
Art Appreciation	Art Gallery	Learning	Year round
Religion	Mosque	Meditating/worshiping	Year round
Religion	Church	Meditating/worshiping	Year round
Religion	Temple	Meditating/worshiping	Year round
Beauty	Scenic View	Observing	Year round
Thrill	Airplane	Parachuting	Spring, summer
Business	Conference Hall	Participating	Year round
Business	Convention Hall	Participating	Year round
Business	Trade Show Hall	Participating	Year round
Tournament	Venue	Participating	Year round
Socialize	Nightclub	Partying	Year round
Picnic	Picnic Site	Picnicking	Summer
Religion	Sacred Sites	Pilgrimage	Year round
Tennis	Tennis Court	Playing tennis	Spring, summer, fall
River	Inflatable Raft	Rafting	Spring, summer
Rally	Roads	Rallying auto	Spring, summer, fall
History	Historic Site	Reenacting	Spring, summer, fall
Comfort	Comfort Station	Relieving	Year round
Horses	Trail	Riding, horseback	Spring, summer, fall
Bicycles	Bicycle Trail	Riding, bicycle	Year round
Transportation	Car	Riding, car	Year round
Transportation	Train	Riding, train	Year round
Transportation	Airplane	Riding, airplane	Year round
River	River Boat	River boating	Year round
Water	Pier	Rowing	Spring, summer, fall
Vacation	Recreational Vehicle	RVing	Year round
Sailboat	Sea/Lake/River	Sailing	Spring, summer
Marine Life	Sea/Lake/River	Scuba diving	Summer
Marine Life	Sea/Lake/River	Snorkeling	Summer
Buying	Store	Shopping	Year round
Urban Scenery	Urban Areas	Sightseeing	Year round
Rural Scenery	Rural Areas	Sightseeing	Year round
Exercise	Skating Rink	Skating	Year round
Exercise	Ski Trail	Skiing	Winter, spring

Skimobile	Open Space/Trails	Skimobiling	Winter
Sleep	Hotel	Sleeping	Year round
Snow	Hill	Sledding	Winter
Vacation	Beach	Sunning	Summer
Waves	Sea	Surfing	Summer
Swim	Pool/Sea/Lake/Stream	Swimming	Summer
Trek	Trekking Trail	Trekking	Spring, summer
Vacation	Vacation Home	Vacationing	Year round
Family and Friends	Home	Visiting	Year round
Animals	Zoo	Visiting	Year round
Charity	Nonprofit Project	Volunteering	Year round
Tournament	Venue	Watching	Spring, summer
Water ski	Sea/Lake/River	Water skiing	Summer
Walk	Walking Trail	Walking	Year round
Yacht	Sea/Lake/River	Yachting	Spring, summer, fal

This is an illustrative, not an exhaustive list.

BIBLIOGRAPHY

Abacıoğlu, Muhittin, *İmar Kanunu ve İlgili Mevzuat* (Seçkin Yayıncılık Sanayi ve Ticaret A.Ş., 2000).

Adie, Donald, Marinas—*A Working Guide to Their Development and Design* (Architectural Press Limited, 1977).

Akşit, İlhan, *The Blue Sailing* (Akşit Kültür Turizm Sanat Ajans ve Ticaret, Ltd., 1995).

Akşit, İlhan, *Ancient Civilizations and Treasures of Turkey* (Akşit Kültür Turizm Sanat Ajans ve Ticaret, Ltd., 2000).

Ali, A.Yusuf, *The Holy Qur'an, Translation and Commentary* (Amana Corp., 1983).

Alpözen, T. Oğuz, *Bodrum Castle—Museum of Underwater Archeology* (Celsus Publications, 2002).

Alkpözen, T. Oğuz, Yenseni,Uğur, and Hamza, M. Oğuz, *Bodrum* (*Halicarnassus* (Rehber, Basım Yayın Dağıtım Reklamcılık ve Ticaret A.Ş., 2000).

Apestegui, Cruz, *Pirates of the Caribbean, 1493–1720* (Chartwell Books, 2002).

Arseven, Celal Esad, *Les Arts Decoratifs Turcs* (Librairie Hachette, 1954).

Ashley, Caroline and Harold Goodwin, *Pro-Poor Tourism: What's Gone Right and What's Gone Wrong?* (Overseas Development Institute, London, 2007).

Ashley, Caroline, De Brine, Peter, Lehr, Amy, and Wilde, Hannah, *The Role of the Tourism Sector in Expanding Economic Opportunities* (Harvard University, John F. Kennedy School of Government, Economic Opportunity Series, 2007).

Atıl, Esin, *The Age of Sultan Süleyman the Magnificent* (National Gallery of Art, Washington, DC, and Harry N. Abrams, New York, 1987).

Axtell, Roger E., *Do's and Taboos Around the World* (Parker Pen Company, 1993).

Baggett, Jerome P., *Habitat for Humanity* (Temple University Press, 2001).

Bahn, Paul G., *Lost Cities—50 Discoveries in World Archeology* (Barnes & Noble, Inc., 1997).

Baskin, C. W. (trans.), *Central Places in Southern Germany* (Prentice-Hall, 1966).

Bass, George F., *Shipwrecks in the Bodrum Museum of Underwater Archeology* (Donmez Offset-Ankara, 1996).

Baykara, Taşkın, *Rakkamlarla Marmaris ve Yöresi* (Marmaris Ticaret Odası, İstatistik ve Araştırma Geliştirme Bölümü, 2001).

Bennett, Oliver, Roe, Dilys, and Ashley, Carolyn, *Sustainable Tourism and Poverty Elimination Study* A Report to the United Kingdom Department for International Development (April 1999).

Beshers, James M., *Urban Social Structure* (Free Press of Glencoe, 1962).

Beyard, Michael D., Braun, Ray, McLaughlin, Herb, Philips, Patrick, and Rubin, Michael, *Developing Urban Entertainment Centers* (Urban Land Institute, 1998).

Boissevain, Jeremy, "Coping with Mass Cultural Tourism: Structure and Strategies," *International Gazette of Anthropology*, pp. 1–12, 2006).

Bolwell, Dain, and Weinz, Wolfgang, *Reducing Poverty through Tourism* (International Labor Office, Geneva, Switzerland, 2008).

Bornstein, David, *How to Change the World—Social Entrepreneurs and the Power of New Ideas* (Oxford University Press, 2004).

Bryden, John M., *Tourism and Development—A Case Study of the Commonwealth Caribbean* (Cambridge University Press, 1973).

Buckley, Ralf, *Adventure Tourism* (CABI, Oxfordshire, UK, and Cambridge, MA, 2003).

Burbon, Fabio; Lavagno, Enrico, *The Holy Land* (White Star S.r.l, 2001).

Burton, Robin, *Sailing the Great Races* (Chartwell Books, Inc., 1979).

Business, The Ultimate Resource (Perseus Publishing—Bloombury Publishing Plc, 2002).

- Byrd, Drayton, *Managing 1:1 Marketing*
- Elkington, John, *Environmental Management*
- Anonymous, *Other*

Çağlayan, Adnan, *Glass, the Eternal Beauty* (Penajans DMB&B—Şişe Cam, 1990).

Caribbean and Mexico Cruises 2004–2005 (Princess Cruises, 2003).

Carnegie Endowment for International Peace, National Commission on America and the New World, *Changing Our Ways* (Carnegie Endowment for International Peace, 1992).

Cattaneo, Marco, and Trifoni, Jasmina, *The Great Book of World Heritage Sites by UNESCO*

- *Ancient Civilizations* (WMB Publishers, 2004).

- *Nature Sanctuaries* (White Star Publishers, 2003).

- *The Treasures of Art* (White Star Publishers, 2002).

Chant, *Christopher, The World's Railroads* (Chartwell Books, Inc., 2000).

Chaplin, Lois Trigg, *The Story of Callaway Gardens* (Callaway Gardens Resort, Inc., 2000).

Christaller, Walter, *Die zentralen Orte in Süddeutschland* (*The Central Places in Southern Germany*) (Gustav Fischer, 1933).

Churchill, Winston S., *The Second World War* (TAJ Books Ltd., 2003).

Çini, Rıfat, *Kütahya Çiniciliği* (Celsus Yayıncılık, 2002).

Conservation International and George Washington University, *Tourism Rapid Assessment Tool Concept Paper* (Rural Agricultural Income and Sustainable Environment Program, U.S. Agency for International Development, undated).

Cooley, Charles H., *The Theory of Transportation* (doctoral dissertation, University of Michigan, 1894).

Cooper, Chris, Fletcher, John, Fyall, Alan, Gilbert, David, and Wanhill, Stephen, *Tourism: Principles and Practice* (Pearson Education Trans-Atlantic Publications, 2008).

Contracting, Chapter 489 (General Laws of the State of Florida).

Critical Path Method (CPM), Scheduling Basics, Parts I–II (Chichester Management Systems, Inc., 1998).

Csörnyei, Sandor, ed., *Bains, Piscines et Plage de Budapest* (Editions Pannonia, 1971).

Dallen, Timothy J., *Shopping Tourism, Retailing and Leisure* (Channel View Publications, Clevedon, UK, 2005).

deBlij, H. J., and Murphy, Alexander B., *Human Geography—Culture, Society, and Space* (John Wiley & Sons, Inc., 2003).

De Chiare, Joseph, and Callander, John Hancock, eds., *Time-Saver Standards for Building Types* (McGraw-Hill Book Company, 1990).

Destination Cayman, 2003 (Ralston Publications Ltd., 2003).

Developing Island Countries (United Nations, 1974).

Dick Pope Sr. Institute of Tourism Studies, *Economic Impact of the Tourism Industry in Osceola County Florida* (University of Central Florida, 2008).

Downes, John, and Goodman, Jordan Elliot, *Barrons's Finance and Investment Handbook* (Barrons's, 1986).

Duggal, Vijay, *CADD Primer—A General Guide to Computer Aided Design and Drafting— Cadd, CAD* (Mailmax Publishing, 2000).

Duncan, Otis Dudley, Scott, W. Richard, Liberson, Stanley, Duncan, Beverly, and Winsborough, Hal H. *Metropolis and Region* (Johns Hopkins University Press, 1960).

Elderhostel—Discover America 2004 (Elderhostel, Inc., 2003).

Elliott, James, *Tourism: Policies and Public Sector Management* (Taylor & Francis, Inc., 1997).

Encyclopedia of Discovery—Science and History (Fog City Press, 2002).

Enhancing the Economic Benefits of Tourism for Local Communities and Poverty Alleviation (World Tourism Organization, 2002).

Erimez, Salih, *Tarihten Çizgiler (Sketches from the Past)* (Paper and Printing Works, Inc., Istanbul, 1941).

Ertem, Tuncer, ed., *Bodrum Ev Stili ve Kültürü* (Celsus Publications, 2000).

Export Programs, A Business Directory of U.S. Government Resources (U.S. Department of Commerce).

Fayez, Zuhair H., *Saudi Arabia—A Cultural Perspective* (Zuhair Fayez and Associates, 1988).

Fout, Xavier, and Carey, Benjamin, *Marketing Sustainable Tourism Products* (United Nations

Environment Programme, Nairobi, Kenya, 2005).

Friedmann, John, and Alonso, William, eds., *Regional Development and Planning—A Reader* (MIT Press, 1964).

From Plan to Market, World Development Report (World Bank and Oxford University Press,1996).

Gannon, Martin J., *Understanding Global Cultures* (Sage Publications, Inc., 2004).

Gardiner, Robert, ed., *The Age of the Galley— Mediterranean Oared Vessels Since Pre-Classical Times* (Conway Maritime Press, 1995).

Gardner, A. Dudley, *Architecture of the Ancient Ones* (Gibbs Smith Publisher, 2000).

Geographica—The Complete Illustrated Atlas of the World (James Mills-Hicks/Mynah, 2001).

Giedion, Sigfried, *Space, Time and Architecture* (Harvard University Press, 1954).

Goeldner, Charles R., and Ritchie, J. R. Brent, *Tourism: Principles, Practices and Philosophies,* 11th ed. (John Wiley & Sons, Inc., 2009).

Gökalp, Şerafettin, *Kat Mülkiyeti Kanunu* (İnkılap Kitapevi, 1995).

Goldstein, Joyce, *Mediterranean—The Beautiful Cookbook* (HarperCollins Publishers, 1994).

Goodman, William I., and Freund, Eric C., eds., *Principles and Practice of Urban Planning,* 4th ed. (International City Managers Association, 1968).

Graham, Scott, *Handle with Care—A Guide to Responsible Travel In Developing Countries* (Noble Press, Inc., 1992).

Guide for Local Authorities on Developing Sustainable Tourism (World Tourism Organization, 1998).

Guide to Estimating Cost for Golf Course Construction (Golf Course Builders Association of America, 1998).

Gunn, Clare A., *Vacationscape—Designing Tourist Regions* (University of Texas Press, 1972).

Gunn, Clare A., and Var, Trugut, *Tourism Planning: Basics, Concepts, Cases* (Taylor & Francis Books, Oxford, UK, 1993).

Gunn, Eileen P., "Would You Please Take My Money" (*Fortune,* March 2, 1998).

Hagen, Toni, *Nepal* (Kummerly and Frey, 1961; updated and reissued by Oxford University Press and IBH Publishing Co., 1971).

Hannau, Hans W., *The Caribbean Islands* (Argos, Inc., 1972).

Harder, Christian, *Arc View—GIS Means Business* (Environmental Systems Research Institute, Inc., 1997).

Hardin, Steven, *The Alamo 1836—Santa Ana's Texas Campaign* (Osprey Publishing, 2001).

Harney, Andy Leon, ed., *Reviving the Urban Waterfront* (Partners for Livable Places, National Endowment for the Arts, Office of Coastal Zone Management, 1981).

Hatt, Paul K., and Reiss, Albert, Jr., eds., *Cities and Society* (The Free Press of Glencoe, 1957).

Hellander, Paul, and Humphreys, Andrew, *Jerusalem* (Lonely Planet Publications, 1999).

Higgins, Benjamin, *Economic Development— Principles, Problems and Policies* (W. W. Norton & Company, 1959).

Hillary, Sir Edmund, "My Story" *(National Geographic,* May 2003).

Hirai, Kiyoshi, *Feudal Architecture of Japan* (Weatherhill/Heibonsha, 1980).

Hirschfelder, Arlene, *Native Americans* (Dorling Kindersley Publishing, Inc., 2000).

His Majesty's Government of Nepal with the assistance of a German technical assistance team, *Physical Development Plan for Kathmandu Valley* (United Nations Development Programme, 1969).

His Majesty's Government of Nepal, *Nepal Tourism Master Plan* (Department of Tourism, 1972).

Hoebel, E. Adamson, *Anthropology: The Study of Man,* 4th ed. (McGraw-Hill Book Company, 1972).

Hoebel, E. Adamson, and Frost, Everett Lloyd, *Cultural and Social Anthropology* (McGraw-Hill Book Company, 1976)

Honeck, Dale, *LDC Poverty Alleviation and the Doha Development Agenda: Is Tourism Being Neglected?* (World Trade Organization, 2008).

Hook, Jason, and Pegler, Martin, *To Live and Die in the West—The American Indian Wars* (Osprey Publishing Ltd., 1999).

Hoover, Edgar M., *The Location of Economic Activity* (McGraw-Hill Book Company, 1948).

Howe, Jeffrey, general ed., *The Houses We Live In* (Thunder Bay Press, 2002).

Howell, David W., *Passport: An Introduction to the Travel and Tourism Industry* (South-Western Publishing Co., 1993).

Hudman, Lloyd, and Jackson, Richard, *Geography of Travel and Tourism* (Thomson Delmar Learning, 2003).

Huxhold, William E., *An Introduction to Urban Geographic Information Systems* (Oxford University Press, 1991).

Hybers, Twan, ed., *Tourism in Developing Countries* (Edward Elgar Publishing, Ltd., Chelterham, UK, 2007).

Imaging the Region—South Florida Via Indicators and Public Opinions (Florida Atlantic University/Florida International University Joint Center for Urban and Environmental Problems, 2001).

Inskeep, Edward, *Tourism Planning: An Integrated and Sustainable Development Approach*, VNR Tourism and Commercial Recreation Series (Van Nostrand Reinhold, 1991).

Isard, Walter, *Location and Space-Economy* (MIT Press, 1956).

Isard, Walter, et al., *Methods of Regional Analysis: An Introduction to Regional Science* (MIT Press, 1960).

Istanbul—A Glimpse Into the Past (Research Center for Islamic Society, Art and Culture, 1989).

İstatistiklerle Türkiye, 1997 (T. C. Başbakanlık Devlet İstatistik Enstitüsü, 1997).

Jennings, Gayle, and Nickerson, Norma Polovitz, eds., *Quality Tourism Experiences* (Elsevier Butterworth-Heineman, Oxford, UK, 2006)

Joint Ventures, Chapter 19 (General Laws of the State of Florida).

Jordan, David, *Wolfpack—The U-Boat War and the Allied Counter-Attack 1939–1945* (Barnes and Noble Books, 2002).

Kamu Arazisinin Turizm Yatırımlarına Tahsisi Hakkında Yönetmelik (T. C. Resmi Gazete, Sayı 18031, 28 Nisan 1983).

Kastarlak, Bulent I. *Tourism and Its Development Potential in Massachusetts* (Commonwealth of Massachusetts, Department of Commerce and Development, 1970).

Report 1: Tourism and Its Development Potential in Massachusetts

Report 2: Tourism and Its Development Potential in Massachusetts (Summary)

Report 3: Characteristics and Geographic Distribution of Tourist Attractions in Massachusetts (Volume I—Computer Maps)

Report 4: Characteristics and Geographic Distribution of Tourist Attractions in Massachusetts (Volume II—Data Matrices)

Report 5: Inventory of Tourist Facility Mixes by Municipalities and Regions in Massachusetts

Kastarlak, Bulent I., "Planning Tourism Growth" (*The Cornell Hotel and Restaurant Administration Quarterly*, February 1971).

Kastarlak, Bulent I., *Tourism and Urban Development Plan for Gandaki/Lumbini Region, Nepal* (unpublished report to the United Nations, 1972).

Kastarlak, Bulent I., *An Evaluation of the Bicentennial Celebrations in Boston, Massachusetts* (unpublished report to the Boston Redevelopment Authority, 1976).

Kastarlak, Bulent I., *Tourism and Its Development Potential in the Eastern Caribbean* (nine unpublished country reports to the United Nations, 1976–1978).

Kastarlak, Bulent I., *Review of Average Room Rates and Average Occupancy Rates for Proposed Suite Hotel, Huntsville, Alabama* (unpublished report, 1995).

Kastarlak, Bulent I., *Center for International Trade, Technology and Culture* (unpublished report, 1997).

Kastarlak, Bulent I., *Project Planning and Control System* (*PP&C*) (unpublished report, 1998).

Kastarlak, Bulent I., *Wadi Mousa Wastewater Treatment Project—Recreational Reuse Option, Kingdom of Jordan* (unpublished report to USAID, 2000).

Kastarlak, Bulent I., *Waterfront-Downtown Destination Area, Boynton Beach, Florida, USA* (unpublished report, 2001).

Kastarlak, Bulent I., *Parsel Kullanım Fizibilitesi ve Mali Analizi, Marmaris, Turkey* (unpublished report, 2002).

Kastarlak, Bulent I., *Business Plan and Financial Analysis for a Four Star Hotel, Istanbul, Turkey* (unpublished report, 2003).

Kastarlak, Bulent I., *Business Plan and Financial Analysis for Hotel Yazgan, Istanbul, Turkey* (unpublished report, 2003).

Kastarlak, Bulent I., and Barber, Brian, *Master Plan of the Driftway Resort Community, Golf Course, Marina, and Hotel, Scituate, Massachusetts* (unpublished report, 1984).

Kastarlak, Bulent I. and Barber, Brian, *Tourism Development Master Plan for Quincy, Massachusetts* (unpublished report, 1988).

Kindleberger, Charles P., *Economic Development* (McGraw-Hill Book Company, 1958).

Kingston, Ross K., ed., *Cruise Ship Tourism* (CABI Bookshop Series, Oxfordshire, UK, and Cambridge, MA, 2006).

Kıyı Kanunu, No. 3621 (T. C. Resmi Gazete, 4 Nisan 1990).

Kotter, John P., "What Leaders Really Do" (*Harvard Business Review*, May–June 1990).

Kültür Ve Turizm Bakanlığı Teşkilat ve Görevleri Hakkında Kanun (T. C. Resmi Gazete, Sayı 25093, 29 Nisan 2003).

Lavery, Brian, *Smithsonian Ship: The Epic Story of Maritime Adventure* (DK Publishing Co., 2004).

Law for the Encouragement of Tourism No. 2634 (Republic of Turkey, Ministry of Culture and Tourism, 1982). Available at http://goturkey.kultur.gov.tr/turizm_en.asp?bel geno=9274.

Leven, Charles L., Legler, John, and Shapiro, Perry, *Analytical Framework for Regional Development Policy* (Regional Science Studies Series, MIT Press, 1970).

Lewis, Bernard, *What Went Wrong?* (Oxford University Press, 2002).

Lewis, Bernard, *The Crisis of Islam* (Modern Library, 2003).

Lewis, James P., *Fundamentals of Project Management* (American Management Association, 1995).

Liens, Generally, Chapter 713 (General Laws of the State of Florida).

Life of the Emperors and Empresses in the Forbidden City, 1644–1911 (China Travel and Tourism Press, 1986).

Lösch, August, *Die räumliche Ordnung der Wirtschaft* (Jena: Gustav Fischer, 1940)

Lukas, Scott A., *Theme Park*, Objekt Series (Reaktion Books, Ltd. 2008).

Lundberg, Donald E., Krishnamoorthy, M., and Stavenga, Mink H., *Tourism Economics* (John Wiley & Sons, Inc., 1995).

Macauley, David, *Cathedral* (Collins, 1983).

Macauley, David, *Mosque* (Houghton Mifflin Harcourt Co., 2003).

Matson, Brad, *Jacques Cousteau: The Sea King* (Random House, 2009).

Malmberg, Melody, *The Making of Disney's Animal Kingdom Theme Park* (Hyperion, 1998).

Mancini, Mark, *Cruising—A Guide to the Cruise Line Industry* (Delmar Learning, 2004).

March, James G., and Simon, Herbert A., *Organizations* (John Wiley & Sons, Inc., 1958).

McWatters, Mason R., *Residential Tourism, (De)Constructing Paradise*, Tourism and Cultural Change Series (Channel View Publications, Ltd., 2009).

Merton, Robert K., "Bureaucratic Structure and Personality," Social Forces *(May 1940)*.

Middleton, T. C., Fyall, Alan, Morgan, Michael, and Ranchhod, Ashok, *Marketing in Travel and Tourism*, 4th ed. (Elsevier; Butterworth-Heinemann, Oxford, UK, 2009).

Miller, Russell, *The East Indiamen* (Time-Life Books, 1980).

Miracle, Barbara, "Venture Capital: Who's Got It, How to Get It," *Florida Trend* (February 1995).

Mitchell Beazley International Ltd., ed., *The World Atlas of Architecture* (Portland House, Encyclopaedia Universalis, 1984).

Mitchell Beazley International Ltd., ed., *The World Atlas of Archeology* (Portland House, Encyclopaedia Universalis, 1985).

Moscow (Bonechi-Welcome Books, 1994).

Mumford, Lewis, *The Culture of Cities* (Harcourt, Brace and Company, 1938)

Murphy, Peter E., *Tourism: A Community Approach* (Thompson Learning, Belmont, CA, 1986).

National and Regional Tourism Planning (World Tourism Organization, 1994).

Newbey, Eric, *The Rand McNally–World Atlas of Exploration* (Mitchell Beazley Publishers Ltd., 1975).

Norgay, Jambling Tenzing, and Coburn, Brighton, *Touching My Father's Soul: A Sherpa's Journey to the Top of Everest* (Harper, 2001).

North American Industry Classification System (U.S. Executive Office of the President, Office of Management and Budget, 1997).

North, Nelson L., and Ring, Alfred A., *Real Estate Principles and Practices* (Prentice-Hall, Inc., 1960).

Obermeyer, Nancy J., and Pinto, Jeffrey K., *Managing Geographic Information Systems* (Guilford Press, 1994).

O'Looney, John, *Beyond Maps: GIS and Decision Making in Local Government* (International City Managers Association, 1997).

Overseas Adventure Travel—Call to Adventure 2002 (Overseas Adventure Travel, 2002).

Özdemir, Kemal, *Piri Reis* (Başkent Ofset Cultural Publications, 2003).

Palm Beach County Visitors Guide (Palm Beach County, Florida, Convention and Visitors Bureau, 2002).

Pegden, C. Dennis, Sadowski, Randall P., and Shannon, Robert E., *Introduction to Simulation Using SIMAN* (McGraw-Hill Book Companies, 1995).

Peters, Michael, *International Tourism: The Economics of Development of the International Tourist Trade* (Hutchinson and Company, London, 1969).

Pitt, Barrie, consultant ed., *The Military History of World War II* (Military Press, 1986).

PKF Consulting, *Hotel Development* (Urban Land Institute, 1996).

"Planner's Notebook: Tourism Planning" *Journal of the American Planning Association* (Summer 1988).

Pleasure Boating—Sail and Power: Construction, Handling, Navigation, Racing, Cruising (A.B. Nordbok, 1977).

Poorvu, William J., and Cruikshank, J. Jeffrey, *The Real Estate Game* (The Free Press, 1999).

Powers, Tom, *Marketing Hospitality* (John Wiley & Sons, Inc.,1990).

Prideaux, Bruce, and Cooper, Malcolm, eds., *River Tourism* (CABI, Oxfordshire, UK, and Cambridge, MA, 2009).

Primavera (CD-ROM)
- Project Planner 3.0
- Sure Trak Project Manager 3.0
- Webster for Primavera 2.0
- Enterprise
- Expedition

Privatization—Toward More Effective Government (Report of the U.S. President's Commission on Privatization, 1988).

Ramsey, Charles G., and Sleeper, Harold R., *AIA Architectural Graphic Standards* (John Wiley & Sons, Inc., 1981).

Ratcliff, Richard U., *Real Estate Analysis* (McGraw-Hill Book Company, 1960).

Recommended Guide for Bidding Procedures and Contract Awards (American Institute of Architects, Associated General Contractors of America, 1995).

Regional Economic Planning—Techniques of Analysis for Less Developed Areas (European Productivity Agency of the Organisation for European Economic Co-Operation, 1961).

Ritchie, J. R. Brent, and Crouch, Geoffrey I., *The Competitive Destination: A Sustainable Tourism Perspective* (CABI Publishing, Oxon, UK, 2003).

Roberts, David, *Journey to Petra and the Holy Land* (Casa Editrice Bonechi, 2000).

Rosenbaum, Lisa T., ed., *Lynn Harbor: Planning for Coastal Development* (MIT Seagrant Program, 1978).

Sail Boston, 1992 (Collector's Edition of Tall Ships, 1992).

Samuelson, Paul, *Economics*, 12th ed. (McGraw-Hill Book Company, 1985).

Scarpari, Maurizio, *Ancient China* (White Star S.r.l, Publishers, 2000).

Schwanke, Dean, ed., *Resort Development Handbook* (Urban Land Institute, 1997).

Searjant, R.B., ed., *The Islamic City* (UNESCO, 1980).

Sekler, Eduard, Allchin, Raymond, Borel, Paul, Chayabongse, Chamras, Jest, Corneille, Kussmaul, Friedrich, Saba, Hanna S., and Tunnard, Christopher, *Master Plan for the Conservation of the Cultural Heritage in the*

Kathmandu Valley (United Nations Development Programme, 1977).

Selling Destinations—Geography for the Travel Professional (Delmar Learning, 2004).

Selznick, Philip, *TVA and the Grass Roots: A Study in the Sociology of Formal Organizations* (University of California Press, Berkeley, 1947).

Sezen, Gürol, *Bin Çeşit Istanbul ve Boğaziçi Yalıları* (Ak Yayınları, 1989).

Sherwood, David, "Costa Rica Sees Tourism's Environmental Dark Side" (*Christian Science Monitor*, April 16, 2008).

Siliotti, Alberto, *The Discovery of Ancient Egypt* (Chartwell Books—White Star, S.l.i., 1998).

Simon, Herbert A., *Administrative Behavior: A Study of Decision-Making Processes in Administrative Organizations* (doctoral dissertation first published in 1947; 4th ed. published by The Free Press, 1997).

Sorensen, Helle, *International Travel and Tourism* (Delmar Publishers, 1997), *Sources of Finance for Trade and Investment in the NIS* (BISNIS, U.S. Department of Commerce, 1997).

Sözen, Metin, *The Evolution of Turkish Art and Architecture* (Haşet Kitabevi A.Ş., 1987).

Standard Land Use Coding Manual (Urban Renewal Administration, HHFA, 1965).

Standard & Poor's DRI, *The Role of Metropolitan Areas in the National Economy* (DRI/McGraw-Hill Book Companies, 1998).

Sterling, Paul, *The Turkish Village* (John Wiley & Sons, Inc., 1965).

Stevens, Stanley F., *Claiming the High Ground—Sherpas, Subsistence, and Environmental Change in the Highest Himalayas* (University of California Press, 1993).

Stevens, Stanley F., "Tourism, Change, and Continuity in the Mount Everest Region, Nepal" (*Geographical Review*, October 1993).

Stevens, Stanley F., "Sherpas, Tourism, and Cultural Change in Nepal's Mt. Everest Region" (*Journal of Cultural Geography*, 1991).

Stevens, Stanley F., "Tourism and Deforestation in the Mt. Everest Region of Nepal" (*Geographical Journal*, September 2003).

Strategic Planning (Video) (Chichester Management Systems, Inc., undated).

Sumner-Boyd, Hilary, and Freely, John, *Strolling through Istanbul* (Redhouse Press, 1983).

Sustainable Development in a Dynamic World, World Development Report (World Bank and Oxford University Press, 2003).

Swarbrooke, John, Beard, Colin, Leckie, Suzanne, and Pomfret, Gil, *Adventure Tourism: The New Frontier* (Elsevier Science, Oxford, UK, and Burlington, MA, 2003).

Taylor, Jane, *Petra* (Aurum Press Ltd., 2002).

Terranova, Antonino, *The Great Skyscrapers of the World* (White Star, S.l.i, 2003).

The Book of London (Automobile Association, 1983).

The Local Government Guide to Geographic Information Systems: Planning and Implementation (International City Managers Association, 1991).

The New Imperial War Museum (London, 1992).

The Tier System Managed Growth Program (Palm Beach County, Florida, 1999).

The World Bank—Annual Reports for 1986 through 2009 (World Bank, Washington, DC).

Throckmorton, Peter, ed., *The Sea Remembers—Shipwrecks and Archeology* (Smithmark Publishers, 1991).

Tinbergen, Jan, *The Design of Development* (Johns Hopkins University Press, 1958).

Tinbergen, Jan, *Development Planning* (World University Library, 1965).

Tourism and Culture (United Nations World Tourism Organization Seminar Proceedings, 1999).

Tourism and Poverty Alleviation (United Nations World Tourism Organization, 2002).

Tourism Investment Opportunities and Procedures in Turkey (Ministry of Tourism, General Directorate of Investments, 2000).

Tourism Supply in the Caribbean Region (World Bank and The Shankland Cox Partnership, 1974).

Turizm Teşvik Kanunu, No. 2634 (T. C. Resmi Gazete, Sayı. 17625, 16 Mart 1982).

Türkiye Turizm Tesisleri Yönetmeliği (Turizm Dayanışma Vakfı, 2006).

Tyrrell, Timothy J. and Johnson, Robert J., "An Econometric Analysis of the Effects of Tourism Growth on Municipal Revenues and Expenditures" *Tourism Economics,* (Vol. 15. No. 4, 2009).

United Nations Conference on Trade and Development (UNCTAD), *Summary of a Pre-Conference Meeting on Trade and Development Implications of Tourism Services for Developing Countries* (UNCTAD Secretariat, Geneva, November 2007).

Unstead, R. J., ed., *See Inside a Castle* (Grisewood & Dempsey Ltd., 1986).

Van Bieama, David, "The Legacy of Abraham" (*Time*, September 30, 2002).

Viking River Cruises—Exploring the World in Comfort (Viking Cruises, 2004).

Vilenski, Dan, ed., *Jerusalem—Six Reproductions of Rare Maps* (Dan Vilenski, Publisher, undated).

Weber, Max, *The Theory of Social and Economic Organization,* trans. A. M. Henderson and Talcott Parsons (The Free Press of Glencoe, 1947).

Weed, Mike, and Bull, Chris, *Sports Tourism, Participants, Policy and Providers,* 2nd ed. (Elsevier Linacare House, Oxford, UK, and Burlington, MA, 2009).

Werner, Herbert A., *Iron Coffins* (Da Capo Press, 2002).

What Tourism Managers Need to Know (United Nations World Tourism Organization, 1996).

Whipple, A. B. C., *The Clipper Ships* (Time-Life Books, 1980).

Woglom, W. H., with the assistance of W. F. Stolper (trans.), *The Economics of Location* (Yale University Press, 1954).

World Bank, *World Development Report: From Plan to Market* (Oxford University Press, 1996).

World Tourism Leaders' Meeting on the Social Impact of Tourism (United Nations World Tourism Organization, 1997).

Yabancı Sermayeyi Teşvik Kanunu, No. 6224 (T. C. Resmi Gazete, 18 Ocak 1954).

Yat Turizmi Yönetmeliği (T. C. Resmi Gazete, No. 18125, 4 Ağustos 1983).

Yatırımlarda Devlet Yardımları Hakkında Karar (T. C. Resmi Gazete, No. 24810, 9 Temmuz, 2002).

Zhou, Zongqing, *E-Commerce and Information Technology in Hospitality and Tourism* (Thomson Delmar Learning, 2004).

Zhou, Zongqing, and Lin, Li-Chun, "The Impact of the Internet on the Use of the Printed Brochure," *Proceedings of the Council on Hotel, Restaurant and Institutional Education Annual Conference,* New Orleans, Louisiana (July 19–22, 2000).

INDEX